Dynamic WAP Application Development

Dynamic WAP
Application Development

SOO MEE FOO
CHRIS HOOVER
WEI MENG LEE

with
CHRISTINA BIGGS
MIKE JASNOWSKI
IAN MOREAS

MANNING

Greenwich
(74° w. long.)

For electronic browsing and ordering of this and other Manning books, visit http://www.manning.com. The publisher offers discounts on this book when ordered in quantity. For more information, please contact:

Special Sales Department
Manning Publications Co.
32 Lafayette Place   Fax: (203) 661-9018
Greenwich, CT 06830   email: orders@manning.com

⊗ Recognizing the importance of preserving what has been written, it is Manning's policy to have the books we publish printed on acid-free paper, and we exert our best efforts to that end.

Library of Congress Cataloging-in-Publication Data
Foo, Soo Mee
    Dynamic WAP application development / Soo Mee Foo, Christopher
       Hoover, Wei Meng Lee.
       p.   cm.
    Includes bibliographical references and index.
    ISBN 1-930110-08-1
    1. Wireless Application Protocol (Computer network protocol)
    2. Application software—Development. I. Hoover, Christopher. II. Lee,
       Wei Meng. III. Title.
       TK5105.5865 .F66 2001
  004.6'2--dc21   2001030932
                              CIP

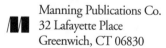

Manning Publications Co.   Copyeditor: Elizabeth Martin
32 Lafayette Place   Typesetter: Dottie Marsico
Greenwich, CT 06830   Cover designer: Leslie Haimes

Printed in the United States of America
1 2 3 4 5 6 7 8 9 10 – VH – 03 02 01

brief contents

contents

preface

In 1999, when the world was still engrossed with building web applications, we noticed an increasing interest and excitement regarding the Wireless Application Protocol (WAP) and its potential. WAP moved very quickly from a relatively obscure protocol to the focus of intense interest among developers who wanted to bring web content to mobile devices. Because people spend much of their time on the move and away from their PCs, the ability to view web content on a mobile device is a very intriguing notion.

Consequently, we started toying with the Wireless Markup Language (WML) and its scripting counterpart, WMLScript. It was soon apparent that building WAP applications (or services, as some put it) is somewhat similar to building web applications. However, WML and WMLScript possess limitations that could easily trip up an uninitiated WAP application developer.

Today, WAP and wireless web technology are still in their infancy. Sources for help and information about WAP, although relatively scarce, are increasing at an amazing rate. The main sources of information are the companies that distribute emulators such as Phone.com, Nokia, and Ericsson, all of which definitely played an important part in educating the public on WAP applications development.

Other information sources are the online communities, including AnyWhere-YouGo.com, ASPToday, and Wireless Developer Network. In addition to featuring WAP articles and resources, these online communities run discussion groups and mailing lists. Close monitoring of these mailing lists shows that developers are frequently asking the same kinds of questions (and getting frustrated when no help is rendered).

This is what led us to write this book which describes the WAP application building process and discusses the common issues faced by developers. And the rest, as they say, is history.

We wrote this book with two main objectives:

First, we hope to share with you our hard-earned experience in developing WAP applications. All of us have made silly mistakes that kept us awake at night. We hope that this book will prevent you from doing the same. Our goal is to make you more productive more quickly.

Second, we aim to equip WAP developers with the skill set and know-how to develop and deploy dynamic WAP applications. To benefit developers who need to incorporate processing at the server side and database access into their applications, we have provided coverage for both server-side and database access technologies. Some of the popular server-side technologies, such as Active Server Pages (ASP), Java servlets, and JavaServer Pages (JSP) are discussed in detail. Database access technologies covered in this book include ADO, OLEDB, ODBC, and JDBC. We have also included a discussion on developing server-side messaging applications using JavaMail.

We hope that you will enjoy this book and find it useful.

acknowledgments

What was originally planned as a six-month project turned out to be much larger and more complex than anyone expected. As with any book, very many people worked tirelessly behind the scenes, paying attention to endless details in order to create the best product possible for our readers. We would like to express our heartfelt thanks to the following:

Marjan Bace, our publisher, who took the bold step of bringing us together for this book. We thank you for the constant encouragement and motivation when the going got tough.

Lianna Wlasiuk, our developmental editor, who was very (very!) patient with us in the many months it took to write. You definitely made this book a better read. Your skill at transforming our writing into useful, readable material is truly amazing.

Susan Capparelle, assistant publisher, for getting the whole project started. We are grateful for the trust you had in us.

Ted Kennedy, review editor, for coordinating all the reviewers and ensuring that this book is of the highest standard.

Mary Piergies, production manager, and her team of Dottie Marsico, Elizabeth Martin, and Jessica McCarty, who polished the raw manuscript into one that we are really proud of.

We do not want to forget all the other folks at Manning Publications who worked behind the scenes on our book. We may not know their names, but we are grateful!

Last but not least, thanks to all our reviewers for their frank and valuable feedback. Your insights and comments on the manuscript in its various stages of development helped improve it immensely. The reviewers were Greg Bridle, Steve Heckler, Ronnie Lackman, Sudhir Menon, Eric Giguere, Warren Hill, Steve Milroy, Jon Skeet, Hemant Sharma, Geoffroy Braem, Gavin Smyth, Dave Bevis, and Alastair Angwin.

Special thanks to Alastair Angwin and Dave Bevis, who in addition to reviewing the manuscript, also looked at it in its final form.

SOO MEE FOO: First of all, I would like to thank the editorial team at Manning for putting in tremendous effort and time to make this book a valuable one. Special thanks must go to Sudhir Menon and his team at StarHub, who had been extremely patient with our queries on certain network operational issues. On a similar note, we are grateful to Teck Kim of Ericsson, as well as Ken and Kheng Wah of Philips for supplying information on their WAP products, some of which are featured in this book. I would also like to mention the co-authors of this book, who were great to work with.

Thanks as well to my brother, Wei Kiang, for his advice on preparing some pictures, and to my parents and Ivan who enjoy seeing my books published.

CHRISTOPHER HOOVER would like to thank Bruce Martin, a great friend and colleague who first introduced me to WAP; my friends Audrey, Ryan, Brad, Jessica, Jenifer, and Aimee (who deserves special kudos for remaining cheerful even as I worked on this book poolside during a vacation). You were all patient even as this project took precedence over other activities.

Thanks guys, I'm very lucky to know you. Finally, thanks to my parents Judy and Jerry Hoover, who (in spite of frequent evidence to the contrary) always believed I'd eventually make something of myself. I'm very lucky to have you, too.

WEI MENG LEE would like to thank the entire Manning production team for their tireless effort to make this book a better one. Special thanks to Mary, Lianna, Dottie, Elizabeth, and Jessica for their patience as our manuscript went through production. This book would not be possible if not for the many people who work tirelessly behind the scenes and whose names do not appear on the cover of the book. My sincere thanks to Soo Mee for taking care of the project while I was away at conferences. Finally, my gratitude to my parents for providing me with a sound education.

CHRISTINA BIGGS would like to thank her husband, Marty, for his love and patience; her co-workers at ateb for being flexible with her work hours; her co-workers at Phuel for getting her started in wireless development; and her parents for everything else.

MIKE JASNOWSKI would like to thank Marjan Bace for picking me out of the morass of developers to contribute to this book, as well as Lianna Wlasiuk for providing valuable feedback and helping make my chapters even better.

Finally, thanks to my wife Tracy and daughter Emmeline for giving me time to work on this book.

IAN MORAES would like to thank his wife, Karen, for her support and encouragement, as well as Anthony and Katie who continually remind me of what is important in life. Finally, thanks to my wonderful role models, my parents.

about this book

This book is written for people who want to delve into the exciting world of WAP application development. It is also suitable for experienced web developers who are making the transition to WAP.

How to use this book

This book is designed to be accessible and instructive to persons very new to WAP (and even new to the Web), as well as provide a valuable reference for the experienced WAP developer. If you are new to WAP, begin with the introduction in part I. This will give you a broad outline of the WAP technologies, as well as tell you what you need to get started with WAP development.

Parts II and III describe two WAP specifications in depth: the Wireless Markup Language (WML), and WMLScript (along with the WMLScript Standard Libraries). Don't let the other WAP specifications put you off, though; markup developers need not know about any of the other WAP specifications in detail. These other specifications exist primarily to shield most developers from the underlying network details.

In addition to WML and WMLScript, part IV of this book covers a markup language that is not part of the WAP specifications suite: the Handheld Device Markup Language (HDML). All three (HDML, WML, and WMLScript) are designed to enable you to control what the user sees on the phone. With the tools you can display text, menus, enable the user to enter data, and send data between servers. Mastery of these three topics is important to successfully developing wireless applications.

The remainder of this book details how to develop application logic that works with a mobile phone to provide useful, compelling services. Because the phone provides very limited processing power, application logic must be kept server side.

To reap the maximum benefit from this book, it would help if you have experience with the Internet and are familiar with terms like TCP/IP and HTML, although it is not mandatory. Also, some basic knowledge of the Java language is required to successfully navigate part VII, which describes the use of Java in wireless application development.

Contents of this book

The book consists of eleven parts.

Part I is an introduction to wireless applications. It provides a short history of the development of WAP technologies, a description of the present state of the wireless Web, and speculates on the future of wireless. Also included is a description of the different technologies that enable the wireless Web, how the wireless Web is experienced (very differently from the "regular" Internet as experienced through a PC), and the platforms and tools available for building wireless applications.

Part II provides a solid foundation in developing applications using WML. It introduces the reader to displaying text and images on the wireless device, navigating through an application, using variables, interacting with a user, and using the "extended" WML elements introduced by Phone.com (but not part of the official WML specification).

Part III introduces WMLScript, a scripting language similar to JavaScript used to make WML code more dynamic and the applications more complex. Chapters 8, 9, and 10 assume the reader is reasonably familiar with WML coding, and has at least a basic understanding of the role of JavaScript in an HTML web page. Part III is a comprehensive look at WMLScript, covering compilation units, functions, blocks, statements, operators, and pragmas.

Part IV provides the reader with an understanding of HDML and the differences between HDML and WML. In spite of the rapid obsolescence of HDML, millions of phones (especially in the U.S.) support only HDML and many existing wireless applications are written in HDML. To reach the largest audience possible, it is mandatory to consider HDML an important markup language. To maintain these applications (or effectively transition them to WML), a working understanding of HDML is necessary.

Part V introduces design principles important to wireless development. Because of the limitations of wireless devices, special care must be taken to ensure your application is usable—not just useful. Chapter 15 describes general design rules as well as common pitfalls to avoid. Chapter 16 discusses the transition of HDML applications into WML: To retain your user base, it's very important to maintain consistent navigation, look and feel, and feature set as applications are recoded in WML.

Part VI introduces the use of Microsoft Active Server Pages for creating dynamic WAP applications. In addition, database access technologies like ADO, OLEDB, and ODBC are covered. This part ends with a look at the common problems encountered by developers.

Part VII presents an alternative to creating dynamic WAP content using Java servlets and JavaServer Pages. This part assumes readers possess some basic knowledge of the

Java language, as it would take another book by itself to cover the language. Developing email applications using JavaMail in conjunction with Java servlets and JavaServer Pages is also explored. Examples are used extensively with tips to help developers avoid falling into some dark pits along the way.

Part VIII introduces the use of XML for wireless content. Chapter 29 provides a brief introduction to XML, XPath, and XSLT. It also introduces the concept of transformations, which is an important aspect of using XML for wireless content. Chapter 30 covers the technologies that enable transformations, namely XML parsers and XSLT processors and shows some examples of using the Microsoft XML parser and the Xerces XML parser. It also shows examples of using the Microsoft XSLT processor and the Xalan XSLT processor. Chapter 31 walks the reader through three complete examples of transformations from XML to HDML, WML, and VoiceXML.

Part IX discusses the use of WAP gateways in real-life deployment as well as for developmental purposes. In particular, the Nokia WAP Server and WAPlite from Infinite.com are featured. Chapter 33 shows how to configure WAP devices that are commonly available. Note that part IX is not intended to be an exhaustive reference on all the WAP gateways and devices available in the market.

Part X serves as a finale to put all the development techniques discussed in this book into two case studies, namely a mobile inventory and ordering system (chapter 34) and a mobile library system (chapter 35).

Part XI includes six appendices with references for WML elements, WMLScript Standard Libraries, HDML elements, setting up a web server to serve WAP content, HTTP/1.1 headers, and Java servlet packages.

Code conventions

A fixed-pitch font is used to denote code as well as programming terms such as elements and attributes, variables, interface names, and other identifiers.

Italics are used to denote file names and definitions.

To improve readability of code examples, a bold Courier font may sometimes be used to call out one or more lines of code. In addition, bold Courier is used to denote graphical user interface (GUI) elements, such as buttons and window names.

To distinguish the HDML code examples from WML code, HDML elements are shown in ALL CAPS.

Code annotations accompany many segments of code. For easier readability, some annotations follow the code and are marked with chronologically ordered bullets, such as ❶, for identification purposes.

Code line continuations are indented.

Source code downloads

All source code for examples presented in *Dynamic WAP Application Development* is available to purchasers of the book from the Manning web site. The URL http://www.manning.com/foo includes a link to the source code files and to the Author Online forum.

Author Online

Purchase of *Dynamic WAP Application Development* includes free access to a private web forum run by Manning Publications where you can make comments about the book, ask technical questions, and receive help from the author and from other users. To access the forum and subscribe to it, point your web browser to http://www.manning.com/foo. This page provides information on how to get on the forum once you are registered, what kind of help is available, and the rules of conduct on the forum.

Manning's commitment to our readers is to provide a venue where a meaningful dialog between individual readers and between readers and the authors can take place. It is not a commitment to any specific amount of participation on the part of the authors, whose contribution to the Author Online forum remains voluntary (and unpaid). We suggest you try asking the authors some challenging questions lest their interest stray!

The Author Online forum and the archives of previous discussions will be accessible from the publisher's web site as long as the book is in print.

about the cover illustration

The figure on the cover of *Dynamic WAP Application Development* is a "Mufti Xefe de la Religion Mahometana" or a professional jurist who interprets Mohammedan law. While the details of his national origin and place of residence are lost in historical fog, there is no doubt that we are facing a man of stature and authority. The illustration is taken from a Spanish compendium of regional dress customs first published in Madrid in 1799. The book's title page informs us:

Coleccion general de los Trages que usan actualmente todas las Nacionas del Mundo desubierto, dibujados y grabados con la mayor exactitud por R.M.V.A.R. Obra muy util y en special para los que tienen la del viajero universal

Which we loosely translate as:

General Collection of Costumes currently used in the Nations of the Known World, designed and printed with great exactitude by R.M.V.A.R. This work is very useful especially for those who hold themselves to be universal travelers.

Although nothing is known of the designers, engravers, and artists who colored this illustration by hand, the "exactitude" of their execution is evident in this drawing. The "Mufti Xefe de la Religion Mahometana" is just one of a colorful variety of figures in this collection which reminds us vividly of how distant and isolated from each other the world's towns and regions were just 200 years ago. Dress codes have changed since then and the diversity by region, so rich at the time, has faded away. It is now often hard to tell the inhabitant of one continent from another. Perhaps we have traded a cultural and visual diversity for a more varied personal life—certainly a more varied and interesting world of technology.

At a time when it can be hard to tell one computer book from another, Manning celebrates the inventiveness and initiative of the computer business with book covers based on the rich diversity of regional life of two centuries ago—brought back to life by the pictures from this collection.

PART I

Introducing wireless development

This introduction to Wireless Application Protocol development provides an overview of WAP technologies, history, and current state (and how that differs from country to country). Popular wireless applications are discussed, and thoughts are offered about the future of this rapidly evolving industry.

This section (chapters 1 and 2) offers an introduction to wireless development as well as to software development kits for building WAP applications. These sections are particularly recommended as a starting point if you are a beginner to wireless development.

C H A P T E R   1

Understanding WAP

1.1   *THE NEXT BIG THING*

Less than a decade ago, the PC-based browser introduced the Internet to the average consumer, spawning a business and communication revolution. If you believe media and technology analysts, the beginning of a *second* Internet-based business and communication revolution is underway. Certainly the numbers are impressive; today, there are more than 300 million cell phones in the world, with analysts estimating more than *one billion* users by 2003. Wireless Internet services (enabled by the Wireless Application Protocol (WAP) technologies that are the subject of this book) have the potential to touch exponentially more people than the PC-based Internet ever will. Hundreds of millions—even billions—of people worldwide without the resources or available infrastructure to use a PC can easily acquire and use a web-enabled cell phone.

The opportunity to participate in this emerging market is not lost on carriers, the companies that build and maintain wireless telephony networks. Major telecommunications network operators worldwide are investing billions of dollars toward building wireless web services for their customers. In the U.S. alone, Sprint PCS, AT&T Wireless, Nextel, and Verizon Wireless are all becoming major investors in wireless web technologies. Traditional Internet companies such as Yahoo!, AOL, Excite, Amazon.com, and countless others are also moving quickly to provide wireless access to their applications.

In spite of the media hype and significant investment, the U.S. remains far behind much of the remainder of the world in providing wireless web services. Europe and Asia (particularly Japan) are far ahead in terms of developing rich, dynamic applications available from a cell phone. Japan alone is home to over 56 million mobile phone users. Internet access through a cell phone is so popular in Japan that its largest wireless carrier, NTT DoCoMo, added one *million* subscribers within just ten weeks, and now provides wireless web services to more than 22 million users. In a single year, NTT DoCoMo built a subscriber base for wireless Internet services almost as large as the entire subscriber base of the U.S.-based Internet service provider (ISP), America Online. Applications available on DoCoMo's wireless Internet service (iMode) are so extensive, and are introduced so rapidly, that *TVGuide*-like publications are sold in train stations to help people keep up with the changes.

Not surprisingly, phone manufacturers are also scrambling to keep up with demand. Most new mobile digital phones, such as those made by Motorola, Qualcomm, Nokia, Ericsson, and the slightly larger-screen smart phones from NeoPoint, are already web-enabled. This is, one analyst observed, nothing short of another revolution—the second coming of the Internet.

Of course, we aren't there quite yet. In spite of marketing messages that promise the ability to carry the Internet in your pocket, today's web-enabled wireless devices don't offer the rich, multimedia experience that is associated with the Internet. If you have seen only the phones available in the United States, however, you might be surprised by the potential of a wireless phone. Much different than the very simple text-based phones in the U.S., some phones available in Japan offer color and rich images. If you doubt that wireless technology will ever offer an experience similar to that on a PC, see figures 1.1 and 1.2.

Sharp, color images, streaming media (both video and audio) and online games are just a few examples of services that will be available through the next generation (3G) wireless device.

Figure 1.1
Video streaming on a cell phone

These Internet-enabled cell phones, now available in Asia, provide an idea of the direction wireless technology is heading in other parts of the world.

Figure 1.2   Internet-enabled cell phones available in Japan

This book provides a guide for those interested in building content and applications that can be accessed by a wireless device. This chapter provides a context and a starting point for this development; it describes the wireless device and its limitations in addition to providing a road map for the absolute beginner.

1.1.1   The phone is different than a PC

Phones available today are not very powerful computing devices that possess limited capabilities; nevertheless, people are sometimes surprised by the phone's spartan display when they first access the wireless Web. The phone's display and processing power are too limited to deliver more than a few lines of text at a time, much less the multimedia available on a PC. Because it's difficult to enter URLs into a phone (the keypad wasn't designed for text entry), the concept of surfing the net, so central on the PC, is much less a part of the wireless Web. Browsing the Internet on a phone is very different from browsing on a PC. In fact, even the term "browsing"—ubiquitous in the PC world—is a misnomer on a phone.

To illustrate the difference between the wireless Web and the PC, consider the image of the Amazon.com home page on a PC (figure 1.3) and on a phone (figure 1.4):

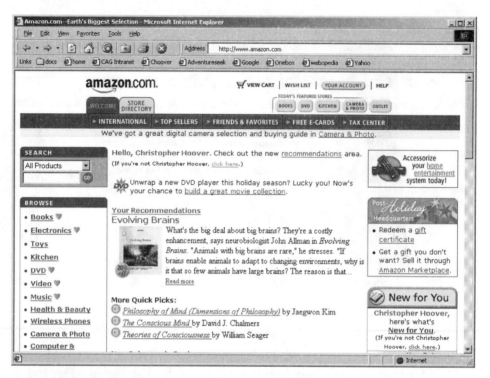

Figure 1.3   Amazon.com's home page on a PC

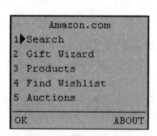

Figure 1.4   Amazon.com's home page on a phone

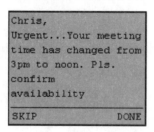

Figure 1.5   Email displayed on a phone

Compare this image to figure 1.4, the Amazon.com home page on a phone.

Make no mistake: Internet-enabled phones are not inferior to the PC, they are simply different tools that excel at different jobs. People tend to use a phone when away from their desk to access concise, specific bits of time-sensitive information (such as stock quotes or flight information). For example, if you are sitting in a taxi and don't have access to your PC, the phone can be an invaluable tool ensuring you don't miss an important email (figure 1.5).

In cases like this, the phone's display characteristics don't matter at all—what matters is that you received important information that might otherwise have been missed. Because of this, it's ridiculous to criticize a phone because it's not a PC. Besides, there are some ways that a phone is *better* than a PC.

1.1.2   The phone is better than a PC

Despite its limitations, the phone offers many unique features unavailable on a PC. Ironically it is the phone's small size—the characteristic toward which most criticism of the wireless Web is directed—that enables these features.

The phone is mobile

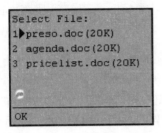

Figure 1.6   Accesssing documents via a phone

The phone goes where the user goes, and can be used to access information when a PC is unavailable. The phone's size and easy mobility make it a very useful device in myriad situations. For example, imagine that you have just arrived at an airport for an important meeting only to discover that your laptop has been damaged beyond repair. If you had an Internet-enabled phone, you could use it to access the server containing your presentation and documents (figure 1.6).

You could further use the phone to select your document and then send it as an attachment to an email address you can access via the Web at a local Internet cafe.

The phone is location-aware

The phone can provide information concerning the estimated whereabouts of a user. Because a phone's location can be estimated by measuring the strength of the phone's signal in surrounding cells, a Yellow Pages application (for example) can make use of this information by automatically delivering results appropriate to the phone's location.

The phone can deliver an alert to a user

In addition to incoming calls, specific events can cause the phone to sound an alert (a short beep, for example, or a flashing light). Alerts can be used with Internet applications to notify a user when a specific event has occurred (when an email from a particular person has been received, for example, or when a particular stock price has dropped below a certain price).

1.2   HOW THE WIRELESS WEB WORKS

Section 1.1 provided a brief description of what the wireless Web looks like on a phone; now let's move to a brief description of how information moves between the Internet and a wireless device. For the remainder of the book, it's assumed that you are familiar with how to use a PC to access the Web, and the fundamental client/server concepts behind the Internet. A comprehensive description of these concepts is beyond the scope of this book; if they are unfamiliar to you, read a beginner's introduction to the Internet.

Despite the difference in display, much of the technology enabling the wireless Web is the same as the technology that enables the PC-based Web. For instance, when you type a URL into a PC, the browser displays content that appears at the URL. On a phone, the procedure is the same: type a URL into the phone's browser and the site at the URL is retrieved and displayed on your phone. There are two important differences between using a phone and using a PC, however:

1 Just as a PC-based browser reads content that is formatted using the HyperText Markup Language (HTML), the phone reads content that is formatted with a specialized wireless markup language, typically either the Wireless Markup Language (WML) or the Handheld Device Markup Language (HDML). Which phones accept which language is discussed in more depth later in this chapter.

2 The PC-based browser communicates directly with the server hosting the requested URL; the phone does not. Because the wireless network on which the phone communicates doesn't understand the Internet (and vice versa), a special translator is needed. This translator, known as a gateway server, is placed between the phone network and the Internet. Rather than communicate directly with the Internet, the phone communicates with the gateway server. In turn, the gateway server sends a request to the URL on the phone's behalf. Upon receiving the content stored at the URL, the gateway server translates the information into a format the phone can understand and sends it back to the phone.

In a nutshell, the wireless Web is identical to the TCP/IP-based Web, with an extra step—the gateway server. Because a wireless network and the Internet use different protocols for communication, they require a translator to communicate with one another. A gateway server is software that sits between the wireless network and the Internet, translating from one to the other (among other things). The gateway server manages the complex interplay of protocols that deliver information from a TCP/IP network to a wireless phone.

Figure 1.7 illustrates these concepts.

Perhaps one day phones will be developed that are able to directly communicate with the net, but until then a gateway server is the door through which all information destined for a wireless device must pass.

NOTE   The gateway server was developed to hide the complexities of the wireless network from the developer. Most developers will build their applications, deploy them to a web server, and access them on a simulator or physical device—with no thought given to the gateway server at all.

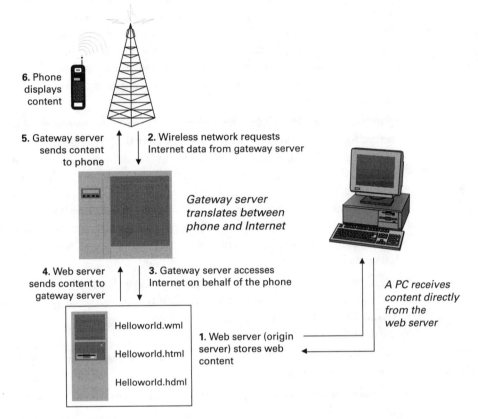

A WAP session

WAP uses a WAP gateway server to intermediate between the Internet and the wireless network.

6. Phone displays content

5. Gateway server sends content to phone

2. Wireless network requests Internet data from gateway server

Gateway server translates between phone and Internet

4. Web server sends content to gateway server

3. Gateway server accesses Internet on behalf of the phone

A PC receives content directly from the web server

Helloworld.wml

Helloworld.html

Helloworld.hdml

1. Web server (origin server) stores web content

Figure 1.7   How a WAP session works

Step-by-step through the wireless Web

Step by step, here is what is happening in figure 1.7.

1   *Origin server*—The WAP document (either HDML or WML) is stored in an *origin server*. Origin servers are conventional web servers—the same servers that contain HTML documents (Netscape Enterprise Server is an example of an origin server). This server may contain static WAP documents (that is, documents that have been developed in WML or HDML and then saved to the server) that are served to a client without any server-side manipulation.

In addition, server technologies can be used to generate WAP documents on the fly—a dynamic WAP application. Microsoft Active Server Pages (ASP) and

Java servlets are two popular server-side technologies that enable a developer to do this. We will see how we can develop dynamic WAP applications using these two technologies in later chapters.

2 *Document request*—To access the Internet, the phone uses the same technology that transmits your voice wirelessly to another phone. Put simply, the phone makes a phone call to an ISP exactly as your PC modem does. There is a difference between calling an ISP over a traditional wireline phone and calling an ISP through a wireless phone: Over the years, the wireless industry has developed a number of incompatible technologies to transmit data, requiring the use of a special WAP gateway server to translate between a particular network technology and the Internet.

3 *Document retrieval*—Once the call is established, the phone asks the gateway server to retrieve a document from a specified URL (the phone uses exactly the same kind of URLs that a PC uses—it sends a request to (for example) http://www.mydomain.com). The WAP gateway, connected directly to the Web using the HTTP protocol, surfs to the specified URL and retrieves the appropriate document from a web server. WAP files are stored on the web server just as any other files are—a WML application, for example, would appear on a web server as MyApp.wml. Similarly, an HDML application would appear on the server as MyApp.hdml.

4 *WAP binary translation*—Once the gateway server has retrieved the file from the web server, the file is translated into WAP binary, a special type of code that a phone can understand (remember, the phone's "language" is different from that used by the Internet).

5 *WAP binary is sent*—If no errors are found, the gateway server sends the WAP binary code to the phone.

6 *Document display*—The phone *parses* (that is, it interprets) the WAP binary and displays the information on the phone.

In brief, then, the phone and the PC access content in the same way—by using a URL to find content on a web server and displaying the content in a browser. In fact, HTML content meant for a PC and WML or HDML content meant for a phone can be stored side by side on the same web server. The server doesn't care if the requesting device is a phone, a PC, or anything else. If you are unsure how to save your content onto a web server, don't worry—we'll explore how a WAP application is created, stored, and served in section 1.4.

1.3 THE WIRELESS APPLICATION PROTOCOL

So far, we've briefly described what the wireless Web looks like from a user's point of view, and we've provided a simplified overview of what's happening behind the scenes. This section takes a closer look at the technologies involved in the transfer of information between a phone and a web server. Collectively, these technologies are referred to as the Wireless Application Protocol, or WAP.

WAP and gateway servers exist because the "language" spoken within the wireless telephony network is different from that spoken by the Internet (that is, the wireless protocols are different from the TCP/IP protocols). In the very early stages of the wireless Web, this communication problem had been addressed by many different (and incompatible) methods; different companies had different proprietary solutions and there was no solution that was clearly better than any other. Potential customers of wireless technology were confused, and demanded a single standard solution.

With the introduction of WAP, this single standard was agreed upon. Founded in 1997 by Motorola, Nokia, Ericsson, and Phone.com (and today made up of over 200 members), the WAP forum was created to unify the myriad proprietary mobile Internet solutions then offered, standardizing the technologies that enable Internet access through mobile phones.

The primary goal of the WAP forum is to bring together companies from all segments of the wireless industry to ensure product interoperability. Without a central body such as the WAP forum, there is a danger that different companies will develop different standards for their products, making application development very difficult. If different brands of cellular phones handled information differently, an application would have to be rewritten to accommodate different phones. This goal has yet to be reached—markup languages other than WML are widely used (including HDML, an obsolete language still in broad use in the United States and described in part IV of this book).

Though many people use WAP interchangeably with WML, the markup language used on the phone, WAP is not a single protocol or specification, but a suite of specifications that together define how data interacts with a phone. These specifications (as defined in the WAP 1.1 specification suite) are summarized in table 1.1.

Table 1.1 Specifications of WAP

Specification	Description
Wireless Application Environment (WAE)	The overall application environment
Wireless Markup Language (WML)	Used to design the user interface on the phone *Described in part II of this book*
Binary XML Content Format	A compression scheme used to encode WML
WMLScript	A scripting language, similar to JavaScript, that enables developers to add logical processes to their WML applications *Described in part III of this book*
WMLScript Standard Libraries	The WMLScript function libraries supported by all WMLScript-enabled browsers *Described in part III of this book, and detailed in appendix B*

Table 1.1   Specifications of WAP (continued)

Specification	Description
WAP Caching Model	The memory cache model used by the browser
Wireless Session Protocol (WSP)	The binary WAP equivalent of HTTP
Wireless Transaction Protocol (WTP)	A protocol that manages individual request-response transactions
Wireless Datagram Protocol (WDP)	A common interface to wireless services
WAP over GSM USSD	Specifies how WAP maps onto USSD, a transport service used in GSM, a digital wireless system
Wireless Control Message Protocol (WCMP)	Used for error tracking over networks that don't support the Internet Control Message Protocol, a message control and error-reporting protocol between a host server and a gateway to the Internet
Wireless Transport Layer Security (WTLS)	The wireless analogue to SSL, the Internet protocol that enables authentication and encryption
Wireless Telephony Application (WTA)	A specification that will allow the integration of calls within WML applications *Integrating calls is described in part II of this book*
Wireless Telephony Application Interface (WTAI)	A specification that will allow the integration of telephony functions, including the address book and call logs, with WMLScript

Again, most of these technologies were developed to hide complexity from developers. For example, you need not worry about WAP-defined Wireless Datagram Protocols, or Wireless Control Message Protocol. Suffice to say that they are working behind the scenes to make wireless Internet access possible.

1.3.1   Why wireless requires new technology

WAP was developed to standardize the protocols used for wireless Internet access, but why was the new protocol set built from the ground up, instead of using the existing set of Internet protocols (HTTP/TCP/IP)? The most important consideration was the limited amount of information a wireless network is able to transfer (wireless networks have limited bandwidth); WAP was designed to minimize bandwidth use. Figures 1.8 and 1.9 compare a "typical" session first using Internet protocols (figure 1.8), and then using WAP protocols.

The same session over WAP protocols (figure 1.9) uses significantly less bandwidth.

WAP is optimized for the bandwidth and device limitations inherent to a wireless network; it can be more efficient than HTTP/TCP because it can integrate many network communications into one.

HTTP/TCP/IP

A typical session, with three requests and three responses. **Bold** items indicate payload. Nonbold items indicate overhead.

User PC

This session consists of 17 packets with 65% overhead (not accounting for DNS, SSL, authentication, or cookies).

1. TCP SYN
→

2. TCP SYN, ACK of SYN
→

3. ACK of SYN, **Data Request**
→

4. Acknowledgement of Request
←

5. **Reply**
←

6. Acknowledgement of Reply
→

7. **Data Request**
→

8. Acknowledgement of Request
←

9. **Reply**
←

10. Acknowledgement of Reply
→

11. **Data Request**
→

12. Acknowledgement of Request
←

13. **Reply**
←

14. Acknowledgement of Reply
→

15. TCP FIN
→

16. TCP FIN, ACK of FIN
→

17. Acknowledgement of FIN
→

Internet Web Server

Figure 1.8   Using Internet protocols

WAT/WTP/UDP

A typical session with three requests and three responses. **Bold** items indicate payload. Nonbold items indicate overhead. *This session consists of 7 packets and 14% overhead.*

WAP Device

1. **Data Request**
→

2. Acknowledgement, **Reply**
←

3. Acknowledgement, **Data Request**
→

4. Acknowledgement, **Reply**
←

5. Acknowledgement, **Data Request**
→

6. Acknowledgement, **Reply**
←

7. Acknowledgement
→

WAP Gateway Server

Figure 1.9   A session using WAP protocols

1.3.2 Common WAP terms

Table 1.2 lists terms that are frequently used within the WAP industry and this book.

Table 1.2   WAP terms and definitions

Term	Definition
Gateway server	The Gateway server stands between the wireless network and the Internet, enabling communication between them.
HDML	The Handheld Device Markup Language was the first markup language developed for the wireless phone. In spite of obsolescence, HDML remains a factor in application development, particularly in the United States.
SDK	A Software Development Kit contains a variety of tools that facilitate the development of applications. Different SDKs are available for different types of applications.
Simulator (or Emulator)	A phone simulator is part of most wireless SDKs. Phone simulators run on a PC and enable a developer to test an application.
SMS	The Short Messaging Service enables transmission of very short messages (up to 160 alphanumeric characters) to a phone.
URL	The Uniform Resource Locator defines the location of a file on the Internet. http://www.manning.com is an example of a URL.
WAP	The Wireless Application Protocol is a set of specifications that enable Internet access on wireless phones.
WAP browser	The software within a WAP device that parses (interprets) input from a gateway server and displays it to the user. The browser also accepts input from a user and delivers it to the server.
WAP device	The hardware that enables wireless access to the Internet. The WAP device most frequently referred to within this book is the mobile phone.
WAP client	Often used interchangeably with "WAP browser," the client refers to the code within the phone that receives information from a server and displays it to the user. The client is also responsible for gathering any user input and delivering it to the server.
WML	The Wireless Markup Language is the markup language specified by the WAP forum. It has succeeded HDML as the preferred markup language for wireless phones.
WMLScript	WMLScript is a scripting language that enables simple client-side logic within a WML application. Based on ECMAScript, it is optimized for a mobile environment.

1.4 *UNDERSTANDING WIRELESS APPLICATIONS*

So far we've briefly looked at what the wireless Web looks like and how it works; the next sections describe how users interact with content delivered through a phone, and the markup languages that are used to define the content.

1.4.1 The card and deck paradigm

Because the phone's display is very small, only a limited amount of information can be displayed at one time. The user is required to react to that display (for example, by pressing "OK" to indicate the display has been read), after which the phone displays another small piece of information. What the phone is showing a user at any given time is referred to as a *card*, the basic level of interaction between a user and a phone (figure 1.10). Several cards can be defined within a single WML file, and that file, with all its cards, is referred to as a *deck*.

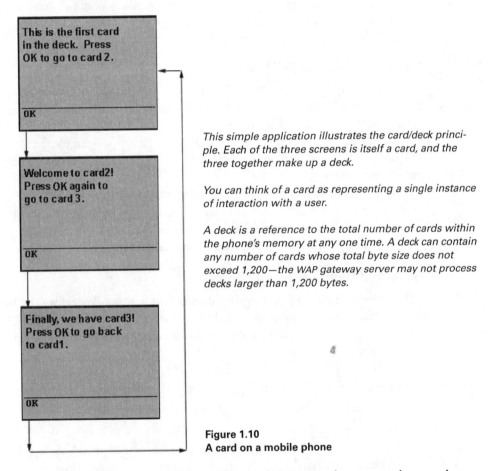

This simple application illustrates the card/deck principle. Each of the three screens is itself a card, and the three together make up a deck.

You can think of a card as representing a single instance of interaction with a user.

A deck is a reference to the total number of cards within the phone's memory at any one time. A deck can contain any number of cards whose total byte size does not exceed 1,200—the WAP gateway server may not process decks larger than 1,200 bytes.

Figure 1.10
A card on a mobile phone

Just as a card is the fundamental unit of interaction between a phone and a user, a deck is the fundamental unit of interaction between a phone and a server. A deck is the smallest unit of WML that can be transmitted to a phone; when a user directs the phone to a particular URL, the phone receives the deck defined by the URL and displays the first card defined by the deck.

Note that an entire application is not (usually) contained within a single deck. The card and deck metaphor is most important as a semantic device, useful when talking or thinking about application development. In fact, although nothing in WML syntax restricts the number of cards you place within a deck, you should plan on developing multiple decks because a phone's limited memory can only contain a small quantity of information at one time.

To ensure a phone isn't overwhelmed with data, the server will not transmit a *compiled* WML deck larger than 1,492 bytes to phones (encountering a larger deck will cause the server to generate an error). Because compiling a deck may increase file size slightly, you should keep the size of all decks smaller than 1,200 bytes to absolutely ensure your file won't overrun the size threshold.

1.4.2   Mobile markup languages

Content displayed on a phone's browser is written in a markup language, exactly as content displayed by a PC-based browser is written in a markup language called HTML. Although the goal of the WAP forum is to standardize all wireless technologies (which includes defining a single universal markup language), the technology is still being developed and many different markup languages designed for wireless phones exist today.

The first markup language developed for the phone (HDML) is obsolete, but still in wide use today within the United States. Much more prevalent worldwide is WML, defined by the WAP forum. Other languages in use include cHTML, or "compact" HTML, used by iMode, the most successful wireless web service in the world.

Handheld Device Markup Language

HDML was the first markup language developed for a mobile device. The first development effort for a microbrowser used a new markup language because HTML didn't have the capacity to manage phone-specific services, such as invoking a phone call, for example.

Although HDML is fast becoming obsolete, you may want to learn it because:

- Millions of phones with browsers that support only HDML have been sold in the U.S., and they remain in circulation. Developing in WML only limits your potential audience.

- Many existing wireless applications available within the U.S. are built using HDML. A knowledge of HDML will smooth the process of transitioning these applications to WML.

Browsers that support only HDML remain very widespread, particularly in the United States and (to a lesser extent) Japan. Millions and *millions* of phones in these countries contain browsers that accept *only* HDML, so it's a good bet that (in the U.S. and Japanese markets, at least) HDML is going to remain a usable skill for some years to come.

It might help to think of the wireless Web today as at a stage similar to the PC-based Web in 1995 or 1996. At that time many sites included a caveat that indicated "This site best viewed with Netscape version 3.0 or above" (or something similar). Because browser technology was moving very quickly, different users had different versions of a browser on their PC—just as many different phones in use today contain different versions of the microbrowser. Of course, phone users today don't have the option of upgrading their browser; they must buy a new phone. Because of this, the paradigm has shifted—instead of requiring the user to upgrade, the onus is on the developer to write applications that support all phones (or consciously exclude some users from accessing the application).

Wireless Markup Language

WML was developed by the WAP forum as a more robust, standards-based, and full-featured successor to HDML. WML is based on the XML standard, that is, WML is a markup language that is designed around a set of guidelines described collectively as XML. Many think that XML-based markup languages are the Next Big Thing in client-side Web development, and all indications show that those people are probably right. If you are interested in more information on XML and the languages that are based on it, a good place to start is the web site at http://www.xml.com.

Other languages

What will remain when both HDML and WML have gone the way of the Commodore 64 computer? Today, the most common bet is that the XML version of HTML (not HDML) known as xHTML will be used. Another possibility is that cHTML (or compact HTML) will become the de facto wireless markup language. cHTML has already enjoyed amazing success in Japan, where it is used in NTT DoCoMo's iMode service. Technology moves very quickly and in unpredictable ways, so the future of wireless markup is anyone's guess. (xHTML isn't a topic in this book, but the curious can learn more about it from http://www.w3.org/TR/xhtml1/, and more about XML in general from http://www.xml.com/.)

1.5 YOUR DEVELOPMENT TARGET: THE MOBILE PHONE

Earlier sections described the technologies that enabled the phone to access information from the Internet, as well as the markup languages that are used to build the content for display on the phone's browser. This section looks at the wireless device itself: the mobile phone.

Other than a cell phone, there are other wireless devices that can access the Internet, such as the Palm Personal Digital Assistant (PDA), the Blackberry pager, and myriad "palmtop" PCs. This book focuses on application development for a wireless phone, however, for two reasons:

- A standard development environment. A WAP application is accessible by any Internet-enabled cell phone. There is no such standard for other devices, however; the Palm and the Blueberry use different application protocols.

- The ubiquity of phones. It's more profitable to develop for phones because there are more cell phone users. For example, Sprint (the third largest wireless carrier in the United States) boasts a subscriber base of some 50 million users. The entire user base of the Palm PDA is less than 5 million. In addition, it is more likely that phone technology will be used outside the U.S. (particularly in less developed countries) than PDAs or palmtop PCs.

1.5.1   WAP development challenges

Mobile phones represent the ultimate constrained computing device. With their limited CPU processing power, tiny amount of memory, short battery life, and restricted user interface, phones are challenging platforms on which to develop useful applications. The phone itself isn't the only challenge; wireless networks are constrained by low bandwidth, high latency, and unpredictable availability and stability. Let's examine some of the development challenges you face as a WAP developer:

Limited bandwidth

A data call from a cell phone can have bandwidth as low as 9,600 bps. This is an important consideration when designing your application; whenever possible, it's important to minimize the number of network round-trips the application requires.

Limited memory and processing power

Your applications must be very lean to perform well on a phone. In fact, they have to be lean to perform on a phone at all—the phone will only compile files smaller than ~1,500 bytes at a time.

Small display

For your application to be usable on the phone, you must design it with the display limitations of the phone in mind. The phone's display size varies from model to model, but keep in mind that although an application that works on a small display will also look fine on a larger display, *the reverse is not true*. To ensure your application is usable by the largest number of people, design your application to work well in a default display size of four lines containing 12 characters each (figure 1.11).

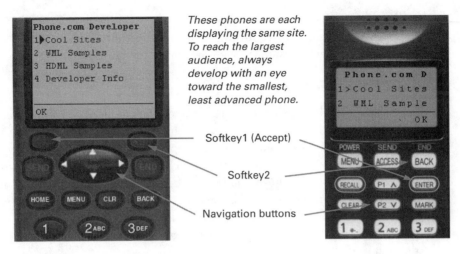

These phones are each displaying the same site. To reach the largest audience, always develop with an eye toward the smallest, least advanced phone.

Softkey1 (Accept)

Softkey2

Navigation buttons

Figure 1.11   A display on a wireless phone

1.5.2   The phone user interface

Entering text on a phone is difficult! The keypad is small, it's awkward to manipulate, and it requires the multiple key presses to cycle to the appropriate letter (for example, a user must press "7" four times to cycle to the letter "s," a difficult task if you are trying to enter "sassafras!" into the phone!

On most web-enabled phones, there are two buttons that are important to highlight: Softkey1 (also known as the Accept button) and Softkey2. Most phones, including the phone on the left in figure 1.11, have these two buttons immediately below the display, and provide an area in the display for labels (the Softkeys are labeled OK and BACK in the image). As the phone on the right in figure 1.11 demonstrates, button positioning is not standardized across phones; just as you should not plan on a particular display size, you should not plan on a particular button layout.

Softkey1

You can think of Softkey1 (figure 1.12) as akin to the Enter key on a computer keyboard—it's what you press when you want to tell the phone "okay, now do something!"

Softkey1 (ACCEPT)   Softkey2

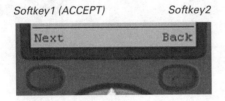

These two buttons are the user's primary interface with the phone. Softkey 1, usually referred to as the Accept button, is the most commonly used button, and typically appears on the left side of the display.

Figure 1.12   The softkeys

Softkey 2

Softkey2 is typically used to invoke secondary functions, such as calling a menu of options, or surfing backward through previously viewed pages.

1.6 GETTING STARTED

If you are a complete beginner to wireless development, don't be intimidated if at this point you feel you have been deluged with information. The concepts will come together once you start building your first applications; and you'll be happy to know that getting started is quite easy. In the next chapter you'll find a discussion of the various SDKs available to help you build wireless applications. For now, you can think of an SDK as a phone simulator that operates on your computer desktop (with some SDKs, that's the literal truth). By downloading and running an SDK on your computer, you'll be able to develop your applications, save them locally, and test them through the SDK simulator.

For example, a very simple application is code that displays Hello World! on the phone. First, you can write the code in any text editor, such as the notepad that appears on a Windows machine. In figure 1.13, the Hello World! code has been written in the Windows notepad, saved to the d: drive as d:/hello.wml, and loaded onto

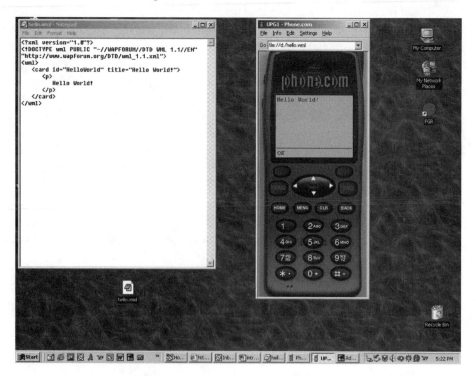

Figure 1.13   Hello World! on a Windows notepad

the phone simulator (part of the Phone.com SDK, described in the next chapter) using the URL file://d:hello.wml. Looks easy, doesn't it? It is.

If you wanted to save your code onto a web server so that it can be accessed over the Internet, simply FTP it to the server instead of saving it to your local machine. If you aren't familiar with file transfer protocol and are unsure how to place files on a web server, the easiest place to begin is with one of the many free hosting services available. A popular hosting service is called Geocities, available for free through Yahoo!. You can check out Geocities at http://geocities.yahoo.com (before you can use the service, it requires that you register with Yahoo!). After registering, you can upload your wireless code onto the host's servers (in this case, Yahoo!'s servers) and access it from any phone browser. See the hosting site for detailed instructions about how this is done.

Once you've uploaded the hello.wml file to the server, you can access it by typing its URL into the phone simulator (or a real phone, for that matter). For example, if you have registered for Yahoo!'s Geocities service as user "Johndoe," the URL for hello.wml might be http://www.geocities.com/johndoe/hello.wml.

1.7 SUMMARY

You should now have a general feel for the components of wireless development: the technology, the markup languages, and the device itself. There exists an enormous potential for mobile applications to touch even remote parts of the world; because web-enabled cell phones are much more ubiquitous worldwide than PCs, the mobile Internet is poised to truly revolutionize how information is exchanged.

The WAP specification is a set of protocols that define how to enable a mobile phone to access the Internet. WAP hides much of the complexity of mobile-enabling the Web, but developers must remain aware of the limitations of their design space: A mobile phone offers limited bandwidth, limited memory, a limited display, and an awkward interface.

The markup languages described in this book are WML, a language developed by the WAP forum and based on XML; and HDML, the first markup language developed for the mobile phone. Both languages use a card and deck paradigm to enable users to access the Internet, and good arguments exist for learning both (even though HDML is rapidly becoming obsolete).

The next chapter begins our discussion of wireless application development with a look at a tool necessary for building WML and/or HDML-based applications: an SDK typically available as a free download from a variety of vendors.

CHAPTER 2

WAP application development platforms

2.1 INTRODUCTION

Before we embark on the exciting adventure of coding for wireless devices, we will first take a look at the tools that can help us jump on the WAP bandwagon without investing too much on resources.

A WAP application development platform contains a suite of tools to aid in your development process. In this chapter, we will focus on the use of emulators that run on the Microsoft Windows operating system to develop WAP applications.

Table 2.1 summarizes the tools that make up a WAP development platform.

Table 2.1   WAP tools

WAP tool	Description
SDK	The SDK contains tools such as, emulators, WML, and WMLScript compilers and editors.
Emulator	Most SDKs contain emulators for you to test the look and feel of your application.
Web server	Web server is essential for applications that use server-side scripts such as, ASP and Java servlets. Appendix D details web server setup.
Text editor or other IDE	The WML text editors aid the developer in creating WML content.
WAP gateway	WAP gateway is optional for WAP development. Chapter 32 covers WAP gateways in more detail.
Mobile phone	Real devices are needed to test your application before deployment. Chapter 33 covers configuration issues for the various devices.

The main steps involved in WAP application development are:

- Developing the WAP application using the tools available. The minimum tool that you need is a text editor.
- Testing the application using available emulators. At this stage, it is rare that you test your application using a real device. Emulators provide an easy and fast tool for debugging your application.
- Deploying an application by uploading the source into a live web server.
- A second round of testing is conducted to ensure that the application runs correctly under real-time condition. In this stage, testing is done using real devices and a WAP gateway (optional).

In this chapter, we will explore two free SDKs. The Phone.com UP.SDK and the Nokia WAP Toolkit come with useful tools that will help you create and test your wireless applications before you deploy them on real devices.

2.2   *WORKING WITH EMULATORS*

Most WAP SDKs contain emulators for testing the look and feel of your application. These emulators resemble the real devices and provide an accurate rendering of the WML decks. Some of the emulated devices are:

- Nokia 7110
- Ericsson R320
- Ericsson R380
- Devices running the Phone.com's microbrowser

Emulators provide a good platform for developing and testing your application because they run directly on the PC and most work without the need for a WAP gateway. Contrast this to using a real device for development—the constant need to connect to a WAP gateway, and using the tiny keypads on a real device is not something fun to do. Emulators get you up to speed quickly.

However, emulators have their limitations. They do not provide the capability to reflect the usability of an application. For instance, text input using emulators is normally done via the keyboard, which is simple to use. In the real world however, the user has to perform input via the tiny keys. An application designed only with emulators in mind is going to fail in the usability testing stage.

The easiest way to test a WAP application is to load the application in an emulator. Although support for HDML is limited, all of the following emulator products support WML:

- UP.Simulator—comes as Phone.com's UP.SDK
- Nokia WAP Toolkit
- Ericsson WapIDE
- Motorola's Mobile Application Development Kit (MADK)

In this chapter, we will cover the use of the emulators that come with UP.SDK 4.0 and Nokia WAP Toolkit 2.0. The majority of the examples in this book will use the UP.Simulator for illustration. Other emulators will be used where there are specific differences in the display.

2.3   UP.SDK

The UP.SDK for Windows is available for free from Phone.com's web site. However, before you download the SDK, you must register for a free developer's account, something we strongly recommend that you do.

UP.SDK 4.0 supports both HDML and WML.

The UP.SDK package contains four components (table 2.2):

Table 2.2   UP.Simulator components

Component	Description
UP.Simulator	Device emulator
Developer documentation	Contains the WML and WMLScript references
Source code of example applications	Sample WAP applications
UP.Link notification library and tools	Tools for sending push messages, and so forth

2.3.1   About UP.Simulator

One of the most robust and easy-to-use emulators is the UP.Simulator, which uses the Phone.com microbrowser, UP.Browser. UP.Browser is also used in many web-enabled mobile devices:

- Ericsson R280
- Nokia 6185
- Motorola Accompli 6188, Talkabout V2288, and Timeport P7389
- Siemens SL-45, S35, C35, and M35
- Sanyo C304A, D301SA, SCP-4000, and TS01

For an updated list of phones that use UP.Browser, point your web browser to http://developer.phone.com/dev/ts/up/phones.html.

2.3.2   Obtaining and installing UP.SDK

The UP.SDK software can be obtained from Phone.com's web site at http://www.phone.com. The downloaded installation file for this version is upsdkW40e.exe.

Installing UP.SDK

Double-click the installation file and work your way through the few simple steps to complete the installation procedure. After installation, you have access to a wealth of information related to WAP. The default directory that contains all the documents and development kit programs is C:\Program Files\Phone.com\Upsdk40.

Starting UP.Simulator

To launch the UP.Simulator (figure 2.1), click the Start button on the task bar and select Programs ⇒ UP.SDK 4.0 ⇒ UP.Simulator.

The emulator consists of two parts:

- A phone browser
- A Phone Information window

The phone browser

The phone browser window displays the simulated phone interface for many different phones. The default phone interface in figure 2.1 is generic. That is, there is no such device in existence. To emulate real device behavior, you can change the "skin" to emulate an actual phone.

For example, you might want to emulate an Alcatel phone (which uses the UP.Browser). To do so, simply click on the File menu and choose the option, Open Configuration. You should see a dialog box with a list of available "skins." Highlight the "skin" for the Alcatel phone, ALAV.pho, and click the Open button (figure 2.2).

Figure 2.1   UP.Simulator windows

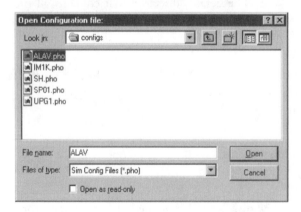

Figure 2.2
Selecting a skin from the Open
Configuration file dialog box

You should see your phone emulator wrapped in a new "skin" (figure 2.3).

You may download the latest "skins" released by Phone.com at http://developer.phone.com/dev/ts/.

Phone Information window

The second component of the emulator is the Phone Information window, which displays what goes on behind the scenes. Consider it your survival kit as it provides very useful hints when you debug your applications. We will take a closer look at it later in this chapter. When we discuss the loading of a WML deck, or dynamic WML content generated using ASP or Java servlets, in later chapters, we will highlight the use of the Phone Information window.

Figure 2.3
The skin for Alcatel handset

2.3.3 Creating and viewing a wireless application

The UP.Simulator (or the UP.SDK, for that matter) does not provide a graphical user interface (GUI) for you to write the source code of your WAP application. If you expect a GUI development environment, like Visual Basic, you are in for disappointment. In developing WAP applications, use your favorite editor to enter the HDML, WML, and WMLScript code. Then, using the emulator, you can test and debug your applications.

Hello world example

Let's try a simple example:

```
<?xml version="1.0"?>
<!DOCTYPE wml PUBLIC "-//WAPFORUM//DTD WML 1.1//EN"
"http://www.wapforum.org/DTD/wml_1.1.xml">
<wml>
    <card id="card1" title="Welcome">
      <p>
         Welcome to the WAP WAP world!!!
      </p>
    </card>
</wml>
```

WML   Let's not be unduly worried about the syntax of the WML code in the example. In part II, we will look into WML in greater detail.

If you save the WML code in a Hello.wml file under the root directory of the local C: drive, enter the following into the Go box (figure 2.4) of the Phone browser:

file://c:/Hello.wml

Figure 2.4
Entering the location of a WML file

If you map the directory containing Hello.wml to a virtual directory, say mydir, accessible by the origin web server sitting on the same host machine as the UP.Simulator, you can also load the document by entering its URL (figure 2.5).

Figure 2.5
Entering the URL of a WML file

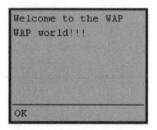

Figure 2.6   The WML deck loaded successfully on the UP.Simulator

For static WAP content, you can use the first method to load your WML deck. The second method is more useful for dynamic WAP content where you use a server-side script like ASP to generate your WML deck. Server-side scripting requires the execution of the web server, hence you need to use the URL to load the deck.

In both cases, you should see the WML deck (Hello.wml) loaded.

Figure 2.6 shows a WML deck loaded on the UP.Browser.

For more information about setting up a web server and creating virtual directories, see appendix D.

Using the Phone Information window

Let's examine the Phone Information window (figure 2.7).

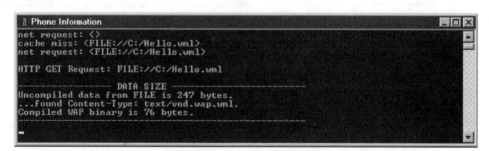

Figure 2.7   The Phone Information window comes with the UP.Simulator

You should notice the following trailing lines:

```
cache miss: <FILE://c:/Hello.wml/>
net request: <FILE://c:/Hello.wml/>

HTTP GET Request: FILE://c:/Hello.wml

-------------- DATA SIZE ---------------
Uncompiled data from FILE is 247 bytes.
...found Content-Type: text/vnd.wap.wml.
Compiled WAP binary is 76 bytes.
----------------------------------------
```

Indicates that the UP.Simulator has just retrieved the WML document, Hello.wml

The size of the uncompiled file is 247 bytes

After compiling the WML document into the WAP bytecode, the size becomes 76 bytes. The bytecode excludes the extra white spaces and user comments

GATEWAY   The UP.Simulator functions both as a WAP browser and a gateway. Chapter 32 discusses WAP gateways and their functionality in detail; compiling a WML document is part of this functionality.

Viewing error messages

Let's be a little adventurous here and create an error in the WML deck:

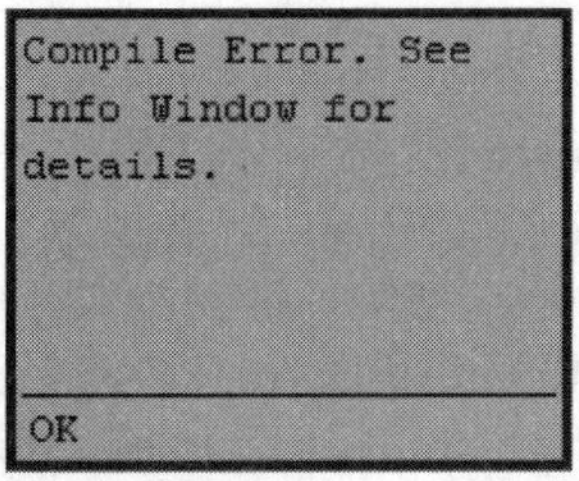

```
Compile Error. See
Info Window for
details.



OK
```

Figure 2.8
An error message

```
<?xml version="1.0"?>
<!DOCTYPE wml PUBLIC "-//WAPFORUM//DTD WML
1.1//EN"
"http://www.wapforum.org/DTD/wml_1.1.xml">
<wml>
    <card id="card1" title="Welcome">
        <p>
            Welcome to the WAP WAP world!!!
        <p>  <!-- the p element is not closed
properly! -->
    </card>
</wml>
```

If you load the file now, a message (figure 2.8) appears in the emulator.

To solve the mystery of the error, let's look at the Phone Information window for clues:

```
======================= WML Errors =====================
WML translation failed.
(7) : error: Invalid element 'p' in content of 'p'. Expected PCDATA | em |
strong | b | i | u | big | small | br | img | anchor | a | table | input |
select | fieldset | do
(8) : error: Close tag 'card' does not match start tag 'p'
(9) : error: Close tag 'wml' does not match start tag 'p'
(10) : error: Expected the end tag 'card' instead of end of file


======================= End Errors =====================
```

The error message rightly points out that the error occurs in line 7.

2.3.4 Debugging your application

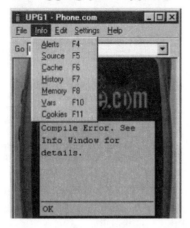

Figure 2.9 Information types for debugging

The Phone Information window provides valuable information for tracing bugs. Besides direct error messages such as the one illustrated in our example, it can display other information such as the content in the memory, the cache, the variables in the application's context, and cookies to help trace more subtle logic errors. To view the types of information that you can choose to display in the Phone Information window, click the Info menu of the UP.Simulator. Do not worry about what each item in the list does. We will explain their functions whenever we make use of them as we walk through examples in the later chapters.

During the testing phase, each time a new document is loaded, we can request a display of the appropriate types of information (figure 2.9) to help us step through the flow of the application logic to verify or trace any suspected error.

2.3.5 Reloading a document in the UP.Simulator

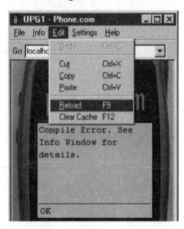

Figure 2.10 The Reload option

When a document that you loaded contains an error, you can invoke your editor to modify the document without exiting the UP.Simulator.

To test the modified document, you must perform an explicit reloading action (figure 2.10) by clicking the Edit menu and invoking the Reload option, or simply by pressing the F9 function key.

2.3.6 Configuring the UP.Simulator

You can configure the UP.Simulator to either talk directly to the HTTP network (HTTP Direct) or through a WAP gateway. The default connection mode is HTTP Direct. In this mode, the emulator will act as both a client and a WAP gateway. In particular, it can receive WML and WMLScript content and compile them into their binary equivalent. This option is useful for development purposes where access to a

WAP gateway is limited. The second option is to configure the emulator to communicate with a real WAP gateway. By doing so, gateway-specific functionality (e.g., cookies support, etc.) can be tested. This option is useful if access to a real WAP gateway is possible and for testing prior to deployment.

To configure the UP.Simulator, click the Settings menu and choose the UP.Link Settings option (figure 2.11).

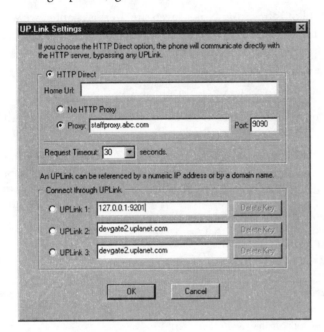

Figure 2.11
UP.Link settings

HTTP Direct connection

To talk directly to the HTTP network, select HTTP Direct. If you are behind a firewall, be sure to supply the Proxy server name and the port number so that you can load WAP applications through the Internet.

UP.Link connection

If you are connecting through a WAP gateway, select one of the three gateways available (UPLink 1, UPLink 2, UPLink 3). For example, if you are connecting to a WAP gateway listening at port 9201 on the same machine as the UP.Simulator, you can specify 127.0.0.1:9201 as shown in figure 2.11 and check the UPLink 1 option.

Chapter 32 will further discuss two specific gateways and how you can connect the UP.Simulator to them.

UP.LINK   *UP.Link* is a WAP gateway from Phone.com. The UP product family of Phone.com consists of the UP.Browser microbrowser, the UP.Link server suite, and the UP.SDK.

The UP.SDK is one of the easiest to use emulators for developing WAP applications. The installation process is also straightforward and requires no other software support like the Java Developer's Kit (JDK). We strongly recommend it to beginners in WAP development.

2.4 NOKIA WAP TOOLKIT

The Nokia WAP Toolkit is free from Nokia's web site. In this chapter, we will describe the important features of the Nokia WAP Toolkit based on version 2.0.

The notable improvements in version 2.0 from version 1.3 are:

- Support for WAP 1.2 Push messages

- Emulation for the 7110 and a WAP 1.2 Blueprint phone

- Inclusion of four editors: WML deck editor, WMLScript editor, Push Message editor, and the WBMP graphics editor

- Inclusion of a WAP gateway that is needed for 7110 emulation (the previous release of the WAP toolkit contains the 7110 emulation that is buggy and requires a separate WAP gateway)

Table 2.3 shows all of the available components.

Table 2.3   Nokia WAP Toolkit components

Component	Description
Developer documentation	Includes the Designer's Guide, Developer's Guide, and the User's Guide
Source code of example applications	Sample codes
Development tools	Push Message, WML, WMLScript, and graphics editors
Phone simulations: Blueprint Phone and 7110 Phone	The emulators for Nokia phones
WAP server simulator	A WAP gateway

2.4.1   Obtaining and installing the Nokia WAP Toolkit

To download the Nokia WAP Toolkit 2.0, point your web browser to http://www.forum.nokia.com/.

The downloaded installation file for this version is a compressed file: NokiaToolkit2_0.zip.

Installing the Nokia WAP Toolkit

Before installing the Nokia WAP Toolkit, you must first install the Java Runtime Environment (JRE) 1.2.2 or later. You can obtain it from the Sun Microsystems, Inc., web site at http://www.javasoft.com/products/jdk/1.2/jre/index.html.

When the JRE is installed, double-click on the installation file for Nokia WAP Toolkit—it should be as straightforward as installing the UP.Simulator. The default directory that houses all the documents and toolkit programs is C:\Program Files\Nokia\WAP_Toolkit_2.0.

Starting the Nokia WAP Toolkit

To launch Nokia WAP Toolkit 2.0, click the Start button on the task bar and select Programs ⇒ Nokia WAP Toolkit 2.0 ⇒ WAP Toolkit.

You should see two windows (figure 2.12).

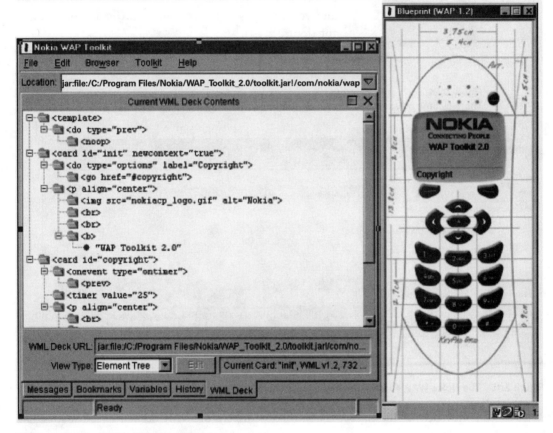

Figure 2.12   The Nokia WAP Toolkit window

2.4.2   Using the Nokia WAP Toolkit

Let us try to load the error-free Hello.wml example that we used with the UP.Simulator. Type the location of the document using either the file or http scheme as explained earlier.

If you retrieve the document from the local disk storage, you may notice that the location specification is more flexible than with the UP.Simulator. We can leave out any slash character after the file: string and before the drive name (figure 2.13).

Figure 2.13   No slash after the filename

You will notice that the name of the first card is automatically appended as #card1 in the Location box and you should see the welcome message in your emulator (figure 2.14).

The Nokia WAP Toolkit window appears as shown in figure 2.15.

Figure 2.14
The welcome message

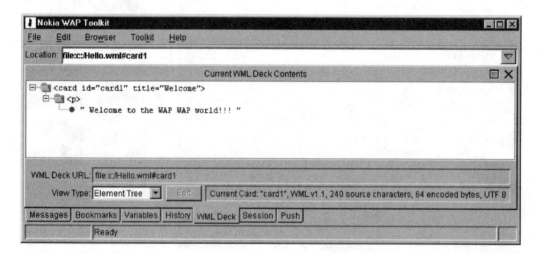

Figure 2.15   The Nokia WAP Toolkit window

Notice that the main emulator window displays the WML deck in a tree-like structure:

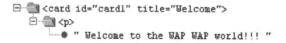

This is the Element Tree view of the document. It depicts the organization of the content in the document. Each WML element tag (e.g., <card>) is represented as a folder, which acts as a container that may contain some other elements (e.g., <p>) or character data (e.g., the string Welcome to the WAP WAP world!!!). The latter is the leaf of a branch in the tree, which cannot contain any other element or data.

To view the same document in other formats, click on the View Type selection list. It shows three other formats: Decoded WML, Bytecode, and Original Source. The original source is what the developer first coded. The bytecode is the compressed code that the gateway sends to the wireless device. The decoded WML is the result of decoding the bytecode, where white spaces and user-given comments in the original source are not preserved.

Notice the document information near the right-hand bottom of the window display in figure 2.15. It is broken out in figure 2.16.

Figure 2.16 WAP document information

As in the UP.Simulator where information about the file size is displayed, here we see that the source file has a size of 240 characters, the bytecode consists of 64 encoded bytes, and the character set used is UTF-8.

2.4.3 Creating and viewing an application

Unlike the UP.Simulator, the Nokia WAP Toolkit provides editors for writing WML and WMLScript code. In addition, an editor for developing WBMP images is provided. You can invoke any of the three editors (but not the Push Message editor) by clicking File ⇒ New of the toolkit (figure 2.17).

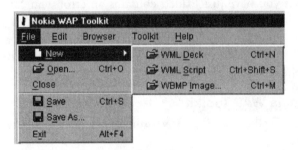

Figure 2.17
Accessing the Nokia WAP editors

2.4.4 Debugging your application

At the bottom of the Nokia WAP Toolkit window, there are seven tabs (figure 2.18).

Figure 2.18 Tabs in the Nokia WAP Toolkit window

The tabs that may be useful for debugging purposes are Messages, Variables, and History. A description of each tab is given in table 2.4.

Table 2.4   Nokia WAP Toolkit debugging tools

Tab	Description
Messages	Shows the messages logged by the microbrowser
Variables	Lists all the variables within the current context
History	Displays the stack of visited URLs or file locations

When the Messages tab is chosen, the content display area of the window will show the messages that the microbrowser logs. You may choose to view at different levels of detail.

When the Variables tab is clicked, the window will list the variables within the current context, together with their values.

The History tab displays the stack of visited URLs or file locations in the current browser context. It is a snapshot of the state of the current browser content, where the most recent document loaded is at the top of the list. The next lower document in the stack is the document that triggers the loading of the document above it, and it is also the document to return to if a Back key is pressed while the document above it is still the current card loaded in the browser.

After identifying an error, tab back to the WML Deck to edit your document.

2.4.5   Reloading a document to the phone simulator

When a document that you have just loaded contains an error, you can toggle to the Nokia WAP Toolkit window to make the necessary modification to the document concerned.

To test the modified document, reload the document by selecting Browser ⇒ Reload Deck via the phone simulator interface.

2.4.6   Configuring the Nokia WAP Toolkit

Unlike the Nokia WAP Toolkit version 1.3, version 2.0 simulates only two phones (figure 2.19). They are:

- Nokia Blueprint phone emulator (supports WAP 1.1 and 1.2)
- Nokia 7110 (supports WAP 1.1)

To select the device to emulate, click on Toolkit ⇒ Select Device.

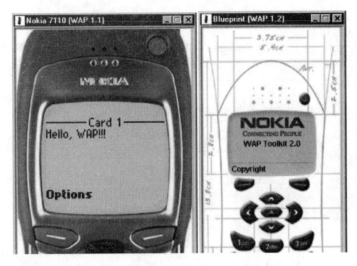

Figure 2.19   Two phones simulated by version 2.0

2.4.7   Blueprint phone emulator

The Nokia Blueprint phone emulator (figure 2.20) allows you to select from two modes of connectivity:

- HTTP Direct
- WAP gateway

To configure the emulator, select Toolkit ⇒ Device Settings.

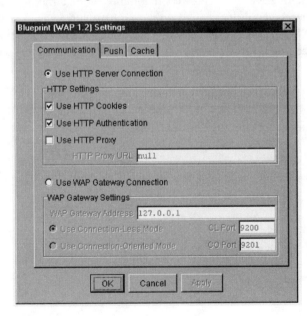

Figure 2.20
The Nokia Blueprint phone
emulator

If you are connecting directly using HTTP, choose the Use HTTP Server Connection option.

If you want to connect using a WAP gateway, choose the Use WAP Gateway Connection option (figure 2.21). In this case, you have to decide the connection, either via a connectionless port or via a connection-oriented port.

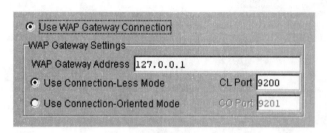

Figure 2.21
Connecting via the
WAP gateway

You should key in the IP address of the machine running the WAP gateway. If your WAP gateway is running on the same machine as your emulator, use the loopback address 127.0.0.1.

WAP GATEWAY   Chapter 32 will cover the installation and use of WAP gateways in greater detail. The chapter will also cover the port number to use for connecting.

2.4.8   Nokia 7110 emulator

The Nokia 7110 emulator requires the use of a WAP gateway. The Nokia WAP Toolkit comes with the WAP Server Simulator, which is a restricted WAP gateway.

NOKIA WAP SERVER   The WAP Server Simulator actually comes with a restricted Nokia WAP server. The restriction imposed is that the gateway can be accessed only locally (i.e., on the same machine as the installed Nokia WAP Toolkit). Also, servlets cannot be added to the gateway. For a comprehensive description of the Nokia WAP server, refer to the accompanying product documentation provided by Nokia.

When the Nokia 7110 emulator is selected/started, the default WAP gateway is automatically started (figure 2.22). If you have problems getting the emulator to work, restart the toolkit before checking the device settings.

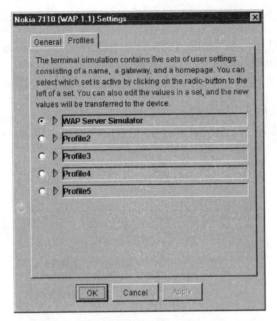

Figure 2.22
The WAP gateway is the default

The Nokia 7110 emulator allows up to five WAP gateway specifications (figure 2.23).

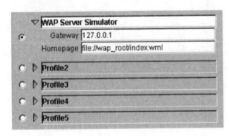

Figure 2.23
Five gateway specifications

2.5   SUMMARY

In this chapter, we have discussed two common WAP application development platforms. The UP.SDK is known for its ease of use and the numerous phones that it can emulate. As new phones running the UP.Browser are launched, you can expect to see more downloadable "skins" for testing on your PC. The downside of using the UP.SDK is its lack of an integrated development environment. For example, you need to rely on a separate editor and also your experience in WAP application building to solve some of the bugs that you may encounter in your development process. UP.SDK provides an information window that helps trace any error that may occur during loading of a card.

The Nokia WAP Toolkit offers an integrated development environment that aids your WAP application development effort. The most valuable part of the toolkit is the emulator for the Nokia 7110. The Nokia 7110 has a huge market share and it is the platform that you are likely to target for your application.

We strongly suggest that you test your application using each of these emulators because the look and feel of your application may differ between emulators. This is important in the real world because your users will be using a wide variety of devices.

This chapter concludes part I. In part II you will learn Wireless Markup Language (WML), the markup language for creating WAP content.

Introduction to WML

Developers use a *markup language* to define how information is displayed on a particular device. HyperText Markup Language (HTML), for example, is used to display information through a browser on a PC.

The Wireless Markup Language (WML), defined by the WAP Forum, is used on WAP devices. WML is XML-based and is supported by most phones worldwide, except within the United States where phones that support only HDML (WML's predecessor, discussed in part IV) remain in wide circulation.

C H A P T E R   3

Getting started with WML

3.1 INTRODUCTION

Welcome to the world of wireless programming using the Wireless Markup Language—or WML. If you are familiar with HyperText Markup Language (HTML) or Extensible Markup Language (XML) development, you should find learning WML relatively painless.

Before you begin, read chapters 1 and 2. Chapter 1 contains general information about wireless applications that will be helpful as you learn WML. Chapter 2 describes the Software Development Kits (SDKs) available for WML development. An *SDK* is a set of programs used by a computer programmer to write applications.

This chapter provides an introduction to WML, describes its syntax and structure, and introduces the basics of displaying and formatting text on a wireless device.

Subsequent chapters will introduce additional skills, including interacting with a user through menus and data entry cards, managing variables, and tapping into functionality offered by external applications.

3.2   WHAT IS WML?

WML is a markup language based on XML, and to fully understand WML we must understand a little about XML. XML is a set of rules for markup languages whose tags describe content instead of how the content is displayed (note that HTML does the opposite—it defines the display without regard for content type). These tags are defined in a set of "rules" called a document type definition, or DTD. In the case of WML, the WAP Forum has created a DTD to define the tags describing the content to be sent to your phone. Thus, a WML document is an XML document that adheres to the specific DTD set up by the WAP Forum.

All XML-based code must begin with a *header* that identifies the code as XML-based and contains a reference to the appropriate DTD. Since a WML document is an XML document, a programmer must reference the DTD in the header. The code that follows is the standard WML header that should appear as the first two lines of your code—it defines the location of the official WML DTD, located on the WAP Forum's web site:

```
<?xml version="1.0"?>
<!DOCTYPE wml PUBLIC "-//WAPFORUM//DTD WML 1.1//EN"
"http://www.wapforum.org/DTD/wml_1.1.xml">
```

The WAP Forum provides information about the WML DTD at http://www.wapforum.org. To learn more about the constantly evolving XML specification, a good place to start is http://www.xml.com.

3.2.1   Opening and closing tags

Similar to HTML, WML defines a set of commands called *tags* that enable you to build a user interface within a WAP browser. Tags are contained within angle brackets (<tag>), and are the basic building blocks of WML. You can use tags to format text, define tasks and functions, set variables, and do all of the other tasks necessary to build an application. In WML, tags are typically used in pairs: The opening tag (<tag>) starts the command, and the closing tag (</tag>) ends the command.

Together, an opening and closing tag is referred to as an *element*. Because it is an XML-based language, WML is somewhat less forgiving than HTML in that WML will generate an error if the code contains an opening tag without a corresponding closing tag. Therefore, this book will always refer to elements, not tags (in practice, the terms are often used interchangeably). This will help as a reminder, hopefully, to always insert a closing tag.

The basic WML code structure is:

```
<elementA>
   <elementB>
```

```
            <elementC>
  .
  .
  .

            </elementC>
        </elementB>
</elementA>
```

To reiterate, each *element* is made up of an opening and a closing tag and a tag is contained within angle brackets (< >). Elements are commands that instructs the browser to perform a particular function. For example, the `<p>...</p>` element instructs the browser to display the text within the element.

Self-closing elements

Elements that contain their functionality in a single tag instead of an opening and closing tag are called *self-closing* and thus do not require a separate closing tag. Self-closing elements use a forward slash (/) to denote the end of the element, and are used if nothing appears between the opening and closing tags. For instance, if you were using a `<go>` element and not passing any variables, then instead of writing:

```
<do type="accept">
  <go href="#display">
  </go>
</do>
```

You should write:

```
<do type="accept">
  <go href="#display"/>
</do>
```

While the first block of code works, the second is more efficient and easier to follow.

Another example is the self-closing element `<br/>`, used to insert a blank line in the display (`<br/>` is described in detail in section 3.4.2). Self-closing elements usually perform some action that is defined by the element itself or its attributes. For additional information on attributes see section 3.4.2.

Nesting elements

All XML-based markup languages, including WML, are *well formed*, meaning that an element opened subsequent to another element must be closed before the original element is closed. For example, if your code contains `<elementA>`, whose content (or code between the opening and closing tags) contains `<elementB>`, you *must* close `</elementB>` before you close `</elementA>`. Similarly, if `<elementB>` contains `<elementC>`, you must close `</elementC>` before closing `</elementB>`. And so on.

Put another way, this code is nested correctly:

```
<elementA>
    <elementB>
```

```
        .
        .
        .
    </elementB>
</elementA>
```

This code will generate a nesting error:

```
<elementA>
    <elementB>
    .
    .
    .
    </elementA>
</elementB>
```

For a practical example, look in section 3.3. Notice how the `<p>` element is nested inside the `<card>` element, which is in turn nested inside the `<wml>` element.

Attributes

WML allows certain *attributes* to be specified within certain elements. An attribute is used to provide details about the element. For example:

```
<card id="HelloWorld" title="Hello World!">
```

The `<card>` element contains two attributes, `id` and `title`. The `id` attribute specifies the name of the card, which can be referenced when navigating in other cards or decks; `title` indicates the text to be displayed at the top of the WAP browser screen. Note that the attribute values (`"HelloWorld"` and `"Hello World!"` in this case) must be contained within a pair of double quotation marks.

 Refer to appendix A for allowable attributes and attribute values for each WML element.

Case sensitivity

WML, like all XML-based languages, is case sensitive. This means that all WML elements must be written in lowercase—`<p>...</p>` is an acceptable WML element, but `<P>...</P>` is not. This rule does not affect the values of attributes (the text in the double quotes) or the actual content of an element (the text between an opening and closing tag). See the example in section 3.3.

White space

WML browsers ignore more than a single consecutive instance of white space.

```
<?xml version="1.0"?>
<!DOCTYPE wml PUBLIC "-//WAPFORUM//DTD WML 1.1//EN"
"http://www.wapforum.org/DTD/wml_1.1.xml">
<wml>
    <card id="HelloWorld" title="Hello World!">
```

```
        <p>
            Welcome to the exciting world of WAP!
        </p>
    </card>
</wml>
```

Would work as well if it were written as:

```
<?xml version="1.0"?><!DOCTYPE wml PUBLIC "-//WAPFORUM//DTD WML 1.1//EN"
"http://www.wapforum.org/DTD/wml_1.1.xml"><wml><card id="HelloWorld"
title="Hello World!"><p>Welcome to the exciting world of
WAP!</p></card></wml>
```

Because WML browsers ignore consecutive instances of white space, you can write your entire code in a single long line, if you wish (although it would be quite difficult). Though the examples used throughout this book use a particular style of indentation and spacing, it is not necessary to use the same style in your code. The examples are formatted in such a way that makes them easier to read—not because WML requires it.

Since more than one space is ignored, what do you do if you want to display multiple spaces on the screen? The answer is to use   to display a space to the screen. More information on formatting text using white space can be found in section 3.4.

Commenting

Code can be hard for people to understand, particularly if someone else wrote the code. The solution is the liberal insertion of *comments*, text that the browser ignores, into your code. Comments make code easier to understand for everyone, yourself included. Reading your own code isn't an exception to this rule. Try it yourself: Write a complete application without comments, go on vacation for a week, and get back into the "flow" of the application when you return. Difficult? You bet. Get into the habit of using comments.

A comment is any text bounded by angle brackets and double hyphens, like this:

```
<-- The browser will ignore all of this text. -->
```

Adding an exclamation point will also work:

```
<!--The browser will ignore all of this text. -->
```

Commenting codes must be repeated for each individual line of text:

```
<-- The first line of ignored text -->
<-- The second line of ignored text -->
<-- The third line of ignored text -->
```

Comments enable you to insert helpful reminders or explanations in your code, and can be helpful in debugging an application; if you suspect a line of code is causing an error, you can easily put comment tags around the offending code.

3 LEARNING BY EXAMPLE: HELLO WORLD!

The ubiquitous "Hello World" application—no programming text is complete without it—will display "Welcome to the exciting world of WAP" in the phone's browser.

If you would like to follow by programming this example as we proceed, simply type the text into a text editor (Microsoft Windows notepad application will do) and save it on a web server as an ANSI file with the extension .wml. Once the code is saved, simply enter the code's URL into a phone (or a phone simulator) to execute it. If you are using a simulator you can also store the file locally on your computer and the phone will execute it when you type the local address into the simulator. For more information on using simulators and real devices, refer to chapter 2. You may prefer to use a WML SDK to enter and edit your code. SDKs enable you to easily build your code and run it through a phone simulator. For information about finding and using an SDK, see chapter 2.

Our "Hello World!" example begins with the XML and DTD definition. Notice that each element is nested properly and each nested element is indicated by an indention. Here is the code:

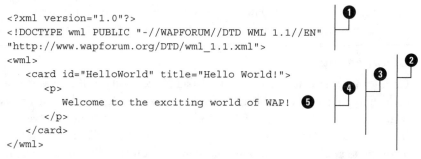

```
<?xml version="1.0"?>
<!DOCTYPE wml PUBLIC "-//WAPFORUM//DTD WML 1.1//EN"
"http://www.wapforum.org/DTD/wml_1.1.xml">
<wml>
    <card id="HelloWorld" title="Hello World!">
        <p>
            Welcome to the exciting world of WAP!
        </p>
    </card>
</wml>
```

Code comments

❶ Specifies the XML version and DTD used in the document.

❷ Defines the markup language used in the document. The <WML></WML> tag pair begins and ends the body of the document and represents a deck.

❸ Defines a card and specifies a card name and title.

❹ Specifies display text using the <p> </p> element.

❺ Text to be displayed.

The "Hello World!" application produces the following output on the various WAP phone simulators currently available on the market. Because different phones display the same code differently you should get into the habit of testing all your WML code using different phones (figures 3.1, 3.2, 3.3).

For more information on WML simulators and WAP SDKs, see part I.

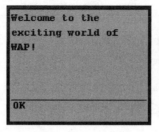

Figure 3.1
Nokia WAP Toolkit

Figure 3.2   UP.Simulator

Figure 3.3
Ericsson WAP IDE SDK

3.3.1   Understanding the code

Let's examine each line of code within the "Hello World!" application. As we learned in section 3.2, a WML document is actually an XML document and must be identified as such. The first element in our example simply instructs the browser that the code following the element is an XML 1.0 document:

```
<?xml version="1.0"?>
```

In section 3.2 we also discussed XML DTDs and their purpose. The next line of code in our program is the header that every WML program must contain. The header defines the URL where the XML DTD is located. In our case, the DTD is located at WAP Forum's web site:

```
<!DOCTYPE wml PUBLIC "-//WAPFORUM//DTD WML 1.1//EN"
"http://www.wapforum.org/DTD/wml_1.1.xml">
```

The following element defines the beginning of the WML deck.

```
<wml>
```

The next element identifies the first (and in this case, only) card within this deck. This `<card>` element uses two attributes: `id` and `title`. The `id` attribute contains the name of the card and can be used for navigation, and the `title` attribute contains the text that will appear at the top of the browser's screen. Also, notice that the `<card>` element is nested inside the `<wml>` element and in the previous full listing is indented slightly to indicate the nesting:

```
<card id="HelloWorld" title="Hello World!">
```

In the next line, the `<p>` element tells the browser to display whatever text follows. The phone will display the text until it reaches the closing element `</p>`. Unlike HTML, WML *requires* the `<p>` element to display text (an empty `<p></p>` element will be ignored). Notice, again, that the `<p>` element is nested inside both the `<card>` and `<wml>` elements and is indented.

```
  <p>
    Welcome to the exciting world of WAP!
  </p>
```

The remaining tags close the `<card>` and `<wml>` tags, respectively. Open tags must be closed in the appropriate order. In this case, the `<card>` element was opened *after* `<wml>` and therefore the `<card>` element is closed *before* the `<wml>` tag:

```
    </card>
</wml>
```

3.4 FORMATTING TEXT

WML enables you to use a variety of font styles and formatting options for text you wish to display to the user.

The following code demonstrates some of the formatting options you can apply to text (bolding, italics, underlining, and inserting a blank line):

```
<?xml version="1.0"?>
<!DOCTYPE wml PUBLIC "-//WAPFORUM//DTD WML 1.1//EN"
"http://www.wapforum.org/DTD/wml_1.1.xml">
<wml>
    <card id="HelloWorld" title="Hello World!">
        <p>
            <b>Welcome</b> to the <i>exciting</i>
                world of <br/> <u>WAP!</u>
        </p>
    </card>
</wml>
```

Again, the text has a different look on each simulator (figures 3.4, 3.5, 3.6).

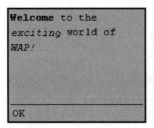

Figure 3.4
The Phone.com browser

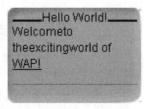

Figure 3.5
The Nokia browser

Figure 3.6
The Ericsson browser

Because WAP is an evolving technology, browsers do not follow a specific standard, and not all browsers support all elements. Notice the Phone.com browser rendered the underlined word as italics, and the Nokia and Ericsson browsers rendered the italics word as unformatted. In addition, the Nokia and Ericsson browsers displayed the title of the application, but the Phone.com browser did not. The Nokia browser didn't render the word spacing correctly (in fact, the spaces are missing). The moral, and one that will be repeated throughout this book, is that you *must* test your application on multiple phones. Testing against different phones is the only way to know if your application is usable by everyone.

3.4.1 Specifying font styles

WML enables you to format text using a variety of font styles, described in table 3.1. Be aware that a display isn't standardized across phones; how the font styles look is determined by the browser and may differ dramatically from one phone to the other. Some phones support only a few font styles, some don't support font styles at all. In each case unsupported font styles are ignored, and the browser will display standard text. Moral to the story: Until obsolete phone browsers disappear from the picture, don't write an application that relies on a particular font style to be useful.

WML enables you to manipulate only the font styles in table 3.1.

Table 3.1   Font attributes for WML elements

WML element	Font attribute
<b></b>	Bold
<big></big>	Large font (how large depends on the phone)
<em></em>	Emphasis. How the text is emphasized depends on the device used. Some phones might emphasize by increasing the size, some might use italics, some might underline, etc.
<i></i>	Italic
<small></small>	Small font (how small depends on the phone)
<strong></strong>	Emphasize strongly! Again, the device determines the specific type of emphasis.
<u></u>	Underline

3.4.2 Inserting a carriage return

WAP browsers will ignore carriage returns; therefore, you must use a special element to move to the next line or to insert a horizontal space on the display. There are two ways to accomplish this task—using <br/> or using <p>...</p>. To use the <p> elements, simply add them to your text:

```
<?xml version="1.0"?>
<!DOCTYPE wml PUBLIC "-//WAPFORUM//DTD WML 1.1//EN"
"http://www.wapforum.org/DTD/wml_1.1.xml">
<wml>
<card>
<p>Hello</p>
<p>Hello</p>
<p>Hello</p>
</card>
</wml>
```

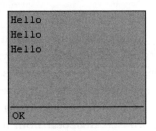

Figure 3.7 A carriage return

The results are shown in figure 3.7.

The <br/> element is a self-closing element that takes the cursor to the next line of the display. If you do not use this element at the end of a line, there will be no carriage return. The next example provides the same result as the previous code:

```
<?xml version="1.0"?>
<!DOCTYPE wml PUBLIC "-//WAPFORUM//DTD WML 1.1//EN"
"http://www.wapforum.org/DTD/wml_1.1.xml">
<wml>
<card>
<p>
Hello<br/>
Hello<br/>
Hello<br/>
</p>
</card>
</wml>
```

This example also renders as shown in figure 3.7.

The next example shows how to create three blank lines after a line of text. Notice that in order to produce three blank lines, you actually need to use four <br/> elements because you have to use one <br/> element to enter a carriage return after the line of text. Here is the code fragment:

```
<p>
The next three lines are blank:<br/>
<br/>
<br/>
<br/>
This line is not blank.
</p>
```

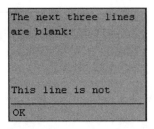

Figure 3.8 Creating three blank lines

Figure 3.8 shows how this example is rendered.

The other way to enter carriage returns is to use the <p>...</p> element. Putting these tags around the text specifies a new paragraph (putting the <p> element around nothing results in behavior identical to <br/>). You can also specify wrapping and alignment using the attributes of the <p> element. Wrapping is discussed in section 3.6 and aligning text is discussed in section 3.5.

3.4.3   Specifying reserved characters

Some text characters are *reserved*; that is, they have special meaning to the browser (<, >, $, ", and & are examples). To use a reserved character in a text display, you must substitute a special code, called an *escape sequence*, in place of the actual character. For example, the escape sequence for an ampersand (&) is &. Using the escape sequences properly is important because if the phone encounters a reserved character in an unexpected location, an error will likely be generated.

To display an ampersand on a phone, enter the escape sequence in the text where the symbol would occur in the sentence. The following will be displayed on the phone as Bill plays golf on Monday & Wednesday:

```
<p>Bill plays golf Monday &amp; Wednesday</p>
```

Table 3.2 shows reserved characters and their corresponding escape sequences.

Table 3.2   Reserved characters and escape sequences

Reserved character	Escape sequence
<	&lt;
>	&gt;
"	&quot;
&	&amp;
$	$$
space	
hyphen	&shy;
Any ASCII character	&#nn; (where nn is the ASCII code)

Figure 3.9
Reserve characters

Use an escape sequence just as you would any other character, remembering to always begin with an ampersand character (&) and end with a semicolon (;). Omit the ampersand and the browser will display the characters in the sequence (instead of the represented character). Omit the semicolon and the phone will display an error.

This code shows how to display reserved characters including several blank spaces. The display is shown in figure 3.9.

```
<?xml version="1.0"?>
<!DOCTYPE wml PUBLIC "-//WAPFORUM//DTD WML 1.1//EN"
"http://www.wapforum.org/DTD/wml_1.1.xml">
<wml>
    <card title="escape chars">
        <p>
            &lt; &gt; &amp; &quot; $$        
        </p>
    </card>
</wml>
```

Because WML ignores multiple spaces, this code example uses the escape sequence ` ` to display them. Note that nbsp stands for nonbreaking space. If you want to allow wrapping in the middle of a series of contiguous nonbreaking spaces, you must insert a regular space at the point you'd like the text to wrap. Note also that some devices, such as the Nokia 7110, tend to ignore the ` ` escape sequence—be sure to test your code thoroughly on different devices to ensure the display is usable.

We'll look at other options available in WML for wrapping text later in this chapter.

3.5 POSITIONING TEXT ON THE DISPLAY

By default, all text within your WML code is left-aligned. To make your text center or right-aligned, simply use the `align="right"` or `align="center"` attributes within the `<p>` element preceding the text.

This code shows how to left-, center, and right-align text. The results are in figure 3.10.

```
<?xml version="1.0"?>
<!DOCTYPE wml PUBLIC "-//WAPFORUM//DTD WML 1.1//EN"
"http://www.wapforum.org/DTD/wml_1.1.xml">
<wml>
    <card id="HelloWorld" title="Hello World!">
        <p>Welcome to the</p>
        <p align="center">exciting world</p>
        <p align="right">of WAP!</p>
    </card>
</wml>
```

Figure 3.10
Left-aligned, centered, and right-aligned text

3.6 WRAPPING TEXT

Keep in mind that the "weakest" phone permits only twelve characters (including spaces) per line; development should be directed to this phone.

Of course, it would be very difficult to develop every application such that only twelve (or fewer) characters are used in a given line. If a line within a card exceeds twelve characters, some phones will not be able to display the entire line at once. WML enables you to control how you want the phone to wrap text using the `mode` attribute of the `<p>` element. The `mode` attribute has two possible values:

- *wrap*—Uses default line wrapping
- *nowrap*—Uses Times Square wrapping

By default, a browser will wrap text to the next line until you specify another mode. Once you specify a mode other than the default, that mode applies to all subsequent lines until reset. For example, if you insert `<p mode="nowrap">` into your text, all subsequent text will appear in Times Square mode until explicitly changed with `<p mode="wrap">`.

We'll look at each of the `mode` values in more detail next.

3.6.1   Default line wrap mode

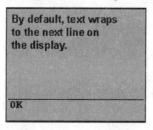

Figure 3.11   Default line wrapping

In default wrap mode, a browser will display as much text on a single line as space permits, and will then wrap the remaining text to the next line, and so on. The browser does not wrap a line midword; rather, it uses the white space to determine where to end the first line and wrap the remaining text to the next line.

Figure 3.11 shows default wrapping.

The default wrapping mode need only be set explicitly when the Times Square mode is already set and you wish to return to default wrapping mode.

3.6.2   The Times Square wrap mode

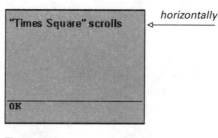

Figure 3.12
Text scrolls right to left

Times Square wrapping mode means that if the text on the line is longer than the width of the display, the text remains on the current line and more text that is not showing will scroll into view every couple seconds. The effect is similar to the way news "runs" on a lighted strip in New York City's Times Square. To modify the default wrapping behavior, set the `mode` attribute of the `<p>` element to nowrap:

```
<p mode="nowrap">
```

Figure 3.12 shows how a message scrolls right to left.

3.7   TABLES

WML enables you to build tables, similar to tables in HTML, in which data can be organized and displayed. One main difference between a table in HTML and in WML is that tables in WML cannot be nested inside one another. You cannot have a table inside a table as you can in HTML. Because the display size on a phone is limited, tables should be used with care so as not to confuse the user. Never forget: Different phones display WML differently; test your code on as many platforms as possible.

3.7.1   Using table elements

To create a table, use the `<table>` element and to specify the number of columns to include in the table, use the `columns` attribute. To specify a row, use the `<tr>` element, and to specify a cell within a row, use the `<td>` element.

It might be easier to visualize this syntax using a template:

```
<table columns="4">
```

`<tr><td>`	`<td>`	`<td>`	`<td>`
`</td>`	`</td>`	`</td>`	`</td></tr>`
`<tr><td>`	`<td>`	`<td>`	`<td>`
`</td>`	`</td>`	`</td>`	`</td></tr>`
`<tr><td>`	`<td>`	`<td>`	`<td>`
`</td>`	`</td>`	`</td>`	`</td></tr>`

```
</table>
```

Note that each row is contained within the `<tr>` element and each cell enclosed within a `<td>` element.

The following code example builds a calendar:

```
<?xml version="1.0"?>
<!DOCTYPE wml PUBLIC "-//WAPFORUM//DTD WML 1.1//EN"
"http://www.wapforum.org/DTD/wml_1.1.xml">
<wml>
    <card id="card1" title="Calendar">
        <p>
            <table columns="7">
                <tr><td> S </td><td> M </td><td> T </td><td> W </td>
                <td> T </td><td> F </td><td> S </td></tr>
                <tr><td> 1 </td><td> 2 </td><td> 3 </td><td> 4 </td>
                    <td> 5 </td><td> 6 </td><td> 7 </td></tr>
                <tr><td> 8 </td><td> 9 </td><td> 10 </td><td> 11 </td>
                    <td> 12 </td><td> 13 </td><td> 14 </td></tr>
                <tr><td> 15 </td><td> 16 </td><td> 17 </td><td> 18 </td>
                    <td> 19 </td><td> 20 </td><td> 21 </td></tr>
                <tr><td> 22 </td><td> 23 </td><td> 24 </td><td> 25 </td>
                    <td> 26 </td><td> 27 </td><td> 28 </td></tr>
                <tr><td> 29 </td><td> 30 </td><td> 31 </td></tr>
            </table>
        </p>
    </card>
</wml>
```

Figures 3.13 and 3.14 show a calendar on the Ericsson and Phone.com browsers.

Figure 3.13   A calendar on an Ericsson phone browser

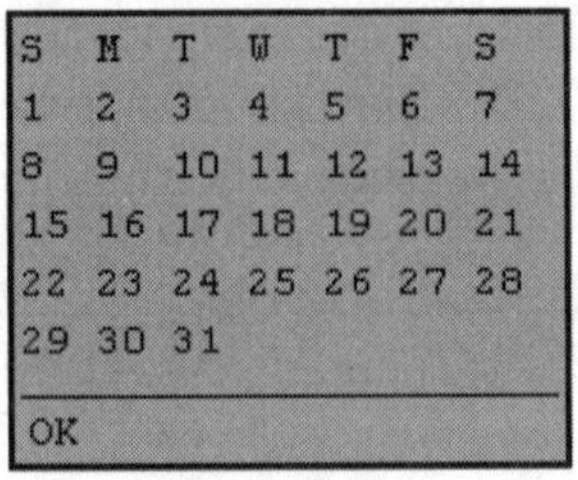

Figure 3.14   A calendar on a Phone.com browser

Note the minor differences in display: The Ericsson browser (figure 3.13) displays a table border, while the Phone.com browser (figure 3.14) does not.

3.8   DEFINING METAINFORMATION

Metainformation is data that affects an entire deck, not just a single card. Metaelements are always placed at the top of the code within the <head> element, outside of any specific card definitions. This section will explain how to use metaelements to control bookmarking privileges, manage caching of decks, and restrict access to a deck.

3.8.1   Using the <head> element

The <head> element specifies information about the deck as a whole, including metadata and access control information. The <head> element is always placed at the top of the deck before any cards are defined. In the example code fragment, content represents deck-level header information contained within either an <access> or <meta> element (or both). These elements are described in detail in the sections that follow.

```
<wml>
<head>
   content
</head>

<card>
.

.

.
</card>
</wml>
```

In this example, any <access> or <meta> elements contained within the <head> element will affect the entire deck. Note that this differs from the <template> element (discussed in chapter 4); data defined within the <template> element is subordinate to conflicting data defined within a card. When using the <head> element, there are no means by which to revoke the metadata within a particular card.

3.8.2   Using the <access> element

When you incorporate a URL into a context—for example by requesting it with a <go> task—you gain access to any variables it uses. This means that an external application could gain access to your user's variables, posing a potential security risk. To control this risk, WML supports *access control*, which enables you to specify whether another application can access your application as part of an activity. For more information on navigating among decks and cards, see chapter 4.

All WML decks are public by default; they grant access to any URL within its domain (URLs outside the deck's domain are *denied* access by default). To specify a particular deck URL that can access a deck, use the <access> element in the deck header.

In the following example, the deck will not allow access to requests from any but the domain defined within <access>. If an attempt is made to access the deck from another URL, an error will be generated. Each deck can have only one <access> element that defines a single domain (and, optionally, a single path). This example shows two applications: one with unlimited access (any other application can redirect a user into it) and a second application that restricts access to a single specified URL.

```
<!--first application with unlimited access-->

<wml>
<card id="firstcard">
 <do type="accept">
 <go href="http://www.mydomain.com/display"/>
 </do>
<p>
 This card navigates to another domain
</p>
</card>
</wml>

<!--second application with restricted access-->

<wml>
<head>
<access domain="http://www.otherdomain.com" path="/home" />    ❶ ❷
</head>
<card id="display">
<p>
The variable is <br/>
$(Melville)!
</p>
</card>
</wml>
```

Code comments

❶ All WML decks are public by default, which means they are accessible by any other application. In this example, the first application is attempting to navigate to another domain (http://www.mydomain.com/display). By default, it can do this.

❷ Because the <access> element within this deck specifies a domain (http://www.otherdomain.com), no other domain may navigate to the deck. If the user of the first deck attempts to navigate to this application, access will be denied.

When access is denied, a message indicating the restriction will be shown to the user. This message may differ from device to device, but will always indicate that access is denied.

Using the domain and path attributes within <access>

The default WML access control settings allow all decks (URLs) in the same domain to access your deck. To restrict access to an application to users coming from a specific location, you identify a specific URL (and optionally a path within the URL) within the <access> element using the domain and path attributes.

When a user attempts to access the restricted deck, the phone compares the values contained within domain and path to the URL of the requesting deck. The domain and path attributes of the requesting deck must match both values in order to access the deck. In addition, the URL and path comparison is a *literal* string match—the phone does not resolve names or aliases into canonical domain names. For example, if you specify domain="123.456.789.012" for your deck, an alias pointing to that domain will not have access to your deck. In this case, you must amend the URL value with a path for it to access your deck. For example: http://123.456.789.012/path. You cannot specify multiple values for either the domain or path attributes.

Table 3.3 demonstrates the results of specifying different values for the domain and path attributes for a deck located at http://site.com/deck.wml.

Table 3.3   Values and attributes and results

Domain attribute	Path attribute	URLs granted access	URLs denied access
domain=default	path=default	http://site.com/deck.wml http://www.site.com/deck2.wml http://site.com/home/app.wml	http://other.com/app.wml
domain="other.com"	path=default	http://other.com/app.wml http://www.other.com/app.wml	http://site.com/deck.wml
domain="www.other.com"	path=default	http://www.other.com/app.wml http://site.www.other.com/	http://site.com http://www.site.com http://www.yetanother.com
domain=default	path="/home"	http://site.com/home/app.wml	http://site.com/app.wml http://other.com
domain="other.com"	path="/home"	http://other.com/home/app.wml	http://site.com/app.wml http://other.com/app.wml

3.8.3   Controlling deck caching using the <meta> element

Just as PC-based browsers use a cache to speed page load time, phones use a memory cache (a storage area within the phone) to reduce perceived latency by preloading cards within a deck. When a phone retrieves a card from the cache, it is presented to the user immediately without the wait associated with retrieving a card from the server. Obviously, the phone cache is much smaller than that available on a PC, and when a phone's memory is exhausted, the oldest decks are dropped from the cache.

The problem with using a cache is that data gets old—in a dynamic application, a cached card might not contain the latest data available from a server. For example, if you are building a program that tracks stock prices (or any other dynamic data, such as sports scores), caching a card "freezes" the data at the moment it is stored. If a user navigates to the cached card, the old data is presented, even if the stock price or score has since been updated on the server.

To address this limitation, WML enables you to define a maximum amount of time a card can be retrieved from the cache before it must be updated directly from the server. When the user navigates to a cached deck, the minibrowser checks the time that has elapsed since the deck was cached and compares it to the maximum cache time indicated by the CONTENT="max-age=[# of seconds]" attribute of the <meta> statement. If the elapsed time is greater than the specified cache time, the phone automatically reloads the deck from the server. Otherwise, it continues to display the cached deck.

Like the <access> element, the <meta> element is always nested within the <head> element. Unlike access, however, multiple instances of <meta> may be used. The following example illustrates the use of a timed cache. Note both the placement of the <meta> element within the <head> element and the use of the forua="true" attribute ("true" is the default value). When forua="true" the meta information will be sent to the user. If forua="false", the metadata information will be removed before the deck by the gateway server:

```
<wml>
<head>
<meta http-equiv="Cache-Control" content="max-age=3600"
      forua="true"/>
</head>

<card id="firstcard">
 <do type="accept">
 <go href="#display">
 </go>
 </do>
<p>
This card navigates to another card
</p>
</card>

<card id="display">
<p>
The variable is <br/>
$(director)!
</p>
</card>
</wml>
```

Specifies whether the information contained within the <meta> element is intended to reach the user. If forua="false", the meta information must be removed by an intermediate agent

Specifies how long (in seconds) the deck can remain in a cache before it must be reloaded from the server

The CONTENT="max-age=[# of seconds]" attribute specifies the maximum time a deck may be cached in seconds. If a deck is particularly time sensitive, set the cache time to 0 so that the phone requests the deck every time the user requests it. If you don't set this attribute for a deck, the phone uses the default cache time, 30 days (2,592,000 seconds).

3.8.4 Controlling bookmarking using the <meta> element

(Note: This bookmarking technique is applicable to the Phone.com gateway *only*.)

Bookmarking a site on a phone saves a particular URL within a special bookmarks or favorites menu so that it can be easily requested—exactly the functionality as bookmarks in Netscape Navigator or favorites in Internet Explorer.

When the user bookmarks a card, the browser adds the URL and associated title to the user's bookmark menu. Accessing the bookmark menu and choosing the bookmark takes the user directly to the associated URL.

All decks default to markable (that is, the deck allows a user to add it to a bookmark file). However, there are circumstances in which you might not wish a user to bookmark a card. For example, a card might require the user to set a series of variables, and would be unusable if bookmarked because the appropriate variables would not be set.

To prohibit a user from bookmarking a deck, use the name and content attributes of the <meta> element using the following attribute values:

```
name="vnd.up.markable"
content="false"
```

The following example illustrates the use of the <meta> element to restrict bookmarking a deck:

```
<wml>
<head>
    <meta name="vnd.up.markable" content="false" />
</head>
<card id="unbookmarkable">
 <do type="accept">
 <go href="#display">
 </go>
 </do>
<p>
This card navigates to another card
</p>
</card>

<card id="display">
<p>
The variable is <br/>
$(director)!
</p>
</card>
</wml>
```

Tells the phone that the deck is not markable—the user will be unable to add it to a bookmark page

You can also use the <meta> element to associate a particular URL with a bookmark. By default, the bookmark is associated with the URL of the active deck. To change the associated URL, include a <meta> element with the name="vnd.up.markable" and the content="*URL*" attribute set, inserting the desired URL as the value of the content option.

In the following example, the URL indicated within the content attribute will be associated with the bookmark:

```
<wml>
<head>
    <meta name="vnd.up.markable" content="http://www.site.com/app.wml" />
</head>
<card id="unbookmarkable">
 <do type="accept">
 <go href="#display">
 </go>
 </do>
<p>
This card navigates to another card
</p>
</card>

<card id="display">
<p>
The variable is <br/>
$(director)!
</p>
</card>
</wml>
```

3.9 SUMMARY

This chapter introduced XML, and showed how WML is defined both by the XML structure rules and by its own DTD. We also discussed how WML elements are used to display and format text on a phone using different fonts, alignment, wrapping, and tables.

It is important to reiterate that different devices can display text differently, and you must make sure that you are not excluding anyone from using your application. Also important is to keep in mind the size of the device display. All development should be done for a default device that can display only about 12 characters horizontally at any given time. By developing for this device, you help ensure that all devices will display your application properly.

In addition, this chapter described how to use the <head> element to control access to a deck, control bookmarking privileges, and control how long a deck may be contained within a phone's cache.

You are now familiar with the basics of WML. From this foundation, the next chapter introduces events and navigation—how to enable a user to move among cards and decks.

C H A P T E R 4

Navigating in WML

4.1 INTRODUCTION

In this chapter, you will learn how to build decks that contain multiple cards and define the way in which the user moves between them. The most basic example of card navigation is a linear movement, starting at card1 and moving sequentially to card2, card3, and so forth. In this example, if a user navigates backward, the cards will simply be displayed in reverse order—card3, then card2, and card1 (figure 4.1).

More often, navigation will not be linear but will be defined by choices that a user makes. The following sections describe how to control the sequence of cards that are displayed to the user.

4.1.1 Navigation basics

Users navigate through the cards that make up your application in a variety of ways—they might choose selections from a menu, enter data, or simply press the Accept button.

Navigation can be very simple. For example, if you wanted to build a series of text display cards (as described in the previous section), the user simply moves back and forth linearly between them (figure 4.1).

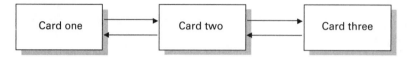

Figure 4.1 Card navigation

By introducing choices to the user, however, you are branching the application. Additional choices within a branch introduce additional complexity. When this happens, a well-defined navigation structure becomes an important topic because the user can easily get lost inside a carelessly designed application. Figure 4.2 shows the complexity that menus add to basic navigation.

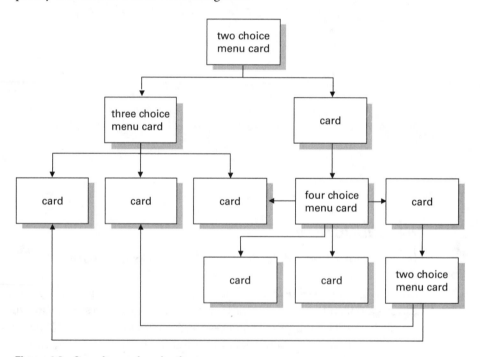

Figure 4.2 Complex card navigation

4.1.2   Planning your WML application

A user's perception of where the current card fits in with the rest of the application is limited because of the restricted display area on the phone. Users can easily become lost within a poorly designed application. As applications become more complex, the chance of losing your users grows significantly. The key to constructing an efficient and easy-to-use WML application is determining the best way to:

- Group your information content into cards and decks
- Create mechanisms that let users navigate between these components

Storyboarding is an excellent method for visualizing your information content and navigation mechanisms. Do this on paper *before* you start developing. These storyboards will save you much time and effort as you build the application in WML.

To effectively create a storyboard for your application, simply draw and label blocks to represent each card in the application, and connect them using arrows which represent the way in which a user navigates through them (figure 4.2). Storyboarding is not a substitute for testing the completed application, however. *Always* conduct user tests of your application; it is the only way to locate and fix problem areas.

4.2 USING THE TASK ELEMENTS

Let's first discuss how to enable the user to move from card to card. We'll start out with an overview of the task elements (table 4.1), and then describe them in-depth in the sections that follow.

Table 4.1 Using task elements

WML task element	Description
<go/> Attributes within <go/> specify to which card the browser should go	Moves forward to a specific card
<prev/>	Moves backward to the previous card
<refresh/>	Refreshes the contents of the current card from the server
<noop>	Remains on the current card and does nothing

4.2.1 Using the <go/> task element

The <go/> element instructs the browser to open a specified URL. The href attribute of the <go/> element is set to the location of the URL to open. As discussed later in this section, the location can be another card, another deck, or a specific card in another deck.

The <go/> element must be nested inside a <do> element in order to associate the <go/> element's task with an action that is taken by a user, such as pressing the Accept button. Here is the structure for the <do> and <go/> elements together:

```
<do type="type">
<go href="location"/>
</do>
```

The `type` attribute of the `<do>` element can be any of those listed in table 4.2 and the `href` attribute can be set to any valid WML card or deck. When the user presses the button defined in the `type` attribute, they will navigate to the location in the `href` attribute.

The following example shows how to navigate between two cards using `<go/>`.

```
<wml>
<card id="card1">              Type="accept" assigns the
<do type="accept">            <go/> task to the Accept button
  <go href="#card2"/>
</do>                                 Defines the URL to which the browser
<p>                                   should navigate. In this case, the URL
   Press the accept button to go to card2   specifies a card within the current deck
</p>
</card>

<card id="card2">
<do type="accept">
   <go href="#card1"/>
</do>
<p>
   Press accept again to go back to card1
</p>
</card>
</wml>
```

Figure 4.3 is what this example looks like.

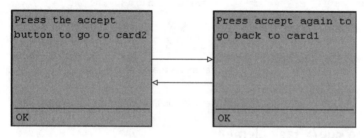

Figure 4.3   Navigation between two cards

NOTE   You can build dynamic applications by sending variables (a name/value pair) from one card to another by defining a `<postfield>` element in conjunction with the URL specified in the `<go/>` element. For more information on sharing variables, see chapter 10.

Specifying where to go

Similar to HTML, WML uses URLs to specify where to navigate. To navigate from card to card within the same deck, or between multiple cards and decks, you simply specify the URL you want to open. For instance, in the `<go/>` element, use a URL to specify the location where you want to send the user next.

To navigate to a card within the same deck, specify the name of the card preceded by a hash (#) mark:

```
#card_name
```

To navigate to a particular deck, specify the deck URL:

```
http://www.mydomain.com/deck.wml
```

To navigate to a particular card within a deck, specify both the deck URL and the card title preceded by a hash mark. (If you do not specify a card, the device automatically displays the first card in the deck.)

```
http://www.mydomain.com/deck.wml/#card_id
```

4.2.2 Using the <prev/> task element

To navigate to the card previously displayed, use the <prev/> element. Backward navigation on a phone is accomplished by "popping" the current URL from the user's history stack, a special area of memory contained within the phone's RAM. (We'll discuss the history stack later in this chapter.)

Similar to the <go/> element, the <prev/> element must also be nested inside a <do> element so that the <prev/> task will be associated with a specific user action, such as pressing the Accept button.

Returning to our simple navigation example, we can replace the <go/> element in the second card with the <prev/> element in order to return to the card immediately previous. The code looks like this:

```
<wml>
<card id="card1">
<do type="accept">
 <go href="#card2"/>
</do>
<p>
   Press the accept button to go to card2
</p>
</card>

<card id="card2">            Type="accept" assigns the
<do type="accept">         <prev/> task to the Accept button
   <prev/>
</do>                       <prev/> sends the user back to
<p>                        the previous card—card1
   Press accept again to go back to card1
</p>
</card>
</wml>
```

From the user's standpoint, this code looks exactly the same as the code in the <go/> element example (figure 4.4).

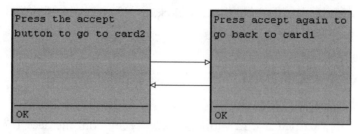

Figure 4.4   Using <prev/> to go back

4.2.3   Using the <refresh/> task element

The <refresh/> element enables the user to reload the current URL from the server. For example, if a card contains time-sensitive data that the user might frequently update (such as a card that displays a stock price), the <refresh/> element is used.

Please note that the <refresh/> element, similar to the <go/> and <prev/> elements, must be nested inside a <do> element so that the <refresh/> task is associated with a specific user action, such as pressing the Accept button.

The following code fragment shows how to refresh a card by pressing the Renew button. The actual stock price is being displayed dynamically using a variable called stockprice. Don't worry about using variables at this point; they are covered in detail in chapter 6. The point here is that the <refresh/> element reloads the stock price every time the user presses the Accept button. Here is the code:

```
<wml>
<card id="stock_quote">
<do type="accept" label="renew">
   <refresh/>
</do>
<p>
   Price= $(stockprice)
</p>
</card>
```

Type="accept" assigns the <refresh/> task to the Accept button

The <refresh/> reloads the card from the current URL

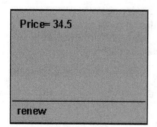

Figure 4.5   Using the <refresh/> element

Figure 4.5 shows what the code looks like on a phone display.

Please note that this code fragment is not usable by itself and is meant only to illustrate the use of the <refresh/> element. It won't update the stock price because the card doesn't define how to retrieve the price (in fact, it doesn't define the value of the variable $(stockprice)). In a real application, this card would likely be called by WMLScript or by server-side code that retrieves the stock price and assigns it to $(stockprice). For more information on variables, see chapter 6; for more information on WMLScript, see chapter 8; and for more information on server-side programming, see parts VI and VII.

4.2.4 Using the <noop> task element

The <noop/> element is odd, but useful. It instructs the browser to do nothing. Sometimes you need to navigate forward and sometimes backward, but once in a while it is useful to stay right where you are! For example, some phones assign backward navigation to Softkey2 by default. If you wish to turn Softkey2 off on these phones, assign a <noop/> task to the key. Additionally, <noop/> can be used to assign values to variables in the background of the application, functionality that will be discussed further in chapter 6.

The <noop/> element is used the same as any of the other navigation elements—it must be nested within a <do> element so that the task (of doing nothing) is assigned to a specified user action, such as pressing the Accept button.

4.3 DEFINING TASKS WITHIN WML

To define navigation within your application, you must use WML elements that enable you to assign a particular navigation action, or the tasks discussed in the previous section, to a particular button on the phone. When a user presses that button, the browser executes whichever task element has been specified (go, prev, refresh, or noop).

Therefore, before we program our application to go somewhere, we must associate a task with a button. There are only a few ways of associating a user's behavior with an action in the program and they will each be covered in the following sections.

4.3.1 Using the <do> element

To associate a task with a button on the phone, use the <do> element. It allows you to program any of the buttons on the phone to some functionality. This is helpful to provide navigation to the user (program the Accept button to take the user to another card when pressed), or you could provide a help screen to the user when the Help button is pressed. The possibilities are endless.

The <do> element has two commonly used attributes—type and label.

Use the type attribute to identify the button with which you want to associate this task. Table 4.2 illustrates the supported values of the type attribute:

Table 4.2 Supported values of the type attribute

Valid type attribute values	Description
Accept	Typically maps to Softkey1; refers to the button used to indicate acceptance
Delete	Maps to the button that deletes an item
Help	Maps to the button that invokes help topics

Table 4.2 Supported values of the `type` attribute

Valid `type` attribute values	Description
Options	Maps to the button that displays a menu of options
Prev	Often maps to Softkey2; refers to the button pressed to navigate backward within the application
Reset	Maps to the Reset button (unsupported by the Phone.com browser)

Use the `label` attribute to set the label that appears on the screen above the button (if you are programming either of the softkeys).

Set the content of the `<do>` element (the text in between the opening and closing `</do>` tags) to the task element that you want to associate with the button.

Here is an example of how you can use the `<do>` element with the `<go/>` task element. In this example, we associate the task with the Accept button. When implemented, the user presses the Accept button to be routed to the card whose address is specified in the `<go/>` element. Details about the `<go/>` element will be covered later in this chapter.

Here is the code:

```
<card id="card1">
<do type="accept" label="next">
 <go href="#card2"/>
</do>
<p>
  Press Next to go to the next card.
</p>
</card>
```

Assigns the action to the Accept button, and labels that button "next"

`<go/>`defines the action that is assigned to ACCEPT

Although different phones have different button layouts, a WAP-compliant device must support the same button types. For example, all phones support the Accept and Previous buttons.

4.3.2 Using the <anchor> element

The `<anchor>` element associates one of the task elements with some text or an image. Similar to the `<do>` element, you specify the task within the `<anchor>` element as well as any text (or image). Here is the structure to use:

```
<anchor title="label"><task/>text</anchor>
```

Similar to the `label` attribute of the `<do>` element, the `title` attribute of the `<anchor>` element specifies the text to be displayed on the screen above the Accept key when the user scrolls to the anchor in the card.

The text in the content of an `<anchor>` element can be any text or it can be an image, specified by the `<img>` element. Using images in anchors and other elements is covered in chapter 5.

There is a special case of the `<anchor>` element in which you don't have to specify the task, only the text in the content. That is the shorter form of `<anchor>`, the

<a> element. The <a> element associates only a <go/> task with an extrinsic event; therefore, you don't have to specify the <go/> element in the content of the <a> element. The structure for the <a> element is:

```
<a href="destination" title="label">text</a>
```

Similar to the <go/> element, the href attribute in the <a> element specifies the location of the next card to load when the link is selected and the Accept button is pressed. The title attribute specifies the text that appears above the Accept button when the link is selected. And, since it is related to the <anchor> element, the text in the content can also be any text or it can be an image specified by the <img> element. More detail about images can be found in chapter 5.

The following example shows how to navigate to different cards using the <do> element and the <a> element. The user has two options in the first card: immediately choosing accept or choosing the linked text card3.

If the user presses the Accept button as soon as the card is displayed, without the card3 link selected, the <do> element navigates to card2.

If the user scrolls down one time (to select the card3 link) and presses the Accept button, the <a> element navigates to card3.

Here is the code:

```
<wml>
<card id="card1">
<do type="accept" label="card2">
 <go href="#card2"/>                      ←   Associates the <go/> task with a
</do>                                          press of the Accept button. Pressing
<p>                                            Accept will navigate to card2
 Press the accept button to go to card2<br/>
 Or go directly to
<a href="#card3" title="card3">card3</a>  ←   Assigns the link to the Accept
</p>                                           button. Pressing Accept with this
</card>                                        link selected will navigate to card3

<card id="card2">
<do type="accept" label="card1">
  <prev/>
</do>
<p>
 This is card2<br/>
 Press OK to go back to card1
</p>
</card>

<card id="card3">
<p>
This is card3<br/>
Press OK to go back to card1
</p>
</card>
</wml>
```

Figure 4.6 shows what the first card of the example looks like. Notice the Accept button is labeled card2—pressing the Accept button at this point would navigate to card2.

If the user scrolls down (by pressing the down arrow on the device) an arrow appears indicating the link is selected, and the Accept button's label changes to card3 (figure 4.7):

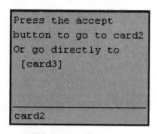

Figure 4.6 Using the <anchor> element

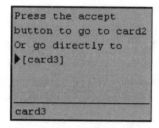

Figure 4.7 Choosing the <anchor> link

NOTE   Just as HTML browsers indicate linked text with a visual cue (typically by underlining the text and displaying it in a different color), phones will cue users to anchored text by differentiating it from surrounding text. In figure 4.7, linked text is placed within brackets, but different phones might use a different display mechanism. There is no standard defined for this cue; some phones might display the linked text by <u>underlining</u> it, others may use another style.

You can use anchors anywhere within a deck that text is acceptable. Note that you cannot use anchors within `<option>` elements (`<option>` enables you to present the user with a menu, thus the text within `<option>` is already associated with a task). For more information about the `<option>` element, see chapter 5.

4.3.3 Placing a phone call with WML

In the excitement of programming Internet content for a device as small and convenient as a phone, we tend to forget the phone's primary functionality—placing a call. One of the greatest features of programming Internet content for a phone is that you can program WML to make a call. The WAP Forum has specified the Wireless Telephony Application Interface (WTAI) for this very reason. WTAI is a specification that is stored within the WAP device and called via the following URL:

```
wtai://wp/mc;number"
```

The number in this URL is, of course, the phone number you wish the phone to dial. In the next example, the card initiates a voice call to the Manning Publications book ordering office by using a `<go/>` task that specifies the WTAI interface in the URL:

```
<wml>
<card>
<do type="options" label="Call">
```

```
<go href="wtai://wp/mc;18002476553"/>
</do>
<p>
Press "Call" to order a book from Manning Publications
</p>
</card>
</wml>
```

When the user presses the `options` key (`Softkey2` on most phones), the phone initiates a call using the number specified in the URL (1-800-247-6553 in this example). When the user hangs up, the phone returns to the same card that initiated the call.

You aren't limited to invoking calls through the `<go/>` element—the WTAI URL can be used within elements just as a regular HTTP URL. For example, the `<option>` element (used to define a menu selection and described in detail in following sections) can use a WTAI URL with the `onpick` attribute so that choosing a menu item will dial a specific number.

4.4 USING MENUS FOR NAVIGATION

Another method for navigating between cards is to use a menu selection. By choosing different menu selections, a user can navigate to different cards, participating in different tasks. This type of navigation can get complicated, so it is important to begin designing this type of navigation using storyboards, as discussed previously in this chapter. It is also important to make sure the user has a logical perception of where they are in the program at all times. Too many branching menus can make for a confusing application.

Using menus for selecting data is covered in chapters 5 and 6. Here we are only going to cover using menus for navigation.

To create a menu for navigation, start with the `<select>` element, which specifies a list of options from which the user can choose. In the case of a navigation menu, no other attributes are needed for the `<select>` element. However, the context of the `<select>` element holds the list of options, represented by `<option>` elements.

The `<option>` element specifies a particular choice in a menu (or `<select>` element). In the case of a navigating menu, the `<option>` element has one attribute that we need to use—`onpick`. Set the `onpick` attribute to the URL of the card to open when the user chooses that option from the menu. Here is the entire structure of a menu:

```
<select>
   <option onpick="location1">text</option>
   <option onpick="location2">text</option>
</select>
```

Obviously, the `onpick` attributes can be set to any valid WML URL, and the text that makes up the content of the `<option>` elements can be used to describe to the user what is going to happen if that option is chosen.

Here is an example that gives the user the option to go to card2 or card3. The card to which a user navigates depends on the menu option chosen. Here is the code:

```
<wml>
<card id="card1">
<p>
   Select a card to go to:          ___ Tells the browser that this
   <select>                        <┘  is a menu
      <option onpick="#card2">Card2</option>  <┐ Tells the browser that this is
      <option onpick="#card3">Card3</option>     a menu option and the
   </select>                                     onpick attribute is the
</p>                                             location to navigate to if this
</card>                                          option is chosen

<card id="card2">
<p>
   You have chosen card2.
</p>
</card>

<card id="card3">
<p>
   You have chosen card3.
</p>
</card>
</wml>
```

Figure 4.8 shows what the user sees.

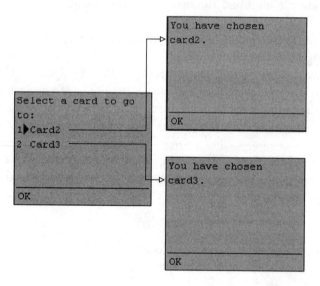

Figure 4.8 Using menus

4.5   *ABOUT BACKWARD NAVIGATION*

On a phone, navigating backward through the history stack pops the card completely off the stack, meaning the top of the history stack is always the card currently displayed. This means that while the `<go/>` element always requires a URL, the `<prev/>` element does not. This also means that a browser can only navigate backward using the history stack; it cannot navigate forward again since the top of the stack is the card being displayed.

4.5.1   About the history stack

Within the phone there is a special area in memory called the *stack*. You can imagine a memory stack as akin to a stack of trays at the front of a line in a cafeteria. As cafeteria trays are added to the stack, trays already in the stack move farther and farther away from the top. As trays are removed, the most recently added tray is removed first. There is no way to access any tray in the stack except for the topmost one—the only way to reach a tray within the stack is to first remove any trays sitting on top of it.

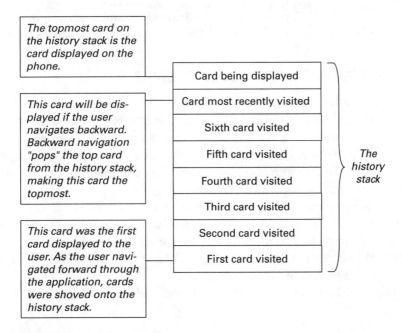

Figure 4.9   The history stack

The phone's memory stack works much the same way—to help visualize this, substitute cards (or, more specifically, URLs) for cafeteria trays in the metaphor. Maintaining a stack of URLs is a simple, useful way to keep track of the history of a user's navigation through cards (which is why the stack is also referred to as the *history stack*). Each time a user navigates forward to a card, the phone pushes that card onto the history stack (figure 4.9). Each time the user presses PREV to navigate backward, the phone pops the current card off the stack, leaving the previous card at the top of the stack.

In figure 4.10, you can see that forward navigation adds a card to the stack and backward navigation removes (or "pops") a card from the stack.

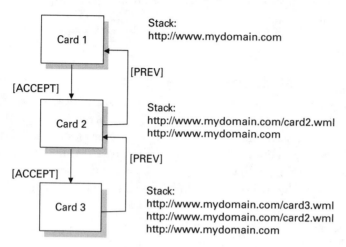

Figure 4.10
Using the history stack

4.6   IMPLEMENTING CARD-LEVEL EVENTS

Until now, we have discussed events that are directly tied to user actions—a user presses a button, which invokes a task. A card-level event, as the name implies, is an event that is inherent to a WML card—it is not directly defined by a specific action performed by the user. Instead of being bound to a user action (such as pressing a button), an intrinsic event is bound to a particular circumstance in a card—if the circumstance occurs, the associated task is invoked.

The difference between a card-level event and an event caused directly by the user can be subtle. To illustrate, imagine a user navigates from card1 to card2 by pressing the Accept button. The button press causes that navigation. Card2, however, might have a card-level event defined that redirects the user to card3—that redirection is not directly related to the button press.

Table 4.3 shows valid WML card-level events, which will be explained in the next few sections.

Table 4.3   WML card-level events

Event	Description
onenterforward attribute of the \<card\> element	Specifies the URL to open if the user navigates to this card through a \<go/\> task
onenterbackward attribute of the \<card\> element	Specifies the URL to open if the user navigates to this card through a \<prev/\> task

Table 4.3 WML card-level events (continued)

Event	Description
ontimer attribute of the <card> element	Specifies the URL to open if a specified <timer> element expires
<onevent> element	Associates one of the previous events with a specific task
<timer> element	Invokes a task automatically after some period of user inactivity

4.6.1 Using the attributes in the <card> element

To associate a card-level event with a task, you may simply insert oneneterforward, onenterbackward, or ontimer with an associated URL into the <card> element.

The onenterforward attribute specifies the URL to navigate to if the user entered this card using a <go/> task. It looks like this:

```
<card onenterforward="location">
```

The onenterbackward attribute specifies the URL to navigate to if the user entered this card using a <prev/> task. It looks like this:

```
<card onenterbackward="location">
```

The ontimer attribute specifies the URL to navigate to if the <timer> element expires. The <timer> element is covered later in this chapter. If looks like this:

```
<card ontimer="location">
```

4.6.2 Using the <onevent> element

An alternative for defining an event in the <card> element is to include the option as part of the <onevent> element. The <onevent> element has one attribute and that is type. Set the type attribute to the event that occurs in order to trigger the <onevent> element's task. The type attribute can be set to onenterforward, onenterbackward, or ontimer. The <onevent> element's structure follows:

```
<card>
<onevent type="option">
  <go href="location">
</onevent>
</card>
```

4.6.3 Using the <timer> element

The previous examples demonstrated another card-level element available in WML—the <timer> element. The <timer> element contains a value attribute that defines a quantity of time (in 1/10 of a second increments). Immediately upon card entry, the timer is initiated and begins to count backward to zero, at which point some task is invoked. There is also a name attribute in the <timer> element. The purpose of the name attribute is to act as a variable to hold the value attribute. You can set the name attribute to anything you like as it is less important to your application, and more important to internal WML processing.

If the ontimer attribute is not specified, either in the <card> element or the <onevent> element, the timer does not have an effect. Also, it is important to note the order that must occur in the <card> element if a <timer> element is used. The order is:

- <onevent>
- <timer>
- <do>

In this example code, the <go/> task is invoked when the 10-second timer expires:

```wml
<wml>
<card id="card1">
<onevent type="ontimer">
  <go href="#card2"/>
</onevent>
<timer name="time" value="100"/>
<p>
   Wait 10 seconds…
</p>
</card>

<card id="card2">
<p>
It has been 10 seconds.
</p>
</card>
</wml>
```

Tells the browser that when the timer expires, send the user to card2

Here the timer is set to a value of 100, which is 10 seconds

Figure 4.11 shows the timer counting down the 10 seconds.

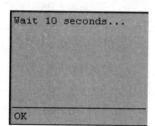

Figure 4.11
Using the <timer> element

4.7   *IMPLEMENTING DECK-LEVEL EVENTS*

Similar to assigning tasks to an entire card, you may want to assign the same task for every card in a deck. For example, you may want to assign a URL containing content to the phone's Help button, making sure that this help is available to the user throughout the deck. One way to accomplish this is to specify identical <do> statements within each <card> statement, each associating the URL containing the help information with the phone's Help button. A more efficient method, however, is to use the <template> element to define behavior that applies to the entire deck.

4.7.1 Using the <template> element

Templates enable you to define a task that applies to the entire deck. The task is defined within a <template> element, and is placed at the top of the deck independent of any cards. Template-level tasks are always subordinate to tasks defined at the card level. For example, if you wish to associate a URL with the Help button for every card in a deck *except one* (for which you would like to associate the Help button with a different URL, to provide context-specific help), simply include a <do> and <go/> statement within the card itself that defines the URL for the Help button.

    In the next example, a <do> task is defined within a template at the top of the code. In the first card, another <do> task is defined. Because card-level events override deck-level events, the <do> task in the first card takes precedence over the template. In the second card, no event is defined, so the event defined in the template becomes active:

```
<wml>
<template>
    <do type="accept" label="done">
        <go href="#card1"/>        ◁─┐ Defines default Accept behavior for
    </do>                            │ the entire deck (go to card1)
</template>

<card id="card1">
<do type="accept" label="card2">
   <go href="#card2"/>           ◁─┐ Behavior defined at the card level
</do>                               │ overrides the default behavior.
<p>                                 │ Pressing Accept will go to card2)
   Press accept to go to card 2
</p>
</card>

<card id="card2">
<p>
   Press accept to go to card 1  ◁─┐ The Accept button navigates to card1
</p>                                │ because the task is defined in the
</card>                             │ <template> element

</wml>
```

4.8 SUMMARY

This chapter described how to enable navigation between cards by assigning navigation tasks to events performed directly by a user, to card-level events (those that are inherent to a card), and deck-level events (those that are inherent to every card in a deck). We also discussed the concept of the history stack and the value of navigating backward in an application.

The next chapter expands on these topics by describing how to present your user with two additional interactive options—a menu from which to make a selection, and an entry form into which to enter data. Capturing and using that data is the topic of chapter 6.

C H A P T E R   5

Getting information

5.1   INTRODUCTION

Chapter 4 described navigation through an application—how to enable a user to interact with an application by moving among the cards that make up a deck. Chapter 5 expands the discussion of user interaction by describing how to develop ways to enter data. In chapter 4 we also discussed how to use menus to allow a user to navigate to different cards. That part of menus will not be covered again here. In chapter 5 we will concentrate on using menus to select data.

After completing this chapter, you should be able to build applications that interact with the user, enabling them to make choices and enter data. You will also learn how to work with images in a WAP application. Carefully used, providing images to supplement or replace text on the phone's display can be a powerful means to improve a user's experience with your application.

5.2   ABOUT MENUS

Because entering data on a phone is difficult, presenting a menu from which users can make selections is one of the most important means by which to interact with users. In some cases, a menu might be creatively used to replace data entry altogether. For example, to avoid forcing the user to enter the name of a state by hand an alternative is to offer a series of menus that move from general to specific—the user would choose an area (northwest, southeast, etc.) and then be presented with a choice of states within the selected area.

5.2.1   Overview of the WML menu elements

Creating a typical menu is a two-step process. First, define the boundaries of the menu with the `<select>` element—all menu items will be contained within `<select>...</select>`. Second, the individual menu selections are defined using `<option>` elements nested within the `<select>` element.

WML includes menu-specific elements (table 5.1).

Table 5.1   WML menu elements

WML Element	Description
`<select>`	All menus are contained within the <select> element, which delimits the menu and whose attributes define the data for the menu. For example, you can assign a value to a variable based on the user's selection within a menu. The name of the variable and its default value are defined within <select>.
`<option>`	Defines the specific choices within a menu. <option> always appears nested within the <select> element.
`<optgroup>`	Nests menus such that selecting a menu item presents the user with an additional menu. An example of this concept: A user would select a large geographic area from a menu, and would then be presented with another menu displaying states within the selected area.

5.2.2   Using the <select> element

To prompt a user to choose one or more items from a specified list, use the `<select>` element. Its attributes are shown in table 5.2.

Table 5.2   Attributes for a `<select>` element

Attribute	Description
Title	Specifies a label for the menu. This attribute is used differently on different devices.
Multiple	Specifies whether the user can choose multiple items. The default is false (meaning that choosing multiple items is not allowed).
Name	Specifies the name of the variable in which the value of the user's choice is stored. In the case of multiple selection lists, the value is stored as a semicolon-separated list.
Value	Specifies the default value to store in the variable specified in the name attribute. In the case of multiple selection lists, the value is a semicolon-separated list.

Table 5.2 Attributes for a `<select>` element (continued)

Attribute	Description
Iname	Specifies the name of the variable that stores the index of the user's choice. The indexes start at 1 and in the case of multiple-selection lists, the values are stored as a semicolon-separated list.
Ivalue	Specifies a string containing the default value for an `iname` variable (in other words, the default index values). Again, in the case of multiple-selection lists, the value is a semicolon-separated list.

In the next section you will see examples of how each of these attributes can be used.

5.2.3   Using the <option> element

Contained within the content of the `<select>` element, which defines the entire menu, are the `<option>` elements, which define specific choices. The `<option>` element contains an attribute, `value`, which enables you to specify a value to assign to the variable that was defined in the `<select>` element's name attribute.

Now let's combine what we know about `<select>` and `<option>` elements to create useful menus. In this first example we use only the name attribute of the `<select>` element and the value attribute of the `<option>` element to create a single-choice list. The user will choose Film, Director, or Actor and the value of each choice will be put in the variable choice. This value can now be used elsewhere in the application. Variables will be discussed in detail in chapter 6. The point here is to learn how to implement menus to get a user's input. Here is the code:

```
<wml>
<card>
<do type="accept">
   <go href="#display"/>
</do>
<p>
   Search for:                          Defines the variable
<select name="choice">         ⤶      as "choice"
<option value="film">Film</option>            ⤶  Sets the variable "choice"
<option value="director">Director</option>       equal to "film"
<option value="actor">Actor</option>
</select>
</p>
</card>

<card id="display">
<p>
   You chose $(choice).       ⤶  Displays the value that
</p>                              the user chose
</card>
</wml>
```

Figure 5.1 displays the result.

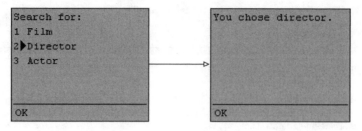

Figure 5.1 Choosing a menu option

To create a multiple-selection list we use the name and multiple attributes of the `<select>` element and the value attribute of the `<option>` element. In this case, the user can choose any or all of the selections (Film, Director, and Actor). The variable, in this case `choice`, will hold the values of the selected items in a semicolon-separated list, which can be used elsewhere in the application. Again, don't worry about the use of the variable; the point is to understand the use of a multiple-selection list. Here is the code:

```wml
<wml>
<card>
<do type="accept">
   <go href="#display"/>
</do>
<p>
   Search for:
<select name="choice" multiple="true">
<option value="film">Film</option>
<option value="director">Director</option>
<option value="actor">Actor</option>
</select>
</p>
</card>

<card id="display">
<p>
   You chose $(choice).
</p>
</card>
</wml>
```

Defines the variable as "choice" and multiple is set to "true"

Sets the variable "choice" equal to "film;director" if both of these are selected by the user

Displays the value that the user chose

Figure 5.2 shows multiple selections.

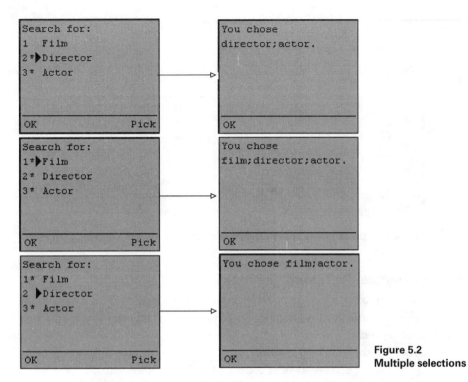

Figure 5.2
Multiple selections

Our final example demonstrates how to use the `iname` attribute of the `<select>` element. In this example, instead of displaying the actual choice that the user makes, we are going to display the indexes that they chose. This information, held in the variable defined in the `iname` attribute of the `<select>` element, can then be used elsewhere in your application. Here is the code:

```
<wml>
<card>
<do type="accept">
<go href="#display"/>
</do>
<p>
    Search for:
<select iname="choice" multiple="true">
<option value="film">Film</option>
<option value="director">Director</option>
<option value="actor">Actor</option>
</select>
</p>
</card>

<card id="display">
<p>
    You chose $(choice).
```

Defines the variable as `"choice"` and multiple is set to `"true"`

Sets the variable `"choice"` equal to `"1"`

Displays the index value that the user chose

```
</p>
</card>
</wml>
```

Figure 5.3 shows the result of using the iname attribute in the <select> element.

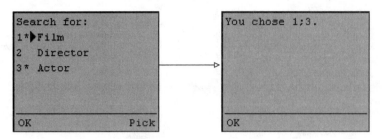

Figure 5.3   Using iname in the <select> element

5.2.4   Using the <optgroup> element

The <optgroup> element enables you to create nested option lists such that a menu option is associated with another menu. That is, the user is presented with a menu, and upon choosing an item from the menu is presented with another (subordinate) menu. In the following example, a user first chooses a set of states (Some states or Other states) and is then presented with a list of states.

Nesting menus can be a good technique for avoiding data entry. As the next code snippet and figure 5.4 show, nested menus allow the user to choose their home state from a series of menus (instead of being prompted with a form inviting the user to enter a state name using the phone's keypad).

```
<wml>
<card>
<do type="accept">
  <go href="#display"/>
</do>
<p>
   Search for:
   <select name="choice">                       Defines the
      <optgroup title="Some states">            first menu
         <option value="ME">Maine</option>
         <option value="NH">New Hampshire</option>    Displays the
         <option value="VT">Vermont</option>           associated menu— its
      </optgroup>                                       choices are specified
      <optgroup title="Other states">                  by each subsequent
         <option value="CT">Connecticut</option>       <option> element
         <option value="MA">Massachusetts</option>
         <option value="RI">Rhode Island</option>
      </optgroup>
   </select>
</p>
```

```
</card>
<card id="display">
<p>
  You chose $(choice).
</p>
</card>
</wml>
```

Here's how the nested menus appear on the phone.

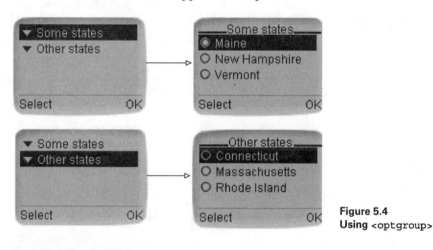

Figure 5.4
Using `<optgroup>`

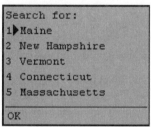

Figure 5.5 `<optgroup>` **on a**
Phone.com browser

NOTE Some devices (specifically those with the Phone.com browser) will not render `<optgroup>` correctly—that is, as different menus presented on separate cards. Instead, they will display all options simultaneously, ignoring the `<optgroup>` element (always test your code on multiple browsers). Figure 5.5 shows how the `<optgroup>` code appears on a Phone.com browser.

5.3 USING INPUT FIELDS

Phone keypads are designed to enable a user to easily enter someone's phone number, not text. Entering text on a phone is not only difficult, but can be dangerous if the user is attempting to enter text while driving. For example, to enter the letter *s* on a phone, you must press the 7 key four times. Now try entering Mississippi on your phone—hard to do! Therefore, limit data entry in your application whenever possible. If you are designing an application that requires text entry, carefully consider whether there is any possible means by which to extract the same information using some other method (with menus, perhaps, or by giving that user an option to set frequently used variables on a PC). In our "Mississippi" example, we could use MS.

5.3.1 Using the <input> element

To enable users to enter data directly into the phone, use the <input> element. For all the attributes that the <input> element supports, see appendix A. For our purposes, the name attribute is all that we need. It specifies the name of the variable that is going to be filled with the data that the user enters. This functionality is similar to data entry on HTML forms. Although forcing a user to enter text into a phone is best avoided, there are circumstances that require it. If you have a secured application, for example, you might require a user to enter a user name and password.

The following example demonstrates using the <input> element to prompt the user for a search string:

```
<wml>
<card id="srchfor">
<do type="accept">
 <go href="#display"/>
</do>
<p>
 Search for: <br/>
 <input name="srchfor"/>    ← Prompts user to enter
</p>                           a search string
</card>

<card id="display">
<p>
 Search for:
  $(srchfor)
</p>
</card>
</wml>
```

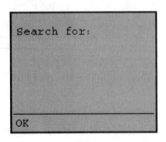

Figure 5.6   Input card on a phone's browser

Figure 5.6 shows the input card. Note that the input field typically is not delimited by a box the way it is on a PC. Many phones or emulators display the input field differently.

There are two important aspects to data entry that a developer should understand: how to enable the user to enter data and what to do with the data once it is entered. Please consult chapter 6 for more information on the latter.

By default, when a phone encounters the <input> element, it requires the user to enter data; you can, however, override this behavior by setting the emptyok attribute to true within the <input> element. Setting this attribute enables the user to navigate beyond the input card without entering any data (without the attribute, nothing will happen if the user presses OK without entering data). For example, let's modify the search form in the earlier example with this attribute:

```
<card id="srchfor">
<do type="accept">
 <go href="#display"/>
</do>
<p>
 Search for: <br/>
 <input name="srchfor" emptyok="true"/>
</p>
</card>
```

The `emptyok = true` **attribute permits the user to continue without entering any data**

In this case, the user can submit a request to the database without entering a search term. The default setting is `emptyok=false`, forcing users to enter a search term before proceeding. Setting the `emptyok` attribute to true is valuable in some applications—for example, a search form submitted without data might return a list of all entries within the database.

5.4   RESTRICTING DATA ENTRY

Because of the limited space available on the phone's display, it can be difficult to effectively describe to a user the type of data the application expects, resulting in data entry that makes no sense to the application. For example, should a birth date be entered as `March 07, 1968`, `030768`, `3/7/68`, or another format altogether?

If your application depends on a specific data format, the `<input>` element provides attributes that restrict users from entering invalid data types.

5.4.1   Formatting input fields

In addition to serving as a prompt for users to enter data, input fields can also require the user to enter data using a specific format. That is, the input field specifies whether the user can enter numbers, letters, or any combination thereof. The `format` attribute of the `<input>` element enables you to specify the type, case, and number of characters the user can enter.

To format an input field, specify a combination of the special characters shown in table 5.3, using the `format` attribute.

Table 5.3   Formatting input fields

Character	Description	Example
A	Allows any uppercase alphabetic character (no numbers)	Format=AAAA Allows four uppercase characters
a	Allows any lowercase alphabetic character (no numbers)	Format=aa Allows two lowercase characters
N	Allows any numeric character (no symbols)	Format=NN Allows two numbers

Table 5.3 Formatting input fields (continued)

Character	Description	Example
X	Allows any numeric, symbolic, or upper-case alphabetic character	Format=XX Allows two of any character except lower-case
x	Allows any numeric, symbolic, or lowercase alphabetic character	Format=x Allows one of any character except upper-case
M or m	Allows any alphabetic character (of any case), and any numeric or symbolic character	Format=Mm Allows two of any character

These formats can be combined to create an infinite number of arrangements as well. For example, entering the attribute FORMAT=NNAA specifies that the user must enter exactly two numbers followed by exactly two uppercase alphabetic characters. When you indicate specific entry, the Accept button will not work (nor will the Accept label be displayed) until the appropriate data quantity and type have been entered.

To enable a user to enter a particular number of characters of a particular type, use the format ntype, where n is the maximum number of characters allowed and type is the character type allowed (*A*, *a*, *N*, *X*, *x*, or *M*). To indicate an unlimited number of entries, use an asterisk (*) in place of *n*. For example, format=N5M enables the user to enter one digit followed by up to five alphanumeric characters, while format=N*M enables the user to enter one digit followed by *any* number of alphanumeric characters.

NOTE   You can use an asterisk or a number only with the **last** character of a format string. For example, the format string 4AN *does not* work. To allow the user to enter four uppercase alphabetic characters followed by a numeric character, you must use the string format=AAAAN.

5.4.2 Preformatting entry data

It is often helpful to place automatic characters that the user cannot edit into an input field. To preformat data, insert a backslash (\) within the format attribute followed by the character that should be automatically generated. When the user enters data, the phone automatically inserts those characters at the positions specified by the backslash.

For example, suppose you use format=\(NNN\). This instructs the phone to automatically insert a left parenthesis before the user has entered anything and a right parenthesis after the user enters three digits (as with an area code).

Similarly, if the user is entering a Social Security number, you might want the phone to automatically place hyphens between the number groupings. The following example shows how you can define specific formatting for a Social Security number using the format attribute of the <input> element:

```
<wml>
<card id="SSN">
<do type="accept">
```

```
    <go href="#display"/>
  </do>
  <p>
   Enter your SSN: <br/>
   <input name="SSN" format="NNN\-NN\-NNNN"/>
  </p>
 </card>

 <card id="display">
 <p>
  Your SSN:<br/>
   $(SSN)
 </p>
 </card>
</wml>
```

Creates a variable into which the value of the input field will be stored. The format attribute automatically inserts a dash (-) in the standard positions for an SSN

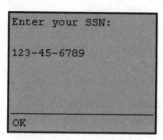

The display will look like figure 5.7 when data entry is complete. The hyphens appear automatically as the user enters data.

Figure 5.7   Preformatting entry data

5.4.3   Ordering input fields

If you create an input form by specifying multiple <input> or <select> statements in a single card, it is likely that many users will not be able to see all fields simultaneously because the phone's display area is too small to contain them all. By setting the order attribute at the card level, you can specify if the phone should display the fields in separate cards or within the same card (through which a user can scroll).

- *<card ordered=true> (the default setting)*—Generally best for short forms containing (mostly) required fields—this choice creates a linear sequence of screens through which users must navigate in a fixed order.

- *<card ordered=false>*—Better for longer forms containing fields that are (mostly) optional or have no sequential order—this attribute value creates a menu that lets users navigate to different fields in any order.

5.5   *IMAGES*

Images are an important part of the PC-based Web, and can be used to great effect on the phone as well. For example, images can be used to supplement or replace text, or to enhance the branding of an application.

Before discussing how to do this, some cautions are in order: Use images thoughtfully—the limitations of the phone (both the small display size and limited memory) require images that are very compact and fit within the context of the application. When using images, remember that an image that works well on a particular model might render the application unusable on a phone with a more modest display. With images, being conservative is the best strategy.

5.5.1 Using the <img/> element

Images are placed on the display with the <img/> element, which must be nested within a <p> element, similar to regular text. The src attribute within the <img/> element defines the location of the image (the URL where the image can be found).

The following example shows how an image might be used in the opening card of a movie directory site:

```
<wml>
<card id="welcome">
<p>
   <center>
     Movie lookup!<br/>
       <img src="http://www.domain.com/movie/splash.wbmp"      Displays the
         alt="Movie Logo"/>                                     image at the
   </center>                                                    indicated URL on
</p>                                                            the phone
</card>
</wml>
```

The resulting image is shown in figure 5.8.

You can make the image a link by nesting it within an <a> element. In the following example, the movie lookup card has been altered such that the image of the move reel is a link:

Figure 5.8
Displaying an image

```
<wml>                                Nesting the
<card id="welcome">                  image within
<p>                                  the <a>
   <center>                          element points
     Movie lookup!<br/>              the image at the
       <a href="#search by">         specified URL
         <img src=http://www.domain.com/movie/splash.bmp
         alt="Movie Logo"/>
       </a>
   </center>
</p>
</card>
</wml>
```

5.5.2 The WBMP image format

Because the common image formats used on the Web (GIF and JPEG in particular) are ill-suited for transmission to phones, the WAP Forum has defined an image format, WBMP (or wireless bitmap) specific for wireless devices. WBMP is a limited format that contains no compression and does not support color.

Tools to convert images to the WBMP format are widely available as downloads. Because WBMP tools are constantly being introduced and updated, any attempt to list them here would be immediately obsolete. Run a search on WBMP tools in your favorite search engine, and you'll find many available.

5.5.3 Using the ALT attribute

Although all WAP-compatible gateways must recognize WBMP as a legitimate MIME type, support for a particular graphic file format (if graphics are supported at all) is not standardized across phone models. Because of this, get into the habit of including the `alt` attribute within the `<img/>` element when you include an image in lieu of text; if a phone can't display the specified image, it will use the text defined in the `alt` attribute instead.

5.5.4 Icons

To include small images within text or alongside a menu, consider using the icons included with many phone models. Use the `localsrc` attribute within the `<img/>` element to specify an icon. (If the icon is not included within the phone's ROM, it is automatically uploaded from the server.)

Figure 5.9   Using icons

Some users might have devices that can present images, but have no icons available either in the device ROM or in its gateway server. You can still provide images to these phones by including both the `localsrc` and `src` attributes together within the `<img/>` element. In this case, the browser uses the `localsrc` attribute first, then the `src` attribute, then the `alt` attribute.

Figure 5.9 shows what happens when an icon is used, and the following example adds a reference for a left-hand icon:

```
<wml>
<card id="welcome">
<do type="accept">
  <go href="#search_by"/>
</do>
<p>
  <center>
    <img localsrc="lefthand" alt="Movie Lookup"/>
    Movie lookup!<br/>
    <a href="#search by">
    <img src=http://www.domain.com/movie/splash.bmp
         alt="Movie Logo"/>
    </a>
  </center>
```

```
</p>
</card>
</wml>
```

5.6 SUMMARY

This chapter discussed how to develop a menu from which the user can select an option, and how to develop an input form into which a user can enter data. Intrinsic to both of these topics is the assignment of a value to a variable. These values can either be associated with a menu selection or entered directly by the user.

Included in this chapter is a discussion on how images can be incorporated into a phone's display to replace or supplement text, enhance a user's experience, or to provide differentiated branding across an application.

Having learned techniques that will assign a value to a variable, the next step is learning to use the variables in a meaningful way. That is the topic of the next chapter.

C H A P T E R   6

Using variables in WML

6.1   INTRODUCTION

The previous chapter covered how to enable users to enter information into the phone. This chapter moves to the next step—how to do something useful with that information.

In this chapter we will start off with a definition of a variable. The complexity of a good WML application is somewhat dependent on a good understanding of what a variable is and how it can be used to allow the user to interact in the easiest possible way with your application.

Also in this chapter we discuss and demonstrate setting a variable three different ways:

- By setting it implicitly in the code itself
- By using input fields and setting the variable according to a user's input
- By setting it according to a user's choice from a selection menu

This chapter also covers the two methods of sending a variable to a server-side process—post and get.

After completing this chapter, you should be able to build applications that reference variables internally and, more importantly, exchange variables with a server-side process. It is the latter functionality—exchanging data with a server-side process—that provides wireless applications with their real power. Because the phone's processing power and bandwidth are very limited, exciting and dynamic WML applications are a collaboration between the WML code and server-side processes (which can be written in C, C++, Java, Perl, or practically any other language). Sending data to, and receiving data from, these processes is the heart of creating a robust wireless application.

6.1.1 Definition of a variable

A *variable*, as the name implies, is a container that holds a piece of information that can change. Think about a little black box sitting inside your mobile device. The name of the box would be the *name* of the variable and the data inside the box would be the *value* of the variable.

An example of common variables used in wireless applications is the gathering and storage of a user's name and password. Two different users who access the same application will enter two different usernames and passwords. Other examples of using variables are a user's selection from a list of search results, or the date on which an online transaction takes place. In each case, the data is dynamic—it can change based on the situation at the time. In WML, variables are always a name/value pair where the name is the variable (username, for example) and the value is the associated data (Joe User, for example).

6.2 ABOUT VARIABLES

A variable consists of a name and a piece of changeable information associated with that name. For example, if a user wants to look up a movie review, he would enter the name of the movie, the director, or an actor in the production. This information would be stored in a variable, and then passed to a process that would look up the information. Much of the time a variable is passed to a WMLScript function to be processed. For more information on using variables with WMLScript, see chapter 8.

In WML, a variable's scope—or area in which it can be used—is the user's application session. This means that a variable is global and can be set or referenced on any card in any deck within an application until the user exits the minibrowser session.

Variables are very useful things; however, they do have certain limitations. The data that is stored in a variable must be escaped or you will get unpredictable results. For example, if there is an ampersand (&) in the content of your variable, it must be represented using the URL escaping sequence &.

Variables can be set either *explicitly* (a value is assigned to a variable based on an event, such as a user entering data), or *implicitly* (the value assigned to the variable is specified by the programmer).

- To define a variable explicitly, the user must complete an activity such as entering data into a form or selecting a menu item; when the activity is completed, the variable value is set.

- To define a variable implicitly within your WML code, use the <setvar> element; assign a name and value to the variable using the name and value attributes, respectively.

Each of these methods will be discussed in more detail later in this chapter.

6.2.1   Naming variables

WML does not explicitly limit the number of variables an application may use, nor is there an explicitly specified limit to the size of the value of a particular variable. There is an implicit limitation to both, however. Remember that there remains a strict limit on the size of the deck that can be sent to a phone—1,492 bytes (with a recommended ceiling of 1,200 bytes for any application, just to be on the safe side). Because of this restriction, you should keep variable names small and limit the value size by setting the maxlength attribute of the <input> element.

There are relatively few guidelines for naming variables in WML:

- Certain characters are not allowed: $, <, >, =, /, \, &, *, #, and white space
- Variable case is significant: Variable_name and variable_name are two different variables
- Variable names should be kept short
- *Valid* variable names are username, user_name, User123, 123User
- *Invalid* variable names are user name, user/name, u$er123, user#123

6.2.2   Referencing variables

Variables can be displayed anywhere within your WML code. You could display the contents of a variable to the screen—perhaps to show the user what they entered or which menu item they chose. You could use the value of the variable in a URL—to send a user to a different location, depending on which menu item is selected. You could use the variable content as a selection item in a list—to provide a user-defined selection menu. The possibilities are almost endless.

To reference a variable, simply enclose the variable name within parentheses and precede it with a dollar sign ($), such as $(variable_name). When the minibrowser processes the WML, the value associated with the variable is substituted and displayed to the user (or used within a process).

When referencing a variable to be used in a URL, if the variable should contain certain reserved characters ("+", ";", "/", "?", ":", "@", "&", "=", or white space), then the variable must adhere to certain URL escaping rules. In other words, the character must be "translated" into its ASCII encoding in order to be used. Most browsers automatically apply the URL escaping rules to the value of the variable, but the following options can be used as well:

- `$(variable_name:escape)` forces *escaping* of symbolic characters
- `$(variable_name:noescape)` forces *no escaping* of symbolic characters
- `$(variable_name:unescape)` forces *removal* of symbolic character escaping

For more information on displaying variables containing reserved characters, see chapter 3.

To illustrate how referencing works, let's look at a two-card example. In the first card, two variables are set (we'll cover setting variables in the next section), and the user is prompted to press OK to see the variable values. In the second card, the variables are referenced (shown in bold) and, once the user presses OK, the values assigned to the variables are displayed. Here is the code:

```
<wml>
   <card>
      <do type="accept">
         <go href="#display">
            <setvar name="Welles" value="Citizen Kane"/>      ⟵⌐ Assigns a value
            <setvar name="Kubrick" value="Clockwork Orange"/>    ⌐ to the variable
         </go>
      </do>
      <p>
         Press OK to view variable values.
      </p>
   </card>

   <card id="display">
      <p>
         Variable Welles =<br/>
         $(Welles)<br/>             ⟵⌐ Displays the value
         Variable Kubrick =<br/>      ⌐ of the variable
         $(Kubrick)
      </p>
   </card>
</wml>
```

The result will look like figures 6.1 and 6.2.

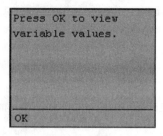

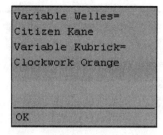

**Figure 6.1 Assigning a
variable value**

**Figure 6.2 Displaying the
value of the variable**

6.3 SETTING VARIABLES

Setting a variable is the act of associating a variable name, which is chosen by the programmer, with a meaningful value, which can be chosen by the programmer or the user. The value of a variable is stored at the moment a user moves from one card to another in an application. There are three distinct ways to set the value of a variable—explicitly, using input fields, and using selection menus.

A programmer may choose to set a variable implicitly if the user should not ever have any contribution to its value—such as setting a default value for a variable that may or may not be changed later in the application. The value of using input fields to set variables is fairly obvious—the variable receives the user's contribution and we use it in the application. For example, a common application is for a user to enter a unique username and password in order to log into an application. In this case, the value of the variable is completely dependent on the user. A selection menu can be just as valuable to the programmer. The programmer can limit the user's input to a menu of choices, while still allowing the user to contribute to the selection. Suppose the user is asked to enter the country in which they live. "United States of America" is a lot to key in on a phone, but with a selection menu, they can choose it with just a couple of key presses.

As you can see, there are several methods for setting variables and the one you use depends on the situation.

6.3.1 Setting variables implicitly

A programmer can set variables implicitly by using the <setvar> element which has two attributes associated with it—name and value. For more information about the <setvar> element, see appendix B. As you might guess, set the name attribute equal to the name of the variable and set the value attribute equal to the value of the variable.

Let's revisit the previous example that demonstrates the correct method of implicitly setting a variable. In this example, the variable Welles is set equal to the value

Citizen Kane and the variable Kubrick is set equal to the value Clockwork Orange. Both variables are displayed on the second card:

```wml
<wml>
   <card>
      <do type="accept">
         <go href="#display">
            <setvar name="Welles" value="Citizen Kane"/>
            <setvar name="Kubrick" value="Clockwork Orange"/>
         </go>
      </do>
      <p>
         Press OK to view variable values.
      </p>
   </card>

   <card id="display">
      <p>
         Variable Welles =<br/>
         $(Welles)<br/>
         Variable Kubrick =<br/>
         $(Kubrick)
      </p>
   </card>
</wml>
```

Assigns the value to the variable implicitly

Displays the value of the variable

6.3.2   Setting variables using input fields

A more common method for setting variables is to set the value of the variable to some sequence of input from the user. To accomplish this, use the <input> element, which was first discussed in chapter 5, but we will expand here.

The <input> element has several attributes, but the most commonly used are:

- *name*—Specifies the name of the variable in which to store the data entered by the user. To set a variable using the <input> element, simply ask the user to input some information, and use the name attribute for the variable name. The string that the user enters will be set to the value when the user advances to the next card.

- *type*—Specifies a label for the input item. Different browsers use this in different ways. If the user is entering a password that shouldn't be seen by anyone standing nearby, set the type attribute equal to password and only stars (*) will be echoed to the screen when the user types in the password.

- *format*—Specifies a data entry format that the user entry must match. Use the format attribute to limit the user to entering a string of a certain format (for three numbers, for example, set the format attribute equal to NNN).

- *emptyok*—Specifies whether the user can leave the field blank. The emptyok attribute can be set to either true or false. If it is set to true, then the user is allowed to leave the variable empty and advance in the application. If it is set to false then some input is required before moving on. The default setting for this attribute is false.

- *maxlength*—Specifies the maximum number of characters a user can enter. The maxlength attribute can be set by the programmer to limit the number of characters the user can enter. This helps to keep variable values small in case your application is pushing the limit of space requirements.

For more information on the attributes of the <input> element, see chapter 5 or appendix B.

In the following example the user is asked to enter the first letter of a favorite movie. This example shows how to store this letter in a variable called letter and then display it to the user in the second card:

```
<wml>
  <card>
    <do type="accept">
      <go href="#display"/>
    </do>
    <p>
      Enter the first letter of your favorite movie: <br/>
      <input name="letter"/>
    </p>
  </card>

  <card id="display">
    <p>
      The letter you entered is $(letter).
    </p>
  </card>
</wml>
```

Enter the first letter of your favorite movie:
 ⟵ Asks the user to enter a letter

<input name="letter"/> ⟵ Stores the letter in the variable

Figure 6.3 shows the result.

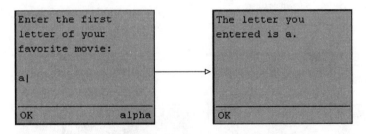

Figure 6.3   Displaying information using a single letter

6.3.3   Setting variables using selection menus

A more complicated, yet just as useful, method for setting a value to a variable is by presenting the user with a list of choices. The variable is set to a value based on the user's choice. To set up the list of choices and the variable, use the <select> element.

To list the actual choices to the user, use the <option> element. The <select> element has several attributes, but the most important is name, which the programmer sets equal to the name of the variable that will be set by one of the values in the list. The <option> element has several attributes also, but the only one we need for setting variables is the value attribute, which the programmer sets equal to the value that is associated with the option. The variable, whose name is in the name attribute of the <select> element, will be set to the value attribute of the <option> element that the user chooses. For more information on the <select> and <option> elements, refer to appendix B.

The following example shows one way that a selection menu can be used. In this case, the user will choose whether they want to search for a movie by the film name, the director, or an actor. The second card displays the user's choice, which is stored in the variable searchby:

```
<wml>

  <card>
    <do type="accept">
      <go href="#display"/>
    </do>
    <p>
      Search in:                            Assigns the name
      <select name="searchby">             of the variable
                                           that will be set
        <option value="Film">Film</option>
        <option value="Director">Director</option>    Assigns the value
        <option value="Actor">Actor</option>          of the option
      </select>
    </p>
  </card>

  <card id="display">
    <p>
      You chose $(searchby).
    </p>
  </card>

</wml>
```

Figure 6.4 shows the result.

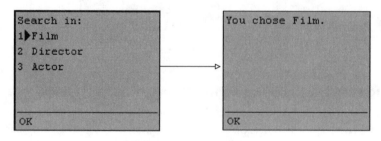

Figure 6.4 Picking a search area

6.4 SENDING VARIABLES TO SERVER-SIDE PROGRAMS

It is often important to enable a user to set a variable and then send that variable to a server-side program for processing. For example, a user might enter a username and password; those values would then be sent to a server-side program that uses the variables to authenticate the user and set the user's permissions. These server-side programs come in the form of ASP, CGI, JSP, and many other scripting and programming languages and are very similar to the server-side code that provides dynamic HTML pages to your browser on your desktop.

The main difference in the WML version and the HTML version is that the WML server-side programs output WML to your phone, while the HTML version outputs HTML to the browser on your computer. Another difference is that in WML, you can use a leading question mark (?) to indicate the URL of the current deck. This is described further in later sections.

Since the server-side program is stored (obviously) on the server, to send a variable to such a program you must send the variable to the URL where the server-side program is located. There are two methods of sending variables to a URL—post and get. Using the post method is preferred because it allows for a larger number of variables to be processed at one time, and permits processing of the data type by the gateway server, ensuring the data is understood by the receiving entity.

As illustrated in figure 6.5, when the mobile device makes a request to the server, the request is transmitted to the WAP gateway, translated into HTTP, and goes to a regular web server. The web server then goes to the URL you requested and executes the server-side functionality. The server then sends the response back to the gateway, where it is sent to the browser on your mobile device.

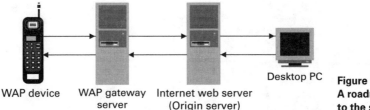

Desktop PC

WAP device   WAP gateway   Internet web server
server   (Origin server)

**Figure 6.5
A roadmap to a request
to the server**

In the example, the variables (username and password) would be sent to a particular URL on the server using either the post or get methods (which are discussed in the next sections). A server-side program, such as ASP, would take the username and password and check it against data that is stored in a database. If the data matches, the server-side program would output a WML document to be displayed on the device, saying that the user is authorized to enter that site. If the data does not match, perhaps the program would return a WML card that tells the user to re-enter the password or simply that access to the site is denied.

For more information on writing the server-side code, refer to parts VI and VII, which discuss creating dynamic applications using both ASP and Java.

6.4.1   Using the post method

As discussed in chapter 4, the `<go/>` element enables you to open a URL when a specified button on the phone is pressed. When sending variables via the post method, simply set the `method` attribute of the `<go/>` element equal to post, and the `href` attribute equal to the URL to which you want to send the user. For more information on using the `<go/>` element, see chapter 4 or appendix B.

To define the variables that you want to send to the specified URL, use the `<postfield>` element within the `<go/>` element's beginning and ending tags. The `<postfield>` element is a self-closing element, as discussed in chapter 3. The `<postfield>` element is similar to the `<setvar>` element, discussed earlier in this chapter, in that it has two important attributes—name and value. Set the name attribute equal to the name of the variable you are passing and set the value attribute equal to the value of the variable you are passing.

The following example combines the code from the previous examples. The user is asked to enter the first letter of a favorite movie and then is presented with a selection menu listing three different methods of searching for that movie—by the film's name, by the director, and by an actor. The example then uses a `<go/>` element with two `<postfield>` elements to send the variables to a server-side process called `movie.asp`:

```
<wml>
  <card>
    <do type="accept">
      <go href="#search"/>
    </do>
    <p>
      Enter the first letter of your favorite movie: <br/>
      <input name="letter"/>
    </p>
  </card>

  <card id="search">
    <do type="accept">
      <go href="#display"/>
    </do>
    <p>
      Search for $(letter) in:
      <select name="searchby">
        <option value="Film">Film</option>
        <option value="Director">Director</option>
        <option value="Actor">Actor</option>
      </select>
    </p>
  </card>
```

```
<card id="display">
    <do type="accept">
        <go href="http://www.mydomain.com/movie.asp" method="post">
            <postfield name="letter" value="$(letter)" />
            <postfield name="searchby" value="$(searchby)" />
        </go>
    </do>
    <p>
        Search for:
     $(letter)<br/>
     in the<br/>
     $(searchby)library
    </p>
    </card>
</wml>
```

**Sets the method to `post`
and `href` to the URL**

**Name/value
pairs to be
sent**

Figure 6.6 shows the results of the search.

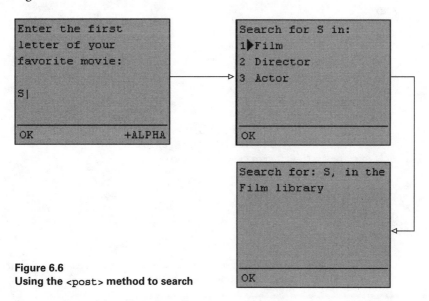

Figure 6.6
Using the `<post>` method to search

The server-side process (called `movie.asp`) can do a number of things using the data from the user. For example, it could search for show times, movie reviews, or video release dates. The possibilities are endless. For more information on server-side programming, see parts VI and VII, which cover dynamic WAP applications using both ASP and Java servlets.

6.4.2 Using the get method

The `get` method is much easier to use to send data than the `post` method. Using the `<go/>` element to send the user to a specified URL, simply append the variables to the URL as a query string. This is exactly the same way a programmer sends data to a server-side process in HTML. More information on specifying the URL can be found in the next section.

Again we use the "movie search" example to demonstrate how the `get` method is used to pass variables. This example shows the user exactly the same screens as in the previous example; the only difference is the method of passing the variables to the server-side process:

```wml
<wml>
  <card>
    <do type="accept">
      <go href="#search"/>
    </do>
    <p>
    Enter the first letter of your favorite movie: <br/>
    <input name="letter" format="A"/>
    </p>
  </card>

  <card id="search">
  <do type="accept">
    <go href="#display"/>
  </do>
    <p>
    Search for $(letter) in:
    <select name="searchby">
       <option value="Film">Film</option>
       <option value="Director">Director</option>
       <option value="Actor">Actor</option>
    </select>
    </p>
  </card>

  <card id="display">
    <do type="accept">
      <go method="get"
        href="http://www.mydomain.com/movie.asp?letter=
          $(letter)&amp;searchby=$(searchby)">
      </go>
    </do>
    <p>
      Search for:
      $(letter), in the<br/>
      $(searchby)library
    </p>
  </card>
</wml>
```

Sets the method to get and href to the URL with the variables appended

To the user, the result looks identical.

6.4.3   Specifying the URL

To specify the correct URL to use for the get method, we must first decide where we want this task to take the user. There are several choices—you can remain on the same card, you can move to a different card, you can pass variables to the same card, you can pass variables to a different card.

To reload the current card, passing no variables, set the href attribute of the <go/> element to a question mark (?). Another way of doing this is to use the <refresh> element, discussed in chapter 4. Here is the structure for using a question mark to reload the same card:

```
href="?"
```

If you need to refresh the current card and pass one or more variables back to the current card in the process, set the href attribute of the <go/> element to a question mark (?), followed by the name of the first variable, followed by the equals sign (=), and followed by the value of the variable. If more than one variable needs to be passed, delimit the "variable=value" combinations with ampersands (&). Keep in mind that you must use the special character element & to specify the ampersand (&) character when using them within URL strings. The string of text that starts with the question mark (?) and ends with the last value is called a query string.

Here is the structure for passing a variable to the same card from which it is originating where var1 is the name of a variable and val1 is the value of the variable:

```
href="?var1=val1"
```

Here is the structure for passing three variables to the same card from which it is originating where var1, var2, and var3 are names of variables and val1, val2, and val3 are their respective values:

```
href="?var1=val1&amp;var2=val2&amp;var3=val3"
```

Now, if you want to send the user to a different card and pass a variable to the card in the process, simply set the href attribute of the <go/> element to the card as usual (discussed in chapter 4), followed by the query string, similar to the previous examples. Here is the structure for passing three variables to another card in the same deck:

```
href="#cardname?var1=val1&amp;var2=val2&var3=val3"
```

Here is the structure for passing a variable to another card in a different deck:

```
href="deckname.wml#cardname?var1=val1"
```

And here is the structure for passing variables to another card in another deck at a different location on the server or on a different server:

```
href:"http://www.mydomain.com/deckname.wml#cardname?var1=val1"
```

6.5   SUMMARY

In this chapter you learned three methods of setting variables, and some of the uses for each method. We discussed using the `<setvar>` element for programmer-specific variables, data input fields to set variables according to a user's input, and selection menus to set variables according to a user's input that is limited by the programmer. Once the variables were set, two methods of passing them to another URL were demonstrated: the `post` method and the `get` method. The `get` method seems simpler than `post`, but the `post` method will be more useful in larger processes with numerous variables to be passed.

The next chapter looks at additional ways variables can be used within extended WML elements defined by Phone.com. These elements are not part of the official WML specification (created by the WAP Forum), and therefore should be used with caution.

CHAPTER 7

Extending WML

7.1 INTRODUCTION

A *context* loosely corresponds to goals a user might have within an application. To reach a particular goal ("check my email" or "read a news article," for example), a user must perform one or more steps that traverse one or more cards, which are in turn held within one or more decks. As the user navigates these cards and decks, setting variables and choosing options, the cards, decks, variables, and values are collectively referred to as a context.

In this chapter we are going to discuss what contexts are in WML, how to implement and navigate them, and how to pass variables between them.

7.2   ABOUT EXTENDED *WML* ELEMENTS

There is certain functionality available within HDML that is not available within WML, most notably the idea of context (called "activities" in HDML, which is covered in detail in chapter 14). To bridge this gap, Phone.com (the original developer of HDML) built additions (called *extensions*, or *extended elements*) to WML that provide developers functionality similar to HDML's activities. These "extended" WML elements have not been approved by the WAP Forum, and are not part of the official WML specification. Nevertheless, all Phone.com browsers support them and many developers might be interested in learning about them.

Properly used, context can be very powerful; it enables a developer to move from application to application seamlessly without losing the *state* of either application (an application's state refers to the contents of its history stack and to the values of variables contained within it).

The extended WML elements that enable context are shown in table 7.1.

Table 7.1   WML extended elements

WML element	Description
<spawn>	Invokes another context (a *child* context) from within an active context (the *parent* context)
<receive>	Receives data sent from a child context
<exit>	Terminates the current context, returning the phone to the parent context. Values may be sent to the parent context with an embedded <send> element.
<throw>	Declares that an exception should be raised. The current context will be terminated (along with any variables and history state) and the phone returned to the parent context. If the parent context does not contain a <catch> element, that context is itself terminated in favor of that context's parent, and so on. If all nested contexts are exhausted without finding a <catch> element, the history stack is cleared and the phone returns to the home deck. As with <exit>, values may be sent to the exception handler with an embedded <send> element.
<catch>	Specifies a course of action to be followed if an exception (an unexpected event, typically an error) is passed by a <throw> task

Because these elements are not part of the WML specification, they are not included in the official WML DTD (the document that defines all the elements being used). To reference the DTD that includes the extended elements, you must precede any code that uses context-related elements with the following header:

```
<?xml version="1.0"?>
<!DOCTYPE wml PUBLIC "-//PHONE.COM//DTD WML 1.1//EN"
"http://www.phone.com/dtd/wml11.dtd" >
```

If you do not reference this DTD, the phone will return an error upon encountering any extended elements.

7.2.1 About context

As mentioned earlier, a context refers to the overall goal of a set of multiple cards and decks. It includes the *state* of the application, defined by its variables and their values, coupled with the contents of the history stack. Figure 7.1 shows a typical login application:

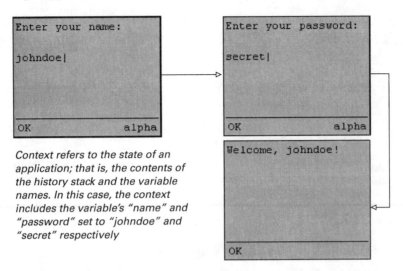

Context refers to the state of an application; that is, the contents of the history stack and the variable names. In this case, the context includes the variable's "name" and "password" set to "johndoe" and "secret" respectively

Figure 7.1   Demonstrating context

In this case, the context has a variable called name, set to the value johndoe, and a variable called password, set to the value secret.

Context also provides scope for variables; that is, a variable and its value are active only within a specific context. Within another context, the same variable might contain a different value—although it is usually a good idea to name all the variables in your application differently to avoid confusion.

7.2.2 Managing state in nested contexts

As the user navigates into nested contexts, the phone preserves the *state* of each context. The state includes attributes such as the context's variables and its card history stack. For example, let's say the user entered his name "Sam" within a context, and the name was associated with the variable first_name. When the user navigates to a nested activity and then returns to the original activity, Sam remains associated with first_name—even if the nested context contained a variable first_name with the value George.

Chapter 4 describes the *history stack,* a record of the cards the user visits, which is maintained by the phone's browser. When using context, the history stack is expanded such that it maintains a record of visited *contexts* (including all cards within that context), not visited cards.

When the phone navigates from one context to another, the state of the original context is maintained because the history stack records the entire user interface state of the calling context, including its variable values and any visited cards within the context.

When the user returns to the original context, the phone pops the nested context off the stack. This restores the calling context (and its user interface state) to the top of the stack.

7.3 IMPLEMENTING CONTEXT

Let's begin with some general rules to follow when implementing a context in WML:

- To implement navigation *within* a context, use the `<go>` and `<prev>` elements, as discussed in chapter 4.

- To implement navigation to a *child* context, use the `<spawn>` element to request the first card in the child context.

- To implement navigation *from* a child context *back* to the context that called it, use the `<exit>` element.

- To return the phone to its parent context (in case of an error in the child context), use the `<throw>` and `<catch>` elements.

7.3.1 An example: variable state in a context

Let's illustrate context in action with an example. In the code that follows, the `<spawn>` element invokes a child context by navigating to the URL indicated within `<spawn>` and pushing the new context onto the top of the history stack. Even though the cards within each context are part of the same deck, their state (that is, both the values of variables and the navigation history within each context) remains independent.

From the users' point of view, the first card instructs them to press OK to view some variables. When they press the Accept button, they navigate to the second card, which shows them that the variable called `actor` equals the value `Orson Welles` and the variable called `director` equals the value `Stanley Kubrick`.

On pressing OK here, users perceive that they have been returned to the first card; in reality, they have arrived at a card called `newcontext` that is spawned when the user exits the second card, and that represents a new context entirely.

The new card instructs users to press OK to view some variables. When they press the Accept button, they navigate to another card that shows them the variable called `actor` equals the value `George Peppard` and the variable called `director` equals the value `William Friedkin`.

Upon pressing OK at this card the user returns to the original context and will again see the first set of variable values, whose state was stored when the user moved to the new context and was retrieved when the user returned to the first context.

Here is the code:

```
<?xml version="1.0"?>
<!DOCTYPE wml PUBLIC "-//PHONE.COM//DTD_WML_1.1//EN"
"http://www.phone.com/dtd/wml11.dtd">
<wml>
<card id="firstcontext">
<do type="accept">
   <go href="#display">
     <setvar name="Actor" value="Orson Welles"/>
     <setvar name="Director" value="Stanley Kubrick"/>
   </go>
</do>
<p>
   Press OK to view variable values.
</p>
</card>

<card id="display">
<do type="accept">
   <spawn href="#newcontext" onexit="#display"/>
</do>
<p>
   Parent context:<br/>
   Variable actor=<br/>
   $(Actor)<br/>
   Variable director=<br/>
   $(Director)
</p>
</card>

<card id="newcontext">
<do type="accept">
   <go href="#newdisplay">
     <setvar name="Actor" value="George Peppard"/>
     <setvar name="Director" value="William Friedkin"/>
   </go>
</do>
<p>
   Press OK to view variable values.
</p>
</card>

<card id="newdisplay">
<do type="accept">
   <exit/>
</do>
<p>
   Child Context:<br/>
   Variable actor=<br/>
   $(Actor)<br/>
   Variable director=<br/>
```

Points to the Phone.com DTD

Invokes a child context when the associated task (in this case, pressing the Accept button) is performed

The variable names are the same in the first and second context, but each context associates different values for the same variable name

Exits the child context and returns the user to the parent context

```
    $(Director)
</p>
</card>
</wml>
```

This example demonstrates two contexts that are invoked within a single deck. In the parent context, two variables are set with specific values. The `<spawn>` element is then used to invoke a child context in which the same variables are set to different values. Because state is maintained, moving back and forth between contexts displays the different values for each variable.

Figure 7.2 shows the result:

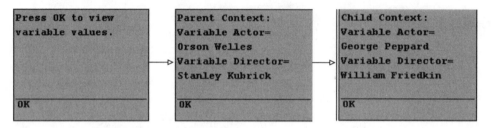

Figure 7.2   Same variables in different contexts

7.4   *NAVIGATING BETWEEN CONTEXTS*

By using nested contexts, you can leverage the functionality of another application, as Figure 7.3 demonstrates (a restaurant application leverages a driving directions application). When the child application (driving directions) returns the user to the parent application (restaurant lookup) the user will find that the *state* of the parent context has been maintained—that is, variables and their associated values within the parent context have not been lost.

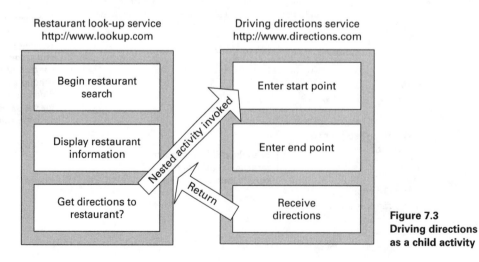

**Figure 7.3
Driving directions
as a child activity**

7.4.1 Returning from a child context to the parent

There are several ways a nested (child) context can allow a user to return to a calling (parent) context:

Using the <exit> element (nested within a <do> element)

If you use the `<exit>` element as the task in a `<do>` element, the associated user action will direct the user back to the parent context.

```
<do type="options" label="Done">
   <exit/>
</do>
```

Specifying an exception with the <throw> task

An exception is an unexpected event (typically an error). By including the `<throw>` element, you are instructing the phone to navigate to a specific URL in the case of an exception.

```
<throw name="error">
   <send value="incorrect value entered"/>
</throw>
```

Specifying a <prev/> task in the first card of the child context

Navigating backward out of a context will pop that context from the history stack.

```
<do type="options" label="Done">
   <prev/>
</do>
```

7.4.2 Returning to the calling card

If you do not include either a `<catch>` element or the `onexit` attribute of the `<spawn>` element within the parent context, the phone will return the user to the same card that invoked the child context—the user is returned to the first card on the history stack that appears after the child context is popped off the history stack.

In some cases, this might not be appropriate. For example, if the parent card provides a list that was modified by the child context, returning directly to the parent card would be undesirable because the list would be obsolete. Fortunately, you can modify the default navigation such that the phone returns from a child context to a location different than the invoking card.

7.4.3 Returning to a specific card

To specify a particular card to which a user will navigate upon returning from a child context, use the `onexit` attribute of the `<spawn>` element. The `onexit` attribute specifies which card to go to if the child context is exited with the `<exit>` element.

For example, to return to the card that is called `specific_card`, use the following <spawn> statement:

```
<spawn href="#child" onexit="#specific_card"/>
```

7.4.4   Using the <throw> and <catch> elements

The <throw> element indicates that an exception should be raised, usually because there was an error of some kind. Throwing an exception terminates the current context and destroys all variables and state information for that context. Values can be sent to an exception handler using the <send/> element within the <throw> element like so:

```
<throw name="error1">
  <send value="Incorrect value entered"/>
</throw>
```

If an exception is thrown and the parent context does not contain an exception handler (a <catch> element), that context is also terminated and the exception is rethrown to that context's parent and so on until an exception handler is found or all parent contexts have been terminated. If this is the case the phone will reset to a reliable state, usually the home page (the page you see when you start your browser).

An exception handler is defined by a <catch> element. The name attribute of the <catch> element is used to specify the name of the exception (to differentiate it from any other exceptions that may possibly be defined in the same card). If no name is defined within the <catch> element, it will handle all exceptions. Values that were sent using the <send> element in the <throw> statement are received with the <receive/> element within the <catch> statement like so:

```
<catch name="error1" onthrow="#errormsg">
  <receive name="throwvalue"/>
</catch>
```

The onthrow attribute of the <catch> element is used to bind the <catch> element to a particular task. Should the <catch> element be used, the user would be redirected to the URL defined in the onthrow attribute.

In other words, if an exception is thrown with a name attribute equal to error1 and the browser finds a parent context with the catch element containing the name attribute equal to error1, then any data that was sent from the <throw> element's <send> statement is received at the <catch> element's <receive/> statement and the browser is redirected to the URL specified in the onthrow attribute of the <catch> element.

Same example: with exception handling

Let's revisit our previous example with some added exception handling to illustrate how to use the <throw> and <catch> elements. Now, the user can press softkey2, labeled `Cancel`, in the child context, and it will throw an exception, which will be handled by a `<catch>` statement in the parent context.

Here's the code:

```
<?xml version="1.0"?>
<!DOCTYPE wml PUBLIC "-//PHONE.COM//DTD_WML_1.1//EN"
"http://www.phone.com/dtd/wml11.dtd">

<wml>
<card id="firstcontext">
<do type="accept">
   <go href="#display">
      <setvar name="Actor" value="Orson Welles"/>
      <setvar name="Director" value="Stanley Kubrick"/>
   </go>
</do>
<p>
   Press OK to view variable values.
</p>
</card>

<card id="display">
<do type="accept">
   <spawn href="#newcontext" onexit="#display">
      <catch>
         <receive name="status"/>
   </catch>
   </spawn>
</do>
<p>
   $(status)
   Parent context:<br/>
   Variable actor=<br/>
   $(Actor)<br/>
   Variable director=<br/>
   $(Director)
</p>
</card>

<card id="newcontext">
<do type="accept">
   <go href="#newdisplay">
      <setvar name="Actor" value="George Peppard"/>
      <setvar name="Director" value="William Friedkin"/>
   </go>
</do>
<p>
   Press OK to view variable values.
</p>
</card>

<card id="newdisplay">
<do type="accept">
```

Catches all exceptions and receives data in a variable called status

```
  <exit/></do>
<do type="options" label="Cancel">
  <throw name="error1">
    <send value="Cancelled"/>
  </throw>
</do>
<p>
  Child Context:<br/>
  Variable actor=<br/>
  $(Actor)<br/>
  Variable director=<br/>
  $(Director)
</p>
</card>
</wml>
```

Indicates that the user is throwing an exception and sends the value Cancelled to the exception handler

7.5 PASSING VARIABLES BETWEEN CONTEXTS

WML provides several methods for passing information between contexts:

- *Sending variables to a child context*—A context can use the <setvar> element to set variable values for a nested context. For more information on <setvar>, see chapter 6.

- *Receiving values from a child context*—When a child context returns to a parent context, it can use the <send/> element to return values to variables specified in the <receive/> element of the <spawn> statement of the parent context.

7.5.1 Sending variables to a child context

Setting variables within a child context is no different from setting variables within a single context application—you must explicitly define the variable using the <setvar> element. As you recall from chapter 6, the syntax for the <setvar> element is:

```
<setvar name="var1" value="val1"/>
<setvar name="var2" value="val2"/>
  .
  .
  .
<setvar name="varN" value="valN"/>
```

The child context uses the variable names to reference variables that the parent context specifies in its <setvar> element; it must know the names of the variables to use them. For example, this code segment uses <setvar> to set the variable Welles equal to the value Kane within the child context:

```
<card id="newcontext">
<do type="accept">
<go href="#newcontext2">
<setvar name="Welles" value="Kane" />
```

```
</go>
</do>
<p>
This card sets the variable within the child context.
</p>
</card>
```

Remember that you can pass variable information from one context to another, but changing a variable within a context does not affect the status of variables within any other context. For example, if you declare the variable name to have the value Sam, within a parent context, passing the variable to a child context would result in each context containing *distinct* variables whose values happen to match. Changing the value of name in either context to George would *not* affect the other context, in which name would still contain the value Sam.

7.5.2   Receiving values from a child context

To accept return values from a child context, you must tell it to send the variable to the parent context by using the <send> element. A sent variable must have a place to go, so you must inform a parent context to expect a variable delivered from the child context by including the <receive/> element in the calling context.

For example, imagine that you are writing an application for travelers, and you would like to provide users with weather information for cities worldwide—information available from a different application. To do this, you would use the <receive/> element within the parent context (the travel application) and the <send> element within the child context (the weather application). The travel application would include a spawn element calling the weather application as follows:

```
<spawn href="http://www.weather.com/phoneapp.wml">
  <receive name="weatherinfo"/>
</spawn>
```

And the weather application would include a send element:

```
<exit>
  <send value="$(forecast)"/>
</exit>
```

Each <send/> element specifies a value to return to the parent context. When the child context exits, the phone uses the values in the <send/> elements to set the corresponding <receive/> variables.

Notice that the <send/> element does not contain a name attribute. To save memory, the phone associates <send/> elements with <receive/> elements one-to-one by position instead of matching <send/> and <receive/> by name. That is, the phone assigns the first value in a series of <send/> elements to the variable that occupies the first position in a series of <receive/> elements. The second <send/> value is associated with the second <receive/> variable, and so on. If the <send/> element series doesn't provide a corresponding value for a variable in the

`<receive/>` elements, the phone clears the variable so that it has no value. This concept is illustrated in figure 7.4.

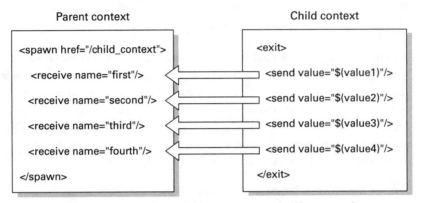

The send and receive variables are not matched by name; they
are associated by position. The first variable passed by `<send>`
sets the first variable defined by `<receive>`, and so on.

Figure 7.4 Receiving values from the child context

7.6 SUMMARY

This chapter discussed how context is used within a WML application. Using context can enable a developer to move from application to application seamlessly without losing the state of either application. Context is a useful tool if you are building an application that can benefit from the functionality available within other applications.

It's important to reiterate that all the new elements described in this chapter are *not* part of the official WML specification. Until these elements are accepted into the WML specification, you shouldn't consider context as WML at all—it is a set of elements defined only by Phone.com. To use context, you must reference the DTD located at the Phone.com site, not the official DTD available within the WAP Forum.

In the next part of this book, we will discuss more ways of adding even more useful complexity and functionality to your WML applications—by using WML's own scripting language, WMLScript.

Introduction to WMLScript

Although a markup language such as a Wireless Markup Language (WML) defines how information is displayed to the user, it has no capacity to execute logical functions based on a user's interaction with that content. While sophisticated logic should be performed server-side, it is often useful to perform simple logical tasks client-side using a scripting language.

Similar in concept and execution to JavaScript (the scripting language used to enable basic logic functions within HTML) WMLScript enables basic logic functions to be included in WML. Common tasks performed through WMLScript are basic mathematical functions, checking user input for errors (for example, did the user enter five numbers to indicate a ZIP code?), and very simple user authentication as well as myriad other useful functions.

CHAPTER 8

Getting started with WMLScript

8.1 INTRODUCTION

Just as HyperText Markup Language (HTML) enables a developer to control how content (text, images, and so forth) is displayed through a desktop browser, Wireless Markup Language (WML) enables a developer to format and present information through the browser on a wireless device. Although WML is good at managing content display, it offers little to enable dynamic interaction with a user; specifically, it does not possess such functionality as logic (if x, then y) or basic mathematics (a = x + y).

One important method to introduce logic into a web site is to embed these more advanced logical functions within server-side code (which can be ASP, CGI, etc.), and invoke this code from within WML. This solution is ideal for most algorithms, but is too bandwidth and labor intensive to be the best solution for very simple logic or mathematic tasks.

A better solution for simple tasks would work directly with the markup language—a relatively straightforward, easy-to-learn scripting language that provides certain important logical and mathematical services and can be embedded directly within the markup code. Years ago, Netscape met this need for HTML programmers with JavaScript. In the HTML world, JavaScript is just what the doctor ordered—it's powerful, flexible, and easy to learn, so people can become productive with it very quickly.

WAP developers face many of the same challenges as their HTML counterparts, and the need for a WAP solution similar to JavaScript quickly became apparent to the WAP Forum. It can be argued that WAP developers have an even more compelling need for an embedded scripting language—server-side logic on the phone is even more expensive than it is on a PC. Forcing a phone application to make a server hit for every logical branch might render the application unusable as it struggles within "real life" network congestion.

To address these issues, the WAP Forum introduced WMLScript, a lightweight scripting language derived from ECMAScript, which is derived from JavaScript. In designing WMLScript, WAP developers kept the most powerful features of other scripting languages, but removed all those features that were unnecessary for the phones' limited development capacity.

This chapter introduces WMLScript. Discussed are the benefits, the structure, the syntax, and how to use variables to add logic to your application. The three chapters in this section assume that you have read the previous chapters on WML and/or have a working knowledge of WML programming.

8.1.1 Overview of WMLScript

WMLScript can add logical functionality to your WML applications. You can add a more advanced user interface, add intelligence for the client, access some of the device's peripheral functionality, and reduce the amount of bandwidth needed to transfer data between the server and the client. WMLScript also allows you, the programmer, to create more usable error-checking routines and better ways of debugging code.

If you've ever programmed in any other language, you'll easily catch on to programming in WMLScript. Similar to other programming languages, WMLScript uses statements, operators, functions, and pragmas to provide the programmer with infinite functionality. WMLScript has a standard set of functions, called libraries, which provide ready-to-use logic and functionality to the programmer. A quick reference for the libraries is provided in appendix B.

8.1.2 Using WMLScript files

If you are new to scripting languages, you won't immediately become a WMLScript whiz just by reading this (or any other) book—you must practice. No book can teach a person how to code in a scripting language; you must sit down and try it out to learn anything.

At the risk of belaboring an obvious point, WMLScript can be used to supplement only a WML application—it is incompatible with HDML! That caveat aside, it's easy to use WMLScript within a WML application—simply write your WMLScript using any text editor, and save it to a server with a .wmls extension (be sure to save the file in simple ANSI format). Because the WMLScript is invoked from within the WML through the WMLScript file's URL, you can save your WMLScript file on any server location you like. To avoid confusion, consider creating a folder within the same directory in which WML code is stored. Name the folder `application_wmls` and store within it all the WMLScript files used by a particular application.

Here is a brief example of how to invoke a WMLScript. This code fragment calls the function, `addtwonumbers`, which is defined in the WMLScript file add.wmls. Don't worry about the syntax here, the point is simply to see that calling a WMLScript function from a WML file is as easy as specifying the WMLScript filename, followed by a hash mark (#) and the function name:

```
<go href="add.wmls#addtwonumbers(var1, var2)"/>
```

WMLScript, unlike JavaScript, is not embedded directly within the markup code. Instead, WMLScript is contained within a separate file whose URL is referenced within the WML. The phone first loads the WML code from the server; only when the WMLScript URL is referenced within the WML code is the WMLScript file loaded from the server to the phone.

The phone loads WMLScript and WML files separately for a couple of reasons:

- To make it easier for developers to stay within the 1,500k-upload limit imposed by the gateway server.

- To reduce the initial amount of time needed to load the WML deck into the phone (which improves the perceived performance of the application).

8.2   STRUCTURE AND SYNTAX

WMLScript is based on ECMAScript, and uses a very similar structure. A WMLScript file is delivered to the phone as a *compilation unit*. In turn, the compilation unit is made up of one or more *functions*, which contain one or more *blocks* (defined by braces and in which variables are scoped). In turn, blocks contain one or more *statements*. Table 8.1 defines terms in figure 8.1 more clearly:

Table 8.1   Terms of WMLScript structure

Term	Definition
Compilation unit	A collection of functions contained in a file
Function	Accepts a query and returns a result. Functions can be invoked by other functions within the same compilation unit or by WML code.

Table 8.1 Terms of WMLScript structure (continued)

Term	Definition
Block	Braces, {}, define a block of WMLScript. The braces define the scope of the variable within that block—calling a variable outside of its scope will generate an error. All WMLScript functions contain at least a single block and must be bounded by at least a single pair of braces.
Statement	A single command within WMLScript; always ends with a semicolon

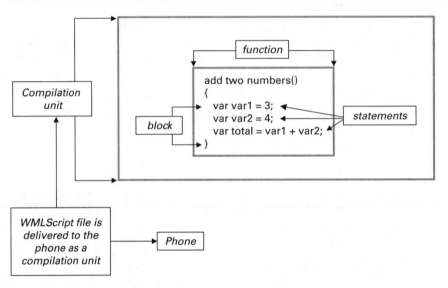

Figure 8.1   Diagram of a function

Case sensitivity

WMLScript, like WML, is case sensitive. Var is a different variable than var in WMLScript. All language keywords, variables, and function names must be properly capitalized. Text that is to be output or values of variables are unaffected by case.

White space

Just as with WML or HDML, the phone's browser ignores spaces, tabs, new lines, and so forth within a WMLScript document, except those that are part of string constants. You can structure your code using as much or as little white space as you desire in order to format it in a way that makes it easiest for you and your colleagues to follow.

Commenting

A *comment*, text ignored by the browser, generally is used by the programmer to explain code and document concepts. WMLScript supports two kinds of comments:

- *Single line*—Begin with a double slash (//) and end with the end of the line. The browser ignores any text on the line following the double slash.

      //This is a single line comment

- *Multiline*—Begin with a slash star (/*) and end with a star slash (*/). The browser ignores any text that is between the slash star (/*) and the star slash (*/).

      /* This is a
      multiline comment*/

Reserved words

Reserved words (also known as *keywords*) are words that have a special meaning in WMLScript and cannot be used as variable or function names. The following list provides all the keywords for the current WMLScript version:

access	extern	name
agent	for	path
break	function	return
continue	header	typeof
div	http	url
domain	if	use
else	isvalid	user
equiv	meta	var
		while

Also avoid using these reserved words in your applications, as they will be used in a future version of WMLScript:

case	enum	sizeof
catch	export	struct
class	extends	super
const	finally	switch
debugger	import	throw
default	private	tr
do	public	

If you are familiar with other programming languages, here is a list of common keywords that are *not* reserved in WMLScript:

delete	null
in	this
lib	void
new	with

8.3 ABOUT VARIABLES

Variables, as defined in chapter 6, are symbolic names for values. WMLScript supports only variables that are declared inside functions or passed as function parameters. Just as in WML, variables used within WMLScript can be set to different types of data. For example, a variable can be set to an integer (for instance, the number 4). Similarly, a variable can be set to a text string (for instance, the text string four). The type of data contained within a variable determines how the phone acts upon the data. A phone will use the *string* variable `true` differently than it would the *boolean* variable `true` (as opposed to `false`).

Thus WMLScript needs to understand the data type contained by a variable to accurately use the variable. Unfortunately, WMLScript does not have an intrinsic ability to check data type—WMLScript is *weakly typed*. This means that data type is not explicitly defined within the variable name, and only very limited type checking is performed automatically by WMLScript.

This is an important consideration because data type is a common source of errors within WMLScript. WMLScript uses a single variable to define all variable types, and carelessly used variables can cause the phone to become confused as to how the variables should be acted upon. To avoid bugs, keep your WMLScript simple and ensure variable types are used consistently throughout the code.

WMLScript recognizes five data types (table 8.2).

Table 8.2   WMLScript data types

Data type	Description
Boolean	Either true or false. Defines whether or not a condition meets specified criteria.
Integer	A whole number. WMLScript understands numbers between –2,147,483,648 and 2,147,483,674.
Float	WMLScript understands floating point variables between 1.17549435E-38 and 3.40282347E+38.
String	A series of text characters. "This is a string" is a string, as can be the number "234." In the latter case, adding a "1" to the string variable would return "2341," not "235."
Invalid	Returned if the variables result in an invalid data type.

8.3.1   Declaring variables

Variables must be declared prior to first use. *Declaring* a variable means that you must give the variable a name and assign a value before you can do anything with it. The syntax for declaring a variable is shown in figure 8.2. (Statements used to define a variable are detailed in chapter 9.)

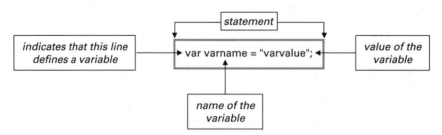

Figure 8.2   Diagram of a variable definition

In this statement, `var` indicates that the statement defines a variable, `varname` is the name of the variable, and `varvalue` is the explicit value of the variable. Instead of explicitly setting a variable value, you can instead use an expression—for example:

```
var varname = var1 + var2;
```

This statement would set the variable `varname` equal to the sum of `var1` and `var2`.

Scope of variables

The *scope* of a variable is the segment of an application in which a variable can be referenced. The scope equals the function that the variable is declared in. This means that a variable name must be unique in that function, but can have the same name as a variable in another function without consequence.

Accessing variables

Obviously, if the scope of a variable is bounded by the function in which it is declared, then you cannot access a variable outside of that function. To access a variable, simply call the variable by name and the value for that variable will be substituted.

In this example we define two variables, `var1` and `var2`, and set them equal to integers, 3 and 4. Then we add the two integers by adding the variables and setting them equal to a third variable, called `total`:

```
var var1 = 3;
var var2 = 4;
var total = var1 + var2;
```

The variable `total` now has a value of 7.

8.3.2 Data type assumptions

WMLScript makes some assumptions about type (table 8.3). In general, data type errors are among the most common in WMLScript. You can depend on a data type assumption being incorrect much of the time.

Table 8.3 Data type assumptions

If WMLScript sees this:	This data type is assumed:	Which may contain these values
var a = true;	Boolean	True and false
var a = 45;	Integer	–2,147,483,648 to 2,147,483,647
var a = invalid;	Invalid	This variable is a literal denoting an invalid value that may result from a floating point overflow
var a = 98.6;	Float	+/- 1.17549435E-38 to +/- 3.402823476E+38
var a = "Hello!";	String	Enclosed by single or double quotes

8.4   FIRST LOOK: ADDING TWO NUMBERS

Before we look at each part of WMLScript in depth, let's begin with an example. It's not necessary to fully understand the code at this point, but it will provide a basic idea of how WMLScript is structured and thus form a foundation for understanding the specifics.

In the example, the user is presented with two entry cards, each soliciting the entry of a single integer. After entering the second number and pressing OK, the user is presented with the sum of the two numbers, compliments of the WMLScript function.

8.4.1   The WML code: add.wml

Here is the WML code, with which you should be familiar:

```
<?xml version="1.0"?>
<! DOCTYPE wml PUBLIC "-//WAPFORUM//DTD WML 1.1//EN"
"http://www.wapforum.org/DTD/wml_1.1.xml">

<wml>
<card id="first">
<do type="accept">
  <go href="#second"/>
</do>
<p>
 Enter a number: <br/>
 <input name="var1"/>
</p>
</card>

<card id="second">
<do type="accept">
  <go href="add.wmls#addtwonumbers(var1, var2)"/>
</do>
<p>
 Enter another number: <br/>
 <input name="var2"/>
</p>
</card>

<card id="third">
<do type="accept">
  <go href="#first"/>
</do>
<p>
 Your numbers add to $(var3)
</p>
</wml>
</card>
```

first (margin annotation for the first card block)

second. (margin annotation for the second card block)

third. (margin annotation for the third card block)

In this example, we start with the WML code, which should be familiar to you. In particular, see how the second card invokes the WMLScript with a URL, just as another card or deck would be invoked.

8.4.2　The WMLScript code: add.wmls

Here is the WMLScript code, which you will learn more about in the chapters ahead:

```
extern function addtwonumbers()
{
var a = WMLBrowser.getVar("var1");
var aInt = Lang.parseInt(a);

var b = WMLBrowser.getVar("var2");
var bInt = Lang.parseInt(b);

var c = aInt + bInt;

WMLBrowser.setVar ("var3", c);
WMLBrowser.go ("add.wml#third");
}
```

When the WMLScript file add.wmls is called from add.wml, a function called addtwonumbers is used and the two values that we got from the user are passed into the function. After the function executes, it returns the user to the third WML card and returns the resulting value. Don't be concerned with understanding the code at this point; just try to get a feel for what WMLScript looks like and how it works with WML.

8.4.3　The result

Figures 8.3, 8.4, and 8.5 show how the application appears. First, the user is asked to enter a number (figure 8.3). The next card (figure 8.4) requests the user enter another number. The final card (figure 8.5) displays the sum of the two numbers.

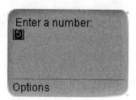

Figure 8.3
The first card

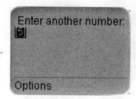

Figure 8.4
The second card

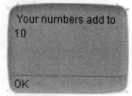

Figure 8.5
The final card

8.5　SUMMARY

This chapter introduced WMLScript and described its benefits and basic attributes. You should have a general sense of the type of functionality offered by WMLScript, as well as an idea of the structure and syntax of the language.

In the next two chapters we will look at the components of WMLScript in detail, beginning with statements, the basic building block of WMLScript. After that we'll move into putting those statements together to create some useful functionality.

CHAPTER 9

Using WMLScript statements and operators

9.1 INTRODUCTION

Chapter 8 introduced the basic structure of WMLScript: compilation units that are made up of one or more functions; functions are in turn made up of one or more blocks; blocks are in turn made up of one or more statements. Statements perform the grunt work of a function by using special keywords and expressions to manipulate data.

In this chapter we will discuss statements and operators. We will learn what a statement is, how it is used to add complex functionality to your program, and discuss the different types of statements in detail. We will also define an operator, explain how to use it to provide logic to your program, and discuss the types of operators. A quick reference at the end of this chapter summarizes all the operators and how to use them.

132

9.1.1 What a statement does

Statements are the engines powering WMLScript, and the specific functionality a statement can perform is almost limitless. In general, however, statements perform one of six general functions:

- *Declare variables and assign them a value*—The statement var a = 5 declares the variable a and assigns a value of 5 to it.
- *Manipulate variables*—WMLScript can change the value type of a variable (from a string to an integer, for example), perform mathematical functions on a variable, and send variables back to a WML application.
- *Check for a condition and act on it*—WMLScript can control the flow of the program, acting in one way or another based on the state of the application. For example, you can instruct WMLScript to check the state of a variable (e.g., is variable A less than 10?), and act based on that state (if variable A is less than 10, perform function foo. If not, perform function bar).
- *Receive variables from and return variables to a WML application—*
  - Call another function and use the returned value.
  - Break the flow of a program.

  You can terminate the WMLScript, stop the execution of a loop, or exit the current function.

Here are some example statements. Note that you must close a statement with a semicolon (;). This is a mandatory syntax rule. Excluding the semicolon will result in an error.

Example 1: variable statement

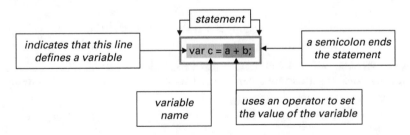

Figure 9.1   Diagram of a variable statement

In figure 9.1, the statement declares a variable named c and assigns it a value equivalent to the values of variables a and b added together. Note that for this statement to work, both variables a and b would also have to be declared and defined elsewhere within the WMLScript (using two additional statements).

Example 2: statement using a function

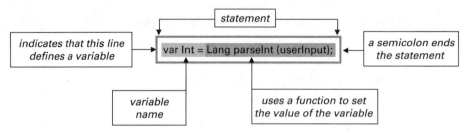

Figure 9.2   Diagram of a statement using a library function

The statement diagrammed in figure 9.2 declares a variable called `Int`. To assign a value to `Int`, this statement calls the library function `Lang.parseInt`, which converts a string value into an integer value (for more information, see the next chapter). In this case, the value of `userInput` is converted to an integer and assigned to `Int`.

Example 3: conditional statement

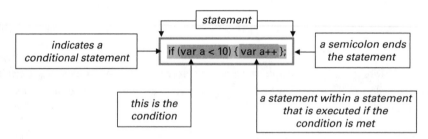

Figure 9.3   Diagram of a conditional statement

The final example, figure 9.3, is a statement that checks if the value of variable `a` is less than 10. If so, the value of `a` is incremented up a single digit. For more information on operators such as `++`, see the operators section at the end of this chapter. Not only does this illustrate a conditional statement, it also shows a statement within a statement (`a++` is itself a statement).

Each of these statements falls within a particular *statement type*, described in section 9.2.

9.1.2   What an operator does

Operators are predefined functions built into the WMLScript language. The name of the function is the *operator* and the variables that are passed in are the variables on either side of the operator. The operator performs some functionality on the variables and returns a result.

For example, the expression a + b uses the operator + and the variables a and b. The functionality of this operator is obviously to add the two variables together and return the result. Not all operators are this obvious. All the operators are summarized in section 9.3 and detailed in section 9.4.

9.2   STATEMENT TYPES

Table 9.1 lists the statement types available within WMLScript. In particular, note the statement types while, for, and if. They are *control constructs*; statements that imbue WMLScript with its real power—the power to make decisions and act on them.

Table 9.1   Statement types

Type	Description
block	A collection of statements enclosed in curly braces ({}) that are treated as a single statement
break	Interrupts a loop initiated by either the for or while control construct
continue	Terminates the execution of a block of statements in a while or for loop and continues the execution of the loop at the next iteration
empty	A placeholder similar to the WML noop task
expression	Describes a statement that defines and sets values to variables or performs mathematical functions, or calls other functions
for	A control construct that performs an operation over and over until a condition is met
if	A control construct that branches depending on whether a particular condition is true
return	Specifies a return value for a function—function *always* returns a value
variable	Defines a variable
while	A control construct that maintains a particular condition only while another condition remains true

Next we look at each statement type and how they appear within a WMLScript function.

Block statements

A block statement is a collection of statements enclosed in braces ({}) and treated as a single statement. Block statements are often called compound statements. Here is an example:

```
{
var x = 0;
var y = Lang.abs(b);
popUp("Reminder!");
}
```

Break statements

The break statement is used to terminate a for loop or a while loop (both defined earlier). It invokes the execution of the statement immediately following the terminated loop.

This example adds an addition condition to the while example used earlier. Here, a random number is generated and a while loop invoked until the value of the number equals 1. In this case, however, the loop will be broken if the value reaches 34.

```
 var  anyNumber = Lang.random (100);
while (anyNumber > 1)
{
   if (index == 34)
   {
     break;
   }
   anyNumber--;
}
```

NOTE   It is an error to use a break statement anywhere outside a for or while loop.

Continue statements

The continue statement terminates a for or while loop and continues execution at the next iteration. If it is a while loop, the continue statement returns to the condition. In a for loop, the continue statement jumps to the update expression (the third expression in a for loop).

This example uses a while statement to evaluate the value of a variable. If the value is less than 5, it is incremented. The value is then added to another variable unless the value is 3, in which case the continue statement returns to the condition, skipping the step that adds the two variables, and continues the loop. Here is the code:

```
var index = 0;
var count = 0;
while (index < 5)
{
   index++;
   if (index == 3)
   {
     continue;
   }
   count += index;
}
```

Empty statements

The empty statement acts just as a <noop> card—it is used where a statement is needed but no operation is required. Here is an example of an empty statement:

```
while (!user(ready)) ;
```

This statement waits until the user() function returns true. Until that time, no operation is needed, so an empty statement is inserted—a space and the semicolon. Note that the user function returns a value (true or false) and that value is assigned to the variable ready which is independent of any variables within the user function.

Expression statements

An expression statement is used to assign values to variables, perform mathematical functions, and call other functions. Examples are:

```
str = "Hello" + userName;
userNumber = 4;
userNumber++;
firstCounter = counter, secondCounter = counter * 10;
Dialogs.alert("That's an invalid number, you goof!");
```

For statements

The for statement is a control construct that consists of three optional expressions and a statement. The syntax is:

```
for (expression; expression; expression) statement;
```

- *The first expression* is typically used to declare a counter variable (or initialize an existing variable as a counter variable).

- *The second expression* is used to evaluate the variable and return a boolean (or invalid response). If the expression returns a true, the statement is invoked; if the expression returns a false or invalid, the loop terminates and the next statement is invoked. The second condition is optional (a true is returned if it is omitted).

- *The third expression* is used to manipulate the variable in some way. Typically, the third expression is used to increment or decrement the variable, or update it in a specific way. After the third expression is executed, the loop returns to the second expression for evaluation of the (recently updated) variable.

This example generates a random number and checks to see if the number is 1. If not, another random number is generated:

```
var userNumber = Lang.random (50)
for (userNumber; userNumber != 1; userNumber = Lang.random(50))
{
Dialogs.alerts ("You're not number one!");
}
Dialogs.alerts("You're number one!");
```

If statements

An if statement contains an expression and one or two statements. It first evaluates the expression and if the expression evaluates as true, the first statement is executed. If the expression is false or invalid the statement following the `else` keyword is executed. Here is the structure for an `if` statement:

```
if (Expression)
{
   statement
}
else
{
   statement
}
```

Note that the second condition (indicated by the `else` preceding it) is optional. An `if` statement can be structured as follows:

```
if (Expression)
{
   statement
}
```

In the following example, the statement looks to see if the variable `userNumber` contains the same value as the variable `winnerNumber`. If true, the `Dialog.alert` function is invoked, sending the message `You won!` to the user. If false, the second condition is invoked, sending the message `You didn't win`.

```
if (userNumber = winnerNumber)
{
   Dialogs.alert ("You won!");
}
else
{
   Dialogs.alert ("You didn't win.");
}
```

Return statements

Use the `return` statement to specify a return value for the function. By default, a function returns an empty string. Here is the structure for a `return` statement:

```
return Expression;
```

In the following example, a random number is generated and if it is more than 10 then invalid is returned; otherwise the variable userNumber is incremented and returned:

```
var  anyNumber = Lang.random (100);
if (anyNumber > 10)
{
   return invalid;
}
else
{
   return userNumber++;
}
```

Variable statements

A `variable` statement is used to declare a variable, which can then be manipulated (`expression` statements are a typical way to manipulate variables described in a `variable` statement). Variables can either be initialized to a specific value or to an empty string (`""`). Here is the structure for declaring a variable:

```
var variableName = variableValue;
```

Examples include:

```
var str = "Hello " + userName;
var userNumber = 4;
var newUsernumber = userNumber++;
var secondCounter = firstCounter * 10;
```

While statements

The `while` statement evaluates a condition, and if the condition is true, executes a statement. As soon as the statement is executed, the condition is re-evaluated. This loop continues until the condition is evaluated as false. The syntax is as follows:

```
while (Expression)
{
   Statement
}
```

One example of this is the same one used in the `empty` statement:

```
while (!user(ready)) ;
```

Of course, any statement can be executed following a `while` statement:

```
while (!user(ready))
{
   Dialogs.alert ("Please get ready!");
}
```

In the following example, a number is randomly generated. As long as the random number is greater than 1, a loop is invoked that decreases the value of the variable by one. When the variable value reaches 1, the loop ends and the next statement is invoked.

```
var  anyNumber = Lang.random (100);
while (anyNumber > 1)
{
   anyNumber--;
}
Dialogs.alert("Finally got to one");
```

9.3 OPERATORS

An *operator* is a symbol that expresses an action or a relationship. You are almost certainly familiar with some operators even if the term is unfamiliar. I'll prove it: Given this expression, 4 + 5 = 9 < 22, the +, =, and < symbols are operators.

WMLScript has 45 operators. Each falls within one of the following categories:

- Arithmetic
- Assignment
- Comma
- Comparison
- Conditional
- Logical
- String
- isvalid
- typeof

Each operator category is summarized in this section and detailed in the quick reference at the end of the chapter.

Arithmetic operators

WMLScript supports all the basic mathematic functions; addition, subtraction, multiplication, floating point division, and integer division. You can also perform more advanced numerical manipulations, such as extracting integer division remainders, bitwise rotations (with optional zero fill), pre- and post-increments and decrements, negations, and bit negations.

Assignment operators

You can assign a value to a variable with a simple declaration (such as var a = 5;). WMLScript enables you to go one step further by supporting variable assignment with operations such as divide and assign, shift and assign, and so forth. Examples include var a += 5; or var a *= 5;. In the first example, the a and 5 are added, and the total is assigned to a. The second example is similar, except a and 5 are multiplied before the resultant value is assigned to a.

Comma operators

Use a comma operator to combine several expressions into one. The result of the comma operator is the value of the second operand. Commas that are used to separate parameters in a function call or a variable declaration are *not* comma operators. If you want to use a comma operator in one of those cases you must put the comma operator expression in parentheses.

The following example shows that the comma operator returns the value of the second operand and also that the expression must be in parentheses when used in a function call. The function in the last line evaluates to myFunction("Name", 9);. Here's the code:

```
var a = 2;
var b = 3, c = 3;
myFunction("Name", 3*(b*a, c));
```

The following example shows a more useful reason for using comma operators—performing a task (in this case incrementing a variable) while returning the value of a different variable. Here is the code:

```
for (a=100, b=1; b < 10; a++, b++)
{
//… do something …
}
```

Comparison operators

Comparison operators compare values. We have already used some comparison operators such as < and >. Comparison operators follow these rules based on the data type of the variable:

- *Boolean*—True is larger than false.
- *Integer*—Comparison based on given integer values.
- *Floating-point*—Comparison based on given floating-point values.
- *String*—Comparison based on the order of character codes of given string values.
- *Invalid*—If at least one of the operands is invalid, the result of the comparison is invalid.

Here are some examples of using comparison operators:

```
if (myHeight < yourHeight);
if myHeight == yourHeight;
```

Conditional operators

Conditional operators assign a value to a variable based on the evaluation of a Boolean statement. Conditional operators use a colon and question mark (: and ?) and act similar to an if statement. The structure follows:

```
var result = expression1 ? expression2 : expression3;
```

In this case, expression1 is being evaluated and if the result is true, the expression2 is executed and expression3 is ignored. If the value of expression1 is false then expression2 is ignored and expression3 is executed.

In this example, if the variable question is set to true, the variable answer will be set to false, and if the variable question is set to false, the variable answer is set to true. Here is the code segment:

```
var answer = question ? false : true;
```

Logical operators

WMLScript supports the three basic logical operations AND, OR, and NOT. When evaluating a logical AND expression, WMLScript evaluates the operands in order; if the first operand is FALSE the expression is FALSE and the second operand is not evaluated. Using the same logic, when evaluating a logical OR expression, if the first operand is TRUE the expression is TRUE and the second operand is not evaluated. In either expression, if the first operand evaluates to INVALID, the expression is INVALID.

String operators

String operators function on, you guessed it, strings. There are only two string operators, + and +=. Both concatenate string variables. For more functionality with strings, refer to the string library, covered in chapter 10.

The following example illustrates how to use the += operator to concatenate two string variables. After this statement executes, the variable str will have a value of Hello Christina:

```
var greeting = "Hello ";
var myname = "Christina";
greeting += myname;  // greeting now equals "Hello Christina"
```

isvalid operators

The isvalid operator checks the validity of a variable or an expression.

The isvalid operator returns:

- True if the result of an expression is valid or if a variable is of a valid type
- False if the result of an expression is not valid or if a variable is not of a valid type

The isvalid operator does not convert the result from one type to another. The following is an example of an isvalid operator:

```
var str = "123";
var ok = isvalid str;  // true
var tst = isvalid (1/0);  // false
```

typeof operators

The typeof operator returns an integer based on the type of a given expression. It does not convert from one type to another; it simply describes the current type.

Here are the supported return values:

- *0*—expression is an integer
- *1*—expression is a floating-point
- *2*—expression is a string
- *3*—expression is a boolean
- *4*—expression is invalid

9.4   OPERATOR QUICK REFERENCE

Tables 9.2–9.7 show the supported operators and the operation each performs.

Table 9.2   Assignment operators

Operator	Operation
=	assign
+=	add (numbers)/concatenate (strings) and assign
-=	subtract and assign
*=	multiply and assign
/=	divide and assign
div=	divide (integer division) and assign
%=	remainder (the sign of the result equals the sign of the dividend) and assign
<<=	bitwise left shift and assign
>>=	bitwise right shift with sign and assign
>>>=	bitwise right shift zero fill and assign
&=	bitwise AND and assign
^=	bitwise XOR and assign
|=	bitwise OR and assign

Table 9.3   Arithmetic operators

Operator	Operation
+	add (numbers)/concatenation (strings)
-	subtract
*	multiply
/	divide
div	integer division

Table 9.4   Complex binary operators

Operator	Operation
%	remainder, the sign of the result equals the sign of the dividend

Table 9.4   Complex binary operators (continued)

Operator	Operation
<<	bitwise left shift
>>	bitwise right shift and sign
>>>	bitwise shift right with zero fill
&	bitwise AND
|	bitwise OR
^	bitwise XOR

Table 9.5   Basic unary operators

Operator	Operation
+	plus
-	minus
--	pre-or-post decrement
++	pre-or-post increment
~	bitwise NOT

Table 9.6   Logical operators

Operator	Operation
&&	logical AND
||	logical OR
!	logical NOT (unary)

Table 9.7   Comparison operators

Operator	Operation
<	less than
<=	less than or equal
==	equal
>=	greater than or equal
>	greater than
!=	inequality

9.5   SUMMARY

This chapter described how to use statements, the fundamental building blocks of WMLScript. Statements are the workhorses of the code that, when combined into a block and used inside a function, provide logical and mathematic resources.

We also discussed the different kinds of operators and how to use them to make your WMLScript functions more dynamic.

Together, statements and operators can make up functions. How functions work, and how to use WMLScript's comprehensive library of prebuilt functions, is the topic of the next chapter. The next chapter will also cover pragmas—a directive that generates specific behavior from a compiler.

CHAPTER 10

WMLScript functions and pragmas

10.1 INTRODUCTION

In chapter 9 we discussed using statements and operators to perform specific functionality that makes WMLScript a more useful language. In this chapter we will cover functions and pragmas.

Just as a function is made up of one of more statements, a WMLScript compilation unit is a collection of one or more functions. A *function* is a piece of code that tells the phone to do something such as "add these numbers" or "compare this data with that data." A function is a block of code that takes an input and returns a result. In this chapter we will discover ways of declaring and using functions in order to make a much more complex program.

A *pragma* is a type of function that is defined at the beginning of file, before any other function declarations, and provides information throughout the entire compilation unit. In this chapter we will learn types of pragmas: `url`, `access`, and `META`.

10.2 FUNCTIONS

Invoking a function's name accesses the services provided by a function; that is, a function is a named procedure that performs a distinct service.

Some examples of services a function might perform:

- Get two variables from a WML application, add them together, and return the result.
- Get a variable from a WML application, determine if it is valid, and send to user's particular card based on the validity of the variable.
- Generate a message and display it on the phone.
- Generate a random number.
- Compare two pieces of data and return a result indicating whether the two pieces of data match.

When you write a WMLScript file, it will contain from one to *n* functions. A WMLScript compilation unit can contain any number of functions, but remember to keep the memory limitations of the phone in mind. Some of these functions are called directly from the WML application; some are called by other functions. These functions can work together to perform a single service, or a number of different services, for the WML application.

You can also define custom functions that perform services necessary to your particular application, and you do it by including a series of statements within the body of the function, as described in the previous chapter.

10.2.1 Function declarations

The following characteristics provide an overview of function rules, with a more detailed explanation in the paragraphs that follow:

- Functions always return a value.
- Ask a function a question; get an answer. The default return value is an empty string (`""`).
- Functions always act as individual entities and cannot be nested.
- Function names must be unique within a compilation unit.
- Names can be any alphanumeric character, and may include the underscore character (_). Names cannot begin with a number.
- Variables are passed from one function to another by value (not by name).

- You must specify a variable name to receive the value.

- Functions must pass exactly the same number of arguments (that is, the same number of values) that are declared in the receiving function.

- Function parameters (values included in parentheses immediately to the right of the function name, to which values sent by an invoking entity are assigned) behave like local variables that have been initialized before the function body is executed.

Functions have names, and are invoked from within a WML application by indicating the URL of the WMLScript and the name of the function preceded by a hash mark (#)—exactly the same way a particular card within a WML deck is invoked. For example, a WML card can invoke a function called `addTwoNumbers` within a WMLScript called `mywmlscript.wmls` as follows:

```
<card>
<do type=accept>
   <go "href=http://www.mydomain.com/mywmlscript.wmls#addTwoNumbers" />
</do>
</card>
```

Function syntax looks like this (This is what the entire compilation unit looks like if it contained only one function):

```
extern function myFirstFunction (optional parameters)   ❶
{
first statement;        ❷     The body of the
second statement;              function is
}                              contained within
                               braces ({})
```

Code comments

❶ (optional) `Extern` indicates that this function may be invoked from outside the compilation unit (a WML deck, for example). Without the extern, this function would only be accessible in other functions within this file.

   `function` describes what you are looking at—a function!

   `myFirstFunction` is the name of this function.

   (optional) The variables within the parentheses contain values that are sent to the function by the invoking entity (another function or WML code).

❷ A function is made up of one or more statements, which are segmented by semicolons (;).

10.2.2   Local functions

By default, functions can only be invoked by local functions—functions within the same compilation unit (put another way, by default a function cannot be invoked from a WML application, nor can it be invoked from another compilation unit). To make a unit accessible to WML applications (as `myFirstFunction` is in the previous example), you must include the term `extern`. In the following example, the extern at the beginning of the `genrandom` function indicates that it may be

invoked by a WML application or by a function within another co[...]
Removing `extern` renders the function accessible only by other fu[...]
the same compilation unit.

```
extern function genrandom ()
{
   return Lang.random(5);
}
```

You can name a function almost anything, as long as the name contains only alphanumeric characters, the underscore symbol (_), and does not begin with a number. The big exception to this is a prohibition on the use of reserved words—words that have special meaning to WMLScript and might cause unpredictable behavior if used in unintended ways. For a list of reserved words, see chapter 8.

The parentheses to the right of the function name contain a comma-separated list of argument names. When values are passed to the function from an external source (a WML application or from another function, for example), the values are assigned to the names in this list in exact order. The number of values sent to the function must match exactly the number of arguments (*parameters*) specified within the parentheses.

10.2.3   External functions

An *external function* is one that can be invoked from functions external to the compilation unit, and are designated by preceding the function declaration with `extern`. An external function acts as an entry point to your WMLScript—only through an external function can a WML application invoke the services contained within the script. Obviously, then, each WMLScript must contain at least one external function to be useful.

Also, you can invoke functions external to an active compilation unit by placing the URL pragma within the compilation unit. Pragmas will be discussed later in this chapter.

10.3   LIBRARY FUNCTIONS

Many common services are available to you through predefined functions built directly into WMLScript. Just as you can invoke the services of another function within the same compilation unit by referencing its name, you need only type the library function name to invoke its service. These predefined functions are arranged into seven libraries of related functions (table 10.1). For a complete list of all functions supported in the libraries, see appendix B.

Table 10.1   WMLScript function libraries

Library	Description
Console	includes more user-interface functions
Dialogs	includes typical user-interface functions
Float	includes floating-point functions that are typically used in applications

Table 10.1 WMLScript function libraries (continued)

Library	Description
Lang	includes functions that are closely related to the WMLScript language core
String	includes typical string functions
URL	includes functions for handling absolute and relative URLs
WMLBrowser	includes functions for interacting with a WML application

You can invoke a function by indicating its library and the function name, separated by a dot. For example, let's build a simple function that generates two random numbers, adds them together, and sends the result back to a WML application:

```
extern function addNumbers()  ❶
{

var a = Lang.random(20);  ❷
var b = Lang.random(20);  ❸
var c = b + a            ❹
WMLBrowser.setVar ("number", c);  ❺

}
```

Code comments

❶ Begins a function called addNumbers, which can be invoked externally. If the "extern" label was missing, the WML application couldn't invoke this function. The empty parentheses are required, but ignore them for now.

❷ Declares a variable called a and defines it with a random number from 0–20. Generating this number is the random function, which lives in the Lang function library. Note that if you wanted to generate a random number from 1–20, you would instead type Lang.random(19)+1.

❸ Declares another variable, named b, and again invokes the random function to give it a value.

❹ Adds the two random numbers together and assigns that value to a variable named c.

❺ Invokes the setVar function from the WMLBrowser library, which sends the value within c back to the WML application, where it will be associated with the number variable. If there is no number variable within the WML application, the function will fail.

Console library

This library is available only through the Phone.com SDK and contains functions that enable you to output a message to the SDK Phone Information Window. These messages are used for debugging and will convert any value to a string and output it to the window.

Dialogs library

The dialogs library contains functions that enable you to send to the user a message that alerts, confirms, or prompts. Dialogs functions are typically invoked based on the value of another function. For example, you might have a function that checks user input for validity. If found invalid, you could use the alert function in the dialogs library to send an alert prompting the user to re-enter the data and then the `lang.exit` function to return the user to the WML application.

Float library

The float library contains a set of common floating point mathematical operations. There is a catch to using functions within the float library—not all devices support floating point operations, and float functions can only be used if float is supported. If a function in this library is used on a phone that does not support floating-point operations, the function will return invalid as a response.

To be on the safe side, include the `lang.float()` function, which returns a `true` if the device supports floating point operations, and `false` if not. Based on this information, you can invoke the float function or redirect the user to an alternative algorithm.

Lang library

The lang library contains a set of functions that perform services that are core to WMLScript functionality. Functions within this library can perform such services as aborting the execution of the WMLScript and assessing certain characteristics of the user's device (such as the character set supported by the WMLScript interpreter and whether the user's device supports floating point operations).

Among the useful functions contained within the lang library is the `lang.parseInt(variable)` function, which converts the value of `variable` into an integer. This is useful because variables received from WML applications default as a string, making them impossible to manipulate mathematically. For example, let's say that a WML application prompted a user to enter a number; the user enters 15" which is then passed to a WMLScript compilation unit. Unless the number is converted to an integer using the `lang.parseInt` function, WMLScript will "see" the number as a string array—a character 1 "followed by a character 5". The `parseInt` function turns the string into the number 15.

String library

The string library contains a set of functions that enable you to manipulate text characters (a string is an array of characters). In WMLScript, each character in a string has a number associated with it, beginning with zero (0) for the first character. For example, in the string Frog, F=0.

An interesting facility of some functions within the string library is to find individual words (or other groupings of characters) within a string by specifying a special *separator* by which *elements* in a string can be separated. For example, using a space as a separator enables WMLScript to recognize individual words. In this case, the elements (words) between the separator (spaces) can be manipulated by specifying the separator and the element index. The first element in a string has an index zero (0). Each instance of a space in the string separates two elements.

URL library

The URL library contains a set of functions that, when invoked with a URL, will return the value of a particular aspect of that URL. For example, the URL.getFragment function will respond with the fragment within the specified URL, if any exists. Similarly, getBase, getHost, getParameters, and getPath return the value of the base, host, parameters, and path of the specified URL (if any exist). If the value doesn't exist, the function will return an empty string.

WMLBrowser library

The WMLBrowser library contains a set of functions that enable you to interact with a WML application. Functions within this library enable you to receive variables from (and send variables to) a WML app, find the current active card within the WML deck, change WML contexts (or clear a context), go to a specified URL, or return to the card previous to the one that invoked the WMLScript.

The WMLBrowser library functions will be among your most-used functions. This library is the key to weaving your WML code with WMLScript.

10.4 PRAGMAS

Just as you can use the <template> tags to define deckwide information in a WML application, you can define compilation-unit-wide information in WMLScript using pragmas. In WMLScript, there are three types of pragmas, all beginning with the keyword use: url, access, and meta.

10.4.1 URL pragma

The url pragma points to the URL of another compilation unit and gives it a local name. Functions within that remote compilation unit can then be called by referencing the local name and the desired function (see the section on functions for more information).

For example, imagine you have compilation units named wmlscript1.wmls and wmlscript2.wmls saved on a server. Let's imagine further that wmlscript1.wmls contains a single function called validateNumber, and that wmlscript2.wmls contains three functions, addTwoNumbers, subtractTwoNumbers, and divideTwoNumbers.

The first compilation unit might be called within the WML deck to validate a number entered by the user. If your program demanded that simple mathematics be performed on this number, you could use the functions contained within `wmlscript2.wmls` using the `url` pragma.

In the following example, the `url` pragma is placed in the beginning of the compilation unit and defines the compilation unit at `http://www.mydomain.com/wmlscript2.wmls` as `Math`. Notice the pragma is called by the `use` command. Functions within `wmlscript1.wmls` can now reference functions within `wmlscript2.wmls` by using the name `Math`.

```
use url Math "http://www.mydomain.com/wmlscript2.wmls";

function validate (num1, num2)
{

return Math#addTwoNumbers (num1, num2);

}
```

By calling `Math#addTwoNumbers`, this function invokes the `addTwoNumbers` function within the URL defined within the `url` pragma. The content of `wmlscript2.wmls` is loaded into the phone, verified, and the specified function (`addTwoNumbers`) is executed.

10.4.2 Access pragma

Any developer can invoke the functions within your WMLScript compilation unit unless you protect it using the `access` pragma. The `access` pragma restricts access to a compilation unit to every entity except those originating within the specified URL.

In the following example, notice again that the pragma is called using the `use` command, in this case, any referring URL within the `mydomain.com` domain:

```
use access domain  "mydomain.com";
```

The pragma in the following example specifies a path. In this case, http://www.mydomain.com/wap/apps/george/test/happy.asp would be allowed access, but http://www.mydomain.com/test.asp would not.

```
use access domain "mydomain.com" path "/wap";
```

10.4.3 Meta pragma

Similar to the `<meta>` tag in HTML, the `meta` pragma enables you to define metainformation about a particular compilation unit. It's up to the user agent how the metadata is used (or even if it used)—WMLScript simply provides a facility to descript metadata; it doesn't say what to do with it.

The `meta` pragma has three attributes:

- Property
- Content
- Scheme

Three properties—name, http equiv, and user agent—are supported. Content is a value attributed to the property; scheme is an optional value that can be used to interpret the property value.

A name property specifies information that is used by the origin servers and ignored by the user agent.

In the following example, the pragma is called with the use command. In this case, the name property specifies content (designer) and scheme (John P. Doe). This information, and all information indicated by the property name, is not meant for the end user—in fact, the WMLScript specification precludes a network server sending any compilation unit with meta name pragmas to an end user.

```
use meta name "designer" "John P. Doe";
```

An http equiv property is used when the content should be interpreted as an HTTP header. In this case, content should be converted to a WSP or HTTP response header if the compilation unit is compiled before it arrives at the user agent.

In the following example, the pragma instructs the compiler to send an HTTP header containing the indicated keywords:

```
use meta http equiv "Keywords" "Fun, Games, WAP, phone, wireless";
```

A user agent property is the opposite of the name property in that it is specifically used to send data intended for the end user. The WMLScript specification requires that this information be sent to the end user and not be modified or removed by any intermediary agent.

In the following example the pragma instructs the server to send the indicated meta data to the user

```
use meta user agent "Build" "16.4";
```

Notice that none of the pragmas say anything about how the information is used: they merely describe the data and indicate the intended recipient. How, and whether, the data is acted upon is independent of the WMLScript.

10.5 AN EXAMPLE APPLICATION— GUESSING A NUMBER

In this section we will start with a high-level view of the application itself, and then look at the WML code. Because chapters 3–7 are devoted to WML, we won't spend a lot of time discussing the code here. Next, we'll examine the WMLScript file. After looking at the specific code, we will view what the results should look like on a phone or simulator.

10.5.1 About the example application

In this example the user is asked to guess a number between 1 and 6. When the user enters a number, he is directed to the WMLScript that compares the user's guess to a random number between 1 and 6. If the user's guess is wrong then he is redirected to a card that tells him that his guess is wrong and shows him the correct random number. If the user guessed right, he is redirected to a card that tells him that he has guessed correctly.

Figure 10.1 shows the flow chart describing the application.

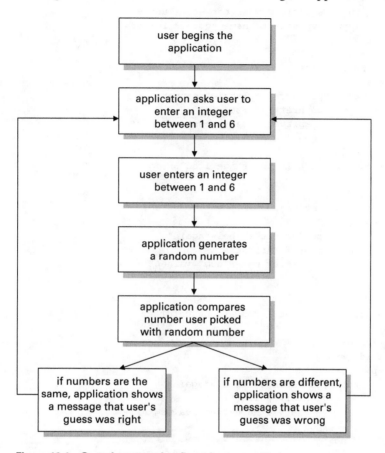

Figure 10.1   Guessing a number flow chart

10.5.2   The WML code

```
<?xml version="1.0"?>
    <!DOCTYPE wml PUBLIC "-//PHONE.COM//DTD WML 1.1//EN"
    "http://www.phone.com/dtd/wml11.dtd">
<wml>
    <card id="first">
        <onevent type="onenterforward">
        <refresh>

        <setvar name="guess" value=""/>
```

```
                            </refresh>
                            </onevent>            ⎤ Calls the function
                <p>                              ⎥ rolldie() from
                    <do type="accept" label="enter">   ⎥ the external
                        <go href="pred.wmls#rolldie()"/>  ◁⎦ WMLScript file
                    </do>                         pred.wmls
                    Enter a whole number between 1 and 6
                    <input type="text" name="guess" format="N"/>
                </p>
                </card>
                <card id="invalid">
                <p>
                    <do type="accept" label="reenter">
                        <go href="#first">
                            <setvar name="guess" value=""/>
                        </go>
                    </do>
                $(guess)is not in the range 1 to 6
                </p>
                </card>
                <card id="gotit">
                <p>
                    <do type="accept" label="again">
                        <go href="#first">
                            <setvar name="num" value=""/>
                        </go>
                    </do>

                    $(guess) is right!  You are psychic!
                </p>
                </card>
        <card id="wrong">
            <p>
                <do type="accept" label="again">
                    <go href="#first">
                            <setvar name="num" value=""/>
                    </go>
                </do>
            Sorry, $(guess) is wrong.  I rolled a $(roll)
            </p>
            </card>

        </wml>
```

10.5.3   The WMLScript code

```
extern function rolldie()              ⎤ Calls the getvar
{                                      ⎥ function in the built-in
                                       ⎥ WMLBrowser library to
var userGuess = WMLBrowser.getVar("guess");  ◁⎦ retrieve the user's guess
var userGuessInt = Lang.parseInt(userGuess);  ◁⎤ Calls the parseInt function in
var max = 6;                              ⎥ the built-in lang library to
var min = 1;                              ⎦ convert the string into an integer
```

```
var wrongGuesses = 0;
var rightGuesses = 0;
var dieRoll = Lang.random (5)+1;
  if ((userGuessInt < min) || (userGuessInt > max))
  {
  Dialogs.alert("The number " + userGuessInt + " is not valid!"); ←─┐
      WMLBrowser.go("pred.wml#first");
  }
  else {
  if (dieRoll != userGuessInt){
      wrongGuesses++;
      WMLBrowser.setVar ("roll", dieRoll);
      WMLBrowser.setVar ("wrong", wrongGuesses);
      WMLBrowser.go ("pred.wml#wrong");}
  else
  rightGuesses++;
  WMLBrowser.setVar ("right", rightGuesses);
  WMLBrowser.go ("pred.wml#gotit");
  }
}
```

Calls the `alertn`
function in the built-
in dialogs library to
let the user know
that the input was
not valid

10.5.4   The result

Now that we've seen and discussed what the application should do and how it does it,
let's see it in action. Again, one of the best ways to learn to program is to try it yourself.
If you do so and run this program on your phone or simulator, you'll find the output
to be similar to figure 10.2 (dependent of course on the integer that you enter):

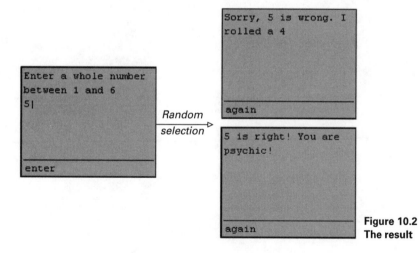

Figure 10.2
The result

10.6 SUMMARY

This chapter completes the discussion of WML's scripting language WMLScript. WMLScript is based on the ECMAScript scripting language, and is used to provide basic logic and mathematic functions to WML applications.

WMLScript provides a set of standard libraries with many predefined functions that are available for use within your WMLScript code. These libraries are contained within the WMLScript compiler and thus reside on the phone itself—no bandwidth issues are inherent to using library functions.

WMLScript is supported to varying degrees from device to device, and provides very limited error-handling resources. Because of this, WMLScript complexity should be minimized, and all applications should be tested on a wide variety of devices—used carefully WMLScript can be a useful tool, but be aware of its limitations and weaknesses or you risk imposing a frustrating and unworkable application on at least some of your users.

PART IV

Introducing HDML

The Handheld Device Markup Language (HDML) was the first markup language developed for the phone, and was made obsolete as soon as Wireless Markup Language (WML) was developed by the WAP Forum. It remains an important language, however, because millions of phones that support only HDML were circulated and remain in active use, particularly in the United States.

Developers working exclusively for the U.S. market may consider building their application in HDML because even the most up-to-date phones support both HDML and WML. By using HDML, developers ensure that all users will have access to their work, and not just those with WML-enabled phones (the HDML-WML translation engines within some gateways do not provide an optimal user experience).

Many thousands of active HDML applications exist, and a working knowledge of the language is necessary for developers to update them, or to translate them into WML.

In this segment of the book, the focus is on building interactivity and using variables with HDML.

C H A P T E R   1 1

Getting started with HDML

11.1   INTRODUCTION

The Handheld Device Markup Language (HDML) was the first markup language developed specifically for the cell phone, and is rapidly becoming obsolete in favor of Wireless Markup Language (WML). The rapid evolution of technology is testimony to the intelligence and imagination of the men and women in the computer industry, but it also has an unfortunate side effect—older technology doesn't go away quickly; it remains a consideration even as more powerful successors are developed. For example, when Microsoft developed its Windows™ operating system, it had to ensure that its previous generation operating system, MS-DOS, was also supported—there were too many applications written for MS-DOS to ignore. Similarly, HDML will remain in widespread use, at least within the United States, for some time.

In this chapter, you will be introduced to HDML—why it is a necessary skill for wireless developers to learn and where it is most frequently used; in addition, this chapter will introduce HDML development with a discussion of how to display and format text on a phone.

The HDML section assumes a working knowledge of WML, or at least that you've read the chapters on WML. Since HDML is being replaced by WML, learning HDML with a familiarity with WML aids when translating between the two languages and when debugging.

11.1.1   Why learn HDML?

There are two reasons that knowledge of HDML is useful:

- *Until recently, most phones sold in the U.S. did not recognize WML*—They contained an HDML-only browser. Many HDML-only phones are still in use.

- *Many existing applications in the U.S. are written in HDML*—Converting them to WML (or any other language) will be made easier with knowledge of HDML.

Most gateway servers have translation capabilities such that they can convert an HDML application into WML before sending it to a WML-enabled phone, or they can convert a WML application into HDML before sending it to an HDML-enabled phone. In either case, knowledge of HDML will be helpful when programming and debugging.

U.S. and (some) Japanese phones support HDML

Phones that support HDML are very widespread, particularly in the United States and Japan. (The most popular service available in Japan, however, is iMode, which uses cHTML, not HDML or WML.) Millions and millions of phones in these countries contain browsers that accept only HDML, so it's fairly certain that HDML is going to remain an important language for some years to come. Even as WML phones become ubiquitous, many HDML applications will require recoding into WML. Knowledge of HDML can make that transition much easier for the developer.

Much of the rest of the world supports WML

HDML isn't nearly as important in Europe because the overwhelming majority of WAP-enabled phones in Europe contain browsers that support only WML. Bottom line: If you are 100 percent sure that the applications you are developing will be accessed by people using only WML-enabled phones, you can probably skip learning HDML.

11.2   HDML SYNTAX AND STRUCTURE

If you have any experience developing web pages with HyperText Markup Language (HTML) or WML, HDML syntax will look very familiar. If you aren't familiar with the syntax used in markup languages, an overview of HDML syntax is in order.

Elements

Similar to HTML and WML, HDML syntax is made up of elements (sometimes called tags) that are bounded on either side by less-than and greater-than symbols (also referred to as angle brackets), like this:

```
<element>        ⤶ The "element" tells the browser to do something
(whatever data being operated on by <element> is inserted here)
</element>        ⤶ The "/element" (note the slash) ends the command
```

Note that the action of the element is cancelled by placing a slash (/) in front of the element name, like this: `</element>`. Similar to WML, elements are the building blocks of HDML, and are used to tell the browser to do things. For example, the following elements tell the browser to center the text:

```
<CENTER> This text is centered </CENTER>
```

Some elements define a single command and don't need closing elements. For example, this element instructs the browser to navigate to a URL when a specific button is pressed:

```
<ACTION TYPE=" ACCEPT" DEST="http://www.mydomain.com/mycard">
```

We'll look at the `<ACTION>` element in more detail in chapter 12. Notice that this self-contained element is different than a self-contained element in WML in that you do not end a self-contained element in HDML with a slash (`<element/>`) as you do in WML. For more information on self-contained elements in WML, see chapter 3.

Attributes

Many elements contain *attributes* that enable you to specifically refine precisely how you would like the element to behave. For example, by itself, `<ACTION>` tells the phone to perform an action, which isn't very helpful unless you also define an action to perform. Attributes let you make those kinds of definitions—enabling you to specifically define the action to be performed.

Using the <HDML> header element

Unlike WML, HDML does not use a document type definition (DTD). (HDML is not an XML-based language.) A header element that describes the location of a DTD is therefore not necessary. It's a good idea, however, to nest your code within the `<HDML>...</HDML>` element.

The HDML element is ignored by the phone browser, but should nevertheless be included for the *WAP gateway*—the component that manages communication between the WAP phone and the Internet. Most servers have translation capabilities such that they can send an HDML application to a WML-enabled phone. By indicating immediately that your application is HDML, you enable the server to quickly perform the appropriate transformation.

Use the version attribute in the `<HDML>` element to indicate which version of HDML your application is using. The latest release by Phone.com is HDML version 3.0. Phone.com virtually replaced any older versions of HDML with the newer one, so it supports and maintains only version 3.0. No further versions will be developed although Phone.com will continue supporting and maintaining the latest version indefinitely. Here is an example HDML header, which we will use for the remainder of the book:

```
<HDML VERSION="3.0">
```

Case sensitivity

Unlike WML, HDML is *not* case sensitive, which means that the `<ACTION>` element used in the previous example could be written as `<AcTiOn>`, or `<action>`, or `<ActIOn>` and it wouldn't make any difference to the browser. Of course, no strict rule exists without exceptions: In HDML, case *is* important when defining variables. See chapters 12 and 13 for more information about variables.

Because HDML is not case sensitive, HDML elements are shown in ALL CAPS in this book to help distinguish the HDML code examples from WML code.

White space

Similar to WML, HDML ignores any white space after a single space. If you insert more than one contiguous new line, carriage return, tab, or space, the browser will render them all into a single space. This is good news—it means you can write your HDML using as many spaces and carriage returns as you like, and it won't matter. Thus, if you find it easier to read HDML code if it has a lot of white space, go ahead. The browser won't care. You can see examples of this fact throughout this book—the formatting used is meant to enhance readability, and is not necessary when building an application.

11.2.1 Commenting HDML code

Code can be hard for people to make sense of, particularly if someone else wrote it. The solution is the liberal insertion of *comments* into your code (comments are text that the browser ignores). Comments make code easier to understand for everyone, you included. Try it yourself: Write a complete application without comments, put it aside or go on vacation, and then pick it up a week or so later. You will likely find that it is very difficult to get back into the "flow" of the application. Get into the habit of using lots of comments.

A comment is any text bounded by angle brackets and double hyphens, like this:

```
<-- The browser will ignore all of this text. -->
```

This will also comment the text:

```
<!--The browser will ignore all of this text. -->
```

Similar to WML but unlike WMLScript, there is no way to comment out more than one line without repeating the commenting codes for each individual line of text:

```
<-- The first line of ignored text -->
<-- The second line of ignored text -->
<-- The third line of ignored text -->
```

Comments enable you to insert helpful reminders or explanations into your code, and can also be a helpful debugging method; if you suspect a line of code is causing an error, you can easily put comment tags around the offending code (i.e., you can "comment it out").

11.2.2 The card/deck paradigm in HDML

Similar to WML, HDML uses the card/deck concept. HDML explicitly defines each card as one of three (table 11.1).

Table 11.1   HDML card types

Card type	Description
DISPLAY card	Displays text to a user
CHOICE card	Provides the user with a menu
ENTRY card	Enables the user to enter data into the phone

Instead of defining each card within the <card>...</card> element as in WML, HDML uses <DISPLAY>...</DISPLAY>, <CHOICE>...</CHOICE>, or <ENTRY>...</ENTRY>. Figures 11.1–11.3 picture each type of card.

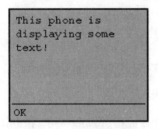

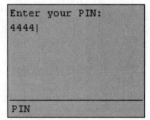

Figure 11.1   DISPLAY card   Figure 11.2   CHOICE card   Figure 11.3   ENTRY card

- Phones display text using a DISPLAY card (figure 11.1).
- Phones display a list of choices using a CHOICE card (figure 11.2).
- Phones enable the user to enter information using an ENTRY card (figure 11.3).

11.3   AN EXAMPLE: HELLO WORLD!

The following very simple example of HDML code is the ubiquitous "Hello World!" application—no programming text is complete without it. The goal of the application is simple: It will display "Welcome to the exciting world of WAP" in the phone's browser.

If you would like to follow by programming this example as we proceed, simply type the text into a text editor (Microsoft Windows notepad application will do) and save it on a web server as an ANSI file with the extension .hdml. Once the code is saved, simply enter the code's URL into a phone (or a phone simulator) to execute it.

Our "Hello World!" example begins with the HDML header and uses a DISPLAY card. Notice that each element is nested properly and each nested element is indicated by an indention. Here is the code:

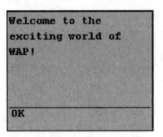

Figure 11.4   Hello World! application

```
<HDML VERSION="3.0">
    <DISPLAY>
        Welcome to the exciting world of WAP!
    </DISPLAY>
</HDML>
```

Figure 11.4 shows "Hello World!" on the simulator. Remember that different phones display the same code differently. Get into the habit of testing all your code using different phones.

11.4   FORMATTING TEXT

The DISPLAY card simply displays text for the user to read. Remember to first define the deck with <HDML> and </HDML> tags.

To display text on a DISPLAY card, use the <DISPLAY>...</DISPLAY> elements. The following example shows how to do this:

```
<HDML VERSION="3.0">      ⌐ All decks begin with the HDML tag      Displays any text between
    <DISPLAY>         ◄─────────────────────                      here and </DISPLAY>
        It was the best of times…   ◄──────────┐ Text for display
    </DISPLAY>  ◄──────────────┐ Closes the
</HDML>     ◄┐ End of deck      │ DISPLAY card
```

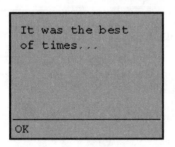

Figure 11.5   Displaying text

Figure 11.5 shows a text display on a phone.

HDML provides a variety of elements to specify how text is wrapped and scrolled, and how it is placed on the phone display. Unlike WML, HDML does *not* support different fonts. If you want to display bold or italic text using HDML you're out of luck. HDML was designed that way: The phone's display is small, and different fonts (especially combinations of fonts) can be very hard to read.

11.4.1 Specifying reserved characters

Just as in WML, the characters <, >, ", $, and & have special meaning to the phone. If you wish to include them in a display, you must use an *escape sequence*, a special code that *represents* the character.

You will recall from the previous section that the phone concatenates multiple instances of white spaces into one. One use of an escape sequence is to force the phone to display all the white space you wish by including   (the escape sequence for "nonbreaking space,") within your text.

Don't ignore the "nonbreaking" part of "nonbreaking space." If you want to allow wrapping in the middle of a series of contiguous nonbreaking spaces, you must insert a regular space where you want to allow wrapping.

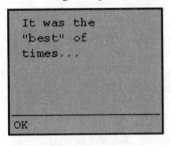

Figure 11.6   Displaying quotes

This example uses the " escape sequence to insert quotation marks within the text. The result is shown in figure 11.6.

```
<HDML VERSION="3.0">
  <DISPLAY>
It was the &quot;best&quot; of times…
  </DISPLAY>
</HDML>
```

Table 11.2 illustrates each reserved character and the escape sequence to use should you want to output it to the screen.

Table 11.2   Reserved characters

Instead of	Use the escape sequence
<	&lt;
>	&gt;
"	&quot;
&	&amp;
$	&dol;
space	
Any ASCII character	&#nn; (where nn is the ASCII code)

Use an escape sequence just as you would any other character, remembering to always begin with an ampersand character (&) and end with a semicolon (;). Omit the ampersand and the browser will display the characters in the sequence (instead of the represented character). Omit the semicolon and the phone will display an invalid deck error.

11.4.2 Positioning text on the display

Text on a phone is left aligned by default. Of course, there might be instances where that doesn't work for you, and HDML offers two additional elements to help you position your text. The following code fragment demonstrates these elements, <CENTER> and <RIGHT>:

```
<CENTER> This text is centered </CENTER>
<RIGHT> This text is right aligned </RIGHT>
```

HDML also contains predefined tab stops, which can be used to create aligned columns of text by inserting <TAB> statements in the text. Because the phone display area is small, use tabs with caution—carelessly inserting tabs (particularly within centered lines) can result in a bizarre display.

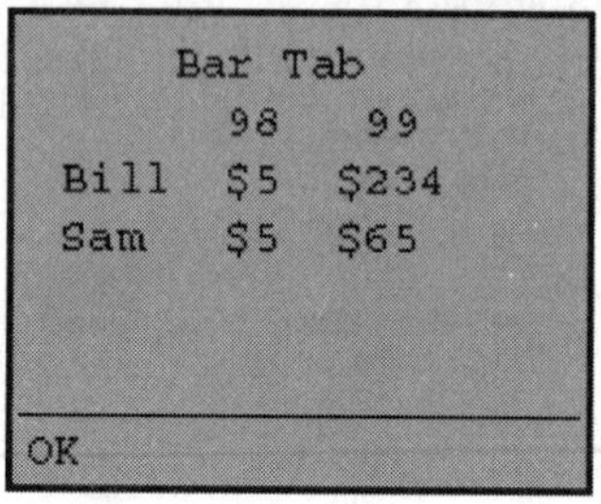

```
        Bar Tab
            98    99
   Bill   $5  $234
   Sam    $5  $65



OK
```

Figure 11.7   Table example

Tabs are the closest HDML comes to supporting tables on the phone (WML has more robust support for tables). In HDML, contiguous lines containing tabs are treated as rows in a table, with the number of columns equal to the number of tabs in the line with the most tabs. Column width is set to accommodate the column's largest cell.

The following code example demonstrates a simple use of the <TAB> element to simulate a table. It is displayed in figure 11.7.

```
<HDML VERSION=3.0>
    <DISPLAY>
        <CENTER>Bar Tab</CENTER>          �})  Centers text
        <TAB>98<TAB>99                     ◄──────────────────
        Harry<TAB>&dol;5<TAB>&dol;234                            Preset tab stops
        Sam<TAB>&dol;5<TAB>&dol;65   ◄} &dol; is an escape      give some
    </DISPLAY>                             sequence for $        formatting
</HDML>                                                          control
```

11.5   *WRAPPING TEXT*

If a horizontal line of text within a card is longer than a phone's display size, the text will wrap. HDML provides two options:

- *You can do nothing*—By default, the phone wraps text around to the next line. If the line is so large as to exceed the length of the second row as well, it will be simply wrapped to a third line, and so on. A phone does not wrap a line mid-word; rather, it uses white space to determine where to wrap the line.

- *You can "Times Square" the text by using the* <LINE> *element*—A phone will display as much text within a <LINE> element as possible, show that text for about two seconds, and then automatically scroll horizontally. The effect is similar to a marquee, thus the name Times Square. Note that you can use the <WRAP>

element to revert text from <LINE> mode back to wrap mode (because <WRAP> is the browser default, you need not specify it otherwise).

The following code example demonstrates the Times Square mode:

```
<HDML VERSION="3.0">
  <DISPLAY>
     <LINE>It really truly was </LINE>
     <CENTER>the best</CENTER>          ↵ Centers text          Indicates
     <RIGHT>of times</RIGHT>            ↰ Right justifies text   Times Square
  </DISPLAY>  |#1                                                wrap
</HDML>
```

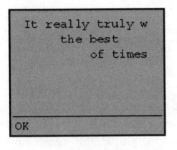

Figure 11.8   Text wrapping

Figure 11.8 shows how the code will appear on the phone. After a short pause the remainder of the first line is displayed without any change in subsequent lines.

As a comparison, the following example uses the <WRAP> element. Remember that <WRAP> is the default mode; it needn't be explicitly included in your code (it was included in this code to highlight the difference in the two modes).

```
<HDML VERSION="3.0">
  <DISPLAY>
     <WRAP>It was the best of times… </WRAP>   ↵ Wraps text
     <BR>It was the worst of times…           ↰ Adds a line break
  </DISPLAY>
</HDML>
```

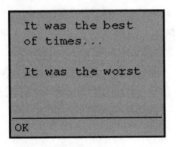

Figure 11.9
Default text wrapping

Default wrapping produces text aligned like figure 11.9.

Wrapping text to the next line is the default mode for all formatted text in display, entry, and choice cards.

11.5.1   When to wrap versus Times Square

Initially, the user-interface specialists thought that Times Square mode was very difficult to read, and thus was to be avoided. This has changed—recent usability studies revealed that people were not terribly disconcerted by Times Square *if used sparingly and thoughtfully.*

What does "sparingly and thoughtfully" mean? It means:

- *Don't overuse Times Square mode*—If every line on a phone's display is blinking back and forth it can be disconcerting and difficult to read. As a user attempts to focus on a single line of text, the movement of the other text within the display will tend to attract the eye away from the line being read. Particularly when the user is doing something in addition to using the phone (such as driving), liberal use of Times Square can render the display almost unreadable.

- *Use Times Square for information that is intuitively connected*—For example, if you choose to display a stock symbol and the market price for that symbol in Times Square mode, the text would flash intuitively between the symbol and the price. On the one hand, if an entire news story were rendered in Times Square mode, the scrolling text would retain little context and lose meaning.

11.6   SUMMARY

This chapter introduced HDML as the first markup language developed for wireless devices. A predecessor to Wireless Application Protocol (WAP), HDML is becoming obsolete; however, you can benefit from knowledge of HDML because many devices in use within the United States accept only HDML and because many applications developed in HDML will likely require translation into WML—an understanding of HDML concepts can simplify this process considerably. For information on converting HDML into WML, see chapter 16.

The basics of HDML were then introduced, beginning with an explanation of how text is displayed and manipulated on the phone using the <DISPLAY> card. Alignment and wrapping of text was also discussed.

The next chapter deals with user interaction—how HDML enables movement between cards and decks, and how HDML enables a user to make a selection from a menu through the <CHOICE> card, and how HDML enables a user to enter data through the <ENTRY> card.

CHAPTER 12

Building interactivity with HDML

12.1   INTRODUCTION

So far we've discussed how to display static text on a browser using display cards. In this chapter, we move to the next step—enabling the use of hyperlinks to move between cards and decks. This chapter also introduces two additional card types:

- The CHOICE card enables you to present the user with a list of options.
- The ENTRY card enables the user to enter data into the phone, similar to a form on an HTML site.

These cards let the user interact with the application by selecting data from a menu or entering data into a form.

12.2 HDML *INTERACTION BASICS*

Accept   Softkey2

Figure 12.1 Softkeys

When a user surfs to an HDML site, the phone moves to the URL and displays the first card it finds. It will then wait for a user to press a button (or enter text and *then* press a button). Similar to WML, the most often used button on a phone is Accept, also referred to as Softkey1. On most phones, the Accept button appears on the left side of the phone immediately below the display (figure 12.1).

Accept is as close to a PC-style enter key as the phone possesses. *Softkey2*, the button opposite Accept (on the lower right of the phone display), is typically assigned tasks that are less frequently used. In figure 12.1, the Accept key prompts the user to acknowledge the display (the OK in the display refers to the Accept button). Notice that Softkey2 is assigned a less frequently used task: navigating to the previous card in the deck (thus the PREV in the display).

12.2.1 Assigning actions to the Accept button

To enable users to interact with the phone, you must assign the Accept button an action to perform when it is pressed. If no task is assigned, the user will navigate to the last URL encountered (the card immediately previous to the card being displayed).

HDML provides two elements for specifying the card to which the phone should navigate when a button is pressed:

- *The <ACTION> element assigns a URL to a button*—When the button is pressed, the phone will invoke the associated task.

- *The <A> element assigns a URL to a selection of text and a button*—(That is, it's a text link, identical to those within an HTML site). When the button is pressed *and* the appropriate text is highlighted, the phone will invoke the associated task.

The following code example demonstrates card-to-card navigation using both the <ACTION> and <A> elements. The first card displays text, and the Accept button is associated with a task that navigates to the second card. Similarly, the second card displays text with an Accept button associated with the third card. The third card, in turn, associates the Accept button with the first card. The result is displayed in figure 12.2.

```
<HDML VERSION="3.2">
  <DISPLAY>
<ACTION TYPE=ACCEPT TASK="GO" DEST="#card2">      Assigns the GO task to
                                                   the Accept button
     It was the best of times      Destination of
  </DISPLAY>                        ACTION in the
                                    first card
  <DISPLAY NAME=card2>
     <A TASK=GO DEST=#card3>It was the worst of times
```

```
    </DISPLAY>

    <DISPLAY NAME=card3>
        <A TASK=GO DEST=#card1> Review
    </DISPLAY>
</HDML>
```

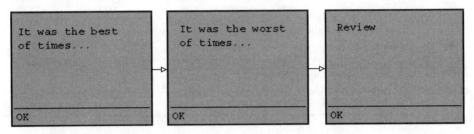

Figure 12.2 Actions assigned to the Accept button

The <ACTION> and <A> elements will be discussed more thoroughly in the sections to come.

12.3 *USING THE <ACTION> ELEMENT*

The <ACTION> element associates a task with a button. It has three important attributes (table 12.1).

Table 12.1 <ACTION> **tasks**

Attribute	Description
TASK	Defines the task
TYPE	Defines the button
DEST	Defines the URL

Take a look at the following code fragment as an example. The elements and attributes are shown in table 12.2.

```
<ACTION TASK=GO TYPE=ACCEPT DEST=http://www.domain.com>
```

Table 12.2 **Elements and attributes in sample code**

Elements/Attributes	Description
ACTION	An element that tells the phone to do something by associating a button press with a URL
TASK	An attribute that defines the action to be performed (in this case, go means navigate to another card)
TYPE	An attribute that defines what button to associate with the task (in this case, the Accept button). For a complete listing of supported type values, see appendix C

Table 12.2   Elements and attributes in sample code (continued)

Elements/Attributes	Description
DEST	An attribute that defines the URL to which to navigate when the button defined in the type attribute (in this case, the Accept button) is pressed

The TASK attribute of the <ACTION> element can perform many jobs. Table 12.3 lists valid values for the TASK attribute and the sections that follow provide a detailed look at each.

Table 12.3   Valid values for the TASK attribute

Task attribute value	Description
GO	Requests the URL specified by the DEST option
GOSUB	Pushes a new activity onto the stack and requests the URL specified in the DEST option
PREV	Displays the previous card in the activity history
RETURN	Returns from a nested activity to the parent activity with the return values specified by the RETVALS option
CANCEL	Cancels the current activity, requesting the URL specified be the parent activity's CANCEL option
CALL	Switches the phone to voice mode and dials the number specified by the NUMBER option
NOOP	Does nothing (useful for disabling default behavior of the specified action)

Each of these tasks is discussed in more detail in the following sections.

About the GO task

The GO task is the most commonly used task in HDML. Setting the task attribute of the <ACTION> element to GO invokes the task when the user presses the button defined in the type attribute.

The GO task requests the URL specified by the DEST attribute. If you use the GO task, you can only specify a relative URL for the DEST attribute.

Other attributes that can be used in the <ACTION> element when the GO task is used:

- DEST
- SENDREFERER
- REL
- POSTDATA
- VARS
- ACCEPT_CHARSET
- METHOD

For more information, see appendix C.

About the GOSUB task

The GOSUB task pushes a new activity onto the stack and requests the URL specified by the DEST option. For more information, see chapter 14.

Eleven other attributes can be used in the <ACTION> element when the GOSUB task is used:

- DEST
- VARS
- SENDREFERER
- FRIEND

- RECEIVE
- ACCEPT_CHARSET
- REL
- METHOD

- POSTDATA
- CANCEL
- NEXT

See appendix C for more information on these attributes.

About the PREV task

The PREV task displays the previous card in the activity history. If the current card is the first card in the current activity, PREV has the same effect as CANCEL.

There are no other attributes that can be used in the <ACTION> element when the PREV task is used.

About the RETURN task

The RETURN task returns the user from a nested activity to the previous activity with the return values specified by the RETVALS option. For more information about activities and the use of the RETURN task, see chapter 14.

Other options that can be used in the <ACTION> element when the return task is used are:

- DEST
- VARS

- SENDREFERER
- ACCEPT_CHARSET

- REL
- METHOD

- POSTDATA

For more information on these attributes see appendix C.

About the CANCEL task

The CANCEL task cancels the current activity, requesting the URL specified by the previous activity's CANCEL option. If no CANCEL option is specified, the phone requests the current card in the previous activity. For more information about activities and the use of the CANCEL task, see chapter 14.

Other options that can be used in the <ACTION> element when the RETURN task is used are:

- DEST
- CLEAR

- SENDREFERER
- ACCEPT_CHARSET

- REL
- METHOD

- POSTDATA

For more information on these attributes see appendix C.

About the CALL task

The CALL task switches the phone to voice mode and dials the number specified by the NUMBER attribute, which replaces the DEST attribute.

Remember that the phone has a great built-in feature—it can make a phone call! HDML enables you to tap into the phone's most fundamental feature. The following code fragment demonstrates this by dialing 555–1212 when the user presses Accept:

```
<DISPLAY>
        <ACTION TYPE=ACCEPT TASK=CALL NUMBER=5551212>

        Press OK to dial a number.
</DISPLAY>
```

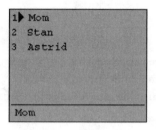

Figure 12.3   CHOICE card

Notice that the format is identical to the GO task, with the exception that the DEST attribute is replaced with the NUMBER attribute.

Calls can also be invoked within a CHOICE card (see section 12.5 for information about the CHOICE card), as shown in the following code fragment. Once again, this example replaces the DEST attribute with NUMBER. Figure 12.3 shows that this code displays identically to any other choice card.

```
<CHOICE>
<CE LABEL=Mom TASK=CALL NUMBER=555-4545>Mom
<CE LABEL=Stan TASK=CALL NUMBER=555-3333>Stan
<CE LABEL=Astrid TASK=CALL NUMBER=555-0999>Astrid
</CHOICE>
```

This displays identically to any other CHOICE card.

About the NOOP task

The NOOP task indicates the browser should do nothing; useful for disabling the default behavior of the specified action, similar to the <NODISPLAY> element.

NOOP has no associated attributes in the <ACTION> element.

12.4   USING THE <A> ELEMENT

The <A> element is similar to the <ACTION> element, but instead of associating a task with a button press, the <A> element associates a task with text (similar to linked text on an HTML page or the anchor element in WML). Using the <A> element, a button can be associated with a task when the user selects specific text. The following code fragment demonstrates the syntax of the <A> element:

```
<A TASK=GO TYPE=ACCEPT DEST=http://www.domain.com>
Selecting this text and pressing ACCEPT will navigate to the indicated URL.
</A>
```

In this example,

- The <A> element is used instead of <ACTION>.
- This prompts the phone to associate the action with all text between the <A> and closing </A> elements.

- The TASK attribute defines the action to be performed (in this case, go means navigate to another card).
- <A> uses the same tasks as <ACTION>.
- The TYPE attribute defines what button to associate with the task (in this case, Accept).

The DEST attribute defines where to go when the button is pressed.

12.4.1 Using the DEST attribute

When used with both <ACTION> and <A>, the DEST attribute defines where the phone navigates when the action is invoked. The DEST attribute is similar to the href attribute in the <GO> or <A> elements in WML. Using DEST, you can navigate to:

- A specific card within the same deck
- The first card within another deck
- A specific card within another deck

Navigating to a specific card within the same deck

To navigate to a card within the same deck, simply specify the card in DEST by indicating the card name preceded by a hash symbol (#), like this:

```
<ACTION TASK=GO TYPE=ACCEPT DEST=#card>
```

When using the hash symbol in your DEST attribute, ensure that the destination card (in our example, the destination card is #card) contains a corresponding NAME attribute or you'll get an error—the phone won't be able to find the card!

Navigating to the first card within another deck

Navigate to the first card within another deck by specifying the deck URL as follows:

```
<ACTION TASK=GO TYPE=ACCEPT DEST=http://www.domain.com>
```

Navigating to a specific card within the same deck

To navigate to a specific card within another deck, specify *both* the URL and the card name (again preceded by a hash mark):

```
<ACTION TASK=GO TYPE=ACCEPT DEST=http://www.domain.com#card>
```

12.5 USER INPUT CARDS

Another way for a user to navigate to a different card is by using input cards. There are two types of input cards—CHOICE and ENTRY.

CHOICE cards allow a user to choose a selection from a list and based on that selection, the user will have either set a variable and proceeded to a different card or navigated to a specific card. Setting a variable using a CHOICE card will be covered in chapter 13. For now we will concentrate on using a CHOICE card for navigation.

ENTRY cards allow a user to enter input from the keypad, then navigate to a new card after entering data. Setting a variable using ENTRY cards will be covered in more detail in chapter 13. For now we will concentrate on the ability of ENTRY cards to send a user to a specific location.

12.5.1   CHOICE cards

Anyone who's ever tried to enter text into a phone understands the value of a CHOICE card. Text entry on a phone is awkward, especially when people are often doing something in addition to using the phone. A CHOICE card in HDML is very similar to using a <SELECT> element in WML.

In the next example, the developer could have chosen to have the user enter Film, Director, or Actor instead of providing them as selections. Offering a selection menu by using a CHOICE card makes it much easier to interact with the phone. In the following code example, the user is offered a menu containing three selections:

```
<HDML VERSION=3.0>
    <ACTION TYPE=ACCEPT TASK=GO DEST=#Film>        ❶

    <CHOICE>
        <CE LABEL=Film TASK=GOSUB DEST=#Film>Film              ❷   Defines a
        <CE LABEL=Drctr TASK=GOSUB DEST=#Director>Director     ❸   CHOICE
        <CE LABEL=Actr. TASK=GOSUB DEST=#Actor>Actor           ❹   card
    </CHOICE>

    <DISPLAY NAME=Film>
      <ACTION TYPE=ACCEPT TASK="RETURN">
      You chose film.
    </DISPLAY>                                              RETURN
                                                           sends the
    <DISPLAY NAME=Director>                                user back
      <ACTION TYPE=ACCEPT TASK="RETURN">                   to the
      You chose director.                                  parent
    </DISPLAY>                                              activity

    <DISPLAY NAME=Actor>
      <ACTION TYPE=ACCEPT TASK="RETURN">
      You chose Actor.
    </DISPLAY>
</HDML>
```

Code comments

❶ ACTION assigns a task to a button. The dest= attribute defines the default selection.

❷ The <CE> element defines choices within the menu.

❸ The LABEL attribute changes the button label.

❹ The DEST attribute defines the destination URL when selection is chosen.

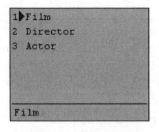

Figure 12.4   CHOICE card

Figure 12.4 displays the code on the phone.

The card in the example displays three choices, each with its own <CE> element. The <CE> element in HDML is similar to the <option> element in WML. Notice the <CE> element contains the LABEL attribute, which enables you to define the text that appears just above the Accept button when a user highlights a selection (the LABEL attribute is optional; the default label is OK). This is similar to the title attribute of the <option> element in a WML selection list.

Just as in the <ACTION> element, the TASK and DEST options define what happens when the user selects a menu option and the destination URL. For example, to duplicate using the onpick attribute in the <option> element in WML, use a GO task and set the dest attribute equal to the desired location in the <CE> element in HDML.

Users choose from among displayed choices by pressing the up/down arrow keys on their phone. As the user scrolls between choices, the carat (>) moves from choice to choice to indicate which is selected, and the ACCEPT label changes to the label specified within the selection's LABEL attribute. When the user presses the Accept button, the phone executes the task specified by the selection.

Some points to keep in mind when using CHOICE cards:

- By default, the left side of the menu within a <CHOICE> card is numbered. If the user presses a keypad number associated with a menu choice at any time while the card containing the link is on the screen, the phone executes the task specified by the link *right away*—the user need not press Accept.

- Each <CE> choice can contain a TASK that defines the action to perform when the choice is selected. These <CE> tasks take precedence over the ACCEPT action defined at the deck level. For example, if you associate the Accept button with http://www.somewhere.com at the beginning of the choice card using the <ACTION> element, the task will be ignored in favor of the task specified within the <CE> element.

- CHOICE cards can do more than point the user to a card (or deck) associated with the menu item. Menu items can be associated with values that are assigned to a variable when the item is selected (for more information see chapter 13), and a variety of different actions can be associated with the TASK option.

12.5.2   ENTRY cards

Entering text on a phone is difficult. Numbers, of course, are less difficult—phones are designed to enable a user to easily enter a series of numbers. If you are designing an application that requires text entry, carefully consider whether there is any possible means by which to extract the same information some other method—with menus, perhaps. Another alternative to text entry on a phone is text entry on a PC. In this case, a form would be presented to a user on a PC; when a user enters data into the form, the data is stored on a server that is subsequently accessed by the phone.

Imagine you are building a restaurant look-up service that requires the user to first enter the city in which to search. Instead of requiring the user to enter a city on the phone, you can instead build a PC interface that enables the user to enter a series of frequently searched cities that is then stored in a database. When the user accesses the service on a phone, that database is read and the cities are presented to the user as a menu.

Although requiring a user to enter text into a phone is best avoided whenever possible, there are circumstances that make it the only option. If you have a secured application, for example, you might require a user to enter a name/password combination. An <ENTRY> card enables a user to enter data directly into a phone, similar to HTML forms. An <ENTRY> card is similar to using the <input> element in WML.

The following code fragment demonstrates the syntax for the <ENTRY> card—it should look quite familiar:

```
<ENTRY NAME=search_for KEY=srchfor DEFAULT=film>
Search for:
<ACTION TYPE=ACCEPT TASK=GO DEST=#display>
</ENTRY>
```

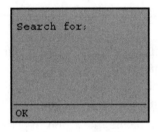

Figure 12.5   ENTRY card

Figure 12.5 shows how the phone will display the card.

The phone displays the text associated with the NAME attribute (Search for:). The user then enters data using the phone's keypad. The KEY attribute defines a variable name with which the user's data will be associated.

Notice the <ACTION> element within this example. By including the <ACTION> element, you are telling the phone to accept the data that the user has entered, assign it to the variable defined by KEY, and go to the URL indicated in the <ACTION> element.

It is possible that the user will choose not to enter any data at all, but simply press Accept. If your application requires a default value to be associated with the variable defined by KEY, you can specify a default value by using the DEFAULT attribute. The default value will be displayed and can be edited by the user.

12.6   CONTROLLING TEXT ENTRY

The Entry card's FORMAT attribute is similar to the format attribute of the <input> element in WML—it enables you to specify the type and case of characters the user can enter. When FORMAT is defined, the user is restricted to a specific type of entry (alphanumeric, alpha only, number only, five numbers only, etc.). Table 12.4 summarizes the values accepted by the FORMAT attribute.

Similar to formatting entry data in WML, entering the option FORMAT=NNAA forces the user to enter exactly two numbers followed by exactly two uppercase

Table 12.4   Format specifiers

Attribute	Description	Example
A	Allows any uppercase alphabetic character (no numbers)	FORMAT=AAAA
a	Allows any lowercase alphabetic character (no numbers)	FORMAT=aa
N	Allows any numeric character (no symbols)	FORMAT=NN
X	Allows any numeric, symbolic, or uppercase alphabetic character	FORMAT=XX
x	Allows any numeric, symbolic, or lowercase alphabetic character	FORMAT=x
M or m	Allows any alphabetic character (of any case), and any numeric or symbolic character	FORMAT=mm

alphabetic characters. When you indicate specific entry, the browser will not display the ACCEPT label until the appropriate data quantity and type have been entered.

You may enable a user to enter 0–*n* characters of a particular type by specifying *n* followed by type, using an asterisk (*) to indicate any number of entries. For example, N5M enables the user to enter a digit followed by up to five alphanumeric characters, and N*M enables the user to enter a digit followed with any number of alphanumeric characters.

NOTE   Use a number only in combination with the last character of a format specifier string. For example, a specifier such as 4AN does not work. To allow the user to enter four uppercase alphabetic characters followed by a numeric character, you must use the specifier AAAAN.

The following example demonstrates the use of FORMAT to enable a user to enter four numbers only:

```
<HDML VERSION=3.0>
    <ENTRY KEY=code FORMAT=NNNN>   ◁┘
        <ACTION TYPE=ACCEPT LABEL=PIN TASK=GO DEST=#PIN>
        Enter your PIN:
    </ENTRY>
    <DISPLAY NAME=PIN>
        Your secret PIN is $(code).
    </DISPLAY>
</HDML>
```

Defines what type of data the user may enter—in this case, the user may enter four numbers

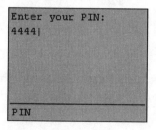

Note that the user can enter only *exactly* four numbers. Until that happens, the Accept button will not invoke anything (and on most phones the label will not appear over the Accept button until the FORMAT criteria is met). The code display is in figure 12.6.

**Figure 12.6
Formatting input**

12.6.1 Entering different types of data

Because the buttons on phones must support a wide variety of data (not only numbers, but uppercase text, lowercase text, and symbols such as @), phones typically have a built-in method for switching from one text entry mode to another. Some also support smart text entry, which tries to guess (without having to press the same key repeatedly) the word the user is attempting to enter.

HDML supports the following text entry modes, only some of which may be supported within a particular model. Selecting a particular mode defines the type of output rendered by the keypad when using it to enter data:

- *alpha*—lowercase alphabetic characters
- *ALPHA*—uppercase alphabetic characters
- *SMART*—Tegic (T9) entry
- *NUM*—numeric characters
- *SYM*—symbols

If you don't use a FORMAT specifier, users can toggle through all modes supported by their phone by using the Soft1 key. If you specify a format using a FORMAT specifier, the phone only allows the user to toggle through the modes allowed by the FORMAT specifier.

Be default, if FORMAT is not specified, the phone enables the user to press Accept and proceed to the next card at any point in an entry card, without regard to the data entered (if any). By contrast, if you use a FORMAT specifier that requires a minimum number of characters (such as NAAN or mm*m) the user can't proceed to the next card until he has entered all the characters required by the specifier. To override and allow the user to proceed without entering anything, specify the entry card option, EMPTYOK=TRUE.

On occasion, you might wish to place automatic characters, which the user cannot edit, into the entry field. For example, if the user is entering a date, you might want the phone to automatically place hyphens or slashes between the month, day, and year. To do this, insert the character between the other FORMAT characters, preceding it with a backslash (\). When the user enters data, the phone automatically inserts the characters at the specified positions.

For example, suppose you insert the following into your <ENTRY> element:

```
FORMAT=\(NNN\)\-
```

This instructs the phone to automatically insert a left parenthesis before the user has entered anything and a right parenthesis and a dash after the user enters three digits (as with an area code).

12.7 USING IMAGES

Images are an important part of the PC-based Web, and can be used to great effect on the phone as well. Use them carefully; the physical limitations of the phone (both the small display size and limited memory) require images that are very compact and fit within the context of the application. Just as with text, it is important to take all types of phones into account when using images—an image that works well on one phone might render the application unusable on a phone with a more modest display. With images, being conservative is the best strategy.

12.7.1 About images

Images are *big*—it takes a huge amount of data for a computer to display an image correctly. In fact, they are so big that if raw images were sent back and forth across the Internet the network would immediately become overwhelmed. To address this, many image *compression algorithms* have been developed that reduce the amount of data being sent over the Internet.

A compression algorithm takes the data that makes up a particular image and performs a mathematical operation on it such that the resultant image data set is smaller. A very shallow overview of this process follows (a comprehensive description of data compression technology is beyond the scope of this book):

1 *An image is compressed using a data compression algorithm*—You are likely familiar with images that have been compressed using the most common algorithms: the files contain the .gif or the .jpg suffix.

2 *When a computer requests an image over the Internet, the compressed image is sent.*

3 *In order to use the image, the receiving computer must understand the compression technology used on the image*—For example, if the received image is compressed using the *.gif format, the receiving computer must understand how to uncompress .gif images. If the compression is unrecognized, the image cannot be displayed.

4 *The receiving computer decompresses the image and displays it.*

Common image formats used on the Web (GIF and JPEG for example) are ill-suited for transmission to phones—the data isn't compressed enough for the very limited bandwidth available to a wireless device. Because of this, the WAP Forum has defined an image format called WBMP (or wireless bitmap) specific for wireless devices. The WBMP format is similar to another common Internet compression format (BMP), and most wireless gateways can automatically convert images from a BMP format into WBMP before sending the image to the phone. You can create BMP images using most any commercially available imaging software.

12.7.2 Placing images within HDML

To display an image in HDML, use the <IMG> element. For more information on using images in a WAP application and the WBMP image format, see chapter 5. Similar to WML, you must include the SRC attribute within the <IMG> element in

HDML—this attribute defines where the phone can find the image. In the following code fragment, the image contained within the specified URL will be fetched and sent to the phone:

```
<IMG SRC=http://www.domain.com/tiger.wbmp>
```

If a phone can't display the indicated image, it will display the text defined in ALT instead. The following code fragment adds to the previous example with an ALT attribute:

```
<IMG SRC=http://www.domain.com/tiger.wbmp ALT=tiger>
```

In HDML, images can be used within a CHOICE card (WML does not support the use of images within selection menus). In the following example, two images are used in lieu of text in a CHOICE card:

```
<HDML VERSION=3.0 PUBLIC=TRUE>
<DISPLAY NAME=welcome>
    <ACTION TYPE=ACCEPT TASK=GO DEST=#search_by>
    Movie lookup!<BR>
    <IMG SRC=http://www.domain.com/movie/splash.bmp       Displays the text, then
        ALT=Movie Logo>                                   a line break, then the
</DISPLAY>                                                 image referenced by
                                                          the URL

<CHOICE NAME=search_by KEY=srchby>                        Choices appear as
  <ACTION KEY=srchby TYPE=ACCEPT ICON=righthand           images. If images
   TASK=GO DEST=#display>                                 aren't supported,
        Search by:                                        ALT= text will be
          <CE LABEL=film VALUE=film>                      displayed
          <IMG SRC=../movie/film.bmp > Film
          <CE LABEL=direc VALUE=dir>
          <IMG SRC=../movie/dir.bmp >Director
</CHOICE>

<DISPLAY NAME=display>
      <ACTION TYPE=ACCEPT TASK=GO DEST=#search_by>
        Searching for:
          $(srchby)              $(srchby) displays the value
</DISPLAY>                        of the variable srchby
  </HDML>
```

Figures 12.7 and 12.8 display images on a phone screen.

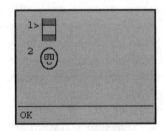

Figure 12.7
Image displayed on screen

Figure 12.8
Using images in a menu

12.7.3 Using icons

If you wish to include small images within text or alongside a menu, many phones have built-in icons that you can use instead of uploading an image from a server. To do this, use the ICON=icon_name attribute within the IMG element. (If the icon is not included within the phone's ROM, it is automatically uploaded from the server.) The following code will display an icon in lieu of a button label:

```
<ACTION KEY=srchby TYPE=ACCEPT ICON=righthand TASK=GO DEST=#display>
```

You can include an <IMG> statement anywhere in formatted text:

- In display text in CHOICE, DISPLAY, and ENTRY cards
- In choice items on a CHOICE card
- In softkey labels

12.8 SUMMARY

This chapter covered the elements that enable navigation between cards and between decks, how to provide the user with a selection menu, and how to enable the user to enter data into forms.

Techniques covered how to control the data entered by a user, and the chapter ended with a discussion of the history stack and the use of images and icons to enhance a simple text display.

Enabling the user to select from a menu and enter data involves variables—the storing of dynamic information within name/value pairs that can be used by the application in a meaningful way. The use of variables within HDML is the topic of the next chapter.

C H A P T E R   1 3

Using variables in HDML

13.1 INTRODUCTION

HDML applications, like all applications, make liberal use of *variables*. A variable, as the name implies, is a changeable piece of data used by the phone. Imagine a black box inside your phone that has a name and that holds some specific information. A variable is just that—a container that has a name and that holds a piece of dynamic information associated with that name. For example, if one were to write: color = red, the variable name is color, which is associated with the dynamic value red. Defining the value of a variable is known as *setting* a variable.

In the previous chapter you learned how to enable users to interact with your application through menus and data entry forms. Interacting with the phone through these devices is the means by which a user sets values to application variables. In this chapter, you will learn the use of variables in HDML—the means through which to set values to variables, and how to send variables to, and receive them from, other applications.

This chapter assumes you understand the concept of a variable (from chapter 6) and will cover setting and referencing variables and ways in which to send variables to server-side programs in HDML.

13.2 ABOUT VARIABLES IN HDML

Some notes on variables:

- Variables can be substituted into formatted text *or* into HDML elements.
- Variables remain within a phone's memory for the duration of an activity (for more information on activities, see chapter 14).
- Variables can be defined explicitly within the HDML or can be set by the user through CHOICE or ENTRY cards.
- Variables are referred to within HDML by placing the variable name in parentheses and preceding it with a $ sign: $(variable).

Similar to WML, the value of a variable can be used in a variety of ways (table 13.1).

Table 13.1 Using variable values

Common uses of variable values	Example
As formatted text	Var_name = "Hello World!"
As attribute values	Var_name = "src=image.wbmp"
As menu choices	Var_name = "red"
To provide default values in CHOICE and ENTRY cards	Var_name = "male"
As a destination URL	Var_name = "http://www.mydomain.com"

Variables are scoped to *activities*. You can reference a variable anywhere within the activity in which it is set; you can't reference it in other activities. For more information on activities, see chapter 14.

Variables can be set either *explicitly* (the value assigned to the variable is specified by the programmer) or *implicitly* (a value is assigned to a variable based on an event, such as a user entering data):

- To define a variable explicitly within your HDML code, use the VARS attribute of the <ACTION> element and the variables will be set when the user activates the <ACTION> element (for instance, by navigating to the next card).
- To define a variable implicitly, the user must complete an activity such as entering data into a form or selecting a menu item. When the activity is completed, the variable value is set.

Each of these methods will be discussed in more detail later in this chapter.

13.2.1 Naming variables

There are only a few rules regarding the name you choose for a variable (and they are the same as the WML naming conventions discussed in chapter 6):

- The following characters are not allowed: $, <, >, =, /, \, &, *, #. Using these characters within a variable name will throw an error.

- Unlike HDML elements, case matters when naming variables: `Variablename` and `variablename` are two different variables.

- Keep names short, as they will be stored in device memory.

- Here are some *valid* variable names: `username`, `user_name`, `User123`, `123User`.

- Here are some *invalid* variable names: `user name`, `user/name`, `u$er123`, `user#123`.

13.2.2 Referencing variables

As shown in table 13.1, variables can be displayed anywhere within your HDML code. You could display the contents of a variable to the screen—perhaps to show the user what he entered or which menu item he chose. You could use the value of the variable in a URL—to send a user to a different location, depending on which menu item he selects. Or you could use the variable content as a selection item in a list—to provide a user-defined selection menu.

To reference a variable within your HDML code, place its name inside parentheses and preceed it with a dollar sign ($): `$(variable_name)`. When the browser processes the HDML, the value associated with the variable is substituted and displayed (or used within a process).

When referencing a variable to be used in a URL, if the variable contains certain reserved characters ("+", ";", "/", "?", ":", "@", "&", "=", or white space), it must adhere to certain URL escaping rules. In other words, the character must be "translated" into its ASCII encoding in order to be used. Most browsers automatically apply the URL escaping rules to the value of the variable, but the following options can be used as well:

- `$(variable_name)` attempts to do what is right—depending on the context, it escapes nonalphanumeric characters according to URL conventions

- `$(variable_name:esc)` forces *escaping* of symbolic characters

- `$(variable_name:noesc)` forces *no escaping* of symbolic characters

For more information on displaying variables containing reserved characters, see chapter 11.

Let's look at an example in order to see how a variable can be referenced. In the following example code fragment, imagine that the variable name has been set with the value `Sam`. The following DISPLAY card will display the string `Hello, my name is` followed by the value of the variable name, which in this case is `Sam`.

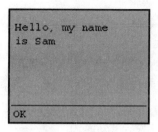

```
<DISPLAY>
    Hello, my name is $(name)
</DISPLAY>
```

When the phone processes this code, the value associated with the variable name is substituted and displayed to the user (or used within a process), as is figure 13.1.

Figure 13.1
Displaying a variable

13.3   *SETTING VARIABLES EXPLICITLY*

Variables can be set explicitly by including a VARS attribute within the <ACTION> element of a card using the following syntax where variable1, variable2, and variable3 are variable names and value1, value2, and value3 are their respective values:

```
VARS=variable1=value1&variable2=value2&variable3=value3
```

Note that the variables are set when the action element is invoked. This procedure is most commonly used to set a variable to a specific value in order to make it the default value, or if you are going to use it as a constant throughout the compilation unit. In the next example, the VARS attribute is used to explicitly set two variables (var1 and var2), the values of which are set when Accept is pressed.

```
<HDML VERSION=3.0>
  <DISPLAY>
    <ACTION TYPE=ACCEPT TASK=GO DEST=#card2
      VARS=var1=George&var2=Sam>        Sets the value of var1
    Press OK to view variable values.    to George and the
  </DISPLAY>                             value of var2 to Sam

  <DISPLAY NAME=card2>
    $(var1)
    <BR>
  $(var2)
  </DISPLAY>
</HDML>
```

Figure 13.2 shows the first card. Pressing OK displays the variable values (figure 13.3).

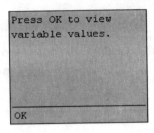

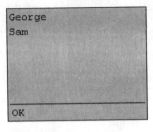

Figure 13.2
Sets the variables

Figure 13.3
Displays the variables

13.3.1 Using the <NODISPLAY> card

To explicitly set variables without requiring the user to perform an action, not even pressing Accept, use the <ACTION> element within a <NODISPLAY> card. <NODISPLAY> is not displayed to the user, and the phone automatically invokes the task defined by <ACTION>.

The following example expands the previous example with the addition of a <NODISPLAY> card, used to set two additional variables.

```
<HDML VERSION=3.0>
   <DISPLAY>
      <ACTION TYPE=ACCEPT TASK=GO DEST=#card2
         VARS=var1=George&var2=Sam>
      Press OK to view variable values.
   </DISPLAY>

<NODISPLAY NAME=card2>
   <ACTION TYPE=ACCEPT TASK=GO DEST=#display
   VARS=var3=Bill&var4=Jim>
</NODISPLAY>

   <DISPLAY NAME=display>
      $(var1)
      <BR>$(var2)
      <BR>$(var3)
      <BR>$(var4)
   </DISPLAY>
</HDML>
```

Sets the variable var1 equal to George and var2 equal to Sam using VARS

This <NODISPLAY> card is not seen by the user, but it sets the variable var3 equal to Bill and var4 equal to Jim

Shows that all four variables have been set

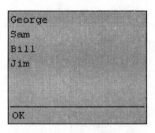

Figure 13.4 Variables displayed

Figure 13.4 shows the display of the sample code. Take care when using NODISPLAY cards. Even though the user does not see them, they require just as much overhead as any other card and can diminish performance just as rapidly. They can give the user the appearance that his application is running slow.

13.4 *SETTING VARIABLES IMPLICITLY*

An implicit variable is one whose value is set as a result of a user's actions. For example, if a user is provided with a CHOICE card that offers a menu of movie genre, you can indicate that whatever choice made on the card be associated with the variable (genre). Later, you can insert the variable style into a DISPLAY card and the phone will display the associated value (e.g., western) in the display.

13.4.1 Using the CHOICE card

To implicitly set a variable using a CHOICE card, set the KEY attribute of the <CHOICE> element equal to the name of the variable that you are setting. Next, set the VALUE attribute of the <CE> element equal to the value that you want to set the variable to (should the user choose that selection from the menu).

The following example illustrates how to use a CHOICE card to implicitly set a variable. A menu is provided, and the variable choice is set to a specific value as a result of the user's selection:

The attribute KEY is set to the variable choice which will be set to a value depending on the user's choice

```
<HDML VERSION=3.0>
<CHOICE NAME=choose KEY=choice>
    <CE LABEL=Film TASK=GO VALUE=film DEST=#display>Film
    <CE LABEL=Director TASK=GO VALUE=dir DEST=#display>Director
    <CE LABEL=Actor TASK=GO VALUE=Actor DEST=#display>Actor
</CHOICE>

<DISPLAY NAME="display">
The value of the variable "choice" is $(choice)
</DISPLAY>
</HDML>
```

If the user chooses this menu item, the variable choice will be set to the value film

Figure 13.5 shows the choices and figure 13.6 shows the value of the choice.

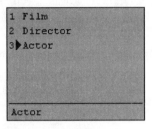

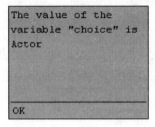

Figure 13.5   CHOICE card   **Figure 13.6   Value of choice**

13.4.2   Using the ENTRY card

Similar to the CHOICE cards, variables can also be set implicitly using an ENTRY card. To set a variable using the ENTRY card, simply set the KEY attribute of <ENTRY> equal to the name of the variable. When the user enters data and invokes the <ACTION> element (for example, by navigating to the next card), the value of the variable will be set to the data that the user entered.

The following example illustrates using an ENTRY card to implicitly set a variable. An entry field is provided to the user, and the variable srchfor is set to a specific value as a result of the user's entered data after they press Accept:

```
<HDML VERSION=3.0>
   <ENTRY NAME="search_for" KEY=srchfor>          ←——  The NAME attribute
     <ACTION TYPE="ACCEPT" TASK="GO" DEST="#display">    defines the entry field
   Enter a letter:                                       and the KEY
    </ENTRY>                                              attribute defines the
                                                          variable name
   <DISPLAY NAME="display">
     <ACTION TYPE=ACCEPT TASK=GO DEST="#search_by">
       variables entered:
       $(srchfor)    ←⌐ Displays variable value
   </DISPLAY>
 </HDML>
```

The ENTRY card is shown in figure 13.7 and the choice of variables is displayed in figure 13.8:

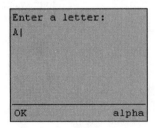

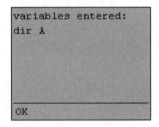

Figure 13.7   ENTRY card   **Figure 13.8   Value entered**

13.5 PUTTING IT ALL TOGETHER

This five-card example uses three different methods to set variables:

- implicitly through a <CHOICE> card
- implicitly through an <ENTRY> card
- explicitly using a <NODISPLAY> card

In the first card of this example, the user is asked to choose a letter. After entering a letter, the user can then press Accept which takes him to the second card.

The second card presents the user with a menu from which they can choose Film or Director. After choosing one of the menu items, he is directed to the third card.

The third card displays the user's menu choice so that he can confirm his selection. When the user presses Accept, he is passed to the fourth card.

The fourth card is a NODISPLAY card that sets the variable secret to the value hi! and secret1 to the value howareya!. After setting those variables the user is directed to the fifth card.

In the fifth card the user is shown all of the values of the variables that were set during the session.

13.5.1 The code

Here is the HDML code which yields the result described in the next section:

```
<HDML VERSION=3.0>
   <ENTRY NAME=letter KEY=letter FORMAT=A>          The variable "letter"
     Choose a letter:                               is set to the data that the
     <ACTION TYPE=ACCEPT TASK=GO DEST=#search_by>   user enters
   </ENTRY>

   <CHOICE NAME=search_by KEY=srchby>               The variable "srchby" is
       Search $(letter) for:                        set to the value in the
       <CE LABEL=film VALUE=film TASK=GO            VALUE attribute of the
       DEST=#search_for>Film                        choice the user makes
       <CE LABEL=director VALUE=dir TASK=GO
       DEST=#search_for>Director
   </CHOICE>

                                   The variable "srchby"
                                   was set in the previous
   <DISPLAY NAME=search_for>       CHOICE card by the user and
       Search for:<BR>             is displayed here
         $(srchby)
       <ACTION TYPE=ACCEPT TASK=GO DEST=#nodisplay>
   </DISPLAY>
                                             The variable secret is
                                             set to the value "hi!"
                                             and secret1 is set to
   <NODISPLAY NAME="nodisplay">              the value
     <ACTION TYPE="ACCEPT" TASK="GO" DEST="#display"   "howareya!" without
       VARS=secret="hi!"&secret1="howareya!">         the user's knowledge
   </NODISPLAY>
```

```
<DISPLAY NAME=display>
    <ACTION TYPE=ACCEPT TASK=GO DEST=#display>
    Searching for:
      $(letter)
      $(srchby)           All the variables are
      $(secret)           displayed here
      $(secret1)
  </DISPLAY>
</HDML>
```

13.5.2   The result

These HDML code displays are illustrated in figure 13.9.

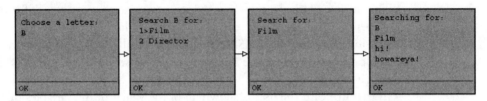

Figure 13.9   Example application using ENTRY, CHOICE, DISPLAY, and NODISPLAY cards

Although this example may seem silly, the concept is extremely useful in many applications. A variety of DISPLAY, ENTRY, and MENU cards can be used to access a large movie database from which users could look up times and locations of movies that are playing. The NODISPLAY card can be helpful to set variables such as password or any thing that you don't want the user to see. The possibilities are endless.

13.6   SENDING VARIABLES TO SERVER-SIDE PROGRAMS

We have learned to assign a value to a variable, and then use the variable within the HDML code. Even more useful is the ability to assign a value to a variable and send that variable outside the HDML code (to a server-side ASP, for example) for processing. If you are building your movie database you might require a method to send user selections to a database for processing. More information on the concept and uses of passing variables to server-side programs can be found in chapter 6.

As in WML, there are two ways to send data to the server:

- The POST method
- The GET method

HDML does not explicitly set a limit to the amount of variables you can export, but take care that you don't exceed the byte limits of the gateway server—keep your code to 1,200 bytes or below.

13.6.1 Using the POST method

Although query string arguments are a common method of sending variables to a URL within the PC-based Web, it is not recommended that you use this method in an HDML application. Using POST to send data enables the wireless gateway server to perform any transposing of data from the phone's character set to a character set understood by your application.

The POST method in HDML is very similar to that in WML. However, in HDML you simply set the METHOD attribute of the <ACTION> element equal to POST, and put the necessary variable = value pairs in the POSTDATA attribute.

Here is an example of sending two variables, searchby and searchfor, to an activity using the POST method:

```
<HDML VERSION=3.0>

  <ENTRY NAME=letter KEY=letter FORMAT=A>
    Choose a letter:
    <ACTION TYPE=ACCEPT TASK=GO DEST=#search_by>
  </ENTRY>

  <CHOICE NAME=search_by KEY=srchby>
      Search $(letter) for:
      <CE LABEL=film VALUE=film TASK=GO
      DEST=#search_for>Film
      <CE LABEL=director VALUE=dir TASK=GO
  DEST=#search_for>Director
  </CHOICE>

  <ENTRY NAME=search_for KEY=srchfor>
    Search for:
    <ACTION TYPE=ACCEPT TASK=GO DEST=#display>
  </ENTRY>

  <DISPLAY NAME=display>
    <ACTION TYPE=ACCEPT TASK=GOSUB
    METHOD=POST
    POSTDATA="srchby=$(srchby)&srchfor=$(srchfor)"
    DEST="http://www.mydomain.com/movie.asp">

    Searching for:
    $(srchby)
    $(srchfor)
  </DISPLAY>

</HDML>
```

Tells the browser to send data via a server POST command

Defines the URL to which data should be sent

Sends data to a URL via a POST command. Amend the POSTDATA command with any variable/value pairs that you wish to send via POST

13.6.2 Using the GET method

Another way you can send data externally is to use the GET method, which is similar in HDML and WML. Simply amend the destination URL with string arguments.

Here is an example of how to amend the URL specified in the DEST attribute with the appropriate string variables:

```
DEST=www.mydomain.com/movie.asp?srchby=$(srchby)&srchfor=$(srchfor)"
```

13.7 SUMMARY

This chapter discussed the implicit and explicit use of variables within HDML, and how variables may be passed from one HDML application to another. The next chapter expands this discussion to explore how HDML enables the developer to organize variables logically in such a way that a user can navigate outside an application and return without the loss of state within the original application.

C H A P T E R   1 4

Activities, bookmarks, cache, and access control

14.1   INTRODUCTION

This chapter introduces *activities*, a concept similar to the WML context available through Phone.com's extensions to WML. For more information on WML contexts, and how the phone history stack enables both context and activities, see chapter 7.

   In this chapter we will discuss how HDML activities work, how to set up cards and decks so that the user can bookmark them (similar to bookmarking on a web browser), and how to prevent the phone from caching them (in the case of dynamic content).

14.2 HOW ACTIVITIES WORK

As with WML contexts, activities enable you to structure your service to enable you to scope your variables and ease the development of a logical user interface:

- *Scoping variables*—Using activities, activity *A* may transfer control to activity *B* without activity *A* losing state. When activity *B* terminates, the user is returned to activity *A* to find all variable values have been maintained. This concept is portrayed in figure 14.1.

- *Easing user interface design*—Because user interface naturally flows from the logical structure of the application, using activities can simplify the task of ensuring the user experience is logical and intuitive.

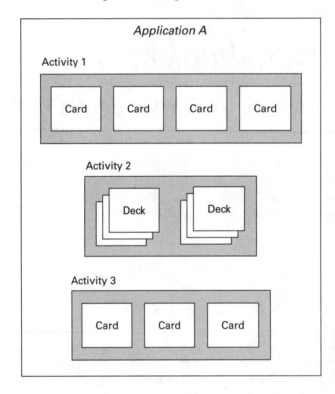

**Figure 14.1
Multiple activities in an
application containing
multiple decks**

Activities are independent of deck and card structure: A single deck might contain multiple activities, or a single activity might contain multiple decks. For example, a single application might contain three activities; each activity may itself contain a single deck or multiple decks.

In a common example, a Yellow Pages service might provide activities such as "Find a seafood restaurant in Detroit" and "Find the number of Barney's Restaurant in New York." A developer might want to access a driving directions application from the Yellow Pages application, but ensure that the Yellow Pages state (including user name, password, and restaurant search terms) remains set (figure 14.2).

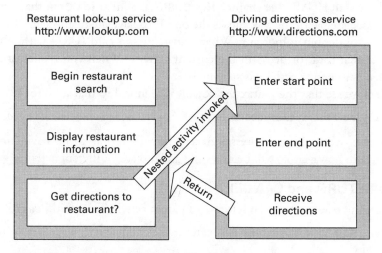

Figure 14.2   Driving directions as a child activity

As the user navigates into nested activities the phone preserves the *state* of the original activity. The state includes attributes such as the activity's variables and its card history stack. In the example, a user might receive driving directions and decide that traffic is too heavy on the roads leading to the restaurant. When the user returns to the restaurant lookup application, state has been maintained—the variables (location, style of cuisine, etc.) need not be re-entered.

14.3   NAVIGATING BETWEEN ACTIVITIES

Just as GO and PREV tasks are used to enable navigation from card to card within a single activity (or deck), navigation between activities uses tasks as well (table 14.1).

Table 14.1   Tasks for navigating between activities

Task	Description
GOSUB	Spawns a nested activity
RETURN	Returns from a nested activity to the parent activity; typically associated with the completion of a user's goal within an activity
CANCEL	Returns from a nested activity to the parent activity; typically associated with the user exiting an activity before reaching the activity's goal

Each of these tasks is discussed in the next sections.

14.3.1 Using GOSUB

HDML calls an activity through the GOSUB task (for more information about defining tasks within HDML, see chapter 12). GOSUB is similar to GO, in that pressing the button associated with the task causes the phone to navigate to another URL. The difference is subtle, but important: When you request a card (URL) with GO, you are including that card (or deck) in the current activity. When you request a card with GOSUB, a new, nested activity is spawned.

Here we see that the syntax for GOSUB is identical to that used for GO:

```
<ACTION TYPE=ACCEPT TASK=GOSUB DEST="http://www.mysite.com/next.hdml">
```

In this case, when the user presses Accept he will appear to be navigating to just another card; however, he will be accessing a completely different activity.

14.3.2 Using RETURN and CANCEL

There are three ways a user can return to a parent activity from within a child activity:

- Navigate backward past the first card in the child activity to return to the parent activity.

- Invoke a RETURN task within the child activity to be returned to a card in the parent activity, which is specified, in the NEXT attribute of the ACTION element which invoked the child activity in the first place.

- Invoke a CANCEL task within the nested activity to be returned to the card that invoked the child activity (with no return values or state changes).

By default, each method will return the user to the card in the parent activity that invoked the nested child activity. HDML provides two methods—RETURN and CANCEL—to return a user to a parent activity. These methods enable a developer to define navigation based on whether the user completed the task or wants to cancel the activity.

If the user completed the child activity, he should use a RETURN task on the final card of the child activity to send the user back to the parent activity. Here is an example ACTION element using RETURN:

```
<ACTION TYPE="ACCEPT" TASK="RETURN" LABEL="OK">
```

If the user cancels the child activity, he can use a CANCEL task on the current card to send the user back to the parent activity:

```
<ACTION TYPE="SOFT2" TASK="CANCEL" LABEL="ESC">
```

An example application that might use nested activities may include an email application that lists the emails in your inbox. Each task (such as reading an email, deleting an email, etc.) is a child activity. You, as the programmer, may choose to program this application so that when the user reads an email, a RETURN task will exit the email activity and move a read email to another folder. You use a CANCEL task to exit the activity and return the user to the inbox (or list of emails) without moving the read email to another folder.

Figure 14.3 shows the flow of these activities. The action starts on the left with the first (parent) activity—a list of emails. The user then chooses one of the emails to read, thus spawning a child activity. From here, the user can either press OK or ESC. By pressing ESC, the programmer uses the CANCEL task to send the user back to the original inbox without removing the read email. If the user presses OK while reading the email, the programmer uses the RETURN task to send the user back to the inbox, but the email he was reading has been removed.

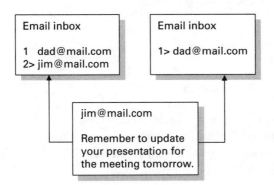

Figure 14.3
Email example diagram

Use RETURN just as you would any other task. It is correlated with the NEXT=*URL* attribute specified with GOSUB in the calling activity, where *URL* is the card to which the phone navigates when the RETURN task is invoked. If NEXT isn't specified, the phone will return the user to the calling card.

If a NEXT attribute is specified within the calling card, the user will be returned to the specified URL. For example, the nested activity might be called by the following code, which specifies a NEXT=*URL* (remember, DEST=URL defines the URL of the nested activity itself):

```
<ACTION TASK=GOSUB NEXT="#delemail" DEST="#reademail">
```

If NEXT is not specified, the user is by default returned to the calling card.

CANCEL offers the same functionality as RETURN, correlated with the CANCEL=*URL* option within the calling card. Just as with the NEXT=*URL*, the phone navigates to the card specified within *CANCEL=URL* when the CANCEL task is invoked within the nested activity.

```
<ACTION TYPE=SOFT2 TASK=CANCEL LABEL=ESC>
    With the calling card specifying the URL with the CANCEL attribute:
<ACTION TASK=GOSUB NEXT=#delemail CANCEL=#inbox DEST=#reademail>
```

14.3.3 Example: calling external applications

Imagine a City Guide service that prompts the user to enter the name of a city in the U.S. Upon entering the city name, the City Guide displays a page offering the selected city's weather and local news (figure 14.4).

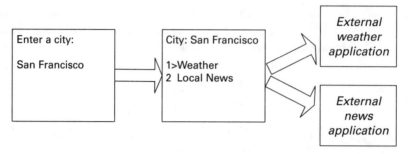

Figure 14.4   Diagram of a city guide application

In this example, let's say that the City Guide application does not have the ability to determine the weather or local news for a particular application; rather, it must leverage the functionality of two other applications to receive this information.

To get the information, the City Guide application:

1 Prompts the user to enter a city

2 Invokes a weather application using the GOSUB task

3 The weather application receives the location variable from the City Guide application, finds the weather information for the city, and displays it to the user. The user presses OK, and returns to the City Guide via a RETURN task. The user returns to the City Guide application, which retains the selected city (San Francisco, in figure 14.4) in its variable store.

If an activity is cancelled, the phone returns the user to the parent activity by default. HDML allows you to define a URL other than the default by inserting the CANCEL= [URL] option in the task element.

14.3.4 Example: providing help with activities

Some phone models feature a specific Help key, and HDML enables you to define what text is displayed when that button is pressed. To set some functionality to the Help button, simply set the TYPE attribute of the ACTION element equal to HELP. This is similar to setting the functionality of the Accept button by setting the TYPE attribute of an ACTION element equal to ACCEPT.

Unless you specifically define HELP for a particular deck (or a specific card), the Help button defaults to a message that informs that user that no help is available.

This three-card example begins with a card that shows the user that this is "card one". After pressing Accept the user is directed to card2 which displays the message that it is card two.

When the user presses Help at card2, a child activity is spawned and the user is directed to the third card, help1.

At the third card, a help message is displayed. If the user presses Accept they are returned to the card that called the child activity (because no NEXT attribute was defined when calling GOSUB).

Here is the code:

```
<HDML VERSION=3.0>

    <DISPLAY NAME=card1>
    <ACTION TYPE=ACCEPT TASK=GO DEST=#card2>
        This is card one.
    </DISPLAY>

    <DISPLAY NAME=card2>
    <ACTION TYPE=HELP TASK=GOSUB DEST=#help1>      ← This is where the child
        This is card two.                            activity is spawned
    </DISPLAY>

    <DISPLAY NAME=help1>
        <ACTION TYPE=ACCEPT TASK=RETURN LABEL=OK>  ← This is where the child
    This is the help display for card two.            activity returns to the
    </DISPLAY>                                         parent activity
</HDML>
```

When building help decks, remember that the user expects to immediately return to the original application upon reading the appropriate help. Don't force a user to scroll backward through help cards to return to an application; to keep navigation intuitive, you should always use the GOSUB task in HELP actions.

14.4 USING VARIABLES IN ACTIVITIES

A variable is available to any card within an activity, but *only* within that activity. Variables can be sent between activities using the attributes in table 14.2.

Table 14.2   HDML attributes for sending variables between activities

HDML attribute	Description	Code example
VARS	Sends variables to a child activity	`<ACTION TYPE=ACCEPT TASK=GOSUB DEST="#child" VARS="var1=John&var2=Doe">`
RETVALS	Returns variables to a parent activity	`<ACTION TYPE=ACCEPT TASK=RETURN DEST="#parent" RETVALS=$(somevar); $(anothervar)>`
RECEIVE	Specifies variables that will be set by data received through RETVALS	`<ACTION TYPE=ACCEPT TASK=GOSUB DEST="#child" VARS="var1=John&var2=Doe" RECEIVE=firstname; lastname>`
CLEAR	Clears all variables within a parent activity	`<ACTION TYPE=ACCEPT TASK=RETURN CLEAR=TRUE>`

Each attribute is discussed in more detail in the following sections.

14.4.1 Using VARS

Include the VARS attribute simultaneously with the GOSUB task to send variables to the activity defined within the DEST attribute. VARS syntax does not change when it is used with GOSUB as shown here:

```
VARS=var1=value1&var2=value2
```

The following code fragment includes VARS used with a GOSUB task. The variables in the VARS attribute will be active within the nested activity:

```
<DISPLAY>
    <ACTION TYPE=ACCEPT TASK=GOSUB DEST="#nested_activity"
      VARS="var1=John&var2=Doe">
            This card sends the indicated variables to the nested activity.
</DISPLAY>
```

14.4.2 Using RETVALS

The RETVALS attribute returns a variable to a parent activity. Use RETVALS to set values defined by the RECEIVE attribute within the calling card. RETVALS uses the following syntax:

```
RETVALS=a;b;c
```

Data sent via RETVALS are associated with variables on a one-to-one basis with RECEIVE—the first value is associated with the first variable and so on. This is in contrast with the VARS attribute, which sends variables by name.

The following code fragment demonstrates how RETVALS is used by a card within a nested activity:

```
<DISPLAY>
    <ACTION TYPE=ACCEPT TASK=RETURN DEST="#parent_activity"
      RETVALS=$(somevar); $(anothervar)>
            This card sends the indicated variables to the nested activity.
</DISPLAY>
```

Values sent via RETVALS set the value of variables defined by the RECEIVE attribute within the parent activity. If RECEIVE variables are not defined within the parent activity, the variables will be lost. RECEIVE assigns data received from RETVALS on a one-to-one basis. If you wish to send only the first and third variables defined within RECEIVE, insert another semicolon to hold the place:

```
<DISPLAY>
    <ACTION TYPE=ACCEPT TASK=RETURN DEST="#parent_activity"
      RETVALS=$(somevar);; $(anothervar)>
        This card sends the indicated variables to the nested activity.
</DISPLAY>
```

14.4.3 Using RECEIVE

The RECEIVE attribute specifies variables that accept return values from the nested activity returning data through RETVALS. The syntax is as follows:

```
RECEIVE=var1;var2;var3
```

The following code fragment illustrates the use of RECEIVE:

```
<DISPLAY>
    <ACTION TYPE=ACCEPT TASK=GOSUB DEST="#nested_activity"
      VARS="var1=John&var2=Doe" RECEIVE=firstname; lastname>
       The RECEIVE attribute in this card defined variables that will be set
by data sent through RETVALS in the nested activity>
</DISPLAY>
```

14.4.4 Using CLEAR

The CLEAR=TRUE attribute is used within a nested activity to clear all the variables within the activity that called it. The FRIEND=TRUE attribute must be set within the calling activity CLEAR=FALSE by default.

For example, CLEAR=TRUE can be used within an activity that authenticates a user. If a server-side algorithm finds that entered username/password combination is invalid, a <NODISPLAY> card containing CLEAR=TRUE can be invoked—which can send the user back to the name/password entry card having cleared the card of previously entered information. The following code fragment illustrates this <NODISPLAY> card:

```
<NODISPLAY NAME=clear>
    <ACTION TYPE=ACCEPT TASK=RETURN CLEAR=TRUE>
</NODISPLAY>
```

Remember that the FRIEND=TRUE attribute must be set within the parent card for CLEAR=TRUE to work. This helps ensure that rogue applications cannot reset the values of variables within the parent application. The following code example uses FRIEND=TRUE within the calling element:

```
<DISPLAY>
    <ACTION TYPE=ACCEPT TASK=GOSUB DEST="#nested_activity"
      VARS="var1=John&var2=Doe" RECEIVE=firstname; lastname FRIEND=TRUE>
      FRIEND=TRUE ensures that a CLEAR=TRUE attribute used within the
      nested activity will clear all variables.>
</DISPLAY>
```

14.5 BOOKMARKS

Bookmarking a site on a phone means saving a particular URL within a special Bookmarks menu so that it can later be easily requested—exactly the functionality as bookmarks in Netscape Navigator or the Favorites folder in Internet Explorer. When the user bookmarks a card, the browser adds a bookmark (a title and an associated

URL) to the user's bookmark menu. Accessing the bookmark menu and choosing the bookmark returns the user directly to the desired card.

Bookmarks can be indispensable on a phone. On a PC, if you accidentally surf away from a driving directions application, it is inconvenient to have to re-enter the location information. If you are trying to drive a car and—oops!—turn off your phone, you're sunk! You have to pull over and re-enter all that information into the phone. Sunk, that is, unless you had the foresight to bookmark the driving directions results URL.

To set up a bookmark, make sure that the MARKABLE attribute of the specific element is set to TRUE. The default value is FALSE. If you wish to make every card in the deck bookmarkable, set the MARKABLE attribute of the HDML element equal to TRUE. If you wish to bookmark some, but not all, sites, set the MARKABLE attribute of each card TRUE (markable) or FALSE (not markable).

To set the address that a bookmark will access and the name of the bookmark, use the following HDML attributes in a DISPLAY, CHOICE, or ENTRY card:

- *TITLE*—Provides a default bookmark name. If you don't specify a title, the phone uses the card's first line of display text as the default title for the bookmark. The user can edit the bookmark name.

- *BOOKMARK*—Specifies the URL that is added to the bookmark list. If you don't specify this option, the phone uses the card's URL. Set this option only if you want the marked URL to be different from the card's actual URL.

Let's look at an example application in which we are setting bookmarking information for two DISPLAY cards.

In the first card, we set the MARKABLE attribute of the HDML element equal to TRUE, making the entire deck markable. We set the title of the bookmark to Sample Bookmark. When the user chooses to access this bookmark, he will be directed to `http://www.domain.com/bookmark.hdml`, which is set to the BOOKMARK attribute.

In the second card, we set the MARKABLE attribute to FALSE. Since card-level functionality overrides any deck-level functionality, the user will not be able to bookmark the second card.

Here is the code:

```
<HDML VERSION=3.0 MARKABLE=TRUE>      ◁┘ Makes the entire deck markable
    <DISPLAY NAME=card1 TITLE="Sample bookmark"
       BOOKMARK="http://www.domain.com/bookmark.hdml">
       <ACTION TYPE=ACCEPT TASK=GO DEST=#card2>
       You can bookmark this card.
    </DISPLAY>

    <DISPLAY NAME=card2 MARKABLE=FALSE>    ◁┐ Prevents the user from storing
       You cannot bookmark this card.        │ this URL within a bookmark file
    </DISPLAY>

</HDML>
```

14.5.1 Disabling bookmarks

There are circumstances in which you might not wish a user to bookmark a card. For example, a card might require the user to set a series of variables, and would be unusable if bookmarked because the appropriate variables would not be set.

As mentioned in the previous section, to prevent a card from being bookmarked, set the MARKABLE attribute of that card equal to FALSE. To prevent a user from bookmarking any of the cards within the deck, set the MARKABLE attribute of the HDML element equal to FALSE. Remember that deck-level functionality can be overridden by card-level functionality.

14.6 USING THE PHONE'S CACHE

A *cache* is a special area of memory that is used to temporarily store frequently requested data. When a user accesses a card, the browser saves the card in a cache for a preset amount of time. Unless the HDML program specifies differently, the default is 30 days. If the user revisits the card during the time it is saved within the cache, the card can be very quickly loaded from the local cache instead of taking time to reload from the server.

The programmer can set the amount of time that each deck or card is held in the cache. To set the Time to Live (TTL) for the entire deck, set the TTL attribute of the HDML element to the number of seconds you want the deck to be available in cache. To set the TTL for an individual card, set the TTL attribute of the DISPLAY, CHOICE, or ENTRY element to the number of seconds you want the card to be available in cache. Remember that card-level settings override deck-level settings. Also remember that the default TTL in either case is 30 days. If you set the cache time to zero (0), the deck or card will not be cached.

In the following example, we have a DISPLAY card with a cache time of 1,200 seconds, or 20 minutes. This example demonstrates one good reason for not keeping the card cached for a long period: It is used to display a stock price. Stock prices are time-sensitive information and can change frequently.

```
<HDML VERSION=3.0 MARKABLE=TRUE>
<DISPLAY NAME=display TTL=1200>
    <ACTION TYPE=ACCEPT TASK=GO>
        The stock price is:
        $(stockprice)
</DISPLAY>
</HDML>
```

Removes the card from the phone's cache after 20 minutes (1,200 seconds)

Note that the browser ignores the TTL attribute if the user is navigating backward. When a user requests a card by pressing Back, the browser always retrieves a deck from its cache, even if the TTLs have expired or were set to 0. This is an effort to reduce latency—because users typically navigate backward quickly in an effort to reach a <CHOICE> or <ENTRY> card and proceed down a different branch, checking deck TTLs and reloading decks would make backward navigation unacceptably slow.

14.6.1　Using a cache to improve performance

If you know which URLs a user is most likely to request, you can significantly improve performance of your HDML application by using the REL=NEXT attribute in <ACTION>, <A>, and <CE> statements. The REL=NEXT attribute instructs the browser to prefetch the URL specified by the DEST attribute while the user is viewing the current card. If the user subsequently requests the URL, the deck is retrieved directly from the phone's cache, where it has already been loaded. The result is that the user experiences a much smaller delay when traversing from one URL to another.

There is no guarantee that the phone will be able to prefetch the specified URL. For example, if the phone is on a circuit-switched network and the circuit is down, the phone will not open a circuit. If the phone fails to execute the prefetch, it does not retry.

If you specify the REL=NEXT option, the URL is added to the end of the phone's cache. If the user does not request the URL soon after the phone caches it, the phone pushes it out of the cache and caches the other data instead (the alternate card that the user chose).

If several tasks on a card specify the REL=NEXT option, the phone prefetches the URLs in the order in which the tasks are listed.

Next is an example in which the first card has a REL attribute defined in the ACTION element to prefetch the second card and make the program seem to flow faster.

Here is the code:

```
<HDML VERSION=3.0>
<DISPLAY NAME=card1>
    <ACTION TYPE=ACCEPT TASK=GO DEST=#card2 REL=NEXT>        Preloads card2
            Pres OK to check the stock price.                while the user is
</DISPLAY>                                                   looking at card1

<DISPLAY NAME=card2>          Since card2 was preloaded,
      The stock price is:     the phone displays it from the
      $(stockprice)           cache instead of loading it
</DISPLAY>                     from the server
</HDML>
```

14.7　ABOUT ACCESS CONTROL

As mentioned in section 14.4, variable values are available to any deck contained within a particular activity. Put another way, when you direct a user to a particular URL using a GO task, you gain access to any variables within the URL called by GO. Similarly, if another deck sent a user to *your* domain using a GO command, that foreign user gains access to any variables stored within your deck.

This presents a security risk: the possibility that an external application could potentially gain access to your user's variables simply by using a GO command. To control this risk, HDML supports *access control*, which enables you to specify whether another application can access your application as part of an activity.

14.7.1 How deck access works

By default, applications within the same domain can incorporate one another into activities. For example, imagine two decks located in different directories:

```
http://www.domain.com/directory1/deck1.hdml
http://www.domain.com/directory2/deck2.hdml
```

Because both decks are hosted on the same domain, the default access control settings allow you to create an activity that spans both decks.

But applications that live on different domains are, by default, denied access to one another. Imagine the same two decks located in different domains:

```
http://www.domain.com/deck1.hdml
http://www.anotherdomain.com/deck2.hdml
```

By default, these decks are denied access to one another.

In the following example, the first deck is stored at http://www.domain1.com, but the URL in the DEST attribute is set to a deck on a different domain (http://www.domain2.com). The first deck will be denied access to the second and the user will be presented with an error.

```
<HDML VERSION=3.0>
    <ENTRY KEY=name1>
        <ACTION TYPE=ACCEPT TASK=GO
        DEST=http//www.domain2.com/deck2.hdml
        VARS=hello=Hello!>
        Enter your name:
    </ENTRY>
</HDML>
```

This deck is stored at http://www.domainl.com and attempts access to a deck on a different domain: http://www.domain2.com

```
<HDML VERSION=3.0>
    <DISPLAY NAME=display>
        $(hello)
        <BR>$(name1)
    </DISPLAY>
</HDML>
```

This is the deck stored at http://www.domain2.com. Because it lives on a different domain from the deck that attempted to access it from an activity, the original deck is denied access

14.7.2 Controlling deck access

Generally, you don't need to change the default access control settings unless you want to access decks that are on a different URL or you want to restrict access to a deck to URLs with certain paths.

Table 14.3 shows the attributes of the HDML element that allow you to control deck access.

For example, if you want to make the previous example work correctly, you could either set the PUBLIC attribute for the second deck to TRUE, or you could set the ACCESSDOMAIN attribute. The following example shows how to set the ACCESSDOMAIN attribute:

Table 14.3 Attributes of the HDML element

Attribute	Description
PUBLIC	Enables access control for a deck. Setting PUBLIC to FALSE limits the URLs that can include the deck in an activity, according to the ACCESSDOMAIN and ACCESSPATH option settings. Setting it to TRUE allows any URL to link to cares in the deck. Set to FALSE by default.
ACCESSDOMAIN	Specifies the domain of URLs that can include the deck's cards in an activity (when PUBLIC is set to FALSE)
ACCESSPATH	Specifies the base path of URLs that can include the deck's cards in an activity (when PUBLIC is set to FALSE)

```
<HDML VERSION=3.0>
    <ENTRY KEY=name1>
        <ACTION TYPE=ACCEPT TASK=GO
        DEST=http//www.domain2.com/deck2.hdml
        VARS=hello=Hello!>
        Enter your name:
    </ENTRY>
</HDML>
```

This deck is stored at http://www.domain1.com and attempts access to a deck on a different domain: http://www.domain2.com

```
<HDML VERSION=3.0 ACCESSDOMAIN=http://www.domain1.com>
    <DISPLAY NAME=display>
        $(hello)
        <BR>$(name1)
    </DISPLAY>
</HDML>
```

Since the ACCESSDOMAIN attribute is set to http://www.domain1.com the first deck will be able to access the second deck correctly

14.8 SUMMARY

This chapter completes the discussion of HDML with a look at how activities can be used to scope variables and to provide for an easier development of an intuitive, logical user interface. Other topics include management issues—phone cache management, bookmark management, and access management.

It's understandable that a developer might be reluctant to take the time and effort to learn a markup language that, like HDML, is fading into obscurity. Learning HDML is well worth the effort, however, particularly for a developer interested in the U.S. demographic. In the short (and, to a lesser extent, medium) term, HDML will remain the only language accepted by millions of phones in the U.S. Learning HDML provides developers with the knowledge to provide those users with applications, and the tools to easily migrate existing HDML applications into another markup language—an important skill as this still embryonic industry continues to evolve.

PART V

Wireless application design issues

Phones are notoriously difficult to use as an application interface. Their small, limited keypad makes text entry tedious, and the display area provides limited context and can cause users to become lost within applications. The most common complaint heard about the web-enabled phone is that it is "hard to use."

For these reasons, a solid understanding of WAP design concepts is imperative. Careful attention to usability and the application of the simple concepts described here can mean the difference between an application that is used and one that is not—or worse, one that fails.

Ensuring a consistent user experience is also important when transforming an existing HDML application to WML. Users familiar with the HDML interface will find it jarring to access the same application in WML and learn a new interface. Although the two markup languages are conceptually very similar, there are some differences that a developer should keep in mind to ensure a smooth transition from one language to the other.

C H A P T E R   1 5

WAP design principles

Ensuring that a site meets the needs of the user takes time, thought, and testing. Unfortunately, in an industry where speed is of the utmost importance, the needs of the end user are often not a primary consideration (if considered at all). The result is clear to anyone who spends any time at all on the Web: There are a lot of sites offering interesting, useful services that get little traffic because they are poorly designed.

A well-designed user interface is *the* most important variable determining whether a user will return to a site, and, therefore, is the most important variable determining a site's success.

Good design requires initial effort and resources, but it means more than an aesthetic consideration; design makes good business sense and pays significant dividends. This chapter introduces design principles basic to wireless application development; using these principles as rules of thumb and following through with user testing will go a long way toward ensuring your application is judged on the merits of its functionality and features, rather than the user interface.

There are many reasons to invest in careful design and user testing. Well-designed applications:

- *Lower support costs*—Maintaining a support desk is expensive, both in terms of real money (support technicians must be hired and trained) and future revenue potential (resources devoted to supporting users could be used to develop and expand the business). Taking time to design and test applications for usability may significantly lower support costs because fewer users will require support.

- *Are used again and again*—Because the wireless Web is new and interesting to users, most applications have a good chance to get *some* initial notice—even if only to satisfy curiosity. Good design matters because it determines which applications will see repeat business. The success of an application depends on quality design as much as it depends on usefulness.

- *Make users happy*—Even if you don't want to make people happy, there's a very good business reason to bite the bullet and do it anyway. People like using applications that are well designed. A happy user is a return user.

- *Are highly recommended*—People will share a well-designed application with others, boosting your audience. The opposite side of the coin: People will also complain to others about poorly designed applications.

15.1 DESIGN CONSIDERATIONS

Obviously, in designing an application, the developer must keep the user and the device in mind.

15.1.1 The user

Just as an application should be designed with the most constrained device in mind, it should also be designed with the least engaged user in mind—the "typical" user, who doesn't read manuals and wants to find the value of an application very quickly. The following six qualities of the typical user point to a single important truth about wireless application design: Keep it simple and intuitive.

The user doesn't read manuals—No matter how much time and effort you spend crafting informative documents for your application, your efforts will be ignored by the majority of users. Your application should be intuitive—that is, easy to use without any prior knowledge.

The user is impatient—Users will not explore an application looking for functionality. If a feature is not immediately obvious when the application is first opened, the odds are low that a user will find it. If the feature is hidden, the odds are practically nil. Define the valuable features of your application and get to them quickly.

The user is trying to solve a problem—Users will not learn your application just for the sake of learning. They are using your application as a tool to solve a problem.

If users don't quickly find what they need to solve their problem, they will not use the application.

The user is not paying full attention—People typically use cell phones while they are doing something else—buying groceries, standing in line, and driving.

An application that requires attention will not be used.

The user doesn't browse—Phone browsers will be used for information retrieval and vertical applications. Users will not be browsing aimlessly, looking for interesting sites. When users want to browse, they will go to their PC.

The user avoids complexity—As application complexity increases, the demands it places on users' patience, attention and time likewise increase. Complex applications will not be used if similar functionality can be found in a simpler application.

15.1.2   The device

You are building applications for a phone, and phones have a particular set of qualities that you must consider when writing your application. Remember that to a user, the value in a phone is not your application.

The value in a phone *is* the phone. People buy phones; they don't buy wireless Internet devices. People are interested in using their phones primarily to speak to other people, and the phone's Internet connectivity is a secondary consideration at best. This simple truth must be the foundation for all design decisions for wireless applications.

Phones are small—Wireless phones running browsers were designed first as a phone, with a browser added later. Most users purchase phones for their phone characteristics, such as size, weight, and voice quality. Whether the phone has Internet accessibility is (at best) a secondary consideration.

Characteristics that make a great phone are not the same as those that make a great Internet device.

The display is small—Careful thought should be given to how text, images, and menu options are displayed on the phone. Applications developed for small displays typically perform well on phones with large displays. The reverse is *not* true.

Specialty phones with large displays are available, and they will probably become more important as the wireless Web grows in popularity. Develop your application with only these larger phones in mind, however, and you will exclude the vast majority of your audience, who own phones with small displays (averaging 4 lines with 12–16 characters visible per line).

Text input is difficult—Although technology is being developed that should make data input on wireless devices easier (Tegic developed a technology called T9 that makes it much easier to enter data on a keypad), data input on phones remains difficult and tedious. Most phones only have a phone keypad that requires the user to repeatedly press a single number to cycle through the various letters represented by that number (press the number 2 three times for the letter *C*, for example). Try to avoid data entry, especially textual.

Every keystroke hurts—Small display and limited context mean that users can easily get lost in applications. If the main value of your application isn't quickly evident, users will abandon your application. Keep your application hierarchy as shallow as possible.

Users like small phones—Once more—it's a phone first! Users bought the phone for its phone-related qualities, not for the Internet. A user happy with the size and feel of the phone is unlikely to replace it for a better online application. Instead, they are much more likely to stop using the application.

Phones are expensive to use—Phones have low-bandwidth data characteristics. Even when carriers make high-bandwidth wireless solutions available, many phones will still utilize low-bandwidth solutions because they will be cheaper. Assume data slowly comes across in small chunks to the user, and build your applications with that in mind.

Most systems charge the user for each round-trip. If it is a circuit-data network, like most implementations in 1999–2000, the user will pay for the data as they pay for a phone call, getting charged by the minute. When packet technology becomes widely deployed, and for packet networks currently available, users will be charged either by the packet, or a flat rate. Until flat-rate packet fees become a standard competitive position in the market, you should assume your application should try to work with as few round-trips to your website server as possible.

15.1.3   The default phone

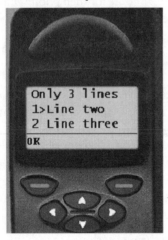

Figure 15.1   A three-line display

The phones you are developing for are small, and applications must be developed with care if they are going to be usable. The default phone you should keep in mind has a small display: only 4 lines containing 12 characters each. The phone in figure 15.1 is even smaller, with only 3 lines!

To help you profile the target phone, make the following assumptions:

Design for a small display—An application designed for a small display looks good if the display is larger, but the reverse is not the case. Always design with small displays in mind: 4 lines containing 12 characters.

There will be two buttons—The phone will have two softkeys (Accept and Softkey2) with labels visible at the bottom of the screen. Take advantage of those labels whenever possible, but remember to limit them to only five characters.

The Accept button is easiest to find and use—Some phones make it more difficult to find Softkey2 functionality. Avoid limiting access to essential features or functionality from Softkey2.

Scrolling will be built in to every phone—A user will always be able to scroll down the display or return to a previous card. You need not design very small cards for fear that some user won't be able to scroll down.

Phone calls may not return to a browser—Assume that once a user places a call the phone will exit the browser and not return.

15.2   DESIGN GOALS AND GUIDELINES

When designing a new application for a phone browser, the application should strive to meet four goals: intuitive navigation, consistency, the fewest number of operations for key activities, and that features be highly discoverable.

Intuitive navigation—A good application design begins with a natural flow. Users think in terms of the problem they are trying to solve, not in terms of how to use the tool to solve the problem. The tool needs to be transparent to the user.

Whenever the user has to stop to figure out how to use the tool, they get side-tracked and frustrated—introducing the risk that they won't find their way, or will forget the problem they are trying to solve. Intuitive interfaces are easier to sell, easier to use, and less likely to render the product useless.

Consistency—A good application leverages consistent metaphors to make it easier for users to intuitively discover how to perform activities. Microsoft's Office Suite is a good example of a series of products that each leverage a single consistent user interface (UI) metaphor. As a result, a user familiar with Word finds PowerPoint much easier and more comfortable to use the first time out than if each application had been developed with a different interface.

Key activities require the fewest operations—An application will have many features, all of which are important, but only about 10 percent will be used 90 percent of the time. For example, a user of a stock application may look up quotes for dozens of stocks before buying or selling a particular one. Understanding what features or activities are key to the user and reducing the steps to accomplish the activities will make the user's experience much more pleasant.

Features should be highly discoverable—A user should be able to figure out how to access all functions within an application without help from other users or from manuals. The placement of less-common features does not necessarily have to be the main path, but should be a short step away from the main path so that they can be found and used when needed.

15.2.1 General design guidelines

The following general principles should be kept in mind when building any wireless application. The overriding principle for all wireless applications is simplicity—the more complexity introduced into an application, the more difficult it is to learn and to navigate.

Keep applications shallow—Try to organize your application to be as flat (hierarchically) as possible, and ensure that the high-value areas of your applications are exposed immediately or with very few keystrokes. Top activities in all applications should not take more than two steps—studies have shown that with each extra step you will lose 50 percent of your users.

Screen real estate is limited, and the most relevant information must always be shown first. For example, one wireless email application was designed to display an email's time stamp as the *first* line when the user selected an email to view. The time stamp is not the most important information in an email header—the subject (or perhaps the sender) is a better choice.

Rely on user preferences as little as possible—Most users will never visit or set their preferences, so defaults for preferences must be designed around the most common user types. Whenever possible, a default behavior should be used instead of preferences. If a preference must be used, then it should be easily discoverable by users.

15.2.2 Navigation guidelines

It can be easy to get lost inside a wireless application because there is so little context provided through the display. The following guidelines help prevent a user getting hopelessly mired within your application.

Design backward navigation carefully—Although the phone follows the same logic as the Internet, users don't think of them as the same. A good example of this is the back key; on a PC, clicking the back arrow cycles the user through the previously viewed page.

Depending on the application, this can be disconcerting on a phone. For example, a study of users working with a Yellow Pages application found that the users expected to be returned to the beginning of the application when they pressed Back (the user was actually cycled backward through the Yellow Pages input fields).

The Back key must take the user to a logical and consistent place in the application, and the design choice should be confirmed through user testing. One way to provide for intuitive navigation is by using the Phone.com extended WML elements to introduce context into your applications, or by using the activities elements available in HDML. If your service will use a Phone.com gateway and browser and will therefore support subroutines through context (HDML) or activities (WML), use them liberally. Don't require the user to hit Back many times. It is incredibly irritating.

Use Softkey2 menus—At certain points, your application may need to provide a menu of actions the user can execute. Do this by specifying an action for Softkey2 such that invoking the Softkey2 action displays a choice card of actions the user can execute.

Softkey2 menus are useful for application navigation as well. If you are building a deep application, build a menu (accessible by Softkey2) that includes an item pointing to the top of the service.

15.2.3 Text guidelines

The following are guidelines related to the display of text on the phone. When editing text for your application, remember: Simplicity wins the day.

Divide lots of text into multiple display cards—The largest deck or digest you can send to a phone in a single response is approximately 1,200 bytes (including the tags). If you have display text that takes up more than 1,200 bytes, divide it into separate DISPLAY cards in separate decks. Specify an ACCEPT action, labeled More, which allows the user to proceed from one DISPLAY card to the next.

The last DISPLAY card should specify an ACCEPT action, labeled Done, which allows the user to return to the card that originally invoked the DISPLAY cards. For example, if the DISPLAY cards display an email message, which the user chose from an email inbox, the Accept key in the last display card should return the user to the email inbox.

Avoid long words—Where you control the data, avoid words longer than ten characters. These words are hard to read on the display if they wrap. This is a particularly important guideline for the title of a CHOICE or data ENTRY card. When a phone displays an option menu or an entry field, it defaults to the first choice (or entry field) on the card. If the title of a CHOICE or ENTRY card is too long to display on a single screen, the phone will scroll some of it off the top of the screen. The user will have to scroll back to read the entire title.

15.2.4 Bookmark guidelines (Phone.com gateway only)

Note that bookmarks are only supported through the Phone.com gateway and browser. Most of the time, it makes sense to enable a user to bookmark all cards within an application—but not all the time. The following guidelines should help you decide whether or not to enable a user to bookmark a card.

Try to make all cards bookmarkable—The user won't understand why something cannot be bookmarked. In particular, try to bookmark lists, find screens, and display screens.

If the bookmark is in the middle of an entry wizard or form, remember to mark to the beginning of the form or wizard—NOT cards within the wizard or form. Bookmarking the center of a form or wizard will confuse the user and may cause incomplete data to be sent to the application processing the entered data.

Don't bookmark edit screens, transient data, or action menus—Make sure it makes sense to enable bookmarking of a particular card or deck. For example, if the user is editing data, there is no sense bookmarking it. The only exception is a useful screen like the final enter stock quote screen, where a user may want to go back and enter quotes.

Always use the title attribute—This makes bookmarking much easier for the user. If you do not specify this option, the default bookmark name is the first line of the card—which usually doesn't provide a meaningful bookmark name.

Title your card carefully—Don't force the user to enter data to make a bookmark informative. If contextual data is associated with a bookmark, use it for the bookmark name. For example, don't use Stock for the bookmark name of a specific stock quote—in this case, if the user bookmarks the IBM quote and the MSFT quote, both bookmarks will appear with the title Stock. Instead, use a variable within the title to define the specific quote being bookmarked: IBM Quote, for example.

Do not allow users to mark URLs that have side effects—If you make a deck markable, the user can create a bookmark that directly requests a card within the deck. Therefore, you should make sure that none of the cards in the deck executes a transaction that user might not want to execute. For example, if a deck contains a card that executes a stock trade make sure that deck is not markable. If the deck is markable, you run the risk of a user bookmarking the stock trade execution card—and automatically invoking a stock trade when the bookmark is selected.

15.2.5 Image rules

Images should be used sparingly within your applications; they are unsupported by many devices and subject to the bandwidth and processing constraints imposed by the phone. The following guidelines will help ensure the images you use enhance your application, rather than defeat it.

Use images to supplement, rather than replace, text—Because image support is not consistent across devices, make sure the text that accompanies an image will still be meaningful if a device cannot display the image.

Use the correct image size—Avoid using splash screen images larger than the device display size. The display size depends on the device. To determine the device's display size, check the HTTP headers of requests from the device.

Specify the <ALT> attribute only for images used as card titles or splash screens—A device that can't display images displays the text specified by the <ALT> option instead. If this text appears in the middle of some display text without the appropriate context, it can be confusing to the user. In particular, avoid specifying the <ALT> option for images in choice items.

15.3 SOFTKEY LABEL GUIDELINES

If there is no recommended softkey label for an action that you want to provide, create your own, subject to the following guidelines:

- Capitalize the first letter of the label; make the subsequent letters lowercase
- Use five characters or fewer

Note that some phone models display labels (table 15.1) in all uppercase, regardless of the case you specify. Other phone models do not display reserved characters in labels at all.

Table 15.1   Recommended softkey labels

Action	Key label	Recommended softkey assignment
Display the next card of extended display text (see *Handling lengthy display text*)	More	ACCEPT
Proceed to the next item (for example, the next news item in a list of news items)	Next	ACCEPT
Complete an activity	Done	ACCEPT
Edit a specified value	Edit	ACCEPT
Execute a search	Find	ACCEPT
Answer a prompt positively	Yes	ACCEPT
Answer a prompt negatively	No	SOFT1
Create an item, record, entry, etc.	New	ACCEPT or SOFT1
Initiate a voice phone call	Call	ACCEPT
Initiate a fax	Fax	ACCEPT or SOFT1
Originate an email message	Email	ACCEPT or SOFT1
Provide a menu of actions the user can execute	Menu	SOFT1
Save a set of preferences	Save	SOFT1

Table 15.2 shows the label to use only in special circumstances and table 15.3 shows labels to avoid.

Table 15.2   Restricted label

Key label	Description
OK	Although this is the default label, attempt to use something more specific.

Table 15.3   Labels to avoid

Key label	Description
Back	HDML provides a key (PREV) that implements this action.
Prev	HDML provides a key (PREV) that implements this action.

Table 15.3   Labels to avoid (continued)

Key label	Description
HELP	Instead, define a HELP action. Any context-sensitive help your application provides should be accessible through the HELP action. For more information, see *Providing help*.
Add	Use New instead.
Sel	Do not use this label.
Linkto	Do not use this label.
Goto	Do not use this label.

15.4   HYPERLINK GUIDELINES

Link as few words as possible: If at all possible, don't allow links to be so big that they wrap beyond two lines (for example, try to keep them shorter than 22 characters, allowing for the 2 brackets on a 12-character display).

Navigational links

Use navigational links at the beginning or end only, not within the data.

- Put navigation links at the top of a card if they're typically used when starting to read the data.
- Put them at the end if they're more often used after reading the data (e.g., after part of a display you can link "[more]" to see more).
- Keep them shorter than 12 characters.
- Use <LINE> mode if the links are longer than 12 characters.
- The Accept button should invoke a task related to the whole card, not some data within it. Use links inline to the data for data links. (For example, don't put the [call] link at the end for calling an embedded phone number. Instead, link the embedded phone number in the data.)
- The total visible text should be 500–800 characters.
- If the text, including links, is longer, use a [More] at the end to link to additional text. Use the first softkey for More if there are no other actions allowed on the data.
- Use titles where they add context to the data.

15.5   OTHER RULES

We are nearing the end of our rules for WAP design.

Menu rules

There are only a few guidelines for menus:

Phones number only the first nine items in CHOICE cards (if they add numbers to the list at all). Because of this, limit numbered choices to nine items per CHOICE card, plus a "More" item that allows the user to navigate to other menu cards. In addition, menu titles should contain fewer than 12 characters—it can be difficult for a user to navigate a menu if the title wraps to multiple lines.

Data entry rules

Entering data on a phone is difficult—the keypad is small and very limited. Whenever possible, present the user with a selection menu instead of forcing data entry. If there is no means to avoid data entry (such as when a user enters a name/password combination), keep the following in mind:

Keep title short—Keep titles to fewer than 12 characters; use Times Square mode if there are more. If the title is a long phrase, for example, Weather for Springfield, Virginia, modify it to be less specific, perhaps just Weather.

If you cannot avoid a long title, truncate it at 22 characters and put ellipses after it (for example, Research Triangle Pa...).

Use data formatting in input cards—Formatting data entry often makes for a more intuitive application, and prevents errors. If you are providing a user with an entry form to enable the entry of hours and minutes, specify the data format such that hrs appears after a user enters a number, and mins after a user enters two additional numbers. A display that contains 3hrs 60mins is much more user friendly than 360.

Table 15.4 shows formatting data types.

Table 15.4   Format specifiers for data types

Data type	Format specifiers
ZIP codes	NNNNN\ 4N (when ZIP+4 is required)
States (U.S.)	AA
Stock ticker symbols	A4A (general)
	A2A (NYSE and AMEX)
	A3A (Nasdaq)
	A4A (options)
Airport symbols	XXX
Telephone numbers	*N
FedEx tracking numbers	NNN\-NNNN\-NNNN\-N
Passwords	mmmmm*m (minimum of five characters)
	mmmmmm*m (minimum of six characters)
	mmmmmmm*m (minimum of seven characters)
	...

Break up big forms to multiple decks—Remember that simple is always better. Breaking up a long data entry form into a series of simpler decks makes the user experience seem less intense. In addition, of course, it prevents data from overflowing buffers.

Don't hide password entry—If you wish, you can enable a security feature on input cards such that each entered character is briefly displayed, then is displayed as an asterisk—similar to many password fields presented on a PC. The difference, of course, is that an error made entering data into a hidden field is relatively easy on a PC, but much more difficult on the phone.

Because of this, avoid using the security feature in input cards. After all, the device is a small phone—it's easy to hide the display from others—and being able to see the data being entered will dramatically reduce user frustration.

15.6   NOKIA BROWSER CONSIDERATIONS

Different WAP phones have very different UI features and layouts. In an ideal world, developers would be able to build different versions of a single application, each designed specifically for a particular browser. Although the majority of phones in the U.S. contain Phone.com browsers, in Europe the Nokia browser is dominant. For developers interested in writing applications for both browsers, it is important to understand the different display of this browser.

Back button

Because Nokia phones often do not have a separate physical Back button, it's good practice to map a back navigation action to the right softkey. (It is a good idea to put this in the <template> section.) For example:

```
<template>
<do type="prev">
<prev/>
</do>
</template>
```

CHOICE cards

Nokia and Phone.com browsers render CHOICE cards differently. In a Phone.com browser, the menu is rendered in a single card from which a user makes a selection, as illustrated in figure 15.2. Notice that Film is the default selection.

The same WML is rendered across a *series* of cards in a Nokia browser. The first card a user encounters is a card containing brackets—identical to the style encountered with an INPUT card (figure 15.3). Because Film is the default selection, it automatically appears in the brackets.

To make another selection, the user first selects Options, and is presented with the screen in figure 15.4.

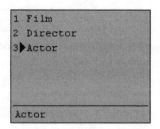

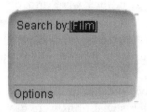

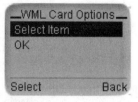

Figure 15.2 Menu selection in a Phone.com browser

Figure 15.3 First step of menu selection in a Nokia browser

Figure 15.4 Second step of menu selection in a Nokia browser

Selecting OK will submit the default entry (Film). Select Item presents the user with a CHOICE menu, as shown in figure 15.5.

The user makes a selection and presses Select. The new selection (figure 15.6) is highlighted.

Pressing OK returns the user to the original card. To submit the new selection (Directory), (figure 15.7) the user will select Options and then select OK.

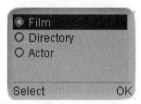

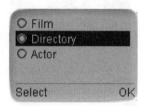

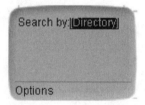

Figure 15.5 Third step of menu selection in a Nokia browser

Figure 15.6 Fourth step of menu selection in a Nokia browser

Figure 15.7 Fifth step of menu selection in a Nokia browser

If you wish, you can ensure more consistent user experience by avoiding the `<select>` element in your WML altogether, instead using a series of `<a>` elements to present a list to the user. Although the selection menu created with `<a>` elements will not be automatically numbered, the resultant navigation will be much the same regardless of the browser.

15.7 SUMMARY

Ensuring your application is well designed—both by taking care during initial development and by user testing once the application is complete—requires extra resources but pays significant dividends in that well-designed applications are used more frequently by more people.

This chapter discussed the qualities of the typical user of an application—a person who lacks the time and inclination to carefully read application documentation or help files, and who will quickly abandon an application if the application's value isn't immediately apparent.

Device considerations were also discussed—a developer should always build applications with the most constrained device in mind (that is, a device with a very small display and limited keypad). An application that runs well in a very constrained device will also run well in a more robust phone, with a large display and many well-marked Softkeys, but the reverse is not true. Designing for a small phone ensures your application will be available to the largest population.

Specific design suggestions were provided for a variety of scenarios, and differences between the Nokia and Phone.com browsers were discussed. These rules should be treated as general rules of thumb and should not be considered gospel. In the end, testing the application with real users is the best means by which to ensure the application is well designed.

The next chapter looks at a specific facet of development and design—repurposing an existing HDML application into WML. There are a variety of challenges that developers face when tasked with building a WML version of an HDML application; the next chapter discusses them, and techniques to better emulate an HDML application's carefully constructed design and user interface in using WML.

CHAPTER 16

Converting HDML to WML

16.1   INTRODUCTION

As WML browsers become more ubiquitous in the United States, developers will frequently be called upon to migrate the existing HDML applications into WML. Because the languages are similar, migration from one to the other needn't be painful. Just as in all things, however, the devil is in the details; it isn't enough to simply duplicate functionality when building a WML version of an HDML application. Users familiar with an HDML application will expect identical navigation and user interface (UI) in the WML counterpart; any differences, however small, will frustrate the user and decrease use of your application. This chapter provides a roadmap for a smooth transition from HDML to WML.

16.1.1   Things to keep in mind

Before addressing specific migration issues, there are some points to keep in mind:

- Automatic HDML to WML translation engines often do not render the optimal UI. It is always best to migrate by hand rather than depend completely on a translation engine.

- WML is XML-based, and therefore requires a stricter syntax than does HDML. In WML, all elements must be lowercase and all attribute values must be contained within quotes. Take care to test your code carefully before deploying it.

- WML is more verbose than HDML, thus WML decks will be larger than their HDML equivalents. Particularly when migrating large HDML decks, take care your WML code does not exceed 1,200 bytes.

- Because HDML code is accepted *only* by a Phone.com browser, it will always render the same way from phone to phone because each phone will contain the same browser.

WML, on the other hand, is accepted by different browsers, each of which may contain different conventions for rendering WML. Test your WML code on different browsers to ensure that navigation remains consistent.

16.2   SYNTAX CONVENTIONS

In general, HDML and WML use a very similar syntax. Because WML is XML-based, it is somewhat more rigid in regard to its syntax requirements than is HDML. After you transform your HDML into WML, you should make sure the new code conforms to the WML document type definition (DTD) standards as well as to XML standards.

WML syntax follows three conventions:

- *WML is case sensitive*—All elements and attributes *must* be lowercase.

- Attribute values *must* have apostrophes around them.

- *All WML decks* must *specify an XML document type declaration at the beginning of each file*—For example, the following document header refers to the official WML DTD, although other DTDs (such as the Phone.com DTD) may be referred to instead.

```
<?xml version="1.0"?>
<!DOCTYPE wml PUBLIC "-//WAPFORUM//DTD wml 1.1//EN"
    "http://www.wapforum.org/DTD/wml_1.1.xml">
```

Cache

In HDML, cache information is defined by the TTL (Time to Live) attribute of the `<HDML>` element. Emulate this in WML by including a `<meta>` element nested within the `<head>` element. Table 16.1 is a side-by-side comparison of the two languages.

Table 16.1   Defining the cache

HDML	WML

<HDML VERSION=3.0 TTL=0> ...	<wml>
	  <head>
	    <meta http-equiv="Cache-Control"
	     content="max-age=0" />
	  </head>
	  ...

Access

By default, HDML decks are private and WML decks are public. Therefore, if the <HDML> attribute PUBLIC=TRUE is indicated, no specific action is required in the WML deck. If the HDML deck does *not* contain the attribute, it is private. To define a WML deck as private, create an <access> element within the <head> element. Table 16.2 is a side-by-side comparison of the two languages.

Table 16.2   Defining access

HDML	WML
<HDML VERSION=3.0 ACCESSDOMAIN=someurl.com ACCESSPATH=/path> ...	<wml> <head> <access domain="someurl.com" path="/path" /> </head>
	...

16.3   BOOKMARKS

Only the Phone.com gateway and browsers support bookmarks on HDML and WML. At present, there is no way to emulate bookmarking on other vendors' gateway and browser products. That said, WML does not have an attribute directly corresponding to the card-level HDML attribute BOOKMARK; instead, bookmarking information must be emulated as a <meta> element within <head> as follows:

```
<meta name="vnd.up.bookmark" forua="true" content="card_id!card_url">
```

Where card_url is the URL to be associated with the bookmark; *card_id* can be omitted if the card is untitled.

Similarly the HDML MARKABLE attribute is emulated in WML as a <meta> element within <head>as follows:

```
<meta name="vnd.up.markable" forua="true" content="card_id!boolean">
```

Where *boolean* is the value of the MARKABLE attribute; if the card isn't titled, *card_id* can be omitted.

Table 16.3 is a side-by-side comparison of the two languages.

Table 16.3 Bookmarking

HDML	WML

`<HDML MARKABLE=TRUE>`
`<DISPLAY BOOKMARK=someurl.com>`
`This is markable text>`
`</DISPLAY>`
 	
`<DISPLAY NAME=CARDTWO`
`    MARKABLE=FALSE>`
`This text is not markable!`
`</DISPLAY>`
`</HDML>`
	`<wml>`
	`<head>`
	`<meta name="vnd.up.markable" forua="true"`
	`    content="true"/>`
	`<meta name="vnd.up.markable" forua="true"`
	`    content="cardtwo!false"/>`
	`<meta name="vnd.up.bookmark" forua="true"`
	`    content="!someurl.com">`
	`</head>`
	
	`<card>`
	`<p>`
	`This is markable text>`
	`</p>`
	`</card>`
	
	`<card id="cardtwo">`
	`<p>`
	`This text is not markable!`
	`</p>`
	`</card>`
	`</wml>`

16.4 EMULATING HDML CARD TYPES IN WML

HDML and WML use the "card and deck" paradigm for building applications. There is a significant difference between the two languages, in that HDML specifically calls out card types within the code, and WML does not.

HDML card types—HDML explicitly defines four card types:

- DISPLAY
- CHOICE
- ENTRY
- NODISPLAY

WML card types—WML has only a single all-purpose card type (defined with the `<card>` element). Specific activities within the card (such as displaying text, providing a menu, etc.) are defined within `<card>` by specific elements. Note that the TITLE attribute within the various HDML cards corresponds to the id attribute in `<card>`.

The following sections discuss considerations for repurposing the various HDML cards.

Emulating <DISPLAY> in WML

Although there is no explicitly defined DISPLAY card in WML, emulating DISPLAY in WML is a straightforward operation: simply include the text on the DISPLAY card within the WML `<p>` element. Table 16.4 is a side-by-side comparison.

Table 16.4   Emulating <DISPLAY>

HDML	WML

<DISPLAY NAME="Justtext"
  TITLE="Displaytext">
This card does nothing but display this
text!
</DISPLAY>
	<card id="Justtext" title="Displaytext">
	  <p>
	  This card does nothing but display this text!
	  </p>
	</card>

Emulating <CHOICE> in WML

In HDML, menus are built by defining a <CHOICE> card and indicating the menu options through nested <CE> elements. WML is similar: define a <card>, then a <p> element. To build the menu, nest a <select> element within <p>, then nest <option> elements to indicate the choices within a menu.

Keep in mind that in a CHOICE card, the title text defaults to WRAP and the CE text defaults to NOWRAP. In WML, then, the <p> element should contain the mode="wrap" attribute for the title text, and the mode="nowrap" attribute for the selection items. Table 16.5 compares the two languages.

Table 16.5   Emulating <CHOICE>

HDML	WML
<CHOICE NAME=menucard TITLE=choose> Make your selection: <CE VALUE=Film> Film <CE VALUE=Director> Director </CHOICE>	<card id="menucard" title="choose"> <p mode="wrap"> Make your selection: </p> <p mode="nowrap"> <select title="choose"> <option value="film">Film</option> <option value="director">Director</option> </select> </p> </card>

Instead of an explicit CHOICE card, menus are defined within WML using <select> and <p> elements nested within the <card> element. A separate <p> element should be included before the menu to contain any title text.

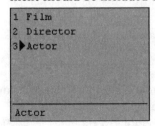

Figure 16.1   Menu on a Phone.com browser

When migrating to WML, it can be a challenge to maintain similar navigation because some browsers render the same WML differently. A selection menu is a good example. The Nokia browser, for example, renders menus indirectly—the user accesses a menu by selecting the Options button on the phone. For example, figure 16.1 shows a WML menu as it appears through a Phone.com browser. Pressing OK selects Film. If the user wanted instead to select Directory, they would scroll to the Directory selection and then press OK (or 2).

The identical code appears very different on a Nokia browser. For the user to change the selection from Film to Directory, the user goes through five steps (figure 16.2).

Step 1: The user is first presented with a screen with the default choice (Film) selected.

Step 2: To change the selection the user selects Options, then Select Item.

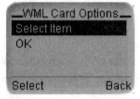

Step 3: Next, the user chooses the new selection and invokes Select.

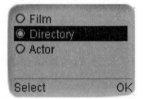

Step 4: The user then returns to the original screen, this time with the new selection highlighted.

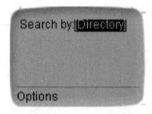

Step 5: To choose this selection, the user must select Options again, returning to the screen in figure 16.3.

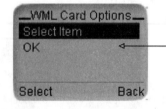

At this point, the user has one more step; scrolling down to OK and invoking Select.

Figure 16.2   A menu on a Nokia browser

Because it is important to retain similar navigation when migrating to WML, there are three strategies when emulating a select card within WML:

- Defining a card in WML that contains *only* the menu field (and pointing the link to that)
- Implementing the menu as a series of links or <do> elements
- Including the menu field within the text of the card that, in the HDML version, contains the link

The appropriate approach should be evaluated on a case-by-case basis.

Emulating <ENTRY> in WML

The <ENTRY> card is emulated in WML by embedding the <p> and <input> elements within a <card> element. Keep in mind that the HDML attribute NOECHO=TRUE (which hides the user input) is emulated though the WML attribute type="password". Because entering data on the phone is difficult enough without using the NOECHO=TRUE or type="password" attributes, it is suggested that these attributes not be used. Table 16.6 compares the languages.

Table 16.6 Emulating <ENTRY>

HDML	WML

<ENTRY NAME=searchfor TITLE=searchfor KEY=entry>
  Search for:
</ENTRY>
	<card id="searchfor" title="searchfor">
	  <p>
	  Search for:
	  <input title="searchfor" name="entry"/>
	  </p>
	</card>

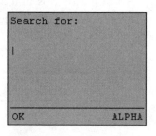

Figure 16.3 An ENTRY card on a Phone.com browser

Considerations for emulating ENTRY card navigation in WML are the same as those for CHOICE. A WML `<input>` field is rendered directly on a Phone.com browser (figure 16.3).

Some browsers (the Nokia browser is an example) will render an entry field *indirectly*—the user accesses the entry field by selecting the options button on the phone (the same navigation system used with selection menus). The steps are shown in figure 16.4.

Step 1: The user is presented with the entry field and selects Options.

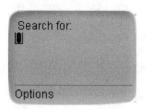

Step 2: The user then selects Edit Selection.

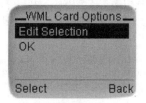

Step 3: The user enters the data using a special text input screen.

Step 4: Finally, the user is returned to the original card.

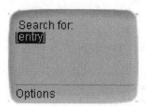

**Figure 16.4
Entering data on a
Nokia browser**

Unfortunately, it is impossible to maintain consistent navigation in this case. An option to consider is emulating the Nokia navigation scheme in your HDML deck by building a display card in HDML that contains a link pointing to the input card.

Although this isn't an ideal compromise, by linking to the input field, the HDML user will experience a somewhat similar navigation as in the Nokia phone. Of course, you should carefully consider whether this option is appropriate if the HDML application is already familiar to many users.

Emulating <NODISPLAY> in WML

In HDML, NODISPLAY cards perform actions (such as initializing variables, or redirecting navigation) without the user's knowledge. To duplicate this functionality in WML, use intrinsic event handlers within the <onevent> element. Table 16.7 is a side-by-side comparison of the languages.

Table 16.7   Emulating <NODISPLAY>

HDML	WML
<NODISPLAY NAME="Card"> <ACTION TYPE=ACCEPT TASK=GO DEST="#card2" VARS="Number=3"> </NODISPLAY>	<card id="card"> <onevent type="onenterforward"> <go href="#card2"> <setvar name="Number" value="3"/> </go> </onevent> </card>

If the HDML NODISPLAY card to be emulated contains the TYPE=PREV attribute, then the <onevent> element should contain the type=onenterbackward attribute. Table 16.8 is a side-by-side comparison.

Table 16.8   Emulating <NODISPLAY> attributes

HDML <ACTION> attribute	WML <onevent> attribute
TYPE=ACCEPT	type="oneventforward"
TYPE=PREV	type="onenterbackward"
If the card does not contain an ACTION with TASK=PREV	<onevent type="onenterbackward"> <prev/> </onevent>

All other attributes and content in the card should be removed.

Emulating TAB using WML tables

HDML doesn't provide robust tools for building tables; instead, a row is indicated by a series of TAB elements ending with a line break. To emulate this in WML, use the table elements <table> <tr> and <td>. Table 16.9 is a side-by-side comparison.

Table 16.9 Emulating TAB using WML

HDML	WML
<DISPLAY>	<card>
One<TAB>Two	<p>
 	<table columns="2">
Three<TAB>Four	<tr><td>One</td><td>Two</td></tr>
</DISPLAY>	<tr><td>Three</td><td>Four</td></tr>
	</table>
	</p>
	</card>

16.5 EMULATING ACTIONS

In HDML, <A> and <ACTION> define tasks. Use of the <A> element (typically used to bind text to the action by creating a link) is very similar in both HDML and WML. The HDML <ACTION> element is emulated by using the <go> element embedded within a <do> element. Table 16.10 is a side-by-side comparison.

Table 16.10 Emulating <A> and <ACTION> tasks

HDML	WML
<A TASK=GO DEST=someurl.com	<a href="someurl.com" title="linkedtext">
LABEL=linkedtext>	This text is linked!
This text is linked!	</a>
</A>	
<ACTION TYPE=ACCEPT	<do type="accept" label="OK">
LABEL=OK	<go href="someurl.com" sendreferer="true"/>
TASK=GO	<server name="name1" value="Fred"/>
DEST=someurl.com	<server name="name2" value="Sam"/>
SENDREFERER=TRUE	</go>
VARS="name1=Fred&name2=Sam">	</do>

Notice that both the HDML <ACTION> element and the WML <do> element contain the type= attribute. They perform the same function in each case, but the attribute names differ somewhat (table 16.11):

Table 16.11 Comparison of attributes

HDML TYPE=	WML type=
ACCEPT	accept
SOFT1	options
PREV	prev
HELP	help
SEND	vnd.up.send (Phone.com gateway only)
DELETE	delete

16.6 EMULATING *HDML* ACTIVITIES IN STANDARD *WML*

HDML uses activities to define variable scope and enable intuitive navigation. Phone.com provides a set of "extended" WML elements that emulate this functionality; standard WML does not. Compared to standard WML, HDML defines a much more refined browser context model; this can have significant implications when repurposing HDML.

HDML context (activities)

The HDML browser context is capable of jumping from one context to another, and getting a new namespace for variables and a new history stack. In the meantime, the parent context state is maintained and can be returned to at any time. In HDML, context can be nested to create a history stack of contexts which can be pushed and popped just as individual cards.

WML context

In WML (not using the Phone.com WML extensions), the context model is not as advanced. Essentially, WML provides a single global context whose state cannot be maintained once exited through the `newcontext` attribute within the `<card>` element. This means that the capability of HDML to "remember" a certain URL to return to is lost, as is the capability to momentarily switch context to protect your variables.

16.6.1 Suggested strategy

Problems will arise when attempting to emulate an HDML application that uses context features. Unfortunately, in standard WML there is no guarantee that a perfect emulation is possible:

- The history stack is deleted when a new context is invoked.
- State is not maintained: Variable space cannot be protected.
- Returning to a URL that (in the original HDML application) appears in a different context.

Using standard WML, the only one of these three problems that anything can be done about is the third—returning to a URL. For example, consider an HDML application that nests a child context within a parent context. When the user completes the necessary task within the child context, the phone returns to the appropriate card within the parent context. Because the parent context is lost in WML, it is possible that the user will get lost and not be able to easily return to the first context. There are three solutions to consider:

- If there is a finite number of possible URLs to which the user can return, you can list them with links. This is a messy solution, prone to mistakes; also, from a design and user navigation point of view, this is not a recommended option.

- Put a `type=onenterbackward` intrinsic event, as shown in the code example below, into each card except the ones to which the user should return.
  Again, this solution is inelegant and not recommended.

```
<card>
    <onevent type="onenterbackward">
<prev/>
    </onevent>
    </card>
```

- Set a local variable with the appropriate address, and call that variable when the user needs to return to the original context.

Although state will not be maintained within the original context, this solution can be used to nicely emulate context navigation.

16.7 WML VERSUS HDML QUICK REFERENCE

Decks and cards

WML element	Syntax	HDML element	Syntax
<wml>	<wml xml:lang="lang" > **content** </wml>	<hdml>	<HDML VERSION="3.0">
<card>	<card id="name" title="label" newcontext="boolean" style="style" onenterforward="url" onenterbackward="url" ontimer="url" > **content** </card>	<display> <entry> <choice> <nodisplay>	<[**card type**] name=(all card types) title=(unused with noop) markable=(unused with noop) bookmark=(unused with noop) format=(entry card only) default=(entry, choice cards only) idefault=(choice card only) key=(entry, choice cards only) ikey=(choice cards only) method=(choice card only) noecho=(entry card only) emptyok=(entry card only)> **content** </[card type]>
<template>	<template onenterforward="url" onenterbackward="url" ontimer="url" > **content** </template>	No equivalent	Intrinsic elements can be emulated by nesting actions within the NODISPLAY card

Decks and cards (continued)

WML element	Syntax	HDML element	Syntax
<head>	<head> content </head>	No equivalent	
<access>	<access domain="domain" path="path" />	Use HDML attributes	<HDML VERSION="3.0" Public=*Boolean* Accessdomain=*URL* Accesspath=*path*>

<meta>	<meta name="name"|http-
	equiv="name"|user-agent="agent"
	  content="value"
	  scheme="format" />
		No equivalent	

Timers

WML element	Syntax	HDML element	Syntax
<timer>	<timer name="variable" value="value" />	No equivalent	

Variables

WML element	Syntax	HDML element	Syntax
<setvar>	<setvar name="name" value="value" />	Use <vars> attribute in <a> or <action> elements	<[a or action] VARS=var1=value+1&var2=value+2> </[a or action]>

Anchored links

WML element	Syntax	HDML element	Syntax

<a href=
  title=>
text
</a>
	<a href="someurl.com" title="linkedtext">
	  This text is linked!
	</a>
		<A TASK=
		  DEST=
		  LABEL=>
		text
		</A>
			<A TASK=GO DEST=someurl.com
			LABEL=linkedtext>
			This text is linked!
			</A>

Events

WML element	Syntax	HDML element	Syntax

<do>	<do type="*type*"
	    label="*label*"
	    name="*name*"
	    optional="boolean" >
	task
	</do>
		<ACTION>	<ACTION TYPE=type TASK=task
			    LABEL=label
			    DEST=dest>

<onevent>	<onevent type="*type*" > **task** </onevent>	<NODISPLAY> <ACTION TYPE=type> </NODISPLAY>	TYPE=PREV TYPE=

Tasks

WML element	Syntax	HDML ACTION attribute	Syntax

<go>	<go href="url"
	    sendreferer="*boolean*"
	    method="*method*"
	    accept-charset="*charset*"
	    content
	</go>
		TASK=GO	<DISPLAY NAME=label>
			    <ACTION TYPE=ACCEPT TASK=GO
			        DEST=#card2>
			    content
			</DISPLAY>

<prev>	<prev> **content** </prev>	TASK=PREV	<DISPLAY NAME=label> <ACTION TYPE=ACCEPT TASK=PREV> **content** </DISPLAY>
<noop>	<noop/>	TASK=NOOP	<DISPLAY NAME=label> <ACTION TYPE=ACCEPT TASK=NOOP> **content** </DISPLAY>

<refresh>	<refresh>
	content
	</refresh>
		CLEAR=*boolean*	<DISPLAY NAME=label>
			    <ACTION CLEAR=TRUE TASK=GO
			        DEST=#card2>
			    content
			</DISPLAY>

Images

WML element	Syntax	HDML element	Syntax

<img>	<img alt="*text*"
	    src="*url*"
	    localsrc="*icon*"
	    align="*alignment*"
	    height="*n*"
	    width="*n*"
	    vspace="*n*"
	    hspace="*n*" />
		<img>	<img alt="*text*"
			    src="*url*"
			    icon="*icon_name*"

User input

Element	Syntax	WML element	Syntax

<input>	<input name="*variable*"
	    title="*label*"
	    type="*type*"
	    value="*value*"
	    default="*default*"
	    format="*specifier*"
	    emptyok="*boolean*"
	    size="*n*"
	    maxlength="*n*"
	    tabindex="*n*" />
		<entry>	<ENTRY
			NAME=*card_name*
			MARKABLE=*boolean*
			TITLE=*card_title*
			BOOKMARK=*mark_URL*
			KEY=*var*
			FORMAT=*fmt_spec*
			DEFAULT=*default_value*
			NOECHO=*boolean*
			EMPTYOK=*boolean*>

<select>	<select title="*label*"
	    multiple="*boolean*"
	    name="*variable*"
	    default="*default*"
	    iname="*index_var*"
	    ivalue="*default*"
	    tabindex="*n*" >
	    content
	</select>
		<choice>	<choice
			NAME=*card_name*
			MARKABLE=*boolean*
			TITLE=*card_title*
			BOOKMARK=*mark_URL*
			KEY=*var_name*
			IKEY=*var_name*
			METHOD=*choice_method*
			DEFAULT=*default_val*
			IDEFAULT=*default_num*>

<option>	<option title="*label*"
	    value="*value*"
	    onpick="*url*" >
	    content
	</option>
		<CE>	<CE
			VALUE=*value*
			LABEL=*key_label*
			TASK=task_type
			DEST=*dest_url*
			REL=NEXT
			METHOD=*get_or_post*
			POSTDATA=*data*
			ACCEPT-CHARSET=*chset*
			VARS=*var_pairs*
			RECEIVE=*var_list*
			RETVALS=*val_list*
			NEXT=*next_url*
			CANCEL=*cancel_url*
			FRIEND=*boolean*
			SENDREFERER=*boolean*
			CLEAR=*boolean*
			NUMBER=*number*>text

<optgroup>	<optgroup title="*label*" > ***content*** </optgroup>	No equivalent	
<fieldset>	<fieldset title="*label*"> ***content*** </fieldset>	No equivalent	

Layout and text formatting

WML element	Syntax	HDML element	Syntax
`<b>`	`<b>` *text* `</b>`	No equivalent	
`<big>`	`<big>` *text* `</big>`	No equivalent	
` `	` `	No equivalent	
`<em>`	`<em>` *text* `</em>`	No equivalent	
`<i>`	`<I>` *text* `</i>`	No equivalent	
`<p>`	`<p align="`*alignment*`"` `mode="`*wrapmode*`" />`	No equivalent	
`<small>`	`<small>` *text* `</small>`	No equivalent	
`<strong>`	`<strong>` *text* `</strong>`	No equivalent	
`<table>`	`<table align="`***alignment***`"` `title="`***label***`"` `columns="`*n*`"/>`	`<RIGHT>` `<CENTER>` `<TAB>`	`<CENTER>`*This text centered* `<RIGHT>` *This text rt.justified* `<LINE><TAB>`*This text indented*
`<td>`	`<td>`***content***`</td>`	No equivalent	
`<tr>`	`<tr>` `<td>`***content***`</td>` `</tr>`	No equivalent	
`<u>`	`<u>` *text* `</u>`	No equivalent	

Escape sequences

WML sequence	Display character	HDML sequence	Display character
`&lt;`	< (less than)	`&lt;`	< (less than)
`&gt;`	> (greater than)	`&gt;`	> (greater than)
`&apos;`	' (apostrophe)	Use ascii	
`&quot;`	" (quote)	`&quot;`	" (quote)
`&amp;`	& (ampersand)	`&amp;`	& (ampersand)

Escape sequences (continued)

WML sequence	Display character	HDML sequence	Display character
$$	$ (dollar sign)	&dol;	$ (dollar sign)
	Nonbreaking space	Use ascii	
&shy;	Soft hyphen	Use ascii	

16.8 SUMMARY

The rapid evolution of technology is testimony to the intelligence and imagination of the men and women in the computer industry, but it also has an unfortunate side effect: Older technology doesn't go away; it remains an important consideration even as more powerful successors are developed. This is as true with wireless technology as it is with any other. Millions of phones with HDML-only browsers are still in use, and thousands of HDML-based applications have been written for them. These applications won't disappear—they must be migrated to WML as HDML browsers become less and less common. This chapter discussed strategies for this migration—methods to streamline development as well as to reduce end user oblivion to any changes taking place to their favorite wireless application.

Dynamic WAP applications with ASP

Although simple logic can be embedded in your WML application using WMLScript, more complex logic must be performed on the server. Active Server Pages (ASP) is one method for building server-side logic that works with the wireless device to deliver a rich, complex application.

ASP is a specification that enables dynamic creation of web pages, including WML pages, through ActiveX scripting—usually VBScript or JScript. When the phone requests an ASP page, the web server generates a deck with WML code and sends it back to the browser. To the user, this process is hidden—the user sees only the final WML code, not the script that generated it.

C H A P T E R 1 7

Introduction to Microsoft Active Server Pages

17.1 OVERVIEW OF MICROSOFT ACTIVE SERVER PAGES

In this chapter we will illustrate the use of Microsoft Active Server Pages (ASP) to develop dynamic web applications. We will explain the capabilities of ASP and how you can use its built-in objects in your development process. Although we will cover ASP version 3.0 in this chapter, most of the concepts are relevant to ASP version 2.0. We will build web applications using ASP in this chapter—not WAP applications—because we want to concentrate on introducing ASP and not get bogged down with the details of using ASP to generate WAP content. Chapter 19 will do just that.

ASP is a server-side technology that enables developers to create dynamic web applications. Among server-side technologies available are:

- Common Gateway Interface (CGI)
- JavaServer Pages (JSP)
- Personal Home Page script (PHP)
- Java servlets

In addition, at least two companies are marketing third-party application servers. They are:

- *Allaire ColdFusion*—ColdFusion is a complete web application server for developing and delivering scalable ebusiness applications. ColdFusion is deployed in addition to a standard web server.

- *Tango Application Server*—Tango, like ColdFusion, sports a GUI interface for rapid web application development. Tango is deployed in addition to a standard web server.

The downside of using a third-party application server is the cost of purchasing it and the added burden it places on the web server (although it may be run on a separate server).

ASP provides a viable option for web developers who are deploying their applications on Windows NT Server 4.0 or Windows 2000 Server. ASP support is integrated with the web server (Microsoft Internet Information Server), which is free with the Windows operating system.

The current release of ASP is version 3.0, available on Internet Information Server (IIS) version 5.0 running under Windows 2000.

If you are running Windows NT Server 4.0, IIS 4.0 can be installed from the NT Option Pack. The version of ASP under IIS 4.0 is version 2.0. Table 17.1 summarizes the versions of ASP.

Table 17.1 Versions of ASP

Operating system	Web server	ASP version
Microsoft Windows 95/98	Microsoft Personal Web Server	2.0
Microsoft Windows NT 4.0 Workstation/Server	Internet Information Server (IIS) 4.0	2.0
Microsoft Windows 2000 Professional/Server	Internet Information Server (IIS) 5.0	3.0

For developers who do not have access to Windows NT, Microsoft supplies the Personal Web Server (PWS) for development use on Windows 95/98. PWS is available on the Windows installation CD or as a free download from Microsoft's web site. PWS also is included in the Windows NT Option Pack.

DID YOU KNOW?   Microsoft Personal Web Server is sometimes called the poor man's web server.

17.1.1 Browser independence

ASP is a server-side technology and as such is browser-independent. Unlike client-side JavaScript or VBScript, which may or may not work depending on the user's browser, ASP is totally transparent to the web browser. In fact, ASP protects code from being scrutinized by anyone surfing your site. The page that users see is always HTML since the server has done all the processing on the server-side.

17.1.2 ASP support for non-Microsoft web servers

ASP is free, as are the web servers that support it, but what happens if you are not running on the Microsoft platform? You have two alternatives:

- Utilizing other server-side technologies, such as Java servlets
- Purchasing a third-party plug-in that supports ASP

If you are running a UNIX box or the Apache web server, you can use ASP to develop dynamic web applications through the use of a third-party plug-in, such as one developed by Chili!Soft.

Chili!Soft ASP provides full ASP support for web servers from Apache, Lotus, Netscape, O'Reilly, and Microsoft, running on HP-UX, Linux, Windows NT, Sun Solaris, and IBM AIX.

The plug-in is available at http://www.chilisoft.com.

A simple ASP example

In this chapter, we will use a web browser to illustrate ASP concepts. It is easier for the beginner to learn ASP by first building a web application, rather than working with WAP applications right away. The concepts that you learn in this chapter will come into play when we discuss WAP application development in later chapters.

Here is a very simple ASP example:

```
<HTML>
<TITLE>Simple ASP Example</TITLE>
<BODY>
The time now is
<% = time %>          ASP scripts are delimited by
</BODY>               the "<%" and "%>" tags
</HTML>
```

To view this example in a web browser:

- Save the ASP document in the example in the Publishing directory on your web server. You must enable the SCRIPT permission of your web-publishing folder. See appendix D for information about setting up the PWS and IIS web servers.
- Open the document in a web browser. You should see a screen similar to figure 17.1.

The time that appears is dependent on the time that you request this page. Do you see why we use the word *dynamic*?

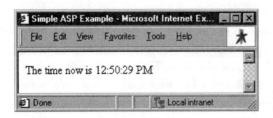

Figure 17.1
A simple example of ASP

As this chapter develops, we will look in more detail at how ASP documents are processed. We will also discuss built-in objects and how to use them.

17.2 PROCESSING ASP DOCUMENTS

ASP documents require the web server to perform additional work. In addition to the standard request and response process, the web server must interpret the scripts embedded within an ASP document. Figure 17.2 shows how an ASP document is processed.

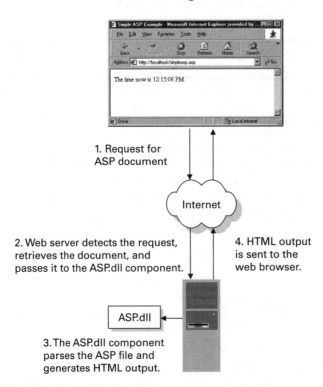

1. Request for ASP document

Internet

2. Web server detects the request, retrieves the document, and passes it to the ASP.dll component.

4. HTML output is sent to the web browser.

ASP.dll

3. The ASP.dll component parses the ASP file and generates HTML output.

Figure 17.2
Processing an ASP document

17.2.1 Writing ASP scripts

When it comes to ASP scripting, you have a number of choices. The default scripting language is VBScript. If you are familiar with other scripting languages like JScript, you can either configure your web server accordingly, or specify the preferred language in your ASP document. In this chapter, we will be using VBScript for ASP scripting. If you are familiar with Visual Basic, then VBScript will not be new to you, except that you have to live with some limitations.

For a crash course in VBScript, log on to http://www.w3schools.com.

Understanding the simple ASP document

When the web server receives a request for an ASP document, it passes the document to the ASP parser, which parses the document from beginning to end looking for special ASP tags (<% %>). All statements contained within these tags are interpreted as ASP script (which may be VBScript or JScript). The ASP script is then executed.

Returning to our simple example, this line appears:

```
<% = time %>
```

The function time() returns the current time according to the web server's internal clock. The output generated by the ASP script is then sent back to the web browser as HTML code.

The web browser receives this HTML code:

```
<HTML>
<TITLE>Simple ASP Example</TITLE>
<BODY>
The time now is
6:10:03 PM        ⟵  The value for the time() function is
</BODY>              returned within the HTML code. The HTML
</HTML>              returned is dependent on the ASP script
```

Since it receives only an HTML page, the web browser is unaware that the document is generated dynamically.

17.3   THE ASP 3.0 OBJECT MODEL

ASP includes built-in objects to make the development of server-side applications easy. For example, the Request object enables you to retrieve the name/value pair sent by the server. Without the built-in objects, you must write low-level routines to achieve your objective. ASP built-in objects shield developers from such complexities.

ASP 3.0 augments ASP 2.0 with additional objects, methods, and properties. We will highlight the differences between versions when we discuss various objects and their respective collections, methods, properties, and events.

NOTE   *ASP built-in objects and custom objects*—The designers of ASP have included built-in objects that simplify the task of developing dynamic applications. Using the built-in objects, your applications can easily include support for many features such as extracting data that the client has sent to the web server or performing page redirection. The built-in objects shield you from much of the underlying complexity and allow you to concentrate on building your application.

To further extend the functionality of your web server with ASP, you can write custom objects. A *custom object* is known as an ASP component. Although writing ASP components is beyond the scope of this book, there are many good resources available. *Developing ASP Components* by Shelly Powers, (O'Reilly & Associates, Inc.) is a good tutorial on building ASP components.

17.4 WORKING WITH BUILT-IN ASP OBJECTS

ASP 3.0 has six built-in objects:

- *Request*—Retrieves the values that the web browser passed to the web server during an HTTP request.
- *Response*—Sends output to the web browser.
- *Application*—Enables the sharing of information among users of an application. All the ASP files in a virtual directory (and its subdirectory) are defined to be an application.
- *Session*—Allows information about each user to be stored on the server side. Makes use of cookies.
- *Server*—Extends the functionality of the web server by allowing components to be instantiated and used.
- *ASPError*—Allows information about errors that have occurred in an ASP script to be obtained. New in ASP 3.0.

Figure 17.3 depicts the use of the various objects.

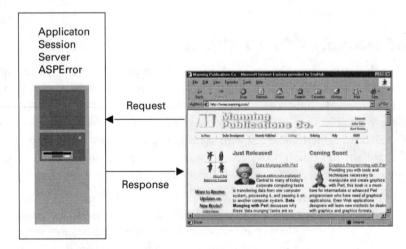

Figure 17.3   How ASP 3.0 objects work

The Application, Session, Server, and ASPError objects are used on the server side. The Request and Response objects are used in the communication between the web browser and server.

17.4.1 Retrieving values using the Request object

The Request object is used to retrieve values sent from the client to the server. Consider the case where you have an HTML document using the <FORM> tag.

```
<HTML>
<TITLE>A Simple HTML Form</TITLE>
<BODY>
    <FORM Method="POST" Action="process.asp">
       Name : <INPUT Type="text" name="Name"><BR>
       <INPUT Type="Submit">
    </FORM>
</BODY>
</HTML>
```

The name/value pair to be sent to the server

Here is the source code for the ASP document:

```
<HTML>
<TITLE>Hello</TITLE>
<%
    Response.Write "Hello, " & Request.Form("Name")
%>
</HTML>
```

The value of the name/value pair using the Response and Request objects

When viewed using the web browser, we see that the name has been passed and retrieved by the web server (figure 17.4).

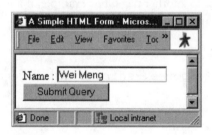
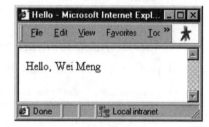

Figure 17.4   What the web server retrieves

Request.Form collection

We use the `Request.Form` collection to retrieve the value that has been sent to the server using the POST method. The name/value pair to be retrieved is indicated within the form collection.

```
Response.Write "Hello, " & Request.Form("Name")
```

Request.QueryString collection

If you use the GET method instead of POST, use the `Request.QueryString` collection.

```
Response.Write "Hello, " & Request.QueryString("Name")
```

17.4.2   Displaying a message to the browser

Once the value is retrieved, we want to display a message to the web browser.

Response.Write() method

In our case, we use the `Response.Write()` method to write a string to the client.

```
Response.Write "Hello, " & Request.Form("Name")
```

The web browser will then receive an HTML document:

```
<HTML>
<TITLE>Hello</TITLE>
Hello, Wei Meng
</HTML>
```

We can also rewrite the process.asp document using the `<% =variable %>` inline tag:

```
<HTML>
<TITLE>Hello</TITLE>
Hello,
<% =Request.Form("Name") %>      ←┐ Retrieves the variable's value
</HTML>
```

17.4.3   Redirecting pages using Response

At times, you will want to direct a user to another page. For example, if a user has not logged in you will want to redirect him to the login page.

Response.Redirect method

To perform page redirection, use the `Response.Redirect` method. For example:

```
<% Response.Buffer=True %>
<HTML>
<TITLE>A Page Redirection Example</TITLE>
<BODY>
<%
    Response.Redirect "another.asp"      ←┐ Redirection using the
%>                                        | Response object
    User won't see this page...
</BODY>
</HTML>
```

When you load this page using the web browser, the web server processes this page, encounters the redirect method, and redirects the browser to the file `another.asp`.

Redirection using the Server object

Besides using the `Response.Redirect` method, you could use either `Server.Execute` or `Server.Transfer`, new methods in ASP 3.0.

We will take a closer look at these two methods in section 17.7 when we discuss the Server object.

17.4.4 Buffering data using the Response object

One interesting feature of the previous example on page redirection is this line:

```
<% Response.Buffer=True %>
```

Response.Buffer property

We use the `Response.Buffer` property to ensure that the web server buffers the output until the processing is done—before any HTTP headers are sent to the web browser. In IIS 4.0, buffering is disabled by default (figure 17.5). In IIS 5.0, buffering is enabled by default.

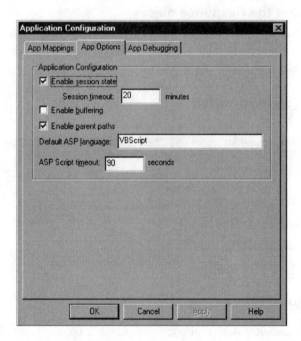

Figure 17.5
Buffering is disabled by default

To see how buffering works, let's set the buffering to `False`.

```
<% Response.Buffer=False %>
```

You will see the following error:

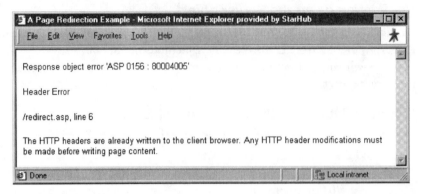

Figure 17.6   A Response object error

The error occurs because, before the web server has finished parsing the ASP document, the HTTP headers have been sent to the client. And when the web server finally redirects the web browser to another page, it is too late.

17.4.5   Setting cookies using the Response object

A *cookie* is a block of data sent by a web server and stored on the client side. Cookies allow a web server to identify a particular user and allow customization of pages based on the identity of the user.

Figure 17.7 shows how a cookie is set on the client side and how a web server can make use of cookies to customize web pages.

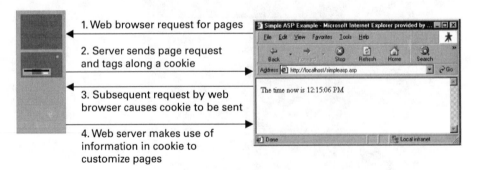

Figure 17.7   Cookies help customize web pages

A cookie can contain information about users. Once a cookie is set, it will be passed back and forth between the client and the server.

Response.Cookies collection

To set a cookie using ASP:

```
<% Response.Buffer=True %>
<HTML>
```

```
<TITLE>A Cookie Example</TITLE>
<BODY>
<%
    Response.Cookies("Name")="Lee Wei Meng"
    Response.Cookies("Name").Expires="August 15, 2000"
    Response.Cookies("Name").Path = "/"
%>
   A cookie has just been set on your computer...
</BODY>
</HTML>
```

Uses the Cookies collection
of the Response object to
set a cookie

We specify the name (`"Name"`) of the cookie inside the cookie collection and assign a value to it.

```
Response.Cookies("Name")="Lee Wei Meng"
```

We set the cookie's expiration date.

```
Response.Cookies("Name").Expires="August 15, 2000"
```

We indicate the cookie's path.

```
Response.Cookies("Name").Path = "/"
```

The `Response.Cookie` collection causes a `Set-Cookie` header to be sent to the browser when the web browser requests this document:

```
Set-Cookie:Name=Lee+Wei+Meng
```

Since it modifies the HTTP header, the processing must be buffered and hence we need to set the `Response.Buffer` property to `true`.

Request.Cookies collection

To retrieve the value of a cookie that has been set on the client, use the `Request.Cookie` collection:

```
<% Response.Buffer=True %>
<HTML>
<TITLE>A Cookie Example</TITLE>
<BODY>
   Getting the values from a Cookie... Hello,
<%
    Response.Write Request.Cookies("Name") & "!"
%>
</BODY>
</HTML>
```

Retrieves a
cookie's value

17.4.6   Managing data caching using the Response object

Web pages are typically cached on web browsers. The advantage to caching web pages is reducing the time taken to request a web page from the origin server when the requested page is in the browser's cache. However, ASP pages should not be cached as this may defeat the reason we use ASP in the first place. We use ASP to create dynamic pages and if the pages are cached, it is very likely that what the user receives is outdated. This is not good if the information sought is stock prices.

Caching on the browser is just one of the problems. A proxy server may also cache web pages. A *proxy server* is a server that acts on behalf of web clients to request web pages from origin servers. A proxy server should not cache ASP documents because, again, outdated information may be provided. By default, ASP instructs the proxy server not to cache pages generated by ASP.

Figure 17.8 shows the positioning of the proxy server.

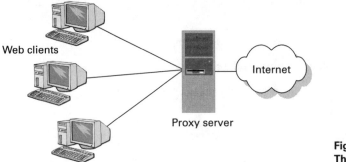

Web clients

Internet

Proxy server

Figure 17.8
The proxy server

Let's now look at how we can control caching on web browsers and proxy servers.

Response.Expires property

To prevent web browsers from caching ASP documents, we use the `Response.Expires` property.

```
<% Response.Expires = -1 %>
```

The `Expires` property indicates the time (in minutes) before the page expires. You can set it to a value of 0 to force the page to expire immediately. However, due to time differences, this method may not work correctly. To be sure, set it to a value of –1.

Response.CacheControl property

To prevent proxy servers from caching the ASP document, use the `Response.CacheControl` property. By default, ASP sets the `Response.CacheControl` property to `"private"`. This indicates that proxy servers should not cache the page. If for some reason you need to cache an ASP document, set the `CacheControl` property to `"public"`, like this:

```
<% Response.CacheControl="public" %>
```

17.5 ENABLING INFORMATION-SHARING USING THE APPLICATION OBJECT

In ASP, the Application object allows users of your web site to share information. An application in ASP is defined to be the set of all ASP files in a virtual directory (including its subdirectory).

17.5.1 Setting application variables

Let's look at an example to see the use of the Application object.

```
<HTML>
<TITLE>Using the Application object</TITLE>
<BODY>
<%
    Application("HighestBid") = 200
%>
</BODY>
</HTML>
```

◁┐ **Creating an Application variable using the Application object**

Assume that the ASP document in the example resides in our Application1 virtual directory: http://localhost/application1/application.asp.

When the document is retrieved, the Application variable ("HighestBid") is set to 200. When another user retrieves another ASP document from the same virtual directory, he will also see the value of the application variable "HighestBid", which is 200 (figure 17.9).

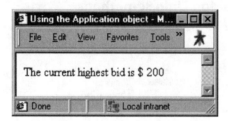

Figure 17.9
Using the Application object

Here is the source code for the ASP document:

```
<HTML>
<TITLE>Using the Application object</TITLE>
<BODY> The current highest bid is $
<% =Application("HighestBid") %>
</BODY>
</HTML>
```

Let's now increase the highest bid by $50:

```
<HTML>
<TITLE>Using the Application object</TITLE>
<BODY>
<%
```

```
      Application("HighestBid") = Application("HighestBid") + 50
%>
</BODY>
</HTML>
```

The bid will now become $250 (figure 17.10).

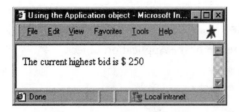

Figure 17.10
Increasing the bid

If two users ask for this ASP document at the same time, our application variable
may not be incremented correctly because both may get the same value and, after
incrementing, the application variable HighestBid will only be incremented once.

Table 17.2 illustrates what happens if two users access the ASP page concurrently:

Table 17.2   Accessing concurrently

Value of HighestBid	User1	User2
Before incrementing	200	200
After incrementing	250	250

17.5.2   Application.Lock and Application.Unlock methods

To address this concurrency problem, the Application object comes with two methods: Lock and Unlock.

```
<HTML>
<TITLE>Using the Application object</TITLE>      Locks all
<BODY>                                           application
<% Application.Lock          ◄──────────────     variables
    Application("HighestBid") = Application("HighestBid") + 50  ◄─┐
    Application.Unlock   ◄─┐ Unlocks all                          Increments
%>                         application                            the
</BODY>                    variables                              application
</HTML>                                                           variable
```

Before the application variable is incremented, a lock is obtained so that other users
cannot access it. Once it is incremented, we can unlock it, allowing access. Note that
the method locks all the application variables; you cannot selectively choose the variables to lock. If you do not specify the Unlock method, the application variables will
be automatically unlocked when the page processing is completed.

Removing application variables

In ASP 3.0, there are two additional methods in the Application object: `Contents.Remove` and `Contents.RemoveAll`.

Application.Contents.Remove method

The `Contents.Remove` method allows you to selectively remove the Application variables that have been created.

For example:

```
<%
    Application.Contents.Remove("HighestBid")
%>
```

removes the Application variable `HighestBid`.

Application.Contents.RemoveAll method

To remove all Application variables, use the `Contents.RemoveAll` method:

```
<%
    Application.Contents.RemoveAll
%>
```

17.5.3 Scope of the application

In the section on the Application object, we discussed the definition of the ASP application. Figure 17.11 illustrates what we meant by that.

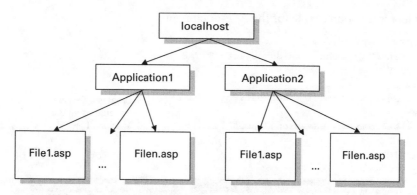

Figure 17.11   The role of virtual directories

Consider the following virtual directories on our web site.

- http://localhost/application1/
- http://localhost/application2/

All the files under the virtual directory Application1 are defined as an application. Similarly all the files under Application2 are defined to be another application. So, all the application variables created by files under the Application1 virtual directory will be kept separate from those created by files under the Application2 virtual directory (even if they have the same name).

17.6   MAINTAINING STATE

As you are aware, the HyperText Transfer Protocol (HTTP) is a stateless protocol, meaning the web server treats each HTTP as an independent request, and it makes no attempt to retain information about the request.

This limitation poses a challenge for web application developers. In order for a web application to be useful, there must be a way for the web server to track the activities performed by the previous request, such as adding an item to a shopping cart in an ecommerce web application.

17.6.1   Setting session variables

ASP provides the Session Object for maintaining state information. Here is an example:

```
<HTML>
<TITLE>Tell us your name</TITLE>
<BODY>
<FORM Method="POST" Action="Session.asp">
   Name : <INPUT Type="Text" Name="Name">
   <INPUT Type="Submit" Value="Send">
</FORM>
</BODY>
</HTML>
```

Here is the source code for the ASP document:

```
<HTML>
<TITLE>Using the Session object</TITLE>
<BODY>
<%
   Session("Name") = Request.Form("Name")    ⟵  Creates a Session
%>                                                variable using the
   Welcome, <% =Session("Name") %>               Session object
</BODY>
</HTML>
```

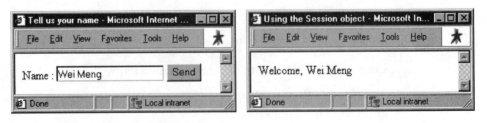

Figure 17.12   Using the Session object to store a name

In figure 17.12, we store the user's name in a Session object using the following statement:

```
Session("Name") = Request.Form("Name")
```

Like the Application object, the Session object stores the session variables in the web server's main memory. However, unlike the Application object, the Session object creates a separate set of variables for *each* user that connects to the web server. That is, if there are 100 users connecting to the web server, 100 sessions are created and there will be 100 sets of session variables created. For this reason, beginners are advised to use the Session object sparingly.

Storing userID and password information

The previous example did not do justice to the Session object. A more common use of the Session object is in storing information about a user, like his login ID and password. Once a user is authenticated, we can use the Session variable to remember the userID and make use of it in other pages.

```
<%
    Session("UserID") = Request.Form("UserID")
    Session("Password") = Request.Form("Password")
%>
```

17.6.2   Implementing sessions

So how are Sessions implemented? Actually, the Session object makes use of cookies. The first time a user requests an ASP document from a web site, ASP will generate a unique number called the SessionID. This SessionID identifies a user's session and is sent to the client as a cookie.

This SessionID is used as a key to reference the Session variables created by the web server.

If the user's browser does not support cookies, or if the user deliberately turns off cookie support, you will not be able to use the Session object in your application.

By default, a session will be terminated after twenty minutes if the user has not requested any other pages from the web server. Once a session is terminated, the next time a user requests another file from the same web server, a new session will be started.

Session.SessionID property

To explicitly identify a session, use the Session.SessionID property.

```
<% =Session.SessionID %>
```

Session.Timeout property

To explicitly set the expiration time of a session, use the Session.Timeout property. The following example sets the session to expire in ten minutes.

```
<%
   Session.Timeout = 10
%>
```

Session.Abandon property

To end a session prematurely before the expiration time, use the `Session.Abandon` method.

```
<%
   Session.Abandon
%>
```

When a `Session.Abandon` method is called in a page, the session is not killed until the last statement in the page has been processed:

```
<%
   Session("Pagecount")=100
   Session.Abandon
   Response.Write Session("PageCount")
%>
```

You would expect the last statement to return an empty string because the session has been abandoned. However, the session is not killed until the last statement is processed and thus you would still see a value of 100 returned by the session variable. A subsequent attempt to reference the same session variable will result in an empty string.

Removing session variables

Like the Application object, ASP 3.0 provides two methods to remove Session variables. They are `Contents.Remove` and `Contents.RemoveAll`.

Session.Contents.Remove and Session.Contents.RemoveAll

```
<%
    Session.Contents.Remove("Password")    ← Removes a single
                                             session variable
    Session.Contents.RemoveAll    ← Removes all
%>                                  sessions
```

17.7 USING THE SERVER OBJECT

The Server object provides the web developer a way to access the methods and properties on the web server. One of the most common uses of the Server object is to create an instance of a component on the web server.

Server.CreateObject method

For example,

```
Set conn = Server.CreateObject("ADODB.Connection")
```

The `Server.CreateObject` method allows a component to be instantiated. It is a very powerful means to extend the functionality of your web application. We will see more uses of this method in chapter 18, where we discuss database connectivity.

ASP 3.0 includes two new methods in the Server object. They are `Server.Execute` and `Server.Transfer`.

17.7.1 Server.Execute method

The `Server.Execute` method calls another ASP document and executes the statements contained within. In a sense, `Server.Execute` is similar to calling a procedure in a programming language. Here is the code for Page1.asp:

```
<HTML>
<TITLE>Demonstrating the Execute method</TITLE>
<BODY>
     I am now in Page 1 <BR>
<%
   Server.Execute("/manning/Page2.asp")          Executes the content
%>                                                 of another file
     Back in Page 1
</BODY>
</HTML>
```

Here is Page2.asp:

```
<%
   Response.Write "I am now in Page 2 <BR>"
   Response.Write "Bringing you back to Page 1 ... <BR>"
%>
```

Load Page1.asp and you will see a screen similar to the one in figure 17.13.

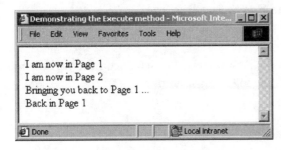

Figure 17.13
The `Server.Execute` method

The `Server.Execute` method will cause the content of Page2.asp to be executed by the ASP parser. After Page2.asp is parsed, control is transferred back to Page1.asp.

```
Server.Execute("/manning/Page2.asp")
```

17.7.2 Server.Transfer method

How about the `Server.Transfer` method? Consider the following example:

```
<HTML>
<TITLE>Demonstrating the Transfer method</TITLE>
<BODY>
      I am now in Page 1 <BR>
<%
   Server.Transfer("/manning/Page2.asp")
%>
      This line will not be displayed
</BODY>
</HTML>
```

Performs server redirection

And the code for Page2.asp

```
<%
   Response.Write "I am now in Page 2 <BR>"
   '---execution will stop here---
%>
```

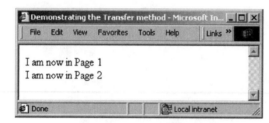

Figure 17.14
The Server. Transfer method

Note that the `Server.Transfer` method transfers the control to the target ASP document (figure 17.14). Control will not be transferred back to the calling document after the processing on the target document is done.

17.7.3   Server. Transfer versus Response. Redirect

What is the difference between the `Response.Redirect` and the `Server.Transfer` methods?

The difference lies in client awareness of which document has been retrieved (figures 17.15 and 17.16). In the following examples:

```
<% Response.Buffer = True %>
<HTML>
<TITLE>Demonstrating the Redirect method</TITLE>
<BODY>
<%
   Response.Redirect "/manning/target.html"
%>
</BODY>
</HTML>
```

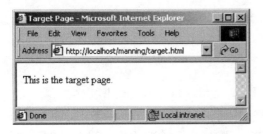

Figure 17.15
The target page

Notice that the URL displays the `target.html` document.
If we use the `Server.Transfer` method:

```
<% Response.Buffer = True %>
<HTML>
<TITLE>Demonstrating the Transfer method</TITLE>
<BODY>
<%
    Server.Transfer "/manning/target.html"
%>
</BODY>
</HTML>
```

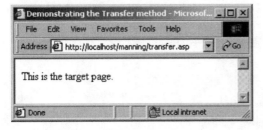

Figure 17.16
The transfer method

Notice that the URL remains the same as the original document.

17.8   HANDLING APPLICATION AND SESSION EVENTS USING THE GLOBAL.ASA FILE

Microsoft IIS contains the file global.asa which provides an avenue for the developer to service events generated by the web server. Such events are related to the Application and Session objects.

The general format of this file is:

```
<SCRIPT LANGUAGE="VBScript" RUNAT="Server">

Sub Application_OnStart()

End Sub
Sub Application_OnEnd()

End Sub

Sub Session_OnStart()
```

```
End Sub

Sub Session_OnEnd()
End Sub

</SCRIPT>
```

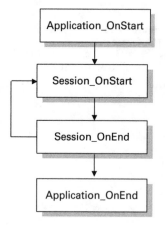

Figure 17.17   The sequence of events in the global.asa file

Four events can be serviced:

- *Application_OnStart*—Triggered before the first session is generated. This event is fired when the web server starts up. Activated only once.

- *Application_OnEnd*—Triggered when the web server shuts down. This event will not be fired if the web server crashes.

- *Session_OnStart*—Triggered when a session is created.

- *Session_OnEnd*—Triggered when a session ends.

Figure 17.17 depicts the sequence of events.

The global.asa file must be stored in the root directory of an application. A very common error is to have multiple global.asa files scattered all over the virtual directories on a web site.

Figure 17.18 shows a virtual directory structure:

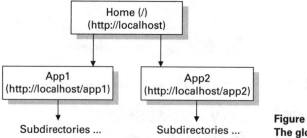

**Figure 17.18
The global.asa file in the root**

As figure 17.18 illustrates, the global.asa file must be placed in the root of the application. That is, in App1 and App2. If you place it in the subdirectories, the events in global.asa would not be serviced.

17.9   IDENTIFYING A CLIENT TYPE

The ability to identify a client type is important. This is especially true with WAP programming. At the moment, WAP browsers render WML in different manners. It is important in designing WAP applications that page customizations be made so that different WAP devices can display the pages correctly.

When a client requests a web page, information about the client is sent to the web server and stored in a set of variables known as the *environment variables*. Appendix D lists the complete set of environment variables.

17.9.1 Request.ServerVariables collection

To retrieve the value of a particular environment variable, we use the `Request.ServerVariables` collection.

```
<% =Request.ServerVariables("HTTP_USER_AGENT") %>
```

Here we are displaying the user's browser type. If you use Microsoft Internet Explorer 5.0, the user agent looks something like this:

```
Mozilla/4.0 (compatible; MSIE 5.0; Windows NT; STARHUB)
```

Because IE 5 is customizable, the user agent string for your browser may be slightly different.

Netscape 6.0 will display the following user agent:

```
Mozilla/5.0 (Windows; N; WinNT4.0; en-US; m14) Netscape6/6.0b1
```

17.10 ERROR HANDLING IN ASP

Before ASP 3.0, error trapping in ASP was done through the use of VBScript's Err error object.

VBScript Err object

Consider the following example:

```
<HTML>
<TITLE>Using the Err object</TITLE>
<BODY>
<%
    total = 30
    num = 0                          Division by
    average = total / num    ◁——┘  zero error
    Response.Write "Average is :" & average
%>
</BODY>
</HTML>
```

The code will cause a run-time error and the error message will be sent to the web browser (figure 17.19). This is certainly not a way to impress your site visitors.

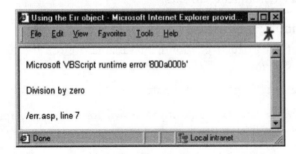

Figure 17.19
A division by zero error

To prevent the ASP parser from generating a run-time error, we can modify our program to "trap" the error:

```
<HTML>
<TITLE>Using the Err object</TITLE>
<BODY>
<%
    On Error Resume Next           Traps the error
    total = 30                     in VBScript
    num = 0
    average = total / num          Checks the source
    if Err.Number>0 then           of the error
        Response.Write "Error : " & Err.Description
    else
        Response.Write "Average is :" & average
    end if
%>
</BODY>
</HTML>
```

The statement:

```
On Error Resume Next
```

Instructs the ASP parser to ignore all errors and continue processing the script. It is now the ASP developer's responsibility to detect when an error can occur. In our case, we do such detection immediately after the decision statement. If an error occurs, the VBScript built-in object Err will contain information about that error.

The Err.Number property will contain the error number:

```
if Err.Number>0 then
```

while the Err.Description property will contain the description of the nature of the error (figure 17.20).

```
Response.Write "Error : " & Err.Description
```

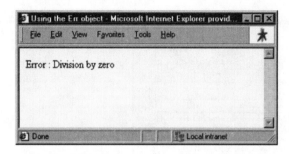

Figure 17.20
Custom error message

After an error has occurred and its remedies taken, clear the error by using the `Err.Clear` method. Alternatively, insert another `"On Error Resume Next"` statement to clear away the last error.

17.10.1 ASPError object

In ASP 3.0, a new built-in object `ASPError` handles errors trapping. When an error occurs, the web server will generate a 500;100 custom error and perform a `Server.Transfer` operation to transfer control to a default file named 500–100.asp. The task of this file is to handle the errors that occurred in the ASP document. The information of the error made is available in the `ASPError` object. Within the 500–100.asp document, a call is made to the `Server.GetLastError()` method. The `Server.GetLastError()` method returns an `ASPError` object.

```
Set objASPError = Server.GetLastError
```

Using the `ASPError` object, all error information can be retrieved and displayed.

17.10.2 ASPError.ASPDescription property

For instance, the error description could be retrieved from the `ASPError.ASPDescription` property.

```
Response.Write Server.HTMLEncode(objASPError.ASPDescription)
```

You may want to create your own custom error-handling document (figure 17.21). To do so, modify the Custom Errors entry in your web site's property window (in IIS 5.0). Look into the 500–100.asp file for more details.

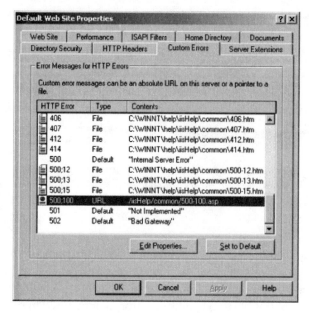

Figure 17.21
Creating custom error messages in IIS 5.0

17.11 SUMMARY

In this chapter, we have taken a whirlwind tour of the Microsoft ASP technology. For those developers new to server-side technologies or ASP, this chapter should get you up to speed quickly.

Note that we have illustrated the examples in this chapter using the web browser. From our experience, it provides a better platform for debugging ASP scripts, allowing you to become familiar with ASP rather than be concerned about the errors that may be generated by the WAP browser.

In chapter 19, we will use ASP with WML to generate dynamic WAP content.

C H A P T E R   1 8

Database connectivity with ADO

In this chapter, we will look at database technologies and how we can use them to create data-aware WAP applications.

Databases play an integral role in the area of ecommerce and mcommerce, (mobile commerce). Databases enable users to store information in an organized fashion and allow information to be stored, retrieved, modified, and deleted. The use of databases in ecommerce and mcommerce is important, as customers' transactions need to be stored and retrieved for processing.

This chapter will get you started on database programming. We will introduce the language used to perform operations on databases as well as highlight technologies for building ecommerce applications.

The intention of this chapter is not to teach you everything on databases but to prepare you for building data-aware WAP applications.

18.1 DATABASE TERMINOLOGY

We first need to define terms that we will be using throughout this chapter as well as several other chapters in this book. To explain these terms, we will make use of some of the examples presented in chapter 31, a case study.

Imagine you are a publisher. You want to store information about each book title in a database. For each title, you want to store the following information:

- *ISBN*—The International Standard Book Number that identifies a book
- *Title*—The full title and any subtitle of the book
- *Authors*—The author(s) of the book
- *Publishers*—The publisher of the book
- *Qty*—The number of books printed or ordered by a vendor
- *Price*—The list price of the book

You list each item in a table illustrated in figure 18.1.

ISBN	Title	Authors	Publisher	Qty	Price
1884777651	Distributed Programming with Java	Qusay H. Mahmoud	Manning	100	49.99
188477766X	Java Servlets by Example	Alan R. Williamson	Manning	50	55.99
1884777678	Java Foundation Classes	Stephen C. Drye and	Manning	45	50
1884777716	Server-Based Java Programming	Ted Neward	Manning	200	60
1884777813	Python and Tkinter Programming	John E. Grayson	Manning	22	56.99
1884777848	Swing	Matthew Robinson ar	Manning	45	56
1884777856	Database Programming for Handheld Devi	Kouros Gorgani	Manning	23	49.99
1884777902	3D User Interfaces with Java 3D	Jon Barrilleaux	Manning	44	34.99
188477797X	Java 3D Programming	Daniel Selman	Manning	55	77
1884777996	Web Development with JavaServer Pages	Duane K. Fields and	Manning	33	60
1930110030	Domino Development with Java	Patton, Anthony	Manning	44	56

Figure 18.1 A publisher's database

- A *field* is a column. ISBN, Title, and Authors are fields.
- A *record* contains information about a book. In figure 18.1, each row is a record.
- A *recordset* is a subset of a bigger set of records.
- The *table* is a set of all records.
- In figure 18.1, the ISBN field is unique. That is, no two titles can have the same ISBN. A field that has this unique property is known as a *key*.

Figure 18.1 illustrates a table for storing book titles. As a publisher, you may also have a table that stores information about bookstores that order books from you (figure 18.2):

CHAPTER 18 *DATABASE CONNECTIVITY WITH ADO*

BookStoreID	Name	Discount
S66533	Best Books	30
S87653	Knowledge Books	25
S87664	AMK Books	40
S98877	GE BookStore	30

Figure 18.2
Information on bookstores

The BookStores table contains three fields:

- *BookStoreID*—A unique ID that identifies a bookstore
- *Name*—The name of the bookstore
- *Discount*—The discount rate given the bookstore

Multiple tables form a database. When the tables are related, the database is called *relational*. We will talk more about table relationships in the next section.

18.1.1 Relationships

The Staff table (figure 18.3) stores staff login information.

StaffID	Name	Password
fsm	Foo Soo Mee	uyer8346
lwm	Lee Wei Meng	secret

Figure 18.3   Keeping track of the staff

It contains three fields:

- *StaffID*—The unique identifier for staff
- *Name*—The name of the staff
- *Password*—The password for the staff (used for logging on)

The Reservations table (figure 18.4) stores bookstore reservation information.

BookStoreID	ISBN	Qty	Date
S66533	1884777996	4	8/12/00-1:13:24 PM
S66533	1884777996	2	8/12/00-1:30:31 PM
S87653	1884777651	6	8/13/00-8:35:31 PM
S87653	188477766X	4	8/18/00-1:10:39 PM
S87664	1884777651	6	8/11/00-1:44:47 PM
S87664	1884777651	2	8/18/00-1:44:24 PM
S87664	1884777996	1	8/21/00-3:05:45 PM

Figure 18.4
Reservations table

The Reservations table contains four fields:

- *BookStoreID*—Identifies a particular bookstore
- *ISBN*—Stores the ISBN of the book reserved by the bookstore
- *Qty*—The quantity of the book ordered
- *Date*—Date of reservation

The four tables—Titles, BookStores, Staff, and Reservation—have a relationship (figure 18.5).

From figure 18.5 you can see that BookStores and Titles are each related to Reservations. The keys in each table are shown in bold.

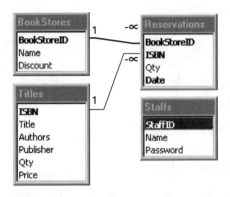

Figure 18.5 The relationship of the four tables

The line connecting the BookStores table to the Reservations table indicates a one-to-many relationship (shown by the 1-∞ symbol). It means that the BookStoreID field in the BookStores table is a key, whereas in the Reservations table, BookStoreID is not (and hence it can appear multiple times). This makes sense, as we can expect a bookstore to make more than one reservation. The same goes for the relationship between the Titles and Reservations tables. A bookstore can reserve the same title at different times and hence ISBN is not unique in the Reservations table.

18.2 STRUCTURED QUERY LANGUAGE

We use Structured Query Language (SQL) to retrieve and modify information in the database.

By using SQL, you can:

- Retrieve record(s)
- Insert/Delete/Update record(s)
- Obtain summary information about records in tables

Table 18.1 shows four common SQL statements (note that SQL statements are not case sensitive):

Table 18.1 Common SQL statements

Statement	Function
SELECT	Retrieves a set of records (of fields)
INSERT INTO	Adds a group of records to a table
UPDATE	Sets the value of field(s) in a table
DELETE FROM	Removes a set of records from a table

SELECT statement

Here are three examples of SQL SELECT statements:

```
SELECT * FROM Titles
```

Selects all the records from the Titles table (all fields of the record are retrieved).

```
SELECT ISBN, Price FROM Titles WHERE ISBN='1234-54-33-44'
```

Selects records from the Titles table whose ISBN is "1234-54-33-44" (only the ISBN and the Price fields of the record are retrieved).

```
SELECT * FROM Titles WHERE Title LIKE '%Java%'
```

Selects all the records from the Titles table whose Title field contains the word "Java."

INSERT INTO statement

The SQL INSERT INTO statement adds a group of records to a table:

```
INSERT INTO Staffs (StaffID, Name, Password) VALUES
    ('LeeWM','WeiMeng Lee','secret')
```

Inserts a new record into the Staffs table with three values
    StaffID='LeeWM', Name="WeiMeng Lee", and Password='secret'

UPDATE statement

```
UPDATE Staffs SET Password='topsecret' WHERE StaffID='LeeWM'
```

Updates the Password field of the Staff's table whose StaffID has the value of "LeeWM".

DELETE FROM statement

```
DELETE FROM Staffs WHERE StaffID='LeeWM'
```

Deletes the record from the Staff's table whose StaffID field has the value of "LeeWM".

18.3 THE OPEN DATABASE CONNECTIVITY TECHNOLOGY

Open Database Connectivity (ODBC) technology provides a common interface for accessing heterogeneous SQL databases. ODBC is based on SQL as a standard for accessing data. This interface provides maximum interoperability: A single application can access different SQL database management systems (DBMSs) through a common set of code. This enables a developer to build and distribute a client/server application without targeting a specific DBMS. Database drivers (low-level routines that "talk" to the database) are then added to link the application to the user's choice of DBMS.

Some of the benefits of ODBC are:

- Applications are not tied to a proprietary vendor's API
- SQL statements can be explicitly included in source code or constructed on the fly at run time
- Applications can ignore the underlying data communication protocols
- Data can be sent and received in a format that is convenient to the application
- ODBC is designed in conjunction with the emerging international ISO Call-Level Interface standard
- There are ODBC database drivers for fifty-five of the most popular databases

Put simply, ODBC allows a programmer to concentrate on data retrieval without worrying about the database in use.

In a scenario where a programmer is writing an application to access data from a Microsoft Access database, over time the company may need to upgrade to a multiuser DBMS, say Microsoft SQL Server. ODBC ensures that the change of the DBMS will not affect the application code. The only change needed is the connection string that links to the database.

18.3.1 Components of ODBC

Figure 18.6 shows the components of ODBC and how an application program makes use of it to link to the database.

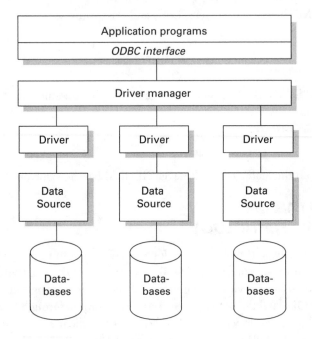

Figure 18.6
Linking to a database

Application programs

Application programs perform processing and call the ODBC functions to submit SQL statements and retrieve results. Examples of application programs are an inventory control system, accounting system, and so forth.

Driver manager

The driver manager loads drivers on behalf of an application. In Windows 95, the driver manager is a dynamic-link library (DLL) called ODBC32.dll.

Driver

The driver processes ODBC function calls, submits SQL requests to a specific data source, and returns the result to the application. If necessary, the driver modifies an application's request so that the request conforms to syntax supported by the associated DBMS. Examples of drivers are MS Access driver, MS SQL Server driver, Oracle driver, and so forth.

Table 18.2 shows database drivers in Windows 95.

Table 18.2   Windows 95 database drivers

Database	Drivers
Microsoft Access	None (Included in MSJET35.dll)
Microsoft Access	MSRD2X35.dll
Dbase	MSXBSE35.dll
Microsoft Excel	MSEXCL35.dll
Microsoft FoxPro	MSXBSE35.dll
Paradox	MSPDOX35.dll
Text	MSTEXT35.dll

Data source

Data source is the data the user wants to access and its associated operating system, DBMS, and network platform (if any) used to access the DBMS.

18.3.2   Setting up a data source name

A data source name (DSN) is a file that contains information on accessing a particular database.

By completing the following steps, it is easy to create a DSN on Windows 95/98:

1   Select Start-> Settings -> Control Panel.

Figure 18.7   Opening the control panel

2 From Control Panel (figure 18.7), select ODBC Data Sources (32 bit).

The ODBC Data Source Administrator window (figure 18.8) appears.

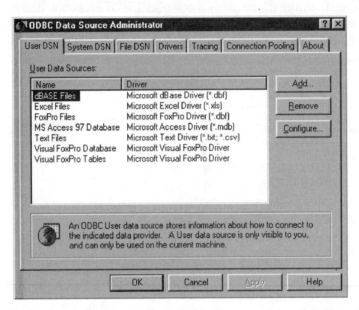

Figure 18.8   The ODBC Data Source Administrator window

3 Choose one of the following tabs:

- *User DSN*—Creates a DSN for use by the currently logged-on user
- *System DSN*—Creates a DSN for the system (regardless of who is logged on)
- *File DSN*—Creates an ODBC file data source. The file DSN can be shared by users who have the same driver installed.

For this example, we will create a User DSN (figure 18.9).

4 From the User DSN tab, Click Add. A list of available drivers appears:

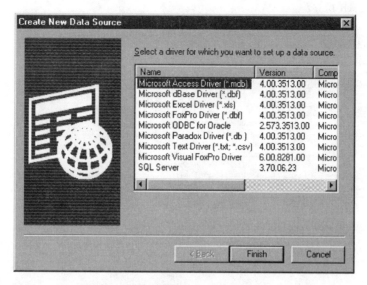

Figure 18.9   Creating a user DSN

5 To create an MS Access DSN, select Microsoft Access Driver (*.mdb) and then click Finish.

6 Enter the Data Source Name and Description, and then choose Select to select a database to point to (figure 18.10).

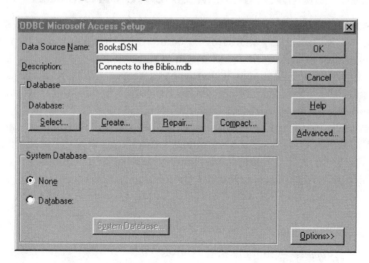

Figure 18.10   Selecting a database

7 Click OK when you are done.

Your DSN is created and it appears in the Data Source Administrator dialog box (figure 18.11).

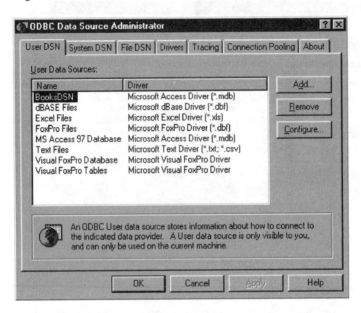

Figure 18.11
The Data Source Administrator

To make use of this DSN, simply use it in the connection string when you connect to a database. We will talk more about this in later sections.

18.4 OBJECT LINKING AND EMBEDDING DATABASES

ODBC has become the de facto standard for standards-based client/server database access. ODBC provides a standards-based interface that requires SQL processing capabilities and is, in fact, optimized for that SQL-based approach.

However, what happens if you want to access data from a non-SQL structured data source? For example, Microsoft Exchange Server does not store its data in a relational manner.

Object linking and embedding databases (OLE DB) builds upon the success of ODBC, but extends it to a component architecture that delivers higher level data-access interfaces, providing consistent access to SQL, non-SQL, and eventually unstructured data sources across the enterprise and the Internet. In fact, for access to SQL-based data, OLE DB still uses ODBC, as it is the most optimized architecture for that area.

OLE DB components consist of:

- *Data provider*—Contains and exposes data
- *Data consumer*—Uses data
- *Service component*—Processes and transports data (such as query processors and cursor engines)

To make use of OLE DB, you must download the Microsoft Data Access Components (MDAC) from http://www.microsoft.com/data/download.htm.

How all the pieces fit

So what is OLE DB and why should developers and organizations be interested? OLE DB is a component-based solution for accessing data from heterogeneous data stores. It provides a single API for operating against SQL and non-SQL data sources, such as mail and directories.

Figure 18.12 shows how the pieces fit together. At the top layer is the application program. You may be using Microsoft Visual Basic, Visual C++, or VBScript for your application. Depending on your language choice, you can either communicate directly with OLE DB or through ActiveX Data Objects (ADO). At the OLE DB layer, communication can be through ODBC or direct to the data source.

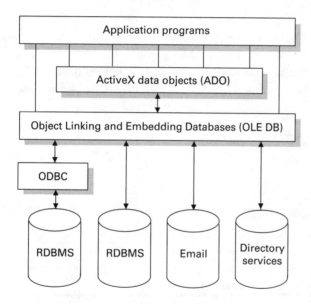

Figure 18.12
Fitting the pieces together

OLE DB provides bindings for C and C++ programmers, and for other programming languages that can use C-style function calls. However, scripting languages, such as Visual Basic, do not provide pointer data types (address variables), and thus cannot use C-style bindings and make direct calls to an OLE DB. The solution for a developer who writes code using a scripting language is to use ADO, a collection of objects that can operate over OLE DB and use OLE DB data providers.

Because ADO will eventually be capable of operating over OLE DB, ODBC, and JDBC (Java Database Connectivity), it will be a high-level solution for connecting to a wide variety of data stores.

In the next section, we will look at ADO in more detail.

18.5 ACTIVEX DATA OBJECTS

ADO—the current version is 2.6—provides an easy-to-use interface to the OLE DB.

Depending on the software installed on your machine, you may have other versions of ADO (table 18.3).

Table 18.3 Versions of ADO

Software installed	Version
IIS 3.0	ADO 1.0
IIS 4.0 / PWS	ADO 1.5
Windows 98	ADO 1.5
Visual Studio 6.0	ADO 2.0
Office 2000, IE 5.0	ADO 2.1
Windows 2000, IIS 5.0	ADO 2.5

To determine the version of ADO installed on your system, download the Component Checker Tool provided by Microsoft at:

http://www.microsoft.com/data/download.htm.

To obtain the latest version of ADO—part of MDAC—download the latest MDAC at http://www.microsoft.com/data/download.htm.

Commonly used ADO objects

ADO contains five objects:

Object	Description
Connection	Represents a connection to a data source
Command	Allows you to execute a command against a data source
Recordset	Stores the results (records) returned from an executed command
Record	Represents a row of a Recordset, or a directory or file in a file system
Stream	Represents a binary stream of data

In the sections that follow, we will concentrate on the use of the Connection and Recordset objects.

18.5.1 Database connection types

The three most common methods of connecting to a database are

- System DSN
- File DSN
- DSN-less

System DSN

A system DSN is a data source that is local to a computer, rather than dedicated to a user. The system, or any user having privileges, can use a data source set up with a system DSN.

File DSN

A file DSN is a file-based data source that may be shared among all users who have the same drivers installed, to have access to a database.

DSN-less

For connection without using a DSN, there is no need to set up the DSN on the server. All you need is a connection string that contains the appropriate information about the database you are connecting to. Connection strings are discussed later in this chapter.

And the winner is?

Which connection method is best? For a web environment, where concurrency is an important issue, the DSN-less method provides the best performance. The system DSN method poses a performance hit whenever a connection is made, as the system needs to check the registry for each connection attempt. The file DSN method poses a huge bottleneck to web sites as the file containing the connection must be opened multiple times when connections are made. The speed of opening, reading, and writing a file limits the performance of file DSN.

18.5.2   Cursors

As an ADO programmer, you must understand cursors. A *cursor* basically controls how a recordset can be navigated. Think of a cursor as a pointer to a record in a recordset (figure 18.13).

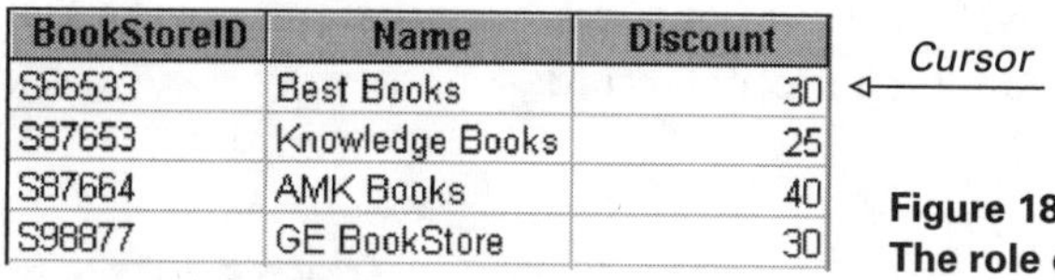

BookStoreID	Name	Discount
S66533	Best Books	30
S87653	Knowledge Books	25
S87664	AMK Books	40
S98877	GE BookStore	30

Cursor

Figure 18.13
The role of the cursor

ADO provides four types of cursors:

Cursor type	Description
adOpenForwardOnly	Allows only forward navigation. The cursor does not allow changes to be made to the recordset. Since it does not need to track changes to the database, this cursor is extremely efficient and is the default cursor.

Cursor type	Description
adOpenKeySet	Allows forward and backward navigation through the recordset. It also allows changes to be made to the recordset. However, you won't be able to see new records added by other users (although you can see changes) to the recordset. Records deleted by other users are inaccessible to you.
adOpenDynamic	The most flexible of the cursor types. It allows you to navigate in both directions and at the same time see changes to the database (new or deleted records). However, speed and efficiency are sacrificed for this kind of flexibility.
adOpenStatic	Also known as the disconnected cursor. Once the recordset is retrieved, the connection to the database can be disconnected. The downside to this cursor is that newly added or deleted records are not reflected in the recordset.

You will see more uses of cursors in the next few sections.

18.6 DATABASE ACCESS USING ASP

Let us now take a more detailed look at how we can use ASP and ADO for database access. Specifically, we'll write code that will enable us to complete basic database access tasks such as:

- Retrieving records
- Adding a record
- Updating a record
- Deleting a record
- Navigating the recordset
- Searching for a record
- Displaying multiple records in an HTML page

18.6.1 Retrieving records from a database

The following code shows how to create a web page that queries the Staff table, discussed in an earlier section, for a specific record:

```
<HTML>
<TITLE>Example of ADO</TITLE>
<BODY>
<%
    Dim conn, rs
    Set conn = Server.CreateObject("ADODB.Connection")
    Set rs   = Server.CreateObject("ADODB.Recordset")
    conn.open "DRIVER={Microsoft Access Driver (*.mdb)};DBQ=" &
        Server.MapPath("Publishers.mdb") & ";"
    sql = "SELECT * FROM Staffs WHERE StaffID=
        'lwm' AND Password='secret'"
```

Creates the Connection object

Creates the Recordset object

Opens the database connection

Forms the SQL statement

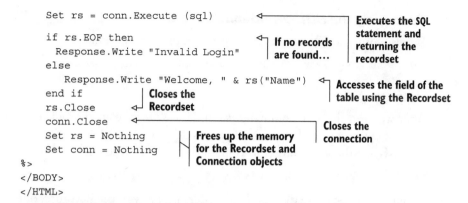

```
Set rs = conn.Execute (sql)                    ◄──────────    Executes the SQL
                                                              statement and
if rs.EOF then                        ◄─┐  If no records      returning the
  Response.Write "Invalid Login"        │  are found...       recordset
else
    Response.Write "Welcome, " & rs("Name")  ◄─┐  Accesses the field of the
end if              ┌─ Closes the             │  table using the Recordset
rs.Close          ◄─┘  Recordset
conn.Close        ◄──────────────────────┐  Closes the
Set rs = Nothing      ┌─ Frees up the memory   connection
Set conn = Nothing    │  for the Recordset and
%>                    └  Connection objects
</BODY>
</HTML>
```

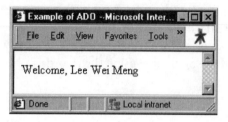

Figure 18.14   An example of ADO

If the table contains a record with an ID and password that match those specified in the SQL statement, the display will be similar to figure 18.14.

Let's look at the code line-by-line to show you how you can use ADO to access your database. (For a more in-depth example, see chapter 20.)

Creating ADO objects

First, we create two objects: Connection and Recordset.

```
Dim conn, rs
Set conn = Server.CreateObject("ADODB.Connection")
Set rs   = Server.CreateObject("ADODB.Recordset")
```

Opening the connection

Next, we open the connection to the database. Note that we are using the Microsoft Access driver. The `Server.MapPath` method will return the absolute path of the database. The `Open` method of the Connection object performs the connection process. The string supplied to the `Open()` method is known as the Connection string.

```
conn.open "DRIVER={Microsoft Access Driver (*.mdb)};DBQ=" &
    Server.MapPath("Publishers.mdb") & ";"
```

Recall that earlier we created a DSN to point to a database. In this case, if we create a DSN named Pub, we can make use of this DSN in the Connection string:

```
conn.open "Provider=MSDASQL.1;Persist Security Info=False;Data Source=Pub"
```

> **DSN**   We won't be making much use of DSN in this chapter, as it is not efficient in the web model.

Specifying the SQL command

We also form the SQL command to perform the data retrieval.

```
sql = "SELECT * FROM USER WHERE StaffID='lwm' AND Password='secret'"
```

Retrieving data

After we form the SQL command, we use the `Execute` method of the Connection object to perform the data retrieval. The `Execute` method will return a recordset (if any). We use the `rs` recordset to contain the returned recordset.

```
Set rs = conn.Execute (sql)
```

In our example, we use the `EOF` (end-of-file) property of the Recordset object to see if the `Execute` method returns any record. If the `EOF` property is true, it indicates that no records are returned and that the ID and password do not match.

If the recordset is nonempty, we print a welcome message and display the user's name. We access the Name field of the Staff table using the recordset object (`rs`).

```
Response.Write "Welcome, " & rs("Name")
```

Closing the connection

Once the retrieval is done, close the Connection and Recordset objects.

```
rs.Close
conn.Close
```

Releasing memory

Finally, release the memory used by the two objects:

```
Set rs = Nothing
Set conn = Nothing
```

RECORDSET We can also directly use the Recordset object to retrieve records from a database. In this case, we can simply replace the line:

```
Set rs = conn.Execute (sql)
```

With:

```
rs.Open sql, conn
```

We will discuss the Recordset and Connection objects in more detail in the following sections.

18.6.2 Adding a record to a table

It is as important to be able to retrieve records from a database as it is to add records. We will now add a record to the Staff table. Because you can use either the Connection or the Recordset object to add a record, we will show two examples using each object:

Using the Connection object

The following code shows how to add a record using the Connection object:

```
StaffID = "Mike"
Name = "Michael"
Password = "5gg[34*"
sql = "INSERT INTO Staffs Values ('" & StaffID & "','" & Name & "','" &
      Password & "')"
On Error Resume Next     ⤶ Traps the error

conn.Execute(sql)
if err.Number <> 0 then  ⤶ Detects the error code
    Response.Write "Error encountered : " & err.Description ◄
else
    Response.Write "New record added!"
end if
```

Traps the error

Detects the error code

Displays the error description

When adding a record, it is important to ensure that it does not violate the rules of the table. For example, if the `StaffID` "Mike" has already been used (`StaffID` is the key of the table), the operation will result in an error. The ASP parser will abort the script and return an error message to the browser (figure 18.15). This is unsightly. You do *not* want your visitors to know that your script has crashed.

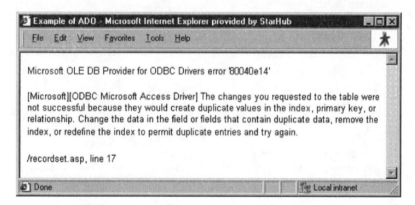

Figure 18.15   A record of failure

To prevent your ASP script from crashing, add the following line to your script before the `Connection.Execute()` method.

```
On Error Resume Next
```

This statement will inform the ASP parser to treat any errors as though they did not happen, after which we will check explicitly if any error has occurred:

```
if err.Number <> 0 then
    Response.Write "Error encountered : " & err.Description
else
    Response.Write "New record added!"
end if
```

The VBScript `Err` error object will contain the information about the error. If the `err.Number` property contains a nonzero, an error has occurred. The `err.Description` property will contain the error message, a good debugging aid during development time.

Using the Recordset object

You can also add a record without using SQL. You can use the Recordset object directly to add a record:

```
<!--#INCLUDE file="adovbs.inc" -->
<HTML>
<TITLE>Example of ADO</TITLE>
<BODY>
<%
    Dim rs
    Set rs = Server.CreateObject("ADODB.Recordset")

    connStr = "DRIVER={Microsoft Access Driver (*.mdb)};DBQ=" &
        Server.MapPath("Publishers.mdb") & ";"

    StaffID = "Mike"
    Name = "Michael"
    Password = "5gg[34*"
    On Error Resume Next

    rs.Open "Staffs", connStr, adOpenStatic,      Uses the Recordset object
        adLockOptimistic, adCmdTable              to open a recordset

    rs.AddNew
        rs("StaffID") = StaffID     Adds a record
        rs("Name") = Name           using the
        rs("Password") = Password   Recordset object
    rs.Update

    if err.Number <> 0 then
        Response.Write "Error encountered : " & err.Description
    else
        Response.Write "New record added!"
    end if

    rs.Close
    Set rs=Nothing
%>
</BODY>
</HTML>
```

Let's take a closer look at the code in our example:

```
<!--#INCLUDE file="adovbs.inc" -->
```

We need to include a reference to the file "adovbs.inc" because it contains the constant values that we will use for the Recordset object. Simply copy this file and save it in the same directory as your ASP file. If you have installed MDAC, you should have this file in your hard disk.

```
Dim rs
Set rs = Server.CreateObject("ADODB.Recordset")

connStr = "DRIVER={Microsoft Access Driver (*.mdb)};DBQ=" &
    Server.MapPath("Publishers.mdb") & ";"
```

Note that in this example, we are not using the Connection object. We are purely using the Recordset object. This is the flexibility of ADO.

```
rs.Open "Staffs", connStr, adOpenStatic, adLockOptimistic, adCmdTable
```

Next, we add a record using the Recordset's `AddNew()` method. The record is added when the `Update` method is called.

```
rs.AddNew
   rs("StaffID") = StaffID
   rs("Name") = Name
   rs("Password") = Password
rs.Update
```

Creating implicit and explicit recordsets

In the first example, we created a recordset using the Connection object:

```
Set rs = conn.Execute (sql)
```

The Connection object creates a recordset *implicitly* and, in this case, the cursor of this recordset defaults to adOpenForwardOnly. As we discussed in the section on cursors, the adOpenForwardOnly cursor does not allow you to make changes to the recordset. Hence, you cannot have something like this:

```
Set rs = conn.Execute (sql)
rs.addnew
...
```

To create a recordset *explicitly*, use the Recordset object:

```
rs.Open "Staffs", connStr, adOpenStatic, adLockOptimistic, adCmdTable
```

The `RecordSet.Open()` method has the following parameters:

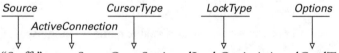

rs.Open "Staffs", connStr, asOpenStatic, adLockOptimistic, adCmdTable

ActiveConnection

The ActiveConnection specifies the connection string for linking to the database:

```
connStr = "DRIVER={Microsoft Access Driver (*.mdb)};DBQ=" &
    Server.MapPath("Publishers.mdb") & ";"
```

Section 18.7 will show other connection strings that you can use.

CursorType

Using a Recordset object enables you to specify the CursorType for the record-set (adOpenStatic).

LockType

LockType specifies the type of record locking to use. LockType can have one of four values:

- *adLockReadOnly*—Indicates that the records are read-only. Changes to the recordset are not allowed.
- *adLockPessimistic*—Indicates that a record will be locked as soon as changes are made to that record. It will only be unlocked after the Update() method is called.
- *adLockOptimistic*—Indicates that a record will only be locked after the update() method has been called. After the updating is done, the record will be unlocked.
- *adLockBatchOptimistic*—Indicates that records are updated in batches. The records that have been changed are not updated until the UpdateBatch() method is called.

Options

The last parameter that we specified is the Options parameter. It can have one of six values:

- *adCmdUnknown*—The default options which indicate that the source is unknown. If this option is used (or not specified), ADO will examine the Source parameter and decide on the type. This option impacts the performance of the database access and should not be used where possible.
- *adCmdText*—Indicates that the Source is an SQL statement
- *adCmdTable*—Indicates that the Source is a table
- *adCmdStoredProc*—Indicates that the Source is a stored procedure
- *adCmdFile*—Indicates a persisted recordset
- *adCmdTableDirect*—Indicates a table name is being used

For more information on ADO, refer to *Beginning ASP Databases* by John Kauffman, Wrox Press.

18.6.3 Updating a record

Updating a record in a table is as easy as adding a record. Here is an example of how a record can be updated in the Staff table:

```
<!--#INCLUDE file="adovbs.inc" -->
<HTML>
```

```
<TITLE>Example of ADO</TITLE>
<BODY>
<%
    Dim conn, rs
    Set conn = Server.CreateObject("ADODB.Connection")
    Set rs   = Server.CreateObject("ADODB.Recordset")

    conn.open "DRIVER={Microsoft Access Driver (*.mdb)};DBQ=" &
        Server.MapPath("Publishers.mdb") & ";"

    StaffID = "Mike3"
    newPassword = "gfgkl4"
    On Error Resume Next

    sql = "UPDATE Staffs SET Password='" & newPassword & "'
        WHERE StaffID='" & StaffID & "'"
    conn.Execute(sql)

    if err.Number <> 0 then
        Response.Write "Error encountered : " & err.Description
    else
        Response.Write "Record Updated!"
    end if

    rs.Close
    conn.Close
    Set rs=Nothing
    Set conn = Nothing
%>
</BODY>
</HTML>
```

Note that the Connection object does not return a recordset after the update.

18.6.4   Deleting a record

To delete a record, you can use either the Connection object or the Recordset object.

Using the Connection object

To delete a record using the Connection object:

```
StaffID= "Mike"
Sql = "DELETE FROM Staffs WHERE StaffID='" & StaffID & "'"
Conn.Execute(sql)
```

Using the Record object

The Recordset object supports the ADO `Delete()` method. To delete a record using the Record object:

```
sql = "SELECT * FROM Staffs WHERE StaffID='" & StaffID & "'"
SET rs = conn.Execute(sql)
rs.Delete
```

If you run the above code snippet, you will get an error (figure 18.16).

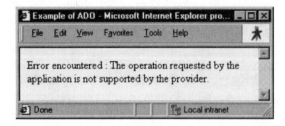

Figure 18.16
Error caused by choosing wrong cursor

Again, the cursor type that we are using causes this error. To solve the problem, simply open the record using the appropriate cursor.

18.6.5 Navigating records

You have seen how record(s) can be added, deleted, and edited in the previous three sections. We now take a look at how records can be navigated.

To navigate records in a Recordset object:

```
<!--#INCLUDE file="adovbs.inc" -->
<HTML>
<TITLE>Example of ADO</TITLE>
<BODY>
<%
    Dim conn, rs
    Set conn = Server.CreateObject("ADODB.Connection")
    Set rs   = Server.CreateObject("ADODB.Recordset")
    conn.open "DRIVER={Microsoft Access Driver (*.mdb)};DBQ=" &
        Server.MapPath("Publishers.mdb") & ";"

    sql = "SELECT * FROM Titles"
    SET rs = conn.Execute(sql)

    if err.Number <> 0 then
        Response.Write "Error encountered : " & err.Description
    end if

    Response.Write "<TABLE Border='1'>
        <TR><TH>ISBN</TH><TH>Title</TH><TH>Author(s)
        </TH><TH>Publisher</TH><TH>Qty</TH><TH>Price</TH></TR>"
    While not rs.EOF
        Response.Write "<TR><TD>" & rs("ISBN") & "</TD>"
        Response.Write "<TD>" & rs("Title") & "</TD>"
        Response.Write "<TD>" & rs("Authors") & "</TD>"
        Response.Write "<TD>" & rs("Publisher") & "</TD>"
        Response.Write "<TD>" & rs("Qty") & "</TD>"
        Response.Write "<TD>" & rs("Price") & "</TD></TR>"
        rs.MoveNext        ←──┐  Navigates forward to
    WEND                      │  the next record
    Response.Write "</TABLE>"
    rs.Close
    conn.Close
    Set rs=Nothing
    Set conn = Nothing
```

```
%>
</BODY>
</HTML>
```

After all the records are retrieved,

```
SET rs = conn.Execute(sql)
```

we use a `While` loop to iterate the records. We check to see if the `EOF` property is true, and if it is not, loop through all the records and display them in a table. To move to the next record, we use the `MoveNext()` method of the Recordset object.

```
While not rs.EOF
    Response.Write "<TR><TD>" & rs("ISBN") & "</TD>"
    Response.Write "<TD>" & rs("Title") & "</TD>"
    Response.Write "<TD>" & rs("Authors") & "</TD>"
    Response.Write "<TD>" & rs("Publisher") & "</TD>"
    Response.Write "<TD>" & rs("Qty") & "</TD>"
    Response.Write "<TD>" & rs("Price") & "</TD></TR>"
    rs.MoveNext
WEND
```

INFINITE LOOP   If you find that your machine is slowing to a crawl after running the previous code snippet, it is likely that you have forgotten to include the line:

```
rs.MoveNext
```

That is, your program is looping infinitely because the record pointer is always pointing to the current record!

Figure 18.17 shows what the program will produce.

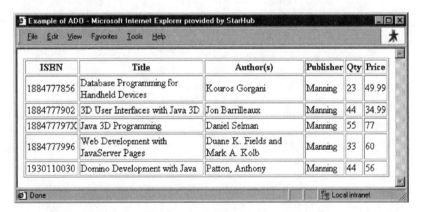

Figure 18.17   Displaying all the records in the recordset

The Recordset object supports three other methods for navigation:

- *MoveFirst()*—Moves to the first record
- *MoveLast()*—Moves to the last record
- *MovePrevious()*—Moves to the previous record

Having said that, you must, of course, use the correct cursor type for your record-set. For a discussion on cursors, refer to the section on cursors earlier in this chapter.

18.6.6 Searching for a record

Once a recordset is retrieved, you can perform searching on it. To search a recordset, use the Find() method of the Recordset object.

The following program uses the Find() method from the Recordset method to search for a record:

```
<!--#INCLUDE file="adovbs.inc" -->
<HTML>
<TITLE>Example of ADO</TITLE>
<BODY>
<%
    Dim conn, rs
    Set conn = Server.CreateObject("ADODB.Connection")
    Set rs   = Server.CreateObject("ADODB.Recordset")
    conn.open "DRIVER={Microsoft Access Driver
        (*.mdb)};DBQ=" &Server.MapPath("Publishers.mdb") & ";"

    rs.Open "Titles", conn, adOpenDynamic, adLockOptimistic, adCmdTable   ❶
    if err.Number <> 0 then
        Response.Write "Error encountered : " & err.Description
    end if

    rs.Find "ISBN = '1884777856'"   ❷

    Response.Write "<TABLE    Border='1'>
        <TR><TH>ISBN</TH><TH>Title</TH><TH>Author(s)
        </TH><TH>Publisher</TH><TH>Qty</TH><TH>Price</TH></TR>"
    While not rs.EOF
        Response.Write "<TR><TD>" & rs("ISBN") & "</TD>"
        Response.Write "<TD>" & rs("Title") & "</TD>"
        Response.Write "<TD>" & rs("Authors") & "</TD>"
        Response.Write "<TD>" & rs("Publisher") & "</TD>"
        Response.Write "<TD>" & rs("Qty") & "</TD>"
        Response.Write "<TD>" & rs("Price") & "</TD></TR>"
        rs.MoveNext
    WEND
    Response.Write "</TABLE>"

    rs.Close
    conn.Close
    Set rs=Nothing
    Set conn = Nothing
%>
</BODY>
</HTML>
```

Creates a connection to the database

Code comments

❶ Opens an explicit recordset. In the earlier example, we specified a connection string for the ActiveConnection parameter (connstr), and in this example, we used a Connection object (conn). They are equivalent. We also use a dynamic cursor (adOpenDynamic). Since we are specifying the name of a table in the Source parameter (Titles), we have to explicitly indicate this in the Options parameter (adCmdTable). If the Options parameter is not specified, the default value is adCmdUnknown.

❷ Uses the Find() method to search for records. To search for a record, we use the Find() method of the Recordset object. The Find() method takes one parameter that is similar to SQL, except that it does not support multi-column searching.

18.6.7 Displaying records across multiple pages

We have seen how to use the Recordset object to navigate records, but so far we have seen only a relatively small recordset (i.e., containing only a few records). However, it is likely that your query may return a large recordset. While displaying a hundred records on a web page is a nonissue, attempting to display a hundred records in a WML card is a big problem! You will exceed the deck size limit on a WAP device.

In this section, we will show you a technique for displaying records across multiple HTML pages.

To retrieve all records from the Titles table and then display three records per HTML page:

```
<!--#include file="adovbs.inc"-->
<HTML>
<TITLE>Records Paging</TITLE>
<BODY>
<%
    Dim conn, rs
    Set conn = Server.CreateObject("ADODB.Connection")
    Set rs   = Server.CreateObject("ADODB.Recordset")
    '---Opens the connection to the database---
    conn.open "DRIVER={Microsoft Access Driver (*.mdb)};
        DBQ=" & Server.MapPath("Publishers.mdb") & ";"
    sql = "SELECT * FROM Titles"

    rs.Open sql, conn, adOpenStatic, adLockReadOnly, adCmdText
    if rs.EOF then
        Response.Write "No title found!"
    else
        recordCount = rs.RecordCount
        rs.PageSize = 3
        PageNo = CInt(Request.Form("PageNo"))
        if PageNo = 0 then
            PageNo = 1
        end if
```

Creates an instance of the Connection object

Creates an instance of the Recordset object

Connects to the database using the DSN-less method

Forms the SQL statement

Opens the recordset using the adOpenStatic cursor

Holds the total record count

Sets the page size to 3

Retrieves the current page number

If loading for the first time, then go to first page

```
        rs.AbsolutePage = PageNo ◄──── Sets the page number using   Displays the
        count = 0                       the AbsolutePage property    total number
        Response.Write "<b>" & recordCount & "                       of records
            title(s) retrieved.</b><br>"                             retrieved
     Response.Write "<i>Displaying titles " &
            ((PageNo-1) * rs.PageSize )+ 1 & " to "
        if (rs.PageSize * PageNo) > recordCount then                 Shows the
            Response.Write recordCount & "</i><br>"                  record
        else                                                        number
            Response.Write ((PageNo-1) * rs.PageSize )+              currently
                rs.PageSize & "</i><br>"                             displaying

        end if

        While not rs.EOF AND count<rs.PageSize
            count = count + 1                                        Displays the
            Response.Write count + ((PageNo-1) * rs.PageSize) &      records in
            ". "& rs("Title") & "<br>"                               the current
            rs.MoveNext                                              page
        Wend

        if not rs.EOF then
            Response.Write "<FORM method='POST'
                action='pagingrecords.asp'>" | #15                  Displays
            Response.Write " <input type='hidden'                   the Next
                name='PageNo' value='" & PageNo + 1 & "'/>"         button
            Response.Write " <input type='submit'
                value='Next " & rs.PageSize & "'>"
            Response.Write "</FORM>"
        end if
        if PageNo>1 then
            Response.Write "<FORM method='POST'
                action='pagingrecords.asp'>"
            Response.Write "<input type='hidden'                    Displays
                name='PageNo' value='" & PageNo - 1 & "'/>"         the Prev
            Response.Write "<input type='submit'                    button
                value='Prev " & rs.PageSize & "'>"
            Response.Write "</FORM>"
        end if
    end if

    rs.Close                          Performs all
    conn.Close                        the standard
    Set rs=Nothing                    housekeeping
    Set conn = Nothing
%>
</BODY>
</HTML>
```

Understanding the code

This example makes use of the following ADO properties:

- RecordCount
- AbsolutePage
- PageSize

To calculate how many records have been retrieved, use the `RecordCount` property of the Recordset object:

```
recordCount = rs.RecordCount
```

It is important that we do not use the default cursor (adOpenForwardOnly). The default cursor allows only one-way record navigation, which does not support the `AbsolutePage` property. In addition, the `RecordCount` property will not register the correct record count if the default cursor were used. Instead, we will use the adOpenStatic cursor.

To set the current page size, use the `PageSize` property. To set the current page, use the `AbsolutePage` property.

You can visualize the records in figure 18.18:

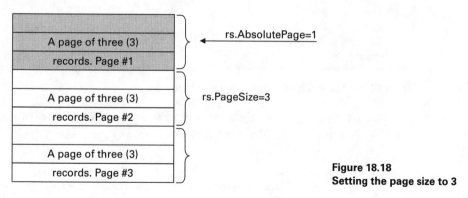

Figure 18.18
Setting the page size to 3

And so, at any one time we display only three records within a single page (figure 18.19):

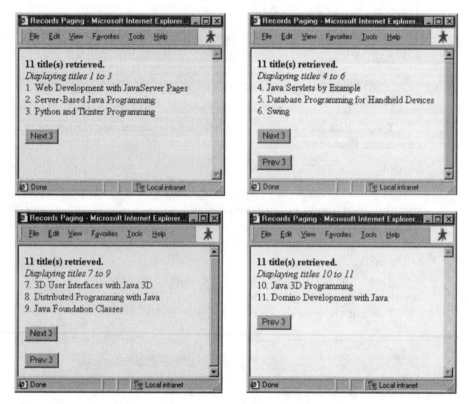

Figure 18.19   The result of setting page size to three

To enable navigation to the next page of records, we use two <FORM> elements in HTML that appear as a Next and Previous button:

```
if not rs.EOF then
  Response.Write "<FORM method='POST' action='pagingrecords.asp'>"
    Response.Write " <input type='hidden' name='PageNo' value='" &
        PageNo + 1 & "'/>"
    Response.Write " <input type='submit' value='Next " & rs.PageSize & "'>"
    Response.Write "</FORM>"
end if
if PageNo>1 then
    Response.Write "<FORM method='POST' action='pagingrecords.asp'>"
    Response.Write "<input type='hidden' name='PageNo' value='" &
        PageNo - 1 & "'/>"
    Response.Write "<input type='submit' value='Prev " & rs.PageSize & "'>"
  Response.Write "</FORM>"
end if
```

If the EOF marker is not yet reached, it means that we should have a Next button. If the page number is greater than one, it means that we must have a Prev button. We also pass the next/previous page number in a hidden field:

```
Response.Write " <input type='hidden' name='PageNo' value='" &
      PageNo + 1 & "'/>"
```

Though this example is illustrated on a web browser, the techniques described are applicable for WAP applications as well. In chapter 20, we will illustrate record paging on a WAP device.

18.7   CONNECTION STRINGS

Up to this point we have been using Microsoft Access as our database. In the real world, you should never deploy your live web site using MS Access because it is not designed for the kind of workload that is expected in an environment like the web. What you need is a database server such as Microsoft SQL Server, Oracle, Sybase or IBM DB2.

To connect to different databases you must use the correct connection string. Here are some sample connection strings that you will likely see in a typical ADO application:

```
{Microsoft Access Driver
(*.mdb)};DBQ=c:\inetpub\manningWap\publishers.mdb;uid=;pwd=;  ❶

PROVIDER=Microsoft.Jet.OLEDB.4.0; DATA SOURCE=
c:\inetpub\manningWap\publishers.mdb;USER ID=;PASSWORD=;"  ❷

Provider=MSDASQL.1;Persist Security Info=False;Data Source=DSNpublishers  ❸
```

Code comments

❶ Using MS Access ODBC Driver—DSN-less.

❷ Using the OLE DB provider for Microsoft Jet—DSN-less.

❸ Using OLE DB Provider for ODBC drivers—System DSN.

For a list of connection strings for the various databases, logon to:
http://www.able-consulting.com/ado_conn.htm?f=ado_conn.htm

18.8   MIGRATING TO A DATABASE SERVER

So far we have used Microsoft Access for all our examples because the average reader might not have access to a database server like SQL Server or Oracle. For those who are enterprise applications developers, we strongly recommend a database server to deploy a WAP application. Microsoft Access, as we said earlier, is not designed for deployment on the web (or for that matter, WAP) environment, where concurrency is a major issue.

In a deployment environment, a database administrator (DBA) maintains the database server. The DBA ensures the security and integrity of the database system and performs routine procedures like backups and performance tuning.

All of the examples in this book can be migrated to a database server. Please refer to your database server documentation or DBA on migrating the databases discussed in this chapter to a database server. In the next section, we will show you how to modify your code if Microsoft SQL Server 7.0 is your database server.

18.8.1　Changing the connection string

The main thing to change is the connection string for the Connection object.

If you have Microsoft Visual Basic 6.0, you can make use of the ADO data control to build your connection string:

1 Create a project in VB.

2 Add an ActiveX component to the project by clicking Project->Components.

3 Select Microsoft ADO Data Control 6.0 (OLE DB) (figure 18.20).

☐ Microsoft ActiveMovie Control
☑ Microsoft ADO Data Control 6.0 (SP4) (OLEDB)　　**Figure 18.20**
☐ Microsoft Agent Control 2.0　　　　　　　　　　　**Microsoft ADO Data Control**

Drop the newly added ADO data control from the Toolbox to the default form (figure 18.21).

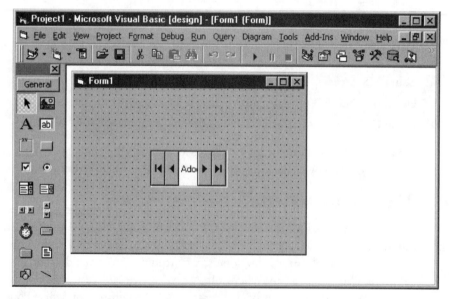

Figure 18.21　Adding ADO data control to the default form

Right-click the ADO data control (on the form) and then select ADODC Properties (figure 18.22).

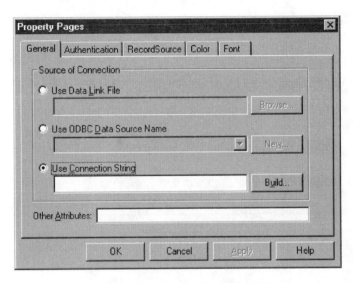

Figure 18.22
The property pages

Click Build to build the connection string.

Follow the instructions on the screen and select the database that you are using. You may also need to indicate the name of the database server and the username and password for accessing the database (figure 18.23).

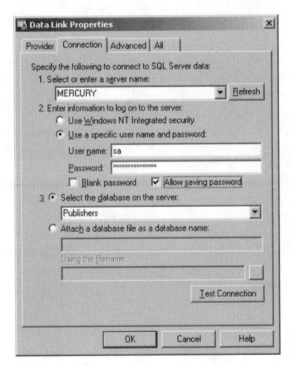

Figure 18.23
Accessing the database

Click OK.

The connection string now appears in the Use Connection String textbox (figure 18.24).

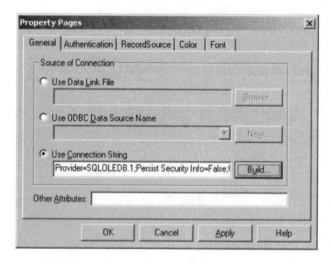

Figure 18.24
The connection string

Using the ADO data control, you can easily build the connection string for the various database servers that you might be using.

18.9 SUMMARY

In this chapter we have covered a large number of technical details for database access. We have only scratched the surface of SQL. We have also talked about various database technologies, in particular ODBC, OLE DB, and ADO.

If you are using ADO for the first time, you might be overwhelmed by its flexibility. For example, to open a recordset you can either use the Connection or Recordset object. And the ability to mix-and-match the cursors and LockTypes can sometimes create headaches for the beginner. Our experience shows that to clear up any doubt you really need to try out some examples. Try using the various cursors and navigate the records and analyze the error messages that you receive. In no time, you will be smiling again!

Chapter 17 and this one provide the foundation for programming with ASP and ADO. The next three chapters will show how to apply this knowledge in a WAP environment. Also, the case study in chapter 34 will make extensive reference to the techniques discussed in this chapter.

C H A P T E R   1 9

Using ASP to generate dynamic WAP content

19.1   INTRODUCTION

In chapter 17, "Introduction to Microsoft Active Server Pages," you learned how to use ASP to create dynamic web applications, and in chapter 18, "Database Connectivity with ADO," you learned how to simplify back-end database access using some of the current database technologies, ADO and OLE DB.

In this chapter, you will use your new skills to create a dynamic WAP application. This chapter will also compare the development processes used to create web and WAP applications.

19.2 CREATING A DYNAMIC *WAP* APPLICATION

Let's now develop our first WAP application using ASP.

```
Firstwap.asp          ❶
<% Response.ContentType = "text/vnd.wap.wml" %>  ❷
<?xml version="1.0"?>
<!DOCTYPE wml PUBLIC "-//WAPFORUM//DTD WML 1.1//EN"
"http://www.wapforum.org/DTD/wml_1.1.xml">
<wml>
 <card id="card1" title="Card 1">
   <p>
     It is now <% =time %> and this is my first dynamic WAP application! ◁┐
   </p>                                                                     ❸
 </card>
</wml>
```

Code comments

❶ Saves our file with a .asp extension. Since this is a dynamic WAP application, we create an ASP document so that the web server can process the scripts in the document.

❷ All .wml files are associated with the WML MIME type (text/vnd.wap.wml) so that the WAP browser can display.

❸ Uses the time() function to return the current time.

This is accomplished by the `Response.ContentType` property:

```
<% Response.ContentType = "text/vnd.wap.wml" %>
```

The only thing that is truly dynamic in this application is the line:

```
It is now <% =time %> and this is my first dynamic WAP application!
```

Here, we are calling the time() function in VBScript, then inserting the value into the WML <p> element.

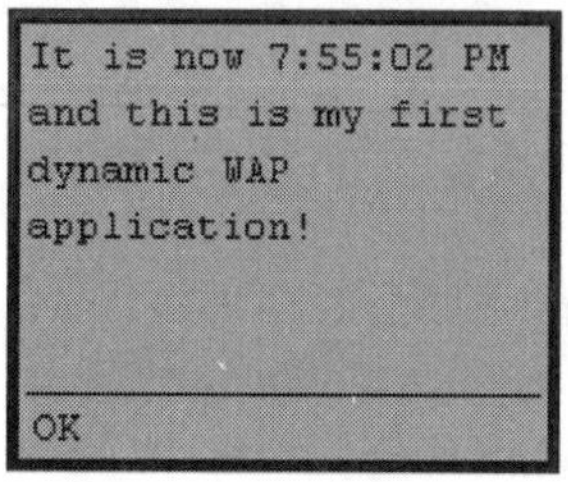

Figure 19.1 Dynamic WAP application

Where is the development environment for developing WAP applications? If you are a Visual Basic or Visual C++ developer, you are accustomed to seeing the helpful integrated development environment (IDE). There aren't many development environments to use for developing WAP applications (though the Nokia WAP Toolkit and the Ericsson WAP IDE provide something similar to an IDE). Our recommendation is to use your favorite text editor to key in the codes.

Depending on the time you run this application, you will see something like figure 19.1.

19.3 *Testing using* WAP *emulators*

How to use WAP emulators is the most frequently asked question on many of the WML mailing lists. Because we have received numerous emails asking how to run a WAP application using one or more emulators, we are going to go through the process of creating a dynamic application, from editing to success—where you can sit back and enjoy watching your application as it runs beautifully in the emulator. Chapter 2, "WAP Application Development Platforms," covers some of the emulators that you can use for your development purposes.

You'll need to complete four steps before you get to the success stage:

- Create and edit an ASP document
- Save the ASP document to the appropriate directory
- Install and run the emulator
- View your application from the perspective of multiple emulated WAP devices

19.3.1 Step 1: editing an ASP document

You may be accustomed to your favorite ASP development tool, such as Microsoft Visual Interdev 6.0. But my favorite is still Notepad (figure 19.2). In any case, edit your ASP document in a text editor (any text editor capable of saving your file in plain text format will do; do not use a word processor such as Microsoft Word to type in your codes) and save it to your web-publishing directory (see step 2).

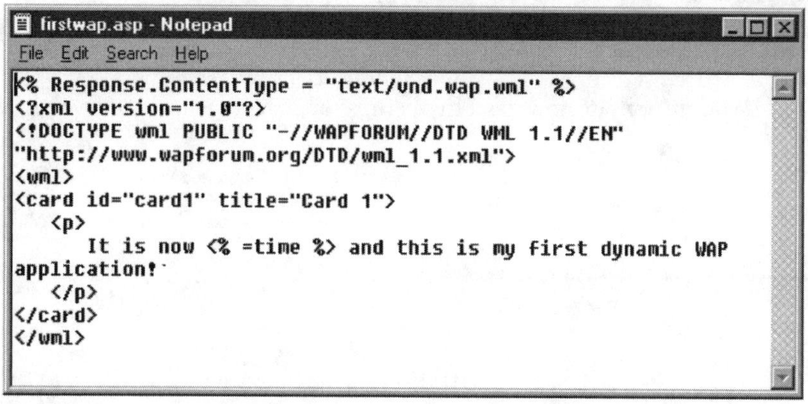

```
firstwap.asp - Notepad
File  Edit  Search  Help
<% Response.ContentType = "text/vnd.wap.wml" %>
<?xml version="1.0"?>
<!DOCTYPE wml PUBLIC "-//WAPFORUM//DTD WML 1.1//EN"
"http://www.wapforum.org/DTD/wml_1.1.xml">
<wml>
<card id="card1" title="Card 1">
    <p>
        It is now <% =time %> and this is my first dynamic WAP
application!
    </p>
</card>
</wml>
```

Figure 19.2   Editing a WAP application in Notepad

19.3.2 Step 2: saving to the web-publishing directory

To execute ASP scripts, you need a web server (see appendix D). For my development use, I like Microsoft Internet Information Server 4.0. My default web publishing (home) directory is c:\inetpub\manningWap\. For the examples in this chapter, I will save all my .wml and .asp documents in my home directory. You may configure your home directory to some other physical directory. In this case do save your files in that particular directory.

Be sure that you have selected the Script permissions (figure 19.3) for this directory; otherwise, the web server will not be able to process the ASP document.

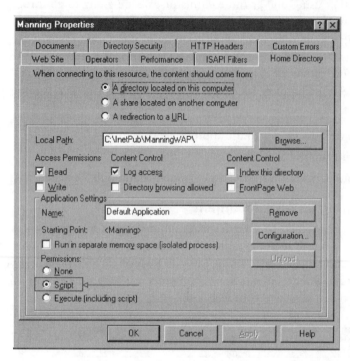

**Figure 19.3
Selecting the Script
permissions**

If you are not sure how to set this permission, refer to your web server documentation.

19.3.3   Step 3: using the emulators

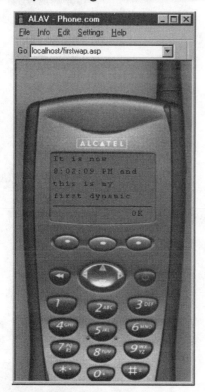

Once your ASP document is saved to the proper directory, test it using the emulators. There are quite a number of emulators available; for this section, I am going to use Phone.com's UP.Simulator to test our application.

After installing the emulator, launch it and open your ASP document. You should see something like figure 19.4.

To view a WML deck or ASP document in the emulator, enter the URL in the Go textbox (figure 19.5).

Figure 19.5   The Go textbox

It's so easy, isn't it? You are on your way to professional WAP development.

Figure 19.4   Using an emulator

19.3.4   Step 4: testing the look and feel

Although this step is optional, I strongly suggest performing it if you are developing applications to be deployed on a variety of devices. One of the nice things about emulators is that they allow you to choose from numerous emulated devices for testing. At the moment, Phone.com provides different browser "skins" to emulate the behavior of different devices. It is good practice to run your application on different devices to see how the look and feel differs.

Figure 19.6 shows how our application looks in various emulated devices:

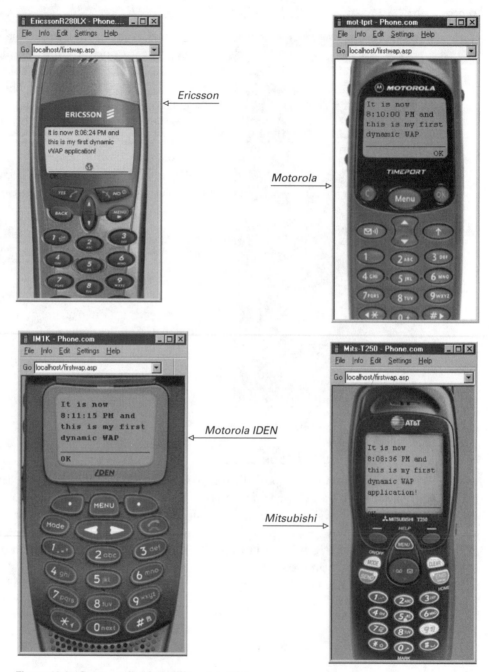

Figure 19.6 Same application, different emulators

You might not notice much difference among the devices for this application. However, if you have a much more complex application, the differences become very noticeable.

Other emulators that you can try are:

- Nokia WAP Toolkit 2.0
- Ericsson WAP IDE 2.1
- Motorola Mobile ADK (MADK)

For more information about downloading and installing emulators, see chapter 2.

19.4 SENDING AND RETRIEVING DATA

A useful WAP application requires participation and input from the user. You may need the user to supply his logon password, or you may need the user to key in a quantity for an item that he is buying using a WAP handphone. In this case, your WAP application must be able to retrieve the data sent from the WAP browser and process it.

19.4.1 Passing values from client to server

Chapter 5 explained entering information using the WML <input> element. However, information that is entered must be sent to the web server for processing before the application can be considered useful.

This WML code allows the user to enter his loginID and password:

```
Login.wml
<?xml version="1.0"?>
<!DOCTYPE wml PUBLIC "-//WAPFORUM//DTD WML 1.1//EN"
"http://www.wapforum.org/DTD/wml_1.1.xml">              Uses the
<wml>                                                   <input>
<card id="card1" title="Card 1">                        elements for
  <p>                                                   text input
    LoginID: <input type="text" name="Login" maxlength="8"/>
    Password: <input type="password" name="Password" maxlength="8"/>
    <do type="accept" label="Login!">               ❶
      <go method="post" href="Authenticate.asp">    ❷
        <postfield name="Login" value="$Login" />
        <postfield name="Password" value="$Password" />   ❸
      </go>
    </do>
  </p>
</card>
</wml>
```

Code comments

❶ Maps a function to a soft key using the <do> element.

❷ Indicates that the information be sent to the server using the POST method.

❸ Once the loginID and password are entered, use the WML `<postfield>` element to send the information to the ASP document named Authenticate.asp (figure 19.7).

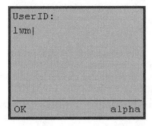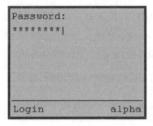

Figure 19.7
Entering the loginID and password

19.4.2 Using the POST method

The POST method sends data to the server in a separate transmission. The client first contacts the document listed in the `href` attribute of the WML `<go>` element, in this case, `authenticate.asp`, and then it sends the data across. To see what goes on behind the scenes when this transmission occurs, you can use the UP.Simulator to test the application and examine the results in the Phone Information window (figure 19.8).

```
Phone Information                                                    _ □ ×

HTTP GET Request: HTTP://LOCALHOST/login.wml
─────────────────── DATA SIZE ───────────────────
Uncompiled data from HTTP is 727 bytes.
...found Content-Type: text/vnd.wap.wml.
Compiled WAP binary is 214 bytes.

cache miss: <HTTP://LOCALHOST/Authenticate.asp?0oc=106>
net request: {
              <HTTP://LOCALHOST/Authenticate.asp?0oc=106>
            >

HTTP POST Request: HTTP://LOCALHOST/Authenticate.asp
POST Data:
UserID=lwm&Password=secret

HTTP Error: 404

─────────────────── DATA SIZE ───────────────────
Uncompiled data from FILE is 238 bytes.
...found Content-Type: text/vnd.wap.wml.
Compiled WAP binary is 77 bytes.
```

Figure 19.8   The Phone Information window using the POST method

From the Phone Information window, you can see that the client first requests the document Authenticate.asp and then sends the data, `Login=lwm&Password= secret`, in a separate transmission.

19.4.3 Using the GET method

Let's modify this application so that it uses the GET method to send data:

```
<go method="get" href="Authenticate.asp">
```

Notice that this time (figure 19.9), the data to be sent is appended to the URL:

```
HTTP GET Request:
HTTP://LOCALHOST/Authenticate.asp?Login=lwm&Password=secret
```

ERROR 404   Do not worry about the HTTP Error: 404 message in figure 19.9. This error occurs because the Authenticate.asp document could not be found in the web-publishing directory.

Figure 19.9   The Phone Information window using the POST method

19.4.4   A common pitfall using the GET method

HTML programmers who are familiar with the GET method often neglect to encode special characters as in:

```
Action="Authenticate.asp?Name=lwm&Password=secret"
```

You might be tempted to do the same in WML:

```
<go href="Authenticate.asp?Name=lwm&Password=secret">
```

If you do, your code will fail. In WAP, the ampersand (&) must be encoded with the special code: &

So your code must be modified as follows:

```
<go href="Authenticate.asp?Name=lwm&amp;Password=secret">
```

19.5   RETRIEVING VALUES SENT TO THE SERVER

Depending on the method you use to send data to the server, you can either use the Request.Form or the Request.QueryString collection to retrieve the values from the server.

19.5.1   Using the Request.Form collection

If you use the POST method to send data, use the Request.Form collection to retrieve the values:

```
<%
Dim Name, Password
Name =Request.Form("Name")
Password = Request.Form("Password")
...
%>
```

If you use the GET method, use the Request.QueryString collection:

```
<%
Dim Name, Password
Name =Request.QueryString("Name")
Password = Request.QueryString ("Password")
...
%>
```

> **POST ERROR**   Before you deploy your application, test it on a real device to ensure that the handset supports the send method that you are using.

19.6   *SESSION SUPPORT IN WAP DEVICES*

If you are an ASP web developer, you are familiar with the Session object discussed in chapter 17. The Session object allows the web server to maintain state between itself and the client. As we also saw in chapter 17, the Session object requires cookie support.

Unfortunately, the current generation of WAP phones does not support cookies. Fortunately, there are simple ways to test whether a WAP device supports cookies.

The first application attempts to set a cookie on the WAP device. The second then attempts to retrieve the cookie value.

```
<% Response.ContentType = "text/vnd.wap.wml"
   Response.Buffer = true        ←⌐ Sets the web server
%>                                  │  buffering to true
<?xml version="1.0"?>
<!DOCTYPE wml PUBLIC "-//WAPFORUM//DTD WML 1.1//EN"
"http://www.wapforum.org/DTD/wml_1.1.xml">
<wml>                                    Sets a cookie
  <card id="card1" title="Cookie">       using the        Sets an
    <p>                                   Cookies          anchor to
      Setting a cookie...                 collection of the  link to
      <% Response.Cookies("Test")= "123" %>  ←⌐ Response object  another ASP
      <a href="getCookieValue.asp">Check Cookie Support</a>  ←⌐ document
    </p>
  </card>
</wml>
```

If the cookie value can be retrieved, the WAP device supports cookies (figure 19.10).

```
<% Response.ContentType = "text/vnd.wap.wml" %>
<?xml version="1.0"?>
<!DOCTYPE wml PUBLIC "-//WAPFORUM//DTD WML 1.1//EN"
"http://www.wapforum.org/DTD/wml_1.1.xml">
<wml>
   <card id="card1" title="Cookie">
      <p>
         <%
            if Request.Cookies("Test") = "123" then
               Response.Write "Cookies Supported!"
            Else
               Response.Write "No Cookie-Support!"
            end if
         %>
      </p>
   </card>
</wml>
```

> **If the Cookies collection "Test" contains the value "123", cookie is supported, else cookie not supported**

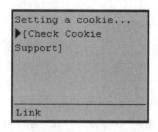 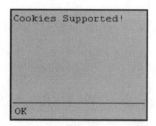

Figure 19.10
Checking for cookie support

WAP GATEWAYS Before you lament the lack of cookie support on current WAP devices, fret not! Some of the WAP gateways actually do the job of supporting cookies for the devices. The WAPlite gateway, discussed in more detail in chapter 27, supports session and persistent cookies. The rule-of-thumb for developing WAP applications at the moment is to forget about cookies!

Emulators often support cookies, so don't be fooled if your application using the Session object seems to work well on an emulator. Test it on a real device!

Once you have verified cookies support, you can use the Session object as discussed in chapter 17.

19.7 *USING ENVIRONMENT VARIABLES*

When developing applications for your services, it is essential that you make an attempt to detect the correct browser type. For example, if you try to access a WAP application from a web browser, you may see something like figure 19.11.

It would be far better if your application could first detect that the user is using a web browser, then redirect him to a web page that explains the error. Using specific environment variables, you can add this functionality to your WAP application.

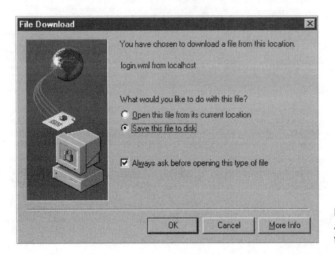

Figure 19.11
Accessing a WAP application from a web browser

19.8 DETECTING WEB AND WAP BROWSERS

A very simple detection method is to check the value of either HTTP_USER_AGENT or HTTP_ACCEPT.

Getting the value of HTTP_USER_AGENT

This code detects whether the user is using a WAP or a web browser based on the value of the HTTP_USER_AGENT environment variable.

```
<% Response.ContentType = "text/vnd.wap.wml"
   Response.Buffer = True %>
<?xml version="1.0"?>
<!DOCTYPE wml PUBLIC "-//WAPFORUM//DTD WML 1.1//EN"
"http://www.wapforum.org/DTD/wml_1.1.xml">
<wml>
<card id="card1" title="Detecting...">
   <p>
      <% if Instr(Request.ServerVariables("HTTP_USER_AGENT"), "Moz") then
           Response.Redirect "nonWML.html"
         Else
           Response.Write "Welcome to the Wireless World!"
         end if
      %>
   </p>
</card>
</wml>
```

If the HTTP_USER_AGENT variable contains the word "Moz", redirect him to nonWML.html, else write a welcome message

If the user is using a WAP browser (in this case, an emulator), a card like the one illustrated in figure 19.12 appears.

If the user is using a web browser, he will be redirected to another page as illustrated in figure 19.13:

Figure 19.12 Using a WAP browser

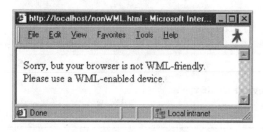

Figure 19.13 Redirecting the HTML user

Getting the value of HTTP_ACCEPT

Another method of differentiating a WAP browser from a web browser is to use the environment variable `HTTP_ACCEPT`.

This is the call via Detect.asp:

```
<% Response.ContentType = "text/vnd.wap.wml"
    Response.Buffer = True %>
<?xml version="1.0"?>
<!DOCTYPE wml PUBLIC "-//WAPFORUM//DTD WML 1.1//EN"
"http://www.wapforum.org/DTD/wml_1.1.xml">
<wml>
<card id="card1" title="Detecting...">
    <p>
        <% if Instr(Request.ServerVariables("HTTP_USER_AGENT"), "Moz") then
            Response.Redirect "HTMLaccept.asp"
        else
            Response.Write "Welcome to the Wireless World!"
            Response.Write "The browser can accept : " &
            Request.ServerVariables("HTTP_ACCEPT")
        end if
        %>
    </p>
</card>
</wml>
```

This is the call via HTMLaccept.asp:

```
<HTML>
<TITLE>HTML Accept</TITLE>
<BODY>
```

```
<% Response.Write "The browser can accept : " &
    Request.ServerVariables("HTTP_ACCEPT") %>
</BODY>
</HTML>
```

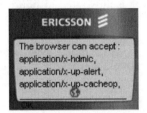

The Phone.com WAP browser accepts documents of the MIME types in table 19.1. (Note that Ericsson phones in the U.S. use the Phone.com's browser shown in figure 19.14.)

Figure 19.14 The Phone.com browser

Table 19.1 Phone.com WAP browser MIME types

MIME type	Description
application/x-hdmlc	HDML compiled
application/x-up-alert	Alert for the Phone.com browser (sent to phone's alert inbox)
application/x-up-cacheop	Clears a Phone.com browser's cache
application/x-up-device	Defines the handset requesting information
application/x-up-digestentry	Obsolete, unsupported type
application/vnd.wap.wml	WML compiled
text/x-wap.wml	WML decks
text/vnd.wap.wml	WML decks
application/vnd.wap.wmlscript	WMLScript compiled
text/vnd.wap.wmlscript	WMLScript uncompiled
application/vnd.uplanet.channel	Obsolete, unsupported type
application/vnd.uplanet.list	Obsolete, unsupported type
text/x-hdml	HDML files uncompiled
text/plain	ASCII text
text/html	HTML files
image/vnd.wap.wbmp	Image in WBMP format
image/bmp	Image in BMP format (dependent on WAP devices, not supported by all)
application/remote-printing text/x-hdml;version=3.1	HDML format version 3.1
text/x-hdml;version=3.0	HDML format version 3.0
text/x-hdml;version=2.0	HDML format version 2.0

The IE5 browser (figure 19.15) accepts the MIME types listed in table 19.2.

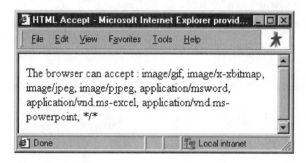

Figure 19.15
The IE5 browser

Table 19.2   IE5 browser MIME types

MIME type	Description
Image/gif	Image in GIF format
Image/x-xbitmap	Image in Xbitmap format
Image/jpeg	Image in JPEG format
Image/pjpeg	Image in PJPEG format
Application/msword	Microsoft Word Application
Application/vnd.ms-excel	Microsoft Excel Application
Application/vnd.ms-powerpoint	Microsoft PowerPoint Application
/	All types accepted

Looking for the string `"text/vnd.wap.wml"` in the `HTTP_ACCEPT` string can help you determine if your user is using a WAP browser.

The `HTTP_ACCEPT` string also indicates whether a WAP device provides image support (image/vnd.wap.wbmp).

In general, it is safer to check the `HTTP_ACCEPT` string as the Microsoft Mobile Explorer is reputed to return a string containing the word "Mozilla" in the `HTTP_USER_AGENT` string!

19.9   *DETECTING WAP DEVICES*

While identifying a WAP browser from a web browser is useful, the real challenge for the WAP developer is detecting the various makes of handsets and devices used to access your WML application.

While WML is a specification defined by the WAP forum, every WAP device renders WML differently. This can produce a different look and feel in your application. As we noted in chapter 15, an application that is designed to work on one device may behave differently on another. To make things worse, different devices have different memory constraints (we will discuss this in a later section).

So how do we effectively identify the WAP browser in use?

Fortunately, every WAP device has a unique identifier string and this string can be retrieved using the environment variable HTTP_USER_AGENT.

This application returns the user agent string of the device being used:

```
<% Response.ContentType = "text/vnd.wap.wml" %>
<?xml version="1.0"?>
<!DOCTYPE wml PUBLIC "-//WAPFORUM//DTD WML 1.1//EN"
    "http://www.wapforum.org/DTD/wml_1.1.xml">
<wml>
<card id="card1" title="User Agent">
  <p>
    <% = Request.ServerVariables("HTTP_USER_AGENT") %>
  </p>
</card>
</wml>
```

Uses the ServerVariables collection of the Request object to access the value of HTTP_USER_AGENT

Figure 19.16 shows the user agent string for three devices:

Figure 19.16   User agent string on three emulations

The emulated devices illustrated utilize Phone.com's WAP browser. Note that each device has a unique user agent string. Remember that certain phones may utilize different browsers in different countries (the Ericsson phone in figure 19.16 is using Phone.com's browser).

Figure 19.17 shows emulators from Ericsson and Nokia. They are currently showing the user agent string:

Figure 19.17 Emulators showing the user agent string

Identifying the browser is simply a matter of looking for the keyword in the HTTP_USER_AGENT string:

```
UAString = Request.ServerVariables("HTTP_USER_AGENT")
if Instr( UAString, "Nokia") then
```

Keyword is "Nokia" for Nokia devices

```
    Response.Redirect "/Nokia/index.wml"
elseif Instr( UAString, "UP") then
    Response.Redirect "/UP/index.wml"
else
```
Keyword is "UP" for devices using Phone.com's browser

Before you deploy your application, it is imperative to check the exact user agent strings for the various devices.

19.10 TESTING USING A REAL HANDSET

While emulators provide a realistic feel of how users will experience your application, nothing beats the real device.

Once you have developed your application, the best thing to do next is test your application on as many emulators as possible. This is important if your target audience is a large group that uses different devices. The vendor-provided emulators are essential for estimating the look and feel of your application in an actual device.

Once you have tested your application using one or more emulators, the next level of testing should involve devices that will most likely be used to run your application. If you are creating an in-house application (e.g., only for internal staff use), it is less tricky since the WAP device used can be determined by company policies. If you are developing a service for a broad group of users, it is worthwhile to get as many WAP devices as possible for testing purposes.

Testing on a real handset can uncover numerous problems:

Problems	Description
Caching	If your application explicitly disables caching on the WAP device, it is important to test this functionality on a real handset, as emulators may not function correctly.
Cookie support	The most notorious culprits in breaking your application are cookies or sessions. Most emulators support cookies, but many actual handsets do not. Remember that when testing for cookie support, the WAP gateway plays a part. For more information about WAP gateways, see chapter 27.
GET and POST methods	Emulators have no problem sending your data to the web server using either the GET or POST method. But when it comes to real handsets, some devices may not function correctly. You will only know if there is a problem by testing your application on a real handset.
Look and feel	For platforms that do not have an emulator such as the Siemens phones (though it uses the Phone.com's browser), testing on the real device is the only way to ascertain the look and feel of your application.
Maximum size of WAP binary	Testing your application on a real handset may help you to uncover the maximum size limit of the WAP device.
Usability	The most overlooked aspect of creating WAP applications. On the emulator, it is easy to enter characters into the phone. Try that on a real handset and you will appreciate this point!

19.11 SIZE CONSTRAINTS OF WAP DEVICES

As you recall, the basic unit of information transferred from the origin server to the WAP device is known as a deck. To minimize the amount of data sent to the WAP device, a deck is compiled into bytecode format known as WAP binary.

Very often, beginning WAP developers tend to overlook the limitations of WAP devices. Because WAP devices have limited memory, the WAP binary that is sent to the device must not exceed its memory capacity. Different devices have different memory constraints. Table 19.3 describes the limitations of some popular WAP devices.

Table 19.3   Limitations of WAP devices

WAP browser	Maximum WAP binary size
UP.Browser 3.2	1492 bytes
UP.Browser 4.x	2048 bytes
Ericsson R320	Approximately 3000 bytes
Ericsson R380	Approximately 3500 bytes
Ericsson MC218	More than 8000 bytes
Nokia 7110	1397 bytes

Failure to adhere to the memory constraint imposed by the device will cause the deck to be incorrectly loaded on the device.

In general, it is useful for developers to detect the kind of devices that the user is using and, based on that information, send different versions of a deck to suit the limitations of the devices.

19.12 CONTROLLING PAGE CACHING

When you load a web page using a web browser, the page is saved to your hard disk so that the next time you request the same page, it is accessed from your hard disk, instead of from the origin server. This is known as *browser caching*.

There is another caching method known as *proxy caching*. Using this method, a dedicated server acts as a go-between from the web surfer to the origin server. The dedicated server is known as a *proxy server*.

An example of proxy caching is when a proxy server caches web pages for an organization. When a user requests a page, it is saved to the proxy server's hard disk. When another user from the same organization requests the same page, the proxy server satisfies the request (figure 19.18).

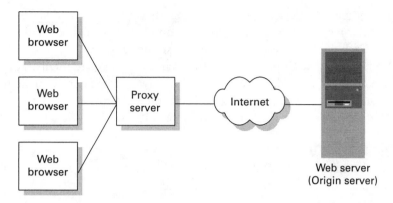

Figure 19.18 Caching at the web browser level and at the proxy server level

As you remember from chapter 1, a WAP device communicates with a WAP gateway. Thus in the WAP caching model, there are three levels of caching (figure 19.19):

- WAP device caching
- WAP gateway caching
- Proxy server caching

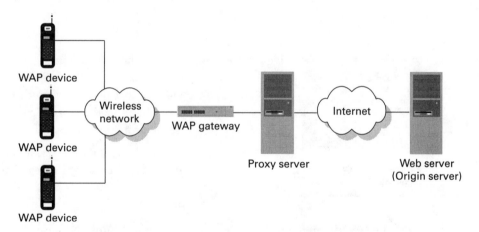

Figure 19.19 Caching at the WAP device level, the WAP gateway level, and proxy server level

The motivation for caching is to reduce the time required to load a document from the origin server. Once a document has been requested and cached, it can be reused. However, if you cache time-sensitive pages, such as stock quotes and weather reports, you are defeating the purpose of caching.

One notable difference between the web model and the WAP model is that WAP is commonly used for dynamic information retrieval. WAP is never intended to replace the web browser as a device for "surfing" the web. Due to the limited size and capability of the WAP device, it is most commonly used to retrieve dynamic data, such as stock information. As such, the information content is highly volatile and time-sensitive. Caching WAP pages in this case makes no sense.

While caching WAP pages has its disadvantages, there are merits. For example, given the limited bandwidth of a WAP device, it would be good to cache frequently accessed static pages. Such pages might include the welcome screen of a site, the login screen for a secure site, and other nonchanging screens.

19.12.1 Disabling caching

To disable caching on a WAP device, use the ASP `Response.Expires` property. This WML deck is not cached when it is loaded:

```
<% Response.ContentType = "text/vnd.wap.wml"
   Response.Expires = -1 %>          <-----------  Causes the deck
<?xml version="1.0"?>                              to expire using
<!DOCTYPE wml PUBLIC "-//WAPFORUM//DTD WML 1.1//EN"  the Expires
    "http://www.wapforum.org/DTD/wml_1.1.xml">       property of the
<wml>                                                Response object
<card id="card1" title="NoCache">
   <p>
       This deck is not cached.
       Time is now <% =time %>
   </p>
</card>
</wml>
```

Figure 19.20   Caching is disabled

Figure 19.20 shows how the application appears using an emulated WAP device.

To convince yourself that the deck is not cached, load it in your WAP emulator and load the same page again (do not use the reload/refresh function in your emulator).

PECULIARITY On the Phone.com browser, if you load the deck and then click the Return key in the Go textbox again, the same deck is loaded from the cache.

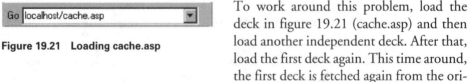

Figure 19.21   Loading cache.asp

To work around this problem, load the deck in figure 19.21 (cache.asp) and then load another independent deck. After that, load the first deck again. This time around, the first deck is fetched again from the origin server.

The `Response.Expires` property sets the time when the deck expires in the WAP device's cache. If you want the deck to expire five minutes after it has been loaded, you can set:

```
Response.Expires = 5
```

A commonly used method is to set

```
Response.Expires = 0
```

However, due to time differences between the server and the client, sometimes this method may not work correctly. To be sure that the deck is not cached, that is, that it expires immediately, set the property to a value of -1.

Be aware that cache control is at the deck level, rather than the card level. Consider the following example:

```
<% Response.ContentType = "text/vnd.wap.wml"
   Response.Expires = -1 %>
<?xml version="1.0"?>
<!DOCTYPE wml PUBLIC "-//WAPFORUM//DTD WML 1.1//EN"
"http://www.wapforum.org/DTD/wml_1.1.xml">
<wml>
   <card id="card1" title="NoCache">
     <p>
         Time in card 1 is now <% =time %>
         <do type="accept" label="Next">
            <go href="#card2"/>
         </do>
     </p>
   </card>

   <card id="card2" title="NoCache">
     <p>
         Time in card 2 is now <% =time %>
     </p>
   </card>
</wml>
```

Although we used the `Response.Expires` property to disable caching, the caching control applies to the deck, not individual cards. This can be seen by the fact that both cards will display the same time (figure 19.22). The time that is inserted is the time the ASP parser interprets the script.

Figure 19.22
Two cards, same time

META ELEMENT Caching can also be implemented using the `<meta>` element. For examples on caching using the `<meta>` element, refer to chapter 3.

19.12.2 Caching on WAP gateways, proxy servers

To control caching on a proxy server, use the `Response.CacheControl` property.

To prevent proxy servers from caching:

```
<% Response.ContentType = "text/vnd.wap.wml"      | Indicates that the ASP document
   Response.CacheControl = "Private" %>      ◄┘  should not be cached
<?xml version="1.0"?>
<!DOCTYPE wml PUBLIC "-//WAPFORUM//DTD WML 1.1//EN"
    "http://www.wapforum.org/DTD/wml_1.1.xml">
<wml>
<card id="card1" title="NoCache">
   <p>
       This deck is not cached by proxy servers.
   </p>
</card>
</wml>
```

To enable proxy server caching, set the `Response.CacheControl` property to `Public`.

```
Response.CacheControl = "Public"
```

Controlling caching on WAP gateways is the same as for proxy servers. The WAP Caching Model specification states that a WAP gateway must "faithfully implement the role of an HTTP/1.1 proxy with respect to caching and cache header transmission."

19.13 SUMMARY

This chapter has touched on creating dynamic WAP applications using ASP. While developing WAP applications is similar to developing web applications, there are a number of points to watch. Detecting the WAP device type and caching are two important topics for any WAP developers.

In part VII of this book, we will look at using Java servlets to develop dynamic WAP applications.

C H A P T E R   2 0

Using ASP to implement data-based WAP applications

20.1   INTRODUCTION

In the previous three chapters you have learned ASP and how it can be used to develop dynamic WAP applications. You have also learned about database technologies to access back-end databases. Let's now put all these pieces together to create a dynamic WAP application using ADO.

20.2   AUTHENTICATION BY EXAMPLE

If you are developing a WAP application that provides services to a select group of users, your application must have some form of user authentication.

Before a user is granted access to your application, he must log on. In this section, we will learn how to prompt a user for logon information, how to authenticate the information, and how to manage invalid logon information and create an account if the user has not registered.

20.2.1 Logging on

A username with password is the most common authentication method. In this example, we will create a WML deck that prompts the user to log on to a Microsoft Access 97 database.

Our database contains a table named Users (figure 20.1).

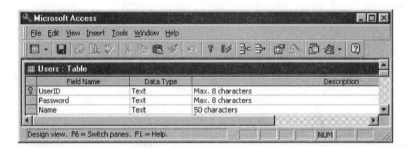

Figure 20.1   The Users table

Our sample table contains two records (figure 20.2):

**Figure 20.2
Two records in a
sample table**

The following WML deck prompts the user to log on:

```
<?xml version="1.0"?>
<!DOCTYPE wml PUBLIC "-//WAPFORUM//DTD WML 1.1//EN"
"http://www.wapforum.org/DTD/wml_1.1.xml">
<wml>
<card id="card1" title="Login">
    <p>
        UserID: <input type="text" name="UserID" maxlength="8"/>
        Password: <input type="password" name="Password" maxlength="8"/>
        <do type="accept" label="Login">
```

**Gets the
UserID and
Password**

**Maps the softkey to the
Authenticate.asp document**

```
<go method="post" href="Authenticate.asp">      ◄───────────┐
    <postfield name="UserID" value="$UserID" />               │    Uses the
    <postfield name="Password" value="$Password" />    ┐      │    POST
</go>                                                   │      │    method to
                                  Uses the <postfield> │      │    send the
                                  element for sending   │      │    information
</do>                             information           │      │
</p>                                                                │
</card>
</wml>
```

Figure 20.3 shows the WML deck when loaded using the UP.Simulator.

Figure 20.3
The WML deck loaded
using UP.Simulator

After the user enters his user ID and password, the ASP program called `Authenticate.asp` is invoked.

20.2.2 Authenticating the logon

Once the user enters a user ID and the password, the data can be sent to the server for checking against the database containing the users' IDs and passwords.

The following ASP document opens a database connection and retrieves the record that contains the `UserID` and `Password`.

```
<% Response.ContentType = "text/vnd.wap.wml" %>
<?xml version="1.0"?>
<!DOCTYPE wml PUBLIC "-//WAPFORUM//DTD WML 1.1//EN"
"http://www.wapforum.org/DTD/wml_1.1.xml">
<wml>
    <card id="card1" title="Verify">
        <p>                                                Creates an
        <%                    Creates an instance of       instance of
        Dim conn, rs       ◄──┘ the Connection object      the
        Set conn = Server.CreateObject("ADODB.Connection")  Recordset
        Set rs   = Server.CreateObject("ADODB.Recordset")  ◄  object
        '---Opens the connection to the database---
        conn.open "DRIVER={Microsoft Access Driver (*.mdb)};  ┐  Connects
          DBQ=" & Server.MapPath("Login.mdb") & ";"           ├  to the
        '---Retrieve the user's record                        ┘  database
        sql = "SELECT * FROM Users WHERE UserID='" &          ┐  Forms the
          Request.Form("UserID") & "' AND Password='" &       ├  SQL query
          Request.Form("Password") & "'"    ┐ Executes the    ┘
        Set rs = conn.Execute (sql)       ◄─┘ SQL query
        if rs.EOF then                                         Login fails if the
            '---means UserID and Password do not match---      recordset.EOF
            Response.Write "Invalid Login"                     marker is true,
                                                               otherwise prints
                                                               welcome message
```

```
        else
            Response.Write "Welcome, " & rs.Fields("Name")
        end if
        rs.Close              │ Closes the Recordset and
        conn.Close            │ Connection objects
        Set rs=Nothing        │ Closes the Recordset
        Set conn = Nothing    │ and Connection objects
%>
</p>
</card>
</wml>
```

If `UserID` and `Password` match the record of logon information, the record is retrieved and the user's name is stored in the recordset's Field collection. Thus, we generate a welcome message.

The `EOF` property checks the recordset to see whether it contains a record. If no record was retrieved, we can be certain that the userID and password do not match and that authentication has failed. Thus, we generate an invalid logon message.

```
if rs.EOF then
    Response.Write "Invalid Login"
else
    Response.Write "Welcome, " & rs.Fields("Name")
end if
```

Figure 20.4 shows the WML card for a valid and invalid logon:

Figure 20.4
Valid and invalid logon

20.2.3 Handling an invalid logon

When a user's logon attempt fails, we can design our application to provide two options:

- Retry the logon process
- Create an account

To allow a user who has not previously registered to register for a new account, we need to modify the code in our ASP program, `Authenticate.asp`.

Let's modify our existing code to add the function for the user to retry the logon process and to register for a new account. The added features are shown in bold:

```
if rs.EOF then '---means UserID and Password does not match---
    Response.Write "Invalid Login. "
```

```
    Response.Write "Do you want to register for a new account ?"
%>
    <do type="options" label="Retry">
        <go href="Login.wml"/>
    </do>

    <do type="accept" label="New">
        <go href="NewAccount.wml"/>
    </do>
<%
else
    Response.Write "Welcome, " & rs.Fields("Name")
end if
```

If the user chooses Retry to retry the logon, loads the login.wml deck

If the user chooses New to create an account, loads the NewAccount.wml deck

Expands user prompt "Do you want to register for a new account?"

Figure 20.5 shows the WML code that was generated by Authenticate.asp.

Figure 20.5 Allowing the user to try again or set up a new account

20.2.4   Entering new account information

When the user opts to set up a new account, the NewAccount.wml deck is loaded.

```
<?xml version="1.0"?>
<!DOCTYPE wml PUBLIC "-//WAPFORUM//DTD WML 1.1//EN"
"http://www.wapforum.org/DTD/wml_1.1.xml">
<wml>
<card id="card1" title="New">
  <p>
      Please select an ID <input type="text"
          name="NewUserID" maxlength="8"/>
      Password: <input type="password"
          name="Password1" maxlength="8"/>
      Confirm Password: <input type="password"
          name="Password2" maxlength="8"/>
      Name : <input type="text" name="Name"
          maxlength="50"/>
      <do type="accept" label="Create">
        <go method="post" href="CreateNew.asp">
            <postfield name="UserID" value="$NewUserID" />
            <postfield name="Password" value="$Password1" />
            <postfield name="Name" value="$Name" />
        </go>
      </do>
  </p>
</card>
</wml>
```

The first <input> element for keying in the UserID

The second <input> element for keying in the Password

The third <input> element for rekeying in the Password

The fourth <input> element for keying in the name

There are four <input> elements in the NewAccount.wml deck (figure 20.6). The user first supplies a user ID, followed by a password. A password confirmation is required to ensure that his password is spelled correctly. In the final step, the user keys in his name.

Figure 20.6   Four input elements to creating a logon record

WMLSCRIPT   Although WMLScript could be used in this example application to confirm the two passwords that the user enters, we are using a simplified example that does not include WMLScript.

20.2.5   Creating an account

Assuming that the two passwords match and the user keys in his name and presses the Create button, the new account is created. The ASP program called CreateNew.asp processes the new account information, saves it to the database, and generates either a confirmation or error message for the user:

```
<% Response.ContentType = "text/vnd.wap.wml" %>
<?xml version="1.0"?>
<!DOCTYPE wml PUBLIC "-//WAPFORUM//DTD WML 1.1//EN"
"http://www.wapforum.org/DTD/wml_1.1.xml">
<wml>
  <card id="card1" title="NewAccount">
    <p>
    <%
    Dim conn
    Set conn = Server.CreateObject("ADODB.Connection")
    '---Opens the connection to the database---
    conn.open "DRIVER={Microsoft Access Driver (*.mdb)};DBQ=" &
       Server.MapPath("Login.mdb") & ";"
    '---Retrieve the user's record
    sql = "INSERT INTO Users (UserID, Password, Name) Values
      ('" & Request.Form("UserID") & "','" & Request.Form("Password") &
      "','" & Request.Form("Name") &"')"
    On Error Resume Next
    conn.Execute (sql)
    if Err.Number<>0 then
      Response.Write "Sorry. Error encountered. Please try again."
    Else
      Response.Write "Thank you, your account is created successfully."
    end if
```

> If an error has occurred, prints an error message, otherwise prints a thank-you message

> **Prevents duplicate UserIDs from crashing the ASP script**

```
      conn.Close
      Set conn = Nothing
%>
</p>
</card>
</wml>
```

The VBScript Err object checks for errors. If an error has occurred, the `Err.Number` property will contain the error code. If there are no errors, `Err.Number` will contain a value of 0. To see a specific description of the error, use the `Err.Description` property.

```
On Error Resume Next
conn.Execute (sql)
if Err.Number<>0 then
    Response.Write "Sorry. Error encountered. Reason: " & Err.Description
else
    Response.Write "Thank you, your account is created successfully."
end if
```

Figure 20.7 shows the WML cards for both the confirmation and error screens.

Figure 20.7
Confirmation and error screens

20.3   UNDERSTANDING MOBILE DATA ENTRY

One of the key limitations of current WAP devices is the difficulty in entering information. And so, when designing your WAP applications, let your user make a selection, rather than asking him to enter textual information manually. To enable users to choose an item rather than entering a choice manually, you can package records using the WML `<select>` element.

20.3.1   Packaging records with the `<select>` element

In this example application, users can book cinema tickets. The application accesses a database table that contains available theaters to allow the user to select a specific one. Figure 20.8 shows a Cinema table.

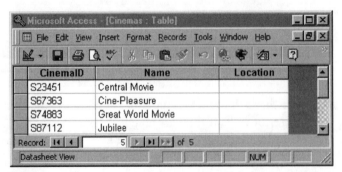

Figure 20.8
A Cinema table

Figure 20.9
An up/down navigational button

The ASP application which follows retrieves all the theaters and generates a WML deck that allows the user to make a selection by navigating the up and down navigational buttons (figure 20.9).

```
<%
    Dim conn, rs
    Set conn = Server.CreateObject("ADODB.Connection")
    Set rs   = Server.CreateObject("ADODB.Recordset")
    '---Opens the connection to the database---
    conn.open "DRIVER={Microsoft Access Driver (*.mdb)};DBQ=" &
        Server.MapPath("Cinema.mdb") & ";"
    '---Retrieve the user's record
    sql = "SELECT * FROM Cinemas"
    Set rs = conn.Execute (sql)
    Response.Write "<select name='cinemas'>"        ← Creates the
    While not rs.EOF                                   <select> element
        Response.Write "<option value='"
        & rs("CinemaID")& "'>" & rs("Name") &        Uses the while
        "</option>"                                   loop to print all
        rs.MoveNext          ←    Moves the           the cinemas
    Wend                           recordset pointer
    Response.Write "</select>"     to the next
    rs.Close                       record
    conn.Close
    Set rs=Nothing
    Set conn = Nothing
%>
```

Figure 20.10
Selecting a cinema

Figure 20.10 shows how the WML looks.

To select an item, simply press the navigational buttons to position at the correct cinema and press the OK button to select it.

What we did in the application was to retrieve all the cinemas in the table and package them using the WML <select> and <option> elements.

```
Response.Write "<select name='cinemas'>"
While not rs.EOF
    Response.Write "<option value='" & rs("CinemaID")&
      "'>" & rs("Name") & "</option>"
    rs.MoveNext
Wend
Response.Write "</select>"
```

Using double quotes correctly—When you use the `Response.Write` method to output WML statements, a pair of double quotes (`" "`) usually encloses attribute values. However, double quotes have special meaning in VBScript. To prevent a conflict with VBScript syntax, replace the double quotes with single quotes (`'`).

For example:

```
Response.Write "<select name="cinemas">"
```

will generate a VBScript error, as the double quotes are not closed properly.

To solve this syntax problem, use either single quotes (`'value'`) or two sets of double quotes (`""value""`) to enclose attribute values. For example:

```
Response.Write "<select name='cinemas'>"
```

or

```
Response.Write "<select name=""cinemas"">"
```

The second statement uses two double quotes to turn off the special meaning of the double quotes.

20.4 RECORD DISPLAY BY EXAMPLE

One of the most common mistakes you can make as a beginning WAP developer is neglecting to check the size of the WML deck. This occasionally happens when you try to display records from a table. In order to prevent this error, always restrict the number of records to be displayed on a card/deck.

Deck size problem—The problem of controlling the size of a deck is a tricky issue. This is because we would not know the deck size until the WAP gateway compiles the deck. And there is no formula to calculate the deck size before and after compilation. As such, the safest best is to try out different numbers of records to squeeze into a deck and derive a figure that generates a compiled size less than the memory capacity of your target device.

In this example application, users can search for a particular title from a books database. The search process may return a huge number of titles in which case we display a set number of records across multiple pages. Figure 20.11 shows the Titles table of our example database:

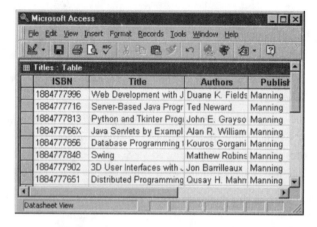

Figure 20.11
A Titles table showing
a books database

20.4.1 Displaying records across multiple pages

Figure 20.12 Searching
for a book

The WML code shown in the next section allows the user to search a database table containing computer book titles (figure 20.12).

When the titles are retrieved, they are displayed across multiple cards (figure 20.13).

By displaying the records across multiple cards, we have achieved two objectives:

- Reduced the size of the deck
- Presented the records in manageable chunks

Figure 20.13 Multiple cards showing book titles

20.4.2 Understanding the code

Let's take a look at the code that lets us retrieve data and display it across multiple cards:

```
<% Response.ContentType = "text/vnd.wap.wml" %>
<!--#include file="adovbs.inc"-->
<?xml version="1.0"?>
<!DOCTYPE wml PUBLIC "-//WAPFORUM//DTD WML 1.1//EN"
"http://www.wapforum.org/DTD/wml_1.1.xml">
<wml>
```

```
<card id="card1" title="Result">
  <p>
  <%
  Dim conn, rs
  Set conn = Server.CreateObject("ADODB.Connection")
  Set rs   = Server.CreateObject("ADODB.Recordset")

  '---Opens the connection to the database---
  conn.open "DRIVER={Microsoft Access Driver (*.mdb)};
      DBQ=" & Server.MapPath("Books.mdb") & ";"

  '---Retrieve the user's record
  sql = "SELECT * FROM Titles WHERE Title LIKE '%" &
      Request.QueryString("searchStr") & "%'"

  rs.Open sql, conn, adOpenStatic, adLockReadOnly, adCmdText

  rs.PageSize = 3
  PageNo = CInt(Request.QueryString("PageNo"))
  if PageNo = 0 then
      PageNo = 1
  end if

  rs.AbsolutePage = PageNo
  count = 0
  While not rs.EOF AND count<rs.PageSize
    count = count + 1
    Response.Write count + ((PageNo-1) * rs.PageSize) &
        ". " & rs("Title") & "<br/>"
    rs.MoveNext
  Wend

  if not rs.EOF then
      Response.Write   "<do type='accept' label='Next'>"
      Response.Write      "<go method='get' href='search.asp'>"
      Response.Write         "<postfield name='PageNo' value='" &
          PageNo + 1 & "'/>"
      Response.Write         "<postfield name='searchStr' value='" &
          Request.QueryString("searhStr") & "'/>"
      Response.Write         "</go>"
      Response.Write   "</do>"
  end if
  if PageNo>1 then
      Response.Write   "<do type='options' label='Previous'>"
      Response.Write      "<go method='get' href='search.asp'>"
      Response.Write         "<postfield name='PageNo' value='" &
          PageNo - 1 & "'/>"
      Response.Write         "<postfield name='searchStr' value='" &
          Request.QueryString("searchStr") & "' />"
      Response.Write         "</go>"
      Response.Write   "</do>"
  end if

  rs.Close
  conn.Close
```

```
        Set rs=Nothing
        Set conn = Nothing
%>
</p>
</card>
</wml>
```

You can run the application by typing the following in the WAP emulator:

http://localhost/search.asp?searchStr=java

Retrieving records

Notice that in this example, we are using the Recordset object's `Open` method to retrieve the records:

```
rs.Open sql, conn, adOpenStatic, adLockReadOnly, adCmdText
```

We opened the recordset using a static cursor (adOpenStatic). If the default cursor (adOpenForwardOnly) was used, this statement would fail. Cursors are explained in chapter 18.

Setting the page size

We next set the size of the page. That is, the number of records to be displayed in a card:

```
rs.PageSize = 3
```

Determining the current page

We next determine the current page of records to be displayed. If the deck is loaded for the first time, PageNo would be 0 and we would set it to the first (1) page.

```
PageNo = CInt(Request.QueryString("PageNo"))
if PageNo = 0 then
    PageNo = 1
end if
```

Setting the current page

We next set the current page of the recordset.

```
rs.AbsolutePage = PageNo
```

Displaying records

Once the page number is set, we can start to display the records in that particular page:

```
count = 0
While not rs.EOF AND count<rs.PageSize
    count = count + 1
    Response.Write count + ((PageNo-1) * rs.PageSize) & ". " &
        rs("Title") & "<br/>"
    rs.MoveNext
Wend
```

Navigating between records

The last step is to provide a Next and a Previous button to allow the user to navigate the records:

```
if not rs.EOF then
    Response.Write    "<do type='accept' label='Next'>"
    Response.Write      "<go method='get' href='search.asp'>"
    Response.Write        "<postfield name='PageNo' value='" &
        PageNo + 1 & "'/>"
    Response.Write          "<postfield name='searchStr' value='" &
        Request.QueryString("searchStr") & "'/>"
    Response.Write        "</go>"
    Response.Write    "</do>"
end if
if PageNo>1 then
    Response.Write    "<do type='options' label='Previous'>"
    Response.Write      "<go method='get' href='search.asp'>"
    Response.Write        "<postfield name='PageNo' value='" &
        PageNo - 1 & "'/>"
    Response.Write          "<postfield name='searchStr' value='" &
        Request.QueryString("searchStr") & "'/>"
    Response.Write        "</go>"
    Response.Write    "</do>"
end if
```

NOTE   We can also rewrite the above statements without using the WML `<postfield>` element:

```
Response.Write      "<go href='search.asp?PageNo='"&
    (PageNo+1) & "/>"
```

20.5 SUMMARY

We have illustrated the concepts that we learned in the previous few chapters with examples. We have also shown some of the techniques to use when developing WAP data-based applications.

By mastering this chapter as well as chapters 17–19 and 21, you can take on Case Study 1 (chapter 34) with relative ease.

C H A P T E R   2 1

Troubleshooting your ASP/WAP application

21.1   ERRORS AND PROBLEMS

So far, we hope that you have been successful in getting your web server to generate dynamic WAP applications and that you are getting comfortable and geared up for more challenges ahead.

However, it is likely that you may encounter ASP-related errors or difficulties in generating WAP content correctly. In this chapter, we will share some of our debugging experiences for problems that may trip up a beginning WAP developer.

We will be using Phone.com's UP.Simulator for debugging purposes. In particular, the Phone Information window is especially helpful for tracing the source of error.

In the next couple of sections, we will look at some of the common problems (figure 21.1) that you may encounter when developing WAP applications. The sources of

338

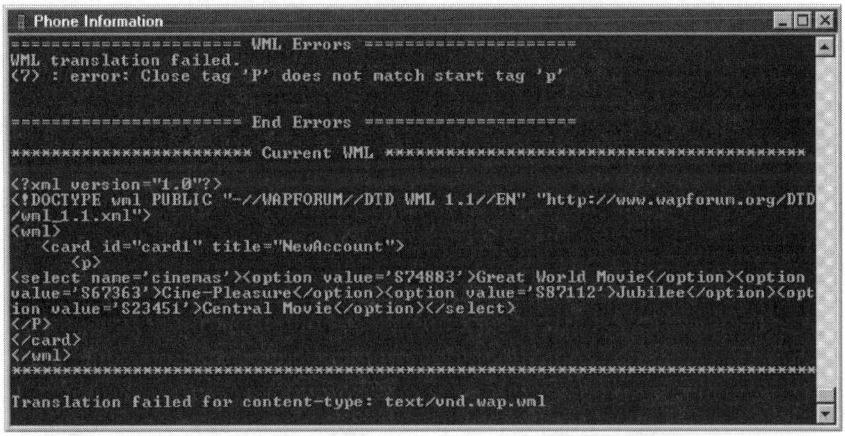

Figure 21.1   Common generating errors

error may be due to ASP, or simply the result of incorrect configuration of emulators or gateways. We also include some of the errors that may result when you deploy your applications in the real world.

21.1.1   ASP script errors

If your ASP script contains errors and bugs (which are likely), the ASP parser would be unable to interpret the script correctly and would halt. When the parser halts, it generates error messages and sends them to the WML compiler for compilation to WAP binary. There are a couple of reasons for ASP to fail on your web server. You could be using an older version of MDAC and trying to connect to a database in your application. In this case, the server may fail to create an ADO object. Or, you could have a run-time error such as a division-by-zero error.

Problem

This message in your emulator (UP.Simulator) is usually a good indication that the deck received does not adhere to the WML DTD rules:

```
Compile Error. See Info Window for details.
```

This message is caused by the error messages that are sent as part of the deck.

Let's consider the following simple example:

```
<% Response.ContentType = "text/vnd.wap.wml"
   Response.Buffer = True %>
<?xml version="1.0"?>
<!DOCTYPE wml PUBLIC "-//WAPFORUM//DTD WML 1.1//EN"
    "http://www.wapforum.org/DTD/wml_1.1.xml">
<wml>
<card id="card1" title="Error...">
```

```
    <p>
        <% Dim a
        a = 5/0  ◄───────────── We are trying to
        Response.Write a         perform a division-by-
        %>                       zero operation here
    </p>
</card>
</wml>
```

Examining the Phone Information window yields the following explanation:

```
<?xml version="1.0"?>
<!DOCTYPE wml PUBLIC "-//WAPFORUM//DTD WML 1.1//EN"
"http://www.wapforum.org/DTD/wml_1.1.xml">
<wml>
<card id="card1" title="Error...">        The error was caused
    <p>                                    by the VBScript run
        <font face="Arial" size=2>         time, which means it
<p>Microsoft VBScript runtime </font>      was generated during
  <font face="Arial" size=2>error '800a000b'  interpretation of the
</font>                                    ASP document
<p>
<font face="Arial" size=2>Division by zero</font>  ◄── Error reported by the
<p>                                                     VBScript run time
<font face="Arial" size=2>/error.asp</font>
  <font face="Arial" size=2>, line 9</f
ont>
```

```
Translation failed for content-type: text/vnd.wap.wml
```

The division-by-zero error caused the ASP parser to halt and send the error message to the WML compiler.

Solution

To prevent the VBScript from crashing the program when an error occurs, simply insert the statement On Error Resume Next before any VBScript statement:

```
<% Dim a
  On Error Resume Next
  a = 5/0
  Response.Write a
%>
```

The use of the On Error Resume Next statement is to inform the VBScript interpreter to ignore any errors that occur and resume execution. To report the error, you can use the Err object to check for the error.

```
<% Dim a
  On Error Resume Next
  a = 5/0
  if Err.Number <> 0 then
      Response.Write "An error has occurred, due to : " & Err.Description
```

```
      end if
      Response.Write a
%>
```

In this code segment, we use the `Number` and `Description` property of the Err object to check for the occurrence of errors. If an error has occurred, the `Number` property will contain a non-zero number and the `Description` property will contain the cause of the error.

21.1.2   MIME type errors

A common problem when using ASP to generate WAP content is failing to set the correct MIME type. WML decks have the MIME type `text/vnd.wap.wml`. In chapter 1, we saw that for files ending with the .wml extension, we can associate the WML MIME type with the web server (or the operating system). However, for ASP documents (with file extension .asp), we need to explicitly set the WML MIME type.

Problem

This error message in your emulator is likely caused by the incorrect MIME type:

```
Content-Type Error. See Info Window for Details
```

If your ASP document does not set the WML MIME type correctly, the default MIME type is text/html. This error message from the Phone Information window of the UP.Simulator illustrates this:

```
---------------- DATA SIZE -----------------------
Uncompiled data from HTTP is 227 bytes.
...found Content-Type: text/html.              | The MIME type
                                               | is text/html
Content-Type: text/html. Content follows:      |

<?xml version="1.0"?>
<!DOCTYPE wml PUBLIC "-//WAPFORUM//DTD WML 1.1//EN"
"http://www.wapforum.org/DTD
/wml_1.1.xml">
<wml>
<card id="card1" title="Error...">
   <p>
       Hello Wireless world!
   </p>
</card>                                        | Though the WAP emulator
</wml>                                         | is receiving the correct
End Content-Type: text/html.                   | WML deck, the MIME type
                                               | is not correct
No translator for content-type: text/html   <-|
```

Sometimes, an ASP script error will also trigger a content-type error as this example shows:

```
<% Response.ContentType = "text/vnd.wap.wml"
   Response.Buffer = True %>
<?xml version="1.0"?>
```

```
<!DOCTYPE wml PUBLIC "-//WAPFORUM//DTD WML 1.1//EN"
"http://www.wapforum.org/DTD/wml_1.1.xml">
<wml>
<card id="card1" title="Detecting...">
   <p>
       <% if Instr(Request.ServerVariables("HTTP_USER_AGENT"),
          "Moz") '—then missing-
             Response.Redirect "HelloHTML.asp"
         else
             Response.Write "Welcome to the Wireless World!"
         Response.Write "The browser can accept : " &
            Request.ServerVariables("HTTP_ACCEPT")
         end if
         %>
   </p>
</card>
</wml>
```

The "then" keyword is missing

The Information window returns the following error message:

```
---------------- DATA SIZE ----------------------
Uncompiled data from HTTP is 417 bytes.
...found Content-Type: text/html.          ◄───

Content-Type: text/html. Content follows:
 <font face="Arial" size=2>
<p>Microsoft VBScript compilation </font>
     <font face="Arial" size=2>error '800a03f9'</font>
<p>
<font face="Arial" size=2>Expected 'Then'</font>    ◄
<p>
<font face="Arial" size=2>/detect.asp</font>
   <font face="Arial" size=2>, line 8</font>
<pre>if Instr(Request.ServerVariables(&quot;HTTP_USER_AGENT&quot;),
  &quot;Moz&quot;)
----------------------------------------------------------^</pre>
End Content-Type: text/html.

No translator for content-type: text/html
```

The MIME type is text/html ... but you have to look further down

The missing "then" keyword is the culprit

Solution

When using ASP to generate a WML deck, remember to use the Response.ContentType property to set the MIME type:

```
<% Response.ContentType = "text/vnd.wap.wml" %>
```

If you are saving the WML deck directly with the .wml extension, you have to set the MIME type explicitly on your web server or operating system. Appendix D, "Setting Up Microsoft PWS and IIS" will show you how.

We have heard that some gateways refused to work if the "<" character from the string

```
<?xml version="1.0"?>
```

is not the first character to be received. This is because the line

```
<% Response.ContentType = "text/vnd.wap.wml" %>
```

will generate a carriage return. In such cases, simply append the line with the first ASP statement like this:

```
<% Response.ContentType = "text/vnd.wap.wml" %><?xml version="1.0"?>
```

21.1.3 Emulator problems

There was once a saying about a particular operating system: "It is a feature, not a bug." Perhaps we have come to terms with the fact that bugs in software—including WAP emulators and microbrowsers—are here to stay. Perhaps there should be three additional buttons on your handphone: CTR, ALT, and DEL! We have tested some of the WAP handsets and are pleased that making them hang is not a difficult task at all. Suddenly you have a handphone that needs to be rebooted once or twice a day!

Problem

Sometimes you may encounter errors from your emulator and, despite checking the source line by line, word by word, you still cannot solve the problem.

Solution

Our best advice is to close the emulator and relaunch it. Most of the time this will solve your problem. If the problem persists after relaunching the emulator, reboot your machine.

21.1.4 Web server and gateway configuration problems

WAP emulators typically offer two connection methods: HTTP direct or WAP gateway. Generally, connecting using HTTP direct should not pose too much of a problem. Connecting through a gateway is trickier.

Problem

Connecting through a gateway can cause a few potential problems:

- The gateway is using an incorrect proxy setting
- The port number of the gateway is not specified correctly
- Web server internal error 500

Solution

Refer to chapter 29.

21.1.5 Logical errors

It is called an error, but it isn't one. Suppose you load up a deck expecting to see time-sensitive information such as a stock quote. However, the information on the deck displays the same stock information from a day ago. Why is it displayed again? Why doesn't it change?

Problem

The problem here is that the previously loaded decks have been cached. When the deck is requested again, it is loaded from the cache instead of being fetched from the Origin server.

Solution

You must disable caching in the deck. Setting the HTTP response header to cause the deck to expire immediately after loading will solve the problem. Chapter 19 will show how to disable WML deck caching using the <meta> element as well as using ASP.

21.1.6 User interface issues

As stressed throughout this entire book, user interface, in particular usability of WAP applications is of paramount importance. While your application may work and display perfectly in one device, it may break in another device.

Problem

Your application runs perfectly on one device but appears differently on another device.

Solution

The problem stems from the different look and feel of the various WAP devices available in the market at this moment. As the WML specification is more concerned about functionality, the implementation aspect is left to the device manufacturers. As such, the behavior of each application varies across devices. One way to solve the problem is to maintain multiple sets of WML decks (each catering to a particular device) and during execution time detect the device type that the user is using. The environment variables HTTP_ACCEPT and HTTP_USER_AGENT will contain information about the content type acceptable to the device as well as the device type. Of course, the downside to this approach is redundancy. It is not feasible to maintain multiple sets of WML decks given that there are so many different devices available.

Another solution is to mark up your content using XML and use the XSLT stylesheet to dynamically transform your content to produce the WML deck that can be best displayed on the target device. Part VIII of this book will discuss XML and XSLT in more detail.

21.1.7 Detecting the user device

Earlier we discussed the use of the environment variables HTTP_ACCEPT and HTTP_USER_AGENT. So when do you use them and which one do you use?

Problem

You have used the following code to detect users using web browsers:

```
if Instr(Request.ServerVariables("HTTP_USER_AGENT"), "Mozilla") then
    '---user is using a web browser
else
    '---assume user is using WAP browser
end if
```

In essence, you are looking for the keyword "Mozilla" in the environment variable HTTP_USER_AGENT.

Some time after deployment, some user complains that your application is not working correctly on his device. Upon further probing, it is discovered that this group of users is using devices running the Microsoft Mobile Explorer (MME). Because MME returns a user agent string containing the word "Mozilla", it managed to "sneak" into the part of the code where we assumed the user is using a web browser.

Solution

Besides checking HTTP_USER_AGENT to differentiate between web and WAP browsers, it is more accurate to check the HTTP_ACCEPT string for the list of MIME types supported by the device. The following snippets of code illustrate this:

```
if Instr(Request.ServerVariables("HTTP_ACCEPT"), "WML") then
    '---assume user is using WAP browser
else
    '---user is using a web browser
end if
```

However, the best solution is to test both environment variables as some devices can support both WML and HTML contents (e.g., Microsoft MME). And so you can decide whether to send WML or HTML to the device.

21.1.8 Memory problems

Memory issues are an overlooked factor when troubleshooting your WAP application. Real devices have finite memory installed. Different devices have different memory capacity.

Problem

Your application works all right on some devices but fails on others. You have tested on many devices but somehow your application fails on one particular model.

Solution

It is likely that you have run into a memory overflow error on that particular device. Remember that the memory fitted on the device varies from model to model and it is possible that the size of the WAP binary produced by the WAP gateway has exceeded the memory capability of your device. Since some devices have more memory than others, you may not get an error on the other devices. Testing using emulators is unlikely to reveal this problem.

To solve this problem, always try to ensure that your deck size is kept to its minimum. You can always use the Information window that is displayed when the UP.Simulator is launched to check for the WAP binary size. If the WAP binary size can be kept within the limit of 1000 bytes, your application is pretty safe.

21.1.9 Redirection problems

Almost all the microbrowsers currently available on the market support client-side redirection. Client-side redirection is easily accomplished in ASP using the `Response.Redirect()` method.

Problem

Deck redirection will not work correctly if you are not careful. Consider the following:

```
Response.Redirect "Login.wml"
```

The code snippet quite simply instructs the client to fetch the deck "Login.wml" from the current directory. Suppose your current directory is in "/email" and so essentially you are redirecting to "/email/Login.wml". Testing on your emulator (in HTTP Direct mode) reveals no problem. However, when you test it on a real gateway, you may have some surprises! The redirection may suddenly cease to work.

The reason is that some WAP gateways may interpret the relative path of redirection as an absolute one. So the redirection is interpreted by the gateway as:

```
Response.Redirect "/Login.wml"
```

where in actual fact it should be:

```
Response.Redirect "/email/Login.wml"
```

Solution

The safest way for redirection to work correctly is to code using absolute path. While this method is not advisable where portability of code is concerned, it is necessary in order to prevent the redirection from failing.

21.1.10 Performance problems

Performance is another area that is often overlooked when developing WAP applications. When testing your application using the emulators, you would not be able to get a realistic feel of the actual performance of your application. It is only through field-testing and deployment that you discover the actual performance of the application.

Problem

You discover after deploying your application that the speed of your application is slow. This is something that you do not experience during development time.

Solution

The real reason for the sluggish performance is that real devices have to download the WAP binary through a connection that is limited to a low bandwidth (typically 9600 bps). The size of the WAP binary plays an important part in improving the performance. In general, try to reduce the size of the WML deck as much as possible so as to reduce the size of the WAP binary generated.

In addition, you might be using XML and XSLT to tailor your content for the different devices. As XSLT transformation on the server side is a processor intensive process, it may slow down your web server quite drastically when there are multiple users connected at the same time. In such cases, you might want to utilize techniques like XSLT caching on the server side. XSLT caching is beyond the scope of this book. Please refer to Part VIII for more information on using XML and XSLT to develop WAP applications.

21.1.11 WMLScript support

In the web environment, it is common to have scripting on the client side so that the content is interactive and a round-trip delay to the server can be avoided. Similarly, in the WAP environment, WMLScript is sometimes used to provide client-side input validation. However, the current implementation of WMLScript is still not stable. In our development process, we have discovered that the support of WMLScript on the client side cannot be taken for granted. Not all devices support WMLScript. In addition, the implementation of WMLScript on some devices seems shaky.

Problem

You have coded an application using WML and WMLScript. The WMLScript portion works all right on one emulator but sometimes behaves erratically on another. Also, your users have reported that on some devices your application does not behave properly.

Solution

In our opinion, it is safe to refrain from using WMLScript for client-side scripting if you are developing an application for the public where the likelihood of using different devices to access your application is high. If you are developing an intranet application where you have more deterministic control over the type of devices used, WMLScript seems a safe bet. To really build robust applications, it is imperative that you check the MIME type supported by the client through the use of the

`HTTP_ACCEPT` environment variable. Even then, implementation bugs might cause your application to fail.

21.1.12 Cookies problem

While cookies are commonly used in web applications, it is a big no-no for current WAP applications. If you come from a web development background, it is likely that you would use cookies for maintaining states between decks. Unfortunately, most current WAP devices do not support cookies on the client side.

Problem

You have developed your killer WAP application and everything runs perfectly on all the emulators that you have been using. You have even tailored your content for the different devices. However, when your application runs on the real device, it breaks! You have learned that it is due to the lack of cookie support on the real device and hence the application cannot work correctly.

SESSION OBJECTS   Note that Session objects in ASP make use of cookies for maintaining state. Hence, if cookies support is not available, the Session object will fail.

Solution

There are a number of ways to solve this problem. First, most of the gateways support cookies on behalf of the device. That is, if your user connects to a device that supports cookies, it is possible to maintain state between decks using cookies. However, if you use this approach, your application is now dependent on the WAP gateway that is being used. Users who are using another WAP gateway that does not support cookies will not be able to view your application correctly.

One way to maintain state between decks (without the use of third-party application servers) is to pass values from deck to deck. This can be accomplished using the `<postfield>` element.

21.2   SUMMARY

In this chapter, we have looked at potential problems that beginners to WAP may encounter. It is impossible to detail every single problem that you are likely to see; hopefully we have provided you with some pointers to prevent you from tripping.

PART VII

Dynamic WAP applications with Java technologies

Active Server Pages, discussed in part VI, are not the only means through which a developer can enable the delivery of dynamically generated WML decks. Java, a language developed by Sun Microsystems, is also well suited for the task.

Originally developed for hand-held devices and set-top boxes, Java was later modified by Sun to take advantage of the Web. Today, Java is a mature general purpose programming language with a number of features that make the language well suited for WML development. Some of Java's features include well-designed, portable, object-oriented APIs such as Java servlets, JavaServer Pages (JSP), and JavaMail.

Java servlets and JSP facilitate the dynamic generation of web pages while JavaMail supports accessing services and content on email servers that can then be presented through a WML deck.

C H A P T E R   2 2

Introduction to Java servlets

22.1   OVERVIEW OF SERVLETS

The Java servlet is a server-side technology used in web-based applications. It is an alternative to the Microsoft Active Server Pages (ASP) discussed in part VI.

This chapter provides an overview of the Java servlet as well as its deployment in a typical traditional web-based application. It highlights the relevant application programming interface (API) and methods used to illustrate how a servlet works in a typical web-based application. We do not intend to provide detailed coverage of the servlet technology and servlet programming here.

The next chapter explains how servlets may be extended to provide solutions to dynamic Wireless Application Protocol (WAP) applications.

22.1.1   What are servlets

As with many other server-side technologies such as Common Gateway Interface (CGI), ASP, server-side JavaScript, and Personal Home Page scripting (more commonly called PHP), servlets enable a web application developer to incorporate back-end processing on the fly, yielding results to client requests dynamically. In the case where the servlet needs to pass the dynamic response to the client browser via the web server, the servlet must generate the HyperText Markup Language (HTML) code that the client browser can interpret. The generated data stream should contain the appropriate content type (e.g., text/html) in the HyperText Transfer Protocol (HTTP) header.

Figure 22.1 shows the role of a servlet in a typical web-based application involving back-end database access:

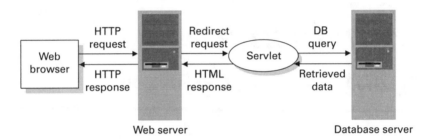

Figure 22.1   The role of a servlet in a web-based application

In web-based applications, a servlet is often invoked as a result of an applet making a request from the client browser, or through the submission of an HTML form by the client. The requested servlet is then loaded and executed at the server side to accomplish the commissioned task such as retrieving information from a database. Note that the servlet in question does not necessarily reside on the same host machine as the web server.

There are various ways that a servlet may be invoked. We shall discuss them later in the chapter.

22.1.2   Why servlets

The Java servlet is specifically designed to overcome some of the well-known problems of existing alternative server-side technologies. In particular:

- A servlet is a lightweight task that can be executed in the form of a thread.
- A servlet shares the same memory space as the server responsible for loading it.
- A servlet can remain in the memory, unlike a CGI process which terminates once it has finished executing.

With these features in place, servlets offer three advantages.

Portability—As the developing programming language used is the Java language, servlets are portable across different host machine platforms as well as different operating systems. That is, you can run your servlets on any machine where there is a Java virtual machine (JVM).

Scalability—Servlets can run as lightweight threads to handle multiple client requests. This will avoid the enormous resource burden imposed on the host as compared to running the same number of CGI processes.

Performance—A servlet can be initialized once and reside in memory to service subsequent client requests without having to be loaded and initialized for each request.

22.2   SOFTWARE USED FOR DEVELOPMENT

Before we lead you deeper into the use of Java servlets, we shall first specify in this section the software that we use in this book for developing and running the servlet-related applications. The suggested software is by no means the only possible tool. You should consult books on servlet programming as well as relevant web sites such as http://java.sun.com/ to get updated information on available tools for the platform on which you wish to develop your servlets.

A few categories of software to consider are the operating system, Java Developer's Kit (JDK), Java Servlet Development Kit (JSDK), web server, servlet loader, database management system, and Java Database Connectivity (JDBC) driver for database connectivity. The software used in the various categories is:

- The operating systems used in this book are Windows NT 4.0 and Windows 98.

- JDK 1.2.2 is used to develop the Java code in a servlet. You can download the latest JDK from http://www.java.sun.com/.

- JSDK 2.2 is used to support the Java servlet classes and interfaces used. It can be downloaded from http://www.java.sun.com/products/servlet/index.html.

- The web servers used are Microsoft Internet Information Server (IIS) on Windows NT and Microsoft Personal Web Server (PWS) on Windows 98.

- Since neither web server supports servlets natively, we need to install a third-party servlet loader. JRun, which can be downloaded from http://www.allaire.com/, is chosen. An example of a web server that supports servlets natively is the Java Web Server (JWS).

- For the database system, we will use both Microsoft SQL 7.0 and Microsoft Access.

- The component that enables a Java servlet to communicate with a database system is the JDBC API. A JDBC driver is required to bridge the gap between the Java code and the database. We will use the JDBC-ODBC bridge in this book for the simple reason that it comes with the JDK used and that no other vendor-dependent software needs to be downloaded. The latter reason is important in helping us to stay as unbiased as possible in product selection. We will discuss JDBC in greater detail in the next chapter.

There are many other Java development tools that you should seriously look into when you are ready to develop large-scale enterprise applications. These tools will shield you from much of the low-level programming discussed in the next few chapters. Typically, these tools may incorporate an integrated development environment (IDE), graphical user interface (GUI), as well as libraries and wizards to ease the job of a developer. Some of these rapid application development (RAD) tools include Kawa by Allaire, IBM's VisualAge for Java, and Visual J++ from Microsoft.

There are some products classified as (Java) application servers that provide a framework and a wealth of utilities and tools for building enterprise applications. They incorporate the support for many other enabling technologies such as Enterprise JavaBeans (EJB), JDBC, and distributed computing platform. Some useful utilities include code generation for performing a task, as well as ease of deploying the enabling technologies supported. This category includes products such as Inprise's AppServer, BEA WebLogic Server, and Enhydra Application Server.

22.3 SERVLET FRAMEWORK

Figure 22.2 outlines the hierarchy of the interfaces and classes for developing servlets. Please refer to appendix F for a full listing of the interfaces and classes.

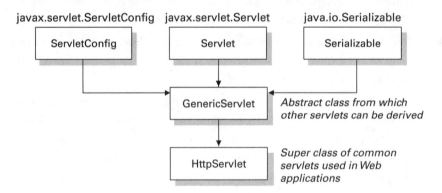

Figure 22.2 Servlet hierarchy

The top-level containers in figure 22.2 are three interfaces, namely `ServletConfig`, `Servlet`, and `Serializable`, from which servlet classes are implemented. The first two interfaces belong to the javax.servlet package and will be discussed further in this chapter, while the third is an interface in the java.io package.

A class that implements the `Serializable` interface implies that an instance of the class (i.e., object) can be written to a stream and the recipient of the serialized object can receive it as an object instead of a stream of unrelated data fields.

We will now explore the core of the servlet hierarchy:

Using the Servlet interface

All servlets are implemented from this interface. It defines the following methods:

```
init()         ⎤
service()      ⎬  life-cycle methods
destroy()      ⎦
getServletConfig()
getServletInfo()
```

The life-cycle methods are elaborated in the next section where the life cycle of a typical servlet is discussed.

Use the getServletConfig() method to obtain the start-up information of the servlet which is passed to the init() method. Use the getServletInfo() method to return a string containing information about the servlet such as author, copyright, and version.

A servlet, however, typically subclasses (using extends in Java) GenericServlet (which implements the Servlet interface) or HttpServlet, a descendant of GenericServlet. We will look at the latter two classes next and see how we can declare a servlet.

Using the GenericServlet abstract class

This abstract class eases the task of writing a servlet. It provides the necessary life-cycle methods and configuration methods required of a servlet. In the simplest implementation, the developer needs only implement the service() method, a life-cycle abstract method that characterizes the application domain.

GenericServlet is an abstract class that extends java.lang.Object and its declaration follows:

```
public abstract class GenericServlet
        implements Servlet, ServletConfig, java.io.Serializable
```

The GenericServlet class consists of numerous methods, among which are the life-cycle methods mentioned earlier: init(), service(), and destroy().

The following shows the declaration of a servlet, FirstServlet, by extending GenericServlet:

```
public class FirstServlet extends GenericServlet {
    . . . . . . . .
}
```

Using the HttpServlet abstract class

This abstract class extends the GenericServlet class to provide a convenient framework for handling the HTTP protocol.

The declaration of `HttpServlet` is:

```
public abstract class HttpServlet extends GenericServlet
        implements java.io.Serializable
```

To declare a servlet, `WebServlet`, by extending `HttpServlet`:

```
public class WebServlet extends HttpServlet {
       . . . . . . .
}
```

22.4   LIFE CYCLE OF A SERVLET

The life cycle of a servlet has three events:

- Servlet is loaded into memory by a server, then initialized
- Servlet processes client requests
- Servlet is removed by server

The life-cycle method involved for each stage is init(), service(), and destroy() respectively.

22.4.1   Initializing a servlet

Loading a servlet into memory is associated with an initialization process. A servlet can be loaded once but accessed many times by continuing to reside in the memory. The servlet is also initialized only once—at the time of loading. This improves the performance in responding to subsequent requests directed to the servlet.

If the servlet developer does not wish to implement any initialization tasks specific to the servlet in question, the init() method provided in GenericServlet can be executed:

```
private transient ServletConfig config;        ❶
public void init(ServletConfig config)
                 throws ServletException {
   this.config = config;
   log("init");         ❷
}
```

Code comments

❶ The transient (unserializable) `ServletConfig` object, *config*, is initialized by the parameter passed to the init() method. The parameter contains the servlet's start-up configuration and initialization parameters. This is necessary so that the appropriate information can be correctly returned when it is being queried via the getServletConfig() method at a later point during the lifetime of the servlet.

❷ The log() method is called to log a specified string message into the servlet log file. In fact, the method also logs the class name together with the message as shown in its definition in GenericServlet:

```
public void log(String msg) {
    getServletContext.log(getClass().getName() + ": " + msg);
}>
```

However, there are some well-justified reasons that the developer may want to override this method:

- Initialization of some application-specific variables using some of the initialization parameters
- Management of some resources, such as shared data stores

Overriding init()

This example shows a way of overriding the init() method:

```
public void init(ServletConfig config)
                 throws ServletException {
    super.init (config);        ❶
    String temp = config.getInitParameter("startValue");      ❷
    int counter = Integer.parseInt(temp);
}
```

Code comments

❶ The base class's init() method is first called to keep the servlet's configuration information as the private ServletConfig object, *config*, from which configuration information may be retrieved whenever it is needed. If this step is omitted, the developer should write his own code to store the configuration information if he may need such information at a later point in time.

❷ Next, the value of an initialization parameter, *startValue*, is extracted and stored as an integer variable named *counter*, which is specific to the servlet in question.

Note that in implementation, you need to include the appropriate if statement or try-catch Java code to handle any logic error or exception. For example, it may not make sense for temp in the application to be null, which occurs if startValue does not exist. In the assignment statement for counter illustrated above, the parsing method, parseInt(), will give rise to a NumberFormatException exception if temp is null.

22.4.2   Servicing client requests

The service() method in a servlet is responsible for handling the incoming client requests. A multithreading mechanism is used to handle multiple client requests simultaneously. It is the developer's responsibility to make sure that access to shared resources is properly synchronized to achieve data integrity.

The Servlet interface contains a declaration of service():

```
public void service (ServletRequest req, ServletResponse res)
                throws ServletException, IOException;
```

A `ServletRequest` object, *req*, encapsulates information of the client request to the servlet while the `ServletResponse` object, *res*, contains results to be returned to the client.

The most common methods to which `service()` delegates HTTP requests are `doGet()` and `doPost()`. The `doGet()` method of `HttpServlet` should handle the HTTP request with data passed in via the HTTP GET method. On the other hand, the `doPost()` method handles the HTTP request with data passed in via the HTTP POST method.

Other methods that handle other types of HTTP requests are `doDelete()`, `doPut()`, `doOptions()`, and `doTrace()`, of which the latter two are normally not overridden.

Typically, the `doGet()` or `doPost()` method is overridden to handle the following tasks:

- Retrieve data from the incoming request.
- Set the HTTP header information as deemed appropriate—for example, the content type of the response to be sent back to the client.
- Generate the rest of the response data as a Java writer stream or Java output stream.
- If the writer is used to write the response data, make sure that all necessary HTTP header information is set before any response data is output since the latter activity will cause the HTTP header to be flushed any time.

22.4.3 Termination

The `destroy()` method releases all servlet resources, including database connections. It also provides the last chance to write or commit persistent data by writing data into files or the database, and to make final log entries into relevant log files.

As in the case with the `init()` method, if the servlet developer does not wish to implement any specific tasks in this method, the `destroy()` method provided in `GenericServlet` can be executed.

22.5 INVOCATION OF A SERVLET

In a typical web-based application, a servlet can be invoked in a few different ways. Consider a compiled servlet, `MyServlet.class`, placed under the servlet directory expected by the servlet loader used, and at the host www.myHost.com. Furthermore, the servlet expects a parameter, *name*, to be passed via the HTTP GET request method when it is called.

- The servlet can be invoked through the specification of the URL of the servlet `class` at a browser interface (figure 22.3):

Figure 22.3 Specification of servlet's URL in the Address input box of the browser interface

- The same servlet may be invoked via an HTML form that takes in a username input using a simple text input box. The servlet's URL is specified through the `action` attribute of the `<FORM>` tag in the `html` document and the default request method, `GET`, is used:

```
<FORM action="http://www.myHost.com/servlets/MyServlet">
    Name: <INPUT type="text" name="username" size="50">
          <INPUT type="submit">
          <INPUT type="reset">
</FORM>
```

- A server-side-include document (with extension shtml) may also be used to invoke the servlet through the `<SERVLET>` tag:

```
<HTML>
<H1> Welcome To My First Servlet </H1>
    <SERVLET
       name="testServlet"
       code="http://www.myHost.com/servlets/MyServlet">
       <param name="username" value="Soo Mee">
    </SERVLET>
</HTML>
```

In the last case, the shtml document is parsed, and the servlet specified as an attribute of the `<SERVLET>` tag is loaded and executed. The results or response of the servlet will then be sent to the requesting client together with the rest of the HTML code.

22.6 HANDLING REQUESTS WITH SERVICE METHODS

When a servlet is invoked due to an HTTP request, the servlet loader will load the servlet into memory if it is not already loaded. The request is then handled by the appropriate service method, `doGet()` or `doPost()`.

Service methods typically perform the following tasks:

- Retrieving inbound parameter values
- Processing the values as required by the application
- Sending the results to the requesting client

This section will discuss how the parameter values passed to the servlet can be retrieved for further processing, as well as how the servlet generates a response to the client.

22.6.1 Retrieving parameters from the client

In section 22.5, we have seen how parameters can be passed to a servlet during the invocation of the servlet for processing. Before the servlet can process parameter values, it first retrieves them explicitly using either the getParameter() method or the getParameterValues() method. The signatures of both methods are specified in the ServletRequest interface, which the HttpServletRequest class extends:

```
public String getParameter(String name);
public String[] getParameterValues(String name);
```

The getParameter() method is used for parameters that have only one value.

The getParameterValues() method is used for parameters that may have more than one value. All the possible values constitute the array of strings returned by the calling of the method.

For example, consider the following form with two form elements, username and interests, where the first is submitted as a text string while the second consists of possible multiple strings, depending on what the user chooses from the selection list:

```
<FORM action="http://localhost/servlet/RegisterServlet">    ❶
    Name: <INPUT type="text" name="username" size="50">    ◄──  This
    <BR>                                                         defines a
    Tell us your interests:                                      text input
    <SELECT name="interests" multiple size="1">                  box to
        <OPTION value="Cycling">Cycling</OPTION>      This defines  capture
        <OPTION value="Gardening">Gardening</OPTION>  a selection   input for
        <OPTION value="Reading">Reading</OPTION>      list of four  username
        <OPTION value="Swimming">Swimming</OPTION>    options of
    </SELECT>                                         interests
    <BR><BR>
    <INPUT type="submit">    ◄──  This defines a button that the user can click to
    <INPUT type="reset">          submit the form together with the values of the
</FORM>                           username and interests form elements
```

Code comments

❶ The action attribute of the <FORM> element specifies the servlet to execute when the user submits the form.

This code shows how the servlet, RegisterServlet, retrieves the values of the *username* and *interests* elements:

```
String name = request.getParameter("username");
String[] intts = request.getParameterValues("interests");
```

If the user selects *Cycling* and *Swimming* as his interests, the parameter, `interests`, would have the values `Cycling` and `Swimming` as assigned in the HTML code. When retrieved into *intts* in `RegisterServlet`, we have the following:

```
intts[0] = "Cycling"
intts[1] = "Swimming"
```

Also, the expression, `intts.length`, will be evaluated to the value 2.

In the previous example, if the following is used to retrieve the interests of the user, only the first selected interest is retrieved:

```
String intts = request.getParameter("interests");
```

22.6.2 Responding to the client

One important reason that a servlet, or any server-side program for that matter, is used is to generate dynamic responses to the client. A typical HTTP response consists of a *status line*, a *header*, and a *body*.

For example, to generate a response to a client, the Multipurpose Internet Mail Extensions (MIME) content-type value in the HTTP header has to be set to the appropriate value so that the content in the body can be interpreted correctly. Some examples of the content-type value are: `text/plain`, `text/html`, `image/gif`, `video/mpeg`, and so forth.

To set the MIME type and character set, use the `setContentType()` method. The signature of this method is specified in the `ServletResponse` interface, which the `HttpServletResponse` class extends:

```
public void setContentType(String type);
```

In addition to content type, two other methods may be used:

- `setHeader()` is used to set a header field with a specified name to some string value
- `setDateHeader()` is used if the value is a *date* type (expressed in terms of milliseconds since the epoch)

The signatures of the two methods are:

```
public void setHeader(String name, String value);
public void setDateHeader(String name, long date);
```

To generate the body content, specifically HTML content for an HTML browser, a servlet makes use of a stream object. A servlet basically uses a writer stream object or an output stream object to send out data. The output stream can be used to write binary data while the writer stream is used to write formatted text characters. Both the `getOutputStream()` method for obtaining an output stream and the `getWriter()` method for getting a writer stream are declared in the `ServletResponse` interface:

```
public ServletOutputStream getOutputStream() throws IOException;
public PrintWriter getWriter() throws IOException;
```

The servlet uses one of the following declarations depending on the type of stream the developer chooses to work with:

```
PrintWriter out = response.getWriter();
ServletOutputStream out = response.getOutputStream();
```

A precaution: If a writer is used, the content type must be set before calling the getWriter() method in order to use the character set specified by SetContentType(). If an output stream is used, the content type must be set before the output stream is used to output other information.

22.6.3 Generating dynamic HTML content

We shall now use a simple example to illustrate what we've learned about the interaction between an HTML-enabled client and a servlet. We shall design a commonly seen registration page, which consists of a form that prompts the user to enter a user name and to choose his interests. Upon submission of the form, the servlet, RegisterServlet, is invoked. The servlet's tasks include retrieving the user's information and displaying it in the browser via dynamically generated HTML content.

We can reuse the form presented earlier in the first HTML page that will be loaded to interact with the user:

```
<HTML>
<!-- register.html -->
<HEAD><TITLE> Registration </TITLE></HEAD>
<BODY>
<H1>Member Registration</H1>
<FORM action="http://localhost/servlet/RegisterServlet" method="get">
   Name: <INPUT type="text" name="username" size="50">
   <BR>
   Tell us your interests:
   <SELECT name="interests" multiple size="1">
      <OPTION value="Cycling">Cycling</OPTION>
      <OPTION value="Gardening">Gardening</OPTION>
      <OPTION value="Reading">Reading</OPTION>
      <OPTION value="Swimming">Swimming</OPTION>
   </SELECT>
   <BR><BR>
   <INPUT type="submit">
   <INPUT type="reset">
</FORM>
</BODY>
</HTML>
```

When a user accesses this HTML document in a web browser, a Member Registration form appears (figure 22.4). In the example, the user enters the username, Soo Mee, and chooses two options, Cycling and Swimming, from the list of interests. (The user makes multiple selections by pressing the control (CTRL) key when choosing items from the list.)

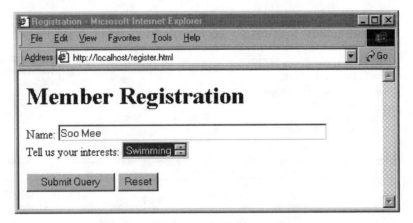

Figure 22.4   The Member Registration page

When Submit Query is clicked, the following servlet is invoked. Note that the service method responsible for handling the request using the get HTTP request method is doGet().

```
/* Registration processing : RegisterServlet.java */
import java.io.*;
import javax.servlet.*;
import javax.servlet.http.*;

public class RegisterServlet extends HttpServlet
{
    /* Servicing client request using HTTP GET method */
    public void doGet (HttpServletRequest  request,          ❶
                       HttpServletResponse response)
             throws ServletException, IOException
    {
        // Retrieve input parameters, username and interests
        String name=request.getParameter("username");        ❷
        String[] intts=request.getParameterValues("interests");   ❸

        // Set content type and other response header fields
        response.setContentType("text/html");                ❹

        // Create a writer stream
        PrintWriter out = response.getWriter();              ❺

        // Output HTML contents
        out.println("<html>");
        out.println("<head><title>Registration</title></head>");
        out.println("<body>");
        out.println("<p>");
```

```
        out.println("Hello, " + name + "!");          ◄─┐ Writes the retrieved
        out.println("</p>");                              │ username value back to the
        out.println("<p>Interests in record:<BR>");       │ client browser for display
        out.println("<ul>");
        for (int i=0; i<intts.length; i++) {             ┐  The for
            out.println ("<li>" + intts[i] + "</li>");   │  loop lists all
        }                                                │  the interests
        out.println("</ul>");                            │  that the user
        out.println("</p>");                             │  has chosen
        out.println("</body>");                          │  earlier
        out.println("</html>");                          ┘
        out.close();
    }
}
```

Code comments

❶ Since `register.html` uses the HTTP GET method to submit the form, the servlet must include the `doGet()` service method to handle the client request when the form is submitted.

❷ Uses the `getParameter()` method of the request object to retrieve the single value of username.

❸ Uses the `getParameterValues()` method of the request object to retrieve multiple values of interests. The values are assigned as an array to the servlet's variable, `intts`.

❹ The application only outputs HTML content. Hence, use the `setContentType()` method of the response object to set the content type to `text/html`.

❺ Uses the `getWriter()` method to create a writer stream object. This object is used to output the body content of the HTTP response message to the client.

The client displays the generated HTML content as shown in figure 22.5.

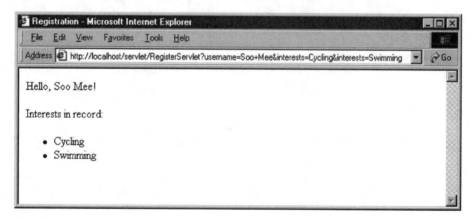

Figure 22.5 Response page generated by RegisterServlet

Two values (`Cycling` and `Swimming`) for the parameter name, `interests`, were passed to `RegisterServlet` as indicated in the `Address` box of the browser in figure 22.5.

If you choose to view the source, the content of the generated page is displayed (figure 22.6).

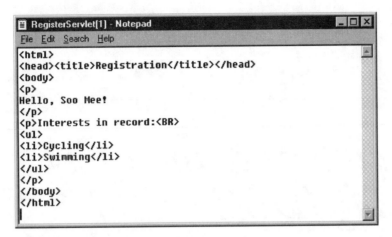

Figure 22.6   HTML code of the response page generated by RegisterServlet

22.7 SUMMARY

This chapter presents a crash course on Java servlets. It explains how a servlet is invoked, how its service method handles a request from the client, and how dynamic HTML content is generated.

In the next chapter, we will look at how a servlet accesses data stored in a database and generates dynamic information based on the result retrieved from the database.

C H A P T E R 2 3

Database connectivity using JDBC

23.1 INTRODUCTION

As most real-life applications of considerable scale need to store some form of application-specific data, a database is often the method of choice to organize and manage the data. Before we look at how a servlet can perform backend processing involving database access, let us first look at how Java works with databases.

The Java Database Connectivity (JDBC™) API enables a developer to write a single version of Java code to access data in different database systems over different operating systems, thus achieving database transparency. The java.sql package contains interfaces and classes for writing code to connect to a database and execute an SQL statement. The Connection and ResultSet interfaces and the DriverManager class are abstractions of concepts for database access across different database systems.

Each database vendor implements its own JDBC driver to bridge the gap between the application code and a database management system (DBMS), making it possible to retain the application code for accessing databases when you need to port your data to a different database management system.

This chapter presents the fundamentals and use of the JDBC 1.0 API, and a brief introduction to the additional features in JDBC 2.0.

23.2   *DATABASE CONNECTIVITY APIs*

The JDBC API tries to achieve the objectives that Microsoft's ODBC (Open DataBase Connectivity) API was designed to provide. The ODBC API offers the ability to connect to various databases on different platforms. However, it is not natural to use ODBC API for pure-Java applications because the ODBC API was developed with the pointer capability of application languages, such as C, in mind. As discussed in chapter 18, applications written in object-oriented languages that do not include support for pointers result in inefficient or inappropriate translation from the application language to the language used at the ODBC driver level.

In fact, Microsoft recognized the problem with the emergence of various programming and scripting languages that differ from the underlying language used in the ODBC API. It has since introduced other APIs such as OLE (object linking and embedding) DB, ADO (ActiveX Data Objects), and RDS (remote data service). Like the JDBC API, these APIs provide similar functionality and object-oriented interfaces to databases that can be used to execute SQL statements. Unlike JDBC, however, these Microsoft-developed efforts are not as portable.

23.3   *TYPES OF JDBC DRIVERS*

JDBC drivers fall into four categories:

Type 1: JDBC-ODBC bridge plus ODBC driver

The JDBC-ODBC bridge is provided in JDK 1.1 and later. The bridge provides database access via the ODBC driver, which must be loaded and configured on the client machine that uses this driver. It is best used when the driver installation is required for small numbers of client machines, or when the JDBC calls are invoked via server-side code and only the machine hosting the server-side code needs to be installed with the driver. It is also a good choice for prototyping purposes.

Type 2: Native-API partly Java driver

These drivers convert JDBC calls into calls that are native to the database system in use. As in the previous case, setup is needed on the client machines. The operating system-specific binary code for native connectivity interfaces must be loaded on each client machine.

Type 3: JDBC-Net pure Java driver

These drivers convert JDBC calls into a DBMS-independent network protocol, which is then translated into a DBMS-specific protocol by a server. The server acts as a middleman that communicates between pure Java clients and different database systems. This driver provides the most flexibility compared to the other alternatives. However, the application making the JDBC calls has no direct access to the DBMS server.

Type 4: Native-protocol pure Java driver

Using this driver type, JDBC calls are converted directly into the network protocol used by the specific DBMS. As most of the protocols are proprietary, the database vendors are the main source of this category of drivers. Since these JDBC drivers do not have to translate database requests into ODBC or a native connectivity interface, or pass the request on to another server, performance is better.

The following web site contains a link to a list of at least 121 available drivers: http://www.java.sun.com/products/jdbc

23.4 BASIC TASKS IN DATABASE ACCESS

The basic tasks performed by a Java application or servlet to access a database are:

- Loading the appropriate JDBC driver
- Establishing a connection to the database
- Formulating and executing an SQL statement

23.4.1 Loading the JDBC driver

The `Class.forName(driver_name)` method may be used to load a specific driver. When it is loaded, the driver creates an instance of itself and registers it with the class, `java.sql.DriverManager`. The `DriverManager` class is responsible for loading all the JDBC drivers found in the system property, `jdbc.drivers`.

For example, the following statement loads the JDBC-ODBC bridge (Type 1 driver): `Class.forName("sun.jdbc.odbc.JdbcOdbcDriver");`

The following example loads a Type 4 JDBC driver from Ashna Incorporated for Microsoft SQL: `Class.forName("com.ashna.jturbo.driver.Driver");`

23.4.2 Establishing a connection to the database

To connect to a database, use the `DriverManager.getConnection(db_url)` method, where `db_url` is the JDBC URL of the database with the following format: `jdbc:<subprotocol>:<dbname>`

The first component in the JDBC URL specification is the protocol used, which in this case is `jdbc`.

`<subprotocol>` specifies a particular database connectivity method such as odbc if an ODBC driver is used, or JTurbo if the JTurbo JDBC driver from Ashna Incorporated is used.

`<dbname>` indicates the database to connect to, possibly with user ID and password as a means of authorization proof to access the specified database. It is specified according to the following format:

```
//host_name:port/database_name;UID=usrid;PWD=passwd
```

Next are some valid examples of the JDBC URL using either the JDBC-ODBC bridge or the JTurbo JDBC driver:

```
jdbc:odbc:myDB
jdbc:JTurbo://myHost/myDB;UID=sa;PWD=admin
jdbc:JTurbo://myHost:1433/myDB
```

Alternatively, the user ID and password can be specified through the getConnection() method as shown in the following examples:

```
Connection conn =
     DriverManager.getConnection("jdbc:odbc:myDB;UID=sa;PWD=admin");

Connection conn =
     DriverManager.getConnection("jdbc:odbc:myDB", "sa", "admin");
```

If JDBC-ODBC is used, we need to associate a data source name (DSN) with the database through the ODBC configuration facility that may be invoked from Windows' Control Panel.

23.4.3 Formulating and executing SQL statements

Once a connection to the database is established, we can construct and execute SQL statements:

```
Statement stmt = conn.createStatement();      ❶
String query = "SELECT Title FROM books";     ❷
ResultSet rs = stmt.executeQuery(query);      ❸
```

Code comments

❶ Uses the createStatement() method of the Connection interface to create a Statement object.

❷ Formulates an SQL statement as a Java string.

❸ Executes the SQL query via the executeQuery() method of the Statement interface. Assigns the result of the query to a ResultSet variable.

Each of the statement strings constructed will be compiled and the driver will perform the value mapping so that the underlying database system can understand it. If the statement is executed multiple times in the application, each time varying only in some parameter values, we can use a precompiled statement to improve the performance. Such a statement is provided as a `PreparedStatement` object.

Here is a simple example:

```
PreparedStatement stmt =
        conn.prepareStatement("SELECT Title FROM books WHERE ISBN=?");   ❶

stmt.setString (1, "188477766X");      ❷
ResultSet rs = stmt.executeQuery();    ❸
```

Code comments

❶ Uses the `prepareStatement()` method of the Connection interface to create a `PreparedStatement` object.

❷ Before using the prepared statement, replace the ? symbol in the statement with the actual value to use. This is accomplished by using one of the value setting methods such as `setString()` or `setInt()`, depending on the data type of the replacing value. The setting method has two parameters. The first is the index of the ? symbol to be replaced in the statement, where the index count starts from 1, running from the left to right of the statement string. The second is the value that is to replace the ? symbol.

❸ This line Executes the SQL query via the `executeQuery()` method of the `PreparedStatement`. Assigns the result of the query to a `ResultSet` variable.

23.5 DATABASE-INDEPENDENT CODE

Any application that contains a `Class.forName()` method with hardcoded driver parameter, or a `DriverManager.getConnection()` method with hardcoded JDBC URL string as described in section 23.4, cannot be independent of the database system used.

To achieve database-independent coding so that the same application code stays intact in the event of a migration of data to a different database, we use a property file. This property file contains information that is relevant to the specific database used. The information must include the driver and the JDBC URL.

Consider the following property file, `DBInfo.properties`, written for a database with properties defined with the names `Driver` and `URL`:

```
Driver=sun.jdbc.odbc.JdbcOdbcDriver     ⟵          Specifies the
URL=jdbc:odbc:myDB   ⟵  Identifies the protocols and    JDBC-ODBC
                        database, myDB, to be used       driver
```

We can access the property file via an `InputStream` or `FileInputStream` of the java.io package, or through the use of the `ResourceBundle` class in the java.util package. We will next present the relevant code that makes use of the two methods.

23.5.1 Accessing properties using InputStream

First, load the property file, `DBInfo.properties`, as an `InputStream`. Load all the properties in the file as a `Properties` object, which provides the `getProperty()` method to retrieve a property that is specified in the property file.

In an application that makes use of the database with DSN, myDB, would include the following lines to take advantage of a property file via an `InputStream`:

```
import java.io.*;   ◄─────────    We need to import this package
import java.util.Properties;       because we need to use one of its
                                   classes: InputStream or
   .                               FileInputStream.
   .
   .
public class processData {
   . . . . . .
   Connection conn = null;
   InputStream inputstream =                    Loads the property file
         ClassLoader.getSystemResourceAsStream  as an InputStream.
         ("DBInfo.properties");                 An alternative is to
   // FileInputStream filestream =              load the files as a
      // new FileInputStream("DBInfo.properties"); ◄┘ FileInputStream.

   Properties db = new Properties ();   Loads the input stream as a
   db.load (inputstream);   ◄───────    Properties object

   Class.forName (db.getProperty("Driver"));
   conn = DriverManager.getConnection (db.getProperty("URL"));  ❶

   . . . . . .
}
```

Code comments

❶ Uses the `getProperty()` method to extract the value assigned to each of the Driver and URL properties specified in the original property file.

23.5.2 Accessing properties using ResourceBundle

The `ResourceBundle` utility class consists of methods to open a property file and to abstract string information for a specified property.

In an application that makes use of the database with DSN, myDB, would include the following lines to take advantage of a property file:

```
import java.util.*;   ◄──    We need to import this package
   .                         because we need to use one of its
   .                         classes: ResourceBundle
   .
public class processData {
   . . . . . .
   Connection conn = null;
   ResourceBundle db = ResourceBundle.getBundle ("DBInfo");  ❶
```

```
Class.forName (db.getString("Driver"));
conn = DriverManager.getConnection (db.getString("URL"));
```
❷

```
      . . . . . .
}
```

Code comments

❶ Uses the `getBundle()` method to open the needed property file named `DBInfo.properties`.

❷ Uses the `getString()` method to extract the value assigned to each of the Driver and URL properties specified in the property file.

23.6 *SERVLET EXAMPLE: LIBRARY BOOK SEARCH*

This section presents an example of a servlet that connects to a library database and retrieves book information. To specify a book to search for, the user enters an ISBN number through a simple HTML form.

The front end—The front-end component is an interface to the user. We shall use a simple HTML document, `search.html`. The document consists of an HTML form, which has an input field named `isbn`, a submit button, and a reset button.

The back end—When the user submits the form after entering the ISBN of a book, the backend retrieving process is performed by a servlet whose source code is kept in `BookSearchServlet.java`.

The database—The database used in this example is implemented using Microsoft Access. In the book searching function, two tables, `books` and `copies`, will be used. The name of the database for this library system is LIBRARY.

23.6.1 Creating the front end

The user enters the ISBN number of the book he is interested in via an HTML form (figure 23.1):

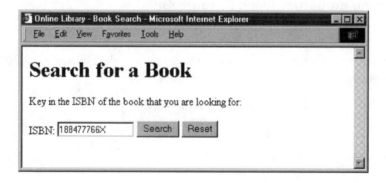

Figure 23.1 HTML form for entering the ISBN of a book to be searched

The HTML code for the user interface page is:

```
<HTML>
<HEAD>
<TITLE>Online Library - Book Search</TITLE>
</HEAD>
<BODY>
<H1>Search for a Book</H1>
Key in the ISBN of the book that you are looking for:
  <FORM action="http://localhost/servlet/BookSearchServlet" method="POST">
      ISBN: <input type="text" name="isbn" size="15">
      <INPUT type="submit" value="Search">
      <INPUT type="reset">
  </FORM>
</BODY>
</HTML>
```

Indicates the servlet to be triggered when the form is submitted through the click on `Search`

Captures the user's input for the ISBN of a book. The name of the field is `isbn`

23.6.2 Creating a data store for book information

In our example, we will use the Microsoft Access database system. Figure 23.2 shows the structure and relationship of the tables used in this example:

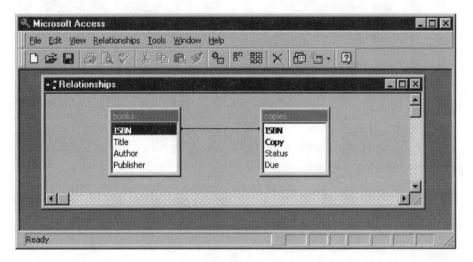

Figure 23.2 Relationships diagram of the tables in the LIBRARY database

The example is a simplified view of database tables used in our library book-searching example. We have omitted details of a sophisticated library system such as accommodation of more than one author, so that we can concentrate on demonstrating the programming features of the servlet.

Creating a data source name

To use a JDBC-ODBC bridge in our servlet to access the database, we must create a data source name for the database. You can associate a data source name, say `myLib`, to the LIBRARY database through the ODBC configuration facility that may be invoked from the Windows Control Panel.

23.6.3   Servlet for retrieving book information

There are two possible responses to the user's request to inquire a book's information and loaning status: one showing the book's details if the book is found in the library's database, the other responding to an unsuccessful search for the requested book. The servlet must be able to handle both cases.

Figure 23.3 shows the response due to a successful search of the database:

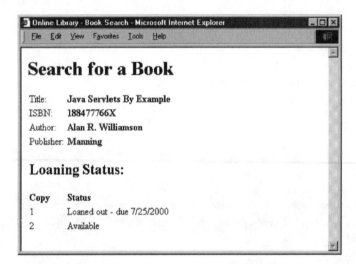

Figure 23.3
Result screen of a
successful search

An example of the response due to an unsuccessful search of the database is shown in figure 23.4.

Figure 23.4
Result screen of an
unsuccessful search

Understanding the servlet code

Listing 23.1 is the code for the servlet invoked upon the submission of the form that captures the ISBN of a book.

Listing 23.1   Code listing of BookSearchServlet

```
/* Library Book Search: BookSearchServlet.java */
import java.io.*;
import javax.servlet.*;
import javax.servlet.http.*;
import java.sql.*;
import java.util.*;

public class BookSearchServlet extends HttpServlet
{
    public void doPost (HttpServletRequest  request,
                        HttpServletResponse response)
            throws ServletException, IOException
    {
        response.setContentType("text/html");

        PrintWriter out = response.getWriter();
        out.println("<HTML><HEAD>");
        out.println("<TITLE>Online Library - Book Search</TITLE>");
        out.println("</HEAD><BODY>");
        out.println("<H1>Search for a Book</H1>");
        out.println("<TABLE>");
        try {
            processSearch(out, request);      ❷
        } catch (Exception e) {
            out.println("Error in processing enquiry SQL.");
        }
        out.println("</TABLE>");
        out.println("</BODY></HTML>");
        out.close();
    }
    protected static void processSearch (PrintWriter out,
                                         HttpServletRequest req)
            throws ServletException, IOException, Exception
    {
        Connection con=null;
        Statement  stmt=null;
        String     query=null;
        ResultSet  rs=null;

        String isbn = req.getParameter("isbn");
        try {

            Class.forName ("sun.jdbc.odbc.JdbcOdbcDriver");
            con = DriverManager.getConnection ("jdbc:odbc:myLib");
            stmt = con.createStatement();

        } catch (Exception e)  {
            System.err.println ("Exception: DB connection...");
            System.err.println (e);
        }
```

Services a request using the HTTP POST method

Sets the content type of output stream generated

Creates a writer stream object ❶

Closes the writer stream after generating the necessary HTML content to the client

Variables for accessing the database

Extracts ISBN from the request form

❸

```
try {
    query = "SELECT Title, Author, Publisher " +           ❹
            "FROM books WHERE ISBN='" + isbn + "'";
    rs = stmt.executeQuery (query);

    if (rs.next()) {                                        ❺
        out.println("<TR><TD width=\"60\">Title:</TD>");
        out.println("<TD><B>" + rs.getString("Title") +
                    "</B></TD></TR>");
        out.println("<TR><TD>ISBN:</TD>");
        out.println("<TD><B>" + isbn + "</B></TD></TR>");
        out.println("<TR><TD>Author:</TD>");
        out.println("<TD><B>" + rs.getString("Author") +
                    "</B></TD></TR>");
        out.println("<TR><TD>Publisher:</TD>");
        out.println("<TD><B>" + rs.getString("Publisher") +
                    "</B></TD></TR>");
        rs.close();
    }
    else {
        out.println("<TR><TD width=\"60\">ISBN:</TD>");     ❻
        out.println("<TD><B>" + isbn + "</B></TD></TR>");
        out.println("<TR><TD>Status:</TD>");
        out.println("<TD><B>Not Found</B></TD></TR>");
        rs.close();
        stmt.close();
        con.close();
        return;
    }

} catch (SQLException e) {
    System.err.println ("Exception: Accessing books table...");
    System.err.println (e);
}

try {   ❼
    query = "SELECT Copy, Status, Due FROM copies " +      ❽
            "WHERE ISBN='" + isbn + "'";
    rs = stmt.executeQuery (query);

    out.println("<TR><TD colspan=\"2\"><BR>");
    out.println("<H2>Loaning Status:</H2></TD></TR>");
    out.println("<TR><TD><B>Copy</B></TD>");
    out.println("<TD><B>Status</B></TD></TR>");
    while (rs.next())         ❾
    {
        out.println("<TR><TD>" + rs.getString(1) + "</TD><TD>");   ❿

        int status = rs.getInt(2);
        if (status == 1)                                   ⓫
            out.println("Available");
        else
            out.println("Loaned out - due " + rs.getString(3));
        out.println("</TD></TR>");
```

```
        }
    } catch (SQLException e) {
        System.err.println ("Exception: Accessing copies table...");
        System.err.println (e);
    }
    finally {        ⑫
        try {
            rs.close();
            stmt.close();
            con.close();
        } catch (Exception e) {
            System.err.println ("Exception: Closing DB connection...");
            System.err.println (e);
        }
    }
}
}
}
```

Code comments

❶ Generates HTML code to display title and page header.

❷ Calls another method, processSearch(), to access database and display detailed book information in a table.

❸ Loads the JDBD-ODBC bridge driver and creates a connection to connect to the LIBRARY database.

❹ Formulates and executes a query to the books table for general information of a book with the specified ISBN.

❺ If a book of the specified ISBN is found, generates code to display its title, ISBN, author, and publisher. It is important to close the ResultSet object that holds the general information of the book retrieved from the books table so that it can be reused.

❻ If no book of the specified ISBN is found, generates code to display the ISBN and a "Not Found" status message. You should then close all the objects used to access the database before exiting the processSearch() method.

❼ Executes only if there was a successful retrieval of a book of the specified ISBN from the books table. Queries the copies table for loaning status of all the physical copies of the same ISBN.

❽ Queries the copies table to retrieve all copies of the book with the specified ISBN that the library owns.

❾ Iterates through each copy of the books with the specified ISBN to determine its loaning status.

❿ Displays the copy number, i.e., rs.getString(1), where 1 indicates the first column or field in a record retrieved from the copies table.

⑪ Checks the loaning status of a copy of a book—the second column or field in a retrieved record. If it is not available, displays the date due for the copy concerned.

⑫ Performs the `finally` block as the last step of the entire `try-catch-finally` block to ensure closing of all the objects used in retrieving information from the database.

Troubleshooting the servlet code

A common error that most beginners make concerning database access via the JDBC API is to overlook the proper closing of the `ResultSet` object before exiting the method. It is a good practice to explicitly include in your servlet code the closing statements for the `Statement` and `Connection` objects as soon as you can release the resources.

Assume that rs is not closed in the `finally` block before exiting the `processSearch()` method in our BookSearchServlet.java example. If your default system debugger is Dr. Watson, an error message (figure 23.5) will be displayed if you invoke the servlet a few times by submitting multiple instances of the HTML form.

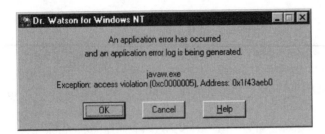

Figure 23.5
Error message box of Dr.
Watson for Windows NT

If you look into the content of the debugger's log file such as drwtsn32.log, assuming Dr. Watson for Windows NT is the debugger, it shows:

```
Application exception occurred:
        App: java.exe (pid=194)
        When: 2/8/2001 @ 22:12:39.520
        Exception number: c0000005 (access violation)
```

When this occurs, check and make appropriate modification to your code and recompile the servlet. You may need to restart the servlet loader.

23.7 JDBC 2.0 FEATURES

The example we use in this chapter makes use of very basic database access functionality that is found in JDBC 1.0.

JDBC 2.0 provides features to support more SQL types and sophisticated processing, as well as improves performance. JDBC 2.0 is compatible with JDBC 1.0. All applications developed using JDBC 1.0 should run well with JDBC 2.0 drivers.

JDBC 2.0 consists of two packages:

- *java.sql*—referred to as JDBC 2.0 Core API, is an extended java.sql of JDBC 1.0
- *javax.sql*—the JDBC 2.0 Optional Package API

Enhancements made in JDBC 2.0 Core API are:

- Scrollable cursor of a `ResultSet`
- Support for new SQL data types such as BLOb (Binary Large Object) and CLOb (Character Large Object)
- Support for user-defined types
- Batch processing of updates to database so as to improve performance by reducing overhead in sending a request, especially to a remote database server

The JDBC 2.0 optional package API facilitates the implementation of a middle-tier Java application or servlet in accessing remote databases by leveraging on some other Java standards extensions such as Java Naming and Directory Interface (JNDI) and Java Transaction Service (JTS). Its features:

- Bind a database *handle* to a simple name for a data source that was registered with a JNDI naming service, thus avoiding the need to register drivers using `DeviceManager` and get a connection using URLs
- Create and maintain a pool of database connections to be allocated to client requests
- Manage transactions where an atomic transaction may involve multiple data sources that may reside on very different platforms

You can find links to documentation of both the core and optional packages at:
http://java.sun.com/products/jdbc/index.html

23.8 SUMMARY

In this chapter, we saw how a Java servlet establishes a connection to a database through the use of an appropriate JDBC-ODBC bridge or JDBC driver. We also learned how to use the JDBC API to load the JDBC driver, make connections to the data source, formulate and execute an SQL query statement, and manipulate the result set and generate HTML code to display the retrieved data in the result set. We also touched on the new features in JDBC 2.0 API.

In the remaining five chapters in this part of the book, we will develop servlets in WAP-based applications with WML front-end instead of HTML front-end on the client or user agent.

CHAPTER 24

Using Java servlets to generate dynamic WAP content

24.1 GENERATING DYNAMIC *WAP* CONTENT

You have seen in part VI how Microsoft ASP technology is used to generate dynamic WML content in a WAP-based application. The concept of performing the same task using Java servlets is much the same.

The main issues undertaken by a typical snippet, be it an ASP document or a Java servlet, that is capable of performing backend processing as well as generating results for a WML-enabled client dynamically are:

- Retrieving the values of WML variables from the calling or referring context
- Specifying the correct content type of the WML deck to be generated

- Overriding specific header information, such as the caching mechanism, as necessary
- Generating valid WML content to form a well-defined WML deck

This chapter will explain how to invoke a servlet and how to use a servlet to process client requests and generate dynamic WML content.

24.2 THE ROLE OF THE SERVLET

Before we plunge into writing servlets, we should first look at where the servlet fits in the whole picture of a typical WAP-based application (figure 24.1):

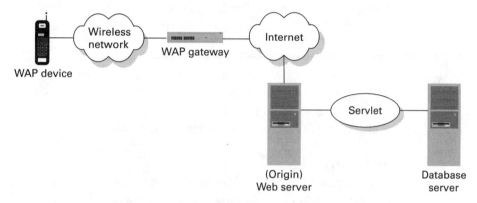

Figure 24.1 Components in a WAP-based application system

As discussed in chapter 22, a servlet processes a client request that is passed from the web server. In a WAP-based application environment, the web server receives the client (i.e., WAP device) request from a remote WAP gateway via the Internet. Alternatively, the WAP gateway and the web server can reside on a single machine. The setup and infrastructure regarding the connectivity of the various components is covered in greater detail in part VIII. Recall that the application-level protocol used in the communication between the WAP gateway and the web server is HTTP. The servlet must understand an HTTP request message that is redirected to it from the web server, as well as generate an HTTP response message to be returned to the client via the web server.

This is exactly what a servlet is doing in a web-based application environment described in chapters 22 and 23. However, one major difference lies in the content it generates. In servicing a web-based client, the servlet generates HTML content that the client can interpret. In servicing a WAP-based client, the servlet generates WML content so that the client can understand.

Hence, in addition to any server-side processing an application may require, a servlet must generate an appropriate HTTP response message, which consists of the response header information such as the MIME content type and caching information, as well as the body of the response. The response body that is intended for a WAP client is a WML deck. Both the header information and the body content are generated as an output stream by the servlet.

24.3   GENERATING OUTPUT TO WAP CLIENTS

To generate an HTTP output stream, we can use a servlet that is derived from `HttpServlet`, which defines interfaces and classes that we can use to handle HTTP requests and create HTTP responses. Refer to appendix F for a listing of the interfaces and classes in the `HttpServlet` API specification.

This section will show the specific methods an `HttpServlet` object uses to set the header information and to output the response body to a WAP client.

24.3.1   Writing the response header information

As mentioned in chapter 22, the methods for setting or overriding an HTTP header are included in the `HttpServletResponse` object of an `HttpServlet`. We will revisit two relevant methods in this section. For a list of HTTP response headers that can be used in an HTTP response message, see appendix E.

setContentType()

For the user agent to interpret the received content correctly, we need to set the content-type header field of the response message to the user agent. The servlet uses the `setContentType()` method to accomplish this. A valid content type of a WML message for a WAP browser is `text/vnd.wap.wml`.

The following statement sets the appropriate content type for a response containing a WML deck. The `HttpServletResponse` instance, *response*, outputs the generated content:

```
response.setContentType("text/vnd.wap.wml");
```

setHeader() and setDateHeader()

To set a header field with a string value, use the `setHeader()` method. Use `setDateHeader()` to add a header with a date value.

The following statement sets the value of the `Cache-Control` header field to `no-cache`, signaling to the receiving proxy server not to cache the received message content.

```
response.setHeader("Cache-Control", "no-cache");
```

For more details about the basic issues on caching, see chapter 19.

24.3.2   Writing the response body

After setting the header information, the servlet is responsible for generating all the relevant content in the response body that constitutes a valid WML deck. Recall from chapter 22 that the servlet uses a writer stream (`PrintWriter`) object or an output stream (`ServletOutputStream`) object to generate output data to a client.

To obtain a stream object, the servlet uses one of the following declarations depending on the type of stream you choose:

```
PrintWriter out = response.getWriter();
ServletOutputStream out = response.getOutputStream();
```

Subsequently, use the `print()` method or the `println()` method to write the output messages.

The following servlet code shows how a writer stream generates the XML prologue that is found in a typical WML deck:

```
"PrintWriter out = response.getWriter();"
out.println ("<?XML version=\"1.0\"?>");
out.println ("<!DOCTYPE wml PUBLIC \"-//WAPFORUM//DTD WML 1.1//EN\"");
out.println ("\"http://www.wapforum.org/DTD/wml_1.1.xml\">");
```

24.3.3 Creating a WAP application using a servlet

We will now look at a servlet example that writes a response header and generates a simple WML deck. HelloServlet generates a message that appears in a WML browser:

Listing 24.1 Source code for HelloServlet

```
/* Generate a greeting: HelloServlet.java */
import java.io.*;
import javax.servlet.*;
import javax.servlet.http.*;

public class HelloServlet extends HttpServlet
{
   public void init(ServletConfig config) throws ServletException {
     super.init (config);
   }

   public void doGet (HttpServletRequest  request,
                      HttpServletResponse response)
             throws ServletException, IOException
   {
     doPost (request, response);   ❶
   }

   public void doPost (HttpServletRequest  request,
                       HttpServletResponse response)
             throws ServletException, IOException
   {
     response.setContentType("text/vnd.wap.wml");   ❷

     PrintWriter out = response.getWriter();    ❸

     out.println ("<?XML version=\"1.0\"?>");
     out.println ("<!DOCTYPE wml PUBLIC \"-//WAPFORUM//DTD WML 1.1//EN\"");
     out.println ("\"http://www.wapforum.org/DTD/wml_1.1.xml\">");
```

Initializes the servlet when it is first loaded into memory

Sets the value of the MIME content type of the generated message to the client

Creates a PrintWriter instance

```
        out.println("<wml>");
        out.println("<card id=\"start\">");
        out.println("<p>");
        out.println("Hello, here's a dynamically generated greeting!");
        out.println("</p>");
        out.println("</card>");
        out.println("</wml>");
        out.close();        ◄──┐ Releases the PrintWriter
    }                            object by using the
}                                close() method
```
Generates an output stream that contains the `<wml>` element, the `<card>` element, and the card content

---

Code comments

❶ Handles incoming HTTP GET requests. It consists of only one statement: a call to doPost(). The effect is to redirect HTTP GET requests to doPost(). Hence, we need to write the client request servicing code only in doPost() since in our application, we intend to handle both types of requests in a similar manner.

❷ Originally handles only incoming HTTP POST requests. In our application, it is also called from within doGet() to handle incoming HTTP GET requests.

❸ Prints an output stream that consists of the XML prologue required in a WML deck.

24.3.4   Viewing the result

Using the UP browser emulator (UP.Browser), you can view the WML deck that the HelloServlet servlet generates. To run the servlet:

- Compile the Java servlet and save it under the appropriate directory where the servlet loader you use can locate it.

- Invoke the browser emulator and enter the URL of the compiled servlet, HelloServlet.class, in the Go input box of the browser interface.

- In figure 24.2, for testing purposes, we use localhost as the host of the URL, and the path, /servlet.

Figure 24.2
URL of a servlet residing on the local host

A text message should appear in the microbrowser (figure 24.3).

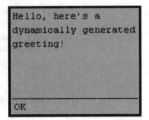

Figure 24.3
Display of WML content generated by HelloServlet

From the emulator, press F5 to display the source content in the Phone Information window. Figure 24.4 shows the dynamic content generated by the servlet and delivered to the client via the WAP gateway. The content is what one would expect to see in a .wml document.

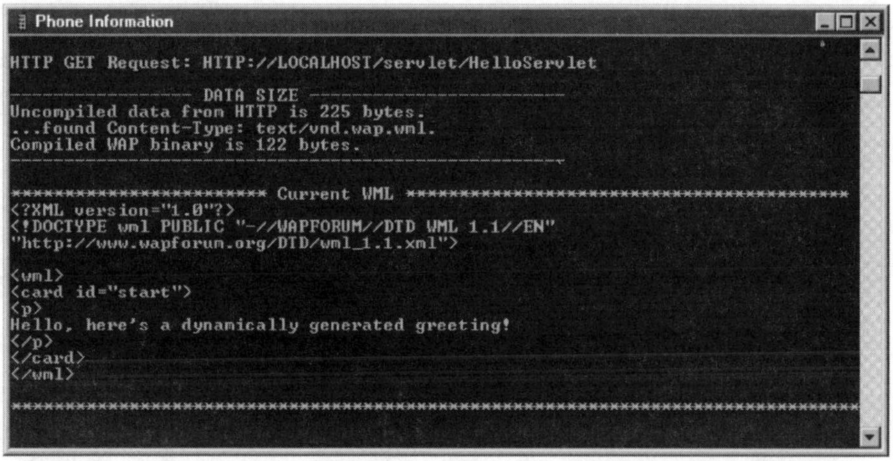

Figure 24.4   Phone Information window displaying the WML code generated by HelloServlet

24.4   INVOKING A JAVA SERVLET

Although you can invoke a servlet by entering its URL directly in the browser interface, it is more often the case that a servlet is invoked from a WML card. You can also pass parameter values from the calling WML card to the servlet. In this section, we will present two other common ways to kick off a servlet.

24.4.1   Calling a servlet from a card

To call a servlet from a card, use the WML <go> or <a> element.

Using the WML <go> element

To see how the WML <go> element works, we will use our HelloServlet example (listing 24.1).

The following code uses the <go> element to invoke HelloServlet when Accept is clicked:

```
<?xml version="1.0"?>
<!DOCTYPE wml PUBLIC "-//WAPFORUM//DTD WML 1.1//EN"
 "http://www.wapforum.org/DTD/wml_1.1.xml">
<wml> <!-- hello1.wml -->
<card id="start" title="hello">
   <do type="accept" label="servlet">
```

Gives the Accept button of the phone interface the label, `servlet`. Clicking this key will kick off the task specified in the <go> element

```
                <go href="http://myHost:port/servlet/HelloServlet" method="get" />
        </do>
        <p>
            Click "servlet" to invoke HelloServlet!
        </p>
    </card>
</wml>
```

Causes the current card to pass control to HelloServlet via an HTTP GET method

The screens in figure 24.5 show what the WML code looks like using UP.Browser.

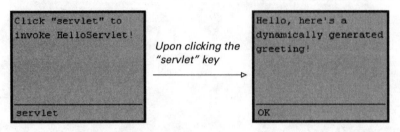

Figure 24.5   Invoking HelloServlet from hello1.wml using the `<go>` element

In our example, if a client invokes the servlet using the HTTP GET method, the request is first passed to the doGet() method, which in turn calls the doPost() method to service the request. In this way, we need only to furnish the code for doPost(), which handles POST requests directly and the GET requests via redirection.

If no appropriate service method can be found in the servlet, the typical error code issued by the origin server is HTTP Error 405.

Using the WML <a> element

The WML deck shows how a servlet can be invoked using the WML `<a>` element:

```
<?xml version="1.0"?>
<!DOCTYPE wml PUBLIC "-//WAPFORUM//DTD WML 1.1//EN"
 "http://www.wapforum.org/DTD/wml_1.1.xml">
<wml> <!-- hello2.wml -->
<card id="start" title="hello">
    <p>
        Navigate to:
        <a href="/servlet/HelloServlet">HelloServlet</a>
        <a href="#end">Ending card</a>
    </p>
</card>

<card id="end">
    <p>
        Thank you for visiting!
    </p>
 </card>
</wml>
```

A link to the servlet, HelloServlet

A link to the last card in the same WML document

Figures 24.6 and 24.7 show what the WML code looks like using UP.Browser.

hello2.wml#start   Generated by HelloServlet

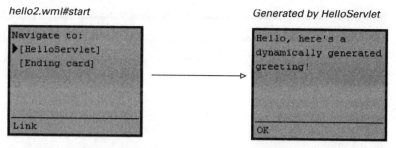

Figure 24.6   Using <a> in hello2.wml to invoke HelloServlet

hello2.wml#start   Generated by HelloServlet

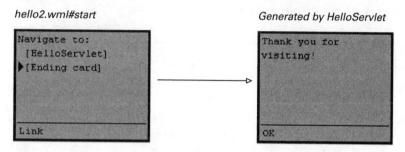

Figure 24.7   Using <a> in hello2.wml to invoke another card in the same WML deck

In general, there is no difference between the use of <go> and <a> unless you need to pass parameters to the referenced servlet as will be discussed next.

24.4.2   Passing parameter values

The way to pass parameters from the calling document to the servlet depends on how the servlet is invoked.

Using explicit query string

One straightforward means to pass parameter values to the referred servlet is to append the variable's name and value pairs as a query string after the URL of the servlet.

Here are four ways of using a query string to pass the values of two parameters, myname and mypwd:

- Supplying parameter values to the Logon servlet via the browser interface:

```
http://localhost/servlet/Logon?myname=susan&mypwd=wap
```

- Supplying parameter values to the Logon servlet via the <a> element:

```
<a href="http://localhost/servlet/Logon?myname=susan&amp;mypwd=wap">
    My login
</a>
```

- Supplying parameter values to the Logon servlet via the `<go>` element:

```
<go href="http://localhost/servlet/Logon?myname=susan&amp;mypwd=wap" />
```

- Supplying parameter values to the Logon servlet via the `onpick` event of the `<option>` element:

```
<option
  onpick="http://localhost/servlet/Logon?myname=susan&amp;mypwd=wap" />
    My login
</option>
```

Using the *<postfield>* element

Another way of passing parameter values from a WML deck to a servlet is through the WML `<postfield>` element, which is used with the `<go>` element.

This code invokes a servlet with the user-input values of two variables, `Name` and `Passwd`, using the `<postfield>` element for each value to be passed to the servlet:

```
<do type="accept" label="servlet">        ❶
   <go href="http://myHost:port/servlet/HelloServlet" method="post">        ❷
      <postfield name="myname" value="$Name" />        ❸
      <postfield name="mypwd" value="$Passwd" />
   </go>
</do>
```

Code comments

❶ Assigns the label `servlet` to the Accept button of the phone interface. Pressing this key will kick off the task specified in the `<go>` element.

❷ Causes the current card to pass control to HelloServlet via an HTTP POST method.

❸ Specifies the name that the servlet must use to retrieve the corresponding value. Here, `Name` and `Passwd` are variables in the card's context, but `myname` and `mypwd` are not visible within the card. The latter two variables can be retrieved from the referenced URL (i.e., HelloServlet) specified in the `<go>` element.

24.5   PROCESSING CLIENT REQUESTS

The way a servlet processes a request from a WML client is identical to the way it handles a request from an HTML client. Typically, a servlet is initialized when it is invoked. It then processes individual requests using the appropriate service method such as `doGet()` or `doPost()`.

In this section, we will use a simple example to illustrate the way a servlet processes a request from a WML client.

24.5.1   Retrieving header information

Just as there are `HttpServletResponse` methods that a servlet can use to set HTTP header information, there are methods that a servlet can use to retrieve HTTP header information from an HTTP request message. For a list of HTTP request headers, see appendix E.

There are four `HttpServletRequest` methods capable of retrieving information about the headers in an incoming request:

- `getHeader("header_name")` returns the value of the specified header as a string.
- `getHeaders("header_name")` returns all the possible values of the specified header as an array of strings.
- `getDateHeader("header_name")` returns the value of the specified header as a *long* number, indicating the number of milliseconds elapsed since midnight, Jan. 1, 1970, UTC. It can be converted into a Java `Date` object.
- `getIntHeader("header_name")` returns the value of the specified header as an integer.

Next is a simple example to retrieve information about the HTTP headers, `Accept` and `User-Agent`. If the user agent is a WML client, the `HTTP_ACCEPT` header should contain the string `text/vnd.wap.wml`, while the `HTTP_USER_AGENT` header provides clues to the type of browser used.

The code illustrates how a servlet determines whether to respond with WML content specifically for the UP browser or WML content for other WML-enabled browsers.

```
String acceptHeader = request.getHeader("Accept");          ❶
String useragentHeader = request.getHeader("User-Agent");

if (acceptHeader.indexOf("wml") != -1 )                     ❷
    if useragentHeader.indexOf("UP") != -1)

        generateDeckforUP();        ❸
else
    response.sendRedirect ("http://host/WML/nonUP.wml");     ❹
}
```

Code comments

❶ Uses the `getHeader()` method to retrieve both the headers, HTTP_ACCEPT and HTTP_USER_AGENT.

❷ Uses the `indexOf()` method to check if the retrieved headers contain the key substrings that indicate support for WML content and use of a UP browser.

❸ If both of these conditions are satisfied, invokes an arbitrary method, `generateDeckforUP()`.

❹ If the user agent is not a UP browser but does support WML, it redirects request to a static WML document, non UP.wml.

For more information on the use of headers such as `Accept` and `User-Agent` to help determine the client browser using ASP, see chapter 19.

24.5.2 Retrieving parameter values

To retrieve the values passed from a WML deck to a servlet, use the `getParameter()` or `getParameterValues()` methods discussed in chapter 22.

The following WML deck invokes the servlet, WelcomeServlet, on the local host for retrieving a name value entered by the user. When WelcomeServlet is called, a parameter is passed to the servlet:

```
<?xml version="1.0"?>
<!DOCTYPE wml PUBLIC "-//WAPFORUM//DTD WML 1.1//EN"
 "http://www.wapforum.org/DTD/wml_1.1.xml">
<wml> <!-- welcome.wml -->
<card id="start" title="welcome">
   <do type="accept" label="login">
      <go href="http://localhost/servlet/WelcomeServlet" method="post">
         <postfield name="myname" value="$Name" />
      </go>
   </do>
   <p>

 What is your name?
     <input name="Name" type="text" maxlength="30" />
   </p>
</card>
</wml>
```

Invokes the servlet, WelcomeServlet, via the HTTP POST request method

Parameter name is myname and the value is that entered by the user under the name, Name

Prompts the user to input a value for the variable, Name, as a text field

The result is displayed in figure 24.8.

Listing 24.2 is the source code for the WelcomeServlet.

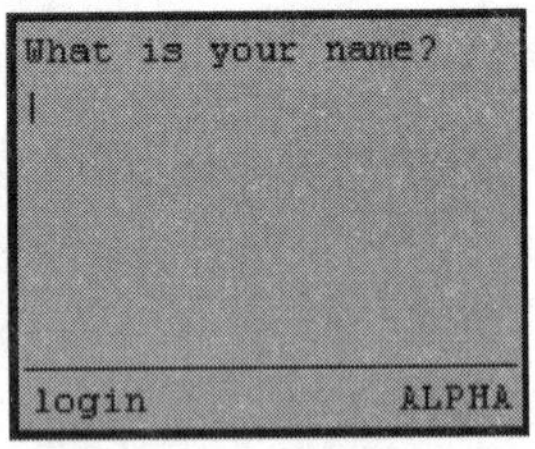

Listing 24.2 Source code for WelcomeServlet

```
/* Library Welcome Message: WelcomeServlet.java */
import java.io.*;
import javax.servlet.*;
import javax.servlet.http.*;

public class WelcomeServlet extends HttpServlet
{
   /* Initialization of servlet */
   public void init(ServletConfig config) throws  ServletException {
       super.init (config);
   }

   /* Redirecting client request that uses HTTP GET method */
   public void doGet (HttpServletRequest  request,
                      HttpServletResponse response)
               throws ServletException, IOException
   {
       doPost (request, response);
   }

   /* Servicing client request using HTTP POST method */
   public void doPost (HttpServletRequest  request,
```

Figure 24.8 Message from the only card in welcome.wml

```
                    HttpServletResponse response)            Sets the
            throws ServletException, IOException            content
                                                            type for
    {                                                       WML
        String username = request.getParameter ("myname"); ❶ content
        response.setContentType("text/vnd.wap.wml");   ◄──┘
        PrintWriter out = response.getWriter();          ❷

        out.println ("<?xml version=\"1.0\"?>");       ◄── Outputs the XML prologue
        out.println
            ("<!DOCTYPE wml PUBLIC \"-//WAPFORUM//DTD WML 1.1//EN\"");
        out.println ("\"http://www.wapforum.org/DTD/wml_1.1.xml\">");

        out.println("<wml>");
        out.println("<card id=\"start\" title=\"welcome\">");
        out.println("<p>");
        out.println("Hello, " + username +
            ", welcome to the XYZ Library!");    ┐ Outputs the
        out.println("</p>");                     │ retrieved user's
        out.println("</card>");                  ┤ name and a
        out.println("</wml>");                   │ welcome
        out.close();                             ┘ message
    }
}
```

Code comments

❶ Retrieves the user's name. Since the parameter name used to pass in the value was myname the servlet must use the same parameter name to retrieve the user's name.

❷ Creates a writer stream instance for use in generating dynamic content.

24.5.3   Understanding the code

Figure 24.9 shows what the WML code looks like using UP.Browser.

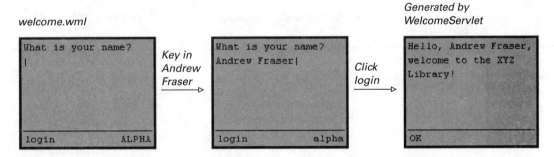

Figure 24.9 Passing name parameter to WelcomeServlet **from** welcome.wml **using** <go> **and** <postfield>

The Phone Information window displays the variable and value sent to the servlet via the HTTP POST request (figure 24.10).

Figure 24.10 Viewing parameter value posted to `WelcomeServlet` in Phone Information window

The variable, myname, has the value `Andrew%20Fraser` where `%20` denotes the hexadecimal value of the ASCII code for the space character.

Next, we shall show another WML deck to illustrate an alternative way to invoke `WelcomeServlet`, namely via the WML `<a>` element. The way to pass in a variable value is through a query string appended to the URL, i.e., the HTTP GET request method.

```
<?xml version="1.0"?>
<!DOCTYPE wml PUBLIC "-//WAPFORUM//DTD WML 1.1//EN"
 "http://www.wapforum.org/DTD/wml_1.1.xml">
<wml> <!-- welcome1.wml -->
<card id="start" title="welcome">
  <p>
    What is your name?
    <input name="Name" type="text" maxlength="30" />
    Navigate to:
    <a href="/servlet/WelcomeServlet?myname=$Name">
      Welcome
    </a>
    <a href="#end">
      Ending card
    </a>
  </p>
</card>

<card id="end">
  <p>
    Thank you for visiting!
  </p>
</card>
<wml>
```

Prompts user to input value for the variable, Name

Creates a hotlink labeled `Welcome` that links to WelcomeServlet

Creates a hotlink labeled Ending card that links to the last card in the same deck

Card referred to in the second hotlink

The use of the second welcome WML document results in similar displays (figure 24.11):

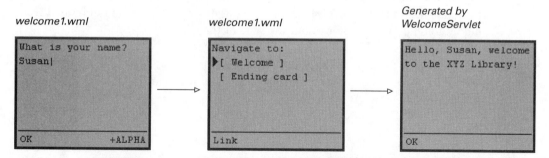

welcome1.wml

```
What is your name?
Susan|



OK              +ALPHA
```

welcome1.wml

```
Navigate to:
▶[ Welcome ]
 [ Ending card ]



Link
```

*Generated by
WelcomeServlet*

```
Hello, Susan, welcome
to the XYZ Library!



OK
```

Figure 24.11 Passing name parameter to WelcomeServlet **from welcome1.wml**

The Phone Information window displays the variable and value sent to WelcomeServlet via a query string attached to the URL of the servlet, using the HTTP GET request method (figure 24.12).

```
Phone Information                                              _ □ ✕
─────────────────────────────────────────────────────────
cache miss: {
                <HTTP://LOCALHOST/servlet/WelcomeServlet?myname=Susan
                >
        }
net request: {
                <HTTP://LOCALHOST/servlet/WelcomeServlet?myname=Susan
                >
        }
HTTP GET Request: HTTP://LOCALHOST/servlet/WelcomeServlet?myname=Susan
─────────────── DATA SIZE ────────────────────────
Uncompiled data from HTTP is 233 bytes.
...found Content-Type: text/vnd.wap.wml.
Compiled WAP binary is 126 bytes.
```

Figure 24.12 WelcomeServlet **is invoked via an** HTTP GET **request**

24.6   SUMMARY

In this chapter, we recapture the main tasks involved in generating dynamic content using server-side technology. Specifically, we see how a Java servlet can be invoked from a WML card as well as the ways of passing parameter values to the servlet.

Once the servlet is loaded, depending on the application on hand, the servlet may need to retrieve the HTTP header information and the incoming parameter values before performing further processing.

To generate output, it requires an output stream or writer object as described in chapter 22. To generate WML output to a WAP client, the servlet needs to set the correct content type, and in order that the client interprets the incoming WML response as intended, the developer is responsible for ensuring in his code the generation of a valid WML deck.

In the next chapter, you will see how we apply what you have learned in this chapter in applications that involve cookie and session, which are commonly used techniques to retain information about the state of the client.

C H A P T E R   2 5

Information tracking

25.1   INTRODUCTION

Keeping track of the state of the client, such as the identity of the user and the content of a shopping cart during a shopping spree at a cybermall, is as easy as using a cookie or the session management mechanism provided by the HttpSession interface of the Java servlet API.

The basic concepts and functionality of cookies are covered in part VI. The structure of a cookie header that can be embedded as an HTTP header field is covered in appendix E.

Here we will demonstrate the use of cookies and session data objects via Java servlets as an alternative to using ASP (explained in detail in part VI). The dynamic WAP content that is generated relies on a cookie or session object to provide the client-side information.

25.2 COOKIE SUPPORT IN SERVLETS

Java servlets implement cookie support in the javax.servlet.http package. This package defines a Cookie class, the addCookie() method, and getCookies() method.

25.2.1 Adding and retrieving cookies

The signatures of the two methods for adding and retrieving cookies are:

```
public void addCookie (Cookie cookie);
public Cookie[] getCookies ();
```

The addCookie() method is defined in the HttpServletResponse interface. It adds a Set-Cookie header for the specified cookie to an outgoing HTTP response message.

The getCookies() method is defined in the HttpServletRequest interface, and it retrieves an array of cookies from an incoming request.

25.2.2 The Cookie class

The Cookie class defines several methods for setting the fields of a cookie. The signature of each method is:

```
public Cookie (String name, String value);
public void setValue (String value);
public void setMaxAge (int expiry);
public void setDomain (String domainUri);
public void setPath (String pathUri);
public void setSecure (boolean flag);
```

The Cookie() method is a constructor of the Cookie class. When a cookie is created, it is given a name (myname, for example) and a value ("Susan" for example). To override the original value of the cookie, use setValue().

setMaxAge() sets the cookie's life span, specified as the parameter, expiry, in seconds. If a negative expiry value is specified, the cookie is not persistent, and will terminate once the browser shuts down.

setDomain() specifies the trailing domain name pattern that the host domain must match before the cookie is presented as part of the client request. For example, if setDomain() sets the domainUri value of a cookie as .myhost.com, then a subsequent request directed to a domain, say, www.myhost.com, will send the cookie's information as part of the HTTP request. On the other hand, www.myhost.com.sg is not a valid domain for the cookie to be sent to. The default domain is the one that originated the message containing the Set-Cookie header field to create the cookie concerned.

setPath() sets the URL or prefix of URL paths for which the cookie is valid. The cookie is sent with the request whose URL begins with the URL path set using this method. The default is the path to the previously requested resource that originated the Set-Cookie header for writing the cookie.

`setSecure()` indicates if the cookie content is to be communicated over a secure HTTP connection. A `flag` value of `true` means a secure communication channel is required.

The Cookie class also provides methods for retrieving the corresponding value and properties that the above methods set for a cookie (table 25.1).

Table 25.1 Retrieving methods

Signature of retrieving method	Description
public String getName();	Returns the name of the cookie
public String getValue();	Returns the value of the cookie
public int getMaxAge();	Returns the maximum specified age of the cookie. If the field was not specified, a negative value is returned.
public String getDomain();	Returns the suffix domain name pattern of hosts for which the cookie is visible
public String getPath();	Returns the prefix of all URL paths for which the cookie is visible
public boolean getSecure();	Returns the boolean value of the 'secure' flag

Browsers may contain bugs in their implementation of support for the optional attributes (i.e., attributes other than name and value). Use the optional attributes with caution and only when necessary.

25.3 UNDERSTANDING COOKIES BY EXAMPLE

We will create a servlet called PutCookieServlet that sets up a cookie for a user agent and create a servlet called GetCookieServlet that retrieves the cookie value and generates a personalized good-bye message.

25.3.1 Creating a cookie

PutCookieServlet retrieves the name of the user input to the system and initiates the creation of a cookie at the WAP gateway to help *remember* this piece of information. The creation of cookie is not visible to the user. The welcome message created by the servlet is visible to the user.

Listing 25.1 is the code for PutCookieServlet:

Listing 25.1 Source code for PutCookieServlet.java

```
/* Creation of cookie: PutCookieServlet.java */
import java.io.*;
import java.util.*;
import javax.servlet.*;
import javax.servlet.http.*;

public class PutCookieServlet extends HttpServlet
{
```

```
/* Initialization of servlet */
public void init(ServletConfig config) throws ServletException {
    super.init (config);
}

/* Redirecting client request that uses HTTP GET method */
public void doGet (HttpServletRequest  request,
                   HttpServletResponse response)
         throws ServletException, IOException
{
    doPost (request, response);
}

/* Servicing client request using HTTP POST method */
public void doPost (HttpServletRequest  request,
                    HttpServletResponse response)
         throws ServletException, IOException
{
    String name = request.getParameter ("username");        ❶
    String encodedname = name.replace (' ', '+');           ❷

    Cookie userCookie = new Cookie ("username", encodedname);    ❸
    userCookie.setMaxAge (-1);
    userCookie.setPath ("/servlet");
    userCookie.setSecure (false);
    response.addCookie (userCookie);        ❹

    response.setContentType("text/vnd.wap.wml");        ❺
    PrintWriter out = response.getWriter();
    out.println ("<?xml version=\"1.0\"?>");
    out.println ("<!DOCTYPE wml PUBLIC \"-//WAPFORUM//DTD WML 1.1//EN\"");
    out.println ("\"http://www.wapforum.org/DTD/wml_1.1.xml\">");

    // Output <wml> element, <card> element, and the card contents
    out.println("<wml>");
    out.println("<card id=\"start\" title=\"Welcome Message\">");
    out.println("<p>");
    out.println("Hello, " + name + ", welcome to the XYZ Library!");
    out.println("</p>");
    out.println("</card>");
    out.println("</wml>");
    out.close();
}
}
```

Code comments

❶ Retrieves user's name from incoming request using getParameter() of the HttpServletRequest interface. The user's name may be input via an <input> element from a WML card. The input value is posted to this servlet when it is triggered via the clicking of some appropriate button defined in the WML card.

❷ Scans the name and replaces all spaces with the `'+'` symbol. (Spaces in cookie values are stored as `'+'` symbols in the HTTP header.)

❸ Creates a cookie instance with the name, *username*, to remember the input user's name. At the same time, other properties of the cookie such as the life span, domain, path, and security option, are specified.

❹ A `Set-Cookie` header in the HTTP response message to be sent to the client. Note that the preparation for writing a cookie ends here. The code that follows this is concerned with displaying a welcome message to the user.

❺ Sets the content type for WML content, creates a Java writer object, and generates a welcome message, which we have explained in detail in chapter 24.

Let us now take a look at the effect of the following fragment of code for setting up value and properties of the cookie:

```
Cookie userCookie = new Cookie ("username", encodedname);
userCookie.setMaxAge (-1);
userCookie.setDomain ("localhost");
userCookie.setPath ("/servlet");
userCookie.setSecure (false);
```

Table 25.2 shows the value and properties associated with a cookie.

Table 25.2   Cookie values and properties

Name / value:	**username** / *value-retrieved-from-referring-card* In our example, we will retrieve the value of this *username* cookie from a WML client, which is responsible for supplying the value of *username*.
Expires:	Cookie expires when the browser is shut down
Path:	/servlet
Domain:	localhost
Secure:	false

The usefulness of a cookie is fully realized only at the time when a server application makes use of the cookie value. In our example, the cookie value that is sent together with a request to any application under the /servlet directory or its subdirectories of the origin server can be retrieved and used by the application.

25.3.2   Retrieving a cookie

The next servlet generates a personalized good-bye message just before a user leaves an application or site. It uses `getName()` to look for the appropriate cookie based on the cookie's name. When the correct cookie is found, the actual cookie value (value of `username` in our example) is retrieved using `getValue()`.

Listing 25.2   Source code for GetCookieServlet.java

```
/* Retrieval of cookie: GetCookieServlet.java */
import java.io.*;
import javax.servlet.*;
import javax.servlet.http.*;

public class GetCookieServlet extends HttpServlet
{
   /* Initialization of servlet */
   public void init(ServletConfig config) throws ServletException {
      super.init (config);
   }

   /* Redirecting client request that uses HTTP GET method */
   public void doGet (HttpServletRequest  request,
                     HttpServletResponse response)
            throws ServletException, IOException
   {
      doPost (request, response);
   }

   /* Servicing client request using HTTP POST method */
   public void doPost (HttpServletRequest  request,
                     HttpServletResponse response)
            throws ServletException, IOException
   {
      String cookieName, nameString="dear reader, ";      ❶

      // Set content type for a WML client
      response.setContentType("text/vnd.wap.wml");

      // Create a writer stream
      PrintWriter out = response.getWriter();

      Cookie[] cookies = request.getCookies();       ◄─┘

      if (cookies != null)  {
         for (int i=0; i<cookies.length; i++)  {
            cookieName = cookies[i].getName();
            if (cookieName.equals("username"))  {
               nameString = cookies[i].getValue().replace('+', ' ')
                     + ", ";

               break;     ◄─┐
            }
         }
      }
      try  {
         goodbyeMessage (nameString, out);     ◄─┘
      } catch (Exception e)  {
         out.println("Error in displaying goodbye message.");
      }
      out.close();
   } // end of doPost()
```

Uses the `getCookies()` **method to retrieve all cookies from the incoming client request**

❷

Exits from the loop once the `username` **cookie is found**

Displays a good-bye message

```
protected static void goodbyeMessage (String nameString,    ③
                                      PrintWriter out)
             throws ServletException, IOException, Exception
{
   // Output the XML prologue
   out.println ("<?xml version=\"1.0\"?>");
   out.println ("<!DOCTYPE wml PUBLIC \"-//WAPFORUM//DTD WML 1.1//EN\"");
   out.println ("\"http://www.wapforum.org/DTD/wml_1.1.xml\">");

   // Output a good-bye message to a WML client
   out.println("<wml>");
   out.println("<card id=\"start\" title=\"Goodbye Message\">");
   out.println("<p>");
   out.println("Bye, " + nameString + "see you again soon!");
   out.println("</p>");
   out.println("</card>");
   out.println("</wml>");

} // end of goodbyeMessage()
}
```

Code comments

❶ Initializes the variable, *nameString*, to "dear reader," which may be overridden if the incoming client request contains a username cookie that carries a more personalized name.

❷ If the incoming request contains cookie(s), the forloop is executed to scan through the list of cookies. For each cookie, getName() extracts the cookie's name and checks if it is the name we are looking for, i.e. username. If such a cookie is found, its value is retrieved using the getValue() method. The value is scanned to convert all '+' characters in the string into spaces.

❸ Generates valid WML content for output to the WAP client. Block-level explanation is provided in the code. For more details, see chapter 24.

25.4   TESTING THE EXAMPLE

To test the cookie's functionality in our servlet example, first compile PutCookieServlet and GetCookieServlet; then save them in the directory that maps onto the virtual directory for servlets as required by your servlet loader.

25.4.1   Invoking PutCookieServlet

Create a simple WML deck, which consists of one card that prompts the user to enter his user name. The card will invoke PutCookieServlet to display a welcome message at the user agent and create a cookie to keep track of the user name. The WML deck may look something like:

```
<wml> <!-- welcome.wml -->
<?xml version="1.0"?>
```

```wml
<!DOCTYPE wml PUBLIC "-//WAPFORUM//DTD WML 1.1//EN"
   "http://www.wapforum.org/DTD/wml_1.1.xml">
 <card id="start" title="Welcome">
   <p>
     What is your name?
     <input name="Name" type="text" maxlength="30" />        ❶
   </p>

   <do type="accept" label="login">
     <go href=
        "http://locahost/servlet/PutCookieServlet" method="post">     ❷
        <postfield name="username" value="$Name" />      ❸
     </go>
   </do>
 </card>
</wml>
```

Code comments

❶ Prompts the user to input his name. The variable name used to capture the user input is Name.

❷ Invokes PutCookieServlet using the HTTP POST method when the Accept key is clicked.

❸ Sends the parameter to PutCookieServlet under the name username and its value is that of the variable Name in the context of the current card.

Key in the URL for welcome.wml in the Go input box of the UP.Phone emulator. Figure 25.1 illustrates how the card looks in the UP.Phone emulator, with the user's input, *Tim Tam*.

After the user enters a name and chooses the login key option, PutCookieServlet generates a welcome message (figure 25.2).

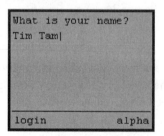

Figure 25.1 Display of the only card in welcome.wml with user's name

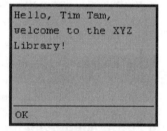

Figure 25.2 WML content generated by PutCookieServlet to the user agent

In your emulator, press F11 to view all the cookies. The cookie set by PutCookieServlet should appear in the Phone Information window (figure 25.3).

```
Phone Information                                          _ □ ×
*************************** Cookies ***************************
Name:     username
Value:    Tim+Tam
Version:  0
TTL:      1160498014 seconds to live
Path:     /servlet
Domain:   localhost
Comment:

***************************************************************
```

Figure 25.3   Viewing cookie information in the Phone Information window

25.4.2   Invoking GetCookieServlet

Create a simple WML deck, which consists of one card that associates clicking Accept, which is labeled goodbye in the screen, with the invocation of GetCookieServlet. The WML deck may look something like this:

```
<wml> <!-- goodbye.wml -->
<?xml version="1.0"?>
<!DOCTYPE wml PUBLIC "-//WAPFORUM//DTD WML 1.1//EN"
    "http://www.wapforum.org/DTD/wml_1.1.xml">
  <card id="start" title="Goodbye">
    <p>
       Click goodbye to leave this site.
    </p>

    <do type="accept" label="goodbye">
      <go href="http://localhost/servlet/GetCookieServlet" method="post" />
    </do>
</card>
</wml>
```

Key in the URL for goodbye.wml in the Go input box of the UP.Phone emulator. Figure 25.4 shows what will be displayed.

Click the goodbye option to invoke GetCookieServlet. The servlet retrieves the username cookie and generates a good-bye message (figure 25.5).

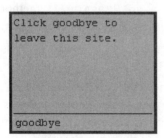

Figure 25.4   Display of the only card in goodbye.wml

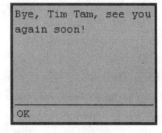

Figure 25.5   A personal good-bye message generated by GetCookieServlet

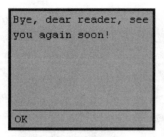

Figure 25.6   A generic good-bye message

If you restart the UP.Emulator and invoke Get-CookieServlet, you should observe the message displayed in figure 25.6. The user is not addressed with his personal name because the username cookie that stores the name information expired when the browser was shut down. Instead, the generic "dear reader" is displayed because that was the initial value of the nameString variable in GetCookieServlet.

The expected message in figure 25.6 was not observed when the UP.SDK 4.0 was used. When the UP.Browser (4.0) restarted, the username cookie still existed. However, with UP.SDK 4.1, the good-bye message was displayed as expected and the cookie was not listed when F11 was clicked.

25.5 SESSION SUPPORT IN SERVLETS

There is an alternative—through the use of the HttpSession interface—to track client-side information.

Session information is tracked using a data object created in the session application layer data. The Java servlet package, javax.servlet.http, provides built-in support for managing such an object. The methods for session management include:

- getSession()
- setAttribute()
- getAttribute()
- getAttributeNames()
- removeAttribute()

For a complete listing of the available methods provided by the HttpSession interface, see appendix F.

getSession()

To retrieve or create a session, use the getSession() method of the HttpServletRequest interface. The signatures of getSession() are:

```
public HttpSession getSession();
public HttpSession getSession (boolean create);
```

The servicing servlet uses this method to retrieve the current valid session associated with the incoming request. If there is no such valid session, a new session is created in the first method and in the second method if the true boolean parameter value is specified; otherwise the null value is returned in the second case if the False boolean value is specified.

setAttribute() and getAttribute()

To bind a name to a data object and to retrieve the value of a name-bound data object, the `setAttribute()` and `getAttribute()` methods of the `HttpSession` interface are used. The data object is where the state of the client, i.e. client-side information, is kept. The signatures of the two methods are:

```
public void setAttribute (String name, Object value);
public Object getAttribute (String name);
```

The name parameter is the name to which an object is associated or bound in the session's application layer data. Hence, the `setAttribute()` method binds the specified object into the session's application layer data with the name given as a parameter. The `getAttribute()` method returns the object that is bound to the specified name.

getAttributeNames()

If all the names used to bind the application layer data objects of a session are required, use the `getAttributeNames()` method of the `HttpSession` interface. The signature of `getAttributeNames()` is:

```
public java.util.Enumeration getAttributeNames ();
```

removeAttribute()

This method of the `HttpSession` interface removes the object that is bound to the specified name in the application layer data of a session. The signature of `removeAttribute()` is:

```
public void removeAttribute (String name);
```

25.6 UNDERSTANDING SESSION MANAGEMENT

Now we will create a simplified shopping cart application that uses the Java servlet API to manage a list of musical instruments. The application will provide a mechanism for the user to request a price quote for the items in the shopping cart.

For simplicity, we assume that quotation of a unit price for each item is sufficient. That is, we need not keep track of the quantity of each item selected. Also, we will not generate final price quotes because that requires database access, which we will discuss in the context of dynamic WAP applications in the next chapter.

25.6.1 Overview of the shopping cart

The application involves the development of two WML decks (shopping.wml and emptyCart.wml) and a servlet (CartServlet).

shopping.wml

This WML deck consists of two cards:

- The first one displays a list of items, (musical instruments in this example) for selection. It provides an option that results in the initiating of a servlet (CartServlet) to add the selected item(s) into a cart using the HTTP POST request method.

- A second card to display a thank-you message.

emptyCart.wml

This WML deck consists of only one card, which displays a message informing the user about the current empty state of the shopping cart. The card also provides an option to make another selection.

CartServlet

This servlet consists of the doPost() and doGet() methods.

The doPost() method is triggered after the user finishes picking his items and wishes to add them to the shopping cart. It:

- Retrieves the items selected by the user.

- Checks for a valid session associated with the current request, and if such session cannot be found, it creates one.

- Adds the retrieved selected items into the session's application layer via the use of a data object.

- Generates an acknowledgement message and the appropriate options that the user can choose to execute next.

The options include continuing with the item selection, in which case the first card of shopping.wml will be invoked; alternatively, the user can opt to request a price quotation for the selected items in the cart. In the latter option, the same servlet is invoked again. However, in this case, the HTTP GET request method is used.

The doGet() method is called when either the user finishes his shopping and wishes to see the price quotes or wishes to empty the shopping cart:

- The method retrieves the option the user made that caused the invocation of the servlet via the GET request method.

- If the option is to clear the shopping cart, the data object responsible for keeping track of the cart's contents will be emptied, and emptyCart.wml will be loaded.

- If the option is to request for price quotation, the servlet will generate a WML card to display the contents of the cart. The generated card also includes options (Confirm and Clear cart) the user can choose to execute next.

25.6.2   Creating WML deck for selecting items

The shopping.wml deck described in section 25.6.1 consists of two cards:

Listing 25.3   WML code for shopping.wml

```
<?xml version="1.0"?>
<!DOCTYPE wml PUBLIC "-//WAPFORUM//DTD WML 1.1//EN"
    "http://www.wapforum.org/DTD/wml_1.1.xml">

<wml>  <!-- shopping.wml -->
<card id="start" title="Select Items">
    <p>
        Pick your choices:
        <select name="items" multiple="true">
            <option value="Accordion"> Accordion </option>
            <option value="Guitar"> Guitar </option>
            <option value="Piano"> Piano </option>
            <option value="Saxophone"> Saxophone </option>
        </select>
    </p>

    <do type="accept" label="Add items">
        <go href="/servlet/CartServlet" method="post">
            <postfield name="items" value="$items" />
        </go>
    </do>
</card>

<card id="end" title="Thank You">
    <p>
        Thank you for visiting!
        We will send you the quotations within 24 hours.
    </p>
</card>
</wml>
```

The start card displays a list of musical instruments for the user to select. Since the `multiple` attribute is `true`, the user is able to select more than one item

Invokes the CartServlet using the HTTP POST method when the user clicks Accept

Assigns all the items selected by the user to the parameter, *items*, and posts it to CartServlet

Displays a thank-you message

Since multiple items may be selected, the parameter, *items*, passed to CartServlet is actually one single string that contains all the selected instruments delimited by a semicolon.

25.6.3   Displaying an empty-cart message

This WML deck is loaded via the CartServlet when the user initiates the option to empty the shopping cart:

Listing 25.4   WML code for emptyCart.wml

```
<?xml version="1.0"?>
<!DOCTYPE wml PUBLIC "-//WAPFORUM//DTD WML 1.1//EN"
    "http://www.wapforum.org/DTD/wml_1.1.xml">

<wml>  <!-- emptyCart.wml -->
<card id="empty" title="Clear Cart">
    <p>
        Your cart is now empty.
    </p>
</card>
```

The only card in this deck displays a simple message to inform the user that the cart is now empty

```
</p>
<do type="accept" label="Select">
   <go href="/shopping.wml#start">        ◄─────────────┐
      <setvar name="items" value="" />   ◄───────┐      │
   </go>              Sets the value of the variable, items, to   The start card of
</do>                empty string before control is passed to   shopping.wml is loaded
</card>              the start card of shopping.wml             if the user clicks Accept
</wml>                                                          to indicate a wish to
                                                               select instruments
```

The card in listing 25.4 provides an option to return to the item selection screen (shopping.wml#start). Before control is passed to the selection screen, the variable, *items*, in the client's WML context is first reinitialized to an empty string using the <setvar> element. This effectively clears the list of items selected so far in the current WML context. The clearing of the data object that keeps track of the shopping cart's contents is handled by the servlet.

25.6.4 Creating the servlet

The servlet for handling the rest of the processing in the application is shown in listing 25.5.

Listing 25.5   Layout of CartServlet.java

```java
/* Retrieval of cookie: CartServlet.java */
import java.io.*;
import java.util.*;
import javax.servlet.*;
import javax.servlet.http.*;

public class CartServlet extends HttpServlet
{
   /* Initialization of servlet */
   public void init(ServletConfig config) throws ServletException {
      super.init (config);
   }

   /* Servicing client requests to add selected items into the cart */
   public void doPost (HttpServletRequest  request,
                  HttpServletResponse response)
            throws ServletException, IOException
   {
      . . . . . . .
   } // end of doPost()


   /* Servicing client requests to generate price quotation */
   /* or empty shopping cart */
   public void doGet (HttpServletRequest  request,
                  HttpServletResponse response)
            throws ServletException, IOException
   {
      . . . . . . .
   } // end of doGet()
}
```

doPost()

This service method handles client requests to add selected items to the shopping cart. Listing 25.6 is the source code of the method.

Listing 25.6 Source code for doPost() of CartServlet.java

```
public void doPost (HttpServletRequest  request,
                    HttpServletResponse response)
          throws ServletException, IOException
{
    HttpSession session = request.getSession(true);       ❶

    String items = request.getParameter ("items");        ❷

    session.setAttribute ("MusicCart", items);            ❸

    response.setContentType("text/vnd.wap.wml");          ❹

    // Generate a WML deck as acknowledgement            ❺
    PrintWriter out = response.getWriter();
    out.println ("<?xml version=\"1.0\"?>");
    out.println ("<!DOCTYPE wml PUBLIC \"-//WAPFORUM//DTD WML 1.1//EN\"");
    out.println ("\"http://www.wapforum.org/DTD/wml_1.1.xml\">");

    out.println ("<wml>");
    out.println ("<card id=\"start\" title=\"Acknowledgement\">");
    out.println ("<do type=\"accept\" label=\"Select\">");
    out.println ("   <go href=\"/shopping.wml#start\" />");
    out.println ("</do>");
    out.println ("<do type=\"options\" label=\"Quote\">");
    out.println ("   <go href=\"/servlet/CartServlet?opt=quote\" " +
                "method=\"get\" />");
    out.println ("</do>");
    out.println ("<p>");
    out.println ("Your selected items have been added to the cart.");
    out.println ("</p>");
    out.println ("</card>");
    out.println ("</wml>");
    out.close();

} // end of doPost()
```

Code comments

❶ The getSession() method of the HttpServletRequest interface checks for a session for the request. It creates one if no such session exists.

❷ Uses the getParameter() method of the HttpServletRequest interface to retrieve the item(s) selected by the user via the start card of shopping.wml.

❸ Adds items selected by the user to the session's application layer data as a data object. Binds the data object to the name, MusicCart.

❹ Sets the content type for the WML content to be generated.

⑤ The rest of the code from this point on concentrates on creating a writer object and generating an acknowledgement message.

doGet()

This service method handles client requests to empty the shopping cart or to proceed with confirmation for price quotation. Listing 25.7 is the source code for the doGet() method.

Listing 25.7   Source code for doGet() of CartServlet.java

```
public void doGet (HttpServletRequest   request,
                   HttpServletResponse response)
         throws ServletException, IOException
{
   String items=null;
   StringTokenizer itemList=null;          ①

   HttpSession session = request.getSession(true);      ②

   String action = request.getParameter("opt");      ③

   if (action.equals("clear"))  {                                          ④
      session.removeAttribute ("MusicCart");
      response.sendRedirect ("http://localhost/emptyCart.wml");
   }

   items = (String) session.getAttribute("MusicCart");      ⑤
   itemList = new StringTokenizer (items.replace(';', ' '));      ⑥

    response.setHeader ("cache-control", "no-cache");

   // Generate a WML deck to display contents of cart
   response.setContentType("text/vnd.wap.wml");      ⑦
   PrintWriter out = response.getWriter();
   out.println ("<?xml version=\"1.0\"?>");
   out.println ("<!DOCTYPE wml PUBLIC \"-//WAPFORUM//DTD WML 1.1//EN\"");
   out.println ("\"http://www.wapforum.org/DTD/wml_1.1.xml\">");

   out.println ("<wml>");
   out.println ("<card id=\"start\" title=\"Confirmation\">");
   out.println ("<do type=\"accept\" label=\"Confirm\">");      ⑧
   out.println ("    <go href=\"/shopping.wml#end\" />");
   out.println ("</do>");

   out.println ("<do type=\"options\" label=\"Clear cart\">");      ⑨
   out.println ("    <go href=\"/servlet/CartServlet?opt=clear\" " +
              "method=\"get\" />");
   out.println ("</do>");

   out.println ("<p>");
   out.println ("Quotation for the following items:");
   while (itemList.hasMoreTokens())                                ⑩
   out.println("<br /> " + itemList.nextToken());
   out.println ("</p>");
```

```
        out.println ("</card>");
        out.println ("</wml>");
        out.close();
} // end of doGet()
```

Code comments

❶ The variable, *itemList*, holds the array of tokens after the single-string *items* is itemized based on the delimiter, namely the semicolon.

❷ Uses getSession() of the HttpServletRequest interface to check for a session for the request. It creates one if no such session exists.

❸ Uses the getParameter() method to retrieve the value of the option made by the user in the previous screen.

❹ If option is "clear", removes the MusicCart data object from the session's application layer data using removeAttribute(), and redirects the request to empty-Cart.wml using sendRedirect().

❺ Retrieves instrument item(s) from the MusicCart data object using getAttribute(). Note that the object returned is cast into a Java String type, which is in turn stored as a list of tokens in *itemList*, whose data type is the Java StringTokenizer.

❻ Sets the value of the cache-control header to "no-cache" to avoid caching the result. This is to ensure that the next request to doGet() displays the most current contents in the cart.

❼ The remainder of the code concentrates on generating a dynamic WML deck to display a list of items in the shopping cart, as well as two possible options, which the user can choose to execute next.

❽ Generates the WML code to associate the invocation of the end card of shopping.wml with the Accept key, labeled Confirm in the display of this generated card.

❾ Generates the WML code to associate the invocation of CartServlet using the GET method with the Options key, labeled Clear cart in the display of this generated card. The invocation involves passing of a parameter, *opt*, with value, clear.

❿ Recovers the individual items by scanning through the list using nextToken() on the StringTokenizer object, itemList.

Common pitfalls

One common error is to use the sendRedirect() method to redirect a request to a card. If we attempt to specify the target of the redirection as a card

```
response.sendRedirect ("http://localhost/shopping.wml#end");
```

we will see the display of the first card of shopping.wml instead, which in this case is the start card. The previous code snippet will display the expected card only if we place the end card to be the first card within the code of shopping.wml.

Note that in `doGet()`, we could also use `false` as the parameter for `getSession()`, in which case we will obtain a null value if there is no existing session for the request. We should then add in the necessary code to handle a `null` return; otherwise an `HTTP Error` code of `500` will be issued when we attempt to execute a `getAttribute()` on a null session.

25.7 A SHOPPING CART EXAMPLE

Now that we have seen the code for the shopping cart example, let's walk through the application.

To run the shopping cart application, first compile CartServlet and save it in the directory that maps onto the virtual directory for servlets as required by your servlet loader. Then, follow these steps:

25.7.1 Selecting items

Start the UP.Simulator and specify the URL for shopping.wml:

http://localhost/shopping.wml (figure 25.7).

Use `Pick` to select Accordion, Piano, and Saxophone. Choose `Add items` by clicking Accept on the phone emulator to add them to the shopping cart. This will invoke CartServlet via the `HTTP POST` request method.

The `doPost()` method generates an acknowledgement (figure 25.8):

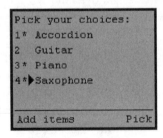

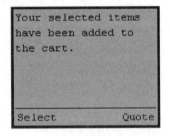

Figure 25.7   User picks three items from the "start" card of shopping.wml

Figure 25.8   Acknowledgement generated by CartServlet

25.7.2 Viewing servlet results

From the UP.Browser emulator, press F5 to display the source code of the current WML content. Next, press F10 to display the values of all the current variables.

The Phone Information window displays the generated WML deck and the value of the *items* variable that was posted to the doPost() method of CartServlet (figure 25.9).

```
Phone Information                                                      _ □ ✕
****************************************************** Current WML *******************
*********************
<!-- WBXML public ID number 0x0004: "-//WAPFORUM//DTD WML 1.1//EN" -->
<wml>
   <card id="start" title="Acknowledgement">
     <do type="accept" label="Select">
       <go href="/shopping.wml#start"/>
     </do>
     <do type="options" label="Quote">
       <go href="/servlet/CartServlet?opt=quote" method="get"/>
     </do>
     <p>Your selected items have been added to the cart.
     </p>
   </card>
</wml>
<>
*********************************************************************************

*********************************************************************************
************************** Current Activity Vars *******************************
vars<items>="Accordion;Piano;Saxophone"
*********************************************************************************
```

Figure 25.9   WML code generated by CartServlet and all WML variables

Notice that *items* is a string that contains all three selected items separated by semicolons.

25.7.3   Navigating from the acknowledgement screen

From the generated acknowledgement screen, if the Select option is chosen, the first selection screen (figure 25.7) will be loaded. The code that dictates this action is found in the generated WML content, which was also shown in figure 25.9:

```
<do type="accept" label="Select">
   <go href="http://localhost/shopping.wml#start" />
</do>
```

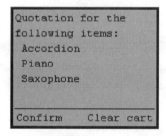

Figure 25.10   Confirmation generated by CartServlet

On the other hand, if the Quote option is clicked, a confirmation screen generated by the doGet() method of the servlet will be displayed (figure 25.10).

The corresponding code for loading the confirmation screen is:

```
<do type="options" label="Quote">
   <go href="/servlet/CartServlet?opt=quote"
     method="get" />
</do>
```

25.7.4 Navigating from the confirmation screen

From the confirmation screen (figure 25.10), if the `Confirm` option is clicked, the card, shopping.wml#end, appears. The relevant code generated by `doGet()` for this option is:

```
<do type="accept" label="Confirm">
   <go href="/shopping.wml#end" />
</do>
```

If the `Clear cart` option is chosen, CartServlet is again invoked to clear the contents of the cart and to display a simple message. The corresponding code generated by `doGet()` is:

```
<do type="options" label="Clear cart">
   <go href="/servlet/CartServlet?opt=clear" method="get" />
</do>
```

To keep the servlet less complex, no further action is implemented to handle the display of price quotes.

Figure 25.11 summarizes the possible navigation paths that you can take when you are at the confirmation screen:

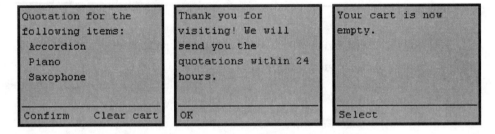

Figure 25.11   Possible navigation paths from the confirmation screen display

25.8   SUMMARY

In this chapter, we show how a Java servlet is used to preserve client-side information, a common requirement in applications that provide personalization services, such as a shopping cart. We discuss two possible mechanisms to accomplish the objective:

- Cookie
- Data object stored as the session's application layer data

In the next chapter, we move on to the database. We will make use of the database access techniques that we learned in chapter 23 and apply them in the context of dynamic WAP applications as discussed in chapters 24 and 25.

CHAPTER 26

Using Java servlets to implement database access

26.1 INTRODUCTION

In chapter 23, we saw how a Java servlet accesses a database. In this chapter, we will incorporate the use of a database in dynamic WAP-based applications. The process is similar except that here, our servlet is required to generate WML content instead of HTML content as used in traditional desktop browsers.

Recall the steps involved in accessing a database using a servlet:

- Load the appropriate database driver
- Establish a connection with the data source
- Formulate and execute SQL statements

415

- The SQL statement may be a query, insertion of new record, modification of existing records, or deletion of records. Refer to chapter 18 for more details on SQL statements.

In the case of a query, the retrieved information, also called the result set, may be further manipulated according to the requirements of the application. For example, the application may need to present the retrieved information in some specific format such as a table.

In this section, we will create a library book inquiry example. We will discuss the requirements of our application and the components that it requires. We will then discuss each component in detail and examine the actual code. Finally, we will present a walk-through of the example.

26.2 OVERVIEW OF THE BOOK INQUIRY SYSTEM

26.2.1 System requirements

The search criterion used in this example is the book title instead of the ISBN used in chapter 23. The user enters the title of a book, which is then used as a search string to retrieve the book from the LIBRARY database.

One of the following actions occurs after a book title search of the database is completed:

- If no book title matches the specified search string, an appropriate not-found message is displayed
- If one book is found, details of the book are displayed immediately
- If there are not more than 10 matches, the list of book titles is displayed; the user is prompted to choose one from the list to view its details
- If more than 10 matches are found, a message is displayed, prompting the user to enter a more precise title to help narrow the search

The book details consist of the:

- Full title
- ISBN
- Author
- Publisher
- Loaning status of all copies of the book in the library catalog

26.2.2 Program components

Table 26.1 shows the components we will include in our application.

Table 26.1 Functional requirements and components of the book inquiry system

Functionality	Component
Prompts user for a new search string	WML card: query.wml#newTitle
Prompts user for a more precise title	WML card: query.wml#modTitle
Displays a not-found message	WML card: contained in notfound.wml
Displays message to prompt user for a more precise title	WML card: contained in narrow.wml
Retrieves books that match the search string and determines a course of action based on the number of successful matches	Servlet: SearchTitleServlet Service method: doPost()
Redirects to a static deck (notfound.wml) if no match is found in the database	Servlet: SearchTitleServlet Redirecting to deck by: doPost()
Redirects to a static deck (narrow.wml) if more than 10 matches are found in the database	Servlet: SearchTitleServlet Redirecting to deck by: doPost()
Retrieves and displays details of a book	Servlet: SearchTitleServlet Method: bookDetails()
Displays a list of matches and prompts the user to select a book from a list of retrieved book titles	Servlet: SearchTitleServlet Method: displayTitles()

26.2.3 LIBRARY database

In this example, we will implement the same LIBRARY database seen in chapter 23 using Microsoft SQL server. It consists of two tables: books and copies. The structure of each and the relationship between the tables are shown in figure 26.1.

To associate a data source name, say `myLibSQL`, with the LIBRARY database, use the ODBC configuration facility found in Windows' Control Panel.

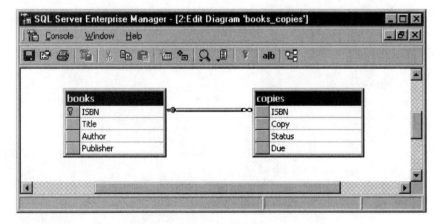

Figure 26.1 Relationships diagram of the LIBRARY database

To achieve portability across database systems, we use a property file DBInfo.properties to store the driver and data source information of the database used. The content of the file is:

```
Driver=sun.jdbc.odbc.JdbcOdbcDriver
URL=jdbc:odbc:myLibSQL
Username=bookuser
Passwd=books
```

26.3 CREATING THE STATIC WML DECKS

This book inquiry system requires three static WML decks:

- query.wml
- notfound.wml
- narrow.wml

Note that the last two WML decks are invoked through redirection from the servlet. Since the target of a redirection via servlet cannot be a card, we are not able to combine the three decks into one.

In the rest of this section, we will look at each deck in detail.

Entering book title: query.wml

The query.wml deck consists of two cards that prompt the user to enter a book title.

The first card prompts the user to enter a new search string. The second prompts the user to modify the title entered previously, specifically to make the title more precise in order to help narrow the search.

The code for this deck is:

Listing 26.1 Source code for query.wml

```
<?xml version="1.0"?>
<!DOCTYPE wml PUBLIC "-//WAPFORUM//DTD WML 1.1//EN"
          "http://www.wapforum.org/DTD/wml_1.1.xml">

<wml>  <!-- query.wml -->

<!-- Enter title -->
<card id="newTitle" title="Book Search" newcontext="true">    ❶
   <p>
      Key in a (partial) book title:
      <input name="title" maxlength="30" />                    ❷
   </p>
   <do type="accept" label="Submit">
      <go href="/servlet/SearchTitleServlet" method="post">   ❸
         <postfield name="title" value="$title" />
      </go>
   </do>
</card>
```

```
<!-- Modify title -->
<card id="modTitle" title="Book Search">
   <p>
      Give a more precise book title:
      <input name="title" maxlength="30" />
   </p>
   <do type="accept" label="Submit">
      <go href="/servlet/SearchTitleServlet" method="post">
         <postfield name="title" value="$title" />
      </go>
   </do>
</card>
</wml>
```

4

5

Code comments

❶ The newcontext attribute of the card is set to true to ensure that each time the user is ready to start a new search session by loading this card, the current URL history stack and variables are first cleared. If the user attempts to advocate a back action after this card is loaded, the microbrowser will navigate out of the current context and the URL from the previous context will be loaded.

❷ Prompts the user for a book title using the <input> element. The input is captured in the variable, title.

❸ When the user clicks Accept, SearchTitleServlet is invoked. The parameter, title, with value entered by the user is posted to SearchTitleServlet.

❹ Prompts the user to give a more precise book title. The input is captured in the variable, title.

❺ When the user clicks Accept, SearchTitleServlet is invoked. The parameter, title, with value entered by the user is posted to SearchTitleServlet.

The display of the first card and an example of the second card are shown in Figure 26.2.

In the second display, the title *Java* results in more than 10 records retrieved from the database. The user is therefore asked to enter a more precise title.

newTitle

modTitle

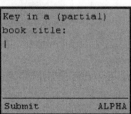

Figure 26.2
Display of the two cards
in query.wml

No match: notfound.wml

notfound.wml#notFound

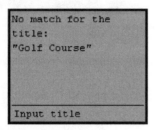

Figure 26.3 Display of the "notFound" card in notfound.wml

The notfound.wml deck consists of a card to display a not-found message. The card also provides a navigation path to the `newTitle` card of the query.wml deck to prompt the user to enter a new title.

Figure 26.3 is a not-found message page, indicating there is no title containing the text string Golf Course in the LIBRARY database.

Listing 26.2 shows the source code for this deck.

Listing 26.2   Source code for notfound.wml

```
<?xml version="1.0"?>
<!DOCTYPE wml PUBLIC "-//WAPFORUM//DTD WML 1.1//EN"
        "http://www.wapforum.org/DTD/wml_1.1.xml">

<wml>  <!-- notfound.wml -->
<card id="notFound" title="Book Search">
  <p>
     No match for the title: <br />
     "$title"
  </p>

     <do type="accept" label="Input title">
        <go href="query.wml#newTitle" />
     </do>
</card>
</wml>
```

Displays the no-match message followed by the title previously entered by the user

Invokes the `newTitle` card of query.wml to prompt user to enter a new title when Accept is pressed

Narrowing the search: narrow.wml

The narrow.wml deck consists of a card to display a message indicating that too many matches were found in the catalog.

The display of the card is shown in figure 26.4 and the code for this deck is shown in listing 26.3.

Figure 26.4 Display of the "narrowSearch" card in narrow.wml

Listing 26.3   Source code for narrow.wml

```
<?xml version="1.0"?>
<!DOCTYPE wml PUBLIC "-//WAPFORUM//DTD WML 1.1//EN"
        "http://www.wapforum.org/DTD/wml_1.1.xml">

<wml>  <!-- narrow.wml -->
<!-- Message to narrow search -->
```

```
<card id="narrowSearch" title="Book Search">
  <p>
    Too many matches found. <br />
    Key in a more precise title to narrow the search.
  </p>

  <do type="accept" label="Input title">
    <go href="http://localhost/query.wml#modTitle" />
  </do>
</card>
</wml>
```

Displays message to inform the user about the overwhelming search results

When Accept is pressed, loads the modTitle card of the query.wml deck

26.4 CREATING THE SERVLET

Besides the two request service methods, doGet() and doPost(), two other methods used are bookDetails() and displayTitles(). They are called by the service methods to perform the appropriate tasks as summarized in section 26.2.2.

Listing 26.4 is the general structure of the servlet:

Listing 26.4 Code layout of SearchTitleServlet.java

```
/* Library Book Inquiry: SearchTitleServlet.java */
import java.io.*;
import javax.servlet.*;
import javax.servlet.http.*;
import java.sql.*;

public class SearchTitleServlet extends HttpServlet
{
    /* Initialization of servlet */
    public void init(ServletConfig config) throws ServletException {
        super.init (config);
    }
    /* Redirecting client request that uses HTTP GET method */
    public void doGet (HttpServletRequest  request,
                       HttpServletResponse response)
            throws ServletException, IOException
    {
        doPost (request, response);
    }
    /* Servicing client request */
    public void doPost (HttpServletRequest  request,
                        HttpServletResponse response)
            throws ServletException, IOException
    {
                        .
                        .
                        .

    }  // end of doPost()

    /* Retrieving and displaying details of a specific book */
    protected static void bookDetails (. . . .)
                    throws ServletException, IOException, Exception
```

Imports the java.sql package

```
    {
            .
            .
            .
    }   // end of bookDetails()

    /* Retrieving and displaying all titles that match the search string */
    protected static void displayTitles (. . . .)
                    throws ServletException, IOException, Exception
    {
            .
            .
            .
    }   // end of displayTitles()
}
```

In the rest of this section, we will look at each of the three methods, doPost(),
bookDetails(), and displayTitles(). We will discuss the functions in detail
and point out their special features.

26.4.1 The doPost() method

The service method doPost() retrieves the title from the incoming client request
and executes a query to the books table of the LIBRARY database based on this title.

The doPost() method will then:

- Redirect to notfound.wml immediately if the result set is empty.

- Call bookDetails() to display the details of the book if there is only a single match.

- Invoke displayTitles() to display the list of titles in the result set if there
  are at least two, but not more than 10 matches.

- Redirect to narrow.wml if the number of matches is too large (i.e., more
  than 10).

The source code for doPost() is shown in listing 26.5.

Listing 26.5 Source code for doPost() of SearchTitleServlet.java

```
public void doPost (HttpServletRequest    request,
                    HttpServletResponse response)
            throws ServletException, IOException
{
    // Variables
    Connection con=null;
    Statement  stmt=null;
    String     query;
    ResultSet  rs=null;
    int        count=0;
    String     ISBNs[] = new String[10];
```

```
String     titles[] = new String[10];
ResourceBundle db = ResourceBundle.getBundle ("DBInfo");      ❶
String username = ((String) db.getString("Username")).trim;

String passwd = ((String) db.getString("Passwd")).trim;

String title = request.getParameter ("title");      ❷
try {
   if (title.length() == 0) {                                    ❸
      String isbn = request.getParameter("isbn");
      bookDetails (isbn, response);
      return;
   }
} catch (Exception e)  {
   System.err.println ("Exception: Calling bookDetails()...");
   System.err.println (e);
}

try  {
   Class.forName (db.getString("Driver"));                       ❹
   if ( (username.length()==0) && (passwd.length()==0) )
      con = DriverManager.getConnection (db.getString("URL"));
   else
      con = DriverManager.getConnection (db.getString("URL"),
                                      username, passwd);

} catch (Exception e)  {
   System.err.println ("Exception: JDBC-ODBC bridge driver...");
   System.err.println (e);
}

try  {                                                            ❺
   stmt = con.createStatement ();
   query = "SELECT ISBN, Title FROM books WHERE Title LIKE '%" +   ❻
            title.trim() + "%' ORDER BY Title";
   rs = stmt.executeQuery (query);

   if (!rs.next())  {                                             ❼
      rs.close();
      stmt.close();
      con.close();
      response.sendRedirect ("http://localhost/notfound.wml");
   }
   else {
      do {                                                        ❽
         ISBNs[count] = rs.getString("ISBN");
         titles[count++] = rs.getString("Title");
      } while (rs.next() && count<10);                            ❾
   }

   if (count == 1)                                                ❿
      bookDetails (ISBNs[0], response);
```

```
        else
            if (rs.next()) {
                rs.close();
                stmt.close();
                con.close();
                response.sendRedirect ("http://localhost/narrow.wml");
            }
            else
                displayTitles (ISBNs, titles, count, response);        ⓬

    } catch (SQLException e)  {
        System.err.println ("Exception: Creating statement object...");
        System.err.println (e);

    } catch (Exception e)  {
        System.err.println ("Exception: Retrieving 'books' table...");
        System.err.println (e);
    }

    finally {        ⓭
        try {
            if (rs != null)   rs.close();
            if (stmt != null) stmt.close();
            if (con != null)  con.close();
        } catch (Exception e)  {
            System.err.println ("Exception: Finally in doPost()...");
            System.err.println (e);
        }
    }

} // doPost()
```

⓫

Code comments

❶ Uses getBundle() to open the property file named DBInfo.properties and retrieve the username and password values.

❷ Uses getParameter() to retrieve the value of title from the incoming request.

❸ If the value of title is left empty, it is an indication that a book was picked from a selection list of multiple possible titles instead of through explicit typing by the user. In this case, we expect the ISBN of the selected book to be passed to the servlet. The servlet therefore retrieves the ISBN from the incoming request and invokes bookDetails() to display the detailed information of this specific book. Since we have no further processing, we explicitly execute a return to exit this servlet.

❹ Loads the jdbc-odbc bridge driver and establishes a connection to the LIBRARY database. Both the driver and database source information are obtained from the property file referenced by db using getString(). If the property file contains a username and password value, use them to establish the connection.

⑤ Creates a `Statement` object and formulates a query statement for retrieving ISBN and title information of books from the `books` table that match the retrieved `title`. Executes the query and assigns the retrieved records to the result set, `rs`.

⑥ The `trim()` method is used to ensure absence of leading and trailing spaces in a string, especially if the string is used as a search string. Also, the SQL `SELECT` query consists of the keyword `LIKE` and the special character `%` before and after the search string. This is the SQL query syntax used for performing a partial match.

⑦ If the result set is empty, closes the `ResultSet`, `Statement`, and `Connection` objects before loading the WML deck, notfound.wml.

⑧ If the result set is not empty, uses two string arrays, `ISBNs[]` and `titles[]`, to buffer the ISBN and title of all the books retrieved from the database for later use in `displayTitles()`. Alternatively, a Java Vector object may be used instead of two string arrays.

⑨ The `rs.next()` method parses through each record of the result set, `rs`. The do loop is controlled by the counter, *count*, which indicates that a maximum of 10 ISBNs and titles will be stored in the `ISBNs[]` and `titles[]` arrays. After the execution of the do loop, the value of *count* serves as an indication of the number of successful matches stored in the result set, `rs`.

⑩ If there is only one successful match stored in the result set, calls `bookDetails()` to display the detailed information of that book.

⑪ If there are more records in the result set after exiting the `doloop`, it means there are more than 10 records in the result set. In this case, we close all the `ResultSet`, `Statement`, and `Connection` objects before loading the WML deck, narrow.wml.

⑫ In this case, at least two, but not more than 10 matches were found. We call the `displayTitles()` method to display all the matching titles.

⑬ The `finally` block is always executed before we exit the `doPost()` method. In this case, we want to ensure that all the objects for accessing the database are properly closed before exiting this servlet.

26.4.2 Database programming issues

In this section, we highlight alternate ways of programming database access, which may improve the code in `doPost()` that we have just seen, provided some conditions are satisfied.

The use of additional memory resources, namely `ISBNs[]` and `titles[]`, in `doPost()` are necessary because the cursor pointing to the rows (i.e., records) in the result set moves only forward. Each time `rs.next()` is called, the cursor moves to the next row, starting from the position before the first row of the result set. However, JDBC 2.0 provides APIs that support moving a cursor backward, and navigation of the cursor to a row with a specified row number. In our illustration, we are unable to take advantage of such cursor operations because the JDBC-ODBC bridge drivers for Microsoft SQL and Microsoft Access are not JDBC 2.0 compliant.

If JDBC 2.0 is used, there is no need to store the result set in string arrays or Vector objects since we can always move the cursor to point to a specific row. We can write the following simple code fragment to determine the number of rows returned in the result set after executing the SQL query:

```
stmt = con.createStatement (ResultSet.TYPE_SCROLL_SENSITIVE,
                            ResultSet.CONCUR_READ_ONLY);
rs = stmt.executeQuery (query);
rs.last();
count = rs.getRow();
```

The statement, `stmt`, is created with two parameters, TYPE_SCROLL_SENSITIVE and CONCUR_READ_ONLY. The first parameter value switches on the capability to scroll forward and backward in the result set while remaining sensitive to changes to the database. The second parameter indicates a read-only capability.

The result set, rs, holds the result after an SQL query, `query`, is executed. The `rs.last()` method moves the cursor to the last row in the result set. The next method, `rs.getRow()`, returns the row number of the current row the cursor is pointing at to the variable, count. Since the cursor is now pointing at the last record, the value of count is also an indication of the number of successful records retrieved from the database.

We can also easily move the cursor to any record in the result set that we are interested in. The following line of code shows how we can set the cursor to point to the second record in the result set:

```
rs.absolute(2);
```

Recall from chapter 22 that the use of a development tool or application server will greatly help to reduce the code that you need to put in manually.

26.4.3 The bookDetails() method

This method is responsible for displaying the general information and loaning status of each of the copies of a book. It is called from within `doPost()` when the application has been able to identify the exact book the user is interested in. `doPost()` passes the ISBN of the book and the `HttpServletResponse` object as parameters to the `bookDetails()` method.

Listing 26.6 is the source code for `bookDetails()`.

Listing 26.6 Source code for bookDetails()

```
protected static void bookDetails (String isbn,
                                   HttpServletResponse response)
            throws ServletException, IOException, Exception
{
   // Variables
```

```
Connection    con=null;
ResourceBundle db = ResourceBundle.getBundle ("DBInfo");
Statement     stmt=null;
String        query1, query2;
ResultSet     rs=null;
PrintWriter out;
int           status;

try {
   Class.forName (db.getString("Driver"));
   if ( (username.length()==0) && (passwd.length()==0) )                ❶
      con = DriverManager.getConnection (db.getString("URL"));
   else
      con = DriverManager.getConnection (db.getString("URL"),
                                         username, passwd);

} catch (Exception e)  {
   System.err.println ("Exception: DB connection...");
   System.err.println (e);
}


try {
   stmt = con.createStatement();                                        ❷
   query1 = "SELECT * FROM books WHERE ISBN='" + isbn + "'";
   rs = stmt.executeQuery (query1);
   rs.next();

   response.setContentType("text/vnd.wap.wml");                         ❸
   response.setHeader("cache-control", "no-cache");

   out = response.getWriter();          ❹
   out.println ("<?xml version=\"1.0\"?>");
   out.println ("<!DOCTYPE wml PUBLIC \"-//WAPFORUM//DTD WML 1.1//EN\"");
   out.println ("\"http://www.wapforum.org/DTD/wml_1.1.xml\">");
   out.println("<wml>");
   out.println("<card id=\"start\" title=\"Book Inquiry\">");

   out.println("<p mode=\"nowrap\">");          ❺

   out.println("\"" + rs.getString("Title").trim() +                    ❻
               "\" <br />");
   out.println("by " + rs.getString("Author").trim() +
               "<br />");
   out.println("ISBN: " + isbn + "<br />");
   out.println("Publisher: " + rs.getString("Publisher").trim()
               + "<br />");
   rs.close();          ❼

   query2 = "SELECT * FROM copies WHERE ISBN='" + isbn + "'";           ❽
   rs = stmt.executeQuery (query2);

   out.println("<table columns=\"2\">");                                ❾
   out.println("   <tr><td><b>Copy</b></td> " +
               "<td><b>Status</b></td></tr>");
```

```
            while (rs.next()) {                                              ⑩
                out.println("    <tr><td>" + rs.getString("Copy").trim()
                            + "</td>");

                status = rs.getInt("Status");      ⑪
                if (status == 1)                                             ⑫
                    out.println("<td>Available</td></tr>");
                else
                    out.println("<td>Due " +
                                rs.getString("Due").trim() + "</td></tr>");
            }

            out.println("</table>");
            out.println("</p>");

            out.println("<do type=\"accept\" label=\"Next search\">");       ⑬
            out.println("    <go " +
                        "href=\"http://localhost/query.wml#newTitle\">");
            out.println("        <setvar name=\"title\" value=\"\" />");
            out.println("    </go>");
            out.println("</do>");

            out.println("</card>");
            out.println("</wml>");
            out.close();
        } catch (SQLException e)  {
            System.err.println ("SQLException: Accessing book details...");
            System.err.println (e);

        } catch (Exception e)  {
            System.err.println ("Exception: Displaying book details...");
            System.err.println (e);
        }

        finally {      ⑭
            try {
                if (rs != null) rs.close();
                if (stmt != null) stmt.close();
                if (con != null) con.close();
            } catch (Exception e)  {
                System.err.println ("Exception: Finally in bookDetails().");
                System.err.println (e);
            }
        }
    } // bookDetails()
```

Code comments

❶ Loads the jdbc-odbc bridge driver and establishes connection to the LIBRARY database based on the information specified by the property file, DBInfo.properties.

❷ Executes an SQL query to retrieve all information (ISBN, Title, Author, Publisher) of the book with the specified ISBN from the books table of the database. Immediately calls `rs.next()` to set the cursor to point to the first and only row in the result set, `rs`.

❸ Sets the appropriate content type for the WML content to be generated. The `cache-control` header is set to `no-cache` to ensure most current result is generated each time a client request to this servlet is invoked.

❹ Creates a writer object. Uses it to generate a WML deck to the client as shown in the rest of the code within the current `try` block.

❺ Sets the `no-wrap` display mode for the display of information that follows.

❻ Writes the title, author, ISBN, and publisher information of the book into the output stream, each on a separate line.

❼ Closes the result set once we have finished processing its contents.

❽ Executes a query to retrieve all information of each physical copy of the book with the specified ISBN. Notice that we reuse the result set variable, `rs`, to hold the results of this second query.

❾ Creates a table with two columns and with headers `Copy` and `Status`. We will tabulate the information of each individual copy of the book with the specified ISBN on a separate row of the table.

❿ Uses a `while` loop and `rs.next()` to step through individual copies of the book. We identify the copy number using the `getString("Copy")` method. The `trim()` method that follows strips off leading and trailing spaces in the string value of `Copy`. The trimmed `Copy` value is displayed as the first field of the new row in the table.

⓫ Retrieves the integer value of the loaning status field of each individual book copy from the result set using the `getInt("Status")` method.

⓬ If the `Status` value of the copy of book is set to 1, outputs the string `"Available"` to reflect its loaning status. Otherwise, retrieves and outputs the due date value from the result set.

⓭ Performs three tasks: (1) Associates the label, `Next search`, with the Accept key to be used in the WML content generated. (2) Associates the action of invoking the card, `query.wml#newTitle`, with the Accept key using the `<go>` element. (3) Generates the code for setting the value of the variable, `title`, to empty string.

⓮ Executed before we exit `bookDetails()` to ensure that all objects created in `bookDetails()` for accessing the database are properly closed before exiting the method.

26.4.4 The displayTitles() method

This method is invoked by `doPost()` if at least two, but not more than ten, matches are found. The parameters passed in are the arrays of ISBNs and titles buffered from the result set, the number of rows determined in `doPost()`, and the `HttpServletResponse` object for sending output stream to the user agent.

Listing 26.7 is the code for displayTitles().

Listing 26.7   Source code for displayTitles()

```
protected static void displayTitles (String ISBNs[],
                                      String titles[],
                                      int count,
                                      HttpServletResponse response)
                   throws IOException, Exception
{
   try {
      response.setContentType("text/vnd.wap.wml");            ❶
      response.setHeader("cache-control", "no-cache");

      PrintWriter out = response.getWriter();            ❷
      out.println ("<?xml version=\"1.0\"?>");
    out.println ("<!DOCTYPE wml PUBLIC \"-//WAPFORUM//DTD WML 1.1//EN\"");
      out.println ("\"http://www.wapforum.org/DTD/wml_1.1.xml\">");

      out.println("<wml>");
      out.println("<card title=\"Book Inquiry\">");
      out.println("<p mode=\"nowrap\">");            ❸

      out.println("   Pick one to view details:");
      out.println("   <select name=\"isbn\">");            ❹
      for (int i=0; i<count; i++) {            ❺
         String isbn = ISBNs[i].trim();
         String title = titles[i].trim();
         out.println("      <option value=\"" + isbn + "\">" +            ❻
                   title + "</option>");
      }
      out.println("   </select>");
      out.println("</p>");

      out.println("<do type=\"accept\" label=\"View\">");            ❼
      out.println("   <go href=\"SearchTitleServlet\">");
      out.println("      <postfield name=\"isbn\" " +
                "value=\"$isbn\" />");
      out.println("      <postfield name=\"title\" " +
                "value=\"\" />");
      out.println("   </go>");
      out.println("</do>");

      out.println("</card>");
      out.println("</wml>");
      out.close();

   } catch (Exception e) {
      System.err.println ("Exception: Displaying book titles...");
      System.err.println (e);
   }
} // displayTitles()
```

Code comments

❶ Sets the content type. The `cache-control` header is set to `no-cache` to ensure most current result is generated each time a client request to this servlet is invoked.

❷ Creates a writer object. Uses it to generate a WML deck to the client as shown in the rest of the code within the current `try` block.

❸ Sets the `no-wrap` display mode for the display of information that follows.

❹ Steps through the `ISBNs[]` and `titles[]` arrays for all matching titles and creates an option within a selection list, enclosed within the `<select>` and `</select>` tags.

❺ Uses a `forloop` to generate the code for transforming each matching title into an option of the selection list.

❻ Displays each title as the label of an option in the selection list, and associates a value, which is the ISBN of the book, with that option.

❼ Performs three main tasks: (1) Associates the label, `View`, with the Accept key to be used in the WML content generated. (2) Associates the action of invoking `SearchTitleServlet` with the Accept key using the `<go>` element. (3) Generates the code for posting the values of two parameters, `isbn` and `title`, to the servlet.

26.4.5 Good practices and common pitfalls

In this section, we summarize good programming practices and common pitfalls, which we also highlight in the annotations of the various code components. Some of them were also mentioned in some earlier chapters.

- To enforce clearing the history and variable stacks in the client's current WML context each time the new Title card is invoked, set the `newcontext` attribute of the card to `true`. Otherwise, the stacks would keep growing in normal circumstances as long as we do not enter new URLs to start a new context. Alternatively, the user needs to keep pressing Back to clear the history stack.

- Include the code for handling the response to pressing Options in each of the screen displays. We omit this practice from a number of our screen designs in order to focus on the implementation of the features of the book inquiry application.

- Include a `finally` block to close all the `ResultSet`, `Statement`, and `Connection` objects created in the method if they are not already closed. Close a `ResultSet` object before reusing it. Failing to do so will cause page fault errors as mentioned in chapter 23.

- Be ready to code the cursor. The cursor to a result set is initially pointing to the location just before the first row. Your application may require you to explicitly call `next()` on the result set to set the cursor to point to the first row. If the JDBC driver you use supports JDBC 2.0, then there is more flexibility in the coding as discussed in section 26.4.2.

26.5 A BOOK INQUIRY EXAMPLE

To test our library book inquiry example, prepare all the WML decks and place them in the appropriate directory. Compile the servlet and save it under the directory that maps onto the virtual directory for servlets as required by your servlet loader. Activate the servlet loader service and the UP.Simulator, and we can start.

Search resulting in too many matches

Key in the URL for `query.wml#newTitle`:

        http://localhost/query.wml#newTitle

Note that you may omit the card name, newTitle, from the URL specification if the card is the first card in the query.wml deck.

A display (figure 26.5) appears, which prompts the user to key in the title of the book to be searched.

Enter the title, *Java* (figure 26.6).

Click Submit. This invokes SearchTitleServlet via the HTTP POST method. The `doPost()` method services the request and finds more than ten titles in the database that contain the `string` Java. It then loads the static WML deck, narrow.wml (figure 26.7).

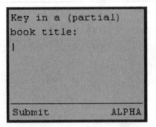

Figure 26.5   Screen display prompting user to enter a title

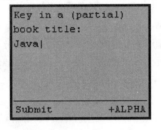

Figure 26.6 Keying in the title

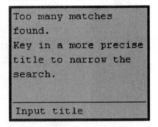

Figure 26.7   Response to user indicating too many matches found

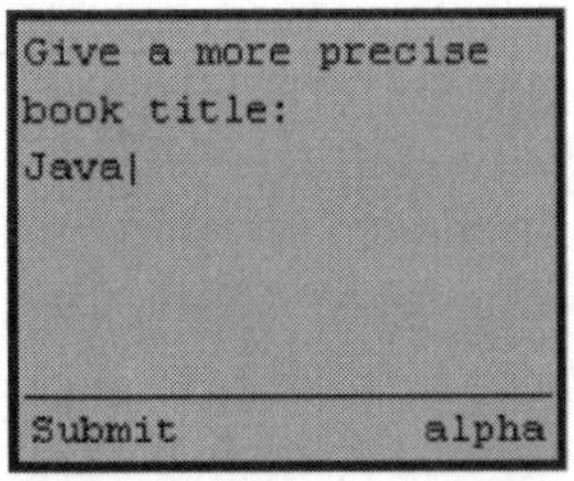

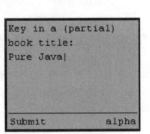

Figure 26.8   Screen display prompting user to give a more precise title

Figure 26.9   Keying in a more precise title

Click Input title. This causes the modTitle card of query.wml to be displayed, showing also the previously entered value of `title` (figure 26.8).

Let's try our luck this time by inserting an additional word, `Pure` (figure 26.9).

Click Submit. This invokes `doPost()` again to handle the request. This time, only one match is found. The `doPost()` method then calls `bookDetails()`, which accesses the database to retrieve more details of the book. It then dynamically generates an appropriate WML deck to the client to display the detailed information in figure 26.10.

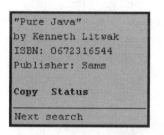

Scroll-down cursor

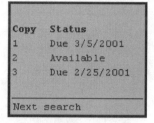

Figure 26.10   Detailed information of the title, *Pure Java*

Note that the user can click the scroll-down cursor to view more information in the next screen. If the `Next search` option is chosen, the newTitle card of query.wml will be loaded to allow the user to enter a new book title for searching.

Before we walk through another search session, let's take a glimpse at the code in the WML deck generated by `bookDetails()` via pressing the F5 key from the UP.Phone emulator. The source code of the generated WML deck is displayed in the Phone Information window (figure 26.11).

```
**************************************************** Current WML ********************
*************************
<!-- WBXML public ID number 0x0004: "-//WAPFORUM//DTD WML 1.1//EN" -->
<wml>
    <card id="start" title="Book Inquiry">
        <p mode="nowrap">&quot;Pure Java&quot;
        <br/>by Kenneth Litwak<br/>ISBN: 0672316544
        <br/>Publisher: Sams<br/><table columns="2">
        <tr>
            <td>
                <b>Copy</b>
            </td>
            <td>
                <b>Status</b>
            </td>
        </tr>
        <tr>
            <td>1</td>
            <td>Due 3/5/2001</td>
        </tr>
        <tr>
            <td>2</td>
            <td>Available</td>
        </tr>
        <tr>
            <td>3</td>
            <td>Due 2/25/2001</td>
        </tr>
        </table>
        </p>
        <do type="accept" label="Next search">
            <go href="http://localhost/query.wml#newTitle">
                <setvar name="title" value=""/>
            </go>
        </do>
    </card>
</wml>
<>
**********************************************************************************
```

Figure 26.11   WML content generated by `bookDetails()` of SearchTitleServlet

Search resulting in three matches

Let us start a new search session with the partial title, *Example* (figure 26.12).

Click Submit. This invokes SearchTitleServlet via the HTTP POST method. The doPost() method makes a query to the database and finds three titles containing the string, Example. It then calls the displayTitles() method to generate a WML deck to display all three titles. The WML deck generated also contains code to provide a View option, which the user can choose to view the details of a title selected from the displayed list.

Figure 26.13 is what displayTitles() would display in this case.

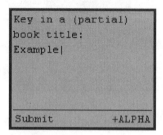

Figure 26.12   User enters a partial book title

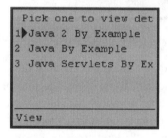

Figure 26.13   Three matches for "Example"

The corresponding WML content in figure 26.13 is shown in the Phone Information window via the F5 key (figure 26.14).

```
▒ Phone Information                                              _ □ ✗
***************************************** Current WML *******************
*******************
<!-- WBXML public ID number 0x0004: "-//WAPFORUM//DTD WML 1.1//EN" -->
<wml>
  <card title="Book Inquiry">
    <p mode="nowrap">Pick one to view details:
      <select name="isbn">
        <option value="0789722666">Java 2 By Example</option>
        <option value="013272295X">Java By Example</option>
        <option value="188477766X">Java Servlets By Example</option>
      </select>
    </p>
    <do type="accept" label="View">
      <go href="SearchTitleServlet">
        <postfield name="isbn" value="$$(isbn:noesc)"/><postfield name="title" v
alue=""/>
      </go>
    </do>
  </card>
</wml>
{}
***************************************************************************
```

Figure 26.14   WML content generated by displayTitles() of SearchTitleServlet

If you pick the third title, *Java Servlets By Example*, and click the View option, notice from the code displayed in the Phone Information window that SearchTitleServlet will be invoked with the isbn value of the chosen title.

The details of the book can be viewed in two screens with the help of the scroll-down and scroll-up cursors (figure 26.15):

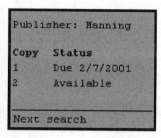

Figure 26.15
Detailed information of book selected from figure 26.13

Also, note that in the first screen, the full title cannot be displayed within one screen. You need to use the scroll-right cursor to view the right-hand portion of the title and the remainder of the author's name.

26.6 SUMMARY

In this chapter, we reviewed the steps involved in accessing the database using the JDBC API. We also discussed in detail an example that retrieved a library book's information based on a title given by the user. A servlet is used to retrieve a book's information and generate WML content to be delivered to the client. We also included highlights of good practices and common pitfalls throughout the discussion of the example code.

In the next chapter, we will introduce you to another server-side technology known as JavaServer Pages (JSP). You will learn how to write simple JSP code and understand the differences between JSP and the other server-side technologies you have seen in this book, namely Java servlet and ASP.

CHAPTER 27

Introduction to JavaServer Pages

27.1 INTRODUCTION

JavaServer Pages (JSP) is a server-side technology for supporting web-based applications. It allows you to embed Java code within an HTML document, just as ASP allows you to embed VBScript or JavaScript code inside HTML documents.

Similarly, we can use JSP in WAP-based applications by embedding Java code in a WML document, allowing us to generate and send dynamic WAP content to a WAP-enabled client. In this chapter, we will learn how JSP works and how it generates WML content. We will also look at the scripting elements and basic coding components used in a JSP document.

27.1.1 How JSP works

A JSP document is also called a JSP page. A JSP document has the extension .jsp. When a WAP-enabled client makes an HTTP request to a JSP document, the following occurs:

1 The origin server receives the HTTP request, recognizes the request type based on the extension, and hands the request over to a *page compilation engine*.

2 The page compilation engine converts the JSP document or page into a Java servlet source file and compiles the latter into a servlet class.

3 If a servlet exists for the JSP page, or the compilation date of the existing servlet is not earlier than the modified date of the JSP page, this compilation process will not be carried out since the existing servlet is up-to-date.

4 The servlet engine loads the servlet class into memory and executes it.

5 Original code within the scriptlet tags (<% and %>) of the JSP page is processed and results are returned to the client as appropriate WML content.

27.2 A JSP EXAMPLE

In this section, we will look at the resources required to process a JSP document and go through a simple example to see how it works.

27.2.1 Resources for running JSP

In the case of a Java servlet, we require a servlet loader, which can load and execute the servlet class when there is a request to the servlet. For JSP, we require a page compilation engine to translate the JSP page to a servlet and then compile it into the corresponding servlet class, in addition to loading the servlet for execution.

Certain web servers provide the page compilation engine required by a JSP page. Some examples are the Java Web Server (JWS) and iPlanet Web Server. Information about them is available at http://www.sun.com/software/jwebserver/ and http://www.iplanet.com/products/infrastructure/web_servers/.

Tomcat works with web servers such as Apache Server as an add-on to support JSP and servlets. JRun is another supplement to web servers such as Apache and Microsoft IIS that do not provide native support to JSP and servlets.

More information about Tomcat is available at http://jakarta.apache.org/tomcat/index.html.

For more information about JRun and to download an evaluation copy go to
http://www.allaire.com/developer/documentation/JRun.cfm
and http://commerce.allaire.com/ download/index.cfm.

27.2.2 Example code

Here is a JSP document that generates a WML deck to prompt the user for input, then prints text as well as the user-input value twice using a `for` loop:

```
<?xml version="1.0" ?>
<!DOCTYPE wml PUBLIC "-//WAPFORUM//DTD WML 1.1//EN"
        "http://www.wapforum.org/DTD/wml_1.1.xml">
```

Prologue, including the document type definition declaration, for WML 1.1

```
<%--greeting.jsp--%>
<% response.setContentType ("text/vnd.wap.wml"); %>
<wml>
    <card id="start" title="Hello">
        <p>
            What is your name?
            <input name="Name" type="text"/>
            <do type="accept">
              <go href="#next"/>
            </do>
        </p>
    </card>
    <card id="next" title="Hello">
        <p>
            <%
                for (int i=0; i<2; i++)
                    out.println ("Good-day, $(Name)! <br />");
            %>
        </p>
    </card>
</wml>
```

Sets the content-type header field in the HTTP response message

Prompts user to input a name

Java `for` loop to output a greeting message together with the name value input by user

Name the document greeting.jsp. Save it into a virtual directory recognizable to the web server, such as the root directory of the web server. (If IIS is used, the root of the web server maps to the /inetpub/wwwroot directory of the drive where IIS is installed.)

27.2.3   Running the example

Invoke the phone emulator and key in http://localhost/greeting.jsp.

Figure 27.1 shows the greeting displayed. Key in the name May (figure 27.2). Click OK and the screen in figure 27.3 will appear.

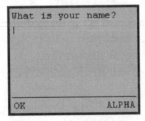

Figure 27.1   Screen display for the start card generated by greeting.jsp

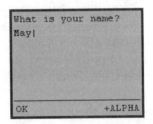

Figure 27.2   User enters the name, May

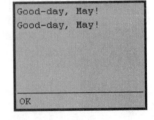

Figure 27.3   User's input is used in the next card for display

Press F5 of the phone emulator and you will see the generated code in the Phone Information window (figure 27.4).

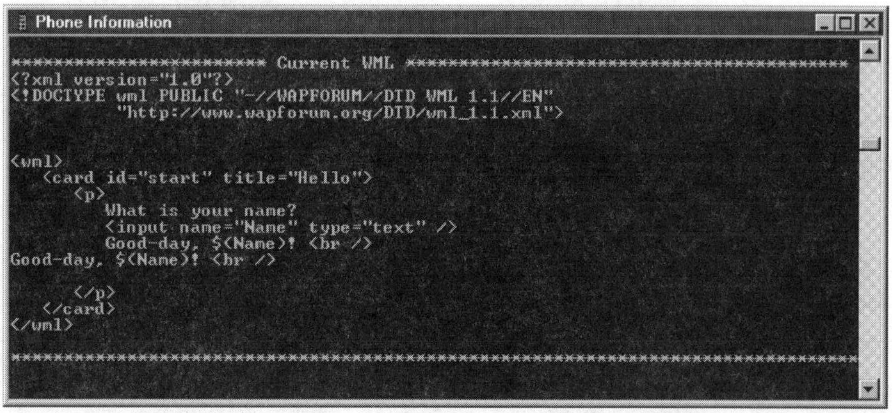

```
****************** Current WML ******************
<?xml version="1.0"?>
<!DOCTYPE wml PUBLIC "-//WAPFORUM//DTD WML 1.1//EN"
          "http://www.wapforum.org/DTD/wml_1.1.xml">


<wml>
    <card id="start" title="Hello">
        <p>
            What is your name?
            <input name="Name" type="text" />
            Good-day, $(Name)! <br />
Good-day, $(Name)! <br />

        </p>
    </card>
</wml>

****************************************************
```

Figure 27.4   Viewing WML content generated by the greeting.jsp in the Phone Information window

Notice in the display that the line with enclosing tags, <%-- and --%>, does not appear and the Java code of a for loop within <% and %> in the original JSP page has been transformed into plain WML code.

27.2.4   Understanding the example

When a request is made to greeting.jsp for the first time, the file is transformed into a servlet source file, then compiled into a servlet class. If you use JRun 3.0, you can find the servlet generated and stored in an appropriate directory (/JRun/servers/default/default-app/Web-inf/jsp).

The page compilation engine generates a servlet that sets the HTTP content-type value to text/html by default. We need to overwrite the default value to text/vnd.wap.wml in the HTTP response to be sent out to the client. To accomplish this, we must include the important statement in the original JSP document that calls response.setContentType().

Notice that we have used two objects—response and out—without declaring them. They are two of several objects that the generated servlet would declare. JSP document developers can use these implicit objects without declaring them in the original JSP page, but the developer who writes the JSP pages must have knowledge of the implicitly declared objects in order to take advantage of the convenience offered by them. In our example, response is an HttpServletResponse object and out is a JspWriter object, which in turn is derived from java.io.Writer.

We will discuss more details of the coding components in the next section.

27.3 *JSP* CONTAINER TAGS

Besides <% and %>, JSP defines other tags used to indicate different intention of the text enclosed. Table 27.1 summarizes the types of JSP scripting elements.

Table 27.1 JSP scripting elements

Scripting element	Description	Example

Scriptlet	A scriptlet consists of executable Java code enclosed within the <% and %> tags.	`<%`
		`    for (int i=0; i<10; i++)`
		`        total += i;`
		`%>`

Comment	Java comments are enclosed within <%-- and --%>, which will not be output to the client. If you want to send any comment in the content to the client, you should use <!-- and --> instead.	`<%-- Iteration starts here --%>`

Directive	Directives are not executable code. Neither will they be output to the client. They are instructions meant for the JSP page. The general format is:
	<%@ directive attribute-value-pairs %>
	
	For a complete list of directives and their associated attributes, refer to the Java-Server Pages specifications, which can be downloaded from:
	http://javasoft.sun.com/ products/jsp/ download.html.
		`<%@ page language="Java"`
		`           contentType="text/vnd.wap.wml"`
		`           info="JSP: Sending greetings"`
		`%>`
		
		The code specifies information concerning the page: the language used (Java), the content type for the WML output, and the text that should be returned when an inquiry is made of the servlet using the `getServletInfo()` method. Note that setting the `contentType` attribute in this way is an alternative to calling `response.setContentType()` to do the task.
		
		`<%@ include file="myPge.jsp" %>`
		The directive specifies inclusion of the file, myPge.jsp, at the time of translation of the page into Java servlet. Any scriptlet inside the included file will be part of the resultant servlet.
		
		`<%@ taglib uri="http://myhost/mytags"`
		`      prefix="wap" %>`
		This directive specifies extension to the current set of JSP tags to include additional tags defined in mytags. To use an element, say `actnow`, defined in `mytags`, the specified prefix must be used:
		`<wap:actnow> ...... </wap:actnow>`

Table 27.1 JSP scripting elements (continued)

Scripting element	Description	Example

Declaration	As in normal programming, variables are declared before use. `<%!` and `%>` are used for declaring global variables as well as methods. Variables can also be declared within scriptlet tags, in which case, they are local variables within the service method of the servlet generated.	`<%! float price = 101.50f; %>`
		`<% int   counter; %>`
		The statements declare two variables. The `float` variable is a global variable while the `int` variable is local to the service method of the servlet.
		
		Invalid example:
		`<% String userID="Jun" %>`
		`<%!`
		`   public String getID() {`
		`      return (userID);`
		`   }`
		`%>`
		The above will cause compilation errors as `userID` is considered undefined within `getID()`. To rectify the problem, declare `userID` using `<%!` and `%>`.

Expression	The text enclosed within `<%=` and `%>` is treated as an expression. The expression is evaluated and its value is returned as a Java String object for output to the output stream.	`<%! int count=10; %>` `<b> counter: <%= count %> </b>`

27.4   *JSP* IMPLICIT OBJECTS

When writing JSP pages, you must declare all variables and methods before using them, unless they are predefined variables (also called implicit objects). Table 27.2 is a list of implicit objects that the generated servlet will declare for you. You can see the declaration statements in the generated servlet source file.

Table 27.2 Predefined variables

Predefined object	Object type	Description
application	javax.servlet.ServletContext	A ServletContext object that may be used to store information that can be shared across servlets in the servlet engine. It is the object returned via the method call, getContext(), of a servlet configuration (i.e., ServletConfig) object.
config	javax.servlet.ServletConfig	The ServletConfig object representing this particular JSP page where the variable is used.
out	javax.servlet.jsp.JspWriter	A JspWriter object for sending data to the output stream.
page	java.lang.Object	Refers to this particular JSP page. It is the object referred to by this in the page.
pageContext	javax.servlet.jsp.PageContext	A PageContext object of a JSP page that is able to store information associated to that page.

Table 27.2   Predefined variables (continued)

Predefined object	Object type	Description
request	Subtype of the generic javax.servlet.ServletRequest object that is protocol-dependent (e.g., javax.servlet.HttpServletRequest, which operates on the protocol, HTTP).	A request object that is associated with the incoming request to the JSP page. This object provides methods to retrieve incoming parameters and HTTP header information.
response	Subtype of the generic javax.servlet.ServletResponse object that is protocol-dependent (e.g., javax.servlet.HttpServletResponse, which operates on the protocol, HTTP).	A response object that is associated with the incoming request to the JSP page. This object provides methods to set HTTP header fields such as the content type.
exception	java.lang.Throwable.	The uncaught Throwable object that caused the invocation of the error page.

27.5   JSP STANDARD ACTIONS

JSP standard actions enable a developer to incorporate common actions into JSP pages. This section briefly describes these standard actions. Refer to the formal JSP specifications for detailed description and usage.

A JSP standard action is expressed in one of two formats, depending on whether it contains any other element tag:

- <jsp:*xxx* .... />
- <jsp:*xxx* ....> .... </jsp:*xxx*>

where *xxx* is a standard action name.

In the second format, the action tags can contain one or more <jsp:param> for defining a property name and value pair. Table 27.3 is an explanation of standard actions.

Table 27.3   JSP standard actions

Standard action	Description	Example
<jsp:forward>	Used to redirect request to another resource such as a servlet or another static JSP page.	<jsp:forward page="Authenticate"> <jsp:param name="myID" value="x123" /> </jsp:forward> Forwards the client request to a servlet named `Authenticate`, and sets the parameter, `myID`, used in the servlet to the initial value, `x123`.
<jsp:include>	Specifies a page to be included in the current JSP page before it is translated into a servlet.	<jsp:include page="common.jsp" flush="true"> <jsp:param name="count" value="100"/> </jsp:include>

Table 27.3   JSP standard actions (continued)

Standard action	Description	Example

<jsp:plugin>	Specifies an HTML object to be embedded (e.g., via the <object> or <embed> tag) in the content generated to the user agent.	<jsp:plugin type="applet"
		    code="chart.class"
		     width="200" height="150">
		  <jsp:paramname="Jan"
		    value="100"/>
		</jsp:plugin>

<jsp:useBean>	Enables a developer to use a Java Bean within the page. The scope of the bean may be beyond the page.	<jsp:useBean id="autoCount"
		    scope="application"
		    class="count.class" />
		The name of the bean instance is `autoCount`. The scope is across the application and the Java class of the bean used is `count.class`.

	Two other related actions used with Java Bean are `<jsp:setProperty>` for setting the value of the bean's property and `<jsp:getProperty>` for retrieving a bean's property value and passing it to the `out` implicit object discussed earlier.	<jsp:setProperty name="autoCount"
		    property="beanName"
		    param="inName" />
		The property, `beanName`, of the bean instance, `autoCount`, is set to the value of the `inName` parameter of the incoming request.
		
		<jsp:getProperty name="autoCount"
		    property="beanName" />
		This retrieves the value of the bean's property named `beanName`.

27.6   *SERVER-SIDE ERROR TROUBLESHOOTING*

Since the JSP document is processed at the server side, when working with JSP pages, errors that occur with JSP will bear the HTTP status code of the server category (*5xx*), if indeed there is an output stream sent to the user agent. The two main types of errors are compilation and run time.

27.6.1   Compilation error

Let us revisit the example we saw in section 27.2.2 and introduce an error in the code as shown in the highlighted line, where the variable i was not declared before its use in the condition check of the for loop:

```
<?xml version="1.0" ?>
<!DOCTYPE wml PUBLIC "-//WAPFORUM//DTD WML 1.1//EN"
     "http://www.wapforum.org/DTD/wml_1.1.xml">

<%--greeting.jsp--%>
<% response.setContentType ("text/vnd.wap.wml"); %>
<wml>
    <card id="start" title="Hello">
      <p>
         What is your name?
```

```
      <input name="Name" type="text"/>
      <do type="accept">
        <go href="#next"/>
      </do>
    </p>
  </card>
  <card id="next" title="Hello">
    <p>
      <%
        for (i=0; i<2; i++)
            out.println ("Good-day, $(Name)! <br />");
      %>
    </p>
  </card>
</wml>
```

This causes an error during the compilation of the servlet generated from the page. The error is caught and the error code indicating server-side error, e.g., 500, is sent to the requesting client. Figure 27.5 is a common error screen.

Figure 27.5 Error code and information displayed in the screen and Phone Information window

If there is error in the Java code embedded in the script, the corresponding servlet generated cannot be compiled successfully, a common cause of a 500 error message. Unfortunately, the error message seen in the Phone Information window is very brief, which is not helpful to our debugging.

To ensure that it is due to the Java coding instead of a setup problem of the origin server, check the directory where the servlet is generated. You can check if the generation time stamp of the servlet source file is the same as that of the compiled servlet class. If the time stamps are different (the compilation time is earlier than the generation time) or the servlet class does not exist, then we can confirm that our Java code is problematic and needs some fixing.

27.6.2   Run-time error

Here is a simple JSP, myPage.jsp, for performing division arithmetic.

```
<?xml version="1.0" ?>
<!DOCTYPE wml PUBLIC "-//WAPFORUM//DTD WML 1.1//EN"
      "http://www.wapforum.org/DTD/wml_1.1.xml">
```

```
<%@ page contentType="text/vnd.wap.wml" %>          ◁┐ Specifies the appropriate
<wml> <!-- myPage.jsp -->                             │ content type header field for
   <card id="start" title="My Page">                  │ the output to the client
     <p>
        This is my JSP page.
     <%! int num=100, divisor=2; %>   ◁┐ Declares and initializes
     <%                                │ two integer variables
        out.println ("Division result: " + (num/divisor));  ◁┐ Prints the
     %>                                                        │ result of
     </p>                                                      │ dividing num
   </card>                                                     │ by divisor
</wml>
```

Figure 27.6 shows the display if the division page is loaded to the UP Simulator.

Now, let us introduce a run-time error by changing the initial value of `divisor` to 0:

```
<%! int num=100, divisor=0; %>
```

When myPage.jsp is reloaded into the phone simulator, we will see an error message (figure 27.7).

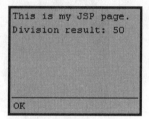

Figure 27.6   Result screen generated by myPage.jsp

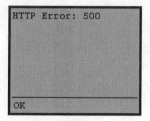

Figure 27.7   Screen showing error code for attempt to divide a number by 0

For run-time errors, we can redirect the handling of the error or exception to an error output page to give more meaningful error messages instead of the 500 status code. To do this, we modify the directive of the example to include the specification of an error output page, say myErrPg.jsp:

```
<%@ page contentType="text/vnd.wap.wml" errorPage="myErrPg.jsp" %>
```

Before we reload myPage.jsp, we must first prepare the error output page, myErrPg.jsp:

```
<?xml version="1.0" ?>
<!DOCTYPE wml PUBLIC "-//WAPFORUM//DTD WML 1.1//EN"
      "http://www.wapforum.org/DTD/wml_1.1.xml">

<%@ page contentType="text/vnd.wap.wml" isErrorPage="true" %>     ◁┐
<wml> <!-- myErrPg.jsp -->                        Sets the isErrorPage flag to
 <card id="start" title="My Error">              true to indicate that this page
  <p>                                                  is an error-handling page
```

```
    Error: <%= exception.getMessage() %>
  </p>
 </card>
</wml>
```

Prints the message pertaining to the error, which is an implicit exception **object**

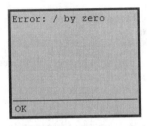

Now, load myPage.jsp once again, and we will see the display in figure 27.8.

Press F5 while at the simulator interface, to see the source code of this error page in the Phone Information window (figure 27.9). It is the page, myErrPg.jsp, populated with the relevant exception message.

Figure 27.8 Display of error via an error-handling page

```
*********************** Current WML ***********************
<?xml version="1.0"?>
<!DOCTYPE wml PUBLIC "-//WAPFORUM//DTD WML 1.1//EN"
         "http://www.wapforum.org/DTD/wml_1.1.xml">

<wml> <!-- myErrPg.jsp -->
   <card id="start" title="My Error">
      <p>
         Error: / by zero
      </p>
   </card>
</wml>
***************************************************************
```

Figure 27.9   Viewing content generated by myErrPg.jsp in the Phone Information window

27.7   SUMMARY

In this chapter, we introduced JavaServer Pages to help ease the development of server-side code using the Java language and servlet technology. Details of declaring common variable objects such as `response` and `out`, as well as compilation of servlets are no longer the responsibilities of the developer. This frees the developer to concentrate on the development of code that concerns implementation of business logic, which could be a huge and complex task.

In the next chapter, we will use JSP to implement an electronic mailing service. You will appreciate the amount of underlying details that are hidden from the developer especially during the debugging stage, so that he can focus on solving the application problem on hand.

CHAPTER 27   INTRODUCTION TO JAVASERVER PAGES

C H A P T E R   2 8

Developing email applications using Java

28.1   INTRODUCTION

Email has become such an important part of our daily lives both at work and at home that many of us use an email application more often than probably any other standard desktop tool. Most of us use a web or a desktop client such as Microsoft Outlook or Lotus Notes for sending and receiving email messages.

Mobile and active users of email applications consider the requirement of using a PC to access emails to be an inconvenience, obviously a problem for those of us who are out of the office or away from home and want to check our email messages quickly. For example, if you are out of the office over your lunch hour and you need to check on an important email message, carrying a laptop with you may not be practical or feasible.

With a wireless device such as a WAP phone, we can now manage our email quickly, anywhere, and at anytime; we are not constrained to using a desktop PC or lugging around a laptop. Thus, email applications have become an important requirement of a wireless application suite.

A WAP email application requires the development of a server-side application infrastructure. Architects and developers who are tasked with developing a server-side architecture in Java to support an email application can use JavaMail, a Java 2 Enterprise Edition (J2EE) platform API. JavaMail increases a developer's productivity by allowing a developer to focus on the business logic of an application rather than on the specifics of email protocols. It does this by providing a layer of abstraction that is designed to support current email standards and future enhancements in a platform and protocol-independent way.

This chapter introduces you to using the JavaMail API for developing WAP email messaging applications. It will cover:

- Email messages
- Email protocols
- JavaMail and the JavaBeans Activation Framework architectures
- JavaMail usage
- JSP to present WML content to WAP email users
- A sample application that uses JavaMail, WML, and JSP to deliver WAP email functionality
- Issues pertaining to WAP email application development

28.2 WHAT IS AN EMAIL MESSAGE?

Before we discuss the JavaMail API, let us explore the concept of an email message. Understanding how a message is structured will help you develop a better appreciation of the JavaMail interface.

An email message's structure is described in terms of two main components: the header and the content.

The message header

Table 28.1 lists the elements in the message header.

Table 28.1   Elements of an email message header

Header element	Description
Sender (from)	The sender's (from) email address
Recipient (to)	The recipient's (to) email address
Date sent	The date the message was sent

Table 28.1   Elements of an email message header (continued)

Header element	Description
Message ID	A message's unique identifier
Subject	The subject of the message

The content is stored in a separate logical structure of a message.

The message content

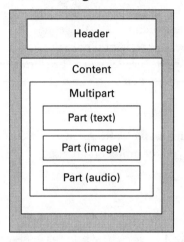

Figure 28.1   Structure of an email message

A *message's content* is the message body and is described in terms of parts. Message content can comprise a single part such as text or a multipart container. The content of a simple text message with no attachments is represented as a single part. The content of an email message with attachments is represented as a multipart object. A *multipart container* serves as a structure with a number of message body parts such as text, audio, and image content, as shown in Figure 28.1.

In summary, the central concepts of a message such as the header, content, multipart, and part are important because, as you will see, they will be reflected in the JavaMail API classes and interfaces.

28.3   OVERVIEW OF EMAIL PROTOCOLS

Now let us explore how messages are sent and received from email servers (figure 28.2). To transfer messages to and from an email server, one uses an *email client*. *Email servers* send and receive email messages across the Internet. These servers store users' messages either permanently or until retrieved by an email client. *Email protocols* are the network mechanisms for sending or retrieving email messages between email clients and servers.

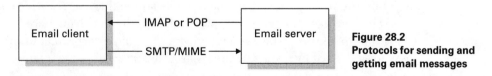

**Figure 28.2
Protocols for sending and getting email messages**

A number of standard email protocols are capable of sending and receiving email messages. In general, email protocols can be placed in two categories:

- Mail transport protocols
- Mail retrieval protocols

Mail transport protocols

Mail transport protocols pertain to transporting messages to email servers. The common protocol for sending Internet email messages is Simple Mail Transfer Protocol (SMTP). The original SMTP specification limited messages to a certain line length and allowed only 7-bit ASCII characters.

The Multipurpose Internet Mail Extensions (MIME) specification builds on SMTP by removing the maximum line length for messages and allowing new types of content, such as images and audio files, to be included in email messages. The MIME specification overcomes SMTP limitations by defining additional fields in a message header to describe new types of content and message structure. MIME defines the *content-type* header to specify the type and subtype of message content. For example, a message with an HTML attachment would have a content-type header set to "text/html." SMTP and MIME are typically used together to send Internet email messages.

Mail retrieval protocols

Mail retrieval protocols pertain to retrieving messages from email servers. To retrieve messages from Internet mail servers, two types of protocols are used:

- POP3 (Post Office Protocol 3)
- IMAP4 (Internet Message Access Protocol 4)

Although POP3 is more widely used, IMAP4 has a number of advantages. First, it supports multiple folders on a remote mail server whereas POP3 supports only the Inbox folder. Second, IMAP supports message status flags such as a flag that indicates whether a message has been previously seen; POP3 doesn't. These types of protocol features are important considerations in designing your application.

In summary, an email client application uses SMTP/MIME to send messages to an email server and uses IMAP or POP to retrieve messages from an email server. JavaMail provides implementations of SMTP, IMAP4, and POP3. For more information on these Internet mail protocols, consult the pertinent Request For Comments (RFC).

28.4 INTRODUCTION TO JAVAMAIL

As an applications developer, if you use the JavaMail API you do not need to learn all the POP, IMAP, or SMTP commands and syntax for sending and receiving email messages. The JavaMail API presents a powerful object-oriented interface in Java that shields you from learning how to use individual email protocols. Let us discuss how this is accomplished by discussing the JavaMail architecture.

28.4.1 JavaMail architecture

The architecture can be described in terms of three main layers (figure 28.3). JavaMail's layered architecture allows clients to use the JavaMail API with different message access protocols (POP3, IMAP4) and message transport protocols (SMTP).

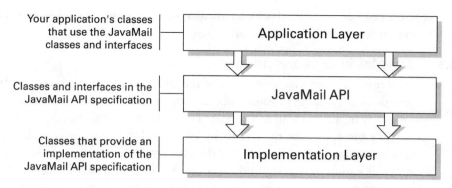

Your application's classes that use the JavaMail classes and interfaces — **Application Layer**

Classes and interfaces in the JavaMail API specification — **JavaMail API**

Classes that provide an implementation of the JavaMail API specification — **Implementation Layer**

Figure 28.3   Overview of JavaMail architecture

Application layer uses the JavaMail API. This layer comprises your application's classes that use JavaMail classes and interfaces to support an email client.

JavaMail API—The second layer is the JavaMail API that defines a set of abstract classes and interfaces for supporting email client functionality. This is the layer that frees a developer from having to deal with specifics of email protocols. JavaMail provides concrete subclasses of these abstract classes for Internet mail. The JavaMail API layer depends on concrete implementations of protocols.

Implementation layer—The implementation layer forms the third layer. Since JavaMail is protocol independent, it's up to service providers to implement specific message retrieval and message transmission protocols according to the JavaMail API. Service provider implementations play a role similar to that of JDBC drivers. A provider registry allows service providers to register their protocol implementations to be used by JavaMail APIs. If you would like to use the JavaMail API but there is no service provider for your email protocol, you can develop a JavaMail implementation for your protocol using the JavaMail Service Provider specification. The JavaMail web site (http://www.javasoft.com/products/javamail/index.html) has more information on third-party service providers and documentation on how to develop a service provider.

28.4.2   JavaBeans activation framework

JavaMail uses another framework to manage a message's content. JavaMail interacts with message content through an intermediate layer called the *JavaBeans activation framework (JAF)*, part of the Glasgow specification (a future release of the JavaBeans component model specification). JAF provides a uniform way of determining the type of a message's content and encapsulating access to it. JAF is implemented as a standard Java extension. Sun provides a royalty-free implementation of JAF that requires JDK 1.1.x or higher.

JAF is used to get and set a message's text and attachments (the message content). JavaMail provides convenient methods to interact with JAF. For example, MimeMessage's setText() method can be used to set a string as a message's content with a MIME type of "text/plain." Another example is MimeMessage's getContent() method, which returns a message's content as a Java object by invoking methods on JAF's DataHandler class.

28.4.3 JavaMail classes and interfaces

Now that you have a basic overview of the JavaMail architecture and JAF, we can discuss the main JavaMail classes and methods needed to support an email client. The simplicity of the JavaMail API is reflected in its choice of abstractions.

We can appreciate the familiarity of these abstractions by considering a typical email scenario and our knowledge of the basic structure of a message. We typically start an email session by logging in using a user ID and password. Then, we can view our messages in our Inbox folder. We can choose to read a message's content, that is, view its parts. We can create a message by entering a recipient's address and a subject and then send the message using some transport mechanism. In this scenario, a number of abstractions such as session, transport, folder, message, address, and part were mentioned. As you will see, we find them modeled as JavaMail API classes and interfaces.

Most of the JavaMail classes and interfaces are in the `javax.mail` package. Classes specific to Internet email such as `MimeMessage` are in the `javax.mail.internet` package. The JAF classes are in the `javax.activation` package. Table 28.2 describes fundamental JavaMail classes and interfaces.

Table 28.2 Important classes and interfaces when using JavaMail and JAF

Class or interface name	Description
Session	This javax.mail class represents a mail session and serves as the main entry point to the JavaMail API. The Session class controls access to the Store and Transport objects.
Transport	This javax.mail class represents a transport agent that sends a message to its recipients using a specific message transfer protocol. Transport is implemented by a service provider.
Store	This javax.mail class defines a message store (a database and an access protocol) for a set of message folders. Folder objects are accessed through a Store object. Store is implemented by a service provider.
Folder	This javax.mail class comprises messages and subfolders in a treelike structure. It also defines methods to delete and retrieve messages. Message objects are accessed through a folder object. Folder is implemented by a service provider.
Message	This javax.mail class models an email message. A message object interacts with its content using JAF. The javax.mail.internet.MimeMessage class extends Message to represent a MimeMessage. Message is implemented by a service provider.
Address	This javax.mail class models an email address. The javax.mail.internet.InternetAddress class extends Address to support Internet email addresses.
Multipart	This javax.mail.Multipart serves as a container for message body parts.

Table 28.2   Important classes and interfaces when using JavaMail and JAF (continued)

Class or interface name	Description
Part	This javax.mail.Part interface represents a message part and is a core interface implemented by Message. The javax.mail.BodyPart is an abstract class that implements Part and models a message part within a message multipart.
DataHandler	Message content is represented as a javax.activation.DataHandler class that wraps around the actual message data. The DataHandler class provides an interface to the JavaBeans Activation Framework.

28.4.4   JavaMail exceptions

An important component of an application's design is how it handles error conditions. For example, if a user enters an invalid user ID or password when connecting to an email server, the application needs to take some action, such as presenting the user with an error dialog. The JavaMail API methods handle error conditions by throwing a number of specific exceptions.

The base class for JavaMail exceptions is javax.mail.MessagingException. MessagingException extends from `java.lang.Exception`. More specific exceptions are listed in table 28.3.

Table 28.3   JavaMail exceptions

Class name	Description
AuthenticationFailedException	Thrown when an invalid user name or password is used in a Store object's connect() operation
FolderClosedException	Thrown when an operation is invoked on a Message and the containing Folder is invalid
FolderNotFoundException	Thrown when a Folder operation is invoked on a Folder that does not exist
IllegalWriteException	Thrown when an attempt is made to update a read-only attribute such as a MIME header of a message
MessageRemovedException	Thrown when an invalid operation is called on a deleted Message
MethodNotSupportedException	Thrown when an operation is not supported by the underlying implementation
StoreClosedException	Thrown when an operation is invoked on a Message object and its associated Store is invalid
SendFailedException	Thrown when a message cannot be sent
NoSuchProviderException	Thrown when a Session attempts to instantiate a Service Provider that does not exist

You should now have an overview of JavaMail and its important classes and interfaces. This discussion used JavaMail version 1.1, a standard Java extension that requires JDK/JRE 1.1.x or higher. The anticipated enhancements in JavaMail 1.2 include new methods for retrieving the default `Session`, new classes, performance improvements, feature enhancements, and bug fixes. For more information on JavaMail 1.2, log on to http://www.javasoft.com/products/javamail/index.html.

28.5 USING JAVAMAIL

Now that you have an understanding of the JavaMail architecture, the main JavaMail classes, interfaces, and exceptions, let us see how JavaMail can be used to perform common email functions. To illustrate, let us consider four core use cases:

- Establishing a session with an email server
- Composing and sending email messages
- Retrieving email messages
- Deleting email messages

28.5.1 Establishing a session with an email server

Before you can send or receive messages, you need to establish a mail session between the mail client, that is, the WAP email application, and the remote email servers. This process involves two steps:

- Initializing the email properties
- Using the email properties to obtain a session

Initializing the email properties

A `Properties` object is first initialized with the email user's configuration data such as SMTP host. A specific email user's properties such as transport protocol, SMTP host, and IMAP host are used to establish a connection to email servers. Other properties need to be set when retrieving messages (using a Store object).

```
// Initialize mail user properties
mailProperties = new Properties();
mailProperties.put("mail.transport.protocol", "smtp");
mailProperties.put("mail.smtp.host", "someSmtpHost");
```

Using the email properties to obtain a session

To manage the email user properties used by the JavaMail API, the Session class is used. To establish a session with an email server, the `Session` object uses the email properties initialized in the first step. The `Session` object is a factory for `Store` and `Transport` objects. The following code uses the mail properties to obtain a `Session` object:

```
// Get a Session object
Session session = Session.getDefaultInstance(mailProperties, null);
// Get a Store object
Store store = session.getStore();
```

The first line of code in the example gets the default `Session` object using the defined mail user properties. The second parameter ensures that subsequent requests for a session are only granted to a caller with the correct `Authenticator` object.

The second line obtains the `Store` object if additional mail properties such as IMAP host, user name, and password had been added to the mailProperties object. The `Store` object is used to retrieve email messages.

One issue to consider as you design the application architecture of your email client is the dependency between your business layer and JavaMail. To reduce tight coupling between the two, the Facade design pattern can be used. For example, mail user configuration can be passed into a Facade to assemble the appropriate JavaMail objects (`Session`, `Transport`, and `Store`) and perform any other initialization such as security. As a result, dependencies between your business layer classes and the JavaMail subsystem are reduced, and your application's business layer can use a simpler, higher-level interface such as `MailFacade.configure(Properties p)`.

A use case pertaining to email server connectivity is support for "disconnected email operation," which involves maintaining email message stores on both the remote server and a local client, performing operations on both stores, and being able to synchronize these two stores. JavaSoft's IMAP provider implements interfaces that can be used for supporting disconnected operation.

For debugging JavaMail, the `Session` object has an operation, `setDebug(dbgFlag)`, to enable or disable the production of debug messages from the JavaMail classes. The argument to `setDebug()` is a boolean value. This debugging output can include the protocol-specific commands such as IMAP commands that are used by a JavaMail service provider to implement a JavaMail method. Studying the debugging output can provide a useful learning and troubleshooting tool for email protocol interactions.

28.5.2   Composing and sending email messages

Once a mail session has been established, an email application can create and send an email message. This process involves three steps:

- Creating a message
- Initializing the message
- Sending the message

Creating a message

First, a `MimeMessage` object needs to be constructed by using the `Session` object.

```
// Create new message
Message msg = new MimeMessage(session);
```

The default `MimeMessage` constructor creates an empty Message object using the current Session object.

Initializing the message

The message object is initialized with the recipient's email address(es), the subject of the message, and the message text. When setting the recipients of a message, a JavaMail class `Message.RecipientType` is used to specify the type of recipient. Currently, you can set three types of recipients: to, cc (carbon copy) and bcc (blind carbon copy).

```
// Initialize the message
msg.setFrom(new InternetAddress(senderEmailAddress));
msg.setRecipients(Message.RecipientType.TO,
    InternetAddress.parse(recipientEmail,false));      ❶
msg.setSubject(subject);
msg.setText(messageText);      ❷
```

Code comments

❶ Parses the comma-separated sequence of addresses in the `recipientEmail` variable into `InternetAddress` objects.

❷ Uses `setText()` to initialize simple text messages.

Sending the message

After the message is created and initialized with the recipient, subject, and message text, the message is ready to be sent. The message is sent using the `Transport` object. Note, we used the `send()` method which is a convenience method of the `Transport` class.

```
// Send message
Transport.send(msg);
```

The `send()` method is a static method of the `Transport` class. We are not required to create an instance of a `Transport` object.

28.5.3   Retrieving email messages

Now that you have seen how a message is created and sent, let's see how messages can be retrieved from an email server. After you've successfully established a mail session, an email client can retrieve your email messages from the email server and display them to a user. This process follows five steps:

- Connecting to the message store
- Opening the folder
- Getting messages from the folder
- Presenting message summary
- Viewing a message's content

Connecting to the message store

First, a connection needs to be established with the message store. Let us assume we want to get messages from our Inbox folder. The `Store` object is used to access the Inbox folder:

```
store.connect();
Folder folder = store.getFolder("INBOX");
```

Other `connect()` methods require parameters such as user ID, password, host name, and port.

Opening the folder

The Inbox folder that we obtained in the previous step needs to be opened.

```
folder.open(Folder.READ_WRITE);
```

A folder can also be opened as `READ_ONLY` which means that the contents of the folder cannot be modified.

Getting messages from the folder

After a folder has been opened, it is used to get message totals and the messages. Note that the `Message` objects returned from the `getMessages()` method call are designed to be lightweight objects. For example, the `Message` objects returned could comprise only message header details. Retrieval of the actual message content is deferred until the message content is used. Thus the `getMessages()` method isn't designed to be a resource-intensive operation.

```
// Getting message totals and messages from a folder
int totalMessages = folder.getMessageCount();
Message[] msgs = folder.getMessages();
```

The operation `folder.getMessageCount()` is called on a folder previously opened. Calling it on a folder that is closed can be expensive and may not be supported by some service providers.

Presenting message summary

A typical email client first displays a summary of messages in the form of header details such as sender (from), recipients (to), subject, and sent date. `Message` objects can provide these details. A summary line for each message can be obtained:

```
Address[] from = msgs[i].getFrom();
Address[] to = msgs[i].getRecipients(Message.RecipientType.TO);    ⟵⎯⎯⎯⎮
String subject = msgs[i].getSubject();                      To get recipients that were
Date d = msgs[i].getSentDate();   ⟵⎯⎯⎮                            carbon copied,
                     Gets the date that the        Message.RecipientType.CC
                     message was sent              could be used as an argument
```

Viewing a message's content

After viewing the message summary, a user can typically decide to view the actual message content in the form of text and/or attachments. A message's content is retrieved in the form of an object. The retrieved object depends on the type of content. If the content is a message with multiple attachments, a `Multipart` object (a container of `BodyPart` objects) is returned. If the `Part`'s content is text, then a simple `String` object is returned. To retrieve a message's content, you can invoke `Part`'s `getContent()` method. Note that `Part` is an interface implemented by Message and BodyPart classes. Due to the limitations of a WAP device, a WAP email application may focus on only displaying a message's text.

```
Object o = part.getContent();
If (o instanceof String) {      ❶
    // we can manage this type of content in a WAP application
} else if (o instanceof Multipart) {      ❷
    // we choose not to manage this type of content in a WAP application
} else if (o instanceof Message) {      ❸
    // we choose not to manage this type of content in a WAP application

}
```

Code comments

❶ Checks whether the message content is text.

❷ Checks whether the message content is a multipart container that needs to be recursively iterated to retrieve the attachments of the message.

❸ Checks whether the message content is a message itself.

Using download algorithms

You've now seen how messages are retrieved using JavaMail. If your application supports both IMAP and POP, you may need to develop different algorithms to download messages, depending on your particular use case and performance requirements. For example, when developing applications for use with low bandwidth clients using POP (which doesn't maintain flags to indicate unread messages), downloading all messages each time becomes a performance issue. Thus you may need an algorithm that uses provider-specific methods to prevent redownloading messages. Depending on your requirements, other algorithms may be needed.

Each of these download algorithms can be encapsulated as Strategy classes (Strategy design pattern) that share a common interface. A Strategy Factory can return strategy objects for downloading messages, depending on particular user configurations. This approach allows you to switch from one download algorithm to another, depending on the user configuration, and avoid having to use protocol-specific conditional statements. For more information on the Strategy and other design patterns, consult *Design Patterns* by Gamma et al. (1995).

CHAPTER 28   DEVELOPING EMAIL APPLICATIONS

When you retrieve messages from a server, a feature that's available in some popular email clients is an Inbox Assistant to process incoming messages such as deleting messages based on user-specified rules. JavaMail doesn't provide direct support for features such as automated message filtering.

28.5.4 Deleting email messages

Another use case for email clients is deleting a message. Using JavaMail, deleting messages from a folder is a two-step process.

- Marking messages to be deleted
- Deleting the marked messages from the folder

Marking messages to be deleted

Messages are marked for deletion by using the Flags class constant. Similarly, the setFlag() operation can also be used to unmark messages.

```
message.setFlag(Flags.Flag.DELETED, true);
```

Deleting marked messages from the folder

Messages that have been marked are deleted from a folder by either explicitly invoking a Folder's expunge() method or closing a folder with the expunge parameter of the close() method set to true.

```
folder.close(true);
```

28.6 JAVASERVER PAGES

We have discussed the JavaMail classes and interfaces for sending and retrieving email messages. Now we need to explore how to present email messages and email menus to a user on a WAP device.

To address this issue, let us turn to another J2EE API. JavaServer Pages (JSP) is a J2EE API that can be used to support the presentation component of a WAP email application. This section will provide a brief overview of JSP as it pertains to the development of a sample WAP email application. For a more detailed discussion, see chapter 27.

As you know, Java servlets and legacy CGI programs allow you to generate dynamic content in response to an HTTP request. However, the intrinsic nature of servlets forces a tight coupling between the presentation logic needed to present the content to a user and the logic needed to interface with the business objects to satisfy a request. For example, a servlet to generate WML is essentially a Java class with WML code embedded in it. Using servlets to produce WML requires nontrivial developer expertise and is not a conducive development environment for WAP page designers.

The JSP specification is a standard extension defined on top of the servlet API that addresses issues associated with using servlets for presentation logic. This is because a JSP can be inherently viewed as a presentation page, such as WML or HTML code, with embedded Java code. Page designers with little Java development experience can develop JSPs. When a request for a JSP page is first made, the JSP is compiled into a servlet, using a process invisible to a JSP designer, to service requests for that page.

At the beginning of each JSP page, you must specify a document prologue in the form of an XML declaration and a document type declaration:

```
<?xml version="1.0"?>
<!DOCTYPE wml PUBLIC "-//WAPFORUM//DTD WML 1.1//EN"
"http://www.wapforum.org/DTD/wml_1.1.xml">
```

A JSP comprises a number of different types of elements such as directives, expressions, scriptlets, comments, and static elements.

Directives

JSP directives are information directed at the JSP engine. Directives are placed in the following `<%@ ... %>` tag. A page directive is used to specify a valid WML MIME type and character set of the JSP using a content type header. A page directive can also be used to specify the packages, such as JavaMail packages, that the JSP imports.

```
<%@ page import="javax.mail.*, javax.mail.internet.*, javax.activation.*"
contentType="text/vnd.wap.wml;charset=ISO-8859-1" %>
```

Scriptlets

JSP scriptlets are code fragments that are executed when a JSP responds to a request. Scriptlets are embedded within the tags `<% ... %>`. For example, to retrieve messages from the `HttpSession` object, the following scriptlet could be used:

```
<%
    Message[] msgs = (Message[]) session.getValue("messages");
%>
```

The `HttpSession` object is an implicit object (it did not have to be created by the page designer) available to a scriptlet.

Expressions

The results of a JSP expression are inserted as a string in a JSP page. An example of an expression is a call to an operation on an object that results in the subject of a message being displayed in a WML card such as:

```
<%=msg.getSubject()%>
```

Comments

JSP comments can be included in a JSP page by placing them within the `<!-- ... -->` tags such as:

```
<!-- Two cards used to accept userid and password -->
```

Static elements

A JSP page can also comprise static elements, that is, no Java code is included in the page. A JSP can simply display a message to a user:

```wml
<wml>
  <!-- Final splash card after user chooses to logout -->
  <card  id="mainmenu">
    <p>
      Thank for you using the WAP email service
    </p>
  </card>
</wml>
```

This brief introduction to JSP should provide you with an overview of the key elements of this technology. We will see JSP elements in more detail in the sample application later in this chapter.

28.7 SAMPLE *WAP* EMAIL APPLICATION

The purpose of this sample application is to show you how the JavaMail API can be used to deliver a WAP email application using JSP, servlets, and WML. Since this example is only provided for illustration purposes, a number of design details such as using enterprise data sources for email configuration and coding details such as extensive error checking have been omitted to ensure clarity of the JavaMail details. However, you can use the overall application architecture as a basis to design your WAP email application.

This section assumes that you have a working understanding of WML, servlets, and JSP because these technologies will be used extensively in this discussion. If not, please refer to the pertinent chapters in this text. This sample JavaMail application enables a WAP user to:

- Log in to a mail server
- Retrieve messages from an email server
- Create and send an email message
- Log out from a mail server

28.7.1 Architecture of WAP email system

The architecture of a WAP email system comprises a number of components:

- WAP phone
- WAP gateway
- Application server comprising servlet, JSP, and JavaMail components
- Email server

To explore this architecture, let us consider a typical scenario. If a WAP user chooses to retrieve email messages from an email server, the following steps need to occur:

1 The WAP user sends this request to the WAP gateway using the WAP protocol.

2 The WAP gateway converts this WAP protocol request and sends an HTTP request to the application server, which comprises a web server.

3 The web server directs the request to a servlet in the application layer that uses JavaMail/JAF to communicate the request to the email server.

4 The JavaMail classes may use a number of different protocols such as SMTP, IMAP, or POP to communicate with the email server. But, in this case, JavaMail uses the IMAP implementation for message retrieval. The email server retrieves the messages.

5 The servlet directs the request to a JSP that uses the downloaded messages to present the message content to a user in the form of a WML deck. The JSP generates a WML deck that is returned for display to a WAP phone.

6 The WML deck is returned to the WAP gateway.

7 The WML deck is encoded and sent back to the WAP device.

The architectural components involved in this scenario are shown in figure 28.4.

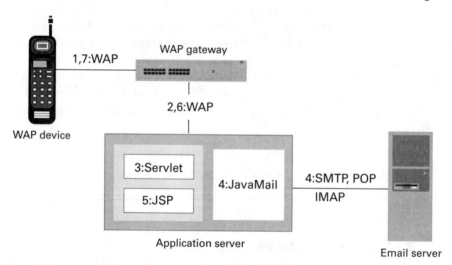

Figure 28.4 Overview of sample WAP email application architecture

28.7.2   Sample application design

Now let us discuss the design of the sample application that uses JSP, a servlet, JavaMail/JAF, and WML. The main components of this application are the JSP that generates the WML, the servlet that processes requests and controls the JSP used to respond to a request, and an email Facade that calls JavaMail methods to perform core use cases such as login, logout, and send a message.

- A JSP component encapsulates the presentation logic in the form of WML and WMLScript. Maintaining the WML code in a JSP, in contrast to a servlet, allows a page designer with WML expertise to more easily enhance and modify the user interface. A servlet selects the JSP page that is used to respond to a request.

- A servlet component responds to requests and determines the type of action to be taken based on input from a WAP user. The servlet interacts with the Email Facade, a business delegate that interfaces with the JavaMail API to satisfy requests from the servlet. Thus, in this architecture, the servlet comprises little to no WML code or logic pertaining to JavaMail. It merely serves as a mediator of requests.

- An Email Facade component encapsulates access to email logic using the JavaMail API. This component can be reused across multiple server-side applications (WAP-based, web-based) that have the same use cases but different presentation mechanisms (WML, HTML).

Thus, the overall architectural flow involves a servlet handling a request from a browser. The servlet uses the Email Facade to satisfy the request. In turn, the Email Facade uses the JavaMail API. The servlet then stores the returned objects such as `Message` objects in the `HttpSession` object. The servlet selects a JSP to present the results of a request to a user. The JSP can use the objects such as `Message` objects from the `HttpSession` object to generate the WML card (figure 28.5).

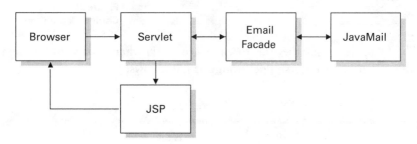

Figure 28.5 Schematic of sample application design

An important architectural consideration is whether to allow components in your application layer components, such as WAP clients and web clients, to reuse the email logic in your business layer. Using a layered architecture and appropriate design patterns can help promote this reuse. For example, different types of architectural components in the application layer can use a Facade to shield the application components clients from the JavaMail API. Both a Java client and a servlet can use the Email Facade to send and receive email messages; a client application would be required to provide only the view and controller components (Model-View-Controller (MVC) design pattern) of this type of mail-enabled application. The view and controller components need to be integrated with the Email Facade to support a WAP email application. When an MVC pattern is applied to this type of server-side development, the servlet acts as the controller responding to requests from the user presentation component, the JSP that generates the WML functions as the view or the presentation component and the JavaMail business objects as the model component. This type of design will be illustrated in this sample application.

To explore this sample WAP email application in more detail, let us discuss each of the three main application components (JSP, servlet, Email Facade).

28.7.3 JSP component

To illustrate the features and flow of this sample application, let us consider the WML cards that are presented to a WAP user as well as the associated JSPs that are used to produce them, that is, the JSPs that comprise the WML code.

Logging in

To log in, this sample WAP application begins by presenting a user two WML cards (figure 28.6).

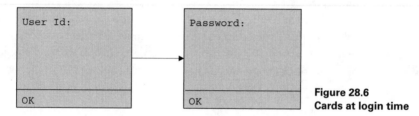

Figure 28.6
Cards at login time

The login deck asks the user to enter a user ID, then a password for email server authentication. A code snippet from this JSP follows:

```
<wml>
<!-- Two cards used to accept userid and password -->
<!-- First card gets user id and then goes to password card -->
   <card id="userIdLogin">          Gets the
      <do type="accept">            user ID of
         <go href="#pwdLogin"/>     the user
      </do>
      <p>
      User Id:
      <input name="userid"/>
      </p>
   </card>

   <!-- This card accepts password and sends values -->
   <!-- to servlet for authentication -->
   <card id="pwdLogin">          Gets the password
     <do type="accept">          of the user
```

```
  <go method="post" href="http://d:9300/servlet/WAPSvlt">
     <postfield name="userid" value="$userid"/>
     <postfield name="password" value="$pwd"/>
     <postfield name="action" value="Logon"/>
   </go>
   </do>
   <p>
   Password:
   <input name="pwd" type="password"/>
   </p>
   </card>
</wml>
```

◁─┐ **Note the use of the `<input>` element's type attribute to mask the password being entered**

Main menu

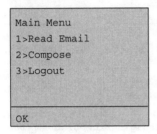

Figure 28.7 The menu screen after login

After a user enters a valid user ID and password, control is passed to the servlet (WAPSvlt) that uses this data to establish a session with a remote mail server. If this process is successful, the main menu screen is presented (figure 28.7).

Selection of any of the main menu options transfers control back to the servlet, (WAPSvlt), for processing the request. A code snippet from this main menu JSP follows:

```
<card  id="mainmenu">
   <!-- Main menu provides options to read messages, send a message -->
   <!-- and logout -->
   <p>
    Main Menu
   <select name="selection">
   <option onpick=
   "http://d:9300/servlet/WAPSvlt/?action=List">Read Email</option>
   <option onpick=
   "http://d:9300/servlet/WAPSvlt/?action=Compose">Compose</option>
   <option onpick=
   "http://d:9300/servlet/WAPSvlt/?action=Logout">Logout</option>
   </select>
   </p>
</card>
```

Actions (List, Compose, Logout) to be performed by the servlet (WAPSvlt) is obtained by the servlet through the request parameter `action`

Reading email

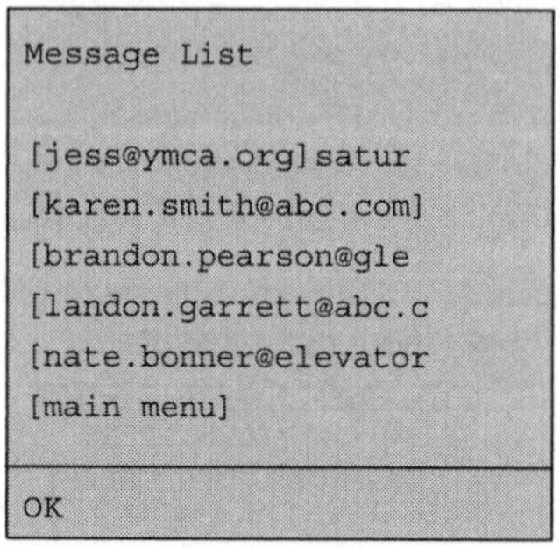

Message List

[jess@ymca.org]satur
[karen.smith@abc.com]
[brandon.pearson@gle
[landon.garrett@abc.c
[nate.bonner@elevator
[main menu]

OK

Figure 28.8   Email message summary screen

Let us assume a user selects the main menu option to read email, that is, the user wants to view a summary of the email messages in the Inbox folder. This would result in a retrieval of the message headers from an IMAP server. For this application, the message header comprises the sender and the message subject. The message list includes an option at the bottom of the list to return to the main menu (figure 28.8).

The JSP scriptlet to display the sender of the message shown in the list of message headers is:

```
<anchor>
  <go method="post"
    href="http://d:9300/servlet/WAPSvlt">
      <postfield name="action" value="read"/>
      <postfield name="msgindex" value="<%=index%>"/>
  </go>
  <%try {
    InternetAddress[] a;

// FROM
    if ((a = (InternetAddress[]) msg.getFrom()) != null) {
      from = a[0].getAddress();
    } else {
      from = "Unknown sender";
    }
  } catch (MessagingException e) {%>
  <%}
  %>
  <%=from%>
</anchor>
```

Uses the message index to identify the selected message whose content is to be retrieved from the server

Note the use of the JavaMail `MessagingException` when obtaining the array of message senders

Displays the address of the first sender of each message

Displays "unknown sender" if the `from` attribute has not been set in the message

Displaying message text

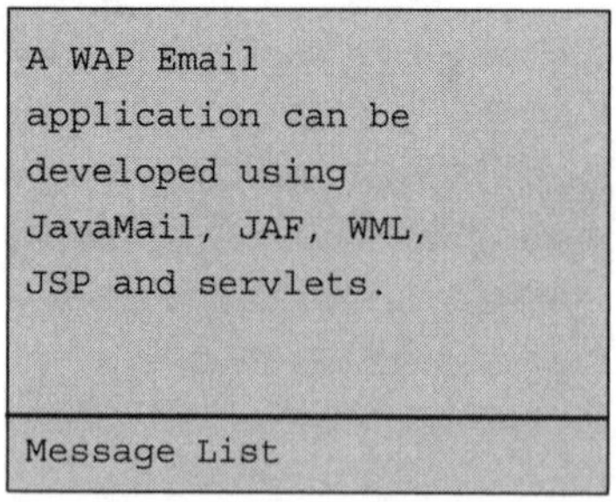

A WAP Email
application can be
developed using
JavaMail, JAF, WML,
JSP and servlets.

Message List

Figure 28.9   The message list

A user can select a header from the message summary list in order to read the message text (figure 28.9). When a specific message is selected, the message text associated with that message is displayed. The screen also has an option to return to the summary list of messages.

The scriptlet that displays a message's text is shown next. A message's text is then placed in the `HttpSession` object by the servlet for retrieval by the JSP when the text is to be added to a WML card. Only text messages are displayed in this sample application. To retrieve the text of a message, with attachments, you need to parse the JavaMail `Multipart` object. This is left as an exercise for enhancing this sample application.

```
<p>
  <% String s = (String) session.getValue("text");%>
  <%=s%>
</p>
```

The JSP obtains the message text from the servlet using the `HttpSession` object.

Two other issues also need to be considered when displaying a message's text. Since dollar signs are not permitted in WML, dollar sign ($) substitution must be performed on a message's text before being included in a card. There is a limit on the size of a deck. A message's text can be significantly larger than the maximum size of a WML deck; therefore, the text may need to be trimmed before being added to a WML card.

Sending email

If the user wishes to compose and send a message, he would need to return to the main menu and select the Compose menu option. Figure 28.10 shows the result.

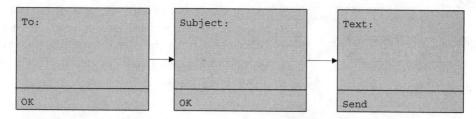

Figure 28.10 Composing an email

The pertinent WML code for these three cards follows.

```
<card id="send">        ←——————   This card is for
  <do type="accept" label= "ok">       entering a recipient of
   <go href="#subject"/>               a message
  </do>
  <p>
  To:
  <input name="to"/>
  </p>
</card>

                            This card is for entering
<card id="subject">    ←—┘   the subject of a message
  <do type="accept">
    <go href="#msgtxt"/>
  </do>
  <p>
  Subject:
```

```
          <input name="subject"/>
      </p>
</card>

<!-- This card accepts message text and sends values -->
<!-- to the servlet for transmission to Email Server-->
<card id="msgtxt">
 <do type="accept" label="Send">
   <go method="post" href="http://d:9300/servlet/WAPSvlt">
       <postfield name="to" value="$to"/>
           <postfield name="subject" value="$subject"/>
           <postfield name="msg" value="$text"/>
           <postfield name="action" value="Send"/>
       </go>
   </do>
   <p>
   Text:
   <input name="text"/>
   </p>
</card>
```

**Servlet retrieves the to,
subject, msg, and
action values from the
request object**

Logging off

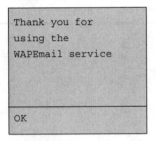

Thank you for using the WAPEmail service

OK

Figure 28.11
The logout card

After a user has entered the text of the message, the message is sent and the user is returned to the main menu. Assuming the user then selects the main menu option to log out, a card (figure 28.11) would be presented to the user.

28.7.4   Servlet component

Now that you have an understanding of the main use cases supported, the user interface design and other presentation components of the application, let us discuss how the servlet, the controller of this application, satisfies requests. The servlet essentially transforms the HTTP requests into calls to the Email Facade that uses the JavaMail API to perform the request.

For this sample application, servicing of HTTP GET requests, using the doGet() method, are forwarded to the doPost() method that supports HTTP POST requests.

```
public void doGet(HttpServletRequest req, HttpServletResponse res)
     throws ServletException, IOException {

     this.doPost(req, res);

}
```

So, for illustration and simplicity, the code for processing an HTTP request is maintained in the servlet's `doPost()` method. Code snippets from the `doPost()` method are shown in the following discussions that describe how the servlet satisfies requests from a WAP email user.

Logging in

For the login use case, the Email Facade is initialized with the user ID and password from `HttpServletRequest`. For this example, the other email configuration parameters are hard-coded. However, enterprise business objects can provide email configuration data of a user, as described later in this chapter. After successful login, the user is presented with the main menu. A JSP identified by the MAIN_MENU_DISPLAY URI produces the main menu card. The `forwardToJspPage()` method uses this URI to forward the request to a JSP page. The `forwardToJspPage()` uses the `forward(req, res)` operation of the servlet's `RequestDispatcher` interface.

```
String url=null;

HttpSession session = req.getSession(true);
String action = req.getParameter("action");

// connect to mail server
if (action.equals(LOGON_ACTION)) {
    String ruserid = req.getParameter("userid" );
    String rpassword = req.getParameter("password" );
    String args[] = {"imap", "myhost",
                     ruserid, rpassword};
    String args[] = {"imap", "myhost",
     server = new EmailFacade(args);
     try {
        server.login();
        url = MAIN_MENU_DISPLAY;
        forwardtoJspPage(url, req, res);
     } catch (Exception e) {
         e.printStackTrace();
     }
 }
```

Determines the type of action requested by a user

If it is a login request, the user ID and password entered need to be retrieved

The user ID and password entered along with hard-coded email configuration data such as protocol name and IMAP host name are used to create an instance of the EmailFacade

Calls the login operation to establish a session with an email server

Reading email

If a user requests a summary of messages (LIST_ACTION) in the Inbox folder of his mailbox, messages are retrieved from an email server and added to the `HttpSession` object. The JSP identified by INBOX_MESSAGE_DISPLAY retrieves the messages from the `HttpSession` object for display.

```
// Display main menu
if (action.equals(MENU_ACTION)) {
    url = MAIN_MENU_DISPLAY;
    try {
        forwardtoJspPage(url, req, res);
```

If the main menu needs to be displayed, the JSP page identified by MAIN_MENU_DISPLAY is used

```
      } catch (Exception e) {
        e.printStackTrace();
      }
    }

// list Inbox messages
if (action.equals(LIST_ACTION)) {
    url = INBOX_MESSAGE_DISPLAY;
    // get messages
    try {
      Message[] msgs = server.getInboxMessages();
       if (msgs != null) {
        session.putValue("messages", msgs);
       }
       forwardtoJspPage(url, req, res);
    } catch (Exception e) {
      e.printStackTrace();
    }
}
```

If the Inbox messages need to be shown, they are retrieved from the server using the EmailFacade. The list of messages is added to the **HttpSession** object so that it can be retrieved by the JSP before the list is displayed

Displaying message text

After viewing a summary of messages, a user may decide to read a specific message. Each message is identified by the message index request parameter. The message array is retrieved from the **HttpSession** object and the text is retrieved. If the content is not a simple text message, the message content is not displayed. The JSP identified by VIEW_MESSAGE_DISPLAY displays the message text.

```
// retrieve email message text for a message
if (action.equals(READ_ACTION)) {
    Message[] msgs = (Message[]) session.getValue("messages");
    String text = "WAP Email could not retrieve message text";
    int msgIndex = 0;
    String index = (String) req.getParameter("msgindex");
    if (index != null) {
        msgIndex = Integer.parseInt(index);
    }
    try {
        Object messageContent = msgs[msgIndex].getContent();
        if ((msgs[msgIndex].isMimeType("text/plain") &&
            (messageContent instanceof String)) {
            text = (String) messageContent;
            forwardtoJspPage(url, req, res);
        }
    } catch (Exception e) {
        e.printStackTrace();

    }
    session.putValue("text", text);
    url = VIEW_MESSAGE_DISPLAY;
    forwardtoJspPage(url, req, res);
}
```

Indicates which message's text is to be displayed

The **isMimeType()** method checks the primary (e.g., "text") and secondary ("plain") content type and returns a **boolean** value. Only simple text messages are displayed

Sending email

The servlet also supports composing and sending a message. Sending a message requires retrieving the message parameters (recipient, subject, test) from the HttpRequest object and calling the sendMessage() operation on the Email Facade.

```
// create a message
if (action.equals(COMPOSE_ACTION)) {
    url = COMPOSE_MESSAGE_DISPLAY;
    forwardtoJspPage(url, req, res);
}
// send a message
if (action.equals(SEND_ACTION)) {
    String rto = req.getParameter("to" );
    String rsubject = req.getParameter("subject" );
    String rmsg = req.getParameter("msg" );
    try {
        server.sendMessage(rto, rsubject, rmsg);
        url = MAIN_MENU_DISPLAY;
    } catch (Exception ex) {
        ex.printStackTrace();
        url = MAIN_MENU_DISPLAY;
    }
    forwardtoJspPage(url, req, res);
}
```

Shows the sequence of three cards to enter a recipient's email address, subject, and text of the message

If the user wants to send a message, we retrieve the message parameters (to, subject, and msg) and call the sendMessage() operation of the EmailFacade

Logging off

A logout request results in a call to close the session with the remote mail server. The final splash card identified by LOGOUT_DISPLAY_JSP displays the statement "thanks for using the WAP email service."

```
// logout of system
if (action.equals("Logout")) {
    try {
        server.logout();
    } catch (MessagingException e) {
    }
    url = LOGOUT_DISPLAY;
    forwardtoJspPage(url, req, res);
}
```

Note that the servlet component comprises no WML-specific code. The WML code is embedded in the JSPs which serve as the view component of the application.

28.7.5   Email Facade

We have seen how the presentation component of a WAP email application is designed and implemented using the JSP and servlet APIs. For example, we use a JSP to display menu options and use a servlet to satisfy requests. The application component that uses the JavaMail API to accomplish requests is the Email Facade. It lacks any coupling with WAP application presentation components so it can support applications with a different presentation component such as an HTML client.

The use of JavaMail classes and interfaces can be seen in the Email Facade. This class is called by the servlet to support the login, retrieve and send messages, and log out use cases. The class is instantiated by passing in email configuration properties to log in to a remote email server. The JavaMail `Session` object uses the email configuration `Properties` object to establish a session with an email server. Here is a code snippet from the class' constructor:

```
mailProperties.put(MAIL_TRANSPORT_PROTOCOL, SMTP);        ❶
mailProperties.put(MAIL_TRANSPORT_HOST, args[1]);         ❷
if (args[0].equalsIgnoreCase(POP3)) {
    mailProperties.put(MAIL_STORE_PROTOCOL, POP3);
    mailProperties.put(MAIL_POP_HOST, args[1]);
} else if (args[0].equalsIgnoreCase(IMAP)) {
    mailProperties.put(MAIL_STORE_PROTOCOL, IMAP);        ❸
    mailProperties.put(MAIL_IMAP_HOST, args[1]);          ❹
}
mailProperties.put(MAIL_USER, args[2]);        ❺
mailProperties.put(MAIL_PASSWORD, args[3]);        ❻
```

Code comments

❶ Specifies SMTP as the mail transport protocol.

❷ Specifies the IP address of the host with the SMTP server as the mail transport host.

❸ Specifies IMAP as the mail retrieval protocol.

❹ Specifies the IP address of the host with the IMAP server as the IMAP host.

❺ Specifies the user ID entered by the user as the user for authentication.

❻ Specifies the password entered by the user as the password for authentication.

Logging in

The `login()` operation uses the properties initialized in the constructor to establish a session with the remote mail server. The Inbox folder is opened so that its messages can be retrieved when requested by the user. A code snippet of this class is:

```
session = Session.getDefaultInstance(mailProperties,
new MailServerAuthenticator(
    (String) mailProperties.get(MAIL_USER),
    (String) mailProperties.get(MAIL_PASSWORD)));
// Get a Store object
store = session.getStore();    ◄────────────
if (store != null) {
    String hostname = ((
  (String) mailProperties.get(MAIL_STORE_PROTOCOL)).equals(IMAP)) ?
    (String) mailProperties.get(MAIL_IMAP_HOST) :
```

Obtains a Store object that implements the IMAP protocol from the JavaMail Session object

```
          (String) mailProperties.get(MAIL_POP_HOST);
        store.connect(hostname,        ←——————————
          (String) mailProperties.get(MAIL_USER),
          (String) mailProperties.get(MAIL_PASSWORD));
        // Open the Folder
        folder = store.getFolder("INBOX");   ←———————
        if (folder == null) {
          System.out.println("The Inbox folder could not be obtained");
        }
      folder.open(Folder.READ_WRITE);   ←——
    }
```

The connect() method uses the user ID and password to connect to an IMAP host

Returns the Inbox folder associated with this Store

Opens the folder in READ_WRITE mode

Reading email

The getMessages() operation retrieves the messages from the Inbox folder when the user selects to read his email. getMessageCount() gets the number of messages in the Inbox folder.

```
if (folder == null) {
  System.out.println("The Inbox folder could not be obtained");
    return null;
}
totalMessages = folder.getMessageCount();
}

if (totalMessages == 0) {
   return null;
}

// Get messages
Message[] msgs = folder.getMessages();
return msgs;
```

Sending email

If a user selects to compose and send the message, the sendMessage() operation is called. In sendMessage(), a MimeMessage is created and its header and content initialized with to, subject, and text parameters entered by the user. The Transport object is used to send this message.

```
// create a new Mime message
Message msg = new MimeMessage(session);
msg.setHeader("X-Mailer", MAILER_LABEL);
msg.setFrom(new InternetAddress(FROM_ADDRESS));
msg.setRecipients(Message.RecipientType.TO,
    InternetAddress.parse(to,false));
msg.setSubject(subject);
msg.setText(text);
    // send the message
Transport.send(msg);
```

The mailer label and the sender's address are hard-coded but could be configured and customized if needed

Logging off

The `logout()` operation of the Email Facade first closes the folder and then the message store. Messages that are marked for deletion are deleted if this argument is true.

```
if (folder != null) {
   folder.close(false);
}
if (store != null) {
  store.close();
}
```

28.7.6 Enhancements to sample application

The sample application is included as an illustration of how JavaMail, along with JSP and servlets, can be used to provide an email application on a WAP device. Thus, this application lacks a number of features that would be needed to deliver a complete WAP email solution:

- Support for additional use cases (reply, forward, delete)
- Global address books
- Logging
- Use of enterprise data sources for email configuration

Typical implementation issues such as more extensive error-checking, thread safety, and use of multiple servlets instead of a single servlet were not addressed to maintain a clear and concise focus on the JavaMail API.

Addressing some of these issues can help you become more familiar with the JavaMail API and, at the same time, help you develop a more useful WAP email application.

28.8 ADVANCED WAP MESSAGING TECHNOLOGIES

Typically, users of WAP messaging applications want to do more than access email. Messaging comes in many forms including voice and fax messages and users may also want to access these types of messages using their WAP phone. Users may also want to use directory services such as access enterprise or personal address books. Notifying users upon deposit of new messages in their remote mailboxes is also a competitive feature of WAP messaging applications. Also, for some users, security of the communication channel is an important consideration when using a messaging application.

To develop a robust WAP email solution that meets these requirements, a WAP applications developer needs to make use of multiple technologies and tools including J2EE APIs, existing enterprise servers, WAP push features, and both WAP and Internet security features. The following sections discuss some of these advanced messaging issues.

28.8.1 Naming and directory services

A WAP email application can have disparate needs such as using global address books (e.g., enterprise directories) when composing and sending email messages, retrieving security credentials of a user from a directory server, obtaining information on resources such as available printers, and locating enterprise computing components.

To address these needs, a WAP email application needs to use naming and directory services. A *naming service* is a mechanism that associates a name with objects and provides a facility to find an object based on a given name. A *directory service* is an extension of a naming service and is typically used to associate attributes with objects. For example, a user object could have attributes such as a user's name, phone number, email address, and fax number. Examples of naming and directory services are Lightweight Directory Access Protocol (LDAP), Network Information Service (NIS), CORBA Naming Service (COS Naming Service) and Domain Naming Service (DNS). A directory service enables a client application to retrieve and modify directory attributes as well as to search a directory using those attributes as a filter.

Using the JNDI API

The Java Naming and Directory Interface (JNDI), a J2EE API, facilitates access to naming and directory services. JNDI allows Java applications to access naming and directory service functionality using a common set of classes and interfaces that are independent of a single naming or directory service protocol. The JNDI API presents a common API by using an architecture that is similar to that of JavaMail. Figure 28.12 shows the JNDI architecture.

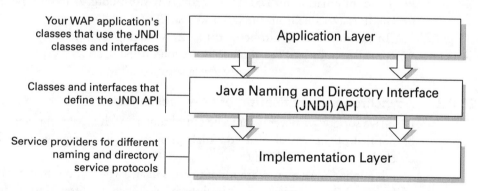

Figure 28.12   The JNDI API architecture

As you can see, there are three main layers. The top layer is the application layer that uses JNDI. The middle layer is the JNDI API that defines a set of classes and interfaces for supporting common naming and directory services functionality. The bottom layer is the implementation layer that comprises service providers for different naming and directory service protocols. The JavaSoft web site has service providers for LDAP, COS Naming, RMI Registry, NIS, DNS, the file system, and Novell's Directory Service.

An LDAP server is a popular choice for maintaining enterprise directories. JNDI can be used by a WAP email application to access an LDAP server (figure 28.13). LDAP is a directory services protocol that enables clients to manage and query a hierarchical repository of entries and attributes. For example, LDAP can be used to locate information pertaining to users (X.509 certificates) and resources (printers). JNDI can also be used by a WAP email application to locate enterprise components such as EJBs. JNDI is used to obtain references to an EJB's home interface, a factory interface for creating, finding, and removing EJBs.

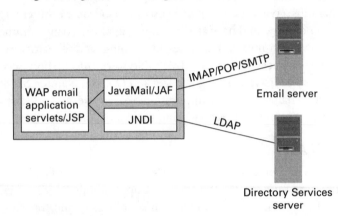

Figure 28.13
Overview of use of JNDI in WAP email application

Directory Services Markup Language (DSML) is an emerging effort to represent directory information using a format that is independent of a specific directory service. For more information on DSML, see http://www.dsml.org. A JNDI service provider for DSML is available from the JNDI web site.

In summary, JNDI can be used to access naming and directory services from a WAP email application. For more information on JNDI, see:

http://www.javasoft.com/jndi.

28.8.2 Asynchronous notification of new messages

In today's society, we never want to be out of touch. With WAP technology a user can be notified of the arrival of a new high priority email message without having to check the mailbox periodically.

Notifying WAP users of important events in an asynchronous manner is a feature of the WAP 1.2 push specification. Push-based architectures differ fundamentally from the more predominant pull-based architectures where an application initiates a request for content from a server. As the name implies, push-based architectures involve server-initiated push events that result in content being pushed to a client without requiring a client to request it.

CHAPTER 28   DEVELOPING EMAIL APPLICATIONS

Push framework for WAP

To support asynchronous notification, WAP has defined a push framework that comprises three main components:

- Push Initiator
- Push Proxy Gateway (PPG)
- WAP device

Let us consider how we can use the WAP push framework to send a notification. The push initiator (mail-based or messaging-based application on an application server) uses the Push Access Protocol (PAP) to push a notification to a mobile user. PAP is a protocol that a push initiator uses to send content to the PPG, another element of the WAP push framework. PAP involves sending XML messages through an existing application-level protocol such as HTTP. A type of WAP content that can be pushed is the WAP service indication (SI) content type, an XML application representing an asynchronous event that is pushed over PAP. The SI comprises a short message such as "you have new email" and a URI of a service such as an email service that is called if the user acts on the notification.

The PPG is a gateway between the wireless and Internet worlds. It is the gate through which push content from the Internet must pass to reach a mobile device. The PPG tries to find the correct device to deliver the content. It can convert an address from a user-specific address (ian.moraes@someserviceprovider.com) to a device-specific address such as Mobile Station International Subscriber Directory Number (MSISDN). The PPG then sends this notification, which may be converted to a format that is optimized for wireless transmission, to a WAP device using the WAP Push Over The Air (OTA) protocol, which is layered above Wireless Session Protocol (WSP). The PPG tries to deliver the notification for a specified period of time. The SI content type allows you to specify an expiration time for a notification. The WAP user who receives the notifications can then decide whether to check for email immediately or at a later time using the URI embedded in the notification message (figure 28.14).

The WAP push specification also supports the notification confirmation service. If confirmation of the notification has been requested, the PPG sends this confirmation after the notification has been delivered to the WAP device.

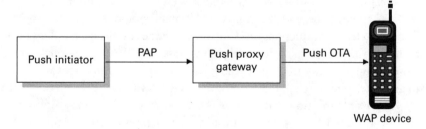

Figure 28.14 Overview of WAP push architecture

If your WAP email application needs to notify a user of important messages, you should consider the use of WAP's push features. More details on the WAP push specification are available at http://www.wapforum.org.

28.8.3 Email configuration

As discussed in previous sections of this chapter, before a user can establish a session with a remote mail server, the appropriate email user configuration information is needed. User configuration data is usually maintained in enterprise data stores so that other non-WAP applications can also use this data.

EJB

Typically, enterprise applications provide a defined interface to manage this data. If you are developing a WAP email application on a J2EE platform, you may be able to access the data using an interface provided by *EJBs*. EJB is the cornerstone of the J2EE platform and provides for a standard server-side component model.

The EJB 1.1 specification defines two main types of components: session beans and entity beans. Session beans are transient and encapsulate the interaction with a client whereas entity beans are persistent and encapsulate the business data. A possible distributed interface might include a Configuration Manager EJB in the form of a session bean that is provided for an email application to create, retrieve, delete, and update user configuration data. Although email configuration data could be represented as an entity bean, it is a good EJB practice for client applications to use a coarse-grained session bean rather than an entity bean directly. If EJBs are not being used to access email configuration data, you may have to use JDBC to access email user data in some relational database. For more information on JDBC, see chapter 23.

If you use appropriate design patterns to design your WAP email application, you should be able to shield your servlets or other classes from the access mechanism of a specific data store. Thus, a change from using JDBC to using EJB or some other mechanism would not result in significant changes to your WAP email application.

28.8.4 Unified communications

Unified communications (UC) is an area with significant market potential. It provides a user with an ability to manage different types of messages (email, voice, fax, and pager) in a consistent way using a variety of devices (WAP device, phone, and HTML client).

UC applications, which comprise WAP email components, need to be able to interface with telephony functions on WAP devices. For example, if a user logs in and receives a summary of email, voice, fax, and pager messages, a WAP UC application might offer a user an opportunity to call the sender of a message. So, you might want to know how to access telephony-related functions on a WAP device using WML or WMLScript.

A possible solution is the use of WAP's Wireless Telephony Application (WTA) specification. WTA is a WAP specification that defines an architecture for WTA applications to use device-specific and network telephony functions in a standard manner.

Wireless Telephony Application Interfaces (WTAI) is a WTA interface that provides WAP content providers with a consistent and device-independent means of accessing telephony-related functions of a WAP phone. The WTA framework comprises the following components:

- WTA user-agent that resides on a device and can perform functions such as making an outbound call or accessing a device-specific address book.

- WTA server that can be simply described as a web server that serves up WTA services and interfaces with the WAP gateway and the mobile network.

- WTAI library that provides device-specific implementations of basic defined telephony functions.

- A repository, which is a persistent store on a WAP device that is used to maintain frequently accessed WTA services

So, if a WAP email application needs to interface with a unified communications server, it can use a URI that identifies an application on the WTA server that interfaces with a back-end unified messaging server. Additionally, to make a voice call from WML, one can use the WTAI WMLScript function `WTAPublic.makeCall(phonenumber)`. WTAI functions may be called as a URI in a WML card or by using WMLScript functions.

For more information on how WTA features can support your WAP application's needs, consult the WTA and WTAI specifications at http://www.wapforum.org.

28.8.5 Security

Although security is a broad topic that cannot be adequately covered here, we can provide a short description of some of the main security mechanisms that need to be considered in order to address the security issues of a WAP email-enabled application.

Typically, the security issues of a WAP messaging application will need to be considered within the context of an overall enterprise security architecture. Security strategies secure architectural components such as WAP devices and secure communication channels such as WAP device to WAP gateway.

Securing architectural components

Securing WAP devices and WAP gateways has been addressed in a separate chapter in this text. A WAP application will typically be deployed on an application server that is inside a corporate firewall. Firewalls are security mechanisms that need to be considered for securing WAP application components within an enterprise network.

A *firewall* is a system or a group of systems that enforces a security policy between two networks. Essentially, firewalls prevent some traffic from reaching a network and allow others depending on the access control policy that has been established. Firewalls are implemented using routers (devices that block traffic based on source and destination IP addresses and ports in IP packets) or application gateways that run proxy servers for TCP/IP services such as telnet, http, and ftp. Firewalls can help protect against unauthorized users trying to log in to the system. However, in general, firewalls cannot prevent email viruses from affecting a WAP application.

Securing communication channels

There are a number of protocols that can be used to secure the communication channels between components in a WAP messaging system:

Secure Sockets Layer (SSL) and Transport Layer Security (TLS)—Protocols may be used to secure the channel between a WAP gateway and an application server. SSL, developed by Netscape, is layered above a reliable transport protocol (TCP) and below application-level protocols (HTTP). SSL supports server authentication, message integrity, and data privacy. The Internet Engineering Task Force (IETF) has proposed a standard based on SSL called TLS that is newer and thus less widely used than SSL.

Wireless Transport Layer Security (WTLS)—WTLS is an optional layer in the WAP protocol stack and operates over the Wireless Datagram Protocol (WDP). WTLS is similar to TLS 1.0, but adapted to the low bandwidth and high latency nature of wireless networks. WTLS provides authentication, data integrity, and data privacy for sending and receiving data between two applications. Most WAP gateways provide WTLS implementations.

S/MIME (Secure/Multipurpose Internet Mail Extensions)—A draft Internet RFC, based on the MIME standard, it provides a way to secure Internet email messages. More specifically, it provides a standard for authentication, message integrity, and data privacy for sending and receiving MIME data. Although JavaMail does not provide specific support for secure email, there are third-party vendors that provide S/MIME components that can be integrated with JavaMail. The JavaMail web site has more information on other third party components.

If you are using the WTA framework in your WAP email application, you need to comply with WTA security requirements. For example, when a WTA user agent establishes a WTA session, it must use a secure WTA port on the WAP gateway. Further, the WAP gateway needs to ensure the authentication of the WTA provider of services.

Depending on your needs, a number of protocols and access mechanisms could be used to support the security requirements of your WAP email application. More information on WTLS and other WAP security details can be obtained at http://www.wapforum.org.

28.8.6   Future direction

The next generation of wireless networks, commonly known as 3G, promises significantly increased bandwidth. This has led to the specification of more sophisticated wireless messaging applications that require this higher capacity. One such emerging application is the Multimedia Messaging Service (MMS).

MMS is an extension of the Short Message Service (SMS) which enables a mobile user to send text messages from one device to another. MMS builds on this concept of device-to-device communication and allows mobile users to send multimedia messages with richer content types such as video and images from one multimedia terminal (multimedia-enabled wireless device) to another or to an email server in a non-real-time manner. These content types are presented to a user in the form of a multimedia presentation. Examples of possible applications of MMS to support personal communication are:

- Sending epostcards to friends or relatives
- Sending a video of an antique to a prospective buyer
- Sending an image snapshot of an upcoming deliverable to a customer

To understand how MMS supports these applications, let us explore the underlying MMS framework. The MMS architecture comprises a number of architectural components:

- MMS user agent
- MMS server
- MMS relay

An MMS user agent supports the creation and retrieval of multimedia messages as well as providing support for presentation of notifications. The multimedia presentation of a message can be facilitated by Synchronized Multimedia Integration Language (SMIL). SMIL is an XML language that allows a synchronized multimedia presentation of independent multimedia content types.

An MMS server manages the storage and handling of multimedia messages and may comprise an email server or a unified messaging server. The MMS relay serves as an intermediary between an MMS server and an MMS user agent. The MMS relay is used to transfer multimedia messages between different messaging systems and can communicate with a WAP gateway to send a message to a device. The MMS relay is considered an origin server in the WAP architectural framework. Figure 28.15 illustrates how these different components might work together.

Although the end-user experience is enhanced and easier with MMS, email messaging and MMS share a number of common features and technologies. To illustrate

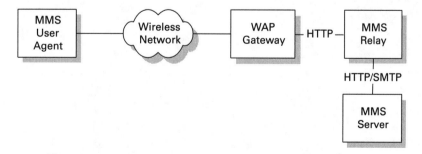

Figure 28.15   Overview of MMS architecture

the similarities, let us consider the use case of composing and sending a multimedia message. When specifying a recipient of a multimedia message, an SMTP-based email address can be used. A multimedia message essentially uses a MIME multipart format to combine different types of content. When the message is sent to an MMS relay, the communication between different MMS relays can be accomplished using SMTP. When a message reaches its destination, the message can be stored in an MMS server. The MMS server can use an email server for multimedia message storage.

This short discussion should provide you with an overview of MMS. Some of the underlying technologies of MMS are familiar email standards. Although still in its infancy, MMS can offer users of person-to-person messaging applications an enhanced user experience. More details on multimedia messaging can be obtained at http://www.3gpp.org.

28.9 SUMMARY

This chapter provided you with an introduction to using JavaMail to develop an email-enabled WAP application. JavaMail/JAF can be used to rapidly develop a WAP email application using an abstract layer without having to perform the difficult task of implementing specific mail protocols and developing an architectural infrastructure to support multiple protocols. The use of multiple J2EE APIs (e.g., JSP, JavaMail/JAF, Java servlets) as well as WML to develop a WAP email application were illustrated through the use of a sample application. Finally, an overview of topics pertinent to WAP email applications development was provided to guide you in your development efforts.

You can obtain more information on JavaMail at:
http://java.sun.com/products/javamail/
More information on the JavaBeans Activation Framework can be obtained from the following site: http://java.sun.com/products/javabeans/glasgow/jaf.html.

PART VIII

Transforming XML into wireless formats

Wireless devices are well suited to deliver well-defined capsules of information, such as news, weather, sports scores, and stock quotes. Much of this information is available to developers in the form of XML feeds through various content providers.

Before these feeds can be delivered to the user, they need to be transformed into a markup language appropriate for the requesting device (WML, in the case of a WAP device). The Extensible StyleSheet Language Transformation (XSLT) enables developers to do this. XSLT utilizes templates to allow developers to apply a single style specification to multiple XML sources.

CHAPTER 29

Introduction to XML, XPath, and XSLT

29.1   INTRODUCTION

In part II, we were introduced to the Wireless Markup Language (WML). We looked at elements for presenting text, accepting user input, and sending the user to another location. In various combinations these elements could form a variety of content for wireless devices. This content could take the form of a WML application that allowed users to check out books from an online library or browse a list of movies playing at the local theater.

In this chapter we are going to look at eXtensible Markup Language (XML), another markup language that can be used to generate content for wireless devices. XML is a platform- and device-neutral markup language for representing data, sometimes called content.

With markup languages such as WML or HTML, you are limited to using a pre-defined set of elements and attributes to create documents. With XML you have no such limitation. You can define your own elements and attributes in any combination. For instance, in XML, you could define an element called `<nextwednesday>` and it would be perfectly acceptable.

But this flexibility comes at a price. Since XML presents a platform- and device-neutral representation of data, it must be transformed into other markup languages that can be understood. For instance, if you had an XML document representing a list of movie showtimes and wanted WAP phone users to be able to browse the movies, you would need to transform it into WML before it could be used. But exactly how do we transform XML into WML?

In this chapter we will also look at two other technologies, XPath and XSLT. XPath (XML Path Language) is a language for addressing different parts of an XML document. XSLT (eXtensible Stylesheet Language Transformations) is a style sheet markup language for transforming XML documents into other types of documents such as XML, WML, or HTML. These technologies will be covered in more detail later in this chapter.

After reading this chapter, you will have a fundamental understanding of what XML is and what it looks like. You will also know what XPath is, what it looks like, and what it is used for. We'll also look at XSLT and how it can be used in conjunction with XPath to transform an XML document in an HTML document.

29.2   TRANSFORMATIONS

Transformation describes the process by which an XSLT style sheet is applied to an XML document to produce an entirely different document. You'll learn more about XSLT style sheets and XML later in this chapter.

Because XML is a neutral representation of data it must be transformed into other usable formats such as WML. For example, a web browser or cell phone may not be capable of displaying an XML document that represents a catalog unless it was in another markup language. Typically, transformations convert XML documents into other markup languages such as HTML or WML, but transformations can also convert XML documents into non-XML-based documents such as PDF or RTF.

In the transformation process, the two input files, the original XML document and the XSLT style sheet remain unchanged, but you end up with a third document. This third document is the result of your transformation. But what determines the content and format of the third document?

What determines this is dependent on things like XSLT template rules and XPath present in the XSLT style sheet. Template rules provide the content that appears in the third document. For instance, if you were transforming an XML document into WML, the template rules would contain WML elements. Template rules require the use of

XPath to determine when the template rule should be instantiated and its contents added. We will discuss the details of each later in the chapter.

As you read the following sections, you will get a better understanding of how XPath works, and how XSLT is used to transform an XML document. You will also see how XSLT uses XPath in the transformation process.

In figure 29.1, we see a typical scenario where transformations are used to present an inventory to clients using different devices. In the scenario, we see three different clients sending in requests to look at a supplier's inventory. Each client has different requirements as to how the inventory should be sent back to them:

- The first client is a hand-held device and must view the inventory as WML.

- The second client is a web browser and must view the inventory as HTML.

- The last client is a back-end system and can view the inventory as XML.

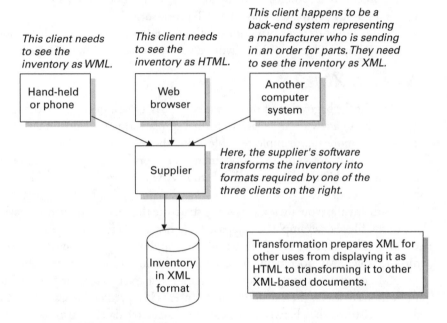

Figure 29.1   The transformation process

As each request comes in, the supplier's software is responsible for a number of things including determining the correct format in which to send the inventory back, transforming the XML inventory into that format, and sending the inventory back to the client.

There are a number of methods that can be used to determine the correct format. For example, the software could examine what type of client is requesting the inventory, or it could require that the client explicitly provide the information to it.

Once the supplier's software knows what format to send it back as, it retrieves the inventory from the database on the far left, and, using an XSLT style sheet and processor, transforms it to the correct format, which is then sent back to the client.

Inside the XSLT style sheet are template rules that instruct the XSLT processor how to transform the XML-based inventory into the correct format. The XSLT processor decides when to use a particular template by matching elements from the XML base catalog to an XPath expression in the XSLT template. XSLT templates and XPath will be covered in more detail in sections 29.4 and 29.5. XSLT processors will be covered in chapter 30.

The important thing to remember is that XML by itself is often not used as is. XML is designed to be device neutral and therefore must be converted into other formats, such as HTML or WML, to be used by web browsers or hand-held devices. The process by which this conversion takes place is called transformation. The transformation process is accomplished using an XML source document, an XSLT style sheet containing XSLT templates, and an XSLT processor.

Before we get to transformations, let's take a detour and learn a little about XML. Understanding the basics of XML will be valuable when writing XSLT style sheets.

29.3   WHAT IS XML?

As we saw at the beginning of this chapter, XML is a markup language that allows representation of data without regard to format or platform. XML documents themselves are nothing more than simple text files. But there are some rules that govern what is—and what is not—an XML document. These rules are spelled out in the XML specification, which can be viewed at http://www.w3c.org, but we will briefly discuss the rules here.

With any file type, there exists some structure that defines how information is laid out in the file. For example, a database table has a structure represented as rows and columns. The columns are given names that applications can use when writing data into the table. XML documents have similar rules about their contents and structure.

XML documents are composed of markup, character data, or both, which allow applications to access their structure and contents in a predictable way. The XML specification distinguishes between markup and character data. It also defines specifications for entities called *elements*. Elements are discussed later in the chapter.

29.3.1   Understanding XML markup

To understand how to read an XML document, one must understand markup. Table 29.1 lists the seven types of markup:

Table 29.1   XML markup types

XML markup type	Description
Document type	Provides document type definition information
Processing instructions	Provides information to applications during parsing

Table 29.1   XML markup types (continued)

XML markup type	Description
Comments	Blocks of text that provide documentation or notes
Entity references	Escaped character sequences used in document
CDATA sections	Character data you do not want treated as markup or to be parsed
Start and end tags <> </>	Defines the beginning and end of elements
Empty element tag </>	Defines an element with no body

XML documents are also composed of *elements* whose start and end are delimited by the start and end tags. There can also be empty elements, which are specified using an empty element tag. We'll discuss elements in detail in section 29.3.2.

Figure 29.2 shows the basic components that make up an XML document:

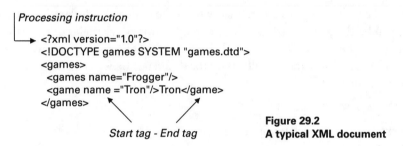

Processing instruction

```
<?xml version="1.0"?>
<!DOCTYPE games SYSTEM "games.dtd">
<games>
  <games name="Frogger"/>
  <game name ="Tron"/>Tron</game>
</games>
```

Start tag - End tag

Figure 29.2
A typical XML document

Now, not all XML documents will be comprised of all seven types of markup. For instance, not all XML documents may have CDATA sections, and not all may have comments.

The following sections will explain each of the types of markup in more detail.

Processing instructions

Processing instructions are a type of markup that is present to pass information to applications. For instance, the `<?xml version="1.0"?>` processing instruction tells the XML parser application that this document's version is 1.0. As you can see, the syntax of a processing instruction is to start and end with a question mark (?) character within angled brackets. Every XML document must begin with the processing instruction `<?xml version="1.0"?>`.

Comments

Like many programming languages, XML includes support for comments. Comments are specified by using the following sequence of characters `<!—comment text goes here -->`. Due to the syntax of the comment, it cannot include the characters "- - " within the comment text. The following block of code illustrates a valid and invalid comment.

```
<?xml version="1.0">
<!- - Classic arcade games - ->
<games>
  <game name="Asteroids"/>
  <game name="Donkey Kong"/>
<!- - Invalid - - Comment - - >
</games>
```

Entities

In the XML specification, *entity* describes a storage unit that refers to components of an XML document such as markup and character data, or it could refer to an entire XML document. Let's look at two types of entities: internal and external.

Internal versus external entities

Internal entity references are defined within the document declaration. Internal entities will be the focus of this section. External entities get their content from another source specified via a URL. External entities will not be covered in this book.

The following examples illustrate the difference between an internal and external entity declaration.

```
<!ENTITY COMPANY "Atari">
```

An external entity declaration looks like:

```
<!ENTITY COMPANY SYSTEM "http://www.mycompany/mycompany.xml">
```

An external entity reference can be used for including the combined contents of two XML documents. For more information about external entities, see http://www.w3c.org.

Internal entity references

An entity reference uses special syntax of an ampersand (&) followed by the name of the entity, followed by a semicolon (;). Entity references are often used to allow special characters to be inserted into your XML document as well as provide a way to repeat often used characters. For example, if we wanted to insert the left-carat (<) character into our document, we would need to use the entity reference representing the left-carat. Another reason we must use this "escape" syntax is that the XML parser would confuse the left-carat with markup. The following XML document shows how to use an entity reference to insert a left-carat into the document

```
<?xml version="1.0"?>
<!DOCTYPE games SYSTEM "games.dtd">
<games>
    <game name="galaga">&lt;</game>
</games>
```

If we did not use the entity reference the parser would throw an error and try to literally interpret the carat (<) as the start of an element. This character must be escaped before it can be used. Fortunately, XML provides built-in entity references that will accomplish what we need (table 29.2).

Table 29.2 XML predefined entity references

Character	Entity reference
<	<
>	>
&	&
'	'
"	"

Declaring internal entities

If we wanted to use our own entities, we need to declare them. You declare an internal entity references much in the same way you do elements and attributes.

For example, to insert the value of a company name in multiple XML documents without having to type it in every XML document explicitly, you could use an entity reference. To do this, we would first define the entity in our games.dtd file:

```
<!ENTITY COMPANY  "Atari">
```

And then reference it in our XML document like this:

```
<?xml version="1.0"?>
<games>
    <game name="asteroids">&COMPANY;</game>
</games>
```

The &COMPANY; is the entity reference to the entity COMPANY. When this entity reference is processed, the value of the game element will be the value of "Atari".

CDATA sections

CDATA sections allow you to include text in an XML document that may contain markup characters. Without a CDATA section, an XML parser would error out upon encountering markup characters.

An XML parser would indicate a problem with the following XML document fragment because the < in the game element (shown in bold) is considered markup:

```
<?xml version="1.0"?>
<!-- Classic Arcade Games -->
<games>
  <game><Asteroids </game>
</games>
```

An XML parser would accept the next example and, most likely, convert the < character to <, the escape character sequence for <:

```
<?xml version="1.0"?>
<!-- Classic Arcade Games -->
```

```
<games>
  <game><![CDATA[ < ]]>Asteroids </game>
</games>
```

CDATA sections are particularly useful if you are creating XML documents that contain source code or JavaScript such as:

```
<?xml version="1.0"?>
<!-- Classic Arcade Games -->
<games>
  <game>Asteroids </game>
  <source>
  <![CDATA[
   <script language="javascript">
     function startGame(){
     this.startGame();
     }
        </script>
  ]]>
  </source>
</games>
```

Character data

In a nutshell, character data is anything that is not considered markup. Character data can be found:

- Between element start and end tags
- As the value of an attribute
- In a CDATA section
- In Figure 29.3, the game element has a value of Asteroids which is considered character data.

```
         Character data
<games>       ↙
  <game> Asteroids </game>
</games>
```

Figure 29.3   Character data in an XML document

Character data, in most cases, is what forms the actual content of your documents through elements and attribute values. Without the character data, you would have an XML document with a series of empty elements. While this may be considered a valid document, it's certainly not as useful.

29.3.2   XML elements

So far we've been looking at XML markup, and how that markup looks in different instances. In the previous section, we looked at comments, processing instructions, start tags, and end tags. But markup alone does not make for a very useful XML document. We need to take the markup and use it to define another entity in the document: the *element*, one of the basic building blocks of any XML document. XML documents are composed of hierarchies of elements, sometimes many levels deep. Elements appear within start and end tags.

Figure 29.4 shows a games element and two game elements, one of which is empty:

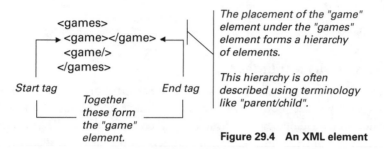

Figure 29.4   An XML element

Elements represent the data of your document. It's what is processed by applications. Elements can contain character data or they can nest other elements. Elements can have a start and an end tag, or they can be empty. Let's take another look at the example shown in figure 29.4 to see how elements work:

```
<games>
    <game>Asteroids</game>
    <game/>
</games>
```

This XML code indicates that one of the game elements has a value of Asteroids and one is empty. It also shows that the games element has two game elements between its start and end tags. Note that an XML document's document type definition (DTD) specifies the allowed combinations of these elements and attributes. This will be discussed in more detail later in this chapter.

Element attributes

Attributes are name-value pairs that occur along with an element within the start and end tags, before the element is closed. The value is enclosed within quotation marks as in name="value".

Attributes are useful for adding information for which an element isn't warranted. In the previous example, we may want to provide what year the game was created. To do this we may add an attribute called year and assign it the appropriate value. It doesn't make sense to add an element just to include this information.

Figure 29.5 shows how to specify an attribute for an element with the addition of the year attribute to the games element.

In figure 29.5, each game element has a name and year attribute.

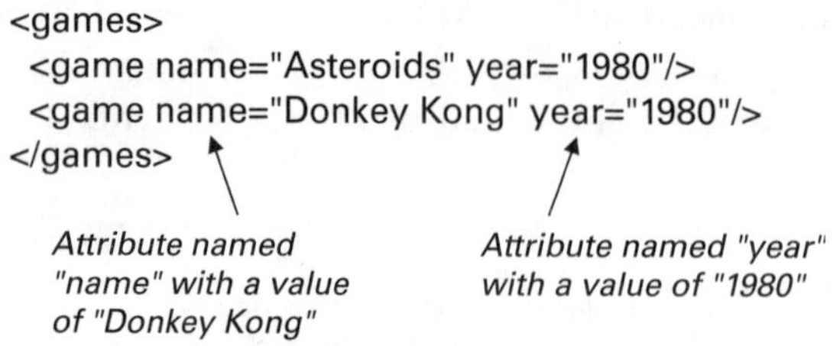

```
<games>
  <game name="Asteroids" year="1980"/>
  <game name="Donkey Kong" year="1980"/>
</games>
```

Attribute named
"name" with a value
of "Donkey Kong"

Attribute named "year"
with a value of "1980"

Figure 29.5
Element attributes

Elements versus attributes

There is no hard-and-fast rule about when to use an attribute and when to use an element. As we saw in the previous section, an attribute could be added if it doesn't warrant an additional element. Let's refine that statement to say, if the attribute you are adding does not provide information that describes the element, it should probably be made into an element.

As an example, look at the following fragment of XML:

```
<games>
  <game name="SuperBomber" year="1980" company="GameCompany"/>
</games>
```

This fragment is probably okay the way it is. However, let's look at the same fragment slightly altered.

```
<games>
  <game name="SuperBomber" year="1980" quantity="10"
lastsold="11/12/1999"/>
</games>
```

The `game` element has a `quantity` and `lastsold` attribute. This seems to be inventory information, which is not describing anything about the game. We should create an element for the inventory of this game. Additionally, if we wanted to keep track of when each copy of the game was sold, it would really get messy trying to add that information as attributes.

The following XML fragment illustrates what the XML document would look like if the inventory information were made into elements.

```
<games>
  <game name="SuperBomber"year="1980">
    <inventory>
        <quantity>10</quantity>
        <lastsold>11/12/1999</lastsold>
    </inventory>
  </game>
</games>
```

But of course this is only one example of how it could be broken down.

Case-sensitivity

XML is a case-sensitive markup language. What this means is that if you define an element named games, and another element named GAMES, they will be treated as different elements.

29.3.3 Document type definition

XML documents by themselves have no real constraints placed upon them. XML does include a DTD, which supplies constraint type information. The DTD is only useful when used with a validating XML parser and the XML specification does not require that a DTD be used when working with the XML document. XML parsers will be covered more in chapter 30. The DTD defines what elements can occur, what order they can occur in, and how many times an element can occur. It also defines constraints for attributes of elements. A DTD indicates these constraints through the use of element and attribute list declarations. A sample DTD may look like the following:

```
<!ELEMENT games (game*)>
<!ELEMENT game EMPTY>
<!ATTLIST game name CDATA #REQUIRED>
```

Figure 29.6 shows the relationship between a DTD and an XML document that references it.

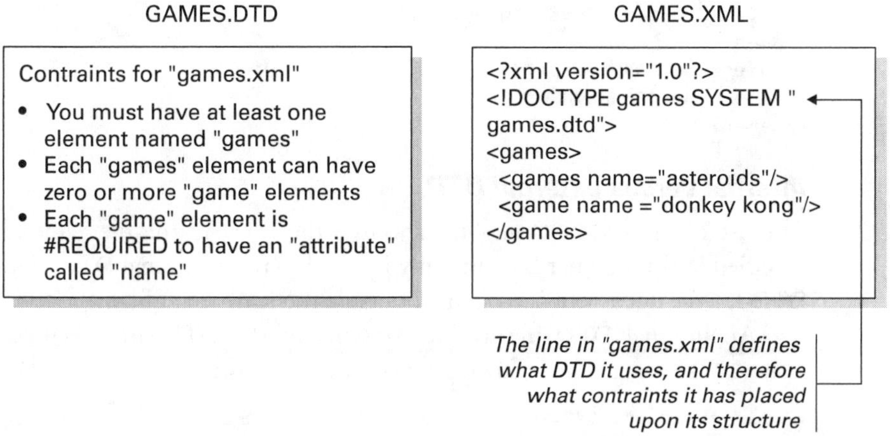

GAMES.DTD   GAMES.XML

Contraints for "games.xml"

- You must have at least one element named "games"
- Each "games" element can have zero or more "game" elements
- Each "game" element is #REQUIRED to have an "attribute" called "name"

```
<?xml version="1.0"?>
<!DOCTYPE games SYSTEM "
games.dtd">
<games>
 <games name="asteroids"/>
 <game name ="donkey kong"/>
</games>
```

*The line in "games.xml" defines
what DTD it uses, and therefore
what contraints it has placed
upon its structure*

Figure 29.6   An XML document and its DTD

Now let's take a look at how we specify a DTD as well as what makes up a DTD.

Specifying a DTD

XML documents indicate what DTD they use by using a document type declaration tag. The following line of code indicates the most common usage of the < !DOCTYPE> tag.

```
<!DOCTYPE root_element PUBLIC\SYSTEM "url">
```

Table 29.3 summarizes the purpose of each component of the < ! DOCTYPE> tag.

Table 29.3   Components of the < ! DOCTYPE> tag

Component	Description
< ! DOCTYPE>	Defines the start of the declaration
Root_element	Specifies which document this DTD belongs to. This value must match the value of the "root" element of the document.
PUBLIC ID	Keyword defined by XML specification, indicates that this DTD is a public DTD
SYSTEM ID	Keyword defined by XML specification; indicates that this DTD is a private DTD
url	Specifies the location of the DTD when an external DTD is used

The SYSTEM keyword and url component are optional. For the official syntax of the < ! DOCTYPE> tag, visit http://www.w3c.org.

<!DOCTYPE> placement

The placement of the < ! DOCTYPE> tag is after the XML declaration <?xml version="1.0"?>, and before the start of the root element of the document. The following block of code shows an XML document with the < ! DOCTYPE> tags. It is placed after the XML declaration, and before the root element, games.

```
<?xml version="1.0"?>
<!DOCTYPE games SYSTEM "games.dtd">
<games>
 <game name="Asteroids"/>
 <game name="Donkey Kong"/>
</games>
```

Internal versus external DTD

The use of the < ! DOCTYPE> tag specifies the DTD in the file games.dtd. A DTD specified in this manner is commonly referred to as an external DTD. This means the DTD for the document is contained outside the XML document.

An internal DTD means the contents of the DTD are specified within the < ! DOCTYPE> tag. The following block of code shows an internal DTD.

```
<?xml version="1.0"?>
<!DOCTYPE games [
<!ELEMENT games (game*)>
<!ATTLIST game name CDATA #REQUIRED>
]>
<games>
 <game name="Asteroids"/>
 <game name="Donkey Kong"/>
</games>
```

Notice the element and attribute list declarations are enclosed in brackets ([ ]). Element and attribute list declarations will be covered in the next section.

Element type declarations

As indicated earlier, a DTD specifies what elements and attributes are allowed, what the allowed combinations and order of those elements are, and what the contents of those elements and attributes are.

Specifying what elements are allowed is done using an *element type declaration*. The following line of code indicates the basic usage of the element type declaration.

```
<!ELEMENT element_name (content)>
```

Table 29.4 summarizes the purpose of each component of an element type declaration.

Table 29.4   Components of the <!ELEMENT> tag

Component	Description
<!ELEMENT	Defines the start of the declaration
Element_name	Specifies the name of the element you are declaring
(content)	This specifies the content of the element. The content can be specified as EMPTY, ANY, Mixed, or children.

Element content values

As indicated in table 29.4, the content of an element can be any combination of four basic values. Table 29.5 summarizes each value.

Table 29.5   Allowed element content types

Element content value	Description
EMPTY	This element can be empty, and as such can be specified using an empty element tag <element/>.
ANY	This element can contain any combination of children and character data.
MIXED	This element can contain both elements and character data. Mixed does not represent an actual value such as "mixed."
children	The names of elements this element can contain as children. Children does represent an actual value such as "children."

You should also note that content is specified between parenthesis in an element type declaration.

Now that we've seen how to define an element type declaration, let's look at examples of element type declarations.

Element type declarations in action

Table 29.6 shows various ways you could use the element type declaration tag.

Table 29.6   Element type declarations

Example	Description
<!ELEMENT games ANY>	Declares an element named games, and specifies that it can have ANY type of element or character data as its children.
<!ELEMENT games (game)>	Declares an element named games and specifies that it can have exactly one child element named game.
<!ELEMENT games (game,game)>	Declares an element named games, and that it can have exactly two child elements, both named game.
<!ELEMENT games (game*)>	Declares an element named games, and that it can have zero or more elements named game.
<!ELEMENT games (game+)>	Declares an element named games, and that it can have one or more elements named game.
<!ELEMENT games (#PCDATA)>	Declares an element called games, and that it can only contain parsed character data (text that is not considered markup).

Child element frequency

In table 29.6, you may have noticed the use of special characters such as an asterik (*) or the plus sign (+). These characters specify the number of times the child element can be present. Table 29.7 summarizes the characters that can be used to specify the frequency of child elements.

Table 29.7   Characters used to denote child element frequency

Character	Description
Missing	If none of the special characters is present, the child can occur exactly once.
?	The child element can occur zero or one times.
*	The child element can occur zero or more times.
+	The child element can occur one or more times.

Child element ordering

You can also specify the order of content and child elements in an element type declaration. To do this, separate child elements and content using either a comma or a vertical bar. Using the comma indicates the elements must appear in the sequence specified. Using the bar indicates the child elements can appear in any order, and only one is required.

```
<!ELEMENT games (child1,child2,child2)>
```

This element type declaration declares an element named games, and has three child elements named child1, child2, and child3. The declaration also says that the elements must appear in the order specified.

```
<!ELEMENT games (child1 | child2 | child3)>
```

This element type declaration declares an element named games, and has three children named child1, child2, and child3. The declaration also says that only one of the elements is required.

Now that we've seen how to declare an element, let's look at how we declare the attributes an element can contain.

Attribute list declarations

To specify what attributes an element can have you must use an attribute list declaration. The following line of code indicates the basic usage of the attribute list declaration tag.

```
<!ATTLIST element_name attribute_name TYPE Default_Value>
```

Table 29.8 summarizes the components of an attributes list declaration.

Table 29.8 ATTLIST declaration components

ATTLIST component	Description
Element_name	The name of the element to which this attribute belongs
Attribute_name	The name of the attribute
TYPE	The type of the attribute. This component can have many values; the one we'll use most often is CDATA.
Default value	The default value of the attribute as CDATA or an XML-defined keyword of #REQUIRED, #IMPLIED, or #FIXED

Attribute type

The type of the attribute can be one of several XML-defined types. But the only one we will discuss here is CDATA, which says this attribute contains character data which does not contain markup. Character data looks like ordinary text:

```
name="Asteroids"
```

Here, the attribute name has a character value of "Asteroids".

Attribute default value

You can also define a default value for an attribute by using a character data value, or one of three keywords. To define an attribute with a default value, you would use a declaration that looks like:

```
<!ATTLIST game name CDATA "Asteroids">
```

But if you don't want to assign a fixed value, you could use one of the three XML defined keywords (table 29.9).

Now let's take a look at some example attribute list declarations.

Table 29.9 Default value keywords

Default value keyword	Description
#REQUIRED	The attribute is required and must have a value.
#IMPLIED	The attribute is not required and thus has no value.
#FIXED	The attribute is required and must have the value specified.

Example attribute list declarations

The following examples show different usages of an attribute list declaration.

```
<!ATTLIST game name CDATA #REQUIRED>
```

This example declares an attribute called name, which belongs to an element named game. It also specifies that it contains character data through the use of the CDATA type, and that it's required through the use of the #REQUIRED keyword.

Another example shows us how to declare an element with a fixed default value.

```
<!ATTLIST game name CDATA #FIXED "Asteroids">
```

This example also declares an attribute of game called name with a fixed value of "Asteroids". This fixed value is specified using the #FIXED keyword.

And finally, let's look at declaring an attribute that is not required. This can be useful if for some reason the value of the attribute cannot be determined.

```
<!ATTLIST games name CDATA #IMPLIED>
```

This example declares an attribute of games called name. It specifies that it is character data, and that it can either be present or not by using the #IMPLIED keyword.

Valid and well-formed documents

For XML documents to be reliable and have integrity, the XML specification has the notion of valid and well-formed documents. One should note that validity is not a requirement for working with XML. Validity supplies the capability to ensure our document contains the information it should.

Valid documents are those that conform to their DTD. *Well-formed* documents are those that conform to basic rules that govern ordering of elements in a document. It ensures that elements are closed out, and closed out in the proper sequence.

Here is an example of a well-formed document:

```
<?xml version="1.0"?>
<!DOCTYPE games SYSTEM "games.dtd">
<games>                         The game elements
    <game name="asteroids"/>    are closed out
    <game name="donkey kong"/>  properly
</games>    ←┐ The games element is
             │ closed out around its
             │ child "game" elements
```

This document meets the criteria of being well formed because it closes out all elements, and closes them out in the proper nested sequence—which means game elements cannot be closed out after the games element has been closed out.

Now let's look at the document's DTD.

```
<!ELEMENT games (game*)>
<!ELEMENT game EMPTY>
<!ATTLIST game name CDATA #REQUIRED>
```

Using the information supplied in the DTD, we can also see that the document meets the criteria for being valid. It includes an element called games. It includes zero or more games elements. And each games element has a #REQUIRED name attribute. It also shows that the game element is nested inside the start and end tags of the games element, meaning the game element is a child of the games element.

Invalid and malformed documents

What would constitute a document that was not well formed or invalid? Any number of things, but for example:

```
<?xml version="1.0"?>
<!DOCTYPE games SYSTEM "games.dtd">
<games>
    <game name="asteroids"/>
</games>
<game name="donkey kong"/>
```

If this document were run through a validating XML parser, it would complain that the last "game" element is in the wrong position. The actual error message is dependent on the parser. Sometimes the error messages are a bit cryptic and don't immediately indicate your document failed validation. But if you run into any problems during parsing, the document format is probably the first place to look.

XML schemas

While the DTD remains the primary mechanism for validating XML documents, the W3C XML schema specification will provide for a richer validation mechanism. It will allow document authors to better indicate the type of data elements are comprised of, such as "string" or "decimal." Currently, everything is treated as character data. The XML schema specification has not yet reached recommendation status. Visit http://www.w3c.org for more details.

In this section, we've looked at what XML is, and what an XML document looks like. XML documents contain markup, elements, attributes, and character data.

We also looked at how to create a DTD to provide constraints to an XML document. A DTD contains element and attribute list declarations, which specify what elements, and attributes, can exist in the document.

Next we will look at XPath, which is a language for addressing parts of an XML document. By addressing parts of an XML document, the values of elements and attributes can be retrieved. This ability to retrieve the value of an element or attribute is fundamental to the transformation process.

29.4 WHAT IS XPATH?

XPath is a language used to address parts of an XML document, as well as to provide common functions for manipulation of strings, numbers, and booleans. The parts of an XML document that XPath can address are things such as elements and attributes. Some of the functions XPath provides allow you to return the portion of a string, or check its length. It also includes functions that convert character data to numeric and boolean.

XPath gets its name from its path notation. XPath uses syntax similar to URLs to address parts of an XML document. A URL might specify a host name followed by a forward slash, then possibly a directory, and then possibly the name of a web page. For example, http://www.amazon.com/default.html. This URL specifies a web site (http://www.amazon.com) followed by a forward slash (/) followed by the name of a web page (default.html) we want to view at that web site.

Now, let's examine an example of an XPath statement:

`/games/game`

Take note of the forward slashes (/) and text between each forward slash. The placement of these elements is part of the XPath syntax. An XPath statement is commonly referred to as an XPath expression. XPath expressions and syntax are covered later in this chapter.

In this XPath statement, the node-test "games" selects the element by that name (`<games>`) followed by a forward slash (/) followed by the node-test "game" which indicates we want to address the "game" nodes of the "games" node. Node-tests are covered in more detail later in this chapter.

Remember, XPath is not a standalone technology. XPath is used by other technologies such as XSLT. It may help to think of XPath as the SQL, or Structured Query Language, of XML. SQL by itself does nothing; it's simply a language for working with databases. Applications use SQL to retrieve rows and columns of a table, and with XPath, you can retrieve elements and attributes of an XML document.

Each of these languages contains syntax and expressions that define *how* you use them to accomplish specific tasks. For example, SQL has the notion of a data model, meaning that SQL expects to work with data organized as tables containing rows and columns. SQL includes functions to work with rows and columns as well. XPath has all of the same concepts. And as you will see in section 29.5, XPath is used by XSLT during the transformation process.

The following sections will elaborate on these XPath concepts:

- Data model
- Expressions
- Functions

After we've gone over these concepts, you should have a fundamental understanding of XPath and how it is used in the context of transformations.

29.4.1 XPath data model

As we mentioned, SQL is designed to work with information organized as tables, rows, and columns. XPath is similar in that it is designed to work with information contained in an XML document organized as a tree. This tree organization or model is referred to as the *XPath data model*. The tree model is organized as a collection of nodes. Each node can have child nodes, and because of the nature of the tree model, each child node can have a parent node. There are different node types such as element node, attribute node, and text node; in all there are seven types of nodes. The node types are listed in table 29.10:

Table 29.10   Node types

Node type	Description
Root nodes	The root of the document
Text nodes	Character data such as the text between an element start and end tag
Namespace nodes	Represents the namespace nodes found with each element
Element nodes	Represents the elements in your document
Attribute nodes	Represents the attributes of your elements and has an Element node as a parent
Processing instruction nodes	Represents processing instructions markup found in the document
Comment nodes	Represents comment markup found in the document

These node types correspond to their representation in an XML document. For example, element nodes are created for each element in the document, attribute nodes for each attribute of an element, and so on. The term node is used to describe an entity in the tree model. A collection of one or more nodes is referred to as a node-set. For example, all of the nodes in a tree could be referred to as a node-set. Figure 29.7 shows how elements in an XML document are represented as nodes in the XPath data model.

It's always important to remember that you are working with a tree. You are not working with a flat structure or a string of text. The tree is composed of nodes and these nodes have relationships with each other. A common metaphor for the relationships between nodes is parent/child. To access child nodes you must access the parent first. The same goes for attributes—you must access the node it belongs to first.

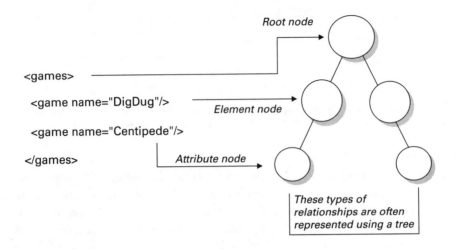

 contains the following labels:

Root node

`<games>`

`<game name="DigDug"/>` — Element node

`<game name="Centipede"/>`

`</games>` — Attribute node

These types of relationships are often represented using a tree

Figure 29.7 XPath data model is comprised of nodes

Now let's look at what it takes to build an XPath expression. XPath expressions may also be referred to as XPath statements, but we'll use the term expression throughout the rest of this document.

29.4.2 XPath expressions

Writing XPath expressions is the way you utilize XPath. XPath expressions are the basic construct in the XPath language and provide the primary mechanism for selecting node-sets to process. XPath expressions can also be used to return values other than node-sets. For instance, if you wanted to see if a node's value matched a certain string, you would probably want to return a boolean value and not the value of the node itself.

XPath expressions evaluate to yield one of four basic types (table 29.11).

Table 29.11 XPath expressions

Xpath expression type	Description	Example
Node-set	A set of Nodes in a source tree	/games
Boolean	A value of true or false	0 or 1, true or false
Number	A floating point number	1.54, 1.0
String	A string of characters	HelloWorld

You can't write down any arbitrary string of text and have it considered an XPath expression. In the following sections, we'll look at how XPath expressions are constructed and rules to remember when using them. We will also look at XPath functions.

You can visit http://www.w3c.org to read the specification in its entirety.

Context

Before diving into the syntax, let's discuss *context*. XPath expressions are evaluated with respect to a context, which is defined in a manner external to XPath. The context is the scope in which the XPath expression can operate (table 29.12).

Table 29.12 Components of an XPath context

Context component	Example
A node (the context node)	If you had the following XPath "/games", the context node would be "games."
A pair of non-zero positive integers (context position, context size)	As you move through a node-set, context position represents the an index into the node-set, and context size is the total number of nodes in the node-set.
A set of variable bindings	A mapping of variable names to values.
A function library	A set of functions that are available such as starts-with, contains.
A set of namespace declarations	A mapping of prefixes to namespace URI. Any prefixes used by the elements in your document; for example xsl:

What this basically says is that, within your expression, XPath determines the scope in which it operates or the fragment of an XML document that satisfies the expression. For instance, if you specified an XPath expression of "/", this would indicate the context of your expression is the "root" node of the document. All subsequent location steps in this XPath expression related to this one would operate under the "root" node. Location steps are discussed in the "Location steps" section. Each time a new part of the XPath expression is evaluated, new contexts may be created and operated under. Figure 29.8 shows how the context changes as different parts of the XPath expression are evaluated.

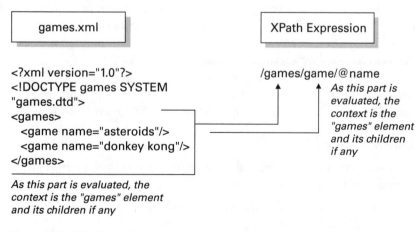

Figure 29.8 XPath context

Context position size and position

When a context is created, it has a size and position. The context size is a number representing the number of nodes in a node-set. It may be helpful to think of it in terms of an array:

Here we have declared an array and can index or print its size by doing something similar to:

```
String data[] = new String[4];
data[2] = "This is a test";
System.out.println(data.length);
```

But unlike arrays, which often are declared and do not change size, the context can change and each context size may be different than the last.

In the example, we accessed the second element of the array using a numeric value. That then allows us to access the value at that position in the array. In XPath, we can use the context position to reference specific nodes a node-set. We can also retrieve the current position at any time. In section 29.4.3 we will look at XPath functions that allow us to work with the position and size of the context.

Location paths

As we mentioned, XPath expressions must conform to certain rules that say how XPath expressions can be constructed. The syntax determines which combinations of characters are an XPath expression and which combinations of characters are not.

*Location path*s are a type of XPath expression for selecting node sets. Location paths are usually constructed using location steps separated by a forward slash (/) character. Location steps are discussed further in the next section. Take the following example:

```
"/games/game"
```

This location path has two location steps. There are two types of location paths: relative and absolute. A relative location path is a sequence of one or more location steps separated by the forward slash (/). An absolute location path consists of the forward slash (/), followed by a relative location path.

There is no rule for which location path you should use; it's simply a matter of what you want to accomplish with the XPath expression. Most commonly though, you will see relative location paths used in most XPath expressions.

Location steps

Location steps are the individual components of a location path. A location step can be composed of three parts:

- An axis, which specifies the relationship between the context node and the nodes selected by the location step
- A node test, which specifies the node type of the nodes selected by the location step

- Zero or more predicates, which use arbitrary expressions to refine the selection of nodes selected even further.

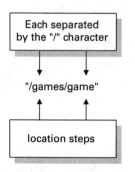

Figure 29.9 Location steps in a location path

The node test is all that is required and sometimes it's all you see in some XPath expressions. Node tests are discussed later in this section. Figure 29.9 shows how location steps are used to build a location path.

The node tests in this example are "games" and "game". If we wanted to further refine our selection, we could have written the expression as follows:

```
"/games/game[@name='asteroids']"
```

This expression would select all game elements that have an attribute of name equal to the string "asteroids." The last part of this location step between the brackets ([ ]) is called a predicate. Predicates are discussed later on in this section.

Axis specifiers

Axis specifiers are often used to explicitly indicate the node-set relationships you want to process:

- *child*—Contains the children of the context node.
- *descendant*—Contains the descendants of the context node. A descendant is a child or child of a child and so on.
- *parent*—Contains the parent of the context node, if there is one.
- *ancestor*—Contains the parent and parents of the parents and so on.
- *self*—Contains the context node itself.

If we wanted to select all children of the games element, we could write:

```
"child::games"
```

Node tests

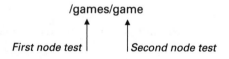

Figure 29.10 XPath node tests

Node tests tell the XPath expression which node type to operate on. A node test is often the name of an element in the source tree.

In figure 29.10, there are two node tests, "games" and "game".

Predicates

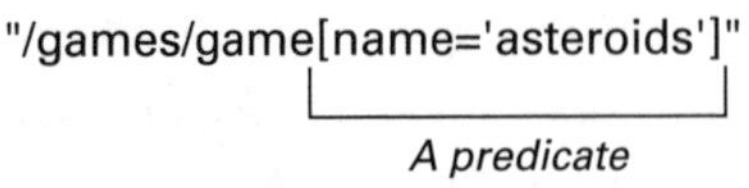

"/games/game[name='asteroids']"

A predicate

Figure 29.11   An XPath predicate

Predicates are another way to further refine the selection of nodes. Predicates are specified between '[' and ']' characters (figure 29.11). We've already seen one example of a predicate in use in the "Location steps" section.

The predicate in this example is "[@name='asteroids']". It tests whether the @name attribute of the context node is equal to the string value of 'asteroids'.

Attributes in XPath expressions

In the section on Predicates, we used a symbol that we haven't used before. The @ symbol is used when you are referring to an attribute of an element. Without this capability to differentiate between an element and attribute, XPath would have almost no way to know when you want to address an attribute. Without using the @ symbol, it's also possible to refer to an attribute using one of XPath's built in abbreviations such as "attribute".

29.4.3   XPath functions

What language would be complete without a function library? XPath functions allow manipulation of common entities such as strings, numbers, and even node-sets. XPath functions are grouped into four categories:

- Node-set functions
- String functions
- Boolean functions
- Number functions

If you are familiar with other programming languages, many of these functions will look familiar and operate in the way you would expect them to. The following sections discuss the more common XPath functions.

Node-set functions

Node-set functions are useful when working against the data model itself (table 29.13).

Table 29.13   Node-set functions

Function	Parameters	Returns	Description
last	None	number	a number equal to the context size
position	None	number	a number equal to the current position in the context
count	Node-set	number	a number equal to the number of nodes in the argument node set

Examples

This example returns the number of game elements under the games element.

```
<xsl:value-of select="count(games/game)"/>
```

This example returns the last game element under the games element. This is done using the value that the last function returns as an index into the game element node set.

```
<xsl:value-of select="games/game[last()]"/>
```

String functions

The string functions (table 29.14) provided in XPath are useful for working with the values of the nodes themselves.

Table 29.14   String functions

Function	Parameters	Returns	Description
string	Object	string	Converts an object to a string using certain rules
concat	Two or more strings	string	A concatenation of two or more strings supplied
contains	String1,String2	boolean	True if the first string contains the second string; otherwise returns false
substring	String,number,number	string	A substring of the first argument starting at the position and going for the length supplied
string-length	String	number	A number equal to the number of characters in the string
starts-with	Node-set	boolean	True if the first string starts with the second string; otherwise returns false

Examples

This example concatenates the text value of each name attribute with the string literal is a classic arcade game.

```
<xsl:value-of select="concat(@name,' is a classic arcade game')"/>
```

This example returns the first four characters of the name attribute of the context node.

```
<xsl:value-of select="substring(@name,1,4)"/>
```

Boolean functions

The boolean functions in XPath (table 29.15) are useful when you don't care about getting a node-set or value but want to test a condition, such as if you wanted to see if the value of a node was blank.

Table 29.15 Boolean functions

Function	Parameters	Returns	Description
boolean	Object	Boolean	Converts an object to a boolean using certain rules
not	Boolean	Boolean	True if its argument is false; otherwise it returns false
true	None	Boolean	Always returns true
false	None	Boolean	Always returns false

Examples

This example returns true if the position of the context node is not equal to the context size. In other words, this node is not the last node in the node-set.

```
xsl:if test="not(position()=last())">
```

This example returns true if the string-length of the value of the "name" attribute is non-zero.

```
<xsl:if test="boolean(@name)">
```

Number functions

The number functions (table 29.16) enable you to work with data that is otherwise treated as character. In XML you cannot represent data as anything other than text, so what happens when you have an XML element representing an employee salary? You may want to produce a total of salaries but need to treat this character data representing the salary as a number. Situations like this are where the number functions come in handy.

Table 29.16 Number functions

Function	Parameters	Returns	Description
number	Object	Number	Takes an object as a parameter and converts it to a number using certain rules
sum	Node-set	Number	Takes a node-set, converts each node's string-value to a number and returns the sum
round	Number	Number	Returns an integer that is closest to the number
floor	Number	Number	Returns an integer that is closest to the number but not larger than the number
ceiling	Number	number	Returns the smallest integer that is not less than the number

Examples

This example prints the name attribute of the context node and then displays total scores by using the sum function to sum the value attribute of each score element. Since the numerical values are actually text values, they are converted to numbers first.

```
<xsl:value-of select="@name"/> high score is
<xsl:value-of select="sum(score/@value)"/>
```

This example first sums the value of each `value` attribute of each `spent` element. Then it rounds the result.

```
<xsl:value-of select="round(sum(spent/@value))"/>
```

In this section we looked at what XPath is and what it is used for. XPath allows you to address individual elements and attributes called "nodes" in XPath. Nodes represent individual components in an XML document.

XPath can also be used to turn the value of an element into a number or boolean, as well as get a portion of the value using one of Xpath's many functions. XPath includes functions for working with strings, numbers, booleans, and node-sets.

In the next section, we will look at XSLT, the language for transforming XML documents into other types of documents such as HTML and WML. XSLT uses XPath expressions when getting the values of nodes, selecting node-sets to process, and during conditional processing.

29.5 *WHAT IS XSLT?*

XSLT is a language for transforming XML documents into documents of other types such as XML, WML, and HTML. The XSLT language is based on XSL. XSLT, therefore, inherits some of the attributes of the XSL language.

Both XSL and XSLT are expressed as well-formed XML documents called *style sheets*. Style sheets are XML-based documents typically used in conjunction with a second document to produce a third. Style sheets contain elements that act as rules and instructions on how to produce the third document and how to determine what goes into it. In transformations, the third document is often referred to as the "result tree." We will explain result trees later in this chapter.

XSL style sheets versus XSLT style sheets

What is the difference between XSL and XSLT style sheets? They are closely related because both use similar elements to define the style sheet, but each uses different elements to define what can go into the style sheet.

XSL style sheets are for formatting XML documents in a manner similar to a cascading style sheet used with HTML.

In an XSLT style sheet, you use a subset of XSL elements defined specifically for transforming XML documents (table 29.17). Thus, for transformations, we really don't need to worry about elements that are used strictly for XSL style sheets.

Table 29.17   Transformation-related XSL elements

Transformation-related XSL elements	Description
<xsl:stylesheet>	Defines a style sheet
<xsl:template>	Defines a template rule

Table 29.17   Transformation-related XSL elements

Transformation-related XSL elements	Description
<xsl:apply-templates>	Instructs the XSLT processor to apply a template to child nodes
<xsl:value-of>	Gets the value of the specified node which could be an element or attribute node
<xsl:for-each>	Loops through a node set
<xsl:if>	Conditionally processes based on a boolean test
<xsl:choose>	Presents a list of choices that can be used to selectively process nodes in a node set

The following code example shows a simple XSLT style sheet.

```
<?xml version="1.0"?>                    ◄————————————       Required XML
<xsl:stylesheet xmlns:xsl="http://www.w3.org                declaration
    /1999/XSL/Transform" version="1.0">     ◄┐ Defines this   since this is
<xsl:template match="/">                        document as an   an XML-based
<html><body>                                    XSLT style sheet   document
<xsl:value-of select="games/game"/>
</body></html>
</xsl:template>                          ┐ Defines the end of
</xsl:stylesheet>                        ◄┘ the style sheet
```

An XSLT style sheet must begin with the `<?xml version="1.0"?>` processing instruction, and must include the `<xsl:stylesheet> </xsl:stylesheet>` start and end tags. Start and end tags were discussed in section 29.3.1.

Template rules

At the start of this section, we talked about how XSLT style sheets contain rules and instructions to determine what goes into the result tree. The XSLT language uses a construct called a *template*, also referred to as a *template rule*, to define what goes into the result tree. We'll use the term template rule throughout this chapter.

How does XSLT know when to use a template rule? Each template rule has a pattern specified that basically says, when something matches this pattern, instantiate this template rule and add its content to the result tree. Template rules are discussed in detail in section 29.5.1. For now though, you should understand that template rules are used to define how you want the transformation to occur, and what you want in your result tree. They are the "rules" for the transformation. They are also used to specify what parts of the XML document will be transformed.

Result tree

XSL transformations work in the context of a source tree and a result tree. Often, the source tree is your input XML document, and the result tree is the output document. Figure 29.12 shows the general role of XSLT in the transformation process.

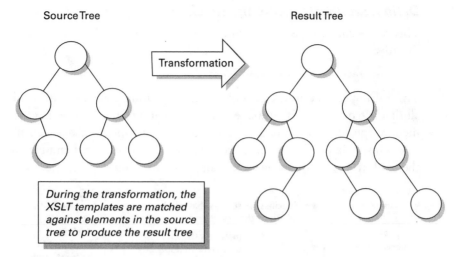

Source Tree

Result Tree

Transformation

During the transformation, the XSLT templates are matched against elements in the source tree to produce the result tree

Figure 29.12 The transformation process takes a source tree and produces a result tree

Other than template rules, XSLT includes support for some common functions such as iterating over a node-set. Node-sets are discussed in section 29.4.1. The remainder of this section is devoted to template rules, common functions, and XSLT syntax. In the following sections we will discuss:

- XSLT template rules
- Generating text
- Repetition
- Conditional processing

After you read about these concepts you should have a fundamental understanding of how XSLT is used to transform an XML document. You should also understand how to create a simple XSLT style sheet and a template rule.

29.5.1 XSLT template rules

As we mentioned in the first part of this section, template rules are how we specify what we want to go into the result tree during the transformation. XSLT style sheets are primarily composed of template rules. Nodes in a source XML document are processed according to the template rules. Templates use "patterns" to indicate when they should be instantiated. Patterns are specified within double quotes after the "match" attribute of the `<xsl:template>` element. Even with no templates specified in a style sheet, XSLT is capable of applying some default templates to produce a default result tree. There is no restriction as to the number of templates in a style sheet.

In the next section, we'll discuss xsl:template and xsl:apply-templates.

Defining rules: the xsl:template element

This XSL element is used to define an XSLT template rule. The basic syntax looks like this:

```
<xsl:template match="pattern"></xsl:template>
```

The XSLT specification defines other attributes of this element, but usually `match` is all that is required. This template rule states that, when encountering the "root" element as specified by the pattern, instantiate this template rule. When this template rule is instantiated, the contents specified between its start and end tags are added to the result tree. The following code example shows a simple template rule.

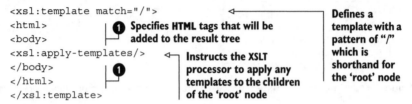

This template rule will be instantiated when the "root" element of the source document is encountered, at which time, the contents between its start and end tags will be written out, and the "apply-templates" element will be processed for each child element of the "root" element. This usually results in the text values of each element being added to the result tree.

If we were using this template rule in an actual XSLT style sheet, and ran a transformation against the following XML document

```
<?xml version="1.0"?>
<games>
   <game> Asteroids </game>
   <game> Donkey Kong </game>
</games>
```

we would end up with a resulting document that looked like this:

```
<html>
<body>
   Asteroids            Text value of the first
                        "game" element
   Donkey Kong          Text value of the second
</body>                 "game" element
</html>
```

You may be wondering how the HTML elements and character data from the XML document made it into the resulting document. This is explained in the next section.

Adding content to the result tree: template instantiation

Instantiation is commonly used to describe the action of taking a template's contents and adding it to the result tree. When a template's pattern is matched, the template is instantiated and its contents are added line by line to the result tree. The contents of a template may contain character data, the markup of other languages such as HTML or WML, or instructions to process any child nodes.

So in the previous template example, we had HTML elements, and an element `<xsl:apply-templates/>` to process any child elements. The `<xsl:apply-templates>` element is discussed in the next section. By using HTML elements in the template, our result tree ends up being an HTML document. If we wanted to produce a WML document, we would have used WML elements in the template instead.

Processing child elements: the xsl:apply-templates element

The `xsl:apply-templates` element is used to recursively process child elements of the context node. It can be used with a "select" attribute or without. This element is shown below with and without the `select` attribute:

```
<xsl:apply-templates/>

<xsl:apply-templates select="node-set expression"/>
```

The following example processes all `<game>` elements, and uses the `<xsl:apply-templates>` element to process any children of `<games>`.

```
<xsl:template match="/games/game">
<html>
<body>
<xsl:apply-templates/>
</body>
</html>
</xsl:template>
```

Using the `select` attribute allows you to specify the node set you want to process. It should match a template you have specified elsewhere in the document.

```
<xsl:template match="game">
 <b><xsl:value-of select="@name"/></b>
</xsl:template>
<xsl:template match="/games">
<html>
<body>
<xsl:apply-templates select="game"/>
</body>
</html>
</xsl:template>
```

If the `select` attribute is not used, then default templates will be applied.

29.5.2 Generating text: the xsl:value-of element

At some point, you will want to be able to retrieve the values of nodes in your source tree. To retrieve the values of nodes in the source tree, the `<xsl:value-of/>` element is often used. This element has a `select` attribute that uses an expression to select nodes to generate text from.

The following example puts the value of each `<game>` element between the `<body></body>` tags:

```
<xsl:template match="/">
<html>
<body>
<xsl:value-of select="games/game"/>
</body>
</html>
</xsl:template>
```

29.5.3 Repetition: the xsl:for-each element

XSLT includes support for looping through node-sets. The `<xsl:for-each/>` element is used to support this type of processing. In the following example, the `<xsl:for-each>` is being used to loop through each game node of the games node-set. It then gets the value of the name attribute of each game node.

```
<xsl:template match="/">
<html>
<body>
<xsl:for-each select="games/game">
 <xsl:value-of select="@name"/><br/>
</xsl:for-each>
</body>
</html>
</xsl:template>
```

xsl:for-each selects all "game" nodes of the "games" node set

XSL to get value of "name" attribute of current "game" node

29.5.4 Conditional processing: the xsl:if and xsl:choose elements

At some point during processing, you may want to check a condition, or determine whether or not to continue processing of a node-set. XSLT supports two types of conditional tests within a template: `<xsl:if>` and `<xsl:choose>`.

The xsl:if element

This element has a `test` attribute that contains an expression that, if it evaluates to true, the contents between the opening and closing `<xsl:if>` tags will be inserted into the result tree.

```
<xsl:template match="/">
<html>
<body>
<xsl:for-each select="games/game">
```

```
<xsl:if test="not(position()=last())">
  <xsl:value-of select="@name"/><br/>
</xsl:if>
</xsl:for-each>
</body>
</html>
</xsl:template>
```

XSL to test if the current node is the last one in the node set

To put all but the last element in the result tree, this code checks the position of the context node in relation to the last node of the source tree. If that condition is true, then the XSLT processor takes the value of the name attribute of the `<game>` element and inserts it into the result tree.

The xsl:choose element

This element uses a combination of `<xsl:when>` elements and a single `<xsl:otherwise>` element to conditionally process. Each `<xsl:when>` includes a test attribute that specifies an expression used to trigger its execution. If the test evaluates to true, the content between its opening and closing tags is inserted into the result tree. If none of the `<xsl:when>` tests succeed, then the `<xsl:otherwise>` kicks in and processes. It does not have a test attribute.

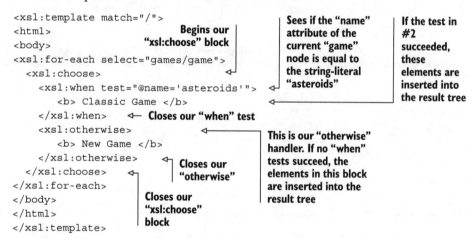

```
<xsl:template match="/">
<html>
<body>
<xsl:for-each select="games/game">
  <xsl:choose>
    <xsl:when test="@name='asteroids'">
       <b> Classic Game </b>
    </xsl:when>
    <xsl:otherwise>
       <b> New Game </b>
    </xsl:otherwise>
  </xsl:choose>
</xsl:for-each>
</body>
</html>
</xsl:template>
```

Begins our "xsl:choose" block

Sees if the "name" attribute of the current "game" node is equal to the string-literal "asteroids"

If the test in #2 succeeded, these elements are inserted into the result tree

Closes our "when" test

This is our "otherwise" handler. If no "when" tests succeed, the elements in this block are inserted into the result tree

Closes our "otherwise"

Closes our "xsl:choose" block

29.6 SIMPLE XSLT STYLE SHEET EXAMPLE

In this chapter we looked at XML, XPath, and XSLT. We learned what an XML document looks like and how we could define constraints on the document using a DTD. Later we'll look at how we can address different parts of an XML document using XPath.

We also saw how we could use XPath in conjunction with XSLT to write style sheets that can be used to transform XML documents. Now we are going to put this knowledge to use by writing a simple XSLT style sheet that will transform an XML document into an HTML document.

For this example, we are going to use an XML document based on the examples used in this chapter. The XML document contains information about games that have been played, and now we must produce a report for the users who played those games.

In this example, we want to create a report that provides:

- Each game that has been played, regardless of when
- Our total scores for each game
- How much money we spent on each game
- How much money in all we have spent

29.6.1 The input document

When working with transformations, the input XML document can be supplied in a number of ways:

- As a simple text file on your hard drive
- As a row in a table from a database
- As a parameter to a function call

In this example, we are going to walk through the transformation and will not be concerned how the source XML document is stored. Listing 29.1 shows the XML document representing our game information.

Listing 29.1 XML input document

```
<?xml version="1.0"?>                              ❶
<!DOCTYPE games[                                    ❷
<!ELEMENT games (game*)>                            ❸
<!ELEMENT game (score,spent)>                       ❹
<!ATTLIST game name CDATA #REQUIRED>                ❺
<!ELEMENT score EMPTY>                              ❻
<!ATTLIST score value CDATA #REQUIRED>              ❼
<!ELEMENT spent EMPTY>                              ❽
<!ATTLIST spent value CDATA #REQUIRED>              ❾
]>                    ❿
<!-- Classic Arcade Games -->                       ⓫
<games>           ⓬
    <game name="Asteroids">            ⓭
      <score value="1234"/>            ⓮
      <spent value="15.30"/>           ⓯
    </game>
    <game name="Donkey kong">
      <score value="1234"/>
      <spent value="20.70"/>
    </game>
</games>
```

Code comments

❶ The XML declaration for our document.

❷ An internal document type declaration for our document.

❸ Element declaration for element name "games" specifying it has zero or more child elements named "game".

❹ Element declaration for element named "game" specifying it has exactly one child element named "score" and exactly one child element named "spent".

❺ Attribute list declaration specifying that the "game" element has an attribute named "name", that it is character data, and is required.

❻ Element declaration specifying that the "score" element is an empty element. That is, it has no children.

❼ Attribute list declaration specifying that the "score" element has an attribute named "value", that it is character data, and is required.

❽ Element declaration specifying that the "spent" element is an empty element. That is, it has no children.

❾ Attribute list declaration specifying that the "spent" element has an attribute named "value", that it is character data, and is required.

❿ The end of the document type declaration.

⓫ Comment markup in the XML document.

⓬ XML element named "games". This is the root element of the document.

⓭ XML element named "game". This represents a single element in the game.

⓮ XML element named "score". This represents the score of the game. This element also has an attribute named "value".

⓯ XML element named "spent". This represents the amount of money spent on the game.

Now that we've looked briefly at the XML document containing our game information, lets look at the style sheet we are going to use to transform it.

29.6.2 The style sheet

Up to this point, we've seen snippets of XSLT, XPath, and templates. We've talked about how these pieces work together during transformations. But XSLT style sheets are more than XPath and XSLT. The XSLT style sheet is the document that contains the XSLT transformation rules and other content. This style sheet is then read into an XSLT processor, which also reads the XML document and then applies the rules and the other elements together with the XML. XSLT processors are covered in chapter 30.

In this sample XSL style sheet, we have two templates defined: one for processing the games element and another to process the game element, and intermingled with the templates are HTML tags. This would lead to the conclusion that we are transforming from XML to HTML. So as the templates are matched and instantiated, HTML tags and the values from the XML input document will be put together to form the result tree.

Listing 29.2 shows our XSLT style sheet:

Listing 29.2 XSLT style sheet

```
<?xml version="1.0"?>
<xsl:stylesheet xmlns:xsl="http://www.w3.org/1999/XSL/Transform"
version="1.0">
<xsl:template match="game">          Defines a template which will be
<tr>                                  used on the "game" element
<td><xsl:value-of select="@name"/></td>
<td align="right"><xsl:value-of select="sum(score/@value)"/></td>
<td><xsl:value-of select="spent/@value"/></td>
</tr>
</xsl:template>                                  Puts the value of the
<xsl:template match="games">    ❶               "name" attribute,
<html>    ❷                                       and the sum of all
<body>    ❸                                       "value" attributes of
<table border="0" cellspacing="4">                the "score" element
<tr>                          HTML tags to define the    into the result tree
<td>Game</td>                 table elements that will
<td>Total Score</td>          hold the report
<td>$ Spent</td>                          Used to apply the template
</tr>                                     specified previously and puts its
<xsl:apply-templates select="game"/>      contents into the result tree
<tr>
<td colspan="2" align="left">Total</td>
<td><xsl:value-of select="sum(game/spent/@value)"/></td>
</tr>
</table>    ❹
</body>    | HTML tags to define the end
</html>    | of our HTML document
</xsl:template>
</xsl:stylesheet>
```

Code comments

❶ Defines a template which will be used on the "games" element.

❷ HTML tag to define the start of the HTML document.

❸ HTML tag to define the start of the body of the document.

❹ HTML tag to define the end of the table.

29.6.3 How XML documents and XSL style sheets work together

Let's describe the transformation that occurs to produce our HTML-based report. The process described here is conceptual and does not detail the actual process used by the XSLT processor.

Reading and validation

The inputs to our transformation are the XML document and XSL style sheet. Both documents are read and go through a process called validation. Validation is described in the "Valid and well-formed document" section. This ensures the documents are well formed and conform to the constraints specified in the DTD. DTDs are discussed in the "Document type declaration" section.

Document processing

Once our XML document and XSL style sheet have been validated, the XSLT processor will begin looking for matches as it encounters elements in the XML input document. So, for example, when the `<games>` element is encountered in the XML document, the template defined in the XSL style sheet to handle that element is run. This will cause some HTML elements as well as values from the XML document to be merged together and placed into the result tree. This process continues until the entire XML document has been processed. You'll learn more about XSLT processors in chapter 30.

The result tree

What you have at the end of the transformation process is a document that contains elements from the XSLT style sheet—namely, the HTML tags, and the text values of the attributes of the elements from the XML document. If you recall, our XML document had an element called `game` with an attribute called `name`. The value of the `name` attribute will appear in the result document as will the values of the `value` attribute from the `spent` and `score` elements.

Figure 29.13 shows the output of the transformation running in Internet Explorer.

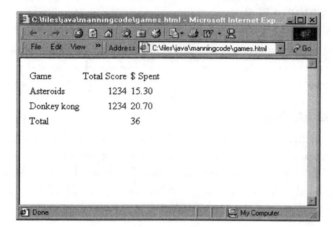

Figure 29.13
The resulting HTML document

We can look at the actual source of the document by selecting View->Source from the Internet Explorer menu bar. Figure 29.14 shows the source of the document.

```
<html>
<body>
<table cellspacing="4" border="0">
<tr>
<td>Game</td><td>Total Score</td><td>$ Spent</td>
</tr>
<tr>
<td>Asteroids</td><td align="right">1234</td><td>15.30</td>
</tr>
<tr>
<td>Donkey kong</td><td align="right">1234</td><td>20.70</td>
</tr>
<tr>
<td align="left" colspan="2">Total</td><td>36</td>
</tr>
</table>
</body>
</html>
```

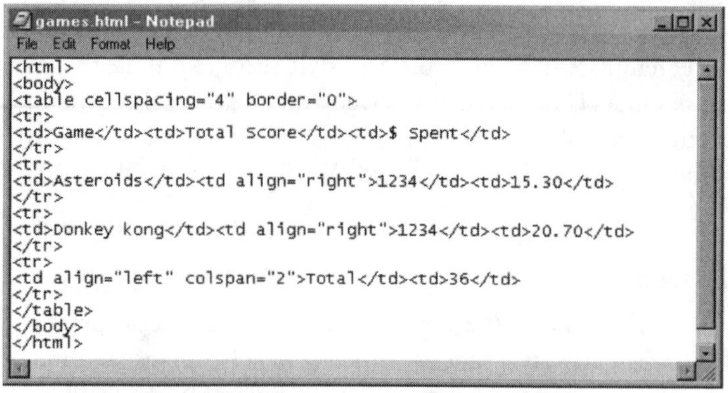

Figure 29.14
The HTML source of the document

As you can see from the previous source listing, the values of the attributes from the `game` elements are reflected in the HTML. We can also see the names of the games as well as the values of the attributes from the `spent` elements.

29.7 SUMMARY

This chapter has given you an introduction to XML, XPath, and XSLT, technologies which allow software developers to write applications for a variety of devices and platforms using a single content source.

We have seen that XML documents are composed of elements, attributes, processing instructions, and comments. XSLT provides a way to take an XML document and transform it into other document types, such as WML, HTML, or even PDF. XSLT template rules define what happens as elements are encountered during processing and what content is added to the result tree. XPath provides the glue between transformations and XSLT style sheets. It's how XSLT knows what to operate on when doing a transformation.

While this chapter introduced the concepts of XML, XPath, and XSLT, it is in no way a complete reference.

For additional information you might look at the following resources: http://www.xml.com, http://www.xmlhack.com, or http://www.w3c.org. The W3C URL is the location of the specifications mentioned in this chapter. These specifications serve as the definitive guides to what XML, XPath, and XSLT are. But a word of warning, they are not for the faint of heart.

Additionally, there are a number of books that more thoroughly discuss the topics of XML and XSLT such as *XSLT Quickly* by Bob DuCharme from Manning Publications, or *XML Bible* by Elliotte Rusty Harold from IDG Books.

With these fundamentals, we can now move on to the next chapter where we will learn about the application modules and technologies that are needed to use XML, XPath, and XSLT—XML parsers and XSL/XSLT processors. We will also look at putting them to work and doing a transformation to HTML!

CHAPTER   3 0

XML parsers
and XSLT processors

30.1   INTRODUCTION

In the previous chapter, we looked at XML, XPath, and XSLT and learned how these languages work together to transform XML documents into other document types. But XML is just a representation of data and, as with any data, we need a way to present it to an application so that it can be used. For instance, a Microsoft Word document needs the Microsoft Word application to be able to read and edit the document. A document that contains VoiceXML markup needs an interpreter and a phone to be useful.

For an XML document to be used by another application such as a word processor, web browser, or XSLT processor, an application module called an XML parser is used. XML parsers read and validate XML documents. They also create a structure that represents the XML document depending on the type of XML parser you are using. Using this structure, most often modeled as a tree, you can retrieve values from and change the structure of an XML document.

We also mentioned that XML documents can be transformed into other document types such as WML and HTML. The application module that does this is called an XSLT processor. Its job is to apply an XSLT style sheet to an XML document, transforming it into a document of another type.

In this chapter, you'll learn:

- What an XML parser is and what it is used for
- What an XSLT processor is and what it is used for
- How an XML parser and XSLT processor are used in transformations
- How to work with two XML parsers and two XSLT processors

After reading this chapter you will have a fundamental understanding of what an XML parser and XSLT processor do. You will also know how to write a simple application using the Microsoft XML parser and Xalan XSLT processor to transform an XML document to an HTML document.

Understanding the role of XML parsers and XSLT processors will be helpful when you start writing your own transformations for real applications.

30.2 *XML PARSERS*

XML parsers are application modules that read XML documents and present them to other applications in a logical structure. XML parsers also validate the structure of XML documents. Why do we need XML parsers? Take an XML document contained in a plain text file, as an example. We could just read this file into a text editor and change its contents by hand. But what if we wanted to present this document to other applications that had no human interaction? These other applications need to access the XML document's structure and contents. But how do we tell these applications about the document's structure and its content? Through an XML parser. XML parsers most commonly use a logical structure called a document object model (DOM) tree to represent an XML document. DOM is discussed later in this chapter.

XML parsers do one other important thing. Since XML is intended to be a neutral representation of data, we must be able to ensure that what is in the document being parsed is actually XML. XML parsers do this for us using a process called *validation*, which applies constraints that have been specified in the XML document's DTD. During validation, the XML parser ensures that the document is structured according to its DTD, and that it contains only valid elements and attributes. For more information about DTDs, see chapter 29.

XML parsers are not required to validate the XML documents they read, and that is why they can run in *validating* and *nonvalidating* modes.

Parsing

XML parsers understand the markup contained in XML documents. They know about start and end tags and concepts of validity and well-formed documents. Because the XML specification dictates a predictable structure for XML documents, parsers can easily read and validate any XML-based document. The process of reading an XML document is commonly referred to as *parsing*.

In the following sections, we will examine two common parsers: MSXML, which is implemented as a COM component, and Xerces, which is Java-based. Regardless of the vendor you choose, be sure that the parser selected conforms to the W3C XML specification as much as possible.

First let's look at DOM and Simple API for XML (SAX).

30.2.1   About DOM and SAX

There are two types of XML parsers, DOM and SAX. DOM parsers read an XML document as a whole and store it as a tree of nodes. SAX parsers read an XML document and generate events for each type of node. Both types of parsers can run in validating and nonvalidating modes whereby the constraints specified in a document's DTD may or may not be checked. There are many implementations of DOM- and SAX-based parsers.

Figure 30.1 shows the different results produced by SAX and DOM parsers.

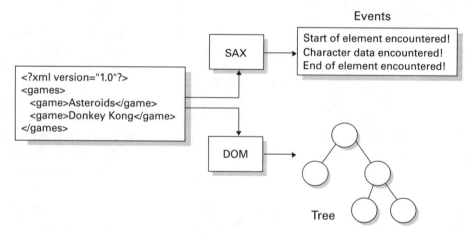

Figure 30.1   SAX and DOM parsers present XML documents differently

DOM

DOM is an API for accessing and modifying the structure and contents of a document. The DOM API is a W3C specification, which can be viewed in greater detail at http://www.w3c.org. DOM-based XML parsers read an entire document into a tree structure and expose the document through the API with objects that closely mimic those nodes found in the tree.

Table 30.1 shows the W3C DOM primary interfaces.

Table 30.1   W3C DOM primary interfaces

Classes and interfaces	Description
org.w3c.dom.Document	Represents the complete document, all elements, and attributes
org.w3c.dom.Element	Represents a single element in the document
org.w3c.dom.ProcessingInstruction	Represents a processing instruction in the document
org.w3c.dom.Attr	Represents an attribute of an element
org.w3c.dom.NodeList	A set of nodes in the DOM tree
org.w3c.dom.Node	The primary data type in DOM
org.w3c.dom.Text	Represents text in a document, such as in an element or attribute value

Figure 30.2 shows how the DOM API exposes a document's structure.

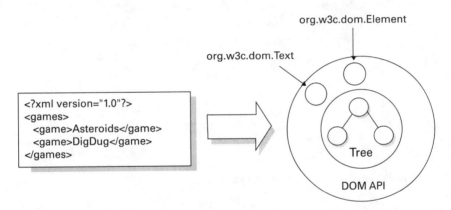

Figure 30.2   The DOM API wraps an XML document and exposes it through classes

Using the DOM API

Listing 30.1 is the source code for using a DOM parser to parse an XML document. It then shows how to use the DOM API to create a Document object representing the XML document.

Listing 30.1   Source for using a DOM parser

```
import org.apache.xerces.*;
import org.apache.xerces.parsers.*;
import org.w3c.dom.*;

import java.io.*;
```

```
import org.xml.sax.*;

public class xercesParse{

   public static void main(String args[]) throws IOException,SAXException{

      DOMParser parser = new DOMParser();
      parser.parse("games.xml");
      Document dom = parser.getDocument();
   }

   public xercesParse(){
      super();
   }
}
```

In the first line of the `main()` method, we create an instance of the DOMParser class. Next, we call the `parse()` method of the DOMParser class, passing in the file name games.xml, which causes the XML document to be parsed. In the last line, we use the `getDocument()` method to retrieve a reference to the XML document. This reference is in the form of a Document object, part of the DOM API.

We could also expand the Java application to access elements of the XML document through the Document object we created. In this application, we reuse all of the code from the previous example, and add the three lines shown in bold.

```
import org.apache.xerces.*;
import org.apache.xerces.parsers.*;
import org.w3c.dom.*;

import java.io.*;
import org.xml.sax.*;

public class xercesParse{

   public static void main(String args[]) throws IOException,SAXException{

      DOMParser parser = new DOMParser();
      parser.parse("games.xml");
      Document dom = parser.getDocument();

      NodeList nodeList = dom.getElementsByTagName("game");

      Node node = nodeList.item(0);

      System.out.println(node.getNodeName());
   }

   public xercesParse(){
      super();
   }
}
```

We use the `getElementsByTagName()` method of the `Document` interface to retrieve all the elements of the document with a name of game. This returns an object called a `NodeList` which contains a set of `Nodes`. `Nodes` and `NodeList` were described in table 30.1. Next, we retrieve the first node from the node list by using the `item()` method of the `NodeList` interface. We pass a zero as the argument, which represents a position in the node list, in this case, zero. It says, "Give me the first node in the list." Next, we print the name of the node using the `getNodeName()` method of the `Node` interface.

SAX

SAX is also an API for accessing the structure and contents of an XML document. The difference between a SAX parser and a DOM parser is that a SAX parser does not create a tree, but rather generates events. As the SAX parser reads in the document, it will generate an event for each type of node it encounters. SAX is not a W3C standard, and does not use any particular object model, but it has become a very popular API for working with XML. Table 30.2 is a list of the more important types of nodes that a SAX parser generates events for.

Table 30.2   Common SAX event types

Event	Description
Start of an element	Fired when the parser encounters <element>
End of an element	Fired when the parser encounters </element>
Attributes	Fired when the parser encounters <element attr="value"...
Character Data	Fired when the parser encounters something like <element> Chardata...

SAX parsers work in conjunction with an event handler that is registered to receive the events as they happen. The event handler is an interface with the type of `org.xml.sax.ContentHandler` that must be implemented by another class. Most often these events generated from using the SAX API to parse an XML document feed into other processes, and are used to build a result tree or do some other processing.

Implementing the `ContentHandler` interface is very similar to the event listening interfaces present in the JDK. For example, when registering as an ActionListener, you must implement the `ActionListener` interface and implement the `actionPerformed()` method. Each time an object that you registered interest in generates an ActionEvent, this method is called. What you do with the result is up to you.

Using the SAX API

Listing 30.2 illustrates the use of the SAX API to parse an XML document. Remember, the SAX API does not create any structure representing the XML document as does a DOM parser. It simply generates events as it parses the XML document.

Creating the ContentHandler class

The first thing we need to do is define a ContentHandler to receive the events from the parse. Recall from the beginning of this section that a SAX parser sends events to a registered ContentHandler. To register the event handler we could build an application that implements the `ContentHandler` interface or create a separate class that implements the interface. The latter is the method we will use for this example.

As you can see, we have a Java class called MyContentHandler which implements the `ContentHandler` interface. We then provide the implementations of the methods from the `ContentHandler` interface in our class. In some of the methods we have put in a `System.out.println` to indicate when a certain method has been called. If you recall from the start of this section, each of these methods corresponds to a certain event type in the SAX API.

Listing 30.2   Source for the ContentHandler

```
import org.xml.sax.SAXException;
import org.apache.xerces.parsers.SAXParser;
import org.xml.sax.Locator;
import org.xml.sax.ContentHandler;
import org.xml.sax.Attributes;

public class MyContentHandler implements ContentHandler{        ❶

    public MyContentHandler(){}

    //* ContentHandler Interface Methods *//

    public void characters(char[] ch, int start, int length){
            String charData = new String(ch,start,length);
            System.out.println("Character Data: " + charData);      ❷
    }
    public void endDocument(){
            System.out.println("End of the XML document");          ❸
    }
    public void endElement(String namespaceURI,
            String localName, String qName){
            System.out.println("End of Element: " + qName);         ❹
    }
    public void startDocument(){
            System.out.println("Start of the XML document");        ❺
    }
    public void startElement(String namespaceURI, String localName,
            String qName, Attributes atts){
            System.out.println("Start of Element: " + qName);       ❻
    }

    //* Less interesting ContentHandler Methods *//

    public void endPrefixMapping(String prefix){}
    public void ignorableWhitespace(char[] ch,int start, int length){}
    public void processingInstruction(String target,String data){}
```

```
    public void setDocumentLocator(Locator locator){}
    public void skippedEntity(String name){}
    public void startPrefixMapping(String prefix,String uri){}

}
```

Code comments

❶ This line Defines our class named MyContentHandler and implements the ContentHandler interface.

❷ Prints out character data encountered during the parse.

❸ Prints out "End of Document" when the end of document is encountered during the parse.

❹ Prints out "End of Element" whenever the end tag of an element is encountered.

❺ Prints out "Start of Document" when the beginning of the document is encountered.

❻ Prints out "Start of Element" whenever the start tag of an element is encountered.

Creating the application

Next, we need to create an application that uses the SAX parser and the MyContentHandler class defined in listing 30.2. The following Java application shows how to use a SAX parser to parse an XML document. In this application, we will also see how to register our ContentHandler we just created to receive events during the parse.

```
import org.xml.sax.SAXException;
import org.apache.xerces.parsers.SAXParser;
import org.xml.sax.ContentHandler;
import java.io.IOException;

public class SAXParse{

    public static void main(String[] args){

        try{

        SAXParser parser = new SAXParser();
        parser.setContentHandler(new MyContentHandler());
        parser.parse("games.xml");

        }catch(IOException ioe){
        System.out.println(ioe);
        }catch(SAXException sax){
        System.out.println(sax);
        }
    }
}
```

We create a SAXParser object in the "main" method of the application. Next, we call the setContentHandler method of the parser object and pass in an instance of the

MyContentHandler class. And finally we call the parse method of the SAXParser object, passing in the file name "games.xml".

Figure 30.3 shows the results of running our Java application using a SAX parser.

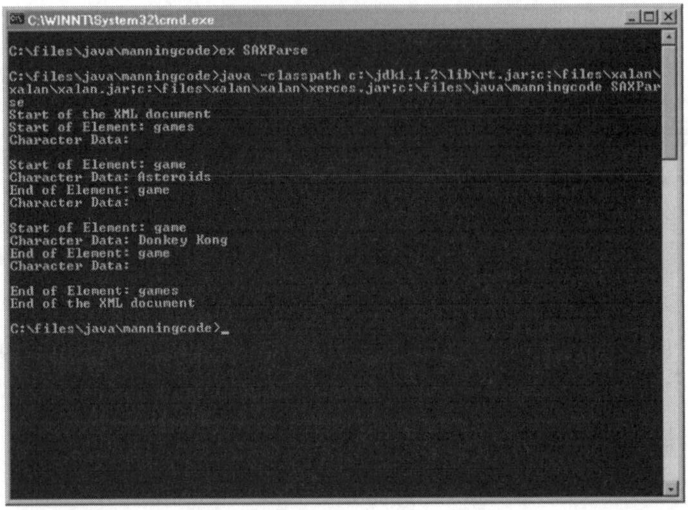

Figure 30.3
The results of using
the SAX API to parse
an XML document

As you can see from the output, we received several different events. We received an event for the beginning of the document, signified by the "Start of XML Document" text printed out. We also received an event for the beginning of the element named "games," and then an event for some character data. But there is nothing shown because the character data encountered is most likely the carriage return and line-feed in our "games.xml" file, which does not print a visible character.

The parsing goes on, with more text being printed out for each event. And finally the parser encounters the end of the document, where the text "End of XML document" is printed out. Why would you want to use the SAX API instead of the DOM API? The SAX API doesn't create anything tangible at the end of the process, so what benefit can it be? There are some cases where using the SAX API would be better than using the DOM API.

For instance, suppose you wanted to parse the XML document into something other than a tree structure. If you recall from the beginning of this chapter, an XML parser's job is to parse an XML document into a structure and present it to other applications. If we used the DOM API, the only choice we have is a tree structure. Using the SAX API, we could parse it into a single variable or into a Java Vector object.

In another case, suppose we wanted to build an application that provided debugging capabilities to XML parsing. Using the SAX API would be ideal for this because we would want to be notified each time a new element or some character data was encountered. You could set breakpoints on certain elements in the XML document, and when you received an event from the SAX parser for this element, the breakpoint would be activated.

Next, we will look at two implementations of XML parsers, the Microsoft XML parser, and the Xerces XML parser.

30.2.2 Microsoft XML parser

The Microsoft XML parser, or MSXML, is a Component Object Model (COM) object that can be used with Active Server Pages (ASP), VBScript, and Visual Basic. It also has a software developer's kit (SDK) for using it from C++. The MSXML parser contains many extensions to the W3C DOM specification, meaning many methods in the parser do not exist in the W3C specification. For a more complete description of the MSXML parser properties and methods, visit http://msdn.microsoft.com. Below is a brief list of methods and properties of the parser:

Object

DOMDocument—The main object that represents the document. This could be an XML document or an XSLT style sheet.

Properties

* `async`—Indicates whether asynchronous download is permitted (read/write)
* `doctype`—Returns the document type node that specifies the DTD (read)

Methods

* `load`—Loads an XML document from the specific location
* `loadXML`—Loads an XML document using the supplied string

Parsing a document

Parsing a document with the MSXML parser can be done in as little as two lines of code. The following example shows how to parse an XML document using MSXML from VBScript.

```
set xmlDoc = CreateObject("MSXML2.DOMDocument")
xmlDoc.load("games.xml")
```

The first line of code creates a DOMDocument object using the `CreateObject` method of VBScript and assigns it to the variable `xmlDoc`. The second line of code calls the `load` method of the DOMDocument object using the name of an XML document, in this case "games.xml" to load and parse the document. There are no further steps required. And after line two is finished executing, the DOMDocument object created in the first line contains the XML document.

30.2.3 Xerces XML parser

Xerces is an XML parser from the Apache Foundation which comes in Java and C++ versions. The Xerces parser uses the W3C DOM API for representing documents, elements, and other types of nodes. It then uses its own API to facilitate parsing, providing both DOM and SAX implementations. For a complete description of all Xerces classes, fields, and methods, visit http://xml.apache.org. The following is a brief list of interfaces, classes, and methods. We will list some of the W3C DOM classes and interfaces also so that they may be seen in the context of the parser being discussed.

DOMParser and SAXParser classes

- *org.apache.xerces.parsers.DOMParser*—This class represents a parser that produces a W3C DOM tree as its output.
- *org.apache.xerces.parsers.SAXParser*—This class represents a parser that implements the SAX APIs.

Methods

- *parse*—This method is inherited from the XMLParser superclass, and is called to perform the parse of the XML document.
- *getDocument*—This method returns an instance of the DOM tree as a Document object.
- *parse*—This method is inherited from the XMLParser superclass and is called to perform the parse of the XML document.
- *startDocument*—This method is implemented from the XMLDocumentHandler interface and is called when the start of the document is encountered.
- *endDocument*—This method is implemented from the XMLDocumentHandler interface and is called when the end of the document is encountered.
- *startElement*—This method is implemented from the XMLDocumentHandler interface and is called when the start of an element is encountered.
- *endElement*—This method is implemented from the XMLDocumentHandler interface and is called when the end of an element is encountered.
- *setContentHandler*—This method allows you to set a custom ContentHandler for receiving SAX events.

W3C DOM Interfaces

- *Document*—This interface represents the whole XML document.
- *getElementsByTagName*—This method returns a NodeList of elements that match the given tag name.
- *createElement*—This method creates an element in the document.
- *createComment*—This method creates a comment in the document.
- *createAttribute*—This method creates an attribute in an element in the document.
- *Element*—This interface represents an element in the XML document.

- *getAttribute*—This method returns the given attribute value.

- *getElementsByTagName*—This method returns a NodeList of child elements that match the given tag name.

- *Node*—This interface represents the data type of everything in the DOM. It represents a single Node in the DOM tree.

- *getNodeName*—This method returns the name of the node.

- *getNodeValue*—This method returns the value of the node, if there is one.

- *getNamedNodeMap*—This method returns a map of the attributes on an element.

Parsing a document

Parsing with Xerces is nearly as straightforward as it was with MSXML. It can be done in roughly two lines of code, not counting imports and class declarations:

```
DOMParser parser = new DOMParser();
parser.parse("games.xml");
```

The first line of code in this example creates an instance of a DOMParser object and assigns it to the variable `parser`. The second line calls the parse method of the DOMParser object, using the name of the XML document as a parameter. To see these lines of code in a full application, see the section titled "Using the DOM API" earlier in this chapter.

In this section we looked at what XML parsers are and how they can be used to parse an XML document. We also looked at how to use the XML parsers that used both the DOM and SAX API.

Next we are going to look at another type of application module, the XSLT processor. The XSLT processor is the application module that uses an XSLT style sheet to transform an XML document.

30.3 *XSLT PROCESSORS*

XSLT processors are application modules that facilitate the transformation process. To transform an XML document, you need more than just XML and an XSLT style sheet, although theoretically you could do the transformation by hand if you had a lot of time. Realistically, just as we need an XML parser to work with an XML document, we need an XSLT processor to do transformations.

XSLT processors understand the markup contained in XSLT style sheets and how to apply the template rules contained within. XSLT processors know how to carry out the following processes:

- Read an XSLT style sheet.

- Read an XML document.

- Apply the transformation rules specified in the style sheet to the XML document.

- Produce an output document.

Figure 30.4 shows the components used during transformation. Each component plays a specific role.

- The XML document serves as the document you are trying to transform.
- The XSLT style sheet provides the content and rules that the XSLT processor uses to perform the transformation.
- The XSLT processor is the application module that uses the XSLT style sheet and XML document to produce the output HTML document.

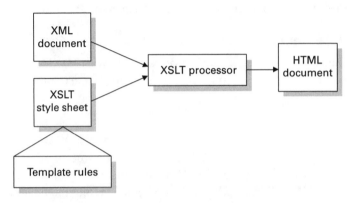

Figure 30.4   Input files an XSLT processor uses to produce an HTML-based output document

The XSLT processor itself does not perform all the steps involved. Rather, it calls other application modules as needed. For example, it calls an XML parser to read in the XML document and XSLT style sheet. XML parsers were discussed in the beginning of this chapter.

One of the key actions carried out by the processor is the application of the template rules. The terms *transformation* rules and *template* rules are somewhat interchangeable, although template rules is the proper technical term. The transformation rules specified in the style sheet are represented using template rules. For an explanation of template rules, see chapter 29.

To better understand how XSLT processors work, let's examine two XSLT processors, MSXML and Xalan.

30.3.1   Microsoft XSLT processor

MSXML also provides XSLT processing. Because the MSXML XSLT processor is contained in the same application module as the MSXML parser, we will not list all properties and methods here again. Please refer to the "XML Parsers" section earlier in this chapter for a description. We will, however, call out one interesting method:

transformNode—Performs the transformation using a source document and the supplied XSLT style sheet.

MSXML in action

Figure 30.5 Result of running transformation using MSXML from VBScript

Here is an example of the MSXML XSLT processor at work from VBScript. In this code, we are performing a transformation. We read in and store the XML document in a DOMDocument object, and do the same for the XSLT style sheet. We then call the `transformNode` method of the DOMDocument object representing the XML document to transform it according to the template rules in the XSLT style sheet. Template rules were discussed in chapter 29. Running this VBScript, would result in the MessageBox shown in figure 30.5.

```
set xmlDoc = CreateObject("MSXML2.DOMDocument")   ❶
xmlDoc.async = false
xmlDoc.load("games.xml")   ❷
set xslDoc = CreateObject("MSXML2.DOMDocument")   ❸
xslDoc.async = false
xslDoc.load("games.xsl")   ❹
MsgBox xmlDoc.transformNode(xslDoc)   ❺
```

Code comments

❶ Creates a DOMDocument object. This will represent the XML document.

❷ Loads and parses the "games.xml" file.

❸ Creates a DOMDocument object. This will represent the XSL style sheet.

❹ Loads and parses the "games.xsl" file.

❺ Calls the transform function of the DOMDocument object, passing the DOMDocument representing our style sheet as the parameter.

30.3.2 Xalan XSLT processor

The Xalan processor is an XSLT processor from the Apache Foundation which comes in Java and C++ versions. This processor uses the Xerces parser to read and validate XSL style sheets. The following is a list of interesting classes and methods used in the processor. For a complete description of the Xalan XSLT processor, visit http://xml.apache.org.

Classes

- *XSLTInputSource*—This class represents an XML or XSL input source.

- *XSLTResultTarget*—This class represents the result of a transformation.

- *XSLTProcessorFactory*—This class is the factory for creating implementations of the XSLTProcessor interface.

XSLTProcessorFactory methods

- *getProcessor*—This method returns a new XSLT processor and XML parser.

- *XSLTProcessor*—This interface represents the transformation processor.

XSLTProcessor methods

- *process*—This method is used to transform the XML input.

- *reset*—This method is used to reset the instance of XSLTProcessor you are using if you want to reuse it.

Xalan in action

Listing 30.3 is a sample using the Xalan XSLT processor to transform the XML document games.xml.

Listing 30.3   Using Xalan to transform an XML document

```
import org.xml.sax.SAXException;
import org.apache.xalan.xslt.XSLTProcessorFactory;
import org.apache.xalan.xslt.XSLTInputSource;
import org.apache.xalan.xslt.XSLTResultTarget;
import org.apache.xalan.xslt.XSLTProcessor;

public class xalantransform
{
  public static void main(String[] args)
    throws java.io.IOException,
           java.net.MalformedURLException,
           org.xml.sax.SAXException
  {
    XSLTProcessor processor = XSLTProcessorFactory.getProcessor();

    processor.process(new XSLTInputSource("games.xml"),
                      new XSLTInputSource("games.xsl"),
                      new XSLTResultTarget(System.out));
  }
}
```

We first get an instance of the XSLTProcessor; this is the Java class that does the transformation. We call its process method, passing the games.xml file, the games.xsl XSLT style sheet, and a parameter specifying where we want the results stored. In this case, we use System.out which means the transformation results will be written on the screen.

30.4 HOW *XML* PARSERS AND *XSLT* PROCESSORS WORK TOGETHER

So far, we've looked at XML parsers and XSLT processors individually, but they do not work to perform transformations of XML documents. While the XML parser does not participate in the actual transform, it does provide necessary functions to the overall process.

XSLT processors use XML parsers to read in and validate:

* A source XML document
* An XSLT style sheet

Making sure the XML document and XSLT style sheet are valid and well formed is a necessary step of the transformation process. Most often though, you don't directly work with the XML parser—it's the XSLT processor's job to make sure it gets called. So, unless you are writing your own XSLT processor, you shouldn't worry that much about the XML parser.

Figure 30.6 shows how a source XML document and XSL style sheet are used by an XSLT processor to produce a result tree. The XML parser's role in this picture is to read and validate both the XSLT style sheet and XML document.

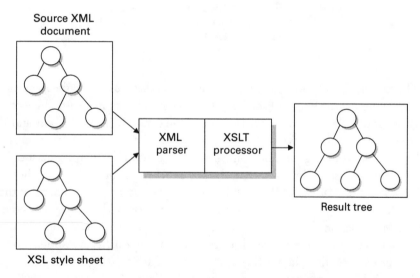

Figure 30.6 An XSLT processor and XML parser work together

The entire process of reading and validating the XML, reading and validating the XSL style sheet, and running the transformation, are usually presented as one step in your code. It all depends on how the XSLT processor was written. In fact, in some cases, you can even specify what XML parser you want the XSLT processor to use.

To further illustrate this relationship, let's modify the Java application from the last section to print out the name of the XML parser being used by the Xalan XSLT processor. Here is the modified source code.

```
import org.xml.sax.SAXException;
import org.apache.xalan.xslt.XSLTProcessorFactory;
import org.apache.xalan.xslt.XSLTInputSource;
import org.apache.xalan.xslt.XSLTResultTarget;
import org.apache.xalan.xslt.XSLTProcessor;
import org.apache.xalan.xpath.xml.XMLParserLiaison;

public class xalantransform
{
   public static void main(String[] args)
      throws java.io.IOException,
             java.net.MalformedURLException,
             org.xml.sax.SAXException
   {

     XSLTProcessor processor = XSLTProcessorFactory.getProcessor();

     XMLParserLiaison xmlLiason = processor.getXMLProcessorLiaison();

     System.out.println("XML parser being used: " +
        xmlLiason.getParserDescription());

     processor.process(new XSLTInputSource("games.xml"),
                     new XSLTInputSource("games.xsl"),
                     new XSLTResultTarget(System.out));

   }
}
```

The first line in bold adds an import statement so that we can use the XMLParserLiaison class in our code. The XMLParserLiaison is a class that acts as a liaison between the XML parser and the XSLT processor. Fully describing the XMLParserLiaison and the use of other XML parsers with Xalan is beyond the scope of this chapter. Visit http://xml.apache.org for more information. The next line in bold adds a call to get the XMLParserLiaison by calling the getXMLProcessorLiaison method of the XSLTProcessor class. On the next line, we add a System.out.println to print the name of the XML Parser. This is done by calling the getParserDescription method of the XMLParserLiaison class.

Figure 30.7 shows the result of running our modified Java application.

From the first line of output "XML Parser being used: XML4J Version Xerces 1.2.2" we can see that we are using the Xerces XML Parser. This line was generated by the call to getParserDescription of the XMLParserLiaison class.

In this section we looked at what XSLT processors are and how they use XSLT style sheets to transform XML documents. We also briefly examined how XSLT processors use XML parsers to read and validate XSLT style sheets.

In the next section, we are going to put this knowledge to use and do a simple transformation from XML to HTML.

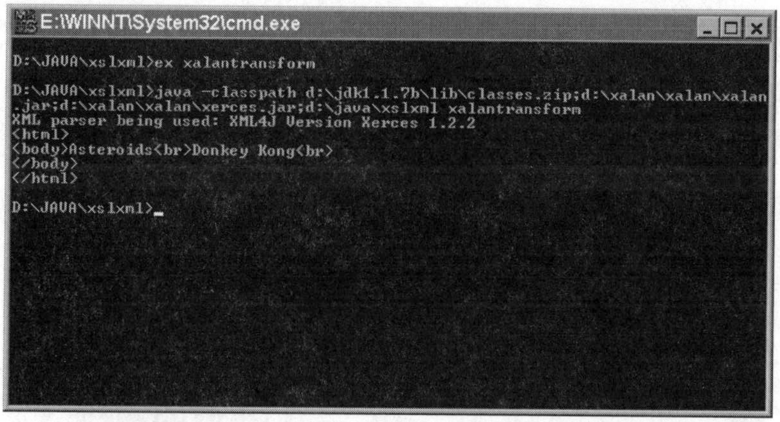

Figure 30.7 Using the XMLParserLiaison class to print the name of an XML parser

For this example, we will be using the Microsoft XSLT processor and ASP to transform an XML document

30.5 *A SAMPLE TRANSFORMATION: XML TO HTML*

In the following section, we will look at two examples covering a transformation from XML to HTML. Given HTML's wide use and easy-to-use markup, it will give us a chance to focus on the transformation process instead of details about the markup language. We will look at more examples in chapter 31.

30.5.1 MSXML and ASP

Our first example will use the MSXML XSLT processor to transform a simple XML document into HTML. The MSXML XSLT processor will be called from an ASP.

The input document

We'll use the following XML document (games.xml) as our input. You should store this XML document in the same directory as the ASP described later.

```
<?xml version="1.0"?>
<!DOCTYPE games[
<!ELEMENT games (game*)>
<!ELEMENT game (#PCDATA)>
]>
<games>
  <game>Asteroids</game>
  <game>Donkey Kong</game>
</games>
```

The style sheet

Our transformation will use the XSLT games.xsl style sheet. It contains one template that is instantiated when the root element is encountered. This template is defined by using the <xsl:template> element. The style sheet should also be stored in the same location as the XML document.

```
<?xml version="1.0"?>
<xsl:stylesheet xmlns:xsl="http://www.w3.org/1999/XSL/Transform"
version="1.0">
<xsl:template match="/">          ❶
<html>
<body>
<xsl:for-each select="games/game">     ❷
 <xsl:value-of select="text()"/><br/>
</xsl:for-each>
</body>
</html>
</xsl:template>
</xsl:stylesheet>
```

❶ Inserts the start of our HTML document with an `<HTML>` tag

❷ Gets the text value of each "game" element

Inserts the end of our HTML document with an `</HTML>` tag

Code comments

❶ Runs when the "games" element is encountered. The "games" element is the root of the XML document.

❷ Runs through this loop for each "game" element in the "games" element.

In our style sheet, you can see that there are HTML tags that will be used to form our HTML document. We are also using the <xsl:for-each> element to loop through each "game" node and the <xsl:value-of> to get the text value of the node. We use the HTML element <br/> to insert a linebreak after each text value is written out. This will make our HTML document more readable.

For a description of nodes, the <xsl:template>, <xsl:for-each>, and <xsl:value-of> elements, see chapter 29.

The Active Server Page

We now need to create the ASP which will call the MSXML XSLT processor to do the transformation. Type the ASP code and save this file in the same location as the (games.xml) file with the name transform.asp.

This ASP script uses the MSXML XSLT processor to load the XML document (games.xml), the XSLT style sheet (games.xsl), and calls the transformNode method of the DOMDocument to complete the actual transformation. See the sections on "XSLT Processors" earlier in this chapter for a description of the MSXML XSLT processor.

```
<%
set xmlDoc = Server.CreateObject("MSXML2.DOMDocument")     ❶
xmlDoc.async = false
```

```
xmlDoc.load(Server.MapPath("games.xml"))        ❷
set xslDoc = Server.CreateObject("MSXML2.DOMDocument")   ❸
xslDoc.async = false
xslDoc.load(Server.MapPath("games.xsl"))        ❹
Response.Write xmlDoc.transformNode(xslDoc)      ❺
%>
```

Code comments

❶ Creates a DOMDocument object which represents our XML document.

❷ Loads the DOMDocument object with the contents of the "games.xml" file.

❸ Creates a DOMDocument object which represents our XSL style sheet.

❹ Loads the DOMDocument object with the contents of the "games.xsl" file.

❺ Calls the `transformNode` method of the DOMDocument object using the DOM-Document object representing our XSL style sheet as its parameter.

The transformation results

Figure 30.8   HTML output from transformation

After you have saved your ASP script, open your web browser and enter the URL of the ASP script (transform.asp). After the script runs, you should see the web page in figure 30.8.

From the View menu, select Source to view the HTML source code (figure 30.9).

Figure 30.9   Source view of HTML generated

As we can see from the Source listing in figure 30.9, our HTML document contains the HTML start tags (<HTML> and <BODY>) defined in our template. Next, we have the text values of each game element from our XML document—in this case, the text values of Asteroids and Donkey Kong. After each of these is the HTML tag <BR/>. We finish the HTML document by using the </BODY> and </HTML> end tags.

Figure 30.10 shows how the template in the XSLT style sheet was used to create the HTML document.

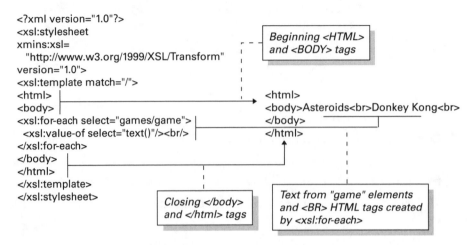

```
<?xml version="1.0"?>
<xsl:stylesheet
xmins:xsl=
   "http://www.w3.org/1999/XSL/Transform"
version="1.0">
<xsl:template match="/">
<html>
<body>
<xsl:for-each select="games/game">
  <xsl:value-of select="text()"/><br/>
</xsl:for-each>
</body>
</html>
</xsl:template>
</xsl:stylesheet>
```

Beginning <HTML> and <BODY> tags

```
<html>
<body>Asteroids<br>Donkey Kong<br>
</body>
</html>
```

Closing </body> and </html> tags

Text from "game" elements and
 HTML tags created by <xsl:for-each>

Figure 30.10   How the template produced the HTML output

30.5.2   Xalan and Java

For our next example of transforming to HTML we'll use the same XML document and XSLT style sheet, but this time we'll use the Xalan processor. This example will use a Java application and Xalan to perform a transformation.

Listing 30.4 uses the same games.xml and games.xsl files for input. Store these files into the same directory as the Java application.

Listing 30.4   Using Xalan to transform an XML document to HTML

```
import org.xml.sax.SAXException;
import org.apache.xalan.xslt.XSLTProcessorFactory;
import org.apache.xalan.xslt.XSLTInputSource;
import org.apache.xalan.xslt.XSLTResultTarget;
import org.apache.xalan.xslt.XSLTProcessor;

public class xalantransform
{
  public static void main(String[] args)
    throws java.io.IOException,
           java.net.MalformedURLException,
           org.xml.sax.SAXException
  {
    // Have the XSLTProcessorFactory obtain a interface to a
    // new XSLTProcessor object.
    XSLTProcessor processor = XSLTProcessorFactory.getProcessor();    ❶
```

```
        processor.process(new XSLTInputSource("games.xml"),     ❷
                           new XSLTInputSource("games.xsl"),     ❸
                           new XSLTResultTarget(System.out));    ❹
    }
}
```

Code comments

❶ Get a new instance of an XSLTProcessor.

❷ Specify the name of the input XML document.

❸ Specify the name of the input XSL style sheet.

❹ Specify the output target, in this case System.out.

When you run this application, the results of the transformation are written to the console window from where you executed the application. This is because we specified System.out as the XSLTResultTarget (figure 30.11). You can find out more about what an XSLTResultTarget is by reading the Xalan documentation.

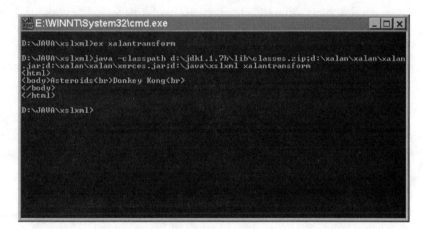

Figure 30.11   The transformation output written to the console window

To write the results of the transformation to a file instead, we would have to make the following changes to our Java application.

```
import org.xml.sax.SAXException;
import org.apache.xalan.xslt.XSLTProcessorFactory;
import org.apache.xalan.xslt.XSLTInputSource;
import org.apache.xalan.xslt.XSLTResultTarget;
import org.apache.xalan.xslt.XSLTProcessor;
import org.apache.xalan.xpath.xml.XMLParserLiaison;

import java.io.FileOutputStream;        ◁─┐  Adds an import for
                                            the FileOutputStream
public class xalantransform{                class
```

```
    public static void main(String[] args)
      throws java.io.IOException,
             java.net.MalformedURLException,
             org.xml.sax.SAXException
  {

    XSLTProcessor processor = XSLTProcessorFactory.getProcessor();

    processor.process(new XSLTInputSource("games.xml"),
                new XSLTInputSource("games.xsl"),
            new XSLTResultTarget(new FileOutputStream("games.html")));

    }
  }
```

The changes to our application are minimal: We added an import statement so that we can use the Java class FileOutputStream. In the line where we call the process() method, we change the third parameter slightly. Instead of creating an XSLTResultTarget and specifying System.out, we change the System.out to a FileOutputStream and specify the name of the file we want to create—"games.html."

When you run this application, instead of seeing the HTML written out to the console window, you will have a file on your hard drive called "games.html" that contains the results of the transformation.

In both of the examples we transformed an XML document containing information about games into an HTML document. Even though we used a different XSLT processor in both examples, we were able to use the same XSLT style sheet. A true testament to standards!

In the next section, we take a look at an advanced feature of the Xalan XSLT processor. Xalan has the capability of providing trace information during the transformation process.

30.6   TRACING THE TRANSFORMATION PROCESS

The transformation process itself is somewhat hidden. We know that something is going on inside the processor because we get a result tree, but we have little control over the process and don't know what happens and when. We don't know when the processor is inserting nodes into the result tree, or has selected a template to instantiate. Wouldn't it be interesting if we could peek inside the process?

With a few lines of code, Xalan can trace the execution of our transform and output information about it. Xalan provides an extensible framework for debugging and tracing style sheets at run time.

30.6.1   Tracing with Xalan

The Xalan tracing framework is contained in the package org.apache.xalan.xslt.trace and includes a relatively small number of classes to facilitate tracing. Following is a brief description of the objects and methods for the tracing framework. For a complete description, visit http://xml.apache.org.

Classes

- *PrintTraceListener*
- *Generated*—Called when a GenerateEvent occurs
- *Selected*—Called when a SelectedEvent occurs
- *Trace*—Called when a Trace event occurs
- *GenerateEvent*—An event generated by the XSLT processor after it generates a new node in the result tree
- *SelectionEvent*—An event triggered by the selection of a node in the style tree
- *TracerEvent*—Parent class of events generated by the tracing execution of XSL processor

Interfaces

- *TraceListener*
- *Generated*—Called when a GenerateEvent occurs
- *Selected*—Called when a SelectionEvent occurs
- *Trace*—Called when a Trace event occurs

30.6.2 Tracing style sheet execution

Let's take our code sample from the "Xalan and Java" section, and add tracing capabilities. We'll first create a class called Tracer that implements the `TraceListener` interface and list the events to System.out. For simplicity's sake, we'll print only the GenerateEvents.

GenerateEvent class

The GenerateEvent class is used to represent an event that is generated when a new node is created in the result tree. For example, when doing a transformation to HTML, an <HTML> tag would be one of the first elements inserted. With tracing enabled, a GenerateEvent would be sent to registered TraceListeners with an event type of `EVENTTYPE_STARTELEMENT`. Table 30.3 is a list of event types that can be generated.

Table 30.3 Xalan GenerateEvent class event types

Event type	Description
EVENTTYPE_CDATA	Generated after a CDATA section is generated
EVENTTYPE_CHARACTERS	Generated for character data with the exception of CDATA and ignorable white space
EVENTTYPE_COMMENT	Generated after a comment has been added
EVENTTYPE_ENDDOCUMENT	Generated when the document ends
EVENTTYPE_ENDELEMENT	Generated after an element ends after its children have been added

Table 30.3   Xalan GenerateEvent class event types

Event type	Description
EVENTTYPE_ENTITYREF	Generated after an entity reference is created
EVENTTYPE_IGNORABLEWHITESPACE	Generated for ignorable white space
EVENTTYPE_PI	Generated for processing instructions
EVENTTYPE_STARTDOCUMENT	Generated when a document begins
EVENTTYPE_STARTELEMENT	Generated when an element starts after its attributes have been processed but before its children

Creating the Tracer class

The Tracer class implements the `TraceListener` interface and implements its methods: `generated()`, `selected()`, and `trace()`. This class will be used to capture events as they happen in the XSLT processor. As we indicated earlier, we will only concern ourselves with generate events, events that get sent when a new node is generated in the result tree.

Listing 30.5   Source for the Tracer class

```
import org.apache.xalan.xslt.trace.*;

public class Tracer implements TraceListener{

  public Tracer(){}

      public void generated(GenerateEvent ev){      ❶
      if (ev.m_eventtype == GenerateEvent.EVENTTYPE_STARTELEMENT){
      System.out.println(ev.m_name +
      " starting element was generated in the result tree");  ❷
      }
      if (ev.m_eventtype == GenerateEvent.EVENTTYPE_CHARACTERS){      ❸
         System.out.println(new String
            (ev.m_characters,ev.m_start,ev.m_length) +
            " character data was generated in the result tree");}
    if (ev.m_eventtype == GenerateEvent.EVENTTYPE_ENDELEMENT){      ❹
      System.out.println(ev.m_name +
         " ending element was generated in the result tree");
      }

  }
  public void selected(SelectionEvent ev){}
  public void trace(TracerEvent ev){}
}
```

Code comments

❶ Implements generated method to capture Generate events.

❷ Prints out a message indicating that the start of an element has been inserted in the result tree.

❸ Prints out a message indicating that character data has been inserted in the result tree.

❹ Prints out a message indicating that the end of an element has been inserted in the result tree.

Updating the Java application

Now that we have our Tracer class, we can update our previous code sample to incorporate the trace capabilities.

Listing 30.6 Updating source to provide tracing output

```
import org.xml.sax.SAXException;
import org.apache.xalan.xslt.XSLTProcessorFactory;
import org.apache.xalan.xslt.XSLTInputSource;
import org.apache.xalan.xslt.XSLTResultTarget;
import org.apache.xalan.xslt.XSLTProcessor;

public class xalantransform
{
   public static void main(String[] args)
     throws java.io.IOException,
            java.net.MalformedURLException,
            org.xml.sax.SAXException,java.util.TooManyListenersException
   {
     // Have the XSLTProcessorFactory obtain a interface to a
     // new XSLTProcessor object.
     XSLTProcessor processor = XSLTProcessorFactory.getProcessor();

        processor.addTraceListener(new Tracer());

     processor.process(new XSLTInputSource("games.xml"),
                       new XSLTInputSource("games.xsl"),
                       new XSLTResultTarget(System.out));
   }

}
```

The first thing we do is modify the main method declaration to throw a `TooManyListenersException` because we did not wrap the call to `addTraceListener` in a try/catch block. Next, we add a line to add our TraceListener to the XSLT processor. This registers an instance of our Tracer class as a listener for trace events.

Figure 30.12 shows the results of running our application with the trace output.

The first several lines of output were generated in response to our trace; the last four lines are our normal transformation output. So as you can see, tracing provides some unique abilities when doing style sheet development and transformations.

Figure 30.12   Output from transform including trace

30.7   STATIC VERSUS DYNAMIC TRANSFORMATIONS

So far, we've seen a few examples of *static* transformations of XML to HTML. We ran an application that used the Xalan XSLT processor to transform an XML document into HTML. The resulting HTML document could then have been saved to a file for later viewing by a web browser.

But in many applications, the content is rarely static. Content such as stock quotes, purchase orders, or movie times may be generated on request. Each time a user sends a request for a stock quote, the application retrieves the current quote and then returns this to the user. Each time the user requests the same quote, it must be looked up each time to ensure that it is accurate.

As we saw in chapter 17, WAP content can be generated dynamically from database queries. This content was not static, meaning the WML cards were created and presented on the fly. If we took that same scenario but generated XML content from database queries instead of WAP content, the process would be similar. However, we can't present the XML document to the user; we must first transform it to WML. This is an example of a dynamic transformation because the resulting WML is created on the fly. The primary difference between dynamic and static transformations is "when" the transform occurs.

Dynamic transformations occur when a client requests a specific XML-based resource from a server, such as an online product catalog. The server then takes the requested resource, and, depending on the type of client requesting, transforms it to the appropriate markup language.

Applications that may be well suited for dynamic transformations are ones that provide real-time content to other businesses. For example, suppose there was a business that provided real-time stock information. Since the information changes so rapidly, the business could not realistically generate static content continuously. Instead, it would transform the XML into the markup language required by each customer as it was requested. This would probably encompass a small set of popular markup languages such as HTML and WML.

Another good example of where dynamic transformations would be well suited is for online financial institutions which may be storing customer information such as portfolio statistics, stocks traded, and financial news. Storing static copies of each customer's information would not only be time consuming but resource consuming. Instead, as each customer requested information about a portfolio, the XML document representing the portfolio would be transformed into the appropriate markup language.

While dynamic transformations offer the ability to generate other formats on the fly, there are costs that should be considered. Transformations can be resource-intensive operations based on the size of your input document, the complexity of the style sheet, and the amount of CPU available to the XSLT processor. You should take this into consideration when using dynamic transformations for your content.

Static transformations occur ahead of time. A developer may determine that the requested resource does not require regular updates. For example, an online catalog application may need to be updated only once a month. Therefore, at monthly intervals, the XML document is updated and the transformation is run. The documents resulting from the transformation are stored in a public location. You may decide to use a static transformation if the resource is too large and would consume too many hardware resources to transform each time or the transformation you wish to do is too time consuming itself.

30.8 COMPILED STYLE SHEETS

Whether you're doing dynamic or static transformations, you may want to consider using a compiled style sheet to improve performance. Compiled style sheets are not a requirement for transformations, but they can help if you use the same style sheet over and over. Consider for a moment that when you are doing a transformation, the style sheet has to first be read in. At the same time, it is being parsed and validated. For small style sheets this may not be as big of a concern. But for larger ones it may bring a noticeable difference in the validation. Also, the actual transformation time may be improved as well. As the processor encounters elements in the source tree, it must find and match those to template rules in the style sheet, and then insert them into the result tree. With a compiled style sheet, this matching and inserting process will be reduced.

Think of a compiled style sheet as analogous to an interpreted program versus a compiled program. In an interpreted program, the interpreter goes line by line. It checks the syntax of each line, and checks to make sure functions you are calling exist and have the proper argument types. This results in a much slower program. Compiled programs do all of these processes before the program runs. In most languages, the compiler checks the syntax, functions, and argument types to ensure they are valid. It then often produces a binary form of your program suitable to run on the target operating system.

So let's assume you've decided to use a compiled style sheet for your transformation. The Xalan processor includes classes and methods that allow you to precompile a style sheet, then reuse it in subsequent transformations.

Utilizing compiled style sheets involves only a few lines of code as illustrated in Listing 30.7.

Listing 30.7 Source for using a compiled style sheet with Xalan

```java
import org.xml.sax.SAXException;
import org.apache.xalan.xslt.XSLTProcessorFactory;
import org.apache.xalan.xslt.XSLTInputSource;
import org.apache.xalan.xslt.XSLTResultTarget;
import org.apache.xalan.xslt.XSLTProcessor;
import org.apache.xalan.xslt.*;

public class xalantransform
{
   public static void main(String[] args)
     throws java.io.IOException,
            java.net.MalformedURLException,
            org.xml.sax.SAXException,java.util.TooManyListenersException
   {
     // Have the XSLTProcessorFactory obtain a interface to a
     // new XSLTProcessor object.
     XSLTProcessor processor = XSLTProcessorFactory.getProcessor();

     StylesheetRoot style = processor.processStylesheet
        (new XSLTInputSource("games.xsl"));

     style.process(new XSLTInputSource("games.xml"),
        new XSLTResultTarget(System.out));
   }
}
```

This application looks very similar to the examples from the "Xalan and Java" section, but has some noticeable differences.

In the first bold line of source code, we create a StylesheetRoot class by calling the processStyleSheet method of the XSLTProcessor class, passing in the name of the style sheet we want to compile. In the next line, we call the process method of the newly created StylesheetRoot class, passing in the file name of the XML document, and the XSLTResultTarget specifying where the transformation results should be written. This is different from the process of the other examples where we called the process method of the XSLTProcessor class, and passing in the same parameters.

Compiled style sheets are required to do transformations, but they do provide opportunities. For example, with compiled style sheets, one could precompile all style sheets used in an application and cache them for later use.

30.9 SUMMARY

In this chapter we looked at XML parsers and XSLT processors and how they are used to transform XML documents. There are two types of XML parsers: DOM and SAX. XSLT processors use the template rules in the XSL style sheet to transform the XML document and produce an output tree. In the next chapter, we'll examine sample transformations that will use different types of input documents to produce transformations to various markup languages.

C H A P T E R   3 1

Implementing transformations

31.1   INTRODUCTION

In this chapter, we will examine transformations to HDML, WML, and VoiceXML. These samples will be presented with a focus on the transformation and creation of style sheets rather than application logic.

Each sample is meant to stand alone, and does not build on any topics presented in other examples. All examples follow a similar pattern of development, which you should pick up on as you do each one. So, if you're interested in doing the VoiceXML example first, go right ahead!

31.2 TRANSFORMATION TO HDML USING MSXML/ASP

In this example, we are going to examine publishing an XML-based product catalog to an HDML-capable client. First we will identify the steps we will go through.

One of the first steps we will take is to examine the XML document and work out how the information should be presented. We don't want to throw the entire catalog at the user at once because it would not make any sense.

Catalogs are usually browsed, page by page, or a user goes to an index and then jumps to a specific page. So, we need to decide what pieces of information we want on each screen. We should also decide if we want to create multiple HDML documents containing the information, in which case we may run multiple transformations. For this example, we are only going to create one HDML document.

Once we have a rough idea of the organization of the catalog, we should sketch out some screens and how the user can navigate between them. These sketches could include what is presented on each screen, and some rough indication of navigational elements.

Once we have an idea of how we want the catalog presented, we should determine what target markup language elements we will use, in this case, HDML elements.

Next we need to start designing the XSLT style sheet to transform the XML catalog into HDML. Our resulting transformation needs to produce not only the data elements of the display, but also the HDML elements that will instruct the HDML client to present the information.

Once we have created the style sheet, we will run the actual transformation. This particular sample uses the Microsoft XML XSLT processor and ASP. The transformation is run when the user requests the ASP page from the web server. The ASP will use MSXML to transform the XML catalog to HDML, and present one HDML document back to the client. The HDML document will contain multiple HDML elements that allow the user to navigate and view the catalog.

31.2.1 Setting up a development environment

Before beginning this example, make sure the following software resources are available and installed.

- PWS or IIS
- Active Server Pages
- UP SDK simulator
- Microsoft XSLT processor/MSXML

31.2.2 Understanding the product catalog

Let's begin by examining what the product catalog is comprised of. Table 31.1 shows the elements of the catalog. By elements I do not mean XML elements, but simply entities in the catalog.

Table 31.1 The product catalog description

Catalog elements	Description
A list of products	All of the products in the catalog.
Product ID and product name	Each product has a name and unique ID.
Product description	Each product has a textual description.
Product inventory	Each product has an inventory.
Inventory quantity and LastSold date	Each inventory contains how many items there are and when the last one was sold.

That's a pretty simple set of information to work with. But knowing what each element is and the relationships between them will be helpful when we start designing the presentation. Now let's look at the XML representation of that catalog.

XML catalog

The following XML document represents the product catalog:

```
<?xml version="1.0"?>
<products>
    <product id="A1" name="Product1">        ❶
       <description>Description</description>    ❷
       <inventory>
          <quantity>500</quantity>              ❸
          <lastsold>01/17/2000</lastsold>
       </inventory>
    </product>
    <product id="A2" name="Product2">        ❶
       <description>Description</description>    ❷
       <inventory>
          <quantity>10</quantity>               ❸
          <lastsold>12/17/1999</lastsold>
       </inventory>
    </product>
</products>
```

Code comments

❶ Represents the products of the catalog; each product has the ID and NAME attribute.

❷ Represents the descriptions of the products.

❸ Represents the inventory for each product; there is a quantity and last sold date.

In figure 31.1 we see how the XML elements and attributes correspond to the catalog elements that were listed in table 31.1:

We should now have a general picture of the product catalog and the elements contained in the catalog. We also have seen what that catalog looks like in XML. With this in hand, let's move onto the next step and decide how we want to present this information to a user.

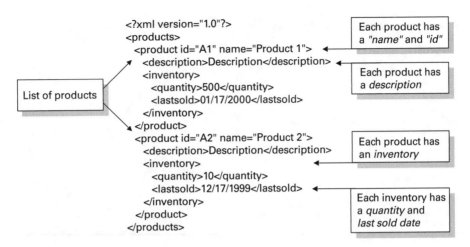

Figure 31.1   Product catalog as XML

31.2.3   Designing the presentation

Determining the presentation of the catalog can be one of the most important steps in the transformation process. A catalog that is hard to navigate, and presents information in an unusual way, would turn away users.

One of the easiest ways to design the flow is to create a storyboard or a flowchart of the screens you think will be needed in the application. This will help sort out what can go on each screen. It can also help to identify possible usability issues with the interface. For instance, let's say you decided to implement the following navigation scheme:

- Present the user with the list of products
- Provide a link to the inventory
- From the inventory, provide a link to the description of the selected product

While this is technically possible, it doesn't make much sense and can be confusing to the user. It would have made more sense to link to the product description first, then provide a link to the inventory. This would help the user make sure he had the correct product first.

Figure 31.2 illustrates the screen flow for this example.

As we stated earlier, we don't want to throw the entire catalog at the user. Not only is this bad usability, but also would make the presentation hard to understand. Remember that we are working with devices that often have screens measuring roughly two inches by two inches. So we need to plan the presentation and navigation accordingly. With this in mind, let's talk about the screen flow.

The first box presents the list of products to the user.

Then, as indicated by the arrow pointing down, we provide a way to navigate to the product description represented by the second box.

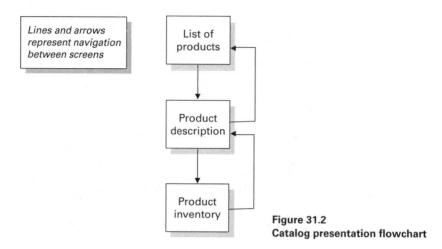

Figure 31.2
Catalog presentation flowchart

From here, we should provide a way for the user not only to move on to the inventory, but also a way for him to move backward. We could provide a link that allows the user to move backward, but for this example, we are going to use the behavior of the Accept key on the device's touch pad to navigate backward. We can do this because the device maintains a history of screens similar to what a web browser does with web pages you visit. By pressing Accept, the user will be sent back to the list of products. While this works for this simple application, you will most likely want to provide an actual link in real applications. You may not be able to count on the previous screen being the one you want.

From the product description, we then want to allow the user to navigate the product inventory represented by the last box in the flowchart. This is the last screen in the application, and from here we can only navigate backward. We will rely on Accept to send us back to the product description screen.

That in a nutshell is the flow of the screens in our example application. We now have an idea of the different screens a user will see when viewing the catalog, and the navigation methods to go between each screen. With this in mind, we will need to determine how to make these screens real. We will examine what elements in HDML we can use to create the screens. First let's talk about how prototyping screens can be useful during this step.

Prototyping the presentation

While the flowchart in figure 31.2 may be sufficient for most uses, some people have a hard time grasping the end result unless they can see an example. To that end, it may make more sense to create a prototype of the screens. To make a simple prototype, create an actual screen using the target markup language which, in this example, is HDML. Take the data from the XML document and use it on the screens. This can give a good sense of what the application will look like before you spend a lot of time doing the rest of the screens.

Figure 31.3 shows what a prototype of the product list screen might look like.

```
<HDML version="3.0">
<CHOICE>
Select a Product
<CE DEST="#A1"TASK="GOSUB"
LABEL="Product1">Product 2</CE>
</CHOICE>
</HDML>
```

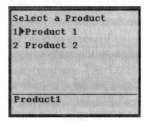

Figure 31.3 Prototype of product list screen

To create this prototype, you would simply type the source HDML using a text editor and save it to a file on your hard drive. Then, load this file into the UP.Simulator or some other device capable of rendering HDML.

31.2.4   HDML elements

We now need to determine the actual HDML elements we are going to use to present the catalog. As seen in chapter 11, HDML uses various elements to display text, accept user input, and present choices. Our output HDML document will need to make use of the elements that display text, provide links to other information, and present choices to the user. Table 31.2 outlines the HDML elements we will need to use.

Table 31.2   HDML elements

Document requirement	HTML element(s)
Displays list of all products	<CHOICE> card
Displays each product in the list	<CE> element to present each product as a choice in the CHOICE card
Displays description of the selected product	<DISPLAY> card
Displays inventory for the selected product	<DISPLAY> card
Displays link to inventory	<A> element to provide a link

We now have a general idea of the elements needed to present the catalog. Before we begin constructing the XSLT style sheet that will take our catalog and transform it to HDML, we will discuss a unique problem that is encountered when transforming XML to HDML.

HDML's unique problem

HDML is not an XML-based markup language; therefore, it does not have the same constraints placed upon its structure. For instance, in XML, all elements must be closed out with an end or empty element tag (`</element>` or `<element/>`)

before it can be considered a valid element. HDML does not enforce this kind of constraint for some elements, such as the `<CE>` element. When an XSLT processor encounters this, it complains that the element is not closed out. This presents somewhat of a problem. We certainly don't want to have to hand-edit our transformed files, and in some cases, we may not be able to.

We could do one of the following:

1 Tell the XSLT processor that this is not an element and ignore the fact that the end tag is missing.

2 Close out the element.

For this example the easiest thing to do is to close out the element. This requires little effort and does not require any special processing tags. It will also keep the document well formed which, even though it is not a requirement of HDML, makes the document easier to understand.

31.2.5 Defining the XSLT style sheet

With a basic idea of the HDML elements we need to produce, we can now start defining the XSLT style sheet. The style sheet will need to contain one `<xsl:template>`. It will also need `<xsl:for-each>` loop blocks to generate the different HDML elements. Since we have multiple products in the catalog, the `<xsl:for-each>` will allow us to generate a set of HDML elements for each product. Table 31.3 summarizes the XSL elements we will use in the style sheet and the purpose each serves.

Table 31.3   XSL elements used

Style sheet element	Purpose
<xsl:for-each>	To loop through the product list
<xsl:value-of>	To retrieve the values of attributes and elements for product descriptions, IDs, and names
<xsl:output>	To make sure the XML declaration is not written out
<xsl:text>	To generate markup characters into the output document
<xsl:template>	To define the template for this style sheet

Beginning the style sheet

You will get to know the first two lines of our style sheet well. They are the XML declaration and `<xsl:stylesheet>` element that declares our document a style sheet.

```
<?xml version="1.0"?>
<xsl:stylesheet xmlns:xsl="http://www.w3.org/1999/XSL/Transform"
version="1.0">
<xsl:output omit-xml-declaration="yes"/>
```

For most markup languages, the first two lines are usually all that will be needed. However, since HDML is not XML-based, we need to make sure that the output document does not contain the XML declaration. To do this, we needed to add the `<xsl:output>` element to our style sheet before any templates are defined. This will prevent the XML declaration from being put into the output document

Defining the template

Before we jump into the product list, we need to first define the template for our style sheet. Recall from chapter 29, templates are used to select elements from the source tree for processing. When the XSLT processor matches a template to an element in the source tree, what is in the template will be inserted into the result tree. To define our template, we need to include the following statement in our style sheet:

```
<xsl:template match="products">
```

This defines the start of the template. Later on we will include a statement that ends or closes out the template. Looking at the template, we see that the `match` attribute has a value of `products`. Recall from chapter 29, the `match` attribute is used to tell the XSLT processor when to use this template. The `products` value is called the pattern. When the XSLT processor encounters the `products` element in the source document, this template will be instantiated.

Starting the HDML document

As another part of this template, we need to include an HDML element that will define the start of our HDML document. We can't start defining HDML elements without specifying the start of the document. Recall from chapter 29, all XML documents have a root element that defines the start of the document, and in most cases, the type of document. Even though HDML is not XML-based, we include the root element with the following statement:

```
<HDML VERSION="3.0">
```

With our template started, we can now start defining the XSL that will produce our first screen.

Displaying the product list

In the "Designing the presentation" section earlier in this chapter, we sketched out the screens we would need to have in the application. The first screen we specified was one that presented a list of products. This block of XSL shows the XSL and HDML elements we will need to produce a list of the products.

```
<CHOICE>
Select a Product
<xsl:for-each select="product">
<CE LABEL="{@name}" TASK="GOSUB" DEST="#{@id}"><xsl:value-of
select="@name"/></CE>
</xsl:for-each>
</CHOICE>
```

We first define a <CHOICE> card element, which if you recall from chapter 11, will present a list of choices the user may select from. After that we enter text to instruct the user to make a selection. This may be obvious to us as developers, but if we just threw up a list of products, the user may not understand what needs to be done.

Next, we need to generate the choices themselves. We do this using the <xsl:for-each> element to loop through all of the product nodes in the source tree. If you recall from chapter 29, XSLT uses XPath in conjunction with the template to select nodes for processing. In this case, we are telling the <xsl:for-each> element to process all of the <product> elements. Why don't we need to specify products/product? Because we are already in the proper context and don't need to specify it again. The proper context (see chapter 29) was set when the template was instantiated.

Each time through the loop, a new product node is selected. At this point we have access to all of its values and attributes. We start by specifying a <CE> element, which is the HDML element for a unique choice in the list. We then set the LABEL attribute of the <CE> element to the value of the name attribute of the product.

Next, set the DEST attribute of the <CE> element equal to the ID attribute of the XML <product> element. The DEST attribute specifies where the user will be sent when this choice is selected. Then, we need to put in the textual value that will be displayed on the screen. For this, we use the <xsl:value-of> element to insert the value of the name attribute of the product element.

After this, we close out the <xsl:for-each> and the HDML <CHOICE> card. We are now ready to move onto the next set of screens.

Displaying product descriptions

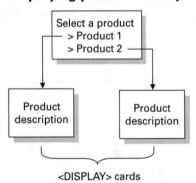

<DISPLAY> cards

Figure 31.4   <DISPLAY> card for each product description

The next set of screens is the product description screens. Unlike the product list screen, we actually need to define multiple screens, one for each product, with the product description on it. Figure 31.4 illustrates the relationship between the product choices and the screens that display the corresponding product descriptions.

This block of XSL shows us how to do this.

```
<xsl:for-each select="product"
<DISPLAY name="{@id}">
 Desc:<xsl:value-of select="description"/> |#3 [LW: OK to split this line of
code?]
<xsl:text disable-output-escaping="yes">&lt;BR&gt;&lt;BR&gt;</xsl:text>
```

```
<A TASK="GO" TYPE="ACCEPT" DEST="#{concat(@id,'INV')}"> View Inventory
</A>
</DISPLAY>
</xsl:for-each>
```

The first line is in a different place than it was the product list section. In the product list section, we were defining a single <CHOICE> card. Here, we need to define multiple <DISPLAY> cards for each product description. So, we have to start with the <xsl:for-each> which also loops through each product element just like the <xsl:for-each> did in the product list section.

Next, we define the <DISPLAY> card. We set its name attribute to the value of the id attribute of the current product node. We need to set it to this value because in the product list, we set the DEST attribute of the <CE> element to the same value. That way, when the user makes a selection, he is taken to the <DISPLAY> card with the corresponding id. Figure 31.5 illustrates how each choice identifies the product description card it needs to send the user to.

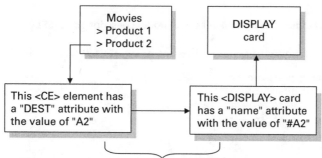

Figure 31.5
<CE> choice "DEST" attribute corresponds to a <DISPLAY> card

The value of "A2" is the value of the product "id" attribute

The text of the <DISPLAY> card consists of the string "Desc:" followed by the value of the product's description node. We retrieve this value by using the <xsl:value-of> to select the description node. Next, insert a couple of blank lines after the description to improve readability because we must also provide a link to the product inventory.

To provide a link to the inventory, we use the <A> HDML element. We set its text value to the string "View Inventory" but we need to set its DEST attribute to a unique value just as we did for the DISPLAY card. But we can't use just the ID, because that would conflict with the <DISPLAY> cards we already defined. Instead, we create a concatenated value using the product id and the string "INV."

We finish by closing out the <DISPLAY> card and the <xsl:for-each> element. Each time this <xsl:for-each> runs, a <DISPLAY> card is generated. We can now move on to the final set of screens, the product inventory.

Displaying product inventory

For the product inventory screens, we are going to follow the same pattern we used for the product descriptions. We are going to generate <DISPLAY> cards for each product with the inventory information on it. Figure 31.6 illustrates how each product description card links to a product inventory card.

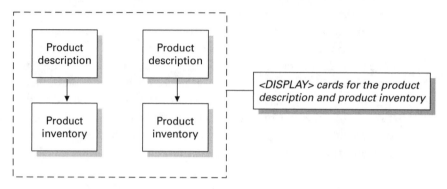

Figure 31.6 Each product description links to a product description <DISPLAY> card

This XSL shows how to generate the inventory <DISPLAY> cards.

```
<xsl:for-each select="product">
<DISPLAY name="{concat(@id,'INV')}">
Quantity:<xsl:value-of select="inventory/quantity"/>
LastSold:<xsl:value-of select="inventory/lastsold"/>
</DISPLAY>
</xsl:for-each>
```

We start with the <xsl:for-each> element to begin the loop through the product nodes.

We define the <DISPLAY> card, using the concatenated value of the product's id attribute and the string literal 'INV.' This corresponds to the value we used for the <A> link on the product description <DISPLAY> card. See the previous section for why we are using a concatenated value.

Next, we define the text that will appear in the <DISPLAY> card. This text begins with the string "Quantity:" followed by the value of the quantity node of the product inventory node. We get this value using the <xsl:value-of> to retrieve the value of the quantity node. We specify this using a value of "inventory/quantity" so that we have the right context. Since the quantity element is not a direct child of the product element in our source document, we need to specify "inventory" so that the XSLT processor will know where to look for the quantity element.

We follow the same pattern when putting the lastSold date into the <DISPLAY> card. We start with the string "LastSold:" and then follow it with the value of the `lastsold` node, again using the `<xsl:value-of>` to retrieve the value of this node.

We then close out the `<DISPLAY>` card and the `<xsl:for-each>`. We now have the XSL to generate a product inventory screen for each product.

Ending the style sheet

We need to produce our HDML product catalog. But first we need to close out some elements that we started earlier in the process. If you remember, we started with `<xsl:stylesheet>` element, then defined an `<xsl:template>` element, and started our HDML document with an `<HDML>` element. We need to finish the style sheet by closing these elements out in reverse order.

```
</HDML>                    ❶
</xsl:template>            ❷
</xsl:stylesheet>          ❸
```

Code comments

❶ Closes out the `<HDML VERSION="3.0">` element and defines the end of the HDML document.

❷ Closes out the `<xsl:template match="products">` element, and ends the definition of the template.

❸ Closes out the `<xsl:stylesheet>` element, and ends the definition of the entire XSL style sheet.

With all of this completed, we are now ready to move on to running the transformation using this style sheet. But first, here is a tip. When creating a style sheet it can be easy sometimes to forget to close out elements, especially when the style sheet is large. To help reduce the possibility of this occurring, it is helpful to immediately close out elements, and then type the rest of the style sheet. For example, you may want to start with a style sheet that looks like this:

```
<?xml version="1.0"?>
<xsl:stylesheet xmlns:xsl="http://www.w3.org/1999/XSL/Transform"
version="1.0">
<xsl:template match="">
</xsl:template>
</xsl:stylesheet>
```

This way, you can just type in between the `<xsl:template>` tags and not worry about forgetting to close out the template or style sheet.

31.2.6   Running the transform

Before we run the transformation, we need to gather the XML document and XSL style sheet pieces together and store them. We also need to create the ASP that calls the XSLT processor. Table 31.4 outlines the files needed for the transformation and how each file should be prepared:

Table 31.4 Preparing the files

File	Description	Do this with it
products.xml	XML catalog	Save in the "wwwroot" folder of your IIS or PWS installation.
products.xsl	XSLT style sheet	Save in the "wwwroot" folder of your IIS or PWS installation.
chap31samp1.asp	ASP	Save in the "wwwroot" folder of your IIS or PWS installation.

Creating the ASP

For this example, we are going to use ASP to invoke the transformation process. From an ASP, we are going to call the Microsoft XSLT processor to do the actual transformation.

```
<%
response.ContentType = "text/x-hdml"
set xmlDoc = Server.CreateObject("MSXML2.DOMDocument")
xmlDoc.async = false
xmlDoc.load(Server.MapPath("products.xml"))
set xslDoc = Server.CreateObject("MSXML2.DOMDocument")
xslDoc.async = false
xslDoc.load(Server.MapPath("products.xsl"))
Response.Write xmlDoc.transformNode(xslDoc)
%>
```

Without the first line of the ASP, the UP.Simulator will not understand what we are sending back to it. The `text/x-hdml` content type tells it that this is HDML. The second line creates a DOMDocument object which will represent the product's XML document. The third line loads the products.xml file into the DOMDocument object. This causes the MSXML parser to parse the document and ensure it's valid and well formed.

The next two lines basically repeat the same process, but this time we specify the products.xsl file. In the final line, we call the XSLT processor to transform the XML product catalog into HDML. This is written back to the client using the ASP Response object.

Viewing the resulting HDML output

Figure 31.7 Navigate to the ASP page

Using the UP.Simulator, navigate it to the location of the chap31samp1.asp file we just created (figure 31.7).

This will display the product list (figure 31.8).

Next, select "Product2" from the list of products, which should display our description for that product (figure 31.9). Recall we generated a `<DISPLAY>` card for product descriptions.

Next, using the arrow keys, navigate to the "View Inventory" link, and press Accept. This will display the inventory for the product (figure 31.10). If you recall, we generated a <DISPLAY> card for product inventory information.

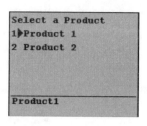

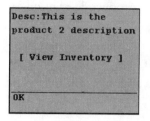

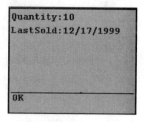

Figure 31.8
The product list

Figure 31.9
The product description

Figure 31.10
The product inventory

The HDML source

If we were to look at the source that was generated after running the ASP page, it would look like the following:

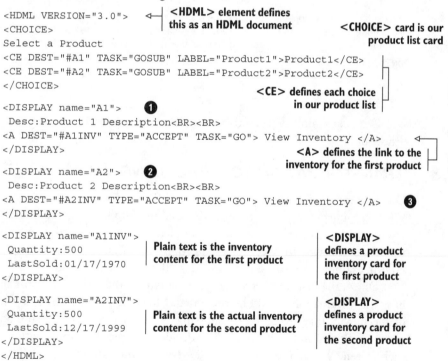

```
<HDML VERSION="3.0">          <HDML> element defines
<CHOICE>                       this as an HDML document          <CHOICE> card is our
Select a Product                                                  product list card
<CE DEST="#A1" TASK="GOSUB" LABEL="Product1">Product1</CE>
<CE DEST="#A2" TASK="GOSUB" LABEL="Product2">Product2</CE>
</CHOICE>
                                        <CE> defines each choice
                                           in our product list
<DISPLAY name="A1">     ❶
 Desc:Product 1 Description<BR><BR>
<A DEST="#A1INV" TYPE="ACCEPT" TASK="GO"> View Inventory </A>
</DISPLAY>                                      <A> defines the link to the
                                           inventory for the first product
<DISPLAY name="A2">     ❷
 Desc:Product 2 Description<BR><BR>
<A DEST="#A2INV" TYPE="ACCEPT" TASK="GO"> View Inventory </A>     ❸
</DISPLAY>

<DISPLAY name="A1INV">
 Quantity:500              Plain text is the inventory       <DISPLAY>
 LastSold:01/17/1970       content for the first product     defines a product
</DISPLAY>                                                     inventory card for
                                                              the first product

<DISPLAY name="A2INV">
 Quantity:500              Plain text is the actual inventory  <DISPLAY>
 LastSold:12/17/1999       content for the second product     defines a product
</DISPLAY>                                                      inventory card for
</HDML>                                                         the second product
```

Code comments

❶ <DISPLAY> defines a product description card for the first product.

❷ <DISPLAY> defines a product description card for the second product.

❸ <A> defines the link to the inventory for the second product.

Troubleshooting

When running this example, you may encounter a few problems. Table 31.5 offers troubleshooting tips.

Table 31.5   Troubleshooting tips

Problem	Solution
UP.Simulator says it can't compile document	Look at the source of the document using the UP.Simulator "info>source" menu option. This will show you if you have a syntax error or some other problem.
UP.Simulator source says there is a syntax error	Look at the HDML that was generated. Spaces in the LABEL element of or / at the end of elements can cause syntax errors. HDML does not have the notion of an empty element tag as in XML.
Microsoft XML parser complains there is no style sheet element	Ensure the MSXML XSLT processor can locate the XSL style sheet file on your file system. You should use "Server.MapPath" to make sure it looks in the right location on the file system.
You can't navigate to the product description or inventory	Look at your XSL style sheet and ensure you provided closing <DISPLAY> tags. This will probably be caught by the UP.Simulator unless you never generated the tags in the first place.

Our next sample delves into XML to WML transformations using the Xalan XSLT processor.

31.3   TRANSFORMATION TO *WML* USING *JAVA*

Our next sample illustrates publishing an XML-based listing of movies and times to a WML-capable client. WML is an XML-based markup language unlike HDML. As we saw in the HDML transformation example, we first described a series of steps we would go through to accomplish the transformation. If you just came from the HDML example, you can skip this section. If not, please read on.

One of the first steps we will take is to examine the XML document and work out how the information should be presented. Movie lists are usually browsed by names of the movies that are currently showing. A list of movies often contains the show times. With that in mind, we need to decide what pieces of information we want on each screen. We should also decide if we want to create multiple WML documents containing the information, in which case we may run multiple transformations. For this example, we are going to create only one WML document.

Once we have a rough idea of the organization of the movie list, we go back to the storyboard, sketching screens and how the user can navigate between them and what will be presented on each, plus a rough indication of navigational elements.

Next, we should determine what *target markup language* elements we will use. The target markup language is the markup language we end up with after transforming the XML catalog to WML. Since WML is our target markup language, we should determine what elements in WML we will need to use to present the information to the user.

Next, we need to start designing the XSLT style sheet with template rules that will transform the XML catalog into WML. The resulting transformation needs to produce not only the data elements of the display, but also the WML elements that will instruct the WML client to present the information.

Once we have created the style sheet, we will run the actual transformation. This particular sample uses the Xalan XSLT processor from a Java application. This transformation will be run to produce a static WML document which will contain multiple WML elements that allow the user to navigate and view the movie list.

31.3.1 Setting up a development environment

For this sample you will need the following already installed on your machine:

- Nokia WAP Toolkit or another emulator capable of rendering WML
- Xalan XSLT processor
- JDK1.2

31.3.2 Understanding the movie list

Let's begin by examining what the movie list is comprised of. The elements in table 31.6 mean entities in the movie list, not XML elements.

Table 31.6 Movie list description

Movie list elements	Description
A list of movies	All of the movies in the list.
Movie name	Each movie has a name.
Movie description	Each movie has a textual description.
Showings	Each movie has a list of times the movie is shown.
Showing	A movies list of showings is comprised of individual show times, which have a day and time.

This is not an overwhelming amount of information to work with, but knowing what each element is and the relationships between them will be helpful when we start designing the presentation.

XML movie list

Listing 31.1 is the source code for an XML document movie list. It has only two movies, but this should be enough for example purposes.

Listing 31.1 Source code for an XML movie list

```
<?xml version="1.0"?>
<movies>
   <movie name="Mission Impossible:2">
      <description>High-Tech spy thriller</description>
      <showings>
         <showing day="Sun" time="01:00pm"/>
          <showing day="Sun" time="03:00pm"/>
         <showing day="Mon" time="01:00pm"/>
          <showing day="Mon" time="03:00pm"/>
         <showing day="Tue" time="01:00pm"/>
          <showing day="Tue" time="03:00pm"/>
         <showing day="Wed" time="01:00pm"/>
          <showing day="Wed" time="03:00pm"/>
         <showing day="Thu" time="01:00pm"/>
          <showing day="Thu" time="03:00pm"/>
         <showing day="Fri" time="01:00pm"/>
          <showing day="Fri" time="03:00pm"/>
         <showing day="Sat" time="01:00pm"/>
          <showing day="Sat" time="03:00pm"/>
      </showings>
   </movie>
   <movie name="Austin Powers">
      <description>International Man of Mystery</description>
      <showings>
         <showing day="Sun" time="01:00pm"/>  |#3
          <showing day="Sun" time="03:00pm"/>  |#3
         <showing day="Mon" time="01:00pm"/>
          <showing day="Mon" time="03:00pm"/>
         <showing day="Tue" time="01:00pm"/>
          <showing day="Tue" time="03:00pm"/>
         <showing day="Wed" time="01:00pm"/>
          <showing day="Wed" time="03:00pm"/>
         <showing day="Thu" time="01:00pm"/>
          <showing day="Thu" time="03:00pm"/>
         <showing day="Fri" time="01:00pm"/>
          <showing day="Fri" time="03:00pm"/>
         <showing day="Sat" time="01:00pm"/>
          <showing day="Sat" time="03:00pm"/>
      </showings>
   </movie>
</movies>
```

Represents the individual movies in the list; each movie has a NAME attribute

Represents the show times for the movie; each showing has a DAY and TIME attribute

Represents the movie's description

In figure 31.11 we can see how the XML elements and attributes correspond to the movie list elements in table 31.6. Note that the XML listed in the figure has been abbreviated to only show one movie.

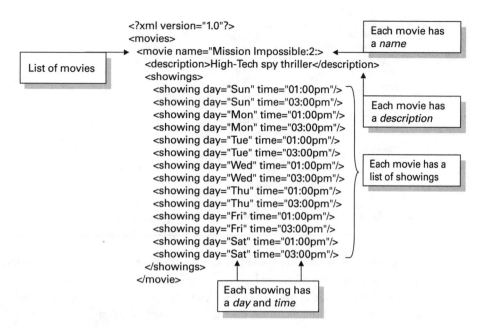

```
<?xml version="1.0"?>
<movies>
  <movie name="Mission Impossible:2:>
    <description>High-Tech spy thriller</description>
    <showings>
      <showing day="Sun" time="01:00pm"/>
      <showing day="Sun" time="03:00pm"/>
      <showing day="Mon" time="01:00pm"/>
      <showing day="Mon" time="03:00pm"/>
      <showing day="Tue" time="01:00pm"/>
      <showing day="Tue" time="03:00pm"/>
      <showing day="Wed" time="01:00pm"/>
      <showing day="Wed" time="03:00pm"/>
      <showing day="Thu" time="01:00pm"/>
      <showing day="Thu" time="03:00pm"/>
      <showing day="Fri" time="01:00pm"/>
      <showing day="Fri" time="03:00pm"/>
      <showing day="Sat" time="01:00pm"/>
      <showing day="Sat" time="03:00pm"/>
    </showings>
  </movie>
```

List of movies

Each movie has a *name*

Each movie has a *description*

Each movie has a list of showings

Each showing has a *day* and *time*

Figure 31.11 Movie list as XML

We should now have a general picture of the movie list and the elements contained in the movie list. We have also seen what that movie list looks like as an XML document. Next we decide how to present this information to a user.

31.3.3 Designing the presentation

Determining the presentation of the movie list can be one of the most important steps in the transformation process.

As we saw in the first example with HDML, if we linked to the inventory from the name of the movie and then the description, we would confuse the user. Instead, we would link from the name of the movie and then to the description. From there we would provide a link to the inventory.

The same design decisions can be applied to this example. We have the same basic flow of information, from a movie, to the description, and then show times.

Figure 31.12 illustrates the screen flow we are going to use for this example.

Again, it's important to keep in mind while doing presentation design that we are working with devices that often have screens measuring roughly two inches by two inches. So we need to plan the presentation and navigation accordingly. With this in mind, let's talk about the screen flow.

The first box presents the list of movies to the user.

Then, as indicated by the down arrow, we provide a way to navigate to the movie's description represented by the second box.

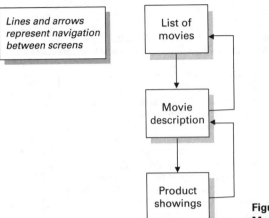

Figure 31.12
Movie list presentation flowchart

From here, we should provide a way for the user not only to move on to the show times, but also a way to move backward. We could provide a link that allows the user to move backward, but for this example, we are going to use the behavior of the Accept key on the device's touch pad to navigate backward. We can do this because the device maintains a history of screens similar to what a web browser does with web pages you visit. By pressing Accept, the user will be sent back to the list of movies. While this works for this simple application, you will most likely want to provide an actual link in real applications. You may not be able to count on the previous screen being the one you want.

From the movie description, we then want to allow the user to navigate the movie showings represented by the last box in the flowchart. This is the last screen in the application, and from here we can only go backward. We will use the method described in the previous paragraph, and click Accept to send us back to the movie description screen.

That in a nutshell is the flow of the screens in our example application. We now have an idea of the different screens a user will see when viewing the movie list, and the navigation he will use to go between each screen. We now need to determine how to make these screens real. We need to examine what elements in WML can be used to create the screens in our example. First let's talk about how prototyping screens can be useful during this step.

Prototyping the presentation

As we saw in the HDML example, prototyping screens from the actual application can help people grasp the end result. You can take a look at "Prototyping the Presentation" from the HDML example to see what prototyping entails. Figure 31.13 shows what a prototype screen for this example would look like.

```
<?xml version="1.0" encoding="UTF-8"?>
<!DOCTYPE wml PUBLIC "-//WAPFORUM//DTD WML
1.1//EN" "http://www.wapforum.org/DTD/wml_1.1.xml">
<wml>
<card title="WAP MoviePhone" id="movielist">
<p> Movies <br/>
<a href="#movie1">Mission Impossible:2</a><br/>
<a href="#movie2">Austin Powers</a><br/>
</p>
</card>
</wml>
```

Figure 31.13   Prototype of movie list screen

To create this prototype, you would simply type the source WML using a text editor and save it to a file on your hard drive. Then, load this file into a WML browser in the Nokia WAP Toolkit, or some other device capable of rendering WML.

31.3.4   WML elements

We now need to determine the WML elements we are going to use to present the movie list. Recall from chapter 3, WML uses various elements to display text, accept user input, and present choices to a user. Our output WML document will need to make use of the elements that display text, provide links to other information, and present choices to the user. Table 31.7 outlines the different WML elements we will need to use.

Table 31.7   WML elements

Document requirement	WML element(s)
Display a list of all movies.	<CARD> element
Display each movie in the list and provide a link to the description.	<A> element. We will also put the text of the movie as the link text.
Display a description of the movie.	<CARD> element
Provide a link to the show times.	<DO> element to assign an action to the accept key <GO> element to actually move the user to the showings <CARD> element
Display a list of showings for a movie.	<CARD> element

We now have a general idea of the elements needed to present the movie list. Let's start constructing the XSLT style sheet that will take our catalog and transform it to WML. For a discussion of WML and its elements, see chapter 3.

31.3.5   Defining the XSLT style sheet

With a basic idea of the WML elements we need to produce, we can now start defining the XSLT style sheet. The style sheet will need to contain two <xsl:template>

elements. We'll also need `<xsl:for-each>` loop blocks to generate the different WML elements. Since we have multiple movies in the list, the `<xsl:for-each>` will allow us to generate a set of WML elements for each movie. Table 31.8 summarizes the XSL elements we will use in the style sheet and the purpose they will serve.

Table 31.8 XSL elements used

Style sheet Element	Purpose
<xsl:for-each>	To loop through the movie list
<xsl:value-of>	To retrieve the values of attributes and elements for movie names and descriptions
<xsl:text>	To generate markup characters into the output document
<xsl:template>	To define the templates for this style sheet

If you've already gone through the HDML example, you will remember that we used a single template to generate our HDML document. In this example, we are going to utilize two templates to generate the WML document, which will be explained later in this chapter.

Beginning the style sheet

You will get to know the first two lines of our style sheet well. They are the XML declaration and `<xsl:stylesheet>` element that declares our document a style sheet.

```
<?xml version="1.0"?>
<xsl:stylesheet xmlns:xsl="http://www.w3.org/1999/XSL/Transform"
version="1.0">
```

For most markup languages, the first two lines are usually all that will be needed.

Defining the first template

We need to define the first template for our style sheet. Recall from chapter 29 templates are used to select elements from the source tree for processing. When the XSLT processor matches a template to an element in the source tree, what is in the template will be inserted into the result tree. To define our first template, we need to include the following statement:

```
<xsl:template match="movies">
```

This defines the start of the first template; later, we will include a statement that ends it. Looking at the template, we see that the match attribute, used to tell the XSLT processor when to use this template, has a value of movies. The movies value is called the pattern. When the XSLT processor encounters the movies element in the source document, this template will be instantiated.

Starting the WML document

As another part of this template, we need to include a WML element that will define the start of our WML document. We can't start defining WML elements without specifying the start of the document. As you recall from chapter 29, all XML documents, have a root element that defines the start, and in most cases, the type, of the document.

Before we define the start of our document, let's define code that will insert a <DOCTYPE> markup into our WML document. This will also tell the WML client what DTD we are using. We need to do this so that the WML browser can validate our WML document. DTDs are used to provide constraints to XML-based documents, and validation is the process by which XML parsers ensure an XML-based document conforms to its DTD.

The following line of code will insert the <DOCTYPE> markup into the WML document.

```
<xsl:text disable-output-escaping="yes">&lt;!DOCTYPE wml PUBLIC "-
//WAPFORUM//DTD WML 1.1//EN"
"http://www.wapforum.org/DTD/wml_1.1.xml"&gt;</xsl:text>
```

After that, we can put in the WML element for the start of the WML document. We do this with the following statement:

```
<wml>
```

With our first template started, we can now start defining the XSL that will produce our first screen.

Displaying the movie list

In the "Designing the presentation" section earlier in this chapter we sketched out the screens we would need to have in the application. The first specified was a screen that presented a list of movies. This block of XSL shows the XSL and WML elements we will need to produce a list of the movies:

```
<card id="movielist" title="WAP MoviePhone">
<p> Movies <br/>
<xsl:for-each select="movie">
   <a href="#{concat('movie',position())}"><xsl:value-of
select="@name"/></a><br/>
</xsl:for-each>
</p>
</card>
```

We first define a <CARD> element, which will present a screen of text to the user. After that we insert text instructing the user to make a selection. This may be obvious to us as the developer, but if we just threw up a list of movies, the user may not understand what to do.

Next, we need to generate the movies themselves. We do this using the <xsl:for-each> element to loop through all of the movie nodes in the source tree. As you recall from chapter 29, XSLT uses XPath in conjunction with the template to select nodes for processing. In this case, we are telling the `<xsl:for-each>` element to process all of the `movie` elements. Why don't we need to specify "movies\movie"? Because we are already in the proper context and don't need to specify it again. The proper context was set when the template was instantiated. Contexts were covered in chapter 29.

Each time through the loop, a new `movie` node is selected. At this point we have access to all of its values and attributes. We start by specifying an `<A>` element, which is the WML element for a link, similar to the HTML anchor tag. We then set its `href` attribute to the value of a pound sign (#), followed by the concatenated value of the string-literal "movie" and a number representing the position of this movie node in the node-set. Getting the position of the node is done using the XPath function `position`. Node-sets and the position function were covered in chapter 29. Next, we need to put in the textual value that will be displayed on the screen. For this, we use the `<xsl:value-of>` element to insert the value of the `name` attribute of the `movie` element.

After this, we close out the `<xsl:for-each>` and the WML `<CARD>` element. We are now ready to move onto the next set of screens.

Displaying movie descriptions

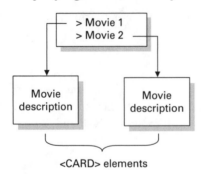

The next set of screens consists of movie description screens. Unlike the movie list screen, we need to define a screen for each movie and its description. On each screen, we also need to provide a link to the showings for that movie. Figure 31.14 shows the relationship between each movie and the movie description card it links to.

This block of XSL shows us how to do this.

Figure 31.14 WML `<CARD>` for each product description

```
<xsl:for-each select="movie">
 <card id="{concat('movie',position())}" title="{@name}">
   <do type="prev" name="Previous" label="Previous">
   <prev/>
   </do>
   <do label="Times" type="accept">
   <go href="#{concat('movie',position(),'showings')}"/>
   </do>
   <p><xsl:value-of select="description"/></p>
 </card>
 <card id="{concat('movie',position(),'showings')}" title="Times">
```

```
    <p><xsl:apply-templates select="showings"/></p>
  </card>
</xsl:for-each>
```

In the movie list section, we defined a single WML card to hold the list of movies. Here, we need to define multiple WML <CARD> elements, one for each movie description. So, we have to start with the <xsl:for-each>, which also loops through each movie element as <xsl:for-each> did in the movie list section.

Next, we define the WML <CARD> element. We set its id attribute to the concatenated value of the string-literal movies, followed by a number representing its position in the node. We need to set it to this value because in the movie list, we set the href attribute of the <A> element to the same value. That way, when the user makes a selection, he is taken to the WML <CARD> with the corresponding id. We also set the card's title attribute to the name of the movie. This way, when the movie pops up on the screen, the screen will be titled with the name of the movie.

Figure 31.15 illustrates how each movie choice identifies the correct movie description card to send the user to.

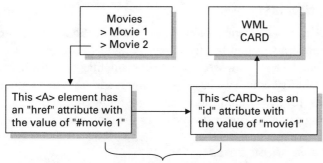

Figure 31.15
<A> href attribute value corresponds to a <CARD> id attribute

Assigning actions to the keypad

Before we insert the description text, we define actions to a couple of keys using the WML <do> element. We set its type attribute to "Previous" indicating this key will be used to navigate backward. We also set its name and label attributes. Setting the label attribute will cause the string "Previous" to be displayed on the screen over the key. Next, we put in a <prev/> element. This will tell the WML client that when the key assigned to this action is pressed, go back to the previous WML card in the history. We then close out the <do> element with a </do> closing tag.

Now we are going to define an action for the second key. This key will be Accept. We are going to assign this key an action that will take the user to the showings for the movie.

We start again with the WML <do> element, setting its type attribute to accept, and its label attribute to "Times". Setting the label attribute will cause the text "Times" to appear over the Accept key.

Within the body of the <do> element, we are going to define another element that will take the user to the card of movie showings. If you recall from the last <do> element we defined, we defined a <prev/> element in the body of the <do> element. This time, we are going to define a <go> element which will instruct the WML client to go to the location defined by its href attribute. We set the href attribute of the <go> element to a concatenated value of the string-literal "movie", a number representing its position in the node-set, and finally a string-literal of "showings". This ends up looking like:

```
<go href="#movie2showings"/>
```

Notice there is no closing <go> tag. Instead we are using an empty-element tag, which was discussed in chapter 29. Now, we need to input text representing the movie description.

Movie description text

The text of the <card> element consists of the value of the movies description node. We retrieve this value by using the <xsl:value-of> to select the description node. Next, we insert a couple of blank lines after the description that will improve readability because we have to also insert a link to the product inventory.

We finish the <card> definition by closing it out with a </card> closing tag. Next, we are going to define the cards to display the movie showings.

Displaying movie show times

We are going to take advantage of the <xsl:for-each> we are using to generate the WML <card> elements for the movie show times. We could just as easily have ended the <xsl:for-each> and defined a new one to generate the cards.

We start by defining a WML <card> element, and set its id attribute to the concatenated value of the string-literal "movie", followed by a number representing its position in the node-set, then a string-literal of "showings." As you recall from earlier in the chapter, we created a <go> element with an href attribute that had the same value. We set the title attribute of the <card> element to the value "Times".

Using a second template: <xsl:apply-templates>

As in the previous sections in this example, you saw how to use the <xsl:value-of> element to insert values from the source tree. In this example, however, we are going to use a different template to insert the values for movie show times. We make use of this second template by using an <xsl:apply-templates> element. We set its select attribute to the value of "showings", which basically means any templates that have the same pattern should be instantiated here. Don't worry about the definition of this template for now. We are going to cover it later in this chapter.

Using the `<apply-templates>` in this case is like making a function call. The results of the function call are inserted into the result tree (figure 31.16).

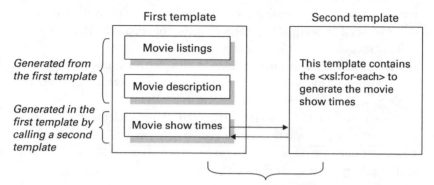

Figure 31.16   Movie show times are generated using <xsl:apply-templates>

We then end the WML `<card>` element, and close out our `<xsl:for-each>`.

Ending the first template

We need to finish this first template by closing out the `<wml>` element and the `<xsl:template>` element using:

```
</wml>
</xsl:template>
```

We still need to define another template to generate the movie showings.

Defining the second template

In the first template, we generated WML `<card>` elements to hold individual movie show times and we specified that we wanted to use a second template to generate the values representing the show times. We start our second template using the familiar `<xsl:template>` element with its `select` attribute set to the value of `"showings"`.

```
<xsl:template match="showings">
```

Generating movie show times

Now we need to put in the actual text representing the movie show times. The following block of XSL shows us how to do this.

```
<do type="accept" label="Back">
    <prev/>
```

```
</do>
<xsl:for-each select="showing">
 <xsl:value-of select="@day"/> @ <xsl:value-of select="@time"/><br/>
</xsl:for-each>  |#3
```

We begin by assigning the Accept key an action that allows the user to go back to the movie description by pressing a key on the keypad. This is done using the WML element `<do>`. The body of the `<do>` element contains a WML `<prev/>` element that will instruct the WML client to go back to the previous WML card in the history. We also assign its `label` attribute a value of `"Back"` providing a visual cue to the user as to its purpose. This is very similar to what we did when we assigned the same key a value to send the user back to the movie list.

Next, we use the familiar `<xsl:for-each>` element to loop through each `showing` node. Within the `<xsl:for-each>` we extract the values of the `day` and `time` attributes of the `showing` node, which puts the show times in the card. We then finish by closing out the `<xsl:for-each>`.

Ending the style sheet

We now have almost all the XSL we need to produce our WML movie list. We need to close out some elements that we started earlier in the process. We started with the `<xsl:stylesheet>` element, and then defined another template with `<xsl:template>`. We need to finish the style sheet by closing these elements out in reverse order.

```
</xsl:template>        ❶
</xsl:stylesheet>      ❷
```

Code comments

❶ Closes out the `<xsl:template match="movies">` element, and ends the definition of the template.

❷ Closes out the `<xsl:stylesheet>` element, and ends the definition of the entire XSLT style sheet.

We are now ready to run the transformation using this style sheet. Before you continue, you may want to read the "Ending the style sheet" section from the HDML example for some tips on style sheet creation.

31.3.6   Running the transform

Before we run the transformation, we need to gather the WML document and XSLT style sheet pieces and store them someplace. We also need to create the Java application that calls the XSLT processor. Table 31.9 outlines some of the steps we need to take.

Table 31.9 Preparing the files

File	Do this with it
XML movie list	Save as a file called "movies.xml" in a directory on your hard drive.
XSLT style sheet	Save the XSL into a file called "products.xsl" in the same directory as the "movies.xml" file.
Xalantransform.java	Save this file into the same directory as the "products.xml" and "products.xsl" files.

Creating the Java application

As the title of this example implies, we are going to use Java in the transformation process. From a Java application, we are going to call the Xalan XSLT processor to do the actual transformation. Listing 31.2 shows the Java application we are going to use:

Listing 31.2 The Java application

```
import org.xml.sax.SAXException;
import org.apache.xalan.xslt.XSLTProcessorFactory;
import org.apache.xalan.xslt.XSLTInputSource;
import org.apache.xalan.xslt.XSLTResultTarget;
import org.apache.xalan.xslt.XSLTProcessor;
import java.io.FileOutputStream;

public class xalantransform
{
  public static void main(String[] args
    throws java.io.IOException,
           java.net.MalformedURLException,
           org.xml.sax.SAXException
  {

    XSLTProcessor processor = XSLTProcessorFactory.getProcessor();

    processor.process(new XSLTInputSource("movies.xml"),
                  new XSLTInputSource("movies.xsl"),
               new XSLTResultTarget(new
                   FileOutputStream("movies.wml")));
  }
}
```

We begin by specifying a number of imports using the Java keyword `import`. This is necessary so our application can find the necessary class in the right packages. Next, we define our class and name it xalantransform. And since this is a Java application, we define the `main` method next.

The next line after the main method is where we create an instance of the XSLT-Processor using the XSLTProcessorFactory class. We do this using the `getProcessor` method of the XSLTProcessorFactory class. For more discussion on the Xalan XSLT processor, see chapter 30.

Next, we call the `process` method of the XSLTProcessor object we just created. We have specified the name of our input file "movies.xml", and the name of the input XSLT style sheet, "movies.xsl". We then specify where we want the resulting transformation to be stored. In this case, we use the Java class FileOutputStream and specify a parameter to its constructor of "movies.wml".

Running the Java application

Save the Java application code and compile it into the directory with the "movies.xml" and "movies.xsl" files. Make sure that the Xalan class libraries are in your CLASSPATH before you try to compile. Also, make sure the Xerces libraries are in your CLASSPATH. As you recall from chapter 29, XSLT processors make use of XML parsers. Xalan happens to use Xerces.

Once you have successfully compiled the application, run it using the Java executable. Again, make sure you have the Xalan and Xerces class libraries in your CLASSPATH before executing this command.

If the application successfully runs, you should have a new file in the same directory as the Java application called "movies.wml."

Viewing the resulting WML output

Using a Nokia phone simulator or browser, load the "movies.wml" file, which will start you at the `movielist` card (figure 31.17).

Then click Show. This should cause the application to be loaded into the phone emulator and present the `movielist` card (figure 31.18).

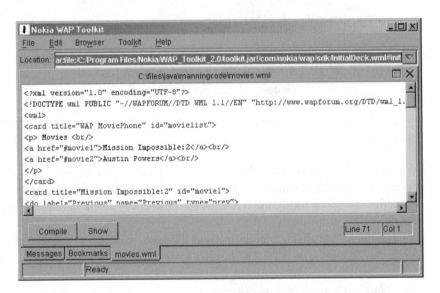

Figure 31.17 Loading the "movies.wml" card into the Nokia WAP simulator

Using the arrow keys on the phone, navigate to the link "Mission Impossible:2" and click Accept. This should bring you to the description of the movie (figure 31.19).

As you can see, we have a description and links to the movie showings indicated by the "Times" label on the first softkey. We also have a link to the previous screen indicated by the "Previous" label on the second softkey. Using your keypad, select the "Times" option, which should display the list of showings for that movie (figure 31.20).

Figure 31.18
The movie list

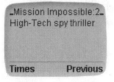

Figure 31.19 The movie description

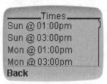

Figure 31.20 The movie show times

Using the arrow keys on the keypad, you can scroll up and down the list of movies. We have also provided an option to navigate back to the description by assigning an action to Accept. This is indicated by the Back label on the screen.

The WML source

If we were to look at the source that was generated after running the Java application, it would look like this:

Listing 31.3 Source of WML movie document

```
<?xml version="1.0" encoding="UTF-8"?>
<!DOCTYPE wml PUBLIC "-//WAPFORUM//DTD WML 1.1//EN"
"http://www.wapforum.org/DTD/wml_1.1.xml">
<wml>                  ❶
<card title="WAP MoviePhone" id="movielist">
<p> Movies <br/>
<a href="#movie1">Mission Impossible:2</a><br/>   ❷
<a href="#movie2">Austin Powers</a><br/>
</p>
</card>
<card title="Mission Impossible:2" id="movie1">
<do label="Previous" name="Previous" type="prev">
<prev/>
</do>
<do type="accept" label="Times">      ❸
<go href="#movie1showings"/>
</do>
<p>High-Tech spy thriller</p>
</card>
<card title="Times" id="movie1showings">
<p>
<do label="Back" type="accept">
```

❶ WML element <CARD> that shows the list of movies

❷

WML element <CARD> that shows the movie

WML element <DO> that assigns an action to a key on the keypad to navigate back one WML card

❸

Text representing the movie description

WML element <CARD> that shows each movie's show times

```
<prev/>
</do>
Sun @ 01:00pm<br/>
Sun @ 03:00pm<br/>
Mon @ 01:00pm<br/>
Mon @ 03:00pm<br/>
Tue @ 01:00pm<br/>
Tue @ 03:00pm<br/>
Wed @ 01:00pm<br/>
Wed @ 03:00pm<br/>
Thu @ 01:00pm<br/>
Thu @ 03:00pm<br/>
Fri @ 01:00pm<br/>
Fri @ 03:00pm<br/>
Sat @ 01:00pm<br/>
Sat @ 03:00pm<br/>
</p>
</card>
<card title="Austin Powers" id="movie2">
<do label="Previous" name="Previous" type="prev">
<prev/>
</do>
<do type="accept" label="Times">
<go href="#movie2showings"/>
</do>
<p>International Man of Mystery</p>
</card>
<card title="Times" id="movie2showings">
<p>
<do label="Back" type="accept">
<prev/>
</do>
Sun @ 01:00pm<br/>
Sun @ 03:00pm<br/>
Mon @ 01:00pm<br/>
Mon @ 03:00pm<br/>
Tue @ 01:00pm<br/>
Tue @ 03:00pm<br/>
Wed @ 01:00pm<br/>
Wed @ 03:00pm<br/>
Thu @ 01:00pm<br/>
Thu @ 03:00pm<br/>
Fri @ 01:00pm<br/>
Fri @ 03:00pm<br/>
Sat @ 01:00pm<br/>
Sat @ 03:00pm<br/>
</p>
</card>
</wml>
```

Text representing the movie show times

Code comments

❶ WML element that declares this a WML document.

❷ WML element <A> that puts the name of the movie in the card as a link to the description of the movie.

❸ WML element <DO> that assigns an action to the Accept key on the keypad to navigate the user to the show times for the movie.

Troubleshooting

When running this example, you may encounter a few problems. Table 31.10 shows some common problems and what you can do about them.

Table 31.10   Common problems and solutions

Problem	Solution
Nokia WAP Simulator says it can't compile document.	Look at the source of the WML document in the Toolkit window. Make sure you have a valid document and well-formed elements.
Nokia WAP Simulator says there is "No declaration for an element".	Look at the WML that was generated and ensure you have valid element names—for instance, if you mistakenly used "<hdml>" as the beginning of your WML document instead of "<wml>".
You can't navigate to the movie description or show times.	Look at your XSLT style sheet and ensure you provided closing <CARD> tags. The Nokia WAP Simulator will probably catch this unless you never generated the tags in the first place.

31.4   TRANSFORMATION TO VOICEXML USING JAVA

The next sample illustrates publishing an XML-based movie list to a VoiceXML capable client. This is very similar to the WML example. But instead of browsing it with a WAP-enabled phone, you will use your telephone to listen to it.

One of the first steps we will take is to examine the XML document and work out how the information should be presented. Movie lists are usually browsed by names of the movies that are currently showing. Then selecting a movie usually lists its times. So with that, we need to decide how we want to organize the information.

Organizing the information for a VoiceXML application is different than the other two examples. There is no visual aspect to this example—it's completely voice driven. Nevertheless, we can apply similar design practices to organizing the information.

We should also decide if we want to create multiple VoiceXML documents containing the information, in which case we may run multiple transformations. For this example, we are going to create only one VoiceXML document.

Once we have a rough idea of the organization of the movie list, we should sketch out some screens and how the user can navigate between them. These sketches could include what is presented on each screen, and some rough indication of navigational elements. Keep in mind that the sketches should be centered on the idea of a conversation between two people. One person introduces the movie list, and the second asks questions of the first person, which the first person responds to. The second person can also make other requests of the first person, which may cause them to repeat information.

Once we have an idea of how we want the movie list presented audibly, we should determine our target markup language elements. The target markup language is the one we end up with after transforming the XML catalog to VoiceXML. Since VoiceXML is our target markup language, we should determine what elements in VoiceXML we will need to use to present the information to the user.

Then we need to start designing the XSLT style sheet with template rules that will transform the XML movie list into VoiceXML. Our resulting transformation needs to produce not only the data elements of the application, but also the VoiceXML elements that will instruct the VoiceXML client to present audio containing each piece of data.

Once we have created the style sheet, we will run the transformation. This particular sample uses the Xalan XSLT processor from a Java application. This transformation will be run to produce a static VoiceXML document. The VoiceXML document will contain multiple VoiceXML elements that allow the user to navigate through the movie list, and make selections using their voice.

31.4.1   An introduction to VoiceXML

VoiceXML is an XML-based markup language which contains tags that allow applications to present audio choices, prompt for input, and present audio to the user. XML is covered in chapter 29. Unlike HTML and WML, VoiceXML is designed to operate minus a visual user interface. It also overcomes some of the limitations of other markup languages due to the types of devices on which they are displayed. Instead of having to abbreviate everything to fit on a tiny screen, we can use full-length text descriptions and introductions to present the application to the user. Other than that, VoiceXML is just like any other markup language.

For more information about VoiceXML, visit the VoiceXML forum at http://www.voicexml.org.

VoiceXML interpreter

With other markup languages such as HTML and WML, there is a visual representation of the document. You can look at HTML pages in a web browser, and look at WML documents in a WAP phone or other device capable of rendering WML.

VoiceXML documents, as we said earlier, have no visual user interface. VoiceXML documents are processed by an application module called the *VoiceXML interpreter*.

Its job is to understand the markup contained in a VoiceXML document. It understands what the different elements mean, and what is supposed to be speech, and what is an element.

From a user's perspective, the primary means of interacting with a VoiceXML application is a phone. So basically, all interaction is between the phone and the VoiceXML interpreter.

A full discussion of the architecture needed to run a VoiceXML application is beyond the scope of this example. The TellMe Studio web site offers everything we will need to run, test, and debug this VoiceXML example. We will talk more about the TellMe Studio web site later in this chapter.

Now that we have a little background on VoiceXML, let's take a brief look at some of the elements used in constructing a VoiceXML document.

VoiceXML elements

Since this is not intended to be a comprehensive VoiceXML tutorial, we will cover elements only as they relate to this sample.

For a complete description of all VoiceXML elements, visit the VoiceXML forum at http://www.voicexml.org.

VoiceXML elements fall into six broad categories that indicate their general area of usage:

- Document elements
- Form elements
- Field elements
- Menu elements
- Event handlers
- Directives

These categories also serve to indicate the general purpose and location in a VoiceXML document. For instance, Form and Menu elements are used to present information to the user and contain other elements that form the logic of the VoiceXML document.

Directive elements are used to direct something to happen, such as go to a certain location, or play a piece of audio.

Event handler elements are used to handle events that occur during processing of a VoiceXML document. For instance, if a user does not give a response to a prompt within a specified period of time, an event handler can be defined to repeat the prompt, or disconnect the user.

Table 31.11 shows a list of the elements we will be using in this example, its category, and a short description of what the element does.

Don't be too worried about remembering what each element does. We'll take a look at each one later in this chapter. What you should take note of is that there are

Table 31.11   VoiceXML elements used in this example

Element name	Category	Description
<vxml>	Document	Identifies a document as a VoiceXML document
<menu>	Document	Presents a list of choices to the user and transitions to the chosen information
<prompt>	Event handler	Plays audio to the user and listens for a response
<audio>	Directive	Plays an audio file or text to speech within a prompt
<pause>	Directive	Pauses the execution for a specified number of milliseconds. This is a TellMe specific tag. The closest equivalent in the VoiceXML DTD would be <break>.
<noinput>	Event Handler	An event-handling element that specifies what to do when the user does not say anything
<reprompt>	Directive	Presents the last prompt presented to the user
<choice>	Menu	Defines one choice in a menu
<form>	Document	This is one of the primary constructs in the VoiceXML language. Forms are similar to <card> elements in WML. They contain grammars, prompts, event handlers, and directives.
<block>	Form	Specifies a block of directives that are executed in document order
<goto>	Directive	Jumps to the specified URL. This can be used to jump to a <form> in the document.

similarities between VoiceXML elements and those in WML or HDML. For instance, in WML, the <card> element is the primary means of presenting information to the user. In VoiceXML, the <form> element performs a similar function. In HDML, the <choice> element is used to present a list of choices to the user, and in VoiceXML, the <menu> element is used to perform a similar function.

Let's take a look at a simple VoiceXML document that uses some of the described elements.

31.4.2   A sample VoiceXML document

To get an idea how these elements are used, let's look at a simple VoiceXML document. Note that the XML declaration and the <!DOCTYPE> have been excluded for brevity.

```
<vxml>
  <form id="hello">
    <block>
        <audio> Hello World </audio>
    </block>
  </form>
</vxml>
```

This document begins with the <vxml> element, indicating that this is a VoiceXML document. Remember, all XML-based documents contain a root element that indicates the type of document it is.

The <form>0 element

Next, we use the VoiceXML `<form>` element to define a single form. Remember that the `<form>` element performs a similar function as the WML `<card>` element. We set its `id` attribute to the value `hello`. The `id` attribute gives the form a name so it can be referenced elsewhere in the document if needed. When working with VoiceXML documents, you will probably see this element a lot.

The <block> element

We then define a `<block>` element, a general-purpose element that must reside inside the closing and ending tags of a `<form>` element. You may also hear the `<block>` element referred to as a *form item*.

Generally speaking, `<block>` elements contain other executable content. They can contain other elements that instruct the VoiceXML interpreter to speak, go to another location, prompt the user for input, or disconnect the user. To say it another way, `<block>` elements contain directives. And as such, this particular `<block>` element contains another VoiceXML element, `<audio>`.

The <audio> element

The `<audio>` element instructs the VoiceXML interpreter to play an audio clip or speak the text that is in between its start and end tags. In the case of this example, the text is "Hello World."

So far, we've had a brief look at VoiceXML. We looked at some elements used in a VoiceXML document, and what those elements are used for. We also did some comparisons between VoiceXML elements and elements from other markup languages such as HDML and WML.

Now let's create a VoiceXML document that presents a list of movies and allows the user to navigate it using his voice.

31.4.3 Setting up a development environment

For this sample you will need the following already installed on your machine:

- Account at TellMe.com
- Xalan XSLT processor
- JDK1.2

31.4.4 Understanding the movie list

Let's begin by examining a movie list. Table 31.12 shows the elements of the movie list. Remember, elements mean entities in the movie list, not XML elements.

This is not an overwhelming amount of information to work with. But knowing what each element is and the relationships between them will be helpful when we start designing the presentation. Now let's look at the XML representation of that movie list.

Table 31.12 The movie list description

Movie list elements	Description
A list of movies	All of the movies in the list.
Movie name	Each movie has a name.
Movie description	Each movie has a textual description.
Showings	Each movie has a list of times the movie is shown.
Showing	A movies list of showings is comprised of individual show times, which have a day and time.

XML movie list

Next is the XML representation of the movie list.

```
<?xml version="1.0"?>          Defines this document
<movies>                       as a "movies" document
  <movie name="mission impossible">          ❶
    <description>High-Tech spy thriller</description>          Represents the
    <showings>                                                 description of
    <showing day="Sunday" time="1:00pm"/>     ❷                the movie
     <showing day="Sunday" time="3:00pm"/>          Represents
    </showings>                                     the showings
  </movie>                                          for this movie
  <movie name="austin powers">
   <description>International Man of Mystery</description>
   <showings>
     <showing day="Sunday" time="1:00pm"/>
      <showing day="Sunday" time="3:00pm"/>
   </showings>
  </movie>
</movies>
```

Code comments

❶ Represents a single movie in the list of movies. The "name" attribute contains the name of the movie.

❷ Represents an individual show time for this movie. Each show time has a day and time.

Figure 31.21 illustrates the relationships between the XML document and the product description seen earlier.

We should now have a general picture of the movie list and the elements contained in the movie list. We have also seen what that movie list looks like as an XML document. Let's move onto the next step and decide how we want to present this information to a user.

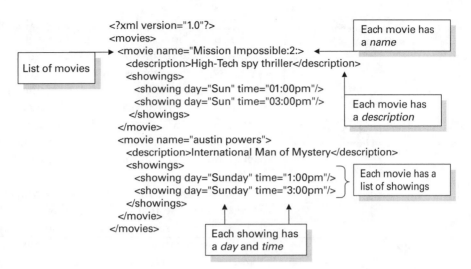

Figure 31.21 Movie list as XML

31.4.5   Designing the presentation

As we saw in the first two examples, constructing a confusing user interface is the last thing we want to do. Therefore the design of the user interface is an important step.

Fortunately we can apply the same design decisions we used in the earlier examples to this one. We have the same basic flow of information, from a movie, to the description, and then show times.

However, with a VoiceXML application, we don't have physical screens from which the user can make selections. So it may help to think of the flow in terms of a conversation between two people. We'll talk more about this later.

Figure 31.22 illustrates the flow we are going to use in this application.

The first box in the flowchart indicates that we will present an introduction, something we need to do so the user knows what to do. If we just started rattling off the names of movies, it would be pretty confusing. Once we provide an introduction, we should pause, and then start speaking the name of each movie. After each movie name is said, we should pause.

After all of the movie names have been said, the system will wait for a reply. But as you will see later, the system can also accept input during this process as well. Meaning, the user could speak the name of the movie he wants before the system finishes saying them all.

If no reply is heard within a system-defined time limit, the user is returned to the beginning and the introduction, followed by each movie name, is repeated.

If a reply is heard, the system will check to see if what was spoken matches any of the movies it knows about.

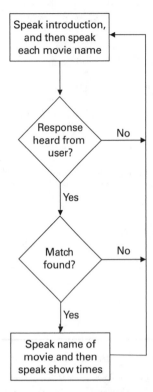

Figure 31.22 Flow of VoiceXML presentation

If a match is found, the system sends the user to the last box in the flowchart, where the name of the movie is spoken to reassure the user he has selected the movie he wants. Then the movie show times are spoken, with a pause between each. After all the show times have been spoken, the system will pause and then send the user back to the first box where the entire process is repeated.

If no match is found, the system sends the user back to the first box in the flow to have the choices spoken again.

As you noticed in several places we provide pauses. This is essential so that the user can understand what is being said, and also has time to respond to prompts.

We also mentioned a system default timeout, which, if reached, will cause an event handler to be executed, which sends the user back to the introduction. For more information on system default timeouts, check the VoiceXML specification at http://www.voicexml.org.

Conversational approach

Designing the flow and presentation of a VoiceXML application can be thought of as designing a conversation between two people. Let's go through a typical exchange that follows the intended flow we just designed.

Person1: "Welcome to VoiceXML MoviePhone"
Person1: <pauses temporarily>
Person1: "Would you like to hear a list of movies?"
Person1: <pause and wait for response from Person2>
Person2: "Yes, I would like to hear the movies"
Person1: "Movies showing today are Mission Impossible, Austin Powers"
Person1: <waits to hear which movie Person2 wants to hear show times for>
Person2: "I want to hear show times for Mission Impossible"
Person1: <determines if Person1 said the name of a known movie>
Person1: "Show times for Mission Impossible are Sunday at 3 pm"
Person1: <pauses temporarily>
Person1: <go back to the introduction>

As we can see from this dialog, it is obvious we need to provide audio prompts to tell the user what to do and we need to wait for the user to respond. We then also need to determine if what he said matches a choice that we know about. And finally, we need to speak the names and times of movies he has indicated interest in.

Now that we have some idea of how the presentation and flow will occur, let's look at the VoiceXML elements that we will use to make this happen.

31.4.6 VoiceXML elements

We now need to determine the actual VoiceXML elements we are going to use to present the movie list. As seen earlier in this chapter, VoiceXML uses elements to prompt the user, provide speech to the user, and accept user input. Table 31.13 outlines the VoiceXML elements we will need to use in our document.

Table 31.13   VoiceXML elements used in this example

Document requirement	VoiceXML element(s)
Speak an introduction	\<audio\> element
Provide a menu of movie selections	\<menu\> element
Pause during speaking	\<pause\> element
Prompt the user	\<prompt\> element
Determine if the user spoke a choice we know about	\<choice\> element
If the user did not say anything, go back to the introduction	\<noinput\> element in conjunction with the \<reprompt\> element
If the user speaks a choice that is not listed	\<nomatch\> element in conjunction with the \<reprompt\> element
Return the user to the introduction after saying the show times	\<goto\> element
Speak each movie's show times	\<audio\> element

We now have a general idea of the elements needed to present the movie list. Let's start constructing the XSLT style sheet that will take our catalog and transform it to VoiceXML.

31.4.7   Defining the XSLT style sheet

The style sheet will need to contain two `<xsl:template>` elements. We'll also need `<xsl:for-each>` loop blocks to generate the different VoiceXML elements. Since we have multiple movies in the list, the `<xsl:for-each>` will allow us to generate a set of VoiceXML elements for each movie. Table 31.14 summarizes the XSL elements we will use in the style sheet and the purpose they will serve.

Table 31.14   XSL elements used

Style sheet element	Purpose
\<xsl:for-each\>	To loop through the movie list
\<xsl:value-of\>	To retrieve the values of attributes and elements for movie names and descriptions
\<xsl:text\>	To generate markup characters into the output document
\<xsl:template\>	To define the templates for this style sheet

Beginning the style sheet

You will get to know the first two lines of our style sheet well: the XML declaration and `<xsl:stylesheet>` element that declares our document a style sheet.

```
<?xml version="1.0"?>
<xsl:stylesheet xmlns:xsl=
    "http://www.w3.org/1999/XSL/Transform" version="1.0">
```

For most markup languages, the first two lines are usually all that will be needed.

Defining the first template

Before we jump into the movie list, we need to define the first template for our style sheet. As you recall from chapter 29, templates are used to select elements from the source tree for processing. When the XSLT processor matches a template to an element in the source tree, what is in the template will be inserted into the result tree. To define our first template, we need to include the following statement in our style sheet:

```
<xsl:template match="movies">
```

This defines the start of the first template. Later, we will include a statement that ends or closes out the template. Looking at the template, we see that the match attribute, used to tell the XSLT processor when to use this template, has a value of "movies". The value is called the pattern. When the XSLT processor encounters the movies element in the source document, this template will be instantiated.

Starting the VoiceXML document

As another part of this template, we need to include a VoiceXML element that will define the start of our VoiceXML document. We can't just start defining VoiceXML elements without specifying the start of the document. As you recall from chapter 29, all XML documents have a "root" element that defines the start of the document, and in most cases, the type of document.

Before we define the start of our document, let's define some code that will insert a `<DOCTYPE>` markup into our VoiceXML document. This will also tell the VoiceXML client what DTD we are using. We need to do this so that the VoiceXML can be validated—the process by which XML parsers ensure an XML-based document conforms to its DTD.

The following line of code will insert the `<DOCTYPE>` markup into the WML document.

```
<xsl:text disable-output-escaping="yes">&lt;!DOCTYPE vxml PUBLIC
    "-//TellMe Networks//Voice Markup Language 1.0//EN"
    "http://resources.tellme.com/toolbox/vxml-tellme.dtd"&gt;</xsl:text>
```

You might notice we are using a DTD from the TellMe Studio web site. This is necessary since we are going to use TellMe Studio software to interpret this VoiceXML document. Normally though, you would most likely see a reference to a DTD from some standards organization such as W3C.

After that, we can put in the VoiceXML element for the start of the VoiceXML document. We do this with the following statement:

```
<vxml>
```

With our first template started, we can now start defining the XSL that will produce our introduction and list of movies.

Presenting the movie list

In the "Designing the presentation" section we sketched out the general flow of the application. As you recall, first we need an introduction; then we speak the name of the movie. This block of XSL shows how we will produce the VoiceXML necessary to present this introduction and list of movies to the user.

```
<menu id="movielist">
<prompt>
<audio> Welcome to VoiceXML MoviePhone</audio>
<audio> After the list, say the name of the movie</audio>
<pause> 300 </pause>
<xsl:for-each select="movie">
<audio><xsl:value-of select="@name"/></audio>
<pause> 300 </pause>
</xsl:for-each>
</prompt>
<noinput>
   <audio> I did not hear your response </audio>
   <reprompt/>
</noinput>
<nomatch>
   <audio> That is not a valid response </audio>
   <reprompt/>
</nomatch>
```

We start by defining a VoiceXML <menu> element and set its id attribute to the string value of movielist. The value of this attribute will be used later to send the user back to the introduction and movie list.

We then define the start of a prompt using the VoiceXML <prompt> element, an event handler element that gives the user some information, and then waits for a response. Event handlers are a category of VoiceXML element that was discussed earlier in this example.

The <prompt> element presents this information through the use of the next set of VoiceXML elements, the <audio> element. Here we use the <audio> element to present an introduction to the user and instruct him to say the name of the movie after he has heard them all. We then insert a <pause> element to provide a nice transition to the list of movies.

We then make use of the <xsl:for-each> element to loop through each movie, and insert both an <audio> element and a <pause> element. These lines of code will provide the spoken list of movies, each followed by a pause.

We end the <xsl:for-each> and then close out the </prompt>. So we have defined the first box on our flow chart: an introduction followed by a list of movies.

But we also indicated that we needed to wait to hear whether or not a response was heard. If the user does not make an audible response during a default period of time, the previous prompt is replayed. We accomplish this by using the VoiceXML <noinput> element. The <noinput> element is categorized as an event handler element.

If no user input is heard, the elements or directives contained within the start and end tags of the <noinput> element are processed. Directives were covered earlier in this example. Within the start and end tags of the <noinput> element, we define an <audio> element which instructs the user that the system did not hear a response. We then use the <reprompt/> element to play the previous prompt over again.

If a response is heard, but it does not match one of the choices, the <nomatch> event handler is run. Within the start and end tags of the <nomatch> element, we define an <audio> element which instructs the user he did not speak a valid response. We then use the <reprompt/> element to play the previous prompt over again.

Up to this point, we have presented an introduction, and a list of movies from which the user can select. But we still haven't seen a way to process the choices, or movie name, the user may speak.

Processing menu choices

The next block of XSL will insert the VoiceXML elements to process the choices from the menu. To process choices in a VoiceXML <menu> element, use the <choice> element. Using the <choice> element does not present the user with three choices as did the <CHOICE> element in HDML from the first example. The <choice> element in VoiceXML simply specifies the allowed choices presented to the user. Therefore, it is important that you indicate to the user what the valid choices are. In the case of this example, we need to tell the user to say the name of a movie.

The VoiceXML <choice> element is categorized as a <menu> element that must be used within the start and end tags of a <menu> element.

```
<xsl:for-each select="movie">
 <choice next="#movie_{position()}">
  (<xsl:value-of select="@name"/>)
 </choice>
</xsl:for-each>
</menu>
```

We start with an <xsl:for-each> element to insert a VoiceXML <choice> element for each movie in the list. Each <choice> element has a next attribute with the value of the pound symbol (#), followed by the position of the movie node in the node-set.

The value of the `next` attribute indicates where to send the user when a match to this choice occurs. Node position and node-sets were covered in chapter 29. The value of the `next` attribute is the `id` of a `<form>` attribute which will be specified later.

The next line inserts the value of the `name` attribute of the current movie node. This is inserted between parentheses. This is the value that will be matched against what the user speaks to determine whether the user's response is valid.

Grammar fragment

In VoiceXML, a *grammar fragment* is a valid utterance by the user that will be recognized by the VoiceXML application software. In our example, the value of the `name` attribute of the current movie node will be used as the speech or grammar fragment. There are other ways to specify valid grammar the user may utilize, but for this example, we will match the user's spoken response to the values of the `name` attribute.

We then close out our `<choice>` element, and the `<xsl:for-each>`. At this point, we can close the `<menu>` element out as well. Figure 31.23 illustrates the use of the `<menu>` and `<choice>` elements.

Up to this point, we have a way to process choices a user may speak, and have specified where to send him if what he says matches a selection. If the user says something, but there is no match, the event handling supplied by the `<nomatch>` element

```
Voice XML document fragment

<vxml>
<menu id="movielist">
<prompt>
<audio> Welcome to VoiceXML MoviePhone</audio>          ⎤
<audio> After the list, say the name of the movie</audio>  ⎥   Present introduction
<pause> 300 </pause>                                       ⎬   and say name of each
<audio> Mission impossible</audio>                         ⎥   movie
<pause> 300 </pause>                                        ⎥
<audio> Austin Powers </audio>                            ⎦
</prompt>
<noinput>
  <audio> I did not hear your response </audio>
  <reprompt/>
</noinput>
<nomatch>
  <audio>That is not a valid response </audio>
  <reprompt/>
</nomatch>
<choice next="#movie_1">      ⎤   If the user says "mission
(mission impossible)          ⎥   impossible" or "austin
</choice>                     ⎥   powers", send them to
<choice next="#movie_2">      ⎬   the location specified in
(austin powers)              ⎥   the "next" attribute
</choice>                     ⎦
</menu>
```

Figure 31.23   Processing choices in a menu

will be invoked, and the user will be told he spoke an invalid choice. After that, he will be sent back to the introduction.

It should be noted that the voice recognition done by the TellMe Studio software is pretty accurate. For instance, speaking "Austin Flowers" will usually result in "Austin Powers" being selected. But if you said a movie name that did not exist, like "The Fifth Element," this would cause the <nomatch> event handling to be invoked.

Now we need a way to present the show times to the user.

Presenting the show times

We now need to create an XSL that will insert the show times for each movie. The following line of XSL shows us how to do this.

```
<xsl:apply-templates select="movie/showings"/>
```

This XSL makes use of the <xsl:apply-templates> element to instantiate a second template at this point in the result tree. This template, to be defined later in this section, will be instantiated when the showings node is encountered in the source tree.

Ending the first template

We need to finish out this first template by closing out the <vxml> and the <xsl:template> elements using:

```
</vxml>
</xsl:template>
```

We aren't quite ready to finish because we still need to define another template to generate the movie showings.

Defining the second template

In the first template, we generated a VoiceXML <menu> element that presented an introduction and list of movies from which the user could select. We also generated a series of <choice> elements to process those selections. But instead of generating the values representing the show times at that point, we specified that we wanted to use a second template to accomplish this. We start our second template using

```
<xsl:template match="movie/showings">
```

This template has its match attribute set to "movie/showings" which means this template will be run for each child of the showings element.

Generating movie show times

Now we need to put in the elements that will present the movie show times for each movie. Listing 31.4 shows us how to do this.

Listing 31.4   Source code for show times

```
<form id="movie_{position()}">
<block>
  <audio> You chose <xsl:value-of select="parent::movie/@name"/></audio>
  <pause> 300 </pause>
  <audio> ShowTimes are </audio>
  <pause> 200 </pause>
  <xsl:for-each select="showing">
     <audio><xsl:value-of select="@day"/>
        at <xsl:value-of select=
        "concat(substring-before(@time,':'),' ',
        substring-after(@time,'00'))"/> </audio>
  </xsl:for-each>
  <goto next="#movielist"/>
</block>
</form>
```

We start by defining a `<form>` element containing the other elements necessary to present the movie show times. If you recall, we have said the `<form>` element is similar to the WML `<card>` element.

We set its `id` attribute to a value of "movie" following its position in the node, set (figure 31.24). As you recall, earlier in the example we created a series of `<choice>` elements, with its `next` attribute set to the same value.

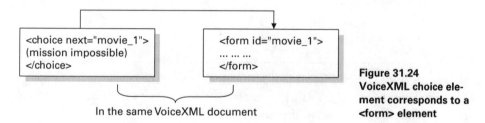

In the same VoiceXML document

Figure 31.24
VoiceXML choice element corresponds to a `<form>` element

We define a series of `<audio>` elements, with the first telling the user which movie he has selected. We use `<xsl:value-of>` to retrieve the name of the movie. We are using an XPath axes specifier of `parent` to access the parent node of the `showings` node and then get the value of the `name` attribute of the current movie node. XPath axes specifiers were covered in chapter 29.

After we say the name of the movie, we insert a `<pause>` element to wait, and then another `<audio>` element to give another audio cue that the movie's show times are about to come. We insert one more `<pause>` element, and then start presenting the times.

We use the `<xsl:for-each>` element to loop through each `showing` node and get its `day` and `time` attribute values. We need to do some special processing on the `time` attribute because we want to make sure that the VoiceXML interpreter can say the correct thing. So, instead of getting a value of `1:00pm`, we use the XPath function `substring-before` to extract the portion of the `time` attribute that occurs before the semicolon. We then use the XPath function `substring-after` to extract the portion that occurs after the double zeros. We then use the XPath `concat` function to concatenate these two values with a blank space. This results in a string value that looks like the following:

```
Sunday 1 pm
```

We enclose this concatenated value in the start and end tags of an `<audio>` element, and then close out the `<xsl:for-each>`.

After the `<xsl:for-each>` we insert a VoiceXML `<goto>` tag that will send the user back to the menu we defined earlier in this example. We set the `next` attribute to the value of `"#movielist"` which is the value of the `id` attribute of the `<menu>` tag defined earlier in this example.

We then finish by closing out the `<block>` element and complete the form by closing out the `<form>` element defined earlier in this section.

Ending the style sheet

We now have almost all the XSL we need to produce our VoiceXML movie list, but we need to close out some elements to be through. We started with the `<xsl:stylesheet>` element, and then defined another template with `<xsl:template>`. We need to finish the style sheet by closing these elements out in reverse order.

```
</xsl:template>        ❶
</xsl:stylesheet>      ❷
```

Code comments

❶ This closes out the `<xsl:template match="movie/showings">` element, and ends the definition of the template.

❷ This closes out the `<xsl:stylesheet>` element, and ends the definition of the entire XSLT style sheet.

We are now ready to move on to running the transformation using this style sheet. Before you continue, you may want to read the "Ending the style sheet" section from the HDML example for tips on style sheet creation.

Before continuing to our transformation, we are going to take a quick detour and introduce one of the tools needed for this sample, TellMe Studio.

31.4.8 Introduction to TellMe Studio

TellMe Studio is one of the most powerful and easy-to-use web-based development services we have seen. In a matter of minutes, you can set up an account and test a simple VoiceXML application. TellMe Studio allows VoiceXML developers a free venue for developing and testing VoiceXML applications which provide tools and documentation for a developer to get up and running quickly. They also have a series of tutorials and sample code that you can use to get started.

To use TellMe Studio, you need to sign up as a developer. The process is simple and only takes a few minutes.

Setting up a TellMe Studio account

To set up a TellMe Studio account:

1 Visit http://studio.tellme.com.

2 Click Setup Account.

3 Once you complete the form and submit it, you should be mailed a notification within a few minutes. In this email will be your developer ID and a PIN.

4 Once you have this, you can sign in and look around.

TellMe Studio scratch pad

One of the first things you will see upon logging in is the scratch pad. The TellMe Studio scratch pad (figure 31.25) is an application that allows you to create, edit, and save VoiceXML documents at TellMe Studio. It includes links to other tools that allow you to do things like check the syntax of your document, record your own audio, and look at your debug log. The scratch pad will automatically check the syntax each time you update the document.

Now that we have briefly looked at TellMe Studio, and we have our style sheet complete, let's run our transformation.

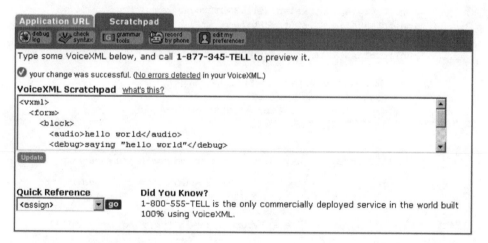

Figure 31.25   TellMe Studio scratch pad

31.4.9 Running the transform

Before we run the transformation, we need to gather the VoiceXML document and XSLT style sheet pieces together and store them. We also need to create the Java application that calls the XSLT processor. Table 31.15 outlines the files needed for the transformation and how you should prepare each file:

Table 31.15 Preparing the files for this example

File	Description file	Do this with it
voicemovies.xml	XML movie list	Save in a directory on your hard drive.
voicemovies.xsl	XSLT style sheet	Save in the same directory as the "voicesmovies.xml" file.
Xalantransform.java	Java application	Save in the same directory as the "voicemovies.xml" and "voicemovies.xsl" files.

Creating the Java application

As with the WML example, we are going to use Java in the transformation process. From a Java application, we are going to call the Xalan XSLT processor to do the actual transformation. Listing 31.5 shows the Java application we are going to use:

Listing 31.5 VoiceXML transformation using Java

```java
import org.xml.sax.SAXException;
import org.apache.xalan.xslt.XSLTProcessorFactory;
import org.apache.xalan.xslt.XSLTInputSource;
import org.apache.xalan.xslt.XSLTResultTarget;
import org.apache.xalan.xslt.XSLTProcessor;
import java.io.FileOutputStream;

public class xalantransform
{
   public static void main(String[] args)
     throws java.io.IOException,
            java.net.MalformedURLException,
            org.xml.sax.SAXException
   {

   XSLTProcessor processor = XSLTProcessorFactory.getProcessor();

   processor.process(new XSLTInputSource("voicemovies.xml"),
                new XSLTInputSource("voicemovies.xsl"),
              new XSLTResultTarget(new
                 FileOutputStream("voicemovies.vxml")));
   }
}
```

We begin the application by specifying a number of imports using the Java keyword `import`. This is necessary so our application can find the necessary class in the right packages. Next, we define our class and name it xalantransform. And since this is a Java application, we next define the `main` method.

The line after the `main` method is where we create an instance of the XSLTProcessor using the XSLTProcessorFactory class. We do this using the `getProcessor` method of the XSLTProcessorFactory class. For more discussion on the Xalan XSLT processor, see chapter 30.

Next, we call the `process` method of the XSLTProcessor object we just created. We have specified the name of our input file voicemovies.xml, and the name of the input XSLT style sheet, voicemovies.xsl. We then specify where we want the resulting transformation to be stored. In this case, we use the Java class FileOutputStream and specify a parameter to its constructor of voicemovies.vxml.

Running the Java application

Save the Java application code and compile it into the directory where the voicemovies.xml and voicemovies.xsl files are. Make sure that the Xalan and the Xerces class libraries are in your CLASSPATH before you try to compile. As you recall from chapter 29, XSLT processors make use of XML parsers; Xalan uses Xerces.

Once you have successfully compiled the application, run it using the Java executable. Again, make sure you have the Xalan and Xerces class libraries in your CLASSPATH before executing this command.

If the application successfully runs, you should have a new file in the same directory as the Java application called voicemovies.vxml.

The VoiceXML source

Listing 31.6 is the VoiceXML source code you should see in the voicemovies.vxml file.

Listing 31.6   VoiceXML source code

```
<?xml version="1.0" encoding="UTF-8"?>
<!DOCTYPE vxml PUBLIC "-//TellMe Networks//Voice Markup Language 1.0//EN"
"http://resources.tellme.com/toolbox/vxml-tellme.dtd">
<vxml>            ❶
<menu id="movielist">        ❷
<prompt>        ◄────────────── Begins prompt
<audio> Welcome to VoiceXML MoviePhone</audio>              Provides
<audio> After the list, say the name of the movie</audio>   introduction
<pause> 300 </pause>       ❸
<audio>mission impossible</audio>        ❹
<pause> 300 </pause>       ❺
<audio>austin powers</audio>       ❹
<pause> 300 </pause>       ❺
</prompt>
<noinput>
<audio> I did not hear your response </audio>        Sends the user back
<reprompt/>                                          to the introduction
</noinput>                                           if he does not say
                                                     anything
```

```
<choice next="#movie_1">            ◁┐ Processes a choice
    (mission impossible)              ┘  the user speaks
</choice><choice next="#movie_2">
    (austin powers)
</choice>                            ┐ Defines the start of a
</menu>                              │ form that presents the
<form id="movie_1">                 ◁┘ movie show times
<block>
<audio> You chose mission impossible</audio>   ◁┐ Indicates the movie that
<pause> 300 </pause>                             ┘  has been selected
<audio> ShowTimes are </audio>
<pause> 200 </pause>
<audio>Sunday at 1 pm</audio>        ┐ Presents the show
<audio>Sunday at 3 pm</audio>        │ times for the movie
<goto next="#movielist"/>           ◁┐ Sends the user back to
</block>                              │ the introduction and
</form>                              │ movie list after he hears
<form id="movie_2">                  ┘ the show times
<block>
<audio> You chose austin powers</audio>
<pause> 300 </pause>
<audio> ShowTimes are </audio>
<pause> 200 </pause>
<audio>Sunday at 1 pm</audio>
<audio>Sunday at 3 pm</audio>
<goto next="#movielist"/>
</block>
</form>
</vxml>
```

Code comments

❶ Defines this as a VoiceXML document.

❷ Defines the start of our menu.

❸ Provides a pause after introduction.

❹ Provides names of movies the user can select from.

❺ Provides a pause after each movie.

With this file created, we are ready to test it out using TellMe Studio.

31.4.10   Testing the application

To test the application, we need to take the VoiceXML document from the voicemovies.vxml file and use it in conjunction with the software at TellMe Studio. The following sections outline the steps to test this application.

Signing in to TellMe Studio

First we need to sign into TellMe Studio using the developer ID and PIN. At the top of the screen is an area where you can specify the ID and PIN, and then click Sign In (figure 31.26).

Figure 31.26   Signing in to TellMe Studio

Saving a document using the scratch pad

After signing in, we need to save our VoiceXML document using the scratch pad.

Just cut and paste the text from the voicemovies.vxml file into the text area in your scratch pad. Then click Update. If the update is successful, a message indicating this will be displayed at the top of the text area. Figure 31.27 illustrates what this will look like at TellMe Studio.

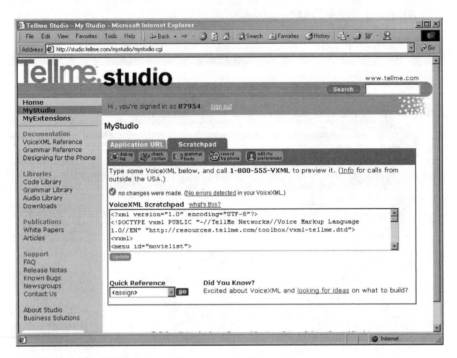

Figure 31.27 Saving the VoiceXML at TellMe Studio

Listening to the VoiceXML document

To test our application, we will need to call the TellMe Studio test line at1-800-555-VXML (1-800-555-8965). This number can be found at the web site as well. You will be prompted for your developer ID and PIN. Once this is entered, the VoiceXML in your scratch pad will be played.

VoiceXML document played

When you call the TellMe Studio test line, you should hear a short introduction indicating the number caller you are. Once you are connected, you will hear your VoiceXML document being played.

You will also be instructed to speak at certain times to make selections. To indicate the speaker in our sample dialogue, we will use "TellMe" for when the TellMe system is responding back to you, and "You" to indicate when you should speak.

- TellMe: "Welcome to VoiceXML MoviePhone"
- TellMe: "After the list say the name of the movie"
- A pause will occur
- TellMe: "Mission Impossible"
- A pause will occur

- TellMe: "Austin Powers"

- A pause will occur

- You: If you don't say anything, the `<noinput>` event handler will run and you will hear "I did not hear your response." You will once again be redirected to the menu at step 1.

- You: If you say something that doesn't match, the `<nomatch>` event handler will run and you will hear "That is not a valid response." You will then be redirected to the menu at step 1.

- You: If you say the name of the movie, "mission impossible" for instance, you will hear "You chose Mission Impossible."

- A pause will occur

- TellMe: "Show times are"

- A pause will occur

- TellMe: "Sunday 1 P.M."

- TellMe: "Sunday 3 P.M."

- A pause will occur

- You will then be redirected back to the main menu, step 1.

Troubleshooting

When running this example, you may encounter a few problems. Table 31.16 shows some common problems and what you can do about them.

Table 31.16   Troubleshooting this sample

Problem	Solution
TellMe Studio scratch pad says it can't compile document	Look at the source of the VoiceXML document in the Toolkit window. Make sure you have a valid document and well-formed elements.
TellMe Studio indicates there is a syntax error	Look at the message TellMe Studio provides. The TellMe Studio scratch pad is pretty good about telling you what is wrong (for instance, if you try to use a directive element in the wrong place). Always make sure you are using the elements in the place they are allowed.
TellMe Studio says it did not understand what you said even if you said nothing	The phone is a very sensitive device. Any background noise can be picked up by TellMe Studio. So, if a noisy co-worker is looking over your shoulder, this could be the culprit.

Figure 31.28 shows how the TellMe Studio scratch pad indicates an error in your VoiceXML document.

Problems with your VoiceXML document are indicated using red text. In this case, we mistakenly typed a `<wxml>` instead of `<vxml>` as the start of our document.

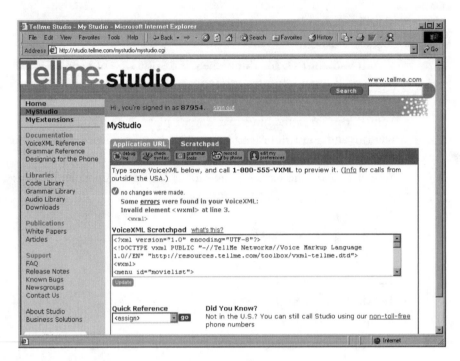

Figure 31.28 TellMe Studio scratch pad indicates a syntax error

31.5 SUMMARY

This chapter has taken you through three complete transformations of XML to HDML, WML, and VoiceXML. We saw step-by-step how to construct each style sheet. In those style sheets, we saw how to construct template rules to process our XML document. Each style sheet followed the same fundamental flow based on the requirements of each sample.

Transformations are an important concept to understand as XML gains dominance as a content format. XML and XSLT are key technologies for publishing content to many wireless devices. And their existence as standards in the industry hopefully will ensure their continued adoption by many software and hardware vendors.

Setting up a testing environment

WAP defines a proxy, called a gateway, that serves to translate requests from a wireless network to the Internet (and vice versa). Before deploying your WAP services, it is important to test them internally—to find bugs in the code and ensure usability.

The next chapters discuss the configuration of a gateway server, as well as the devices that use that server to access the Internet.

CHAPTER   3 2

Using WAP gateways

32.1   INTRODUCTION

Most of the examples presented in the earlier chapters can be tried on emulators using the HTTP direct method. While this is adequate for development purposes, it is imperative that you test your application on a real WAP gateway and WAP device before you deploy your applications. Many of the problems that will surface in real-world deployment using a WAP gateway cannot be easily detected by testing using emulators.

When testing and deploying WAP applications, a developer has two choices: a private gateway or a public gateway. You can either set up your own private gateway or you can use one that is publicly available. A private gateway provides more access control and security than a public one. For testing purposes it is advisable to use a private gateway as it provides you with a better understanding of how a WAP gateway is administered. When deploying WAP applications, you can then use a public gateway. The downside of using a private gateway is the additional cost and administrative work involved. However, by using a public gateway you need to rely on the gateway provider for the availability of the gateway.

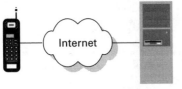

Origin server

Figure 32.1 The Nokia WAP Toolkit emulator contains the gateway functionality

One of the most notorious problems that developers run into when testing their WAP applications has to do with cookie support. On an emulator, cookies are supported nicely (due to the abundant memory available on the PC) but once your application runs on a real device, it is the gateway that your user connects to that determines cookie support. And the problem is you won't have any control (or know) which gateway your user connects to.

In addition, deck redirection using the HTTP Redirect method often causes problems when the application is deployed using a WAP gateway. A redirection to a deck indicated by a relative directory may be interpreted as a redirection to a deck stored in an absolute directory. This problem is highlighted in chapter 21.

These are the kinds of problems that can be uncovered only when using a gateway (through either using an emulator or a real device).

HTTP DIRECT   When this mode is used, the user agent bypasses any gateway and communicates with the HTTP server directly. The gateway functionality is embedded within the emulator.

Testing using real devices and gateways fulfills three objectives (table 32.1).

Table 32.1   Advantages of using a real device and gateway

Testing objective	Advantages of using a real device and gateway
Assess the look and feel of the application.	Device-dependent look and feel can be tested accurately.
Determine actual performance of the application.	Performance issues such as download time can be reflected accurately only through using a real device.
Manage inherent microbrowser/phone characteristics.	Issues like cookie support can be verified.

In this chapter we will take a closer look at two popular WAP gateways: WAPlite and the Nokia WAP server. We will also discuss how to prepare a machine for installing the gateway and the startup and administration features of the two gateways.

32.2   *WAP ARCHITECTURE REVISITED*

So far we have been using emulators for testing our WAP applications. When using emulators, the WAP gateway is actually embedded in the emulator and thus the communication is directly from the emulator to the origin server (figure 32.2). The gateway is therefore transparent to the developer. However, in the real world, most WAP devices do not contain the WAP gateway.

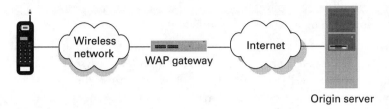

Figure 32.2   WAP architecture

Let's recap the architecture of a WAP client accessing services residing in some origin server on the Internet.

Here, the WAP device is communicating with a WAP gateway through the wireless network and the WAP gateway in turn communicates with the origin server through the Internet.

The roles of a WAP gateway are to:

- Connect the wireless device, such as a mobile phone, to the Internet and intranet applications

- Translate requests from the WAP protocol stack (WSP, WTP, WTLS, and WDP) to the WWW protocol stack (HTTP, SSL, and TCP/IP)

- Translate WAP content into binary content to be sent to the wireless device

- Translate HTML encoding to WML encoding (only applies to some WAP gateways)

- Translate WML encoding to HDML encoding (only applies to some WAP gateways, especially in the U.S.)

The benefits of a WAP gateway are to:

- Reduce the size of the content transmitted to the wireless device by encoding and compressing the WAP content

- Allow WAP content and applications to be hosted on standard WWW servers, thus leveraging the huge investments already made by companies

32.3 *EMULATOR VERSUS GATEWAY*

So far, you have been using the emulator for testing your applications. Why do you need a gateway now? Because:

- *The gateway is a distinct component within the WAP architecture*—While an emulator contains both the WAP microbrowser and the gateway, in a real-life environment your WAP device does not contain the gateway. The WAP device must dial up a WAP gateway and then rely on it to access the requested Internet service.

- *Not all gateways support cookies*—While many emulators provide cookie support, in the real world this support is dependent on the gateway. Some WAP gateways support cookies while others do not. Hence, it is of ultimate importance that you test all your applications that make use of cookies using the gateway you intend to deploy in the actual production environment.

- *Gateways can provide a performance evaluation*—Testing using a gateway provides a better gauge of the overall performance of the system you developed, on the gateway as well as on the device. This is because the request and response cycle involves accessing the various individual components in order to satisfy a client's request.

Besides installing your own gateway, you can make use of some of the public gateways available. These public gateways allow users to connect their WAP devices to access the available WAP services/application on the Internet. While this is an attractive option for companies to avoid hosting gateways, it is not a viable option when access control and uptime of the gateway is of paramount importance. Gateway security, which we will discuss later in this chapter, is another concern for hosting gateway by a third party.

32.4 RUNNING YOUR OWN GATEWAY

The subject of running your own WAP gateway has generated many questions within the developer community. Technically, this is not a very difficult task and you need not purchase expensive hardware in order to run your own gateway, especially for experimental or prototyping purposes.

For this chapter, we will be looking at two WAP gateways:

- WAPlite from Infinite Technologies (http://www.waplite.com)
- Nokia WAP Server (http://www.nokia.com)

To install the WAP gateways, you need a machine that is running Windows 95, Windows 98, or Windows NT, although NT is recommended. For our development purposes and discussion, we use Microsoft Windows NT 4.0.

> **UNIX BOXES** There are a number of WAP gateways running on UNIX boxes. If you are running Linux or UNIX, you should take a look at the following gateways (some are Open Source):
> Java-based gateway: http://www.eigroup.com/products/
> anoncvs/index.jsp
> Kannel: http://www.kannel.org/

32.4.1 Preparing to run a WAP gateway

This chapter focuses on the Microsoft Windows NT platform. We shall first make sure that the following components are installed on our Windows NT host machine:

- Protocol: TCP/IP stack
- Hardware: Modem and a phone line
- Services: Remote Access Services (RAS)

- Web server: Internet Information Server 4.0
- Accounts: User accounts for dialing in

Installing RAS service

The RAS service handles dial-in calls from a real phone device. If you are merely testing a WAP gateway using an emulated phone browser, this service is not necessary. When installing the RAS server, be sure to configure the Port Usage to Dial Out and Receive Calls (if you do not want to dial out, select Receive Calls Only). See figure 32.3.

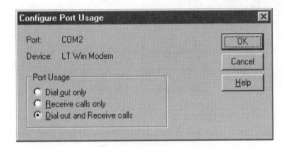

Figure 32.3
Dialog window for configuring the COM port

Creating a user account

You must create a user account for the WAP device to be connected to your server. To grant a user with the dial-up permission, go to Start→Administrative Tools (Common)→User Manager for Domains. Figure 32.4 shows the User Properties dialog box.

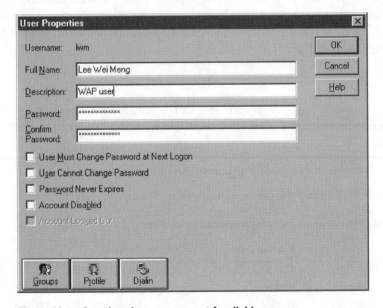

Figure 32.4   Creating the user account for dial-in access

To grant permission, click Dialin. Figure 32.5 shows the Dialin Information dialog box.

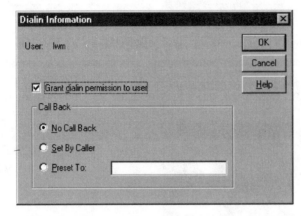

Figure 32.5
Assigning the dialin permission

Check the Grant Dialin Permission to User checkbox; click OK.

That's all you need to do to prepare your machine for running the WAP gateway.

Troubleshooting

You might encounter two problems:

- *Modem not responding*—Be sure that your modem is working properly. A good check is to try to dial out and see if the modem connects to a remote host.

- *RAS not installed properly*—To test if your RAS is installed correctly, try calling your machine with the phone line plugged into the modem. If the modem does not try to make a connection or the RAS reports an error, your RAS is not installed correctly.

32.5 WAP*LITE*

WAPlite is a lightweight WAP gateway that is suitable for development as well as deployment. It includes a WAP 1.1-compatible stack that supports:

- GET and POST methods
- Connection and Connection-Less oriented modes over UDP

Table 32.2 shows the phones and emulators supported by WAPlite.

Table 32.2   Phones and emulators supported by WAPlite

Name	Product type	Remarks
Nokia 7110	Phone	GSM 800/1800
Motorola Timeport P7389	Phone	Tri-band GSM 800/1800/1900
Motorola L-Series+	Phone	Similar to P7389, but GSM 800/1800

Table 32.2   Phones and emulators supported by WAPlite

Name	Product type	Remarks
Ericsson MC218 PDA	PDA	
Ericsson R320s	Phone	GSM 800/1800
Nokia WAP Toolkit v1.2 and v1.3	SDK/Emulator	
Ericsson WapIDE	SDK/Emulator	
Ericsson R380 emulator	SDK/Emulator	
Phone.com v4.0 SDK	SDK/Emulator	
WAPman from Edge Consultants	Palm and Windows browser	

32.5.1   Installing WAPlite

Developers who want to experiment with a real gateway can download a 30-day trial edition of WAPlite at http://www.waplite.com. It comes in two flavors: WAPlite and WAPlite (WTLS version).

WTLS   Wireless Transport Layer Security (WTLS) is a security protocol designed to establish a secure communications channel over wireless networks. For it to work, it must be implemented in both the microbrowser of the wireless device and the WAP gateway.

The following sections are based on the WTLS version of WAPlite. Installing WAPlite is straightforward. Simply run the WLITE-WT.exe program and you will be prompted to specify an installation directory.

32.5.2   Starting WAPlite

The WAPlite gateway is installed as a service. To invoke the WAPlite management screen, select Start→Programs→WAPlite.

Configuring WAPlite

The WAPlite management screen (figure 32.6) contains five tabs: Stats, Options, Restrictions, Log, and Advertising. The last tab is used only if you wish to perform advertising on WAP devices.

The Stats tab provides a good way for you to monitor the number of users who are currently connected to your gateway and the number of requests processed. To start the WAPlite gateway, click Install Service.

The Options tab (figure 32.7) allows you to select the WTLS option as well as the proxy server and session details. We will discuss this in greater detail when we illustrate how we can use an emulator to connect to the gateway.

The Restrictions tab allows you to restrict the devices that are allowed to make connections through the WAPlite server.

The Log tab enables or disables logging to be performed by the WAPlite gateway.

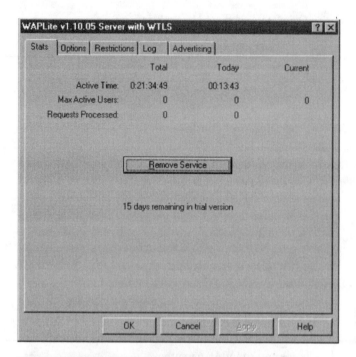

Figure 32.6
WAPlite management screen

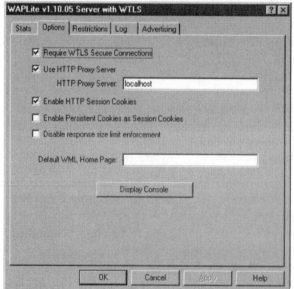

Figure 32.7
Configuring WAPlite

The Advertising tab allows you to configure special advertising messages that will be inserted into WML request/response dialogs issued by the user agent.

32.5.3   Connecting to WAPlite using an emulator

After the installation and configuration of WAPlite, we shall proceed to test the gateway using phone browser emulators. Using a working emulator instead of a WAP-enabled phone for the testing helps to reduce problems that we may encounter. We can more safely attribute any problem encountered during the testing to be related to the WAP gateway setup. After we have verified that the WAP gateway is properly set up, we can then configure a phone to connect to the WAP gateway. How to configure your phone to work with a WAP gateway will be discussed in chapter 33.

NOTE   If you are testing the gateway using emulators, you need not set up RAS.

Let's try using Nokia WAP Toolkit version 2.0. For the Nokia WAP Toolkit, you need to specify in the Toolkit→Preference window that you are connecting using a WAP gateway. We will review how to do this in the next section.

Using Nokia WAP Toolkit

You can download the toolkit version 2.0 from Nokia's web site. Refer to chapter 2 for more details.

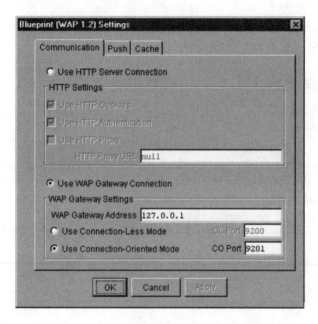

**Figure 32.8
Configuring the Nokia
WAP Toolkit to connect
to the gateway**

To ensure that your Nokia emulator is able to connect to the gateway (figure 32.8), you need to:

* Set the IP address of the WAP gateway. If your gateway is running on the same machine, set it to the loopback address, 127.0.0.1.

- Use either the Connection-Less Mode or the Connection-Oriented Mode to connect to the WAP gateway.
- We use the Connection-Oriented Mode and a port number of 9201 in this example. Table 32.3 shows the port numbers available.

Table 32.3   Port numbers

Port number	Description
9200	Connection-Less Mode
9201	Connection-Oriented Mode
9202	Connection-Less Mode (WTLS)
9203	Connection-Oriented Mode (WTLS)

For the Nokia WAP Toolkit, turn off the secure connection on the WAPlite gateway because secure connection is not supported by the toolkit. Specifying port number 9202 or 9203 will not work. To turn off the secure connection, tab the Options of the WAPlite management screen (figure 32.6) and uncheck Require WTLS Secure Connections (figure 32.9).

To load a deck onto the Nokia WAP Toolkit, enter a valid URL in the Location input box of the interface (figure 32.10).

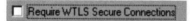

Figure 32.9   Turning off the security option for WAPlite

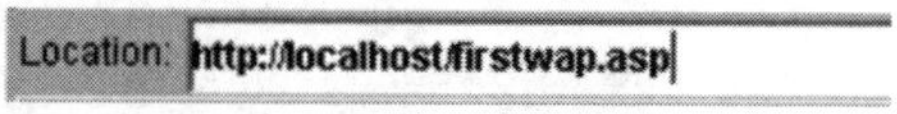

Figure 32.10   Entering the URL at the Location textbox

If the application runs, then the gateway has been installed and configured correctly. What if the application does not run? A common source of error is setting the port number incorrectly. Also, make sure that you are connecting using the correct mode. Figure 32.11 shows the display after a successful installation.

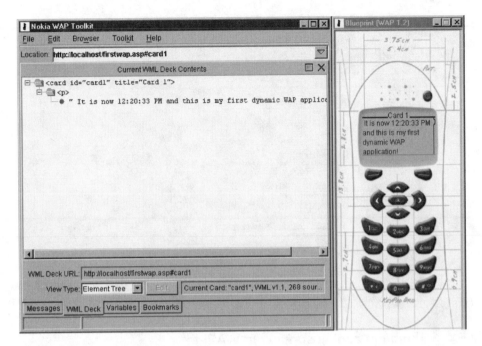

Figure 32.11   Using the Nokia WAP Toolkit

Using UP.Simulator

We shall now test our gateway using another emulator: Phone.com's UP.Simulator.

WTLS   By default, UP.Simulator uses WTLS to communicate with a WAP gateway. If you are using a non-WTLS version of WAPlite, you need to turn off the WTLS support in the UP.Simulator using the –nonsecure option when it is launched. For example:

> C:\phone.com\UPSDK40>upsim -nonsecure.

As in the case of Nokia WAP Toolkit, you need to specify the gateway IP address and the port number for UP.Simulator. To specify the WAP gateway, select Settings →UP.Link Settings (figure 32.12).

The UP.Simulator does not provide an explicit option to specify the port number. If you are using the WTLS version of WAPlite, enter the correct port number (9203 in our case) after the WAP gateway IP address as shown in the interface above in the text box for UPLink 1.

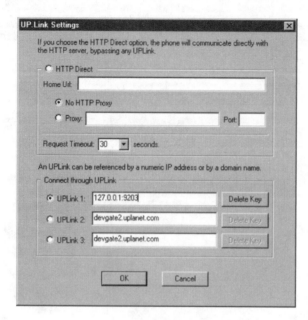

Figure 32.12
Configuring the UP.Simulator
for WAP gateway access

32.5.4 Enabling cookie support in WAPlite

We can enable support for HTTP session cookies in WAPlite under its Options tab (figure 32.13).

Note that there are two kinds of cookies supported: HTTP session and persistent.

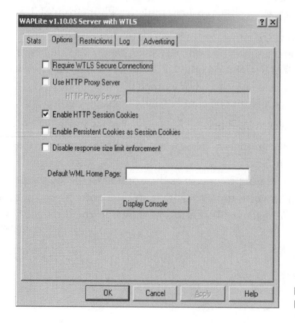

Figure 32.13
Enabling cookie support in WAPlite

By default, WAPlite supports session cookies. However, if the cookie has an expires tag present, the cookie will be treated as a persistent cookie. A session cookie is valid until the user closes the connection; a persistent cookie resides on a hard disk so that it is reusable for subsequent connections. Due to current limitations of WAP, WAPlite does not enable a persistent cookie to be reused for subsequent connections.

Recall that in chapter 17, we mentioned that the ASP Session object requires the support of cookies. In the next example, we are going to verify that we have set up WAPlite to support cookies. If we are able to set a session variable successfully, we can conclude that cookies are indeed supported by the WAPlite we have just set up (figure 32.14).

Figure 32.14 Testing for cookie support using the Session object

The first step is to create a simple ASP file and save it as SetSession.asp:

```
<% Response.ContentType="text/vnd.wap.wml"%>
<?xml version="1.0"?>
<!DOCTYPE wml PUBLIC "-//WAPFORUM//DTD WML 1.1//EN"
"http://www.wapforum.org/DTD/wml_1.1.xml">
<wml>
    <card id="card1" title="Session">
        <p>
            <% Session("Name")="Wei Meng" %>
            Session variable set!
        </p>
    </card>
</wml>
```

Loading SetSession.asp will result in the display shown in figure 32.14.

If the session variable, Name, is set correctly, loading the following dynamic WML content (GetSession.asp) via an ASP script will result in the screen in figure 32.15.

Figure 32.15 Cookie support is present if Session object works correctly

```
<% Response.ContentType="text/vnd.wap.wml"%>
<?xml version="1.0"?>
<!DOCTYPE wml PUBLIC "-//WAPFORUM//DTD WML 1.1//EN"
"http://www.wapforum.org/DTD/wml_1.1.xml">
<% 'GetSession.asp %>
<wml>
    <card id="card1" title="Session">
        <p>
            Hello,
            <% =Session("Name") %> !
        </p>
    </card>
</wml>
```

32.6 Nokia WAP Server

Nokia WAP Server version 1.1 is WAP 1.1-compliant and it may be run on Windows NT, HP-UX, and Sun Solaris.

Features of Nokia WAP Server are:

- It supports connection with WAP phones via various bearers such as short message service (SMS) and circuit switched data (CSD).

- Static WML contents and other backend systems implemented using ASP or Java servlets can be stored locally at the WAP server. Alternatively, the WAP server is able to access an HTTP 1.0 or HTTP 1.1 origin server for the actual contents.

- It supports secure connections via WTLS.

- It supports the HttpSession interface of the Java Servlet API 2.1.

- It is able to support cookies. Note that the wireless device needs to support cookies for meaningful applications.

- It includes the Nokia WAP Toolkit for application development.

> **NOTE** *WAP gateway versus WAP server* Nokia names its WAP gateway a WAP server since it provides both WAP gateway and application server functionality through its support of Java servlets. Note that we use the term WAP gateway and WAP server interchangeably throughout this chapter, as we do not cover the application server aspects of the Nokia WAP Server.

32.6.1 Downloading and installing the Nokia WAP Server

The Nokia WAP Server has been renamed Nokia Activ Server with a few additional features in its version 2.0. However, Nokia Activ Server 2.0 Professional Edition is based on the Nokia WAP Server product, so that Nokia WAP Server can be easily upgraded to Nokia Activ Server 2.0. For more information, visit http://www.nokia.com/.

> **NOTE** Be sure to install Nokia WAP Server on a partition with at least 100MB free space. Failing to do so will render the server unable to start and to generate a string of errors. Be sure to check the free disk space if you encounter errors in starting the server.

Installation of the server is straightforward and you will be appropriately instructed on screen as you proceed.

32.6.2 Starting Nokia WAP Server

Once Nokia WAP Server is installed, simply click on Start→Programs→Nokia WAP Server→Nokia WAP Server (figure 32.16).

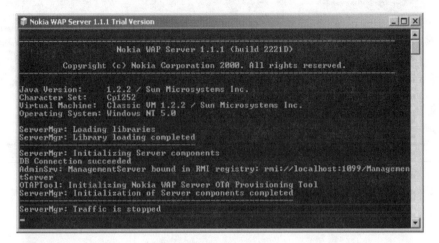

Figure 32.16   Starting the Nokia WAP Server

Once the server is started, bring up the Nokia WAP Server manager for administration. To launch, click Start→Programs→Nokia WAP Server→Nokia WAP Server Manager.

If you are running the WAP server locally, use the default `localhost`; otherwise supply the name of the machine running the gateway. Click Connect (figure 32.17) and you will be prompted with the Login dialog box (figure 32.18).

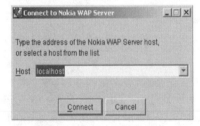

Figure 32.17   Connecting to the Nokia WAP Server host

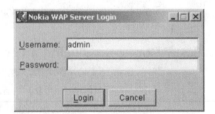

Figure 32.18 Logon to the Nokia WAP Server

You can use the default username `admin` without a password. Click Login to proceed. If the login is successful, you should see the screen in figure 32.19.

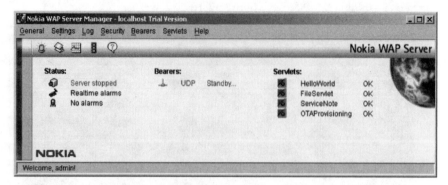

Figure 32.19   Nokia WAP Server manager

The server is stopped by default. To start the server, simply click on the General menu and select Start Traffic (figure 32.20).

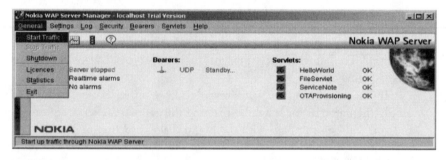

Figure 32.20   Starting the Nokia WAP Server service

32.6.3   Connecting using an emulator

The steps for configuring your emulator to connect to the Nokia WAP Server are similar to the steps used for connecting to the WAPlite gateway. Refer to section 32.5.3 for instructions on configuring the Nokia WAP Toolkit and the UP.Simulator.

32.6.4   Monitoring traffic

There are two ways to monitor traffic in Nokia WAP Server: through the console window and through the statistics window.

Nokia WAP Server console window

When Nokia WAP Server is started, the console window displays the status of the server (figure 32.21). This console window is useful for monitoring the traffic of the

WAP server. For example, if we load a WML deck named index.wml into our Nokia WAP Toolkit:

Figure 32.21 Monitoring the Nokia WAP Server using the console window

The console window reports:

```
127.0.0.1 -> http://localhost/index.wml      ❶
127.0.0.1 <- http://localhost/index.wml, [200], 121ms      ❷
```

Code comments

❶ The request for index.wml from (127.0.0.1).

❷ The response of the file index.wml from localhost. Note that [200] is the status code of the HTTP response and 121ms is the processing time of the deck in milliseconds.

If we do a reload on the emulator, we see the following information on the console:

```
127.0.0.1 -> http://localhost/index.wml                  ❶
127.0.0.1 <- http://localhost/index.wml [c], [200], 20ms      ❷
```

Code comments

❶ The request for index.wml from localhost (127.0.0.1).

❷ The requested file is obtained from the gateway cache [C]. Note that the processing time has been drastically reduced.

When we reload a deck that is already residing in the gateway's cache, the processing time is reduced, as it does not need to compile the WML deck again.

Statistics window

To view the number of requests and other useful information, you can launch the Nokia WAP Server Statistics window by clicking General → Statistics.

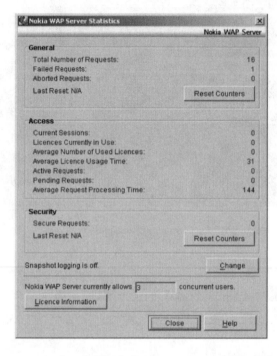

Figure 32.22
Viewing the Nokia WAP
Server statistics

As figure 32.22 shows, you can obtain information such as:

- Total number of requests
- Number of failed and aborted requests
- Average request processing time
- Number of secure requests
- Licensing information

For more information, refer to the documentation provided by Nokia.

32.6.5   Converting HTML and text to WML

One special feature of the Nokia WAP Server is its capability to convert non-WML content into WML decks for loading on a WAP device. In particular, the Nokia WAP Server is able to convert HTML to WML and text to WML.

HTML to WML

Let's test the feature by creating an HTML document, Singapore.html:

```html
<html>
<head><title>Singapore!</title></head>
   Hello Singapore!
   <img border="1" src="singapore.jpg" width="50">
</html>
```

Loading Singapore.html onto a web browser will display a screen shot similar to figure 32.23.

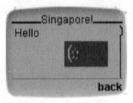

Figure 32.23
Viewing HTML content on a web browser

Let's now load the same HTML document onto the Nokia WAP Toolkit via our Nokia WAP Server (figure 32.24).

Figure 32.24
Using the Nokia WAP
Toolkit to view
HTML content

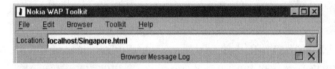

Figure 32.25 is the display obtained if the concept blueprint phone of the toolkit is used.

Note that the Nokia WAP Server converts the HTML content into a WML deck.

Figure 32.25   Viewing
HTML content on the
Nokia WAP Toolkit

```xml
<?xml version="1.0"?>
<!DOCTYPE wml PUBLIC "-//WAPFORUM//DTD WML 1.1//EN"
"http://www.wapforum.org/DTD/wml_1.1.xml">

<!-- Deck Source: "http://localhost/singapore.html#frstcard" -->
<!-- DISCLAIMER: This source was generated from parsed binary -->
<!-- WML content. This representation of the deck contents does -->
<!-- not necessarily preserve original white space or accurately -->
<!-- decode any CDATA section contents, but otherwise is an accurate -->
<!-- representation of the original deck contents as determined -->
<!-- from its WBXML encoding.  If a precise representation is -->
```

```
<!-- required,then use the "Element Tree" or, if available, the -->
<!-- "Original Source" view. -->

<wml>
  <template>
    <do type="prev" label="back">
      <prev/>
    </do>
  </template>

  <card title="Singapore!" id="frstcard">
    <p>
       Hello Singapore!
      <img src="singapore.jpg" alt="IMAGE" width="50"/>
    </p>
  </card>

</wml>
```

Figure 32.26
Non-WBMP graphics may not display correctly
on WAP devices/emulators

NOTE   While the WML deck in the example displays correctly on the Nokia em-
        ulator, it may not display correctly on other emulators/devices, as they
        might not be able to support non-WBMP graphics file formats. For exam-
        ple, when the above is loaded on the Ericsson WapIDE, the image does
        not appear (figure 32.26).

Text to WML

Suppose we have the following text file, Nokia.txt:

```
Please note that the Nokia WAP Server Manager Help pages only assist
you in using the Nokia WAP Server Manager. For more detailed
information on administering the Nokia WAP Server, see the Nokia WAP
Server Getting Started Guide and Nokia WAP Server Administration
Guide.
```

Using the Nokia WAP Toolkit to load the text file through the Nokia WAP Server, we have a browser message log (figure 32.27) and the message displayed on the screen (figure 32.28).

Figure 32.27
Viewing text content using the Nokia WAP Toolkit

Figure 32.28   Text content displayed on the Nokia WAP Toolkit

The WML code generated is:

```
<?xml version="1.0"?>
<!DOCTYPE wml PUBLIC "-//WAPFORUM//DTD WML 1.1//EN"
"http://www.wapforum.org/DTD/wml_1.1.xml">

<!-- Deck Source: "http://localhost/nokia.txt" -->
<!-- DISCLAIMER: This source was generated from parsed binary -->
<!-- WML content. This representation of the deck contents -->
<!-- does not necessarily preserve original white space or  -->
<!-- accurately decode any CDATA Section contents, but otherwise -->
<!-- is an accurate representation of the original deck contents as -->
<!-- determined from its WBXML encoding.  If a precise representation -->
<!-- is required, then use the "Element Tree" or, if available, the -->
<!-- "Original Source" view.-->

<wml>
  <template>
    <do type="prev" label="back">
      <prev/>
    </do>
  </template>

  <card>
    <p>

Please note that the Nokia WAP Server Manager Help pages only assist you in
using the Nokia WAP Server Manager. For more detailed information on
administering the Nokia WAP Server, see the Nokia WAP Server Getting Started
Guide and Nokia WAP Server Administration Guide.

    </p>
  </card>

</wml>
```

Enabling the conversion capability

To enable the conversion capability of Nokia WAP Server, check the appropriate converter checkboxes in the Content dialog box shown in figure 32.29.

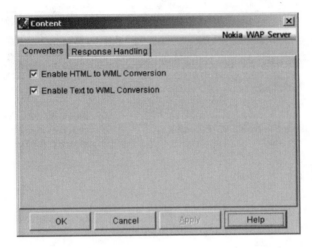

Figure 32.29
Configuring the conversion capability of the Nokia WAP Server

When the conversion capability is enabled, the Nokia WAP Server will not convert the content if the target device supports the content in the native format of the original document. For example, if a target device can support HTML, Nokia WAP Server would not convert the HTML content into WML before sending it to the device.

32.7 HOSTING VERSUS SUBSCRIBING TO WAP GATEWAY

We have seen how simple it is to set up your own WAP gateway. Corporations that choose to offer WAP services can also set up and configure their own WAP gateways according to the requirements and availability of resources.

There are two important reasons why corporations often prefer to set up their own WAP gateway:

- *Full control of the gateway, hardware as well as software, which in turn gives the company the flexibility to reconfigure and fine-tune configuration when new needs arise.*

- *Security*—It is common knowledge that translation of Internet data to the WAP data for wireless transmission, as well as any encryption and decryption applicable to the application in question, are carried out in the WAP gateway. This implies that data from the origin server to the wireless device (and vice versa) would need to be held in the RAM of the machine hosting the WAP gateway. The pessimistic user would take meticulous care to avoid any possible security breach that might take place during the short interval when the data is held in the RAM of the WAP gateway host. As such, an externally hosted WAP gateway is considered undesirable.

Despite the fears of security breaches, it is not uncommon for corporations to leave the gateway out of their existing company network. In the latter case, a company would need to subscribe to a third party, typically a telecommunications company, or *telco*, to host the gateway and to deliver the WAP traffic. The advantages from the corporate point of view include saving manpower and computing resources in administering an additional WAP gateway. On the other hand, the third-party WAP gateway hosting company must ensure a secure transmission channel as well as confidentiality of data that stays in the RAM of the hosting machine for translation, encryption, and decryption.

In the next section, we will look at how a network operator typically deploys a WAP gateway.

32.8 DEPLOYING *WAP* GATEWAY

The objective of this section is to demystify what goes on within the realm of the network operator (also called a telco) that hosts a WAP gateway. Figure 32.30 is an outline of a network diagram that a telco might use to provide a communications channel via a WAP gateway.

There are a number of steps involved in sending a request from a wireless device to an origin server using dial-up through a RAS server.

- Wireless device dials into the RAS server via some base stations and mobile switching center (MSC) based on the wireless device's current location.

- RAS authenticates the user dialing in with the help of Remote Authentication Dial-In User Service (RADIUS) based on user ID and password.

- If the authentication is successful, the dialin device is informed that a session is established with the specified WAP gateway (or gateway supplied as part of the user information by the RADIUS server). Subsequent session communications will be passed to the WAP gateway under the safeguard of the firewall.

- The wireless device next sends its request for some resource residing in the Internet.

- Decompression and decryption may be performed on the WAP request from the wireless device, before it is being translated into an HTTP request and possibly with encryption, depending on the application.

- The HTTP request is sent out as any other HTTP request originated from an HTTP client such as an IE browser.

- The origin server was specified as the target URL in the request originated by the wireless device. It may be one of telco's servers or some other Internet server outside the telco.

- The origin server eventually receives the request and responds accordingly.

- The response would follow a reverse direction flow from that described in the steps above.

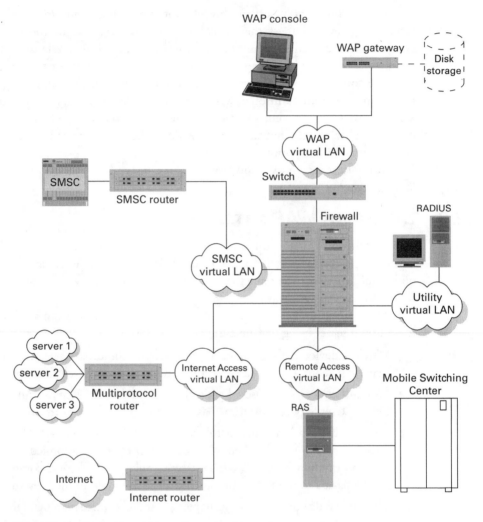

Figure 32.30 Typical network configuration for a telco

The short message service center (SMSC) connections are offered as a means to provide notifications (such as email alerts) to phones that are not connected to the WAP gateway at any particular time.

32.9 SECURITY OF WAP-BASED SYSTEMS

To understand the possible security threats in a WAP-based system, which also include the web-based portion, figure 32.31 presents a big picture of the relevant communications protocols that are used between a wireless device and an origin server.

In the entire request-response cycle, security can be a concern in several areas:

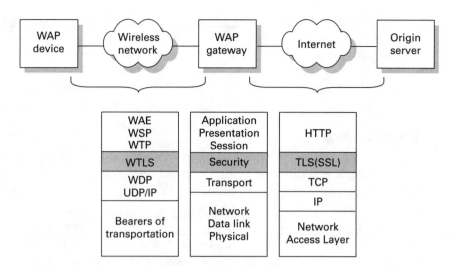

Figure 32.31 Network protocols for a WAP-based system

- *Wireless device*—The device may store information such as certificates and PINs used for some applications. This pretty much means safeguarding the physical phone or module card(s) used in the phone.

- *Communications channel between the user agent and the WAP gateway*—Security protocol must be used to provide a secure channel for data to flow between the device and the gateway to guard against eavesdropping.

- *WAP gateway*—Organization must set up security policy regarding the physical safety of the machine hosting the WAP gateway. Administrative access rights must be carefully granted. Also, before purchasing a gateway, the evaluator must make sure that the time interval when data stays in the RAM as clear text is as short as possible and that flushing of RAM is performed once the data is not needed on the gateway.

- *Communications channel between the WAP gateway and the origin server*—Appropriate security protocol must be used to provide a secure channel for data passing between the gateway and the origin server to guard against information leakage.

- *Origin server*—The issues of physical safety and access rights as mentioned for the WAP gateway apply here as well. The applications stored in the origin server should be organized carefully in directories with the appropriate access rights granted to them. If secure path is needed for clients to access some services on the server using protocol such as secure sockets layer (SSL), which will be discussed later, a certificate must first be installed in the server. Applications should also safeguard its users by implementing user logon and password at the application level.

In this section, our discussion will emphasize establishing secure communications channels, specifically, communication between the WAP-enabled phone and the WAP gateway, as well as communication between the WAP gateway and the origin server. Before we move into details of communications security, we will introduce *cryptography* and *digital certificates*, two enabling technologies that are indispensable in implementing secure channels in this internetworking world, either via wired or wireless networks.

32.9.1 Cryptography

Cryptography involves encryption of plain text into an indecipherable form before transmission in a network so that it is unreadable to any unauthorized users who might be able to capture packets of data traffic from the network. The transformed message is known as *ciphertext*. Encryption is accompanied by decryption to recover the original plain text from the ciphertext. Cryptography is used where privacy, authentication, integrity, or nonrepudiation is needed. Examples include filling out an online income tax form, purchasing goods over the web using a credit card, and sending confidential electronic mail messages.

There are two types of cryptographic algorithms: *symmetric* and *asymmetric*. These algorithms make use of *keys* for encrypting and decrypting data. A key is a string or numeric value that determines the result of transforming a given piece of data using a given cryptographic algorithm.

Symmetric cryptography uses a single key, invariably called a *symmetric key*, *secret key*, or *private key*, for both the encryption and decryption processes. An example is the Data Encryption Standard (DES), which was first approved by the National Institute of Standards and Technology (NIST), U.S., in 1977.

Asymmetric algorithms require a pair of keys—*public* and *private*—to work. The application on hand will decide which key to be used for encryption and the other for decryption. For example, to transmit a confidential message, the sender would encrypt the message with the recipient's public key, and the recipient, upon receiving the encrypted message, will decrypt it using the recipient's own private key. If the sender needs to ensure the recipient that the message received is truly from the sender and that the message has not been tampered with, the sender then uses its private key to create a digital signature, and sends it together with the message to the recipient. The recipient will use the sender's public key to verify the sender's identity as well as to prove the original message was received intact. An example of asymmetric algorithm is the RSA algorithm, which is named after its inventors, Rivest, Shamir, and Adleman.

In general, an asymmetric algorithm is more complex mathematically and the amount of processing involved can slow the response time considerably at both ends. Figure 32.32 illustrates the appropriate use of both asymmetric and symmetric (e.g., RSA and DES) cryptographic algorithms for two parties to exchange confidential messages. Notice that the use of the public cryptography is restricted to the distribution of the secret key. The encryption and decryption of the actual confidential data is via symmetric cryptography. Also, more than one secret key may be used, for example, one for encrypting data from Amy to Zan and the other for data from Zan to Amy.

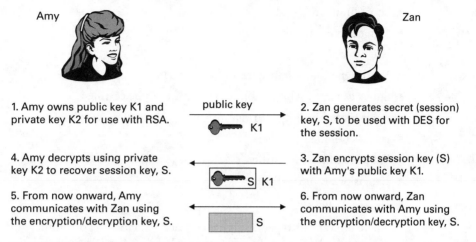

Amy

Zan

| 1. Amy owns public key K1 and private key K2 for use with RSA. | public key → K1 | 2. Zan generates secret (session) key, S, to be used with DES for the session. |

4. Amy decrypts using private key K2 to recover session key, S.

← S K1

3. Zan encrypts session key (S) with Amy's public key K1.

5. From now onward, Amy communicates with Zan using the encryption/decryption key, S.

↔ S

6. From now onward, Zan communicates with Amy using the encryption/decryption key, S.

Figure 32.32 Use of asymmetric and symmetric cryptographic algorithms in sending confidential information

A private key is meant only for the eyes of the owner of the key. A public key is to be used by anyone who wishes to be involved in a secure communication with the owner. One problem with deploying cryptography is the distribution of the key to the various parties involved. The digital certificate provides a solution to the problem. We will discuss digital certificates next.

32.9.2 Digital certificates

A digital certificate is an identification card or passport in the digital world that certifies an entity to which it is bound. An entity here may be a person, a hardware device such as a router, or software such as an HTTP server or WAP gateway. A certificate may be used for various functions:

- Authenticating server or client
- Verifying authenticity of downloaded software
- Controlling access to resources
- Distributing public key

The X.509 standard is the most commonly adopted certificate standard. It is an ITU-T and ISO/IEC certificate format standard. The latest version of the standard is 3.0.

NOTE   ITU-T is an acronym for the International Telecommunication Union-Telecommunication Standardization Sector; ISO stands for the International Organization for Standardization; IEC is the International Electrotechnical Commission.

A typical X.509 v3 certificate contains the following information:

- Version of the X.509 standard used (3, in this case)
- Serial number
- Signature algorithm
- Issuer name
- Validity period: a start date and expiry date
- Subject's name, where subject is the entity to be certified
- Subject's public key information
- Issuer's unique identifier
- Subject's unique identifier
- Extensions (optional)
- Issuer's digital signature

There are various types of digital certificates. The categorization varies from one Certification Authority (CA) to the other, where a CA is a trusted organization that is capable of issuing a certificate.

Table 32.4 lists and describes some common certificate types.

Table 32.4   Some certificate types

Certificate type	Description
Certification Authority (CA) certificate	Contains necessary information such as the public key of a CA, name of the CA, or name of service being certified. It is used to certify other kinds of certificates. Such a certificate can either be self-signed or it can be signed by another CA. For example, VeriSign issues CA certificates that are signed by the VeriSign Public Primary Certification Authority (PCA).
Server certificate	Contains public key of a server, name of the organization that runs the server, and its Internet hostname.
Personal certificate	A personal certificate contains an individual's name and public key, and other information such as individual's email address, postal address, etc.
Software publisher certificate	This category of certificate is used for code signing. For example, before a software developer or vendor uses Microsoft's Authenticode to attach a signature to their program, they need to first apply for a certificate to use Authenticode.

In general, the life cycle of a digital certificate can be summarized as follows:

- A subject to be certified first generates a public-private key pair followed by a certificate request file. For example, the *Key Manager* that is incorporated into Microsoft's Internet Information Server (IIS) can be used to generate a key pair.
- The subject then sends the certificate request to one of the following to apply for a certificate:
  - Locally to a certificate server, such as Microsoft's *Certificate Server*

- To a CA, such as VeriSign
- Via a Local Registration Authority (LRA), such as VeriSign OnSite LRA service
- If all goes well, the subject is informed of its successful application by the appropriate CA.
- The subject installs a certificate from the certificate server/CA/LRA.
- Applications (e.g., browsers) that need to use certificates are required to install the root certificate of the CA if it is not already installed.

Note that root certificates of major public CAs are preinstalled in a browser. Figure 32.33 shows some of the preinstalled CAs in a particular IE browser, which can be viewed using the Certificate Manager by invoking Tools → Internet Options → Content → Certificates from the interface of the IE browser:

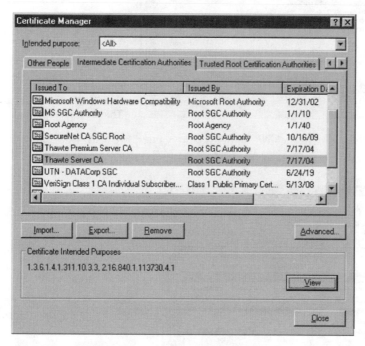

Figure 32.33   Preinstalled certificates shown in the Certificate Manager window

Figure 32.34 shows the details of a certificate, say one that was issued to Thawte Server CA, when we click the View button.

Figure 32.34
Details of a certificate issued to
Thawte Server CA

Scrolling down the list of fields and values, we can view more information (figure 32.35).

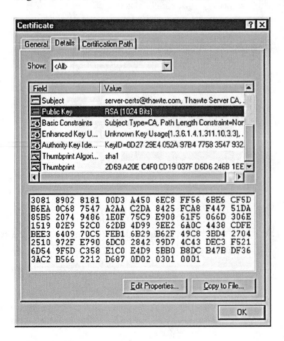

Figure 32.35
More details of the certificate issued
to Thawte Server CA

32.9.3　Security in traditional communications

Traditionally, to protect session data against eavesdropping and malicious tampering, the SSL protocol is used. SSL was first designed by Netscape Communications to provide web security for communications between browsers and web servers. It was implemented as a layer below the HTTP layer for supporting security in web-based applications. Although the main motivation behind SSL was to provide web security, it can be used with other Internet applications such as those running on File Transfer Protocol (FTP) and Net News Transfer Protocol (NNTP).

SSL VERSUS TLS　The Internet Engineering Task Force (IETF) has taken over the development of SSL standards and renamed SSL as TLS (Transport Layer Security) whose first version was released officially in 1999. TLS 1.0 consists of only a few improvements over SSL 3.0, which is the latest version of SSL before the IETF became the overseer of the standard.

Before data is exchanged between the client and server, a handshaking process takes place to establish a secure session. In a typical handshaking process:

- The client (browser) initiates a request for a secure communications channel via a ClientHello message, specifying the highest SSL version, compression methods, and the cipher suite the client supports. The cipher suite contains information on cryptographic parameters such as cryptographic algorithms and key sizes supported.

- The message also contains a session ID and random number serving as a seed for cryptographic computations.

- The server responds with a ServerHello message that contains the version of SSL and cryptographic parameters that both parties should eventually use to transmit sensitive data.

- The server then sends to the client its public key information in plain text in a ServerKeyExchange message or a digital certificate containing its public key. The latter is sent if the application requires server authentication.

- If the server requires client authentication, the server also sends a client authentication request to the client at this point.

- The ServerHelloDone is finally sent to inform the client that the negotiation phase of the handshaking process is completed.

- If there are no appropriate parameters to be used, an error message will be issued.

- The client receives a digital certificate from the server if it needs to authenticate the server.

- The client ensures that the server's certificate is not expired or revoked, and that it was signed by a CA that the client trusts.

- If client authentication is required, the client will now send its Certificate to the server or respond with a NoCertificateAlert message.

- The client sends a key exchange message to pass to the server a *premaster secret*, to allow both sides to agree upon the same secret.

- Depending on the key exchange algorithm used, this can involve generating a session key to be used by both parties to encrypt data during the current secure session. The key information in the ClientKeyExchange message is encrypted using the server's public key before it is sent to the server.

- If client authentication is required, the client generates a CertificateVerify message by using its private key to sign session information so that the server can use the public key sent in the client's certificate to verify the client's identity.

- The client sends a ChangeCipherSpec message to the server and updates its internal state to indicate that subsequent messages it sends will be using the cipher suite agreed upon by both parties.

- The client sends a final message, Finished, containing the result of applying a hash function on the following information: key information, all previous handshaking messages exchanged between the systems, an indicator of the sender being a client.

- This is a last chance for the server to detect any compromise of security from the start of the handshaking process.

- The server receives the client's ChangeCipherSpec message and updates its internal state to indicate that it expects all received data to be secure (using the negotiated cipher suite) from this point on.

- The server receives the client's Finished message and checks against its own computation using the same hash algorithm.

- A mismatch indicates that either the key information or the original handshaking message has been tampered with by an intruder.

- The server sends a similar ChangeCipherSpec message to the client and updates its internal state to indicate that subsequent messages it sends will be using the cipher suite agreed upon by both parties.

- The server sends a similar Finished message to the client.

- The client receives the server's ChangeCipherSpec message and updates its internal state to indicate that it expects all received data to be secure with the negotiated cipher suite.

- The client receives the server's Finished message and checks against its own computation using the same hash algorithm. A mismatch indicates that either the key information or the original handshaking message has been tampered with by an intruder.

- If all is fine at this point, both parties can be assured that data transmitted between them is secure.

Figure 32.36 summarizes the exchange of messages involved in establishing a secure communication session (with client and server authentication) successfully using SSL.

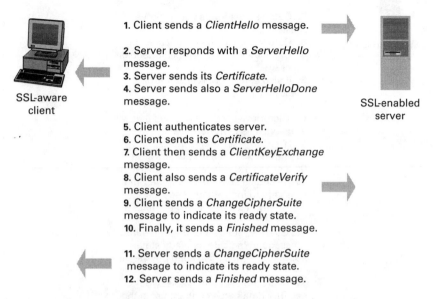

SSL-aware client

1. Client sends a *ClientHello* message.

2. Server responds with a *ServerHello* message.
3. Server sends its *Certificate*.
4. Server sends also a *ServerHelloDone* message.

5. Client authenticates server.
6. Client sends its *Certificate*.
7. Client then sends a *ClientKeyExchange* message.
8. Client also sends a *CertificateVerify* message.
9. Client sends a *ChangeCipherSuite* message to indicate its ready state.
10. Finally, it sends a *Finished* message.

11. Server sends a *ChangeCipherSuite* message to indicate its ready state.
12. Server sends a *Finished* message.

SSL-enabled server

Figure 32.36   Handshaking process of an SSL session

SSL does not mandate the inclusion of server or client authentication. However, most web applications that require security in data transfer, such as payment in an electronic commerce transaction, would require at least authentication of the server to ensure that the server the user is communicating with is the intended merchant for the transaction. Some applications would require authentication of the client, or both client and server. Authentication is accomplished through the use of digital certificates as shown in the previous steps.

32.9.4   Security in WAP client-server communications

The WTLS technology is the counterpart of SSL over the wireless network. For it to work, both parties must implement WTLS. In the context of WAP applications, the two parties are typically a microbrowser and WAP server or gateway. As in SSL, WTLS relies on digital certificates to implement authentication and negotiate a secure communications path between the microbrowser and the WAP server.

We will not go through the protocol in detail. Figure 32.37 illustrates a typical negotiation process between a microbrowser and WAP server that requires authentication of both parties.

Refer to the WTLS specifications by the WAP Forum for more details of the various steps. You can find it at http://www.wapforum.org/what/technical.htm.

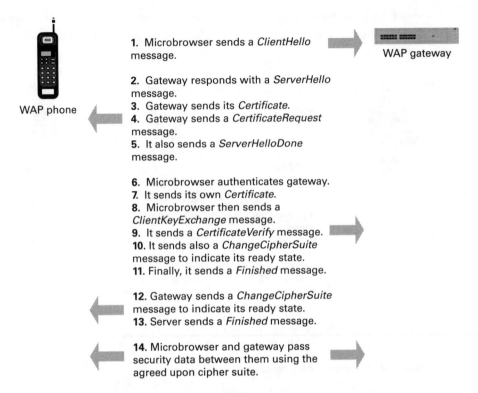

1. Microbrowser sends a *ClientHello* message.

WAP gateway

WAP phone

2. Gateway responds with a *ServerHello* message.
3. Gateway sends its *Certificate*.
4. Gateway sends a *CertificateRequest* message.
5. It also sends a *ServerHelloDone* message.

6. Microbrowser authenticates gateway.
7. It sends its own *Certificate*.
8. Microbrowser then sends a *ClientKeyExchange* message.
9. It sends a *CertificateVerify* message.
10. It sends also a *ChangeCipherSuite* message to indicate its ready state.
11. Finally, it sends a *Finished* message.

12. Gateway sends a *ChangeCipherSuite* message to indicate its ready state.
13. Server sends a *Finished* message.

14. Microbrowser and gateway pass security data between them using the agreed upon cipher suite.

Figure 32.37   Handshaking process of a WTLS session

Here are some constraints when implementing the WTLS protocol:

- Overhead incurred in sending messages (such as certificates) during the hand-shaking process slows down the system since the wireless transmission rate is still rather modest.

- Limited processing power of the wireless device must be taken into consideration when deciding on the cryptographic algorithms that the device must support.

- Limited RAM capacity of the wireless device also restricts the types of cryptographic algorithm to support. Some algorithms require a lot of parameters and thus take up more memory. Storage of client certificates for authentication, as well as private keys, may also be a concern.

Security in wireless communications has become an important issue that needs to be addressed in promoting mobile commerce using wireless devices. Below are some web sites that you may want to visit for available security solutions provided by different organizations:

- http://www.entrust.com/products/wapcerts/index.htm
- http://www.globalsign.com/digital_certificate/wireless_security/index.cfm
- http://www.verisign.com/products/wireless/index.html

32.10 SUMMARY

In this chapter, we walked through the configuration of two WAP gateways, WAPlite and the Nokia WAP Server 1.1. We also explained how to use a WAP gateway to test your applications using emulators as the user agents.

We discussed a high-level network diagram of how network operators typically deploy WAP gateways. Our goal was to dispel common myths that readers may have concerning how WAP requests are eventually delivered and fulfilled via a third-party WAP gateway such as that provided by a network operator.

Finally, we discussed security based on the overall WAP-web architecture we have covered so far. Both SSL and WTLS were explained and various issues of wireless security were discussed. By doing so, we have tried to provide the information you need to develop and deploy secure WAP applications.

In the next chapter, we will look at the issues of configuring some of the popular WAP devices available in the market.

C H A P T E R   3 3

Configuring WAP devices

33.1   INTRODUCTION

As mentioned in the previous chapter, it is of ultimate importance to test your applications using the actual devices and the WAP gateway. This is to make sure that the features you have implemented work—as you expect them to—in the real environment.

After testing your application via an emulated phone and an actual WAP gateway, the next challenge is to launch it using a WAP-enabled phone. The main task to perform here is to set up the parameters to successfully connect to a WAP gateway. The set of parameters to configure vary across different phone models. Basically, they should provide sufficient information about your Internet service provider (ISP) and the WAP gateway to which you are connecting.

Table 33.1 shows the typical parameters that need to be configured to use WAP services.

In this chapter, we will walk through the procedure to configure a WAP phone to work with a WAP gateway. The objective is to give you a general idea of the typical

Table 33.1   Typical connection parameters for using WAP services

Connection parameter	Description
Dial-up number	The number for establishing a connection with your ISP
Dial type	The call type, which may be analog or digital such as ISDN depending on your operator
User ID and password	The attributes of the account for logon to the ISP
Gateway's IP address and port	IP address and port number of a WAP gateway
Default home page	The first page you wish to load when accessing the Internet service

parameters that you need to set to prepare the phone for using WAP services. We will illustrate the configuration setting of a few common models:

- Ericsson R320
- Ericsson R380
- Siemens S35

33.2   ERICSSON R320

The Ericsson R320 phone (figure 33.1) is the first Ericsson phone to contain a WAP microbrowser. Besides its characteristic slim design, a notable aspect is its large screen, which makes for easy reading. Some of its other features and capabilities are:

Figure 33.1   Ericsson R320 WAP phone

- Dual band GSM 900/1800 that helps improve its coverage offered by the network operator
- WAP services
- Built-in data capabilities
- Full graphic display
- Support for full SMS services and input of Chinese names in the phone book through its complete Chinese interface and keyboard

33.2.1   Configuring Ericsson R320 for WAP services

To set up your Ericsson R320 to access WAP services, follow these instructions:

1   Press the right or left arrow until you see the WAP Services menu.
2   Scroll down using the down arrow and select WAP Settings.

3   Select a Profile from 1 to 5.

4   Select Rename.

5   Type a new profile name and click OK.

6   Under WAP Settings, select Edit Homepage or Chg Homepage and type the URL of the deck you want to set as home page, e.g., http://www.developersEd.com/home.wml.

7   Click Yes to save.

8   Select Communication.

9   For Access Type, select GSM Data.

10 Press Yes to save.

11 Select Phone number: If you have an Internet account with a local ISP, enter the dial-up number.

12 Press Yes.

13 For Dial type, select Analog or ISDN (refer to your service provider or telecommunications operator for the exact one to use).

14 Press Yes.

15 For User ID, enter the user ID of your account with the service provider.

16 Press Yes.

17 For Password, enter the password of your account with the service provider.

18 Press Yes.

19 Enter any value in option 5 in the GSM Data menu, Inactive Timeout, to indicate the number of seconds of inactivity before the telephone disconnects, e.g. 300.

20 Press No to return to the previous menu: Communication.

21 Select Gateway.

22 Select GSM Data address and enter the IP address of the WAP gateway, which could be any public WAP gateway.

23 Press Yes.

24 When you are back in the Gateway menu, keep pressing No until you leave the menu mode.

33.2.2   Loading a WML deck

To load a WML deck on your R320, follow these steps:

1   Scroll to the WAP Services menu.

2   Press Yes.

3   Select Homepage to fetch the default home deck that was configured earlier or Enter Address to access any WML deck.

4 Press Yes.

5 If Enter Address was selected, enter the URL containing the desired WML deck (e.g., developersEd.com/home.wml) and press Yes.

If your WAP setting is correct, the appropriate WML card should be loaded and displayed on the phone device.

33.2.3 Options available during browsing

Figure 33.2 Menu showing the browsing options of an Ericsson R320 phone

When you are in a browsing session, you can access the Options menu to choose any option available in the Options page. There are two ways to access the Options menu:

- Press and hold Yes until the Options menu appears.
- Scroll to a screen area that does not contain any link, phone number, or email address and press Yes.

Although the options available depend on the Options page that you access, the Options menu typically provides options that are similar to those in table 33.2. Figure 33.2 shows the browsing options as seen in the phone window.

Table 33.2 Ericsson R320 browsing options

Browsing option	Description
Reload	Refreshes the current WAP page
Add bookmark	Adds the current WAP page to the bookmark list
Send as SMS	Sends the current WAP page as a bookmark to another phone via SMS
New homepage	Sets the current WAP page as homepage
Suspend/Go to Menu	Goes to the WAP Services menu to access bookmarks, etc.
Exit	Exits the browsing session

33.3 ERICSSON R380

The Ericsson R380 phone (figure 33.3) is a compact, dual-band smart phone. It incorporates a built-in Personal Digital Assistant (PDA) and it offers an impressive array of capabilities such as:

- Multilanguage support
- Games
- Unified messaging
- Email, SMS, fax
- Handwriting recognition capability
- Touch screen capability
- WAP services

Figure 33.3 Ericsson R380 WAP phone

The R380 utilizes the EPOC operating system from Symbian. For more information on EPOC and Symbian, go to http://www.symbian.com/.

SYMBIAN   Formerly the software subsidiary of Psion, Symbian was established as an independent company in June 1998 by Ericsson, Motorola, Nokia, and Psion.

Symbian's mission is to set the standard for mobile wireless operating systems and to enable a mass market for wireless information devices.

The company aims to maximize long-term value to its principal customers' businesses by:

- Developing core software, application frameworks, applications, and development tools for wireless information devices
- Evangelizing standards for the interoperation of wireless information devices with wireless networks, content services, messaging, and enterprise-wide solutions

33.3.1   Configuring Ericsson R380 for WAP services

In this section we will illustrate the steps needed to configure your R380 for WAP services.

1. First configure the WAP gateway to dial into for WAP services by selecting the Extras tab. Make the selection by tapping on the touch-screen using the stylus provided.

2. Select the System icon from the main menu (figure 33.4).

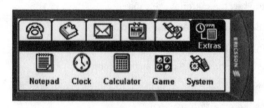

Figure 33.4
Main menu of Ericsson R380

3. Select Preferences from the System configuration screen (figure 33.5).

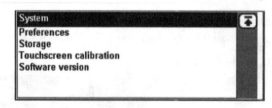

Figure 33.5
System menu of Ericsson R380

4 Select WAP services option (figure 33.6).

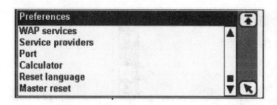

Figure 33.6
Preferences menu of
Ericsson R380

5 Select Gateway in the WAP Services Settings screen (figure 33.7).

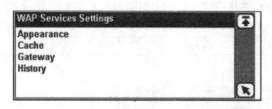

Figure 33.7
WAP Services Settings
menu of Ericsson R380

6 A default gateway would have been set up for you. In our case, we want to configure a new gateway. Select New Gateway (figure 33.8).

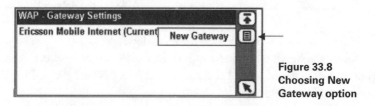

Figure 33.8
Choosing New
Gateway option

7 In the New Gateway screen (figure 33.9), supply the information in table 33.3.

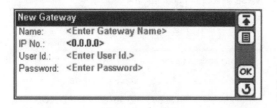

Figure 33.9
Dialog screen for entering information of a new gateway

Table 33.3   Gateway information

Name	Name of the WAP gateway that you are dialing in
IP No.	IP address of the WAP gateway
User ID	User ID that is assigned by your service provider
Password	Password provided by your service provider

Figure 33.10 shows some of the information we provided.

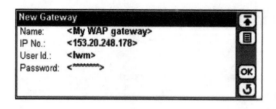

Figure 33.10
Example of a new gateway

The User ID and the Password fields are not always needed. Check with your service provider to see if they are required.

8 Once you have keyed in the information, select Set as Current to set the current gateway as the default (figure 33.11). This gateway will be used for future WAP sessions.

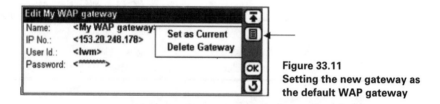

Figure 33.11
Setting the new gateway as the default WAP gateway

Next you need to set the Service Providers.

Select the Service Providers option in the Preferences screen (figure 33.6). Press ▤ on the right-hand side of the screen and select New Service Provider. Supply the information in table 33.4.

Table 33.4 Parameters for setting up a service provider

Name	Name of your service provider
Tel. Number	Telephone number for you to dial in
Bearer capability	Bearer type
Username	Username supplied by your service provider to allow logon
Password	Password supplied by your service provider
Confirm password	Same as password above—to ensure no typo was made

Once the above information is input, press OK to save the configuration. You are now ready to access your WAP gateway!

33.3.2 Loading a WML deck

Ensuring that your gateway setting is correct is a five-step process.

1 Tab on the WAP services menu (figure 33.12).

Figure 33.12
Choosing WAP services
from the main menu

2 Select the Browser icon to launch the WAP browser and you should see the Welcome screen (figure 33.13).

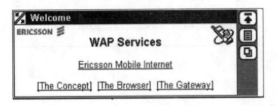

Figure 33.13
Welcome screen of WAP services

3 To load a WML deck from your gateway, press ▤ and select Open Location (figure 33.14).

Figure 33.14
Choosing Open Location

4 When the Go to Location screen appears, enter the URL of the WML deck and press OK (figure 33.15).

Figure 33.15
Entering URL of a WML
deck to be loaded

5   If your gateway is running and the configuration was done correctly, you should see the specified WAP page in your WAP browser (figure 33.16).

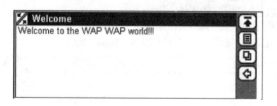

Figure 33.16
Display of hello.wml in the
microbrowser of Ericsson R380

33.4   SIEMENS S35

The Siemens S35 phone is also a dual-band handphone (figure 33.17). Its capabilities include:

- Integrated antenna
- WAP capability
- Infrared interface: IrDA
- Large screen

Figure 33.17   Siemens S35 WAP phone

33.4.1   Configuring for WAP services

The following steps guide you through the procedure to configure your Siemens S35 phone for WAP services:

1   Select Internet from the Menu.

2   Select an unused profile and press OK. (Siemens S35 supports up to five profiles so you can configure your phone to connect to multiple WAP gateways.)

3   Select Settings.

4   Enter a Profile name.

5   Enter the phone number of the server provider that you are dialing in.

6   Change the Call Type to Analog.

7   Enter the Log-in Name for logging into the service provider.

8   Enter the Password for your account with the service provider.

9   Enter the IP address of the WAP gateway that you are using.

10   Enter the IP Port of the WAP gateway you are using, typically one of the following values: 9200, 9201, 9202, or 9203. You may want to refer to chapter 32 regarding the setting of port numbers for a WAP gateway.

11   Set the default home page to be loaded after connection.

12 Set the Linger-time that determines the amount of time to wait before disconnecting due to user inactivity.

13 Press Back to go back to the selected profile menu and select Activate.

33.4.2 Loading a WML deck

Once the configuration of the device is completed, you are ready to load your first WAP page from the gateway.

Perform the following steps to test your setup:

1 Select Internet from the Menu.

2 Select Home to connect to the gateway that you have specified.

3 To load some other specific WAP page, select Navigation from the Menu.

4 Select Go to URL and key in the URL of the WML deck that you want to load from.

If your phone is configured correctly, you should see the specified WAP page loaded.

33.4.3 Setting a home page

To load a default WML deck when the WAP device is connected to the service provider, do the following:

1 Select Internet from the Menu.

2 Select Profiles.

3 Choose the profile that you want to set the home (default) page and press OK.

4 Select Settings.

5 Scroll down the list of options, and select item number 8 (Home) and press OK.

6 Enter the URL of your default home page.

The next time you connect using the profile that you have selected, the default home page would automatically be loaded.

33.5 GENERAL TIPS ON TESTING

This section provides some simple tips to make testing WAP applications on the actual WAP phone less painful.

The first tip concerns minimizing the input required from the user so as to make the testing less tedious. This tip is also applicable to the actual deployment of your WAP applications. The second tip concerns the placement of the WAP gateway, specifically with respect to the RAS server.

33.5.1 Handling entry of long URLs

One of the frustrations in testing WAP applications is entering lengthy URLs. If you disagree, you must be using emulators all along. When testing WAP applications, you don't have the luxury of a keyboard. You have to manually key in the URL using the numeric keypad. While the speed in keying in characters using the numeric keypad will improve over time, we don't think that is the right way to go.

We have thought of a simple method to quickly launch your application without requiring you to spend too much time on the key-pressing task. Consider the following WML deck:

```
<?xml version="1.0"?>
<!DOCTYPE wml PUBLIC "-//WAPFORUM//DTD WML 1.1//EN"
"http://www.wapforum.org/DTD/wml_1.1.xml">
<wml>
  <card id="card1" title="Home">
    <p>
        <a href="http://localhost/currency.wml">Currency Converter</a>
        <a href="http://localhost/calendar.asp">Calendar System</a>
    </p>
  </card>
</wml>
```

Creates a hot link that loads the deck, currency.wml, from the specified host when activated

Creates a hot link that loads the deck, calendar.asp, from the specified host when activated

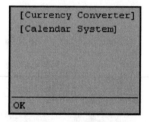

Figure 33.18 A page with two hot links serving as options for loading the appropriate decks

The simple WML deck in the example contains two `<a>` elements. Each defines a link to a WAP application. Imagine that you need to test the two applications using a WAP device (figure 33.18). Using the normal way, you have to connect to the RAS server, followed by manually keying in the URL of the targeted application. This is time-consuming and error prone.

A better approach is to set the WML deck as your default home page. When you connect to your RAS server, the deck is automatically loaded and testing your application is just a couple of clicks away rather than tedious pressing of keys to enter the possibly lengthy URL.

To add more applications, simply add more `<a>` elements linking to your applications.

33.5.2   Connecting WAP devices to gateways

While you may be running your own RAS server and allowing WAP devices to be connected to it, note that it is not necessary for you to run your own gateway. So long as your RAS server is connected to the Internet, you can specify a remote WAP gateway to connect to. The remote WAP gateway may either be a public gateway such as that hosted by a telco or a gateway that is hosted by someone else on a remote machine.

Refer to the diagram in section 32.7 for a clearer picture of the connectivity of the RAS server and the WAP gateway hosted by a telco. If you are setting up your own RAS server, the server will then be in your premises instead of under the roof of the telco.

A common misconception is that the gateway must be installed on the same machine as the RAS server. This is not necessary, though it is common when testing your WAP applications during development.

33.6 SUMMARY

This chapter provided a quick configuration guide for three common handsets. This chapter is not intended to be an exhaustive guide to the configuration of these three devices. The manuals that come with the handsets are reliable sources to refer to when in doubt. You should also consult your network operator on issues such as dialing up or connectivity problems.

The following summarizes the typical parameters that need to be configured to use the WAP services:

- Dial-up number to the service provider
- Dial type or call type (e.g. Analog or ISDN)
- User ID and password to the service provider
- Gateway's IP Address and port number
- Default home page

In the next part of this book, we shall present two case studies demonstrating technologies and programming techniques that were introduced and discussed in considerable length in the earlier chapters.

PART X

Case studies

Often the best way to learn is by example. The case studies in this section describe how the technologies in this book were leveraged to provide solutions for real-world requirements.

C H A P T E R   3 4

Mobile inventory and ordering system

34.1   INTRODUCTION

In this chapter, we will look at a case study of how a business can make use of WAP technology to enhance its effectiveness.

Manning Store supplies quality computer books to retailers. These retailers are the conventional bookstores and supermarkets, which in turn sell to readers like you and me. The sales personnel at Manning Store regularly visit the retail outlets to check that stocks are adequate. Very often the retailers want to check if a particular title is available and how much stock they should order.

To check stock information, each Manning sales representative carries a notebook computer which lists the titles and prices in the publisher's inventory. The information is updated at the end of each day but that does not mean it is current at the time a salesperson makes a call. Titles may be reserved by other clients and the information is not updated until day's end.

An alternative would be to use the Internet for checking the stock information. However, this method is cumbersome and time consuming: An Internet connection must be available and the notebook computer must be booted up and connected.

The desired solution must provide the following functionality at the touch of a button:

- Search for books by ISBN or title
- List the price of a book and its discounted price for a particular bookstore
- List the stock quantity of a title
- List the number of reservations for a title
- View the cover of a book
- Place a reservation for a title
- Change a reservation
- View the reservations of bookstores (retailers)

With WAP, all these are possible. The salesperson could dial in to a WAP gateway provided by a telco and access the WAP application hosted by Manning. In this case study, we will illustrate how we can make use of the concepts covered in earlier chapters to build such an application.

34.2 SETUP

For this case study, we will be using:

- Microsoft Access 97 to simulate a database server
- Microsoft Internet Information Server 4.0 as the web server
- UP.Simulator to emulate a WAP device

34.2.1 Why use Microsoft Access?

We know some hardcore developers are screaming now! Why do we have to choose Access as the database since it is not suitable for multithreaded applications like the web environment? We are aware of this limitation but for the benefit of readers who do not have a database server installed we think that it is more beneficial to base our example on Access. If you are adapting the example used in this case study in the real world, we strongly suggest that a database server like Microsoft SQL Server or Oracle Server be used instead. Anyway, it is not difficult to port the database in this example to a database server.

34.3 DATABASE STRUCTURE

Figure 34.1 shows the database relationships.

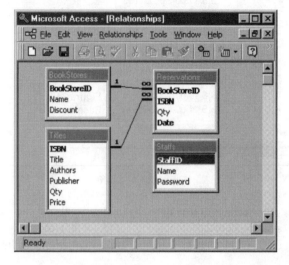

Figure 34.1
Database relationships

There are four tables within the database:

- *BookStores*—Maintains information about bookstores
- *Titles*—Maintains information about the books
- *Staffs*—Staff list and StaffID and password
- *Reservations*—Reservations details

34.4 TABLE STRUCTURE

Figures 34.2 through 34.5 show some of the records in the tables.

BookStoreID	Name	Discount
S66533	Best Books	30
S87653	Knowledge Books	25
S87664	AMK Books	40
S98877	GE BookStore	30

Figure 34.2   BookStores

The BookStores table (figure 34.2) contains the Discount field, which lists the discount rate for each bookstore. Using this field, our application is able to automatically calculate the price of a book for a particular bookstore. This feature allows Manning's salesperson to quickly find out the price of books for a particular bookstore.

The Reservations table (figure 34.3) stores the reservation made by a salesperson for a bookstore. The date of reservation contains the date as well as the time the reservation was made. Note that the date and time are separated by a hyphen. To simplify this case study, we will not be concerned about reservations made by different salespeople. We simply assume the reservations are made by a single salesperson. The focus is on the reservations for the various bookstores.

BookStoreID	ISBN	Qty	Date
S66533	188477766X	3	8/7/00-11:47:33 AM
S66533	1884777716	9	8/7/00-11:47:57 AM
S66533	1884777902	3	8/11/00-2:05:00 PM
S66533	1884777996	7	8/12/00-1:13:24 PM
S66533	1884777996	7	8/12/00-1:13:31 PM
S87653	1884777651	6	8/13/00-8:35:31 PM
S87653	188477766X	4	8/12/00-1:10:39 PM
S87664	1884777651	6	8/11/00-1:44:24 PM
S87664	1884777651	6	8/11/00-1:44:43 PM
S87664	1884777651	6	8/11/00-1:44:45 PM
S87664	1884777651	6	8/11/00-1:44:46 PM

Figure 34.3 Reservations

StaffID	Name	Password
fsm	Foo Soo Mee	uyer8346
lwm	Lee Wei Meng	secret

Figure 34.4   Staffs

The Staffs table (figure 34.4) contains basic information about the salesperson such as, StaffID, Name, and Password.

The Titles table (figure 34.5) contains information on the books in inventory.

ISBN	Title	Authors	Publisher	Qty	Price
1884777651	Distributed Programming with Java	Qusay H. Mahmoud	Manning	100	49.99
188477766X	Java Servlets by Example	Alan R. Williamson	Manning	50	55.99
1884777678	Java Foundation Classes	Stephen C. Drye and	Manning	45	50
1884777716	Server-Based Java Programming	Ted Neward	Manning	200	60
1884777813	Python and Tkinter Programming	John E. Grayson	Manning	22	56.99
1884777848	Swing	Matthew Robinson ar	Manning	45	56
1884777856	Database Programming for Handheld Devi	Kouros Gorgani	Manning	23	49.99
1884777902	3D User Interfaces with Java 3D	Jon Barrilleaux	Manning	44	34.99
188477797X	Java 3D Programming	Daniel Selman	Manning	55	77
1884777996	Web Development with JavaServer Pages	Duane K. Fields and	Manning	33	60
1930110030	Domino Development with Java	Patton, Anthony	Manning	44	56

Figure 34.5   Titles

34.5   SYSTEM FLOW DIAGRAM

Figure 34.6 shows the flow of the WAP application to be discussed in detail in this section.

NOTE   We have tested the example in this case study using the UP.Simulator. As usability is still a tricky issue as far as WAP 1.1/WAP 1.2 is concerned, you may experience some glitches running this example on other emulators or real handsets. If you do, make minor changes to the codes. The main aim of this case study is to illustrate how the concepts that we learned earlier can be pieced together to create a WAP application.

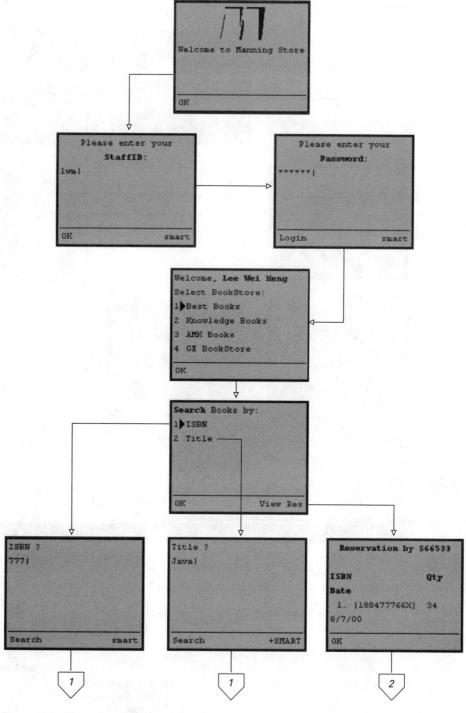

Figure 34.6 Flow of our WAP application (continued on next page)

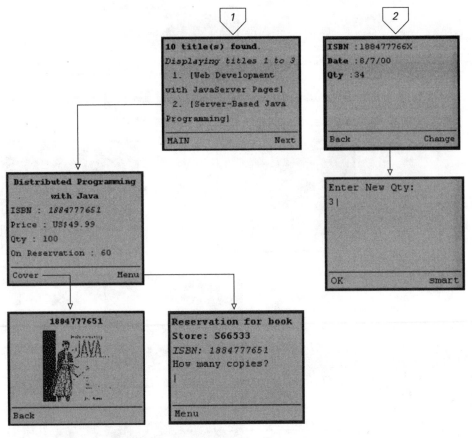

Figure 34.6   Flow of our WAP application (continued)

34.5.1   Welcome deck

The first deck to load for this case study is Welcome.wml.

Listing 34.1   Code for Welcome.wml

```
<?xml version="1.0"?>
<!DOCTYPE wml PUBLIC "-//WAPFORUM//DTD WML 1.1//EN"
"http://www.wapforum.org/DTD/wml_1.1.xml">
<wml>
    <card id="welcome" title="Welcome" ontimer="login.wml">   ❶
        <timer value="10"/>   ❷
        <p align="center">
            <img src="logo.wbmp" alt="Logo"/>        ◄──── Displays
        </p>                                                 the WBMP
        <p align="center">        ◄── The align attribute       file
                                      specifies the positioning
                                      of the paragraph
```

```
          Welcome to Manning Store
      </p>
   </card>
</wml>
```

Code comments

❶ The `<card>` element contains the `ontimer` attribute which indicates the deck to load when the `<timer>` element expires.

❷ The `<timer>` element will expire after 1 second. The `value` attribute is in the unit of 1/10 seconds.

Figure 34.7 shows the welcome card. We used the `<timer>` element to set the expiry time for the card. When the time is up (10 seconds), the Login.wml deck is loaded. We also display the logo of Manning in the WBMP format.

Figure 34.7
The welcome card

34.5.2   The login deck

When the `<timer>` element in the welcome deck expires, the WAP browser loads the login.wml deck.

Listing 34.2   Code for Login.wml

```
<?xml version="1.0"?>
<!DOCTYPE wml PUBLIC "-//WAPFORUM//DTD WML 1.1//EN"
"http://www.wapforum.org/DTD/wml_1.1.xml">
<wml>
<card id="card1" title="Login">
   <p align="center">
      Please enter your <b>StaffID</b>:
         <input type="text" name="StaffID" maxlength="8"/>        ❶
      Please enter your <b>Password</b>:
         <input type="password" name="Password" maxlength="8"/>   ❷
      <do type="accept" label="Login">
         <go method="post" href="Authenticate.asp">       ❸
            <postfield name="StaffID" value="$StaffID" />      ❹
            <postfield name="Password" value="$Password" />
         </go>
      </do>
   </p>
</card>
</wml>
```

Code comments

❶ The `<input>` element for StaffID has a maximum length of eight characters.

❷ The `type="password"` attribute value ensures that the password is not echoed on the screen.

❸ The `href` attribute specifies the deck to load and the `method` attribute indicates using either the GET or POST method.

❹ The `<postfield>` element posts the value from the client side to the server side.

When the salesperson has keyed in his StaffID and password (figure 34.8), the information is sent to the Authenticate.asp document using the POST method.

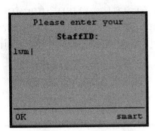

Figure 34.8
Logging to the system

34.5.3 Authenticating the staff login

The salesperson's StaffID and password are authenticated against the database. The authentication source code is in listing 34.3.

Listing 34.3 Code for Authenticate.asp

```
<% Response.ContentType = "text/vnd.wap.wml" %>
<?xml version="1.0"?>
<!DOCTYPE wml PUBLIC "-//WAPFORUM//DTD WML 1.1//EN"
"http://www.wapforum.org/DTD/wml_1.1.xml">
<wml>
    <card id="card1" title="Verify">
        <p>
        <%
        Dim conn, rs
        Set conn = Server.CreateObject("ADODB.Connection")      ◁  Creates an instance of the Connection object ❶
        Set rs   = Server.CreateObject("ADODB.Recordset")   ❶
        '---Opens the connection to the database---
        conn.open "DRIVER={Microsoft Access Driver (*.mdb)};DBQ=" &
            Server.MapPath("Publishers.mdb") & ";"       Forms the connection string to connect to the database. This method is known as "DSN-less" ❷
        '---Retrieve the user's record
        sql = "SELECT * FROM Staffs WHERE StaffID='" &
            Request.Form("StaffID") &
            "' AND Password='" & Request.Form("Password") & "'"    ❷
        Set rs = conn.Execute (sql)     ❸
        if rs.EOF then '---means staffID and Password does not match---     ❹
```

```
        Response.Write "Invalid Login. "
    %>
        <do type="options" label="Retry">        ◁┐  Allows the staff to try
            <go href="Login.wml"/>                  │  the login process again
        </do>
    <%
    else
        Response.Write "Welcome, <b>" & rs.Fields("Name") & "</b><br/>"
    %>
        <do type="options" label="View Res">
            <go href="ViewReservation.asp?bookStoreID=$(bookStore)" />
        </do>

        Select BookStore:                     │  Create a selection list using
        <select name="bookStore">        ◁┘  the <select> element
        <%
            sql = "SELECT * FROM BookStores"
            set rs = conn.Execute(sql)
            While not rs.EOF              ◁─────────────────────────────┐
                Response.Write "<option value='" &                     │
                    rs("BookStoreID") & "'>" & rs("Name")              │
                    & "</option>"                    Displays all the  │
                rs.MoveNext                          bookstores available│
            Wend
        %>
        </select>

        <b>Search</b> Books by:                              Link to the card
        <select name="searchBy">                             to search by ISBN
            <option value=
                "isbn" onpick="searchBy.wml#searchISBN">ISBN</option>  ◁┘
            <option value=
                "title" onpick="searchBy.wml#searchTitle">Title</option> ◁┐
        </select>
    <%                                                       Link to the card
    end if                                                   to search by Title
    rs.Close
    conn.Close
    Set rs=Nothing
    Set conn = Nothing
    %>
        </p>
    </card>
</wml>
```

Code comments

❶ Creates an instance of the `Recordset` object.

❷ Retrieves the record with the specified StaffID and Password.

❸ Uses the `Connection` object to execute the SQL query.

❹ If the recordset EOF property is `true`, indicates Staff could not be found.

If the StaffID and password can be found in the database, the authentication is successful and our application greets the salesperson by displaying his name (figure 34.9).

The salesperson next selects a bookstore. This is essential, as all the functionality of the system after this card would be based on this bookstore. For example, the prices of books selected would be based on the discount rate for that particular bookstore.

Next, the staff is presented with two search options (figure 34.10).

 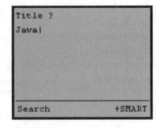

Figure 34.9
Greeting the salesperson

Figure 34.10
Search options

The staff can search for a book by using either the ISBN or part of a title (figure 34.11).

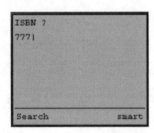

Figure 34.11
Searching either by ISBN or title

```
<b>Search</b> Books by:
<select name="searchBy">
  <option value="isbn" onpick="searchBy.wml#searchISBN">ISBN</option>
  <option value="title" onpick="searchBy.wml#searchTitle">Title</option>
</select>
```

The onpick attribute of the <option> element indicates the deck and card to navigate to when the user chooses that particular option. In this case, the searchBy.wml deck is loaded.

```
<?xml version="1.0"?>
<!DOCTYPE wml PUBLIC "-//WAPFORUM//DTD WML 1.1//EN"
"http://www.wapforum.org/DTD/wml_1.1.xml">
<wml>

  <card id="searchISBN" title="ISBN">    ◄——  The card to search by ISBN
    <p>
```

```
          ISBN ? <input type="text" name="ISBN" maxlength="14"/>
            <do type="accept" label="Search">
               <go href="search.asp" method="post">
                  <postfield name="ISBN" value="$(ISBN)"/>
                  <postfield name="Type" value="ISBN"/>
                  <postfield name="BookStore" value="$(bookStore)"/>
               </go>
            </do>
      </p>
   </card>
```

Links to the search.asp document and sends the information using the `<postfield>` element

```
   <card id="searchTitle" title="Title">    ←── The card to search by Title
      <p>
          Title ? <input type="text" name="Title" maxlength="20"/>
            <do type="accept" label="Search">
               <go href="search.asp" method="post">
                  <postfield name="Title" value="$(Title)"/>
                  <postfield name="Type" value="Title"/>
                  <postfield name="BookStore" value="$(bookStore)"/>
               </go>
            </do>
      </p>
   </card>
</wml>
```

Links to the search.asp document and sends the information using the `<postfield>` element

Once the search criteria have been keyed in, the search.asp document is loaded.

34.5.4   Performing the search

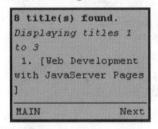

Figure 34.12   Displaying the records found

Depending on the search type, we will build the SQL statement to retrieve the titles from the table. However, the number of titles retrieved may be large, and attempting to list them in a single card will exceed the limit of the size of the WAP binary. This is clearly not feasible.

Hence, in this deck, we split the listing in groups of threes. Every card can display up to a maximum of three titles (figure 34.12).

Listing 34.4   Source code for Search.asp

```
<% Response.ContentType = "text/vnd.wap.wml"    Prevents the deck
   Response.Expires = -1            ←───────┘   from being cached
%>
<!--#include file="adovbs.inc"-->    ←┐ Includes the adovbs.inc file for the
<?xml version="1.0"?>                 │ ADO constants used in the document
<!DOCTYPE wml PUBLIC "-//WAPFORUM//DTD WML 1.1//EN"
"http://www.wapforum.org/DTD/wml_1.1.xml">
<wml>

   <card id="card1" title="Result">
      <p>
```

```
<%
Dim conn, rs
Set conn = Server.CreateObject("ADODB.Connection")
Set rs   = Server.CreateObject("ADODB.Recordset")
'---Opens the connection to the database---
conn.open "DRIVER={Microsoft Access Driver (*.mdb)};DBQ=" &
    Server.MapPath("Publishers.mdb") & ";"

'---determine the search type
if Request.Form("Type") = "ISBN" then
    sql = "SELECT * FROM Titles WHERE ISBN LIKE '%" &          | Select based
        Request.Form("ISBN") & "%'"                            | on ISBN
elseif Request.Form("Type") = "Title" then
    sql = "SELECT * FROM Titles WHERE Title LIKE '%" &         | Select based
        Request.Form("Title") & "%'"                           | on Title
end if

rs.Open sql, conn, adOpenStatic, adLockReadOnly, adCmdText
                                              Opens the recordset using
if rs.EOF then                                 the adOpenStatic cursor
    Response.Write "No title found!"
else
    rs.MoveLast
    recordCount = rs.RecordCount    <- Retrieves the total record count
    rs.MoveFirst    <- Moves to the first record

    rs.PageSize = 3    <- Sets the number of records per page to 3
    PageNo = CInt(Request.Form("PageNo"))
    if PageNo = 0 then     <-| If the deck is loaded for the      Retrieves the
        PageNo = 1           | first time, sets the page to 1     current record
    end if                                                        page number
                                   | Sets the current
    rs.AbsolutePage = PageNo    <-| page number
    count = 0
    Response.Write "<b>" & recordCount & " title(s) found.</b><br/>"
    Response.Write "<i>Displaying titles " &
        ((PageNo-1) * rs.PageSize )+ 1 & " to "
    if (rs.PageSize * PageNo) > recordCount then          Displays the title
        Response.Write recordCount & "</i><br/>"          "Displaying titles
    Else                                                  from x to y"
        Response.Write ((PageNo-1) * rs.PageSize )+
            rs.PageSize & "</i><br/>"
    end if

    While not rs.EOF AND count<rs.PageSize     <-| Displays the current
        count = count + 1                        | list of records
        Response.Write count + ((PageNo-1) * rs.PageSize) &
            ". <a href='DisplayBook.asp?BookStore=" &
            Request.Form("BookStore") & "&amp;ISBN=" &
            rs("ISBN") & "'>" & rs("Title") & "</a><br/>"
        rs.MoveNext
    Wend                                Links to the main page where
                                        the Staff is authenticated again

    Response.Write "<do type='accept' label='MAIN'>"
    Response.Write "   <go href='authenticate.asp' method='post'>"
    Response.Write "      <postfield name='StaffID'
                           value='$(StaffID)' />"
```

```
            Response.Write "          <postfield name='Password'
                                 value='$(Password)' />"
            Response.Write "     </go>"

            Response.Write "</do>"           Displays the Next
            if not rs.EOF then         ◄──┘ Page link
               Response.Write    "<do type='accept' label='Next'>"
               Response.Write      "<go method='post' href='search.asp'>"
               Response.Write          "<postfield name='PageNo'
                                 value='" & PageNo + 1 & "'/>"
               Response.Write          "<postfield name='Type'
                                  value='" & Request.Form("Type") & "'/>"
               Response.Write          "<postfield name='BookStore'
                              value='" & Request.Form("BookStore") & "'/>"
               if Request.Form("Type")="ISBN" then
                  Response.Write         "<postfield name='ISBN'
                        value='" & Request.Form("ISBN") & "'/>"
               else
                  Response.Write         "<postfield name='Title'
                        value='" & Request.Form("Title") & "'/>"
               end if
               Response.Write         "</go>"
               Response.Write    "</do>"
            end if                            Displays the Previous
            if PageNo>1 then            ◄──┘ Page link
               Response.Write    "<do type='options' label='Previous'>"
               Response.Write      "<go method='post' href='search.asp'>"
               Response.Write          "<postfield name='PageNo'
                              value='" & PageNo - 1 & "'/>"
               Response.Write          "<postfield name='Type'
                              value='" & Request.Form("Type") & "'/>"
               Response.Write          "<postfield name='BookStore'
                              value='" & Request.Form("BookStore") & "'/>"
               if Request.Form("Type")="ISBN" then
                  Response.Write         "<postfield name='ISBN'
                              value='" & Request.Form("ISBN") & "'/>"
               else
                  Response.Write         "<postfield name='Title'
                              value='" & Request.Form("Title") & "'/>"
               end if
               Response.Write         "</go>"
               Response.Write    "</do>"
            end if
         end if

         rs.Close
         conn.Close
         Set rs=Nothing
         Set conn = Nothing
    %>
    </p>
    </card>
    </wml>
```

We have made use of the techniques we discussed in chapter 20 on database connectivity to perform paging on the recordsets (figure 34.13).

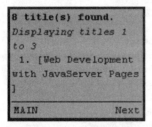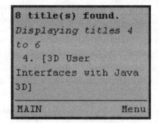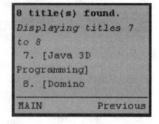

Figure 34.13 Displaying the records in multiple pages

NOTE   *A word about caching*   The HTTP header of –1 is not universally supported. A much safer option when trying to prevent caching is to use the following:

```
Response.Expires = -1
Response.AddHeader "Pragma", "no-cache"
Response.AddHeader "Cache-Control",
    "no cache, must-revalidate"
```

34.5.5   Displaying the book cover

In our case study, the company maintains another set of graphics for the mobile devices. The company has used the current images saved in the JPEG format and a converter to convert them to the WBMP file format. We will talk more about using a WBML converter later in this chapter.

For now, let's look at the codes for displaying the book cover:

Listing 34.5   Code for BookCover.asp

```
<% Response.ContentType = "text/vnd.wap.wml"
   Response.Expires = -1
%>
<?xml version="1.0"?>
<!DOCTYPE wml PUBLIC "-//WAPFORUM//DTD WML 1.1//EN"
"http://www.wapforum.org/DTD/wml_1.1.xml">
<wml>
   <card id="display" title="Book Cover">
      <p align="center">
         <b><% =Request.QueryString("ISBN") %></b><br/>
         <img src="<% =Request.QueryString("ISBN")%>.wbmp" alt="Book Cover"
/>
      </p>
      <do type="accept" label="Back">
         <prev/>
      </do>
   </card>
</wml>
```

Figure 34.14 Displaying a WBMP image

We have used the `<img>` element to display the book cover (figure 34.14).

```
<img src="<% =Request.QueryString("ISBN")%>.wbmp"
    alt="Book Cover" />
```

If the target WAP device does not support graphics, or if a book cover cannot be found, the string "Book Cover" will be shown.

34.5.6 Displaying detailed information

Once the list of titles is retrieved after the search, the detailed information of a book could be displayed if the user selects the link (figure 34.15).

```
3 title(s) found.
Displaying titles 1
to 3
  1. [Java Servlets by
Example]
▶2. [Distributed
Link
```

Figure 34.15 Link to a deck displaying detailed book information

Listing 34.6 Code for Displaybook.asp

```asp
<% Response.ContentType = "text/vnd.wap.wml"
   Response.Expires = -1
%>
<?xml version="1.0"?>
<!DOCTYPE wml PUBLIC "-//WAPFORUM//DTD WML
1.1//EN"
"http://www.wapforum.org/DTD/wml_1.1.xml">
<wml>
   <card id="display" title="Book Info">
      <%
      Dim conn, rs
      Set conn = Server.CreateObject("ADODB.Connection")
      Set rs   = Server.CreateObject("ADODB.Recordset")
      '---Opens the connection to the database---
      conn.open "DRIVER={Microsoft Access Driver (*.mdb)};DBQ=" &
         Server.MapPath("Publishers.mdb") & ";"

      '---Retrieve the Book information
      sql = "SELECT * FROM Titles WHERE ISBN='" &
         Request.QueryString("ISBN") & "'"
      Set rs = conn.Execute (sql)
      if not rs.EOF then '---means the book can be found---
      %>
      <p align="center">
         <do type="accept" label="Cover">
            <go href="BookCover.asp?ISBN=<% =rs("ISBN") %>" />   ◄
         </do>
         <do type="accept" label="Back">   ◄┐
            <prev/>
         </do>
         <do type="options" label="Reserve">   ◄┐
            <go href="#Reserve" />
```

Links to the card that displays the cover image

Goes back to the previous card

Links to the Reservation card

```
        </do>
    <%
        ISBN = rs("ISBN")
        Price = rs("Price")
        Response.write "<b>" & rs("Title") & "</b>"
        Response.Write "</p><p>"                          Displays the
                                                          book
        Response.write "ISBN  : <i>" & rs("ISBN") & "</i><br/>"   information
        Response.write "Price : US$$" & rs("Price") & "<br/>"
        Response.write "Qty   : " & rs("Qty") & "<br/>"

        '---sums up all the reservations
        sql = "SELECT Sum(Qty) as Total FROM Reservations WHERE ISBN='"&
            Request.QueryString("ISBN") & "'"      ← Sums up all the
        Set rs = conn.Execute (sql)                  reservations

        if not isNull(rs("Total")) then
            Response.write "On Reservation : " & rs("Total") & "<br/>"
        end if

        '---retrieve the discount information
        sql = "SELECT Discount FROM BookStores WHERE BookStoreID='" &
            Request.QueryString("BookStore") & "'"   ← Retrieves the
        Set rs = conn.Execute(sql)                     discount rate
        if not rs.EOF then
            Response.Write  "Discounted Price : US$$" &
                round(Price * (1-(CSng(rs("Discount")) / 100)), 2)
                & " (" & rs("Discount") & "% off)"
        end if
    end if
    %>
    </p>
</card>

<card id="Reserve" title="Reservation">      ⌐ Card to prompt for
    <p>                                          ┘ reservation
        <b>Reservation for book Store: $(bookStore)</b><br/>
        <i>ISBN: <% =ISBN %></i><br/>
        How many copies? <input type="text" name="copies" format="3N" />
        <do type="accept" label="Confirm">      ⌐ Links to the reservebooks.asp
            <go href="reservebooks.asp">          ┘ document
                <postfield name="copies" value="$(copies)" />
                <postfield name="ISBN" value="<% =ISBN %>" />
                <postfield name="bookStoreID" value="$bookStore"/>
            </go>
        </do>
        <do type="options" label="Cancel">
            <prev/>
        </do>
    </p>
</card>
</wml>
```

Let's dissect the codes and see how we did it. The result will look like the display in figure 34.16.

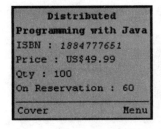

Figure 34.16
Detailed information of a book

First, we perform an SQL operation to retrieve the information of a book.

```
'---Retrieve the Book information
sql = "SELECT * FROM Titles WHERE ISBN='" &
    Request.QueryString("ISBN") & "'"
Set rs = conn.Execute (sql)
```

Once the book information is retrieved, we create the links to the book cover page, previous page, and the reservation page.

```
if not rs.EOF then '---means the book can be found---
%>
<p align="center">
    <do type="accept" label="Cover">
        <go href="BookCover.asp?ISBN=<% =rs("ISBN") %>" />
    </do>
    <do type="accept" label="Back">
        <prev/>
    </do>
    <do type="options" label="Reserve">
        <go href="#Reserve" />
    </do>
```

After that, we list the information of the book:

```
ISBN = rs("ISBN")
Price = rs("Price")
Response.write "<b>" & rs("Title") & "</b>"
Response.Write "</p><p>"

Response.write "ISBN  : <i>" & rs("ISBN") & "</i><br/>"
Response.write "Price : US$$" & rs("Price") & "<br/>"
Response.write "Qty   : " & rs("Qty") & "<br/>"
```

We also need to check the number of reservations for this title:

```
'---sums up all the reservations
sql = "SELECT Sum(Qty) as Total FROM Reservations WHERE ISBN='"&
        Request.QueryString("ISBN") & "'"
Set rs = conn.Execute (sql)
```

```
    if not isNull(rs("Total")) then
        Response.write "On Reservation : " & rs("Total") & "<br/>"
    end if
```

In addition, we need to check the discount rate of the book based on the bookstore.

```
    '---retrieve the discount information
    sql = "SELECT Discount FROM BookStores WHERE BookStoreID='" &
        Request.QueryString("BookStore") & "'"
    Set rs = conn.Execute(sql)
    if not rs.EOF then
      Response.Write  "Discounted Price : US$$" &
          round(Price * (1-(CSng(rs("Discount")) / 100)), 2) &
            " (" & rs("Discount") & "% off)"
    end if
  end if
  %>
  </p>
</card>
```

To reserve a book, pressing Menu will reveal the card in figure 34.17.

Select Reserve to reserve a book.

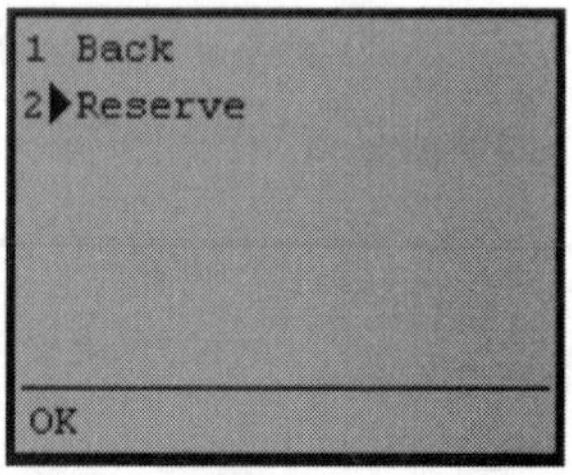

```
<card id="Reserve" title="Reservation">
  <p>
    <b>Reservation for book Store:
        $(bookStore)</b><br/>
    <i>ISBN: <% =ISBN %></i><br/>
    How many copies? <input type="text"
      name="copies" format="3N" />
    <do type="accept" label="Confirm">
      <go href="reservebooks.asp">
        <postfield name="copies" value="$(copies)" />
        <postfield name="ISBN" value="<% =ISBN %>" />
        <postfield name="bookStoreID" value="$bookStore"/>
      </go>
    </do>
    <do type="options" label="Cancel">
      <prev/>
    </do>
  </p>
</card>
```

Figure 34.17
Reserving a book

The card will prompt the salesperson to enter the number of copies to reserve. Once it is done, press Menu and select Confirm (figure 34.18).

 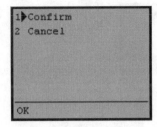

Figure 34.18
Specifying the copy of a book to reserve

Here is the source code for reserving a book.

Listing 34.7   Code for ReserveBooks.asp

```
<% Response.ContentType = "text/vnd.wap.wml"
   Response.Expires = -1
%>
<?xml version="1.0"?>
<!DOCTYPE wml PUBLIC "-//WAPFORUM//DTD WML 1.1//EN"
"http://www.wapforum.org/DTD/wml_1.1.xml">
<wml>
   <card id="reserve" title="Reservation">
      <p>
      <%
      Dim conn, rs
      Set conn = Server.CreateObject("ADODB.Connection")
      Set rs   = Server.CreateObject("ADODB.Recordset")
      '---Opens the connection to the database---
      conn.open "DRIVER={Microsoft Access Driver (*.mdb)};DBQ=" &
         Server.MapPath("Publishers.mdb") & ";"
      '---Insert a new reservation
      sql = "INSERT INTO Reservations VALUES ('" &
         Request.QueryString("bookStoreID")& "','" &
         Request.QueryString("ISBN") & "'," &
         Request.QueryString("copies") & ",'" &
          date & "-" & time & "')"

      On Error Resume Next
      conn.Execute (sql)
      if err.Number <> 0 then
         Response.Write "Reservation failed. Please try again!"
      else
         Response.Write "Reservation successful!"
      end if
      %>
         <do type="Back" label="Back">
             <prev/>
         </do>
      </p>
   </card>
</wml>
```

Forming the SQL to insert a new record

Error trapping to prevent any errors from crashing our script

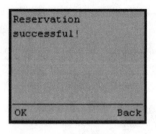

Figure 34.19 The reservation successful card

If the reservation is successful, the salesperson will be notified (figure 34.19).

34.5.7 Viewing reservation information

After the salesperson has selected the bookstore, he has the option of viewing the reservations for that particular bookstore (figure 34.20):

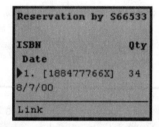

Figure 34.20
Viewing reservations

Listing 34.8 Code for ViewReservation.asp

```
<% Response.ContentType = "text/vnd.wap.wml"
   Response.Expires = -1
%>
<?xml version="1.0"?>
<!DOCTYPE wml PUBLIC "-//WAPFORUM//DTD WML 1.1//EN"
"http://www.wapforum.org/DTD/wml_1.1.xml">
<wml>
    <card id="reserve" title="Reservation">
        <p align="center">
        <%
        Dim conn, rs
        Set conn = Server.CreateObject("ADODB.Connection")
        Set rs   = Server.CreateObject("ADODB.Recordset")
        '---Opens the connection to the database---
        conn.open "DRIVER={Microsoft Access Driver (*.mdb)};DBQ=" &
            Server.MapPath("Publishers.mdb") & ";"
        '---retrieves the reservations
        sql = "SELECT * FROM Reservations WHERE BookStoreID='" &
            Request.QueryString("BookStoreID") & "'"
        Set rs = conn.Execute(sql)
```

◁ **Forming the SQL to retrieve all reservations for the bookstore**

```
      Response.Write "<b>Reservation by " &
         Request.QueryString("BookStoreID") & "</b></p>"
      Response.write "<p><table columns='3'>"
      Response.write
"<tr><td><b>ISBN</b></td><td><b>Qty</b></td><td><b>Date</b></td></tr>"
      counter = 0
      While not rs.EOF  ←——————————┐  Displaying all the
         counter = counter + 1     │  reservations
         Response.Write "<tr><td>" & counter & ". <a
href='DetailedReservation.asp?BookStoreID=" &
Request.QueryString("BookStoreID") & "&amp;ISBN=" & rs("ISBN") &
"&amp;Date=" & rs("date") & "'>" & rs("ISBN") & "</a></td><td>" & rs("Qty")
& "</td><td>" & rs("date") & "</td></tr>"
         rs.MoveNext
      Wend
      Response.write "</table>"
      %>
      </p>
   </card>
</wml>
```

We use the `<a>` element for linking each reservation.

34.5.8   Viewing detailed reservation information

Once a reservation is selected, the detailed information about that reservation is displayed (figure 34.21).

Figure 34.21   Details of the reservation

Listing 34.9   Detailedreservation.asp

```
<% Response.ContentType = "text/vnd.wap.wml"
   Response.Expires = -1
%>
<?xml version="1.0"?>
<!DOCTYPE wml PUBLIC "-//WAPFORUM//DTD WML
1.1//EN"
"http://www.wapforum.org/DTD/wml_1.1.xml">
<wml>
   <card id="reserve" title="Reservation">
      <p>
      <%
      Dim conn, rs
      Set conn = Server.CreateObject("ADODB.Connection")
      Set rs   = Server.CreateObject("ADODB.Recordset")
      '---Opens the connection to the database---
      conn.open "DRIVER={Microsoft Access Driver (*.mdb)};DBQ=" &
         Server.MapPath("Publishers.mdb") & ";"
      '---Retrieve the reservations
      sql = "SELECT * FROM Reservations WHERE ISBN='" &
         Request.QueryString("ISBN") & "' AND BookStoreID='" &
         Request.QueryString("BookStoreID") & "' AND Date='" &
         Request.QueryString("Date") & "'"
```
Forming the
SQL to retrieve
detailed
reservation
information

```
        Set rs = conn.Execute (sql)
        if not rs.EOF then
            Response.Write "<b>ISBN :</b>" & rs("ISBN") & "<br/>"
            Response.Write "<b>Date :</b>" & rs("Date") & "<br/>"
            Response.Write "<b>Qty  :</b>" & rs("Qty")  & "<br/>"
        %>

            <do type="options" label="Change">
                <go href="NewQty.wmls#getNewQty('<% =rs("Qty") %>')">
                    <setvar name="ISBN" value="<% =rs("ISBN") %>" />
                    <setvar name="Date" value="<% =rs("Date") %>" />
                </go>
            </do>
        <%
        end if
        %>
        <do type="accept" label="Back">
            <prev/>
        </do>
        </p>
    </card>
</wml>
```

Link to the WMLScript for changing the quantity of a reservation

If the salesperson wishes to change the quantity of the reservation (figure 34.22), the WMLScript would be loaded:

```
<do type="options" label="Change">
    <go href="NewQty.wmls#getNewQty('<%
        =rs("Qty") %>')">
        <setvar name="ISBN" value=
            "<% =rs("ISBN") %>" />
        <setvar name="Date" value="<% =
            rs("Date") %>" />
    </go>
</do>
```

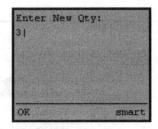

Figure 34.22   Changing the quantity

Listing 34.10 is the source for the WMLScript document:

Listing 34.10   Source code for WMLScript

```
extern function getNewQty(oldQty) {      ❶
    var newQty = Dialogs.prompt("Enter New Qty: ",oldQty);      ❷
    VerifyQty(newQty);      ❸
}
                                    | Internal
function VerifyQty(num) {       ⤶ function
    if (!Lang.isInt(num)) {      ❹
        Dialogs.alert ("Integer expected.");
        getNewQty(num);      ❺
    } else
```

```
        var URL = "ModifyQty.asp?Qty=" + num + "&ISBN=" +          Forms the query
            WMLBrowser.getVar("ISBN") + "&BookStoreID=" +          string to be sent to
            WMLBrowser.getVar("bookStore") + "&Date=" +            the ModifyQty.asp
            WMLBrowser.getVar("Date");                             document
        WMLBrowser.setVar("Qty", num);        ❻
        WMLBrowser.go(URL);    ◁┐ Using the go method from the
    return;                      │ WMLBrowser library to load a deck
}
```

Code comments

❶ An `Extern` function can be called by a WML deck.

❷ Using the Dialog library to prompt the user to key in a number.

❸ Calls the Internal function.

❹ Using the Lang library to verify whether a number is an integer.

❺ If a number is not an integer, call the `getNewQty()` function again.

❻ Using the WMLBrowser library to set a WML variable

We have two functions defined in this document. The `getNewQty()` function is accessible to the WML deck because it has the `extern` keyword. The other function, `VerifyQty()`, is for internal use.

If you are not familiar with WMLScript, refer to part III.

Once the new quantity has been keyed in, we will use the `WMLBrowser.setvar()` method to send the information to the `ModifyQty.asp` document for updating.

```
var URL = "ModifyQty.asp?Qty=" + num + "&ISBN=" +
    WMLBrowser.getVar("ISBN") + "&BookStoreID=" +
    WMLBrowser.getVar("bookStore") + "&Date=" +
    WMLBrowser.getVar("Date");
WMLBrowser.setVar("Qty", num);
WMLBrowser.go(URL);
```

This is the Modifyqty.asp code

Listing 34.11   Code for Modifyqty.asp

```
<% Response.ContentType = "text/vnd.wap.wml"
    Response.Expires = -1
%>
<?xml version="1.0"?>
<!DOCTYPE wml PUBLIC "-//WAPFORUM//DTD WML 1.1//EN"
"http://www.wapforum.org/DTD/wml_1.1.xml">
<wml>
    <card id="card1" title="Modify">
        <p>
        <%
        Dim conn, rs
```

```
     Set conn = Server.CreateObject("ADODB.Connection")
     Set rs   = Server.CreateObject("ADODB.Recordset")
     '---Opens the connection to the database---
   conn.open "DRIVER={Microsoft Access Driver (*.mdb)};DBQ=" &
     Server.MapPath("Publishers.mdb") & ";"
     '---Updates the qty
     sql = "UPDATE Reservations SET Qty=" & Request.QueryString("Qty") & "
         WHERE BookStoreID='" & Request.QueryString("BookStoreID") &
         "' AND ISBN='" & Request.QueryString("ISBN") &
         "' AND Date='" & Request.QueryString("Date") & "'"
     conn.Execute(sql)
     Response.Write "Qty updated!"
     %>
     </p>
   </card>
</wml>
```

Forming the SQL to update the record

Informing the user that the update is successful

NOTE   *WMLScript support*   While WMLScript is similar to JavaScript in that it can perform client-side scripting, its support from WAP devices is far from the support for JavaScript on the web front. Not all devices support WMLScript, and, to make matters worse, some browsers contain bugs in their WMLScript implementation. In such cases, use WMLScript only when you know the target device that your users will be using.

34.6 CONVERTING IMAGE FILES USING A WBMP CONVERTER

Earlier we mentioned that the company maintains a folder containing images of the books in JPEG format. We would like the images to be loaded onto the WAP device so that the salesperson can have a look at the book cover if the need ever arises.

We use the pic2wbmp converter for converting image files to the WBMP format (figure 34.23). This excellent converter is free for download at:

http://www.gingco-newmedia.de.

For installation information and software requirements, refer to the documentation accompanying the software.

Figure 34.23
pic2wbmp image converter

34.6.1   Image types supported by pic2wbmp converter

The pic2wbmp converter supports 10 image formats:

- WBMP
- GIF
- PSD
- XPM
- DIB
- JPEG
- TGA
- ICO
- DDB
- PICT
- TIF
- CUR
- BMP
- PNG
- XBM
- PCX

34.6.2   Converting an image

To convert an image into the WBMP format, click File->Open and select the image that you want to convert (figure 34.24).

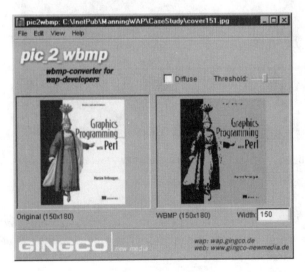

Figure 34.24
Using the pic2wbmp converter to convert image formats

Once the image is loaded, the converter will automatically convert the image into the WBMP format.

You have the option to adjust the intensity of the image by dragging the Threshold slider. Figure 34.25 shows the image quality at various intensity levels.

Figure 34.25   Varying quality can be achieved by adjusting the intensity of the image

For colorful images, use the diffuse option to improve the quality of the image (figure 34.26). Some WAP devices will invert your WBMP files when they are displayed. If you have such consideration, you can invert your WBMP files using the converter (figure 34.27).

Figure 34.26   Optimal image quality using the diffuse option   **Figure 34.27   Inverting an image**

Please note that the images in the preceding figures do not do justice to the original Manning covers. This is due to the fact that the images have been converted into WBMP format so that they can satisfy the memory constraints of the mobile devices, which resulted in loss of quality.

34.6.3 Adjusting the size of the image

Figure 34.28
Specifying the width of an image

The size of the image can be adjusted by changing the width of the image. The width of the image is proportional to its height (figure 34.28).

34.6.4 Saving the WBMP file

Once you are satisfied with the quality of the converted image, you should save it onto your hard disk. The pic2wbmp converter provides a number of save options:

- Saves image as WBMP
- Saves the file in the WBMP file format
- Saves image as WBMP + wml
- Saves the file in the WBMP file format and creates a wml deck for you to test
- Saves image as other file format
- Saves the converted file in another file format other than WBMP

The second save option is helpful for developers who want to test their newly converted image on a WAP device. For instance, we saved the preceding image and the following wml deck is created:

```
<?xml version="1.0"?>
<!DOCTYPE wml PUBLIC "-//WAPFORUM//DTD WML 1.1//EN"
"http://www.wapforum.org/DTD/wml_1.1.xml">
<!-- Source Generated by pic2wbmp Image Converter -->
<!-- http://www.gingco.de/wap -->
<wml>
   <card id="start" title="pic2wbmp">
      <p align="center">
         <img src="cover151.wbmp" alt="pic2wbmp"/>
      </p>
   </card>
</wml>
```

> Using the `<img>` element to display the image

You can then test the image by loading the deck using a WAP device or emulator (figure 34.29).

Figure 34.29   Using the
`<img>` element

34.7 SUMMARY

In this chapter, we illustrated a case study involving an online inventory system. We applied the various concepts that we learned in the earlier chapters (WML, WML-Script, ASP, and ADO) in building the sample case study. We hope that this chapter shed some light on how the various technologies can be integrated to build dynamic WAP applications.

In the next case study, we will look at another WAP application using Java servlets in the back end.

CHAPTER 35

Mobile library system

35.1 INTRODUCTION

In this second case study, we will look at wireless services that a library can mount.

everyWhere Library has decided to implement services that will enable the mobile library users to:

- Look for a book based on the book title
- Check the availability of a book
- Place or cancel the reservation of a book that is out on loan
- Renew a loaned book based on its ISBN
- Contact the library administrator to invoke an interlibrary book loan

35.2 SYSTEM DESIGN

Based on the requirements listed in the previous section, we will draw the system design diagram (figure 35.1) to depict the relevant components as well as the interaction among them, where a component is one of following objects:

- A WML deck or a card in a deck enclosed in a rectangle with solid line
- A servlet or JSP page enclosed in a box with shadow
- A dynamic deck generated by a servlet or JSP page enclosed in a box with dotted line

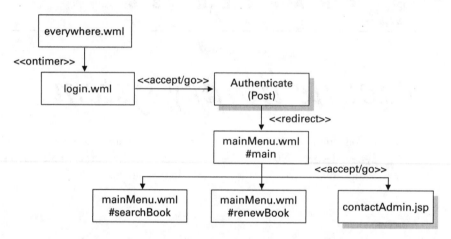

Figure 35.1 First-level component interaction diagram of the mobile library system

35.2.1   Searching for a book

Figure 35.2 expands the book searching function:

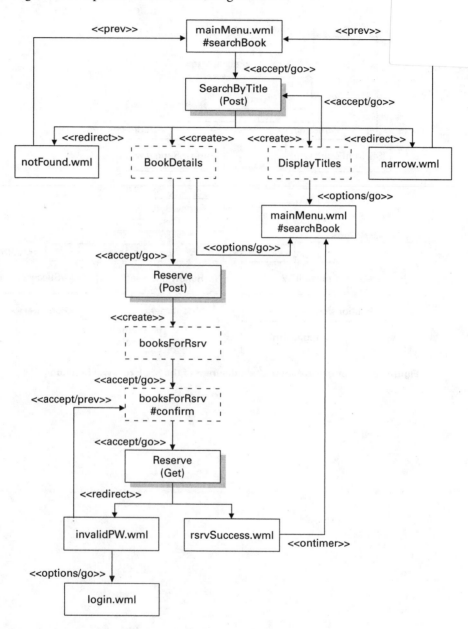

Figure 35.2   Component interaction diagram of the searching function

.2 Renewing a book

Figure 35.3 expands the book renewing function:

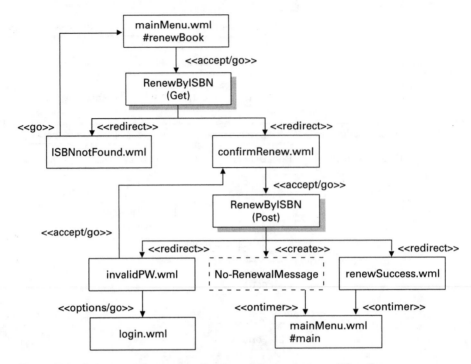

Figure 35.3 Component interaction diagram of the book renewal function

35.2.3 Contacting administrator for interlibrary loan

Figure 35.4 expands the function of contacting the library administrator:

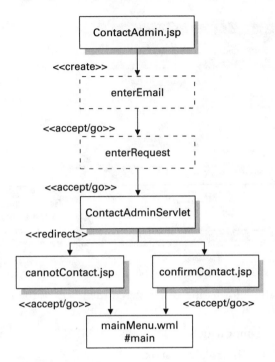

Figure 35.4
Component interaction diagram of the function for contacting library administrator

35.3 SETUP

For this case study, we will be using the following resources:

- Microsoft SQL for creating the library database
- Microsoft Internet Information Server 4.0 for hosting all the Internet services to the users
- JRun 3.0 for loading and running servlets, and compiling JSP pages
- UP.Simulator to emulate a WAP device
- JavaMail v1.1
- JavaBeans Activation Framework

35.4 LIBRARY DATABASE

We will first take a look at the library database. We will look at the relevant tables that we need to implement the services, and the relationship among these tables. We will also look at the structure and contents of each of the tables used in our library application.

35.4.1   Database structure

Figure 35.5 shows the tables used and the relationship among them.

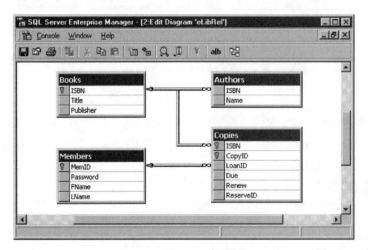

**Figure 35.5
Relationship diagram
of tables in the
library (eLib)
database**

There are four tables used in the library database:

- *Members*—Maintains the information of registered members of the library and their login particulars.
- *Books*—Holds the general information of a book such as ISBN, title, and publisher.
- *Authors*—Stores the author(s) of a given book.
- *Copies*—Maintains the loan status of each physical copy of the book and the ID of any user reserving the book, with at most one reservation per book.

35.4.2   Table structure and contents

In our example, we will design the tables and fill them with data for the walk-through.

Members

Each registered member of everyWhere Library is assigned a unique ID for logging onto the system (figure 35.6). Also, a member needs to key in the password for authentication. We have omitted many other fields, such as address and contact number, that are useful in a real-life library system.

MemID	Password	FName	LName
christopherH	Hoover1	Christopher	Hoover
ianM	Moraes2	Ian	Moraes
soomeeF	Foo3	Soo Mee	Foo
weimengL	Lee4	Wei Meng	Lee

**Figure 35.6
Contents of the
Members table**

Books

The Books table keeps track of the general information of books with a unique ISBN (figure 35.7). In our application, we will keep only the title and publisher in addition to the primary-key field, namely the ISBN.

ISBN	Title	Publisher
188477766X	Java Servlets By Example	Manning
013272295X	Java By Example	Prentice Hall
0672319020	Pure JSP: Java Server Pages	Sams
0789722666	Java 2 By Example	Que
1884777716	Server-Based Java Programming	Manning
0201353407	Java For The World Wide Web	Peachpit Press
0138873089	Java Beans	Prentice Hall
1884777651	Distributed Programming With Java	Manning
0672316544	Pure Java	Sams
1565924843	Java 2D Graphics	O'Reilly
188477797X	Java 3D Programming	Manning
1884777996	Web Development with JavaServer Pages	Manning

Figure 35.7
Contents of the Books table

Authors

ISBN	Name
188477766X	Alan R. Williamson
013272295X	Jerry Jackson
013272295X	Alan L. McClellan
0672319020	James Goodwill
0789722666	Geoff Friesen
1884777716	Ted Neward
0201353407	Dori Smith
0201353407	Tom Negrino
0138873089	Prashant Sridharan
1884777651	Qusay H. Mahmoud
0672316544	Kenneth Litwak
1565924843	Jonathan B. Knudsen
188477797X	Daniel Selman
1884777996	Duane K. Fields
1884777996	Mark A. Kolb

Figure 35.8
Content of the Authors table

The author information is not kept in the Books table because there may be more than one author for a given book. The design principle of a relational database requires that we keep the author(s) of books in a separate table (figure 35.8).

Copies

The library may have more than one physical copy per unique ISBN. The Copies table (figure 35.9) keeps information of each of the copies of a given ISBN. The information to maintain includes the availability of the book and whether it is reserved. If a book is loaned out, the member ID of the borrower is recorded as well as the number of times he has consecutively renewed the book.

In our application we allow only one reservation per physical copy of the book and not more than two consecutive renewals of the same book. Also, if a book is reserved, the current borrower cannot renew the book again.

ISBN	CopyID	LoanID	Due	Renew	ReserveID
188477766X	1			0	
188477766X	2	ianM	5/19/2001	1	christopherH
013272295X	1	ianM	3/21/2001	0	
013272295X	2			0	
0672319020	1			0	
0789722666	1	soomeeF	5/5/2001	0	
1884777716	1	soomeeF	7/19/2001	0	christopherH
1884777716	2	ianM	6/5/2001	0	
1884777716	3	weimengL	5/25/2001	2	
0201353407	1	soomeeF	5/10/2001	0	christopherH
0201353407	2	ianM	6/1/2001	0	
0138873089	1	christopherH	6/1/2001	0	
1884777651	1			0	
1884777651	2	christopherH	5/12/2001	0	
0672316544	1			0	
1565924843	1			0	
188477797X	1	christopherH	5/10/2001	0	weimengL
1884777996	1	christopherH	5/18/2001	0	weimengL
1884777996	2	soomeeF	5/30/2001	0	

Figure 35.9   Contents of the Copies table

35.5   CODE OF THE EXAMPLE

In this section, we will look at the code for searching and reserving books, as well as reading mail. Only significant features will be annotated. For explanation of more trivial code, refer to earlier chapters that cover them in greater detail.

35.5.1   Database properties file

Before we plunge into the core programming, let us first prepare the database properties file that we discussed in chapter 23. The use of such a file enables us to keep our program as independent as possible of the database used, as well as for easier maintenance.

Let's call the properties file eLib.properties:

```
Driver=sun.jdbc.odbc.JdbcOdbcDriver
URL=jdbc:odbc:eLib
```

The Driver property value specifies the JDBC-ODBC driver and the URL property identifies the protocols and database, eLib, to be used.

35.5.2   The welcome deck

The first page of the library is a welcome display, which remains for two seconds before the login card (login.wml) is loaded. The code of the welcome deck is:

```
<?xml version="1.0" ?>
<!DOCTYPE wml PUBLIC "-//WAPFORUM//DTD WML 1.1//EN"
      "http://www.wapforum.org/DTD/wml_1_1.xml">
```

◁ **Prologue, including the document type definition declaration for WML 1.1**

```wml
<wml> <!-- everyWhere.wml -->
<card id="welcome" title="Welcome" ontimer="login.wml">
    <timer value="20" />
    <p align="center">
        <br />
        Welcome to
        <br />
        <b><i>everyWhere</i></b> Library!
    </p>
</card>
</wml>
```

Sets the timer to 20*(l/l0) seconds before loading the card specified by the `ontimer` attribute

Figure 35.10 shows the welcome page that is displayed for two seconds.

Figure 35.10   Welcome page of everyWhere mobile library system

35.5.3   The login deck

This is the deck that contains a login card. The user needs to key in an ID and a password to be authenticated by the system via a servlet, Authenticate, before the user is allowed to make use of the services offered by everyWhere over the air.

The code of the login deck:

```wml
<?xml version="1.0" ?>
<!DOCTYPE wml PUBLIC "-//WAPFORUM//DTD WML 1.1//EN"
        "http://www.wapforum.org/DTD/wml_1_1.xml">

<wml> <!-- login.wml -->
<card id="login" title="Login" newcontext="true">      ❶
    <p>
        <b>Member ID:</b>
            <input type="text" name="MemID" maxlength="15" />
        <b>Password:</b>
            <input type="password" name="Password" maxlength="15" />
    </p>
    <do type="accept" label="Login">
        <go href="http://localhost/servlet/Authenticate" method="post">
            <postfield name="MemID" value="$MemID" />
            <postfield name="Password" value="$Password" />
        </go>
    </do>
</card>
</wml>
```

Prompts user to key in member ID

Prompts user to key in password

❷

Code comments

❶ The value of the newcontext attribute of the card is set to `true`. This causes the user agent to delete current browser context before loading the login card.

❷ When Accept is clicked, the authenticating servlet, Authenticate, is invoked, together with the value of the ID and password that the user has just input.

Figure 35.11 shows the displays you will see for the login process.

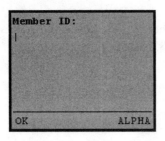 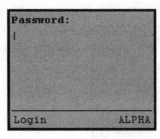

Figure 35.11
User login screens

To invoke the authentication function, the soft-key for Accept (i.e., Login) is pressed after a member enters his password.

35.5.4 Authenticating user login

The authenticating servlet in listing 35.1 is invoked from the login card we saw earlier via the HTTP POST method. The servlet checks the member ID and password keyed in by the user against the Members table of the library database:

Listing 35.1 Source code for Authenticate.java

```java
/* Authenticate.java */
import java.io.*;
import java.util.*;
import javax.servlet.*;
import javax.servlet.http.*;
import java.sql.*;

public class PutCookieServlet extends HttpServlet
{
    /* Initialization of servlet */
    public void init(ServletConfig config)throws ServletException {
        super.init(config);
    }

    /* Redirecting client request that uses HTTP GET method */
    public void doGet (HttpServletRequest  request,
                       HttpServletResponse response)
               throws ServletException, IOException
    {
        doPost (request, response);
```

```
        }
        /* Servicing client request to autheticate user login */
        public void doPost (HttpServletRequest  request,
                            HttpServletResponse response)
                throws ServletException, IOException
        {
            // Variables declaration
            Connection con = null;
            Statement  stmt = null;
            String     query;
            ResultSet  rs = null;
            ResourceBundle db = ResourceBundle.getBundle ("eLib");
            int        err = -1;
            String     id = request.getParameter ("MemID");
            String     pw = request.getParameter ("Password");

            if (id.length() == 0 && pw.length() == 0) err = 0;
            else
                if (id.length() == 0) err = 1;
            else
                if (pw.length() == 0) err = 2;

            try {
                if (err > -1) {
                    loginErr (err, response);
                    return;
                }
            } catch (Exception e) {
                System.err.println ("Exception: loginErr(): empty ID/passwd…");
                System.err.println (e);
            }

            try {
                Class.forName (db.getString("Driver"));
                con = DriverManager.getConnection (db.getString("URL"));

            } catch (Exception e) {
                System.err.println ("Exception: JDBC-ODBC bridge driver…");
                System.err.println (e);
            }

            HttpSession session = request.getSession (true);

            try {
                stmt = con.createStatement();
                query = "SELECT * FROM Members WHERE MemID='" + id +
                        "' AND Password='" + pw + "'";
                rs = stmt.executeQuery (query);

                if (!rs.next()) {
                    rs.close();
                    stmt.close();
                    con.close();
                    loginErr (3, response);
```

err keeps track of the type of error

Uses `getBundle()` **to open eLib.properties**

Retrieves ID and password keyed in by user from the incoming request

Invokes `loginErr()` **to display appropriate login error messages**

Uses `getString()` **to extract value assigned to each of the Driver and URL properties specified in the property file**

Obtains a reference to current session

Queries database to authenticate user based on ID and password supplied by user

```
        }
        else {
            if (session != null) {
                session.setAttribute ("MemID", id);
                session.setAttribute ("MemPW", pw);
                response.sendRedirect ("http://localhost/mainMenu.wml");
            }
        }
```

After user is successfully authenticated, keeps the ID and password in session object and redirects request to mainMenu.wml

```
    } catch (Exception e) {
        System.err.println ("Exception: logingErr(): invalid ID/passwd…");
        System.err.println (e);
    }

    finally {
        try {
            if (rs != null)   rs.close();
            if (stmt != null) stmt.close();
            if (con != null)  con.close();
        } catch (Exception e) {
            System.err.println ("Exception: finally in doPost()…");
            System.err.println (e);
        }
    }

} // doPost()

/* Generate WML deck to display appropriate login error message */
protected static void loginErr (int err, HttpServletResponse response)
{
    String errMsg[] = {"key in both your ID and password.",
                       "key in member ID.",
                       "key in password.",
                       "check your ID and password again."};
```

Defines three possible error messages for the login session

```
    try {
        // Generate WML content to
        // output appropriate error message
        response.setContentType ("text/vnd.wap.wml");

        response.setHeader ("cache-control", "no-cache");
        PrintWriter out = response.getWriter();
        out.println ("<?xml version=\"1.0\"?>");
        out.println
          ("<!DOCTYPE wml PUBLIC \"-//WAPFRORUM//DTD WML 1.1//EN\"");
        out.println ("\"http://www.wapforum.org/DTD/wml_1_1.xml\">");
        out.println ("<wml>");
        out.println ("<card id=\"err\" title=\"Login Error\">");
        out.println ("    <p>");
        out.println ("      Login failed. Please " + errMsg[err]);
        out.println ("    </p>");
        out.println ("    <do type=\"accept\" label=\"OK\">");
        out.println ("       <go href=\"/login.wml\" />");
        out.println ("    </do>");
```

```
        out.println ("</card>");
        out.println ("</wml>");
    } catch (Exception e) {
        System.err.println ("Exception: Displaying login errors…");
        System.err.println (e);
    }
  } // loginErr()

}
```

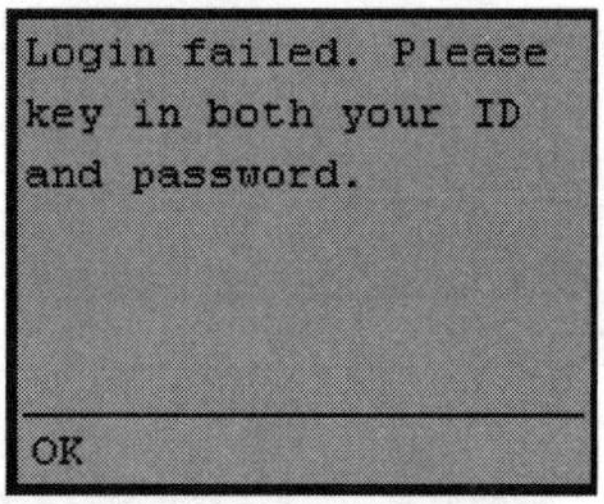

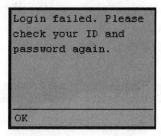

Figure 35.12   Error message displayed if both

Figure 35.13   Error message displayed if login information is incorrect

The servlet first performs error checking. The `loginErr()` method displays error messages based on the error flag values passed in via the variable *err*. Errors handled include:

- Empty member ID input
- Empty password input
- Input member ID not found in the database
- Input password does not match that for the specified member ID

For example, if the user did not key in both the member ID and password, the error message in figure 35.12 will be shown.

If the user did not key in a valid member ID and/or password, the error message in figure 35.13 will be shown.

If the user has been successfully authenticated, the servlet creates a session object to keep track of the member's ID and password. It then sends the deck, main-Menu.wml, to the client.

35.5.5   The main menu deck

The main menu deck consists of three cards:

- *main*—Lists the various services available to the member.
- *searchBook*—Prompts user for a book title and invokes the SearchByTitle servlet to look for the title in the database.
- *renewBook*—Prompts user for ISBN of book and invokes RenewByISBN servlet to update the loaning status of the book and user.

We shall implement the main card in such a way that whenever it is loaded, the current context is cleared to assume a new session of service. This helps prevent the browser's history stack from growing too large since each user agent has a specific depth allowed for the stack.

Also, if the previous page was a login page, this stack clearing also clears away the ID and password variable values keyed in by the user. This is a security measure to prevent cards from extracting such information from the variable stack residing at the user agent.

The main menu presents three possible options to the user:

- *Search*—If the user chooses this option, the searchBook card in the same deck is loaded.

- *Renew*—When the user selects this option, the renewBook card in the same deck is loaded.

- *Mail administrator*—When the user selects this option, ContactAdmin.jsp (the JSP page) is invoked.

The deck design is such that the cards that are likely to be invoked after selections are made in the main menu are included in this same deck. Including probable cards that would be needed next in the same deck ensures a faster response time to the user's subsequent choice of option. Since the third option is considered rare, we can use a different deck to further process this request only when it is selected. In our case, we choose to use a JSP page to handle mailing to the administrator. We will explain the choice of a JSP page instead of a WML deck to handle this request in a later section when we discuss this in greater detail.

Listing 35.2 is the code of this deck:

Listing 35.2 Source code for mainMenu.wml

```
<?xml version="1.0" ?>
<!DOCTYPE wml PUBLIC "-//WAPFORUM//DTD WML 1.1//EN"
      "http://www.wapforum.org/DTD/wml_1_1.xml">

<wml> <!-- mainMenu.wml -->
<card id="main" title="Main Menu" newcontext="true">
   <p>
      Select a service:              The main card displays a
      <select name="service">        selection list of services
         <option value="search" onpick="#searchBook">
            Search for a book</option>
         <option value="renew" onpick="#renewBook">
            Renew a book</option>
         <option value= "mail"
             onpick="http://localhost/jsp/ContactAdmin.jsp">
            Mail administrator</option>
      </select>
   </p>
   <do type="options" label="Exit">       The soft key for Options is
      <prev />                             to exit the library system
   </do>
</card>
```

```wml
<card id="searchBook" title="Book Seach">
   <p>
      Key in (partial) book title:
      <input type="text" name="title" maxlength="50" />
   </p>

   <do type="accept" label="Search">
      <go href="http://localhost/servlet/SearchByTitle" method="post">
         <postfield name="service" value="$service" />
         <postfield name="title" value="$title" />
         <postfield name="isbn" value="" />
      </go>
   </do>
</card>

<card id="renewBook" title="Book Renewal">
   <p>
      Key in ISBN of book:
      <input type="text" name="isbn" maxlength="20" />
   </p>

   <do type="accept" label="Renew">
      <go href="http://localhost/servlet/RenewByISBN" method="post">
         <postfield name="isbn" value="$isbn" />
      </go>
   </do>
</card>
</wml>
```

The searchBook card prompts user to input a (possibly partial) title

The soft key for Accept invokes the SearchByTitle servlet, together with the parameters, `service`, `title`, and `isbn`

The renewBook card prompts user to input the ISBN of the book

The soft key for Accept invokes the RenewByISBN servlet, together with the parameter, `isbn`

While it is wise to place related cards in the same deck, especially if there is a high possibility of navigation occurring among the cards, the size of a deck is also a concern. You should always check the size of the deck during development stage to avoid exceeding the size limit set by various devices. Using Phone Simulator, you can always check the size in the Phone Information window. The Phone Information window indicates 595 bytes of compiled WAP binary content for the deck in listing 35.2.

The main card of the deck in listing 35.2 lists the services offered by everyWhere as shown in figure 35.14.

If the first option is chosen, the searchBook card in the same deck is loaded (figure 35.15).

The second option will load the renewBook card in the same deck (figure 35.16).

If the last option is chosen, a JSP page, ContactAdmin.jsp, is invoked. We will discuss the function of this JSP page in a later section.

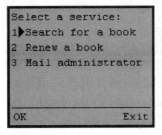

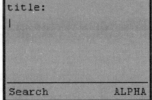

Figure 35.14   Main menu

Figure 35.15   Title entry screen for searching a book

Figure 35.16   ISBN entry screen for renewal of book

35.5.6   Searching by title

When a request is made to SearchByTitle, the servlet executes an SQL query statement to the library database to retrieve all records that contain the input title in the `Title` field of the `Books` table.

The servlet consists of three main methods: `doPost()`, `bookDetails()`, and `displayTitles()`.

We will first present the code of this servlet followed by more in-depth discussion of each of the three methods. Listing 35.3 shows the code of the SearchByTitle servlet:

Listing 35.3   Source code for SearchByTitle.java

```java
/* SearchByTitle.java */
import java.io.*;
import java.util.*;
import javax.servlet.*;
import javax.servlet.http.*;
import java.sql.*;

public class SearchByTitle extends HttpServlet
{
    /* Initialization of servlet */
    public void init(ServletConfig config) throws ServletException {
        super.init (config);
    }

    /* Redirecting client request that uses HTTP GET method */
    public void doGet (HttpServletRequest  request,
                       HttpServletResponse response)
            throws ServletResponse, IOException
    {
        doPost (request, response);
    }
    /* Servicing client request to search a book by title */
    public void doPost (HttpServletRequest  request,
                        HttpServletResponse response)
            throws ServletException, IOException
    {
```

```
// Variables
Connection      con = null;
Statement       stmt = null;
String          query;
ResultSet       rs = null;
ResourceBundle db = ResourceBundle.getBundle ("eLib");
int             count = 0;
String          ISBNs[] = new String[10];
String          titles[] = new String[10];

String title = request.getParameter ("title");    Retrieves title and ISBN
String isbn = request.getParameter ("isbn");       from incoming request
try {
    if (title.length()==0)                      Redirects to main menu if both
        if (isbn.length()==0)                   title and isbn values are empty
            response.sendRedirect ("http://localhost/mainMenu.wml");
        else {
            bookDetails (isbn, response);
            return;                         If no title but an isbn value is
        }                                   found, invokes bookDetails()
} catch (Exception e)  {                     to display details of book
    System.err.println ("Exception: Calling bookDetails()...");
    System.err.println (e);
}

try {
    Class.forName (db.getString("Driver"));
    con = DriverManager.getConnection (db.getString("URL"));

} catch (Exception e)  {
    System.err.println ("Exception: JDBC-ODBC bridge driver...");
    System.err.println (e);                      Retrieves title and ISBN of
}                                                all books from Books table
                                                 whose titles contain the
try {                                            title input by user
    stmt = con.createStatement();
query = "SELECT ISBN, Title FROM Books WHERE Title LIKE '%" +
            title.trim() + "%' ORDER BY Title";
    rs = stmt.executeQuery (query);

    if (!rs.next())   {                                  Redirects to
        rs.close();                             notfound.wml if no match
        stmt.close();                            of the specified title is
        con.close();                             found in the database
        response.sendRedirect ("http://localhost/notfound.wml");
    }                                     Buffers titles and ISBNs retrieved from
    else {                                database to a maximum of 10 records
        do {
            ISBNs[count] = rs.getString("ISBN").trim();
            titles[count++] = rs.getString("Title").trim();
        } while (rs.next() && count<10);
    }                                           If only one record matches
                                                the specified title, calls
    if (count == 1)                             bookDetails() to display
        bookDetails (ISBNs[0], response);       details of book
```

```
          else
          if (rs.next()) {
              rs.close();
              stmt.close();
              con.close();
              response.sendRedirect ("http://localhost/narrow.wml");
          }
          else
              displayTitles (ISBNs, titles, count, response);        ❶

      } catch (SQLException e)  {
        System.err.println ("Exception: Creating statement object...");
        System.err.println (e);

      } catch (Exception e)  {
        System.err.println ("Exception: Retrieving 'books' table...");
        System.err.println (e);
      }

      finally {
        try {
            if (rs != null)   rs.close();
            if (stmt != null) stmt.close();
            if (con != null)  con.close();
        } catch (Exception e)  {
            System.err.println ("Exception: finally in doPost()...");
            System.err.println (e);
        }
      }

  } // doPost()


  /* Retrieving and displaying details of a specific book */
  protected static void bookDetails (String isbn,
                                      HttpServletResponse response)
              throws ServletException, IOException, Exception
  {
      // Variables
      Connection      con = null;
      Statement       stmt = null;
      String          query;
      ResultSet       rs = null;
      ResourceBundle  db = ResourceBundle.getBundle ("eLib");
      PrintWriter     out;
      String          loan, reserve;
      int             reserveFlag=1, reserveAvai=0;

      try {
          Class.forName (db.getString("Driver"));
          con = DriverManager.getConnection (db.getString("URL"));

      } catch (Exception e)  {
          System.err.println ("Exception: DB connection...");
          System.err.println (e);
      }
```

Redirects to narrow.wml if more than l0 matches of the specified title are found in the database

```
try {
    stmt = con.createStatement();
    query = "SELECT * FROM Books WHERE ISBN='" + isbn + "'";
    rs = stmt.executeQuery (query);
    rs.next();
    String title = rs.getString("Title").trim();
    String pub = rs.getString("Publisher").trim();

    response.setContentType("text/vnd.wap.wml");
    response.setHeader("cache-control", "no-cache");

    out = response.getWriter();
    out.println ("<?xml version=\"1.0\"?>");
    out.println
        ("<!DOCTYPE wml PUBLIC \"-//WAPFORUM//DTD WML 1.1//EN\"");
    out.println ("\"http://www.wapforum.org/DTD/wml_1.1.xml\">");
    out.println("<wml>");
    out.println("<card id=\"start\" title=\"Book Search\">");

    out.println("<p mode=\"nowrap\">");

    out.println("\"" + title + "\" <br />");
    out.println("ISBN: " + isbn + "<br />");
    out.println("Publisher: " + pub + "<br />");
    rs.close();

    out.println("By: ");
    query = "SELECT Name FROM Authors WHERE ISBN='" + isbn + "'";
    rs = stmt.executeQuery (query);
    rs.next();
    out.println(rs.getString("Name").trim());
    while (rs.next()) {
out.println(", " + rs.getString("Name").trim());
    }
    out.println("<br />");
    rs.close();

    query = "SELECT * FROM Copies WHERE ISBN='" + isbn + "'";
    rs = stmt.executeQuery (query);

    out.println("<table columns=\"2\">");
    out.println("    <tr><td><b>#</b></td> " +
            "<td><b>Status/Rsrv</b></td></tr>");

    while (rs.next()) {
        out.println("    <tr><td>" + rs.getString("CopyID").trim()
                    + "</td>");

        loan = rs.getString("LoanID").trim();
        if (loan.equals("")) {
            reserveFlag=0;
            out.println("<td>Available</td></tr>");
        }
        else {
            out.println("<td>Due " + rs.getString("Due").trim());
            reserve = rs.getString("ReserveID").trim();
```

Query for retrieving all fields of a book of specified ISBN from the Books table

Starting from here until the end of this try block, output WML content to display details of a particular book

Query for retrieving all author names of a specified ISBN from the Authors table

Use a while-loop to iterate through the set of author records to display their names

Query for retrieving information of all copies of a specified ISBN from the Copies table

Tabulates loaning information of all copies of a specified ISBN

```
                    if (reserve.equals("")) {
                        reserveAvai=1;
                        out.println("</td></tr>");
                    }
                    else
                        out.println(" Rsrv</td></tr>");
            }
        }

        out.println("</table>");
        out.println("</p>");

        if (reserveFlag==1 && reserveAvai==1) {
            out.println("<do type=\"accept\" label=\"Reserve\">");
            out.println("    <go " +
                        "href=\"http://localhost/servlet/Reserve\" " +
                        "method=\"post\">");
            out.println("        <postfield name=\"isbn\" value=\"" +
                        isbn + "\" />");
            out.println("        <postfield name=\"title\" value=\"" +
                        title + "\" />");
            out.println("        <postfield name=\"pub\" value=\"" +
                        pub + "\" />");
            out.println("    </go>");
            out.println("</do>");
        }
        else {
            out.println("<do type=\"accept\" label=\"Next\">");
            out.println("    <go " +
                    "href=\"http://localhost/mainMenu.wml#searchBook\">");
            out.println("        <setvar name=\"title\" value=\"\" />");
            out.println("    </go>");
            out.println("</do>");
        }

        out.println("<do type=\"options\" label=\"Menu\">");
        out.println("    <go " +
                "href=\"http://localhost/mainMenu.wml#main\" />");
        out.println("</do>");

        out.println("</card>");
        out.println("</wml>");
        out.close();

} catch (SQLException e)  {
    System.err.println ("SQLException: Accessing book details...");
    System.err.println (e);

} catch (Exception e)   {
    System.err.println ("Exception: Displaying book details...");
    System.err.println (e);
}

finally {
    try {
```

```
            if (rs != null) rs.close();
            if (stmt != null) stmt.close();
            if (con != null) con.close();
        } catch (Exception e)  {
            System.err.println ("Exception: Finally in bookDetails().");
            System.err.println (e);
        }
    }
} // bookDetails()


/* Retrieving and displaying all titles that match the search string */
protected static void displayTitles (String ISBNs[],
                                     String titles[],
                                     int count,
                                     HttpServletResponse response)
            throws IOException, Exception
{
    try {
        response.setContentType("text/vnd.wap.wml");          ❸
        response.setHeader("cache-control", "no-cache");

        PrintWriter out = response.getWriter();
        out.println ("<?xml version=\"1.0\"?>");
        out.println
          ("<!DOCTYPE wml PUBLIC \"-//WAPFORUM//DTD WML 1.1//EN\"");
        out.println ("\"http://www.wapforum.org/DTD/wml_1.1.xml\">");

        out.println("<wml>");
        out.println("<card title=\"Book Search\">");
        out.println("<p mode=\"nowrap\">");

        out.println("    Pick one to view details:");
        out.println("    <select name=\"isbn\">");
        for (int i=0; i<count; i++) {
            String isbn = ISBNs[i].trim();
            String title = titles[i].trim();
            out.println("        <option value=\"" + isbn + "\">" +
                        title + "</option>");
        }
        out.println("    </select>");
        out.println("</p>");

        out.println("<do type=\"accept\" label=\"View\">");
        out.println("    <go " +
                "href=\"http://localhost/servlet/SearchByTitle\"" +
                " method=\"post\">");
        out.println("        <postfield name=\"isbn\" " +
                "value=\"$isbn\" />");
        out.println("        <postfield name=\"title\" " +
                "value=\"\" />");
        out.println("    </go>");
        out.println("</do>");

        out.println("<do type=\"options\" label=\"Menu\">");
```

```
        out.println
          ("    <go href=\"http://localhost/mainMenu.wml#main\" />");
        out.println("</do>");

        out.println("</card>");
        out.println("</wml>");

    } catch (Exception e) {
        System.err.println ("Exception: Displaying book titles...");
        System.err.println (e);
    }
  }  // end of displayTitles()
}
```

Code comments

❶ Invokes `displayTitles()` if there are fewer than 10 matches to display multiple retrieved records as a selection list.

❷ If all copies of a specified ISBN are loaned out but at least one is available for reservation, generates the `Reserve` option, such that when it is chosen, the Reserve servlet is invoked together with ISBN, title, and publisher posted to the servlet.

❸ Starting from here until the end of this `try` block, outputs WML content to display a list of titles that match the title specified by the user.

❹ Generates a `View` option, which when selected, invokes the same servlet (`Search ByTitle`) together with the ISBN of the selected book.

Let's take a closer look at the three methods in the servlet.

doPost()

This method receives the client's request together with two parameters, `title` and `ISBN`. A client request may be invoked from the searchBook card of main-Menu.wml or it may be invoked from the deck generated by the servlet's own method, `displayTitles()`.

For the first type of request, `doPost()` responds in one of the following ways according to the number of matches found in the library database based on the title input by the user:

- If there is no match found in the Books table of the library database, the method redirects the request to the deck, notFound.wml, which is discussed in the next section.

- If there is only one exact match, `bookDetails()` is invoked to display the details of the book.

- If there are multiple but fewer than 10 matches, `displayTitles()` is called to display the list of titles from which the user can select to view its details.

- If there are more than 10 matches, the method redirects the request to the deck, narrow.wml, to display a message that advises the user to give a more precise title.

For the second type of request, `doPost()` receives a nonempty `ISBN` of the selected book and passes the information to `bookDetails()` to display the details of the book.

bookDetails()

This method retrieves information of a book and generates WML content to display the retrieved information, which includes:

- ISBN of the book
- Title and publisher from the Books table
- Author(s) from the Authors table
- Loaning and reservation status of all the cataloged copies of the book from the Copies table

The following display of details is generated for the book, *Java Servlets By Example*:

- User keys in *Java Servlets* in response to the prompt presented in the searchBook card of the mainMenu.wml deck (figure 35.17).

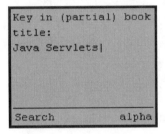

Figure 35.17
User enters *Java Servlets* for searching

- One exact match (*Java Servlets By Example*) is found and `bookDetails()` generates the book information shown in figure 35.18.

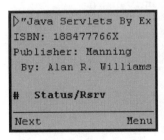 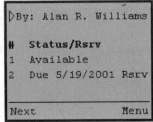

Figure 35.18
Display of book details as a result of the search for title *Java Servlets by Example*

The display of details in figure 35.19 is generated for the book, *Web Development with JavaServer Pages*. Notice that the user is given the choice of making a reservation.

In the previous case, since there was one book still available, the option was not offered. In this case however, all copies have been loaned out and, since copy 2 has not yet been reserved, the reservation option is viable.

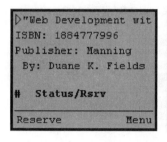 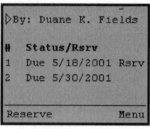

Figure 35.19
Display of details of the book *Web Development with JavaServer Pages*

Clicking the Reserve option will invoke another servlet, Reserve, which will be discussed in section 35.5.8.

displayTitles()

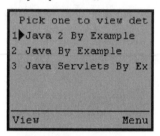

This method generates a WML deck to display all the possible titles found in the library database that match the title input by the user.

The example in figure 35.20 shows the display of several possible titles when the user keys in the search title, *Example*:

Figure 35.20   List of titles that contain the word *Example*

35.5.7   Display-not-found and too-many-matches messages

The two decks, notFound.wml and narrow.wml, are used to display the appropriate warning messages regarding the search results. The first is loaded when the SearchBy-Title servlet cannot find a match for the title specified by the user; the second is loaded when the input title resulted in more than 10 matches.

The code for the notFound.wml deck is:

```
<?xml version="1.0"?>
<!DOCTYPE wml PUBLIC "-//WAPFORUM//DTD WML 1.1//EN"
        "http://www.wapforum.org/DTD/wml_1.1.xml">

<wml>  <!-- notFound.wml -->
<card id="notFound" title="Book Search">
   <p>
      No match for the title: <br />
      "$title"
   </p>
   <do type="accept" label="Input title">
```

```
      <prev />
   </do>
</card>
</wml>
```

When the user chooses to input the title again, the browser merely reloads the previous card instead of loading based on a specified URL. The first method causes the top entry of the URL history stack to pop out, thus reducing the number of entries kept in the stack; the second way loads the specified URL, which becomes the new top entry of the history stack, thus increasing the stack size.

The narrow.wml deck is:

```
<?xml version="1.0"?>
<!DOCTYPE wml PUBLIC "-//WAPFORUM//DTD WML 1.1//EN"
         "http://www.wapforum.org/DTD/wml_1.1.xml">

<wml>  <!-- narrow.wml -->
<card id="narrowSearch" title="Book Search">
   <p>
      Too many matches found. <br />
      Key in a more precise title to narrow the search.
   </p>
   <do type="accept" label="Input title">
      <prev />
   </do>
</card>
</wml>
```

Figure 35.21 shows the display by the two decks which occurred when the user input *Golf* and *Java*:

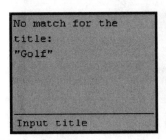 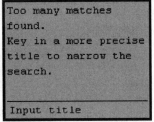

**Figure 35.21
Screen displays for search results of no match and too many matches found**

35.5.8 Reserving a book

The Reserve servlet is used for reserving a book. It may be invoked via the HTTP POST method, or the HTTP GET method. POST requests are serviced by the doPost() method while GET requests are serviced by the doGet() method.

When the user first expresses a desire to reserve a book after viewing details generated by bookDetails() of the SearchByTitle servlet, the Reserve servlet is invoked via the POST method. The doPost() method is responsible for listing the copies of the book of the specified ISBN that are available for reservation. It displays the copies with their due-date information as a selection list. The user can choose any copy, other than the default first copy, to reserve. Upon the selection, the user is prompted to key in his password to confirm his identity. Once this is done, this same servlet is invoked, but this time around, via the GET method.

The doGet() method receives the ISBN, copy ID, and input password. It checks the password against that kept as a session variable when the user first logs on. The reservation is allowed only if the two passwords match, in which case, the doGet() updates the Copies table of the library database accordingly.

Listing 35.4 is the source code of this reservation servlet:

Listing 35.4   Source code for Reserve.java

```java
/* Reserve.java */
import java.io.*;
import java.util.*;
import javax.servlet.*;
import javax.servlet.http.*;
import java.sql.*;

public class Reserve extends HttpServlet
{
    /* Initialization of servlet */
    public void init(ServletConfig config) throws ServletException {
        super.init (config);
    }

    /* Servicing client request to list books available for reservation */
    public void doPost (HttpServletRequest  request,
                        HttpServletResponse response)
            throws ServletException, IOException
    {
        // Variables
        Connection     con = null;
        Statement      stmt = null;
        String         query;
        ResultSet      rs = null;
        ResourceBundle db = ResourceBundle.getBundle ("eLib");
        PrintWriter    out;
        String         copyID, due, reserve;

        String isbn = request.getParameter ("isbn");
        String title = request.getParameter ("title");
        String pub = request.getParameter ("pub");

        try {
            Class.forName (db.getString("Driver"));
            con = DriverManager.getConnection (db.getString("URL"));

        } catch (Exception e)   {
            System.err.println ("Exception: JDBC-ODBC bridge driver...");
            System.err.println (e);
        }
```

Retrieves title, ISBN, and publisher from incoming request

```
try {
    response.setContentType("text/vnd.wap.wml");          ①
    response.setHeader("cache-control", "no-cache");

    out = response.getWriter();
    out.println ("<?xml version=\"1.0\"?>");
    out.println
      ("<!DOCTYPE wml PUBLIC \"-//WAPFORUM//DTD WML 1.1//EN\"");
    out.println ("\"http://www.wapforum.org/DTD/wml_1.1.xml\">");
    out.println("<wml>");
    out.println("<card id=\"start\" title=\"Book Reservation\">");

    out.println("<p mode=\"nowrap\">");

    out.println("\"" + title + "\" <br />");
    out.println("ISBN: " + isbn + "<br />");
    out.println("Publisher: " + pub + "<br />");

    stmt = con.createStatement();
    query = "SELECT CopyID, Due, ReserveID FROM Copies " +
            "WHERE ISBN='" + isbn + "'";
    rs = stmt.executeQuery (query);

    out.println("<select name=\"book\">");
    while (rs.next()) {
        copyID = rs.getString("CopyID").trim();
        due = rs.getString("Due").trim();
        reserve = rs.getString("ReserveID").trim();
        if (reserve.equals(""))
            out.println("   <option value=\"" + copyID + "\">");
                        "Due " + due + "</option>");
    }
    out.println("</select>");
    out.println("</p>");

    out.println("<do type=\"accept\" label=\"Reserve…\">");
    out.println("   <go href=\"#confirm\" />");
    out.println("</do>");

    out.println("<do type=\"options\" label=\"Back\">");
    out.println("   <prev />");
    out.println("</do>");
    out.println("</card>");

    out.println("<card id=\"confirm\">");
    out.println("<p>");
    out.println("   Your password?");
    out.println("   <input name=\"pw\" type=\"password\" />");     ②
    out.println("</p>");
    out.println("<do type=\"accept\" label=\"OK\">");
    out.println("   <go " +                                       ③
                "href=\"http://localhost/servlet/Reserve\" " +
                "method=\"get\">");
    out.println("      <postfield name=\"isbn\" value=\"" +
                isbn + "\" />");
```

Query for retrieving all copies of the book from the Copies table based on specified ISBN

In the selection list, displays due date for each book whose ReserveID field is empty

Generates Reserve link to navigate to the confirm card

```
            out.println("         <postfield name=\"copy\" value=\"$book\" />");
            out.println("         <postfield name=\"pw\" value=\"$pw\" />");

            out.println("   </go>");
            out.println("</do>");
            out.println("</card>");

            out.println("</wml>");
            out.close();

        } catch (SQLException e)  {
            System.err.println ("SQLException: Reservation book details...");
            System.err.println (e);

        } catch (Exception e)  {
            System.err.println ("Exception: Displaying book details...");
            System.err.println (e);
        }

        finally {
            try {
                if (rs != null)   rs.close();
                if (stmt != null) stmt.close();
                if (con != null)  con.close();
            } catch (Exception e)  {
                System.err.println ("Exception: finally in doPost()...");
                System.err.println (e);
            }
        }
    } // doPost()


/* Servicing client request to update ReserveID in the Copies table */
    public void doGet (HttpServletRequest   request,
                       HttpServletResponse response)
              throws ServletException, IOException
    {
        Connection con = null;
        Statement  stmt = null;
        ResourceBundle db = ResourceBundle.getBundle ("eLib");
        String     isbn = request.getParameter("isbn");
        String     copyID = request.getParameter("copy");
        String     pw = request.getParameter("pw");

        HttpSession session = request.getSession(true);
        String loginPW = (String) session.getAttribute("MemPW");    ❹

        if (pw.equals(loginPW)) {    ❺
            try {
                Class.forName (db.getString("Driver"));
                con = DriverManager.getConnection (db.getString("URL"));

            } catch (Exception e) {
                System.err.println ("Exception: JDBC-ODBC bridge driver...");
                System.err.println (e);
            }
```

Retrieves
ISBN, copy ID,
and
password
from
incoming
request

```
                try  {
                    String loginID = (String) session.getAttribute("MemID");
                    stmt = con.createStatement();
                    String update = "UPDATE Copies SET ReserveID='" +      ❻
                                    loginID + "' WHERE ISBN='" + isbn +
                                    "' AND CopyID='" + copyID + "'";
                    stmt.executeUpdate (update);
                    response.sendRedirect("http://localhost/rsrvSuccess.wml");

                } catch (SQLException e)  {
                    System.err.println ("SQLException: Updating ReserveID...");
                    System.err.println (e);

                } catch (Exception e)  {
                    System.err.println ("Exception: Reserving book...");
                    System.err.println (e);
                }

                finally {
                    try {
                        if (stmt != null) stmt.close();
                        if (con != null)  con.close();
                    } catch (Exception e)  {
                        System.err.println ("Exception: finally in doGet()...");
                        System.err.println (e);
                    }
                }
            }
            else
                response.sendRedirect("http://localhost/invalidPW.wml");    ❼

    } // doGet()
}
```

Code comments

❶ Starts generating WML content to display copies of the book available for reservation in a selection list.

❷ The confirm card prompts the user to key in the password in order to process the reservation.

❸ The Reserve servlet is invoked once the user keys in the password and clicks OK. It invokes the servlet using the HTTP GET method.

❹ Retrieves login password from the session object.

❺ This is a check of equality between the login password and the password the user just keyed in.

❻ Updates the Reserve ID to the current user's ID for the record with the specified ISBN and copy ID in the Copies table.

❼ If the password supplied by the user to perform reservation is not the same as the login password, the request is redirected to invalidPW.wml.

Consider again the case in which the user chooses to view the details of the book, *Web Development with JavaServer Pages* (figure 35.22).

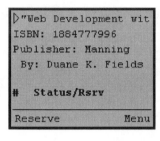
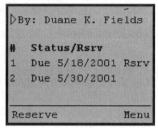

Figure 35.22
Screens showing second copy of *Web Development with JavaServer Pages* is available for reservation

Click the Reserve option and you should see a display generated by the doPost() method of the Reserve servlet (figure 35.23). In fact, the method generates a deck consisting of two cards: start and confirm. The start card was loaded first.

Notice that only the second copy is listed for reservation since the first has been reserved and the library allows only one reservation per physical book. If the user clicks the Reserve navigation link of the previous interface, he will be prompted for a password via the second card, confirm (figure 35.24).

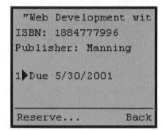
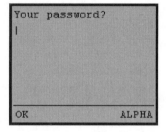

Figure 35.23
Reservation screen

Figure 35.24   User needs to enter password to make reservation

If the user enters a password that is different from that used to perform the login, the servlet redirects the request to a static deck, invalidPW.wml, whose code will be shown later. If the user enters the correct password, he will be greeted with the reservation-is-successful message displayed via redirection to a static deck, rsrvSuccess.wml.

35.5.9   invalidPW.wml and rsrvSuccess.wml

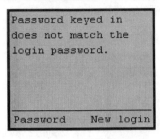

Figure 35.25   Message indicating incorrect password entered for reservation

This section presents two static decks used in the Reserve servlet. The first is used to display a message to inform the user of a mismatch between the input password to activate the reservation and the login password used earlier. The second deck informs the user of the successful reservation.

The display generated by invalidPW.wml is shown in figure 35.25. Here is the code:

```
<?xml version="1.0"?>
<!DOCTYPE wml PUBLIC "-//WAPFORUM//DTD WML 1.1//EN"
        "http://www.wapforum.org/DTD/wml_1.1.xml">

<wml>  <!-- invalidPW.wml -->
<card id="invalidPW">
   <p>
      Password keyed in does not match the login password.
   </p>
   <do type="accept" label="Password">
      <prev />
   </do>
   <do type="options" label="New login">
      <go href="http://localhost/login.wml" />
   </do>
</card>
</wml>
```

The display generated by rsrvSuccess.wml is shown in figure 35.26, and the code is:

```
<?xml version="1.0"?>
<!DOCTYPE wml PUBLIC "-//WAPFORUM//DTD WML
1.1//EN"
http://www.wapforum.org/DTD/wml_1.1.xml">

<wml>  <!-- rsrvSuccess.wml -->
<card id="start"
ontimer="http://localhost/mainMenu.wml#main">
   <timer value="20" />
   <p>
      Reservation is successful...
   </p>
</card>
</wml>
```

Figure 35.26   Message indicating the reservation is successful

If the user requests a search for the book *Web Development with JavaServer Pages* at this point, the status of the second copy of the title is now marked with the `Rsrv` indicator (figure 35.27).

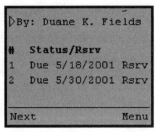

Figure 35.27
The second copy of *Web Development with JavaServer Pages* is now reserved

35.5.10 Renewing books based on ISBN

The design and logical flow of accomplishing this function was shown in the system design section. We have included the book renewal feature to present a complete design of a simple mobile system. We will not present the code for this service here since it will be largely the same as the service for searching and reserving a book.

Book renewal is a valuable service that is well suited for the wireless platform. With increasingly busy schedules, people are often unable to make a trip to the library to renew their books. A wireless renewal service definitely helps to make your use of the library more convenient and it saves you from having to pay fines for overdue books.

Three ways of initiating a renewal service are:

- Prompting the user for the ISBN of the book he wants to renew
- Prompting the user for the title of the book he wants to renew
- Listing all the books currently on loan to the user and prompting him to select a book to renew

Each method has its own merits and we will discuss them briefly. The first method assumes the user has the book and thus supplying the ISBN is not a problem. If the assumption were true, this method would offer the least number of steps to accomplish the task. The second method probably allows partial title matching and the subsequent implementation would be very much the same as the book inquiry and reservation function we saw earlier. The third option requires an additional query to the database to find all the books currently on loan to the user. The advantage is the convenience it offers to the user in specifying the book he wants to renew. This method does not require the user to key in the title or ISBN. Rather, he needs only to pick from a selection list.

Our design is based on the first method. Although we will not show the code here, we will briefly walk you through the book renewing procedure in this section.

Choose Renew a book (figure 35.28) from the main menu (mainMenu.wml#main).

You will be prompted to input the ISBN of the book (mainMenu.wml#renew-Book) (figure 35.29).

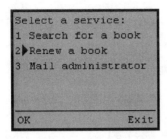

Figure 35.28
Book renewal screen

Figure 35.29   User needs to enter the ISBN of the book to renew

If the user keys in an ISBN that is not found in the Books table, a message (ISBN-notFound.wml) to that effect is displayed (figure 35.30).

If the ISBN entered was found in the database, the user is prompted for his password before the renewal will be processed (figure 35.31).

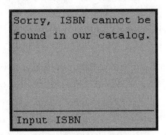

Figure 35.30   Message indicating incorrect ISBN entered

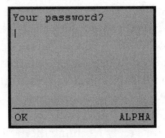

Figure 35.31   User needs to enter password to renew book

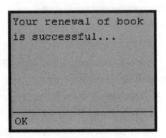

Figure 35.32   Message indicating the renewal is successful

As in the reservation of the book, the password is checked against the login password kept in a session object. Once they are verified to be the same, the Renew servlet will next check that a record exists in the Copies table with the specified ISBN value, and verify that the LoanID value is the member ID used during login (which can be retrieved from the session object). The Renew servlet should then update the Due and Renew fields of the record accordingly. This is followed by a message to the user to inform him of the successful renewal (figure 35.32).

Renewal will not be permitted if:

- The user has renewed the book twice in a row
- There is no record in the Copies table that contains both the specified ISBN and the user's LoanID

The Renew servlet should be able to plug in the appropriate message for display to the user to indicate the reason for his unsuccessful renewal request (figure 35.33).

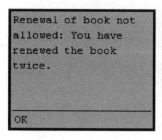
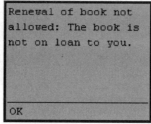

Figure 35.33
Possible reasons for failing to renew a book

35.5.11   Interlibrary book loans

Besides searching and renewing books, a mobile user might want to be able to perform other functions via a mobile device such as suggesting a new book for the library or checking on the availability of a book at a different library.

Suppose a user wants a book that is not found in the mobile library system but can be obtained from a different library that has an agreement with the user's mobile library system. A mobile library user must make a request for an interlibrary loan by contacting the library administrator.

A request for an interlibrary loan can be made through email and the library administrator's reply regarding the availability of the book can also be sent via email.

A mobile library system application needs to provide a way to contact a library administrator. This can be accomplished by using WML and a servlet. These components are described in the rest of this section.

WML

To allow a mobile user to contact the library administrator, a user needs to enter two pieces of information: an email address for the librarian's reply and the name and title of the requested book. This process requires two WML cards.

For this feature of the application, JSP is used to produce the required WML cards. Enhancements to this application, such as including a library ticket number to identify a request, or embedding a date and time in the WML cards, will require generating dynamic content. JSP provides a more flexible way to generate dynamic WML content. The process of contacting a mobile library administrator is supported in the ContactAdmin.jsp:

```
<?xml version="1.0"?>
<!DOCTYPE wml PUBLIC "-//WAPFORUM//DTD WML 1.1//EN"
      "http://www.wapforum.org/DTD/wml_1.1.xml">
<%@ page contentType="text/vnd.wap.wml;charset=ISO-8859-1" %>
<wml>
   <card id="enterEmail">                    ◄————————   Asks the user to enter
      <do type="accept" label="Next">                    his email address
         <go href="#enterRequest"/>
      </do>
      <p>
         Enter your email address:
            <input name="emailAddr"/>
      </p>
   </card>
                                   ┐  Asks the user to
   <card id="enterRequest">     ◄─┘  describe his request
      <do type="accept" label="Send">
         <go method="post"
            href="http://localhost/servlet/ContactAdminServlet">
            <postfield name="email" value="$emailAddr"/>
            <postfield name="msg" value="$msgReq"/>
         </go>
      </do>                      Calls the servlet to process the
      <p>                        request. The email address and the
         Describe your request:  description of the request are
         <input name="msgReq"/>  passed as request parameters so
      </p>                       that they can be used by the servlet
   </card>
</wml>
```

If the Mail administrator option of the main menu is selected, the screens in figure 35.34 are displayed in the sequence shown.

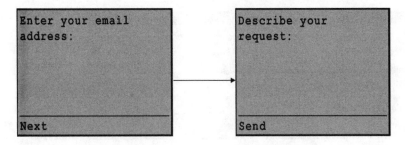

Figure 35.34   Request for email address and request description

If the email message is successfully sent to the mobile library administrator, a user receives a confirmation message as described in the following deck in ConfirmContact.jsp:

```
<?xml version="1.0"?>
<!DOCTYPE wml PUBLIC "-//WAPFORUM//DTD WML 1.1//EN"
      "http://www.wapforum.org/DTD/wml_1.1.xml">
<%@ page contentType="text/vnd.wap.wml;charset=ISO-8859-1" %>
```

```
<wml>
   <card>
      <do type="accept">
         <go href="http://localhost/mainMenu.wml"/>
      </do>
      <p>
         Your request has been sent to the library Administrator.
      </p>
   </card>
</wml>
```

After viewing this confirmation, the user is returned to the main menu

If the email message cannot be sent to the library administrator because the email server is not responding, the user is notified as described in CannotContact.jsp:

```
<?xml version="1.0"?>
<!DOCTYPE wml PUBLIC "-//WAPFORUM//DTD WML 1.1//EN"
      "http://www.wapforum.org/DTD/wml_1.1.xml">
<%@ page contentType="text/vnd.wap.wml;charset=ISO-8859-1" %>
<wml>
   <card>
      <do type="accept">
         <go href="http://localhost/mainMenu.wml"/>
      </do>
      <p>
         Your request could not be processed. Please try again.
      </p>
   </card>
</wml>
```

After viewing the error message, the user is returned to the main menu

Figure 35.35 shows the screens confirming a successful situation and an error message. In both situations, after a user reads the confirmation message, the main menu will be shown.

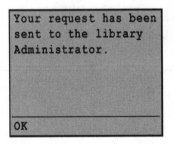
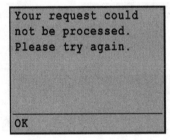

**Figure 35.35
A successful request (left) and an error message**

Servlet

After the user enters the description of a request and sends the message, control is transferred to the ContactAdminServlet servlet to contact the library administrator. The servlet is a mediator of requests. It uses a Facade to the JavaMail API to send an email message to the library administrator. The servlet also forwards requests to JSP pages to provide confirmation messages for a request.

To send an email message to the library administrator, the servlet retrieves two request parameters, namely, the mobile user's email address and the message text describing the nature of the request. The servlet responds to the request in two different ways:

- If the user is able to contact the mobile library administrator through email, the servlet redirects the request to the deck ConfirmContact.jsp.

- If the user is not able to contact the mobile library administrator, the servlet redirects the request to the deck CannotContact.jsp.

In both cases, control from the decks generated dynamically transfers back to the main menu. Listing 35.5 is the source code for ContactAdminServlet.

Listing 35.5   Source code for ContactAdminServlet

```
public class ContactAdminServlet extends HttpServlet {
   private EmailSender server = null; // Facade that interfaces with
                                      // JavaMail
   private static final String SMTP_HOST = "localhost";
   private static final String CONFIRM_CONTACT = "/jsp/ConfirmContact.jsp";
   private static final String CANNOT_CONTACT = "/jsp/CannotContact.jsp";

   public void init(ServletConfig conf) throws ServletException {
      super.init(conf);
   }

   public void doGet(HttpServletRequest req, HttpServletResponse res)
            throws ServletException, IOException {
      this.doPost(req, res);
   }

   public void doPost(HttpServletRequest req, HttpServletResponse res)
            throws ServletException, IOException {

      String url=null;
      HttpSession session = req.getSession(true);
      String email = req.getParameter("email" );
      String msg = req.getParameter("msg" );
         if (server == null)
            server = new EmailSender(SMTP_HOST);
      try {
         server.send(email, "LIBRARY ADMIN REQUEST", msg);
         url =  CONFIRM_CONTACT;
      } catch (Exception e) {
         url = CANNOT_CONTACT;
      }
      forwardtoJspPage(url, req, res);
   }

   private void forwardtoJspPage(String url, HttpServletRequest req,
                              HttpServletResponse res)
              throws ServletException, IOException {
```

Retrieves the user's email address and the description of the request

❶ Creates the Email Facade by passing in the SMTP server's host name

```
      ServletContext sc = getServletContext();
      RequestDispatcher rd = sc.getRequestDispatcher(url);
      rd.forward(req,res);
   }
}
```

Code comment

❶ The Email Facade is used to send an email message by passing in the user's email address, the literal "LIBRARY ADMIN REQUEST" as the subject of the message and the request description as the message text.

Future enhancements can address items such as input validation in the doPost() method. For example, the email address entered can be checked to ensure that it conforms to an Internet email address format such as including the @ symbol. If not, the user can be notified with an appropriate message.

As you can see in the servlet code, there is no use of the JavaMail API by the servlet. The servlet uses the EmailSender class that is a Facade to the JavaMail API. The EmailSender class establishes a new session with an email server and sends a message to a library administrator's email address. Listing 35.6 is the source code for the class.

Listing 35.6   Source code for EmailSender

```
public class EmailSender {
   // mail property constants
   static final String SMTP = "smtp";
   static final String MAIL_SMTP_HOST = "mail.smtp.host";
   static final String MAIL_TRANSPORT_PROTOCOL = "mail.transport.protocol";

   static final String TO_ADDRESS = "admin@mobilelib.org";    ◄── Hard-coded
   static final String MAILER_LABEL = "WAP Mailer";                library
                                                                   administrator's
   private Properties mailProperties =  new Properties();          email address
   private Session session;
   private String smtpHost;

   public EmailSender(String smtpHostName) {
      smtpHost=smtpHostName;
   }

   public void send(String from, String subject, String text)
            throws MessagingException {             Initializes the email
                                               properties with the SMTP
                                                  server's configuration.
      // Get a Session object                  The properties are used
      if (session == null) {                        to obtain a JavaMail
         // initialize mail-user properties to use in      Session object
         // obtaining Session object
         mailProperties.put(MAIL_TRANSPORT_PROTOCOL, SMTP);
         mailProperties.put(MAIL_SMTP_HOST, smtpHost);
         session = Session.getDefaultInstance(mailProperties, null);
      }
```

```
        // create a new Mime message
    Message msg = new MimeMessage(session);      ◄─┐   The MimeMessage
    msg.setHeader("X-Mailer", MAILER_LABEL);           constructor
    msg.setFrom(new InternetAddress(from));            creates an empty
 msg.setRecipient(Message.RecipientType.TO,            Message object
      new InternetAddress(TO_ADDRESS));                using the current
    msg.setSubject(subject);                           Session object
    msg.setText(text);
    // send the message
    Transport.send(msg);      ◄─┐  Uses the JavaMail
 }                               Transport object to
}                               send the message
```

Future enhancements to this system could add a confirmation ticket number to the subject of the email message sent to the library administrator and the confirmation number shown to the user. The use of JSP can facilitate this type of enhancement.

35.6 SUMMARY

This chapter presents you with another case study using WAP and server-side technologies. In this case, we use a mobile library system to illustrate the design of WML decks, as well as the use of servlets and JSP to dynamically generate WML content. Also, the use of the JavaMail API is incorporated into the system to demonstrate how it can be deployed in such a mobile library service.

PART XI

Appendices

The appendices in this segment should serve as a reference for the topics covered in the previous 10 sections. This part of the book covers references for the WML elements, WMLScript Standard libraries, HDML elements, setting up a web server to serve WAP content, HTTP/1.1 headers, Java Servlet Packages, and a list of WAP phones and their features.

APPENDIX A

WML elements

A.1   DECK-LEVEL ELEMENTS

<access>

The <access> element specifies access control information for a WML deck. You must specify this element within the deck header along with any metainformation for the deck (for more information, see <head> element and <meta> element). Each deck can have only *one* <access> element. All WML decks are public by default.

```
<head>
<access domain="http://www.otherdomain.com" path="/home" />
</head>
```

<access> attributes

domain=*friendly_url*	*friendly_url* indicates the URL domain of other decks that can access cards in the deck. The default value is the domain of the current deck.
path=*root_directory*	*root_directory* indicates the URL root of other decks that can access cards in the deck. The default value is "/" (the root path of the current deck), which lets any deck within the specified domain access this deck.

<head>

The <head> element specifies information about the deck as a whole, including metadata and access control information.

```
<wml>
<head>
   content
</head>

<card>
.
.
.
</card>
</wml>
```

In this example, any `<access>` or `<meta>` elements contained within the `<head>` element will affect the entire deck. Note that this differs from the `<template>` element; data defined within the `<template>` element is subordinate to conflicting data defined within a card. When using the `<head>` element, conflicting metadata defined within a particular card is ignores.

<meta>

The `<meta>` element provides metainformation for a WML deck; typically, this information is used by various search engines. This element is specified within the deck header along with any access control information for the deck (for more information, see `<access>` element and `<head>` element). Note that not all devices support every metainformation type.

```
<wml>
<head>
    <meta name="author" content="hoover" />
</head>
```

<meta> attributes

scheme=*name*	Specifies a structure that may be used to interpret the property value. Value may vary depending on the type of metadata.
name=*name*	*name* can be any descriptive term—it is used to describe the metadata.
http_equiv=*name*	Used in place of name, `http_equiv` tells the server to interpret the data associated with the `content` attribute as an HTTP header. As in the name attribute, `name` can be any descriptive term.
content=*metadata*	Specifies the metadata
forua=*boolean*	**true** | false If `true`, this attribute indicates that the author intended the metadata to reach the user. If `forua="false"`, an intermediate agent must remove the `<meta>` element before the document is sent to the client.

<setvar>

The <setvar> element sets a variable to a specified value when the device executes a <go>, <prev>, <spawn>, or <refresh> task.

```
<do type="accept">
        <go href="#display">
            <setvar name="Welles" value="Citizen Kane"/>
            <setvar name="Kubrick" value="Clockwork Orange"/>
        </go>
</do>
```

<setvar> attributes

name=*value*	The name of the variable to set. The device ignores the <setvar> element if *name* does not evaluate to a known variable at run time.
value=*value*	The value to assign to the variable

<template>

A WML deck may contain a <template> element that defines deck-level event bindings, i.e., characteristics that apply to all cards in the deck. You can override these characteristics for a particular card by specifying the same event bindings within the <card> definition.

```
<wml>
<template>
 <do type="accept" label="done">
   <go href="#card1"/>
 </do>
</template>

<card id="card1">
 .
 .
 .
</card>

</wml>
```

<template> attributes

These attributes are each an abbreviated form of the <onevent> element.

onenterforward= *url*	Specifies a URL to open if the user navigates to a card through a <go> task
onenterbackward= *url*	Specifies a URL to open if the user navigates to a card through a <prev> attribute
ontimer= *url*	Specifies a URL to open if a <timer> element expires

\<timer\>

The \<timer\> element provides a method for invoking a task automatically after a period of user inactivity. Any task or user action that activates the card starts the timer, and executing any task element stops it. You can associate only one task per timer, and you can define only one timer per card.

```
<card>
<timer name="time" value="100"/>
<onevent type="ontimer">
<go href="http://www.mydomain.com"/>
</onevent>
<p>Wait 10 seconds…"
</p>
</card>
```

\<timer\> attributes

name= name	The *name* of the variable in which the device stores the timer value
value= number_of_1/10_seconds	You must specify \<timer\> values in units of 1/10 seconds—a value of 50 equals 5 seconds. Specifying a value of 0 disables the timer.

\<wml\>

The \<wml\> element defines a WML deck; only header information is contained outside \<wml\>.

```
<?xml version="1.0"?>
<!DOCTYPE wml PUBLIC "-//WAPFORUM//DTD WML 1.1//EN"
"http://www.wapforum.org/DTD/wml_1.1.xml">
<wml>
   <card id="HelloWorld" title="HelloWorld!">
      <p>
         Welcome to the exciting world of WAP!
      </p>
   </card>
</wml>
```

A.2   CARD-LEVEL ELEMENTS IN WML

\<card\>

A WML deck consists of one or more \<card\> elements, each of which specifies a single interaction between the user and the phone. The phone displays only one card at a time.

Elements nested within a \<card\> element *must* be in the following order: \<onevent\>, \<timer\>, and \<do\>.

With the exception of those three elements, devices display these elements in the order in which you specify them.

```
<card id="display">
<p>
  variable Welles=<br/>

  $(Welles)<br/>
  variable Kubrick=<br/>
  $(Kubrick)
</p>

</card>
```

<card> attributes (default in bold)

id=*cardame*	Specifies a name for the card. The name acts as a URL enabling navigation to that card.
title=*title*	Specifies a brief label for the card, used as the default bookmark name when the user bookmarks the card
newcontext= *boolean*	true | **false** Specifies whether the device should begin a new context whenever the user navigates to the card through a `<go>` task. Specifying `true` removes all context-specific variables and clears the history stack.
ordered=*boolean*	**true**|false Specifies the organization of card content. `True` causes the device to display content in a fixed sequence.
onenterforward= *url*	Specifies a URL to open if the user navigates to this card through a `<go>` task
onenterbackward= *url*	Specifies a URL to open if the user navigates to this card through a `<prev>` attribute
ontimer=*url*	Specifies a URL to open if a `<timer>` element within this card expires

<fieldset>

The `<fieldset>` element allows you to group multiple text or input items within a card. Specifying one or more `<fieldset>` elements lets you control how the device presents card content in order to simplify user navigation. Many phones do not support the `<fieldset>` element; it is recommended the element be avoided.

<fieldset> attributes

title=*label*	Specifies a label for the `<fieldset>` group. Some devices use the label as a title when displaying the `<fieldset>` content; others might use it as a label for a user interface mechanism that enables navigation to the `<fieldset>` content.

<optgroup>

The `<optgroup>` element allows you to group multiple `<option>` (or nested `<optgroup>`) elements within a card. Creating option groups lets you specify control information about how the device should present the card content.

```
<card>
<do type="accept">
    <go href="#display"/>
</do>
<p>
Search for:
<select name="choice">

<optgroup title="Some states">
    <option value="ME">Maine</option>
    <option value="NH">New Hampshire</option>
    <option value="VT">Vermont</option>
 </optgroup>
<optgroup title="Other states">
    <option value="CT">Connecticut</option>
    <option value="MA">Massachusetts</option>
    <option value="RI">Rhode Island</option>
</optgroup>
</select>
</p>
</card>
```

<optgroup> attributes

title=*label*	Specifies a label for the `<optgroup>`. Some devices use the label as a title when displaying the `<fieldset>` content; others might use it as a label for a user interface mechanism that enables navigation to the `<fieldset>` content.

A.3 DEFINING ACTIONS IN *WML*

<anchor>

The `<anchor>` element anchors a task to a string of formatted text, often called a *link*. You can specify a link within any formatted text or image. When a user selects the link and presses Accept, the device executes the task.

```
<card id="card1">
<p>
The word "link" is linked to card3
</p>
<anchor>
<go href="#card3" title="card3">link
</anchor>
</card>
```

<anchor> attributes

title=*label*	A label that identifies the link. If you do not specify the `title` attribute, the device uses the word `"Link"` as the default label. The phone uses the title as the Accept key label when the user selects the link. To ensure compatibility on a wide range of devices, `label` should be a maximum of five characters.

<a>

`<a>` is the short form for the `<anchor>` element. It's used to define implied `<go>` tasks that require a URL specification.

```
<card id="card1">
<p>
The word "link" is linked to card3
</p>
<a href="#card3" title="card3">link</a>
</card>
```

<a> attributes

title=*label*	A label that identifies the link. If you do not specify the `title` attribute, the device uses the word `"Link"` as the default label. The phone uses the title as the Accept key label when the user selects the link. To ensure compatibility on a wide range of devices, `label` should be a maximum of five characters.
href=*url*	The url to which the user will navigate upon selecting the link

<do>

The `<do>` element associates a task with a button on the phone. When the user presses the button, the phone performs the associated `<do>` task.

```
<do type="accept">
 <go href="#card2"/>
</do>
```

<do> attributes

type=*task_type*	Identifies the button that triggers the specified <do> element task (see descriptions in the table below)
label =*label*	A label that appears near the button associated with the task. For example, if you bind a task to the Accept key, the device displays this value as the Accept key label. This label should not exceed five characters.
name=*name*	Specifies a name for the <do> element
optional=*Boolean*	true | false Specifies whether the device can ignore this element

You can specify the following values for the type attribute (all types are reserved except where noted):

Task types

Type value	Perform task if user ...
accept	Invokes ACCEPT mechanism (function key, button, etc.)
delete	Invokes DELETE mechanism (function key, button, etc.)
help	Invokes HELP mechanism (may be context-sensitive)
options	Invokes OPTIONS mechanism (function key, button, etc.)
prev	Navigates to card by invoking PREV mechanism from another card
reset	Invokes RESET mechanism (clears or resets current device state) *The phone.com does not currently support this attribute value.*
unknown	Invokes UNKNOWN mechanism (equivalent to TYPE="") *The phone.com does not currently support this attribute value.*
vnd.*co-type*	Invokes a vendor-specific mechanism where co identifies the vendor and type identifies the action (not reserved)

None of these type values imply a specific user interface mechanism. Some devices map each type to a physical key, while others map them to context-dependent gestures (for example, pressing or press-holding a jog shuttle). Thus, when designing your user interface, keep in mind that you cannot specify (or assume) the particular mechanism that a device will use.

NOTE If you define multiple <do> elements of the same type in one card, you should specify the name attribute for each <do> element in order to uniquely identify each instance of the same type. For example, you might associate the label "menu" with the Options softkey; pressing Options would then provide a menu that includes all <do> elements of the type accept or options.

<go>

The <go> element is a *task* element that instructs the device to open a specified URL. If the URL specifies a particular card, the device displays that card. If the URL specifies a deck, the device displays the first card in that deck.

```
<do type="accept">
 <go href="#card2"/>
</do>
```

<go> attributes

href=*url*	The URL to which to navigate upon invocation of the task
sendreferer= *boolean*	Specifies whether the device should include the deck URL in the URL request. Specifying `sendreferer="true"` causes the device to set the HTTP_REFERER header to the *relative* URL of the requesting deck. If you want to restrict access to trusted services, decks that request specified URLs must set this option to TRUE.
method=*get* (or) *post*	Specifies the method for sending data to the URL. Specifying `method=post` causes the server to transcode variable data to the character set specified by the HTTP headers defined in your application. You should perform this transcoding if non-ASCII characters (specifically UTF-8) exist in the data being passed.
accept-charset= *charset*	Specifies the character encodings that your application can handle. The device uses this attribute to transcode data specified by the postfield element. The server assumes UTF-8 as the default encoding (of which US-ASCII is a subset), so WML services in the United States, Canada, or Australia do not need to use this attribute. You can also omit this attribute if you specify your character set(s) in the HTTP response header. Note that the `accept-charset` attribute overrides any character encodings you specify in the HTTP header. The syntax for this attribute is a comma- or space-delimited list of IANA character sets. For example, accept-charset="UTF-8, US-ASCII, ISO–8859–1". To view the complete IANA Character Set registry, go to http://www.iana.org/.

<input>

The `<input>` element enables the user to enter data into the phone, where it is stored as a value of the variable specified in the name attribute.

```
<card id="srchfor">
<do type="accept">
  <go href="#display"/>
</do>
  <p>
  Search for: <br/>
  <input name="srchfor"/>
  </p>
</card>
```

<input> attributes

name=*variable_name*	The name of the variable in which the device stores the text entered by the user
title=*label*	Specifies a brief label for the input item

type=*text* (or) *password*	Specifies how the device should display text the user enters. Specifying `type=text` causes the text to be visible. Specifying `type=password` causes the text to be masked (for example, replaced by "*" characters). It is recommended that `password` be avoided.
value=*default_value*	Specifies the default value of the variable named in the `name` attribute. If the name variable already contains a value, the `value` attribute is ignored. If the `value` attribute specifies a value that does not conform to the input mask specified by the `format` attribute, the user agent must ignore the `value` attribute.
accesskey =*a number 0-9*	A number (0–9) that appears on the left side of the screen next to the link. If the user presses the corresponding key on the phone keypad, the phone executes the task defined by the link.
format=*data_format*	Specifies a data form that the user entry must match (see Specifying a format).
emptyok=*boolean*	Specifies whether the user can leave the field blank.
maxlength=*number*	Specifies the maximum number of characters the user can enter. If unspecified, the phone imposes a limit of 256 characters.

Specifying a format

You can specify the following values for the `format` attribute:

Tag	Description
A	Any symbolic or uppercase alphabetic character (no numbers)
a	Any symbolic or lowercase alphabetic character (no numbers)
N	Any numeric character (no symbols or alphabetic characters)
X	Any symbolic, numeric, or uppercase alphabetic character (*not changeable* to lowercase)
x	Any symbolic, numeric, or lowercase alphabetic character (*not changeable* to uppercase) .
M	Any symbolic, numeric, or uppercase alphabetic character (*changeable* to lowercase)—for multiple character input, defaults to uppercase first character
m	Any symbolic, numeric, or lowercase alphabetic character (*changeable* to uppercase)—for multiple character input, defaults to lowercase first character

<noop>

The <noop> element is a *task* element that instructs the device to do nothing, i.e., no operation.

```
<do type="delent">
 <noop/>
</do>
```

\<onevent\>

The \<onevent\> element associates an *intrinsic event* with a task. When the intrinsic event occurs, the associated \<onevent\> task is invoked.

```
<card>
<onevent type=onenterbackward>
<go href=http://www.mydomain.com>
</onevent>
</card>
```

\<onevent\> attributes

type=*task_type*	Identifies the intrinsic event that triggers the specified \<onevent\> task.

You can specify the following values for the type attribute:

Type value	Perform task if ...
onpick	User selects or deselects an \<option\> item (see *\<option\> element*).
onenterforward	User navigates to a card through a \<go\> task.
onenterbackward	User navigates to a card through a \<prev\> task or invokes the PREV mechanism (for example, presses the Back key).
ontimer	A specified \<timer\> element expires (see *\<timer\> element*).

\<option\>

The \<option\> element specifies a particular choice within a \<select\> element.

```
<card id="card1">
 <do type="accept">
    <go href="#card2"/>
 </do>
<p>
  Search by:
  <select name="srchby" ivalue="ohmy">
    <option value="lions.">Lions</option>
    <option value="tigers">Tigers</option>
    <option value="bears">Bears</option>
  </select>
</p>
</card>
```

\<option\> attributes

title=*label*	A label that identifies the option; this label usually appears as the Accept key label when the user selects the option. Keep the label to a maximum of five characters.

value=*value*	Specifies the value to assign to the variable defined in the name attribute within the <select> element.
onpick=*url*	Specifies the URL to open if the user selects the option.

<postfield>

The <postfield> element defines name/value pairs that are passed to the HTTP server receiving the <go> request.

```
<card id="display">
<do type="accept">
    <go href="http://www.somedomain.com/some.cgi" method="post">
        <postfield name="$(var1)" />
        <postfield name="$(var2)" />
    </go>
</do>

</card>
</wml>
```

<postfield> attributes

name=*label*	A label that identifies the field.
value=*default_value*	A string specifying the default value for the variable specified by the value attribute.

The element is a *task* element that instructs the device to remove the current URL from the history stack and open the previous URL. If no previous URL exists on the history stack, specifying has no effect.

```
<card id=card2>
<do type=accept>
 <prev/>
</do>
    <p>Pressing accept will navigate backwards</p>
</card>
```

The element is a *task* element that instructs the device to refresh the specified card variables. The device also refreshes the display if any of those variables are currently shown.

```
<card id=card2>
<do type=accept>
 <refresh/>
</do>
    <p>Pressing accept will refresh the card</p>
</card>
```

<select>

The `<select>` element specifies a list of options from which the user can choose. You can specify either single- or multiple-choice `<select>` elements.

```
<card id="card1">
 <do type="accept">
    <go href="#card2"/>
 </do>
<p>
  Search by:
  <select name="srchby" ivalue="ohmy">
    <option value="lions.">Lions</option>
    <option value="tigers">Tigers</option>
    <option value="bears">Bears</option>
  </select>
</p>
</card>
```

<select> attributes

title=*label*	Specifies a brief label for the <select> list. Some devices use the label as a title when displaying the <select> content.
multiple=*Boolean*	Specifies whether the user can select multiple items. Default value is `false`.
name=*variable_name*	The name of the variable in which the device stores the value(s) associated with the option(s) chosen by the user.
value=*default_value*	A string specifying the default value(s) for the variable specified by the `name` attribute. If the `name` attribute already has a value when the user navigates to the <select> element, the device ignores the `value` attribute.
iname=*variable_name*	Identical to the `name` attribute except for the following: The specified variable stores the *index* value(s) associated with the option(s) chosen by the user. The index value associated with each option comes from its *position* in the <select> list, starting with 1. If the user has not selected an option, the index value is 0. The default value is specified by the `ivalue` attribute.
ivalue=*default_value*	Identical to the default attribute except for the following: The specified string contains the default index value(s) for the variable specified by the `iname` attribute.

A.4 TEXT AND IMAGE ELEMENTS IN WML

Note that different phones will display fonts differently—the `<b>` element used on one device may render differently than it will if the identical code is rendered on a different device.

\<b\>

The \<b\> element specifies bold text.

```
<p>
<b>This text is bold</b>
</p>
```

\<big\>

The \<big\> element specifies large font text.

```
<p>
<big>This text is big</big>
</p>
```

\<br/\>

The \<br/\> element specifies a line break.

```
<p>
This text
<br/>
has inserted a line break
</p>
```

\<em\>

The \<em\> element specifies emphasized text.

```
<p>
<em>This text is emphasized</em>
</p>
```

\<i\>

The \<i\> element specifies italic text.

```
<p>
<i>This text is italic</i>
</p>
```

\<img\>

The \<img\> element instructs the device to display an image within formatted text. Note that not all devices can display images.

```
<wml>
<card id=card1>
 <do type=accept>
 <go href=#card2/>
</do>
   <p>
    <center>
    Image!
```

```
  <br/>
  <a href=#search by>
  <img src=http://www.domain.com/movie/image.wbmp alt=Image/>
   </a>
   </center>
    </p>
</card>
</wml>
```

<img> attributes

alt=*alternative_text*	Specifies the text to display if the device does not support images or cannot find the specified image.
src=*url*	The URL of the image to display. If you specify a valid icon for the local `src` attribute the device ignores this attribute.
localsrc=*icon_name*	The name of a known icon. If the device cannot find the icon in ROM (read-only memory), it attempts to retrieve it from the server. If you specify a valid icon (see figure 2.6 for a list of icon names), the device ignores the `src` and `alt` attributes even though they are still required.
align=*top* (or) *middle* (or) *bottom*	Specifies image alignment relative to the current line of text.
hspace=*integer*	Specifies the amount of space to the left and right of the image. The default setting is zero.
vspace=*integer*	Specifies the amount of space to the top and bottom of the image. The default setting is zero.
height=*integer*	Specifies the dimension of the image.
width=*integer*	Specifies the dimension of the image.

<p>

The <p> element specifies a new paragraph and has alignment and line-wrapping attributes.

```
<p align=center>
This text is centered
</p>
```

<p> attributes

align= *left* (or) *right* (or) *center*	Specifies line alignment relative to the display area. Default value is `left`.
mode=*wrap* (or) *nowrap*	Specifies text wrapping mode to use.

<small>

The <small> element specifies small font text.

```
<p>
<small>This text is small</small>
</p>
```

`<strong>`

The `<strong>` element specifies emphasized text.

```
<p>
<strong>This text is emphasized</strong>
</p>
```

`<table>`

The `<table>` element allows you to specify columnar format. WML tables are similar to HTML tables but with fewer capabilities. When defining a table, you have to declare the number of columns, followed by some content. The content can include empty rows and columns.

```
<wml>
   <card id="card1" title="Calendar">
      <p>
         <table columns="3">
            <tr><td> Cell1 </td><td> Cell2 </td><td> Cell3 </td></tr>
            <tr><td> Cell1 </td><td> Cell2 </td><td> Cell3 </td></tr>
            <tr><td> Cell1 </td><td> Cell2 </td><td> Cell3 </td></tr>
         </table>
      </p>
   </card>
</wml>
```

`<table>` attributes

align=*left* (or)*right* (or) *center*	Specifies text alignment relative to the column. Default value is `left`.
title=*label*	Specifies a label for the table.
columns	Specifies the number of columns for the row set. This attribute is mandatory, and specifying a zero value is not allowed.

`<td>`

The `<td>` element is used as a container to hold a single table cell data within a table row. Table data cells may be empty. The user agent should do a best effort to deal with multiple line data cells that may result from using images or line breaks.

```
<wml>
   <card id="card1" title="Calendar">
      <p>
         <table columns="3">
            <tr><td> Cell1 </td><td> Cell2 </td><td> Cell3 </td></tr>
            <tr><td> Cell1 </td><td> Cell2 </td><td> Cell3 </td></tr>
            <tr><td> Cell1 </td><td> Cell2 </td><td> Cell3 </td></tr>
         </table>
      </p>
   </card>
</wml>
```

\<tr\>

The \<tr\> element is used as a container to hold a single table row. Table rows may be empty.

```
<wml>
   <card id="card1" title="Calendar">
     <p>
        <table columns="3">
           <tr><td> Cell1 </td><td> Cell2 </td><td> Cell3 </td></tr>
           <tr><td> Cell1 </td><td> Cell2 </td><td> Cell3 </td></tr>
           <tr><td> Cell1 </td><td> Cell2 </td><td> Cell3 </td></tr>
        </table>
     </p>
   </card>
</wml>
```

\<u\>

The \<u\> element specifies underlined text.

```
<p>
<u>This text is underlined</u>
</p>
```

A.5   PHONE.COM WML EXTENSIONS

These elements are not part of the WML specification. To use them, you must reference the Phone.com DTD in your header.

```
<?xml version="1.0"?>
<!DOCTYPE wml PUBLIC "-//PHONE.COM//DTD WML 1.1//EN"
"http://www.phone.com/dtd/wml11.dtd" >
```

\<catch\> (PHCM)

The \<catch\> element specifies an exception handler that can process an exception passed by a throw task. Parameters sent with the exception are received with the \<receive\> element.

An onthrow event occurs when the exception is caught and can be bound to a task. The onthrow event can be handled with the onthrow attribute or by embedding an \<onevent\> inside the \<catch\> element.

A \<spawn\> element cannot contain more than one \<catch\> element with the same name.

```
<card id="display">
<do type="accept">
<spawn href="#newcontext" onexit="#display">
<catch/>
</spawn>
</do>
<p>
```

```
Parent Context: Variable Actor=<br/>
  $(Actor)<br/>
  Variable Director=<br/>
  $(Director)
</p>
</card>
```

<catch> attributes

name=*name*	Specifies the name of the exception. If the name attribute is missing, the <catch> element will handle any exception.
onthrow=*url*	Specifies the URL to which the phone navigates upon an onthrow event. The onthrow event occurs when an exception matches the <catch> element.

<exit> (PHCM)

The <exit> element declares an exit task, indicating that the current context should be terminated. Values may be sent to the parent context with an embedded <send> element. The exit task causes the current context to be destroyed, including any variable and history state contained in the context.

```
<card id="newdisplay">
<do type="accept">
<exit/>
</do>
<p>
Pressing accept returns to the calling context
</p>
</card>
```

<throw> (PHCM)

The <throw> element declares a throw task, indicating that an exception should be raised. Values may be sent to the exception handler with <send> elements included in the throw. Throwing an exception terminates the current context and causes the context to be destroyed, including any variable and history state contained in the context.

If the parent context does not contain a <catch> element that matches this exception, the parent context is terminated and the exception is re-thrown to that context's parent. This operation repeats until an exception handler is found or all parent contexts have been terminated.

```
<throw name="error">
   <send value="incorrect value entered"/>
</throw>
```

<throw> attribute

name=*name*	Specifies the name of the exception. This name is used to find the correct handler for the exception. The `name` attribute value is case sensitive.

<spawn> (PHCM)

The <spawn> element declares a spawn task, indicating the creation of a child context and invocation of a URL in that child context. If the URL names a WML card or deck, the card is displayed, and the URL becomes the basis for a new history stack in the child context.

When the child context is exited via the exit task, an onexit intrinsic event occurs. The onexit event can be handled with the `onexit` attribute or by embedding a <onevent> inside the <spawn> element. A spawn task can initialize the child context's variables with the <setvar> element, parameters returned from the child context are bound to variables with <receive> elements, and exceptions that occur in child contexts can be caught with the <catch> element.

The spawn element may also contain one or more <postfield> elements. These elements specify information to be submitted to the origin server during the request.

```
<card id="display">
<do type="accept">
<spawn href="#newcontext" onexit="#display">
<catch/>
</spawn>
</do>
<p>
 Parent Context: Variable Actor=<br/>
  $(Actor)<br/>
  Variable Director=<br/>
 $(Director)
</p>
</card>
```

<spawn> attributes

href=*url*	Specifies the destination URL. The URL of the card to display.
onexit=*url*	Specifies the URL to which the phone navigates upon the invocation of an onexit event. The onexit event occurs when the child context is exited with an exit task.
sendreferer =*boolean*	Specifies whether the device should include the relative URL of the requesting deck in the URL request, thus indicating to the receiving URL who is making the request.
method= *get* (or)*post*	Specifies the HTTP submission method. Specifying `method=post` causes the server to transcode variable data to the character set specified by the HTTP headers defined in your application. You should perform this transcoding if non-ASCII characters (specifically UTF-8) exist in the data being passed.

accept-charset=*charset*	Specifies the character encodings that your application can handle. The device uses this attribute to transcode data specified by the post-field element. The server assumes UTF-8 as the default encoding (of which US-ASCII is a subset), so WML services in the United States, Canada, or Australia do not need to use this attribute. You can also omit this attribute if you specify your character set(s) in the HTTP response header. Note that the `accept-charset` attribute overrides any character encodings you specify in the HTTP header. The syntax for this attribute is a comma- or space-delimited list of IANA character sets. For example, accept-charset="UTF-8, US-ASCII, ISO–8859–1". To view the complete IANA Character Set registry, go to http://www.iana.org/.

<send> (PHCM)

The `<send>` element specifies a single value to be included in a parameter block.

The phone creates a parameter block with a single entry for each `<send>` element. Each entry is identified by its position in the parameter block, and the position is derived from the order of the `<send>` elements.

```
<card id="newcontext">
<do type="accept">
<exit>
   <send value="$(varA)"/>
</exit>
</do>
<p>
This card sends the value of varA to the variable defined by the receive
element in the parent context
</p>
</card>
```

<send> attribute

value=*variable_value*	Specifies the data to be sent in this parameter block position. If not specified, the value defaults to an empty string.

<reset> (PHCM)

The `<reset>` element causes all variables in the current context to be cleared. If a task element, `<go>`, `<prev>`, or `<refresh>` contains a `<reset>` element, the reset operation is performed when the task is executed. If the `<catch>` element contains a `<reset>` element, the operation is performed during the `<throw>` task processing.

<receive> (PHCM)

The `<receive>` element is used to receive data sent from a child context. A `<receive>` element without a `name` attribute causes the value in the parameter block to be ignored.

When receiving a parameter block, `<receive>` elements assign a corresponding variable to each value in that parameter block. If there are insufficient values in the parameter block, each additional `<receive>` should be treated as if the parameter block contained an empty string in that position.

```
<card id="firstcontext">
 <do type="accept">
 <spawn href="#newcontext" onexit="#card1">
 <receive name="var1"/>
 </spawn>
 </do>
<p>
A variable sent from the new context will be assigned to var1 as indicated
above
</p>
</card>
```

<receive> attribute

name=*name*	Specifies the variable name. It is an error if the name attribute value is not a legal WML variable name.

<link> (PHCM)

The `<link>` element specifies a relationship between the containing deck and another document. This element must exist inside the `<head>` element.

<link> attributes

href=*url*	Specifies the location of the document being linked to.
rel =	Specifies the relationship between this deck and the document referenced by the href attribute.
sendreferer=*Boolean*	Specifies whether the device should include the deck URL in the URL request. Specifying sendreferer="true" causes the device to set the HTTP_REFERER header to the *relative* URL of the requesting deck. If you want to restrict access to trusted services, decks that request specified URLs must set this option to TRUE.

APPENDIX B

WMLScript function libraries

B.1   FLOAT LIBRARY

ceil

`Float.ceil(value)`

Returns the smallest integer value that is not less than the given value. If the *value* is already an integer, the result is the *value* itself.

> Parameters: *value* = Number
> Return value: Integer or invalid

Float.ceil examples

```
var a = 3.14;
var b = Float.ceil(a);          // b = 4
var c = Float.ceil(-2.8);       // c = -2
```

floor

`Float.floor(value)`

Returns the greatest integer value that is not greater than the given value. If the *value* is already an integer, the result is the *value* itself.

> Parameters: *value* = Number
> Return value: Integer or invalid

Float.floor examples

```
var a = 3.14;
var b = Float.floor(a);          // b = 3
var c = Float.floor(-2.8);       // c = -3
```

int

```
Float.int(value)
```

Returns the integer part of the given value. If the *value* is already an integer, the result is the *value* itself.

> Parameters: *value* = Number
> Return value: Integer or invalid

Float.int examples

```
var a = 3.14;
var b = Float.int(a);            // b = 3
var c = Float.int(-2.8);         // c = -2
```

maxFloat

```
Float.maxFloat()
```

Returns the maximum floating-point value supported by single-precision floating-point format.

> Return value: Floating-point 3.40282347E+38

Float.maxFloat example

```
var a = Float.maxFloat();
```

minFloat

```
Float.minFloat()
```

Returns the smallest nonzero floating-point value supported by single-precision floating-point format.

> Return value: Floating-point 1.17549435E-38

Float.minFloat example

```
var a = Float.minFloat();
```

pow

```
Float.pow(value1, value2)
```

Returns an implementation-dependent approximation to the result of raising *value1* to the power of *value2*. If *value1* is a negative number, then *value2* must be an integer.

> Return value: Floating-point or invalid
> Exceptions: If *value1* == 0 and *value2* < 0, then invalid is returned. If *value1* < 0 and *value2* is not an integer, then invalid is returned.

Float.pow examples

```
var a = 3;
var b = Float.pow(a, 2);          // b = 9
var c = 2.78
var d = Float.pow(c, 3)           // d = 2.783
```

round

`Float.round(value)`

Returns the number value that is closest to the given *value* and is equal to a mathematical integer. If two integer number values are equally close to the *value*, the result is the largest number value. If the *value* is already an integer, the result is the *value* itself.

> Parameters: *value* = Number
> Return value: Integer or invalid

Float.round examples

```
var a = Float.round(3.5);         // a = 4
var b = Float.round(-3.5);        // b = -3
var c = Float.round(0.5);         // c = 1
var d = Float.round(-0.5);        // d = 0
```

sqrt

`Float.sqrt(value)`

Returns an implementation-dependent approximation to the square root of the given *value*.

> Parameters: *value* = Floating-point
> Return value: Floating-point or invalid
> Exceptions: If *value* is a negative number then invalid is returned.

Float.sqrt examples

```
var a = 4;
var b = float.sqrt(a);        // b = 2.0
var c = float.sqrt(5);        // c = 2.2360679775
```

B.2   LANG LIBRARY

abort

`Lang.abort(errorDescription)`

Aborts the interpretation of the WMLScript 1.1 bytecode and returns the control to the caller of the WMLScript 1.1 interpreter with the return *errorDescription*. This function can be used to perform an abnormal exit in cases where the execution of the WMLScript 1.1 should be discontinued because of serious errors detected by the calling function. If the type of the *errorDescription* is invalid, the string `"invalid"` is used instead.

Parameters: *errorDescription* = String
Return value: None (this function aborts the interpretation)

Lang.abort example

```
Lang.abort("Error: " + errVal);  //Error value is a string
```

abs

`Lang.abs(value)`

Returns the absolute value of the given number. If the given number is of type *integer*, an integer value is returned. If the given number is of type *floating-point*, a floating-point value is returned.

Parameters: *value* = Number
Return value: Number or invalid

Lang.abs example

```
var a = -83;
var b = Lang.abs(a);        //b = 83
```

characterSet

`Lang.characterSet()`

Returns the character set supported by the WMLScript 1.1 interpreter. The return value is an integer that denotes a MIBEnum value assigned by the *Internet Assigned Numbers Authority* (IANA) for all character sets.

Return value: Integer

Lang.characterset example

```
var charset = Lang.characterSet();     // charset = 4 for latin1
```

exit

`Lang.exit(value)`

Ends the interpretation of WMLScript 1.1 bytecode and returns the control to the caller of the WMLScript 1.1 interpreter with the given return *value*. This function can be used to perform a normal exit from a function in cases where the execution of the WMLScript 1.1 bytecode should be discontinued.

Parameters: *value* = Any
Return value: None (this function ends the interpretation)

Lang.exit examples

```
Lang.exit("Value: " + myVal);        // Returns a string
Lang.exit(invalid);                  // Returns invalid
```

float

```
Lang.float()
```

Returns true if floating-points are supported, and false if not.

Return value: Boolean

Lang.float example

```
var floatsOkay = Lang.float();
```

isFloat

```
Lang.isFloat(value)
```

Returns a boolean value that is true if the given value can be converted into a floating-point number using parseFloat(*value*). Otherwise false is returned.

Parameters: *value* = Any
Return value: Boolean or invalid
Exceptions: If the system does not support floating-point operations, an invalid value is returned.

Lang.isfloat examples

```
var a = Lang.isFloat (" -123");      // true
var b = Lang.isFloat (" 123.33");    // true
var c = Lang.isFloat ("string");     // false
var d = Lang.isFloat ("#123.33");    // false
var e = Lang.isFloat (invalid);      // invalid
```

isInt

```
Lang.isInt(value)
```

Returns a boolean value that is true if the given *value* can be converted into an integer by using parseInt(*value*). Otherwise false is returned.

Parameters: *value* = Any
Return value: Boolean or invalid

Lang.isInt examples

```
var a = Lang.isInt(" -123");         // true
var b = Lang.isInt(" 123.33");       // true
var c = Lang.isInt("string");        // false
var d = Lang.isInt("#123");          // false
var e = Lang.isInt(invalid);         // invalid
```

max

```
Lang.max(value1, value2);
```

Returns the maximum value of the given two numbers. The value and type returned is the same as the value and type of the selected number.

> Parameters: *value1* = Number; *value2* = Number
> Return value: Number or invalid

Lang.abs example

```
var a = -3;
var b = Lang.abs(a);
var c = Lang.max(a, b);            // c = 3
var d = Lang.max(45.5, 76);        // d = 76(integer)
var e = Lang.max(45.0, 45);        // e = 45.0
```

maxInt

```
Lang.maxInt()
```

Returns the maximum integer value supported by the device.

> Return value: Integer 2147483647

Lang.maxInt example

```
var a = Lang.maxInt();
```

min

```
Lang.min(value1, value2)
```

Returns the minimum value of the given two numbers. The value and type returned is the same as the value and type of the selected number.

> Parameters: *value1* = Number; *value2* = Number
> Return value: Number or invalid

lang.min examples

```
var a = -3;
var b = Lang.abs(a);
var c = Lang.min(a, b);            // c = -3
var d = Lang.min(45, 76.3);        // d = 45 (integer)
var e = Lang.min(45, 45.0);        // e = 45 (integer)
```

minInt

```
Lang.minInt()
```

Returns the minimum integer value.

> Return value: Integer -2147483648

lang.minInt example

```
var a = Lang.minInt();
```

parseFloat

`Lang.parseFloat(value)`

Returns a floating-point value defined by the string value.

> Parameters: *value* = String
> Return value: Floating-point or invalid
> Exceptions: In case of a parsing error, an invalid value is returned. If the system does not support floating-point operations, invalid is returned.

Lang.parseFloat examples

```
var a = Lang.parseFloat("123.4");          // a = 123.4
var b = Lang.parseFloat(" +7.34e2 Hz")     // b = 7.34e2
var c = Lang.parseFloat(" 70e-2 F");       // c = 70.0e-2
var d = Lang.parseFloat("-.1 C");          // d = -0.1
var e = Lang.parseFloat(" 100 ");          // e = 100.0
var f = Lang.parseFloat("Number: 5.5");    // f = invalid
var g = Lang.parseFloat("7.3e meters");    // g = invalid
var h = Lang.parseFloat("7.3e- m/s");      // h = invalid
```

parseInt

`Lang.parseInt(value)`

Returns an integer value defined by the string value.

> Parameters: *value* = String
> Return value: Integer or invalid
> Exceptions: In case of a parsing error, an invalid value is returned.

Lang.parseInt example

```
var i = Lang.parseInt ("1234");            // i = 1234
var j = Lang.parseInt (" 100 m/s");        // j = 100
var k = Lang.parseInt("The larch")         // k = invalid
```

random

`Lang.random(value)`

Returns an integer value with a positive value that is greater than or equal to 0 but less than or equal to the given *value*. The return value is chosen randomly or pseudorandomly with approximately uniform distribution over that range, using an implementation-dependent algorithm or strategy. If the *value* is of type floating-point, `Float.int()` is first used to calculate the actual integer value.

> Parameters: *value* = Integer
> Return value: Integer or invalid
> Exceptions: If *value* is equal to zero (0), the function returns zero; if *value* is less than zero (0), the function returns invalid.

Lang.random examples

```
var a = 10;
var b = Lang.random(5.1)*a;      // b = 0..50
var c = Lang.random("string");   // c = invalid
```

seed

`Lang.seed(value)`

Initializes the pseudorandom number sequence and returns an empty string. If the *value* is zero or a positive integer, then the given *value* is used for initialization; otherwise a random, system-dependent initialization value is used. If the *value* is of type floating-point, `Float.int()` is first used to calculate the actual integer *value*.

> Parameters: *value* = Integer
> Return value: String or invalid

Lang.seed examples

```
var a = Lang.seed(123);      // a = ""
var b = Lang.random(20);     // b = 0..20
var c = Lang.seed("seed");   // c = invalid (random seed left unchanged)
```

B.3   STRING LIBRARY

charAt

`String.charAt(string, index)`

Returns a new string of length **one** containing the character at the specified *index* of the given *string*. If the *index* is of type floating-point, `Float.int()` is first used to calculate the actual integer *index*.

> Parameters: *string* = String; *index* = Number (the index of the character to be returned)
> Return value: String or invalid
> Exceptions: If *index* is out of range, an empty string ("") is returned.

String.charAt examples

```
var a = "Monday, May 24";
var b = String.charAt(a, 0);       // b = "M"
var c = String.charAt(a, 100);     // c = ""
var d = String.charAt(34, 0);      // d = "3"
var e = String.charAt(a, "first"); // e = invalid
```

compare

`String.compare(string1, string2)`

The return value indicates the lexicographic relation of *string1* to *string2*. The relation is based on the relation of the character codes in the native character set. The return value is –1 if *string1* is less than *string2*, 0 if *string1* is identical to *string2*, or 1 if *string1* is greater than *string2*.

Parameters: *string1* = String; *string2* = String
Return value: Integer or invalid

String.compare examples

```
var a = "Hello";
var b = "Hello";
var c = String.compare(a, b);              // c = 0
var d = String.compare("Bye", "John");     // d = -1
var e = String.compare("John", "Bye");     // e = 1
```

elementAt

`String.elementAt(string, index, separator)`

Search *string* for the element enumerated by *index*, and bracketed by *separator*. If the *index* is less than 0, the first element is returned. If the *index* is larger than the number of elements, the last element is returned. If the *string* is an empty string, an empty string is returned. If the *index* is of type floating-point, `Float.int()` is first used to calculate the actual *index* value.

Parameters: *string* = String; *index* = Number (the index of the element to be returned); *separator* = String (the first character of the string used as separator)
Return value: String or invalid
Exceptions: Returns invalid if the *separator* is an empty string ("")

String.elementAt examples

```
var a = "My name is Joe; Age 50;";
var b = String.elementAt(a, 0, " ");     // b = "My"
var c = String.elementAt(a, 14, ";");    // c = ""
var d = String.elementAt(a, 1, ";");     // d = " Age 50"
```

elements

`String.elements(string, separator)`

Returns the number of elements in the given *string* bracketed by the given *separator*. Empty string ("") is a valid element (thus, this function can never return a value that is less than or equal to zero).

Parameters: *string* = String; *separator* = String (the first character of the string used as separator)
Return value: Integer or invalid
Exceptions: Returns invalid if the *separator* is an empty string ("")

String.elements examples

```
var a = "My name is Joe; Age 50;";
var b = String.elements(a, " ");         // b = 6
```

```
var c = String.elements(a, ";");          // c = 3
var d = String.elements(""; ";");         // d = 1
var e = String.elements("a", ";");        // e = 1
var f = String.elements(";", ";");        // f = 2
var g = String.elements(";;,;", ";,");
     // g = 4 separator = ;
```

find

```
String.find(string, subString)
```

Returns the index of the first character in the *string* that matches the requested *sub-String*. If no match is found, integer value −1 is returned. Two strings are defined as a match when they are *identical*. Characters with multiple possible representations match only if they have the same representation in both strings. No case folding is performed.

> Parameters: *string* = String; *subString* = String
> Return value: Integer or invalid

String.find examples

```
var a = "abcde";
var b = String.find(a, "cd");             // b = 2
var c = String.find(34.2, "de");          // c = -1
var d = String.find(a, "qz");             // d = -1
var e = String.find(34, "3");             // e = 0
```

format

```
String.format(format, value)
```

Converts the given value to a string by using the given formatting provided as a format string. The format string can contain only one format specifier, which can be located anywhere inside the string. If more than one is specified, only the first one (leftmost) is used and the remaining specifiers are replaced by an empty string. The format specifier has the following form:

```
% [width] [.precision] type
```

where the `width` argument is a non-negative decimal integer controlling the minimum number of characters printed. If the number of characters in the output value is less than the specified width, blanks are added to the left until the minimum width is reached. The `width` argument never causes the *value* to be truncated. If the number of characters in the output value is greater than the specified width or, if width is not given, all characters of the *value* are printed (subject to the `precision` argument).

The `precision` argument specifies a non-negative decimal integer, preceded by a period (.), which can be used to set the precision of the output value. The interpretation of this value depends on the given type:

Type d specifies the minimum number of digits to be printed. If the number of digits in the *value* is less than precision, the output value is padded on the left with zeroes. The value is not truncated when the number of digits exceeds precision. Default precision is 1. If precision is specified as 0 and the value to be converted is 0, the result is an empty string ("").

Type f specifies the number of digits after the decimal point. If a decimal point appears, at least one digit appears before it. The value is rounded to the appropriate number of digits. Default precision is 6; if precision is 0 or if the period appears without a number following it, no decimal point is printed. When the number of digits after the decimal point is *less* than the number set by the *precision*, extra zeros are added to the right side. For example, the result of String.format ("%2.3f", 1.2) will be ("1.200").

Type s specifies the maximum number of characters to be printed. By default, all characters are printed. When the width is larger than the precision, the width should be ignored.

Unlike the width argument, the precision argument can cause either truncation of the output value or rounding of a floating-point value.

The type argument is the only required format argument; it appears after any optional format fields. The *character* determines whether the given *value* is interpreted as integer, floating-point, or string. The supported type arguments are:

The character d indicates *integer*. The output value has the form [–]dddd, where dddd is one or more decimal digits.

The character f indicates *floating-point*. The output value has the form [–]dddd.dddd, where dddd is one or more decimal digits. The number of digits before the decimal point depends on the magnitude of the number, and the number of digits after the decimal point depends on the requested precision.

The character s indicates *string*. Characters are printed up to the end of the string or until the precision value is reached.

Percent character (%) in the format string can be presented by preceding it with another percent character (%%).

Parameters: *format* = String; *value* = Any
Return value: String or invalid
Exceptions: Illegal format specifier results in an invalid return value

string.format examples

```
var a = 45;
var b = -45;
var c = "now";
var d = 1.2345678
var e = String.format("e: %6d", a);    // e = "e:    45"
var f = String.format("%6d", b);        // f = "   -45"
var g = String.format("%6.4d", a);      // g = "  0045"
var h = String.format("%6.4d", b);      // h = " -0045"
var i = String.format("Do it %s", c);   // i = "Do it now"
var j = String.format("%3f", d);        // j = "1.234567"
var k = String.format("%10.2f%%", d);   // k = "      1.23%"
var l = String.format("%3f %2f.", d);   // l = "1.234567 ."
```

```
var m = String.format("%.0d", 0);    // m = ""
var n = String.format("%7d", "Int"); // n = invalid
var o = String.format("%s", true);   // o = "true"
```

insertAt

`String.insertAt(string, element, index, separator)`

Returns a string with the *element* and the corresponding *separator* (if needed) inserted at the specified element *index* of the original *string*. If the *index* is less than 0, then 0 is used as the *index*. If the *index* is larger than the number of elements, then the element is appended at the end of the *string*. If the *string* is empty, the function returns a new string with the given *element*. If the *index* is of type floating-point, `Float.int()` is first used to calculate the actual *index* value.

> Parameters: *string* = String (original string); *element* = String (element to be inserted); *index* = Number (the index of the element to be added); *separator* = String (the first character of the string used as separator)
> Return value: String or invalid
> Exceptions: Returns invalid if the *separator* is an empty string ("")

String.insertAt examples

```
var a = "B C; E";
var s = " ";
var b = String.insertAt(a, "A", 0, s);    // b = "A B C; E"
var c = String.insertAt(a, "X", 3, s)     // c = "B C; E X"
var d = String.insertAt(a, "D", 1, ";");  // d = "B C;D; E"
var e = String.insertAt(a, "F", 5, ";");  // e = "B C; E;F"
```

isEmpty

`String.isEmpty(string)`

Returns a boolean true if the string length is zero; otherwise returns a boolean false.

> Parameters: *string* = String
> Return value: Boolean or invalid

String.isEmpty examples

```
var a = "Hello";
var b = "";
var c = String.isEmpty(a);        // c = false
var d = String.isEmpty(b);        // d = true
```

length

`String.length(string)`

Returns the length (number of characters) of the given *string*.

> Parameters: *string* = String
> Return value: Integer or invalid

String.length examples

```
var a = "ABC";
var b = String.length(a);             // b = 3
var c = String.length("")             // c = 0
var d = String.length(372);           // d = 3
```

removeAt

`String.removeAt(`*`string, index, separator`*`)`

Returns a new string where the element and the corresponding *separator* (if existing) with the given *index* are removed from the given *string*. If the *index* is less than 0 then the first element is removed. If the *index* is larger than the number of elements, the last element is removed. If the *string* is empty, the function returns a new empty string. If the *index* is of type floating-point, `Float.int()` is first used to calculate the actual *index* value.

> Parameters: *string* = String; *index* = Number (the index of the element to be deleted); *separator* = String (the first character of the string used as separator)
> Return value: String or invalid
> Exceptions: Returns invalid if the *separator* is an empty string ("")

String.removeAt examples

```
var a = "A A; B C D";
var s = "";
var b = String.removeAt(a, 1, s);     // b = "A B C D"
var c = String.removeAt(a, 0, ";");   // c = " B C D"
var d = String.removeAt(a, 14, ";");  // d = "A A"
```

replace

`String.replace(string, oldSubString, newSubString)`

Returns a new string resulting from replacing all occurrences of *oldSubString* in this string with *newSubString*.

Two strings are defined to match when they are *identical*. Characters with multiple possible representations match only if they have the same representation in both strings. No case folding is performed.

> Parameters: *string* = String; *oldSubString* = String; *newSubString* = String
> Return value: String or invalid

String.replace examples

```
var a = "It was the best of times";
var newAdjective = "worst"
var oldAdjective = "best"
var c = String.replace(a, oldAdjective, newAdjective);
    // c = "It was the worst of times"
var d = String.replace(a, newAdjective, oldAdjective);
    // d = "It was the best of times"
```

replaceAt

`String.replaceAt(string, element, index, separator)`

Returns a string with the current element at the specified *index* replaced with the given *element*. If the *index* is less than 0, the first element is replaced. If the *index* is larger than the number of elements, the last element is replaced. If the *string* is empty, the function returns a new string with the given *element*. If the *index* is of type floating-point, `Float.int()` is first used to calculate the actual *index* value.

> Parameters: *string* = String; *element* = String; *index* = Number (the index of the element to be replaced); *separator* = String (the first character of the string used as separator)
> Return value: String or invalid
> Exceptions: Returns invalid if the *separator* is an empty string ("")

String.replaceAt examples

```
var a = "Apples Oranges; Pears";
var s = "";
var b = String.replaceAt(a, "Cherries", 0, s);   // b = "Cherries Oranges;
Pears"
var c = String.replaceAt(a, "Grapes", 5, ";"); // c = "Apples Oranges;
Grapes"
```

squeeze

`String.squeeze(string)`

Returns a string where all consecutive series of white spaces within the *string* are reduced to one.

> Parameters: *string* = String
> Return value: String or invalid

String.squeeze examples

```
var a = "Yippee!";
var b = "It     was    the best of       times.";
var c = String.squeeze(a); // c = "Yippee!";
var d = String.squeeze(b)  // d = "it was the best of times."
```

subString

`String.subString(string, startIndex, length)`

Returns a new string that is a substring of the given *string*. The substring begins at the specified *startIndex* and its length (number of characters) is the given *length*. If the *startIndex* is less than 0, then 0 is used for the *startIndex*. If the *length* is larger than the remaining number of characters in the string, the *length* is replaced with the number of remaining characters. If the *startIndex* or the *length* is of type floating-point, Float.int() is first used to calculate the actual integer value.

Parameters: *string* = String; *startIndex* = Number (the beginning index, inclusive); *length* = Number (the length of the substring)
Return value: String or invalid
Exceptions: If *startIndex* is larger than the last index, an empty string ("") is returned; if *length* <= 0, an empty string ("") is returned.

String.substring examples

```
var a = "FROG";
var b = String.subString(a, 1, 2);      // b = "RO"
var c = String.subString(a, 2, 5);      // c = "OG"
var d = String.subString(BEAR, 0, 2);   // d = "BE"
```

toString

```
String.toString(value)
```

Returns a string representation of the given *value*. This function performs exactly the same conversions as supported by the WMLScript 1.1 language (automatic conversion from boolean, integer, and floating-point values to strings) except that invalid value returns the string "invalid".

Parameters: *value* = Any
Return value: String

String.toString examples

```
var a = String.toString(99);      // a = "99"
var b = String.toString(false)    // b = "false"
```

trim

```
String.trim(string)
```

Returns a string where all trailing and leading white spaces in the given *string* have been trimmed.

Parameters: *string* = String
Return value: String or invalid

trim examples

```
var a = "frog";
var b = "   It was the worst of times   ";
var c = String.trim(a);  // c = "frog";
var d = String.trim(b)   // d = "It was time worst of times"
```

B.4   URL LIBRARY

escapeString

`URL.escapeString(`*`string`*`)`

This function computes a new version of a *string* value in which special characters have been replaced by a hexadecimal escape sequence; a two-digit escape sequence of the form *%xx* must be used. The characters to be escaped are:

- *Control characters:* <US-ASCII coded characters 00-1F and 7F>
- *Space:* <US-ASCII coded character 20 hexadecimal>
- *Reserved:* ; / ? : @ & = + $,
- *Unwise:* ( ) | \ ^ [ ] '
- *Delims:* < > # % "

  The given string is escaped as such. No URL parsing is performed.

  Parameters: *string* = String
  Return value: String or invalid
  Exceptions: If *string* contains characters that are not part of the US-ASCII character set, an invalid value is returned.

URL.escapeString examples

```
var a = URL.escapeString("http://mydomain.com/var?b=\u007f#frog");
//a="http%3a%2f%2fmydomain.com%2fvar%3fb%3d%7f%23frog"
```

getBase

`URL.getBase()`

Returns an absolute URL (without the fragment) of the current WMLScript 1.1 file.

  Return value: String

URL.getbase examples

```
var a = url.getBase();     // a = "http://www.mydomain.com/frog.scr"
```

getFragment

`URL.getFragment(`*`url`*`)`

Returns the fragment used in the given *url*. If no fragment is specified, an empty string is returned. Both absolute and relative URLs are supported. Relative URLs are not resolved into absolute URLs.

  Parameters: *url* = String
  Return value: String or invalid
  Exceptions: If an invalid URL syntax is encountered while extracting the fragment, an invalid value is returned.

URL.getFragment examples

```
var a = URL.getFragment("http://www.mydomain.com/cont#frog");    // a =
"frog"
```

getHost

```
URL.getHost(url)
```

Returns the host specified in the given *url*. Both absolute and relative URLs are supported. Relative URLs are not resolved into absolute URLs.

> Parameters: *url* = String
> Return value: String or invalid
> Exceptions: If an invalid URL syntax is encountered while extracting the host part, an invalid value is returned.

URL.gethost examples

```
var a = URL.getHost("http://www.mydomain.com/path#frog");    // a =
"www.mydomain.com"
var b = UEL.getHost("path#frog");    // b = ""
```

getParameters

```
URL.getParameters(url)
```

Returns the parameters used in the given *url*. If no parameters are specified, an empty string is returned. Both absolute and relative URLs are supported. Relative URLs are not resolved into absolute URLs.

> Parameters: *url* = String
> Return value: String or invalid
> Exceptions: If an invalid URL syntax is encountered while extracting the parameters, an `invalid` value is returned.

URL.getparameters examples

```
var a = URL.getParameters("http://www.mydomain.com/frog;5;66?x=1&y=3");
// a = "5;66"
var b = URL.getParameters("../frog;5;66?x=1&y=3");    // b = "5;66"
```

getPath

```
URL.getPath(url)
```

Returns the path specified in the given *url*. Both absolute and relative URLs are supported. Relative URLs are not resolved into absolute URLs.

> Parameters: *url* = String
> Return value: String or invalid
> Exceptions: If an invalid URL syntax is encountered while extracting the path, an invalid value is returned.

```
var a = URL.getPath("http://www.froggy.com/frog/green/slimey#tadpole");
// a = "/frog/green/slimey"

var b = URL.getPath("../frog/green/slimey#tadpole");   // b =
"../frog/green/slimey"
```

getPort

`URL.getPort(url)`

Returns the port number specified in the given *url*. If no port is specified, an empty string is returned. Both absolute and relative URLs are supported. Relative URLs are not resolved into absolute URLs.

> Parameters: *url* = String
> Return value: String or invalid
> Exceptions: If an invalid URL syntax is encountered while extracting the port number, an invalid value is returned.

URL.getPort examples

```
var a = URL.getPort("http://www.froggy.com:80/frog#flies");   // a = "80"
var b = URL.getPort("http://www.froggy.com/frog#flies");    // b = ""
```

getQuery

`URL.getQuery(url)`

Returns the query part specified in the given *url*. If no query part is specified, an empty string is returned. Both absolute and relative URLs are supported. Relative URLs are not resolved into absolute URLs.

> Parameters: *url* = String
> Return value: String or invalid
> Exceptions: If an invalid URL syntax is encountered while extracting the query part, an invalid value is returned.

URL.getparameters example

```
var a = URL.getParameters("http://www.froggy.com/flies?x=4&y=18");   // a
   = "x=4&y=18"
```

getReferer

`URL.getReferer()`

Returns the smallest relative URL (relative to the base URL of the current file) to the resource that called the current file. Local function calls do not change the referer. If the current file does not have a referer, an empty string ("") is returned.

> Return value: String

```
var referredBy = URL.getReferer();     // referredBy = "frogs.wml"
```

getScheme

```
URL.getScheme(url)
```

Returns the scheme used in the given URL. Both absolute and relative URLs are supported. Relative URLs are not resolved into absolute URLs.

> Parameters: url = String
> Return value: String or invalid
> Exceptions: If an invalid URL syntax is encountered while extracting the scheme, an invalid value is returned.

URL.getScheme examples

```
var a = URL.getScheme("http://www.froggy.com/frog#flies");    // a = "http"
var b = URL.getScheme("www.froggy.com/path#flies");     // b = ""
```

isValid

```
URL.isValid(url)
```

Returns true if the given *url* has the right URL syntax, otherwise returns false. Both absolute and relative URLs are supported. Relative URLs are not resolved into absolute URLs.

> Parameters: *url* = String
> Return value: Boolean or invalid

URL.isValid examples

```
var a = URL.isValid("http://www.froggy.com/");     // a = true
var b = URL.isValid("../frog#flies");     // b = true
var c = URL.isValid("Frogttp://www.froggy.com/flies");     // c = false
```

loadString

```
URL.loadString(url, contentType)
```

Returns the content denoted by the given absolute *url* and the *content type*. The given *content type* is erroneous if it does not comply with the following rules:

- Only one content type can be specified. The whole string must match with only one content type and no extra leading or trailing spaces are allowed.
- The type must be text but the subtype can be anything. Thus, the type prefix must be "text/".

The behavior of this function is the following:

- The content with the given *content type* and *url* is loaded. The rest of the attributes needed for the content load are specified by the default settings of the user agent.

- If the load is successful and the returned content type matches the given *content type*, the content is converted to a string and returned.
- If the load is unsuccessful or the returned content is of wrong content type, a scheme-specific error code is returned.

Parameters: *url* = String; *contentType* = String
Return value: String, integer, or invalid
Exceptions: Returns an integer *error code* that depends on the used URL scheme in case the load fails. If HTTP or WSP schemes are used, HTTP error codes are returned. If an erroneous *content type* is given, an invalid value is returned.

URL.loadString examples

```
var myUrl = "http://www.froggy.com/frogs.vcf";
myCard = URL.loadString(myUrl, "text/x-vcard"); // myCard = contents of
    frogs.vcf
```

resolve

`URL.resolve(baseUrl, embeddedUrl)`

Returns an absolute URL from the given *baseUrl* and the *embeddedUrl*. If the *embeddedUrl* is already an absolute URL, the function returns it without modification.

Parameters: *baseUrl* = String; *embeddedUrl* = String
Return value: String or invalid
Exceptions: If an invalid URL syntax is encountered as part of the resolution an invalid value is returned.

URL.resolve example

```
 var a = URL.resolve("http://frogs.com/","frogs.vcf"); // a =
"http://frogs.com/frogs.vcf"
```

unescapeString

`URL.unescapeString(string)`

The unescape function computes a new version of a *string* value in which each escape sequence of the sort that might be introduced by the URL.escapeString() function is replaced with the character that it represents. The given string is unescaped as such. No URL parsing is performed.

Parameters: *string* = String
Return value: String or invalid
Exceptions: If *string* contains characters that are not part of the US-ASCII character set, an invalid value is returned.

URL.unescapeString example

```
var a = "http%3a%2f%2ffrogs.com%2fflies%3fx%3d99%23flies";
var b = URL.unescapeString(a);
// b = "http://frogs.com/flies?x=99#flies"
```

B.5   WMLBROWSER LIBRARY

getCurrentCard

`WMLBrowser.getCurrentCard()`

Returns the smallest relative URL (relative to the base of the current file) specifying the card (if any) currently being processed by the WML browser. The function returns an absolute URL if the WML deck containing the current card does not have the same base as the current file.

> Return value: String or invalid
> Exceptions: Returns invalid if there is no current card.

WMLBrowser.getCurrentCard example

```
var a = WMLBrowser.getCurrentCard();    // a = "frogs#display
```

getVar

`WMLBrowser.getVar(name)`

Returns the value of the variable with the given *name* in the current browser context. Returns an empty string ("") if the given variable does not exist. Variable name must follow the syntax specified by WML.

> Parameters: *name* = String
> Return value: String or invalid
> Exceptions: If the syntax of the variable name is incorrect, an invalid value is returned.

WMLBrowser.getVar example

```
var a = WMLBrowser.getVar("Animal");    // a = "Bear"
```

go

`WMLBrowser.go(url)`

Specifies the content denoted by the given *url* to be loaded. This function has the same semantics as the GO task in WML. The content is loaded only after the WML browser receives control from the WMLScript 1.1 interpreter after the WMLScript 1.1 invocation is finished. No content is loaded if the given *url* is an empty string ("").

go() and prev() library functions override each other. Both of these library functions can be called multiple times before returning control to the WML browser. However, only the settings of the last call stay in effect. In particular, if the last call to go() or prev() sets the URL to an empty string (""), all requests are effectively cancelled.

This function returns an empty string ("").

> Parameters: *url* = String
> Return value: String or invalid

WMLBrowser.go examples

```
var dest = "http://www.frog.com/frog/green.wml#first";
WMLBrowser.go(dest);
```

newContext

```
WMLBrowser.newContext()
```

Clears the current WML browser context and returns an empty string (""). This function has the same semantics as the NEWCONTEXT attribute in (extended) WML.

Return value: String or invalid

WMLBrowser.newContext example

```
WMLBrowser.newContext();
```

prev

```
WMLBrowser.prev()
```

Signals the WML browser to go back to the previous WML card. This function has the same semantics as the PREV task in WML. The previous card is loaded only after the WML browser receives control from the WMLScript 1.1 interpreter after the WMLScript 1.1 invocation is finished.

prev() and go() library functions override each other. Both of these library functions can be called multiple times before returning control back to the WML browser. However, only the settings of the last call stay in effect. In particular, if the last call to go() or prev() set the URL to an empty string (""), all requests are effectively cancelled.

This function returns an empty string ("").

Return value: String or invalid

WMLBrowser.prev example

```
WMLBrowser.prev();
```

refresh

```
WMLBrowser.refresh()
```

Forces the WML browser to update its context and returns an empty string. This function has the same semantics as the REFRESH task in WML. The function returns an absolute URL if the WML deck containing the current card does not have the same base as the current file.

Return value: String or invalid
Exceptions: Returns invalid if there is no current card

WMLBrowser.refresh example.

```
function anEasyMathProblem(){
```

```
var a = WMLBrowser.getVar("userEntry");
var b = 10.2;
var total = a*b;
WMLBrowser.setVar("userEntry", total);
WMLBrowser.refresh();
}
```

setVar

`WMLBrowser.setVar(name, value)`

Returns true if the variable with the given *name* is successfully set to contain the given *value* in the current browser context; false otherwise. Variable name and its value must follow the syntax specified by WML. Variable value must be legal XML CDATA.

> Parameters: *name* = String; *value* = String
> Return value: Boolean or invalid
> Exceptions: If the syntax of the variable name or its value is incorrect, an invalid value is returned.

WMLBrowser.setVar example

```
var a = WMLBrowser.setVar("favAnimal", "Bears");    // a = true
```

B.6   DIALOGS LIBRARY

prompt

`Dialogs.prompt(message, defaultInput)`

Displays the given *message* and prompts for user input. The default *defaultInput* parameter contains the initial content for the user input.

> Parameters: *message* = string; *defaultInput* = string
> Return value: String or invalid
> Exceptions: N/A

Dialogs.prompt example

```
var a = Dialogs.prompt("zip code:", "94114");
```

confirm

`Dialogs.confirm (message, ok_string, cancel_string)`

Displays the given *message* and two reply alternatives: *ok_string* and *cancel_string*. When the user selects one of the reply alternatives, the function returns `true` for *ok_string* and `false` for *cancel_string*.

> Parameters: *message*=string; *ok_string*=string, empty results in default text (default is implementation-dependent); cancel_string=string, empty results in default text (default is implementation-dependent)

> Return value: Boolean or invalid
> Exceptions: N/A

Dialogs.confirm example

```
function onAbort(){
   return Dialogs.confirm(Sure?, Yes, Well);
   };
```

alert

`Dialogs.alert(message)`

Displays the *message* to the user, waits for confirmation, and returns an empty string.

> Parameters: *message*=string
> Return value: String or invalid
> Exception: N/A

Dialogs.alert example

```
function rightLength (stateCode) {
   if (String.length(stateCode) > 2) {
     Dialogs.alert(Enter two letters only);
   };
};
```

B.7 CONSOLE LIBRARY (FOR USE WITH THE PHONE.COM SDK ONLY)

print

`Console.print(variable_or_string)`

Used for debugging. Converts *variable_or_string* to a string and prints it to the SDK Phone Information window. Remove instances of this function before deploying the application live.

> Parameters: *variable_or_string*= A string or a variable (or both) to be printed to the SDK Phone Information Window
> Return value: String or invalid
> Exception: N/A

Console.print example:

```
var vara = WMLBrowser.getVar("somevar");
var varb = WMLBrowser.getVar("othervar");
var varc = WMLBrowser.getVar("thirdvar");

// begin debugging functions
Console.print("Begin debugging check");
Console.print("vara:" + vara);
Console.print("varb:" + varb);
Console.print("varc:" + varc);
//end debugging functions
```

println

```
Console.println(variable_or_string)
```

Used for debugging. Converts *variable_or_string* to a string and prints it to the SDK Phone Information window. This call is the same as `console.print` except that it adds a new line to the end of the string. Use this function when you want each debug statement printed on a separate line in the Phone Information window. Remove instances of this function before deploying your application live.

> Parameters: *variable_or_string*= A string or a variable (or both) to be printed to the SDK Phone Information Window
> Return value: String or invalid
> Exception: N/A

Console.println example:

```
var vara = WMLBrowser.getVar("somevar");
var varb = WMLBrowser.getVar("othervar");
var varc = WMLBrowser.getVar("thirdvar");

// begin debugging functions
Console.printLn("Begin debugging check");
Console.printLn("vara:" + vara);
Console.printLn("varb:" + varb);
Console.printLn("varc:" + varc);
//end debugging functions
```

APPENDIX C

HDML *reference*

C.1 DECK-LEVEL ELEMENT

HDML defines only one deck-level element—<HDML>. Attributes available within <HDML> provide metalevel data to the deck, including cache control, access control, and bookmarking.

C.1.1 <HDML>

The <HDML> element defines a single deck of cards. In turn, the cards must be defined by including one or more <DISPLAY>, <ENTRY>, or <CHOICE> cards within the <HDML> elements.

Any elements within the <HDML> elements that are not nested within a card specify global settings or actions that apply to all cards within the deck.

```
<HDML VERSION="3.0">
  <DISPLAY>
      You're reading the appendix
  </DISPLAY>
</HDML>
```

<HDML> attributes

VERSION=*HDML version*	The latest version of HDML is 3.0.
TTL=*cache_time*	The number of seconds the phone should cache the deck after it receives it.
	If unspecified, the default cache time = 30 days.

MARKABLE=*boolean*	TRUE = Deck can be marked. Choosing this option also sets PUBLIC option to TRUE.
	FALSE (default) = Deck cannot be marked.
	Note: Specifying the MARKABLE option at the card level supersedes this option at the deck level.
PUBLIC=*boolean*	TRUE = Any deck may access this deck.
	FALSE (default) = Access limited to decks with domains and paths specified by the ACCESSDOMAIN and ACCESSPATH options can link to cards within the deck.
ACCESSDOMAIN=*domain*	When PUBLIC is set to FALSE, this variable specifies the domain of URLs allowed to request cards in the deck .
	DEFAULT = Current deck's domain.
ACCESSPATH=*path*	When PUBLIC is set to FALSE, this variable specifies the base path of URLs allowed to request cards in the deck.
	DEFAULT = / [the root of the current deck's path]; this means that any deck with the domain specified by ACESSDOMAIN can request the deck.

C.2 DEFINING TEXT AND IMAGES

HDML provides only limited control over text display, and does not support any manner of font changes (i.e., bold, underline etc.).

C.2.1 Formatting Text

<LINE>

The <LINE> element starts a new line of text. Text will wrap in Times Square mode (e.g., it will scroll horizontally across the phone's display).

```
<HDML VERSION="3.0">
  <DISPLAY>
     You're reading the appendix.
     <LINE>This line will wrap horizontally across the screen</LINE>
  </DISPLAY>
</HDML>
```

<WRAP>

The <WRAP> element starts a new line of text. Text will wrap to the next line in the display.

```
<HDML VERSION="3.0">
  <DISPLAY>
     You're reading the appendix.
     <LINE>This line will wrap horizontally across the screen</LINE>
     <WRAP>This line will wrap vertically down the screen</WRAP>
  </DISPLAY>
</HDML>
```

<RIGHT>

The <RIGHT> element right-justifies text.

```
<HDML VERSION="3.0">
  <DISPLAY>
      <RIGHT>You're reading the appendix.</RIGHT>
  </DISPLAY>
</HDML>
```

<CENTER>

The <CENTER> element centers text.

```
<HDML VERSION="3.0">
  <DISPLAY>
      <CENTER>You're reading the appendix.</CENTER>
  </DISPLAY>
</HDML>
```

<TAB>

The <TAB> element shifts text a predetermined number of spaces right. The specific width of the tab is dependent on the device.

```
<HDML VERSION="3.0">
  <DISPLAY>
      <TAB>You're
            <TAB><TAB>reading
            <TAB><TAB><TAB>the appendix.
  </DISPLAY>
</HDML>
```

*
*

The element inserts horizontal white space within the display.

```
<HDML VERSION="3.0">
  <DISPLAY>
      You're reading <BR/>
      the appendix
  </DISPLAY>
</HDML>
```

C.2.2   Escape characters

Some text characters are reserved, meaning they have special meaning to HDML. Using them explicitly within a text display might confuse the phone; instead, it is appropriate to substitute an escape character.

Text symbol	Represents
	Nonbreaking space
&lt;	Left angle bracket (<)

Text symbol	Represents
&gt;	Right angle bracket (>)
&quot;	Quotation marks (")
&amp;	Ampersand (&)
&dol;	Dollar sign ($)

<IMG>

On phones that support images, embedding an <IMG> element within any text displays the specified image. Images can be used in lieu of Softkey labels by specifying either the SRC or ICON options within an <ACTION> statement.

```
<HDML VERSION="3.0">
  <DISPLAY>
      This is a picture of
      <IMG SRC=http://www.mydomain.com/tiger.wbmp>
      a tiger!
  </DISPLAY>
</HDML>
```

IMG attributes

ALT=*alt_text*	*alt_text* indicates text to display if the image can't be displayed (if the phone does not support images or the image content can't be found).
SRC=*image_url*	*image_URL* indicates the URL of the image to display. If you specify a valid name for the ICON option, the device ignores this option.
ICON=*icon_name*	*icon_name* indicates the name of a local image to display. If the Phone cannot find the image in ROM, it retrieves it from the server.
	See Figure 2.14 for a list of the icon names you can specify for this option.

C.3   *DEFINING CARDS IN HDML*

HDML defines three different types of cards: a <CHOICE> card that provides a user with a menu; an <ENTRY> card that enables the user to enter data; and a <DISPLAY> card, used to simply display text on the phone.

C.3.1   <DISPLAY>

The <DISPLAY> element defines a card that contains text. Using the <A> element (defined below), selected text can become a link that performs a task when selected.

```
<HDML VERSION="3.0">
  <DISPLAY>
      A display card displays text and images on the phone.
  </DISPLAY>
</HDML>
```

<DISPLAY> attributes

NAME=*card_name*	*card_name* indicates a name for the card. Other cards can specify this name as a destination.
MARKABLE=*boolean*	TRUE = The card can be marked. Sets PUBLIC option to TRUE, even if the option is set to FALSE at the deck level.
	FALSE = The card cannot be marked. Use this option for cards that execute tasks that the user might not want to repeat.
TITLE=*card_title*	*card_title* indicates the default bookmark name that appears when the user marks the card.
BOOKMARK=*URL*	The URL the phone adds to the bookmark list if the user marks the card. If you do not specify the BOOKMARK option, the phone adds the URL of the current card to the bookmark list.

C.3.2   <CHOICE>

The <CHOICE> element defines a card that enables a user to make a selection from a list of options. Each option is contained within a <CE> element and selecting the option performs a task defined within the <CE> element.

```
<HTML VERSION=3.0>
<CHOICE>
        <CE LABEL=First TASK=go DEST=#card1>First Choice
        <CE LABEL=Second TASK=go DEST=#card2>Second Choice
        <CE LABEL=Third TASK=go DEST=#card3>Third Choice
</CHOICE>
</HTML>
```

<CHOICE> attributes

NAME=*card_name*	*card_name* indicates a name for the card. Other cards can specify this name as a destination.
MARKABLE=*boolean*	TRUE = The card can be marked. Sets PUBLIC option to TRUE, even if the option is set to FALSE at the deck level.
	FALSE = The card cannot be marked. Use this option for cards that execute tasks that the user might not want to repeat.
TITLE=*card_title*	*card_title* indicates the default bookmark name that appears when the user marks the card.
BOOKMARK=*URL*	*URL* indicates the URL the phone adds to the bookmark list if the user marks the card. If you do not specify the BOOKMARK option, the phone adds the URL of the current card to the bookmark list.
KEY=*var_name*	*var_name* indicates the variable that receives the value (if any) indicated within <CE> as VALUE (see <CE> variables).
IKEY=*var_name*	*var_name* indicates the default item within a list. If unspecified, the first item is default. After a user selects an item, the user's selection supersedes this variable.

METHOD=*number or alpha*	NUMBER (default) = numbered list.
	ALPHA = unnumbered list.
DEFAULT=*default_val*	*default_val* indicates the default value of the variable specified by the KEY option, ignored if KEY already has a value.
IDEFAULT=*default_num*	*default_num* indicates the index number of the default entry on the choice list. Ignored if the IKEY option is specified.

C.3.3   <ENTRY>

The <ENTRY> element defines a card that enables a user to enter data.

```
<HTML VERSION=3.0>
<ENTRY NAME=callnumber KEY=number>
    Enter a phone number:
    <ACTION TYPE=ACCEPT TASK=CALL NUMBER=5551212>
</ENTRY>
</HTML>
```

<ENTRY> attributes

NAME=*card_name*	*card_name* indicates a name for the card. Other cards can specify this name as a destination.
MARKABLE=*boolean*	TRUE = The card can be marked. Sets PUBLIC option to TRUE, even if the option is set to FALSE at the deck level.
	FALSE = The card cannot be marked. Use this option for cards that execute tasks that the user might not want to repeat.
TITLE=*card_title*	*card_title* indicates the default bookmark name that appears when the user marks the card.
BOOKMARK=*mark_URL*	*mark_URL* indicates the URL the phone adds to the bookmark list if the user marks the card. If you do not specify the BOOKMARK option, the phone adds the URL of the current card to the bookmark list.
FORMAT=*fmt_spec*	*fmt_spec* specifies the data the user enters. The default format is *M (any number of mixed-case alphabetic and numeric characters).
DEFAULT=*default_value*	*default_value* is a string that appears in the entry field when the phone first displays the card, editable by the user.
	If the variable specified by the KEY option has a value, it overrides the value specified by the DEFAULT option.
KEY=*var*	*var* indicates the name of the variable to which the Phone stores the data entered by the user. If the user has already entered data (that is, the specified variable already has a value), the value appears as the default in the entry field.
NOECHO=*boolean*	TRUE = Entered text is hidden from the user, appearing as asterisks (*).
	FALSE (default) = Entered text is not hidden.
EMPTYOK=*boolean*	TRUE = Accepts empty input, even if you have specified a format with the FORMAT option.
	FALSE (default) = Phone will not accept empty input.

C.3.4 <NODISPLAY>

The <NODISPLAY> element defines a card that remains hidden from a user. This card can contain action elements that (typically) set variables or initiate tasks. The action taken by the NODISPLAY card depends on the task that invoked it.

```
<NODISPLAY NAME=card1>
<ACTION TYPE=ACCEPT TASK=GO DEST=#display VARS=var1=Bill&var2=Jim>
</NODISPLAY>
```

<NODISPLAY> actions by invoking task

Invoking task	NODISPLAY action executed by phone
GO	ACCEPT
GOSUB	ACCEPT
RETURN	PREV
PREV	PREV
CANCEL	PREV
RETURN or CANCEL with DEST specifying the NODISPLAY card	ACCEPT
RETURN with the NEXT option of the calling card specifying the NODISPLAY card	ACCEPT
RETURN with the CANCEL option of the calling card specifying the NODISPLAY card	ACCEPT

C.4 ACTION ELEMENTS

Action elements are used to define a task invoked by a user action (a button press).

C.4.1 <A>

The <A> element associates a task with text, which will appear as a link on the phone. Note that <A> cannot be used within a <CHOICE> card (see <CE>).

```
<HDML VERSION="3.0">
  <DISPLAY>
    The next
    <A TASK=GO TYPE=ACCEPT DEST=http://www.mydomain.com>
    word
    </A>
is linked
  </DISPLAY>
</HDML>
```

<A> attributes

Statement	Description
LABEL=*key_label* *Note: key_label* should be five characters or fewer.	When used with the <A> or <CE> element, *key_label* defines the label for the Accept key. The default label is OK. When used with the <ACTION> element, *key_label* defines the label for the function key associated with the task. A label is *required* for all keys except: ACCEPT: **label** is optional (OK is default). PREV: **label** is ignored.
ACCESSKEY=*key_num*	*key_num* indicates a number on the phone keypad (0–9) associated with the link. Pressing the number on the keypad executes the task associated with the link.
TASK=*task_type*	*task_type* indicates the task to execute. Possible values are detailed in section 1.5.
DEST=*dest_url*	*dest_url* indicates the URL to request in GO and GOSUB tasks. If the current activity is nested and the task is a RETURN or CANCEL task, DEST specifies a URL to request upon returning to the calling activity. However, if the calling activity does not designate the current activity as "friendly," the phone ignores the DEST option. The DEST option overrides the NEXT or CANCEL options of the calling activity.
REL=NEXT	Instructs the phone to prefetch the URL specified by the DEST option. The phone loads and caches the URL while the user is viewing the current card. If the user invokes the action (requesting the URL) the phone can retrieve the URL from the cache instead of requesting it from the server. This gives the user a perception of enhanced performance. There is no guarantee that the phone will be able to prefetch the specified URL. For example, if the phone is on a circuit-switched network and the circuit is down, the phone will not open a circuit. If the phone fails to execute the prefetch, it does not retry it. If you specify the REL=NEXT option, the URL is added to the end of the phone's cache. If the user does not request the URL soon after the phone caches it, the phone pushes it out of the cache, and caches other data instead. If several tasks on a card specify the REL=NEXT option, the phone prefetches the URLs in the order in which the tasks are listed.
METHOD=GET (or) POST	If the DEST option specifies a URL, the method used to request the URL: GET or POST. If you do not specify this option, the default, GET, is used. To ensure the server will properly transcode data, it is recommended that you use the POST method instead of the GET method.
POSTDATA=*data*	The *data* to post if the METHOD option specifies POST. If the *data* contains multiple arguments, delimit the arguments with ampersands (&).

Statement	Description
ACCEPT-CHARSET=*charset*	*charset* specifies the character set that the HDML application expects data returned from the phone to use. It can specify character set names, such as the following: utf-8 us-ascii iso-8859-1 shift-jis
VARS=*varpairs*	*varpairs* indicates the list of variables to set for the current activity (if the task is GO) or nested activity (if the task is GOSUB). The variable list must be in query-string format, for example: var1=value1&var2=value2 Variable values must be escaped according to URL-escaping conventions. The phone unescapes the VARS option before setting the value of the variables.
RECEIVE=*var_list*	*var_list* indicates a semicolon-delimited list of variables to which the phone stores the return values from a GOSUB task. The phone stores return values according to ordinal position. For example, if you specify the following option: receive=var1;var2 The phone stores the first return value to var1 and the second return values to var2. If you want to skip a return value, you must include a semicolon as a placeholder.
RETVALS=*val_list*	*val_list* indicates a semicolon-delimited list of values that an activity invoked with GOSUB returns to the invoking activity. The RETVALS option is allowed only with the RETURN task. The values must be escaped according to URL-escaping conventions.
NEXT=*next_url*	*next_url* indicates the URL to request after a nested activity returns. If the FRIEND option in the GOSUB task is set to TRUE, the NEXT option can be overridden by the DEST option in the nested activity's RETURN task.
CANCEL=*cancel_url*	*cancel_url* indicates the URL to request after a nested activity invoked by a GOSUB task cancels. If the FRIEND option in the GOSUB task is set to TRUE, the CANCEL option can be overridden by the DEST option in the nested activity's CANCEL task.
FRIEND=*boolean*	A boolean value specifying whether the nested activity in a GOSUB task is "friendly." A friendly nested activity can use the DEST and CLEAR options in RETURN and CANCEL tasks and override the NEXT and CANCEL options of the calling task. To indicate that the nested activity is friendly, specify TRUE. The default is FALSE.

Statement	Description
SENDREFERER=*boolean*	A boolean value specifying whether the Phone should provide the URL of the current deck when requesting the URL specified by the DEST or NEXT options. If you set it to TRUE, the Phone specifies the deck's URL in the "Referer" header of the request.
	The Phone attempts to use the shortest possible relative URL in the "Referer" header if possible.
	The default value is FALSE.
CLEAR=*boolean*	A boolean value specifying whether a RETURN or CANCEL task from a nested activity unsets all the calling activity's variables. To unset the calling activity's variables, specify TRUE. The default is FALSE.
	The phone ignores the CLEAR option unless the calling activity specifies that the current activity is "friendly."
NUMBER=*number*	For a CALL task, *number* specifies the phone number to call.

C.4.2 <ACTION>

The <ACTION> element associates a task with a function key. Supported function keys are listed in the table below.

```
<HDML VERSION="3.2">
  <DISPLAY>
  <ACTION TYPE=ACCEPT TASK="GO" DEST="http://www.someurl.com ">
    Press the accept button to invoke the action
  </DISPLAY>
</HTML>
```

<ACTION> attributes

Statement	Description
LABEL=*key_label*	When used with the <A> or <CE> element, *key_label* defines the label for the Accept key. The default label is OK.
Note: key_label should be five characters or fewer.	When used with the <ACTION> element, this defines the label for the function key associated with the task.
	Label is *required* for all keys except:
	ACCEPT: **label** is optional (OK is default).
	PREV: **label** is ignored.
TYPE=*button_type*	*button_type* defines the button associated with the task.
	ACCEPT (LABEL optional)
	HELP (LABEL *required*)
	PREV (LABEL ignored)
	SOFT1 (LABEL *required*)
	SOFT2 (LABEL *required*)
	SEND (LABEL *required*)
	DELETE (LABEL *required*)
TASK=*task_type*	*task_type* indicates the task to execute. Possible values are detailed in section 1.5.

Statement	Description
DEST=*dest_url*	*dest_url* indicates the URL to request in GO and GOSUB tasks.
	If the current activity is nested and the task is a RETURN or CANCEL task, DEST specifies a URL to request upon returning to the calling activity. However, if the calling activity does not designate the current activity as "friendly," the phone ignores the DEST option. The DEST option overrides the NEXT or CANCEL options of the calling activity.
REL=NEXT	Instructs the phone to prefetch the URL specified by the DEST option. The phone loads and caches the URL while the user is viewing the current card.
	If the user invokes the action (requesting the URL) the phone can retrieve the URL from the cache instead of requesting it from the server. This gives the user a perception of enhanced performance.
	There is no guarantee that the phone will be able to prefetch the specified URL. For example, if the phone is on a circuit-switched network and the circuit is down, the phone will not open a circuit. If the phone fails to execute the prefetch, it does not retry it.
	If you specify the REL=NEXT option, the URL is added to the end of the phone's cache. If the user does not request the URL soon after the phone caches it, the phone pushes it out of the cache, and caches other data instead.
	If several tasks on a card specify the REL=NEXT option, the phone prefetches the URLs in the order in which the tasks are listed.
METHOD=GET (OR) POST	If the DEST option specifies a URL, the method used to request the URL: GET or POST.
	If you do not specify this option, the default, GET, is used.
	To ensure the server will properly transcode data, it is recommended that you use the POST method instead of the GET method.
POSTDATA=*data*	The *data* to post if the METHOD option specifies POST. If the *data* contains multiple arguments, delimit the arguments with ampersands (&).
ACCEPT-CHARSET=*charset*	*charset* specifies the character set that the HDML application expects data returned from the phone to use.
	It can specify character set names, such as the following:
	utf-8
	us-ascii
	iso-8859-1
	shift-jis
VARS=*varpairs*	*varpairs* indicates the list of variables to set for the current activity (if the task is GO) or nested activity (if the task is GOSUB). The variable list must be in query-string format, for example:
	var1=value1&var2=value2
	Variable values must be escaped according to URL-escaping conventions. The phone unescapes the VARS option before setting the value of the variables.

Statement	Description
RECEIVE=*var_list*	*val_list* indicates a semicolon-delimited list of values that an activity invoked with GOSUB returns to the invoking activity. The RETVALS option is allowed only with the RETURN task.
	The values must be escaped according to URL-escaping conventions.
RETVALS=*val_list*	*val_list* indicates a semicolon-delimited list of values that an activity invoked with GOSUB returns to the invoking activity. The RETVALS option is allowed only with the RETURN task.
	The values must be escaped according to URL-escaping conventions.
NEXT=*next_url*	*next_url* indicates the URL to request after a nested activity returns.
	If the FRIEND option in the GOSUB task is set to TRUE, the NEXT option can be overridden by the DEST option in the nested activity's RETURN task.
CANCEL=*cancel_url*	*cancel_url* indicates the URL to request after a nested activity invoked by a GOSUB task cancels.
	If the FRIEND option in the GOSUB task is set to TRUE, the CANCEL option can be overridden by the DEST option in the nested activity's CANCEL task.
FRIEND=*boolean*	A boolean value specifying whether the nested activity in a GOSUB task is "friendly." A friendly nested activity can use the DEST and CLEAR options in RETURN and CANCEL tasks and override the NEXT and CANCEL options of the calling task.
	To indicate that the nested activity is friendly, specify TRUE. The default is FALSE.
SENDREFERER=*boolean*	A boolean value specifying whether the phone should provide the URL of the current deck when requesting the URL specified by the DEST or NEXT options. If you set it to TRUE, the phone specifies the deck's URL in the "Referer" header of the request.
	The phone attempts to use the shortest possible relative URL in the "Referer" header if possible.
	The default value is FALSE.
CLEAR=*boolean*	A boolean value specifying whether a RETURN or CANCEL task from a nested activity unsets all the calling activity's variables. To unset the calling activity's variables, specify TRUE. The default is FALSE.
	The phone ignores the CLEAR option unless the calling activity specifies that the current activity is "friendly."
NUMBER=*number*	For a CALL task, *number* specifies the phone number to call.
SRC=*image_url*	The URL of an image to display in place of the softkey label. If a valid name is specified for the ICON option, the device ignores this option.
	Because SOFT1 and SOFT2 do not have default labels, you must specify the LABEL option if you use an image for either of these softkeys. The device will use this label if it cannot find the image you specify.

Statement	Description
ICON=*icon_name*	The name of a local image to display in place of the softkey label. If the phone cannot find the image in ROM, it retrieves it from the server.
	Because SOFT1 and SOFT2 do not have default labels, you must specify the LABEL option if you use an image for either of these softkeys. The device will use this label if it cannot find the image you specify.

<ACTION> hierarchy

When a function key is pressed, the phone looks for associated tasks. (It tries to execute an action defined by Rule 1; if Rule 1 doesn't apply, the phone moves on to Rule 2, etc.).

Function key	Rule 1	Rule 2	Rule 3	Rule 4	Rule 5
Accept	Execute selection (if choice card)	If user has scrolled to a link, execute task defined by that link	Execute task defined at card level	Execute task defined at deck level	Display previous card
Prev	Execute task defined at card level	Execute task defined at deck level	Display previous card		
Soft1	Execute task defined at card level	Execute task defined at deck level	Do nothing		
Soft2	Execute task defined at card level	Execute task defined at deck level	Do nothing		
Help	Execute task defined at card level	Execute task defined at deck level	Display no help available		
Send	Execute task defined at card level	Execute task defined at deck level	Do nothing		
Delete	Delete character left of the cursor (if text entry card)	Execute task defined at card level	Execute task defined at deck level	Do nothing	

C.4.3   <CE>

The <CE> element associates a task with a choice on a <CHOICE> card, and appears only within the context of <CHOICE>.

```
<HTML VERSION=3.0>
<CHOICE>
        <CE LABEL=First TASK=go DEST=#card1>First Choice
        <CE LABEL=Second TASK=go DEST=#card2>Second Choice
```

```
    <CE LABEL=Third TASK=go DEST=#card3>Third Choice
  </CHOICE>
  </HTML>
```

<CE> attributes

Statement	Description
LABEL=*key_label* *Note: key_label* should be five characters or fewer.	When used with the <A> or <CE> element, *key_label* defines the label for the Accept key. The default label is OK. When used with the <ACTION> element, this defines the label for the function key associated with the task. Label is *required* for all keys except: ACCEPT: **label** is optional (OK is default). PREV: **label** is ignored.
VALUE=*val*	The <CE> element is contained within a <CHOICE> element, which may contain a variable specified by the KEY option. The value defined by *val* is assigned to that variable.
TASK=*task_type*	*task_type* indicates the task to execute. Possible values are detailed in section 1.5.
DEST=*dest_url*	*dest_url* indicates the URL to request in GO and GOSUB tasks. If the current activity is nested and the task is a RETURN or CANCEL task, DEST specifies a URL to request upon returning to the calling activity. However, if the calling activity does not designate the current activity as "friendly," the phone ignores the DEST option. The DEST option overrides the NEXT or CANCEL options of the calling activity.
REL=NEXT	Instructs the phone to prefetch the URL specified by the DEST option. The phone loads and caches the URL while the user is viewing the current card. If the user invokes the action (requesting the URL) the phone can retrieve the URL from the cache instead of requesting it from the server. This gives the user a perception of enhanced performance. There is no guarantee that the phone will be able to prefetch the specified URL. For example, if the phone is on a circuit-switched network and the circuit is down, the phone will not open a circuit. If the phone fails to execute the prefetch, it does not retry it. If you specify the REL=NEXT option, the URL is added to the end of the phone's cache. If the user does not request the URL soon after the phone caches it, the phone pushes it out of the cache, and caches other data instead. If several tasks on a card specify the REL=NEXT option, the phone prefetches the URLs in the order in which the tasks are listed.
METHOD=*get_or_post*	If the DEST option specifies a URL, the method used to request the URL: GET or POST. If you do not specify this option, the default, GET, is used. To ensure the server will properly transcode data, it is recommended that you use the POST method instead of the GET method.
POSTDATA=*data*	The *data* to post if the METHOD option specifies POST. If the *data* contains multiple arguments, delimit the arguments with ampersands (&).

Statement	Description
ACCEPT-CHARSET=*charset*	*charset* specifies the character set that the HDML application expects data returned from the phone to use.
	It can specify character set names, such as the following:
	utf-8
	us-ascii
	iso-8859-1
	shift-jis
VARS=*varpairs*	*varpairs* indicates the list of variables to set for the current activity (if the task is GO) or nested activity (if the task is GOSUB). The variable list must be in query-string format, for example:
	var1=value1&var2=value2
	Variable values must be escaped according to URL-escaping conventions. The phone unescapes the VARS option before setting the value of the variables.
RECEIVE=*var_list*	*val_list* indicates a semicolon-delimited list of values that an activity invoked with GOSUB returns to the invoking activity. The RETVALS option is allowed only with the RETURN task.
	The values must be escaped according to URL-escaping conventions.
RETVALS=*val_list*	*val_list* indicates a semicolon-delimited list of values that an activity invoked with GOSUB returns to the invoking activity. The RETVALS option is allowed only with the RETURN task.
	The values must be escaped according to URL-escaping conventions.
NEXT=*next_url*	*next_url* indicates the URL to request after a nested activity returns.
	If the FRIEND option in the GOSUB task is set to TRUE, the NEXT option can be overridden by the DEST option in the nested activity's RETURN task.
CANCEL=*cancel_url*	*cancel_url* indicates the URL to request after a nested activity invoked by a GOSUB task cancels.
	If the FRIEND option in the GOSUB task is set to TRUE, the CANCEL option can be overridden by the DEST option in the nested activity's CANCEL task.
FRIEND=*boolean*	A boolean value specifying whether the nested activity specified in a GOSUB task is "friendly." A friendly nested activity can use the DEST and CLEAR options in RETURN and CANCEL tasks and override the NEXT and CANCEL options of the calling task.
	To indicate the nested activity is friendly, specify TRUE. The default is FALSE.
SENDREFERER=*boolean*	A boolean value specifying whether the phone should provide the URL of the current deck when requesting the URL specified by the DEST or NEXT options. If you set it to TRUE, the phone specifies the deck's URL in the "Referer" header of the request.
	The phone attempts to use the shortest possible relative URL in the "Referer" header if possible.
	The default value is FALSE.
CLEAR=*boolean*	A boolean value specifying whether a RETURN or CANCEL task from a nested activity unsets all the calling activity's variables. To unset the calling activity's variables, specify TRUE. The default is FALSE.
	The phone ignores the CLEAR option unless the calling activity specifies that the current activity is "friendly."
NUMBER=*number*	For a CALL task, *number* specifies the phone number to call.

C.5   *TASK* *TYPES*

The TASK attribute is used within an action element to define which specific task is performed when the action is invoked.

Task	Description	Options that can be used with this task (required attributes are in bold)
GO	Redirects the user to the URL specified by the DEST option. If you use the GO task, you can only specify a relative URL for the DEST option.	**DEST**, VARS, SENDREFERER, REL, METHOD, POSTDATA, ACCEPT-CHARSET
GOSUB	Pushes a new activity onto the activity stack and requests the URL specified by the DEST option. When the nested activity returns, the phone puts the nested activity's return values into the variables specified by the RECEIVE option. If the nested activity cancels, the phone requests the URL specified by the CANCEL option.	**DEST**, VARS, SENDREFERER, FRIEND, RECEIVE, NEXT, CANCEL, REL, METHOD, POSTDATA, ACCEPT-CHARSET
PREV	Displays the previous card in the activity history. If the current card is the first card in the current activity, PREV has the same effect as CANCEL.	No attributes are used with a PREV task.
RETURN	Returns from a nested activity to the previous activity with the return values specified by the RETVALS option.	RETVALS, DEST, CLEAR, REL, METHOD, POSTDATA, ACCEPT-CHARSET
CANCEL	Cancels the current activity, requesting the URL specified by the previous activity's CANCEL option. If no CANCEL option is specified, the phone requests the current card in the previous activity.	DEST, CLEAR, REL, METHOD, POST-DATA, ACCEPT-CHARSET
CALL	Switches the phone to voice mode and dials the number specified by the NUMBER option.	NUMBER
NOOP	Do nothing.	

APPENDIX D

Setting up PWS and IIS

This appendix explains how to set up Microsoft Personal Web Server (PWS) and Microsoft Internet Information Server (IIS) 4.0 for web serving, and, in our case, WAP applications deployment.

The use of the web server in the WAP model is to host all the files related to WAP: WML decks, WMLScript documents, WBMP graphics files, and all the server-side files for generating dynamic WAP content. In this appendix, *web site* refers to web and WAP documents.

For comprehensive coverage of the web servers in this appendix, refer to the product documentation.

D.1 MICROSOFT PERSONAL WEB SERVER

Microsoft Personal Web Server is a free web server designed to aid web application developers (in our case, WAP developers) in testing web pages (or WAP applications) before deploying them on the Internet. The use of PWS is for *developmental* use only. Once your web/WAP application is ready to be deployed, you should use a more robust web server, such as Microsoft Internet Information Server (also discussed in this appendix) or Apache. Do *not* deploy your web/WAP application using PWS; it is not designed for deployment purposes.

The primary use of PWS in this book is to execute ASP scripts. We will talk more about setting up a web server to execute ASP scripts when we discuss virtual directories and permissions.

D.1.1 Obtaining PWS

If you are using Microsoft Windows 98, you already have PWS. The PWS installation files are included on the Windows 98 Installation CDs. If you are using Microsoft Windows 95, PWS can be obtained the following ways:

- *Download PWS from the Microsoft web site*—The installation files can be found under the package Windows NT Option Pack.
- *Install PWS from the Microsoft Windows NT Option Pack CD*—The Option Pack CD comes with Microsoft Windows NT Server. The CD also comes with an MSDN subscription.

D.1.2 Installing PWS

Installing PWS is straightforward.

1 Double-click Setup.exe. A setup screen (figure D.1) appears.

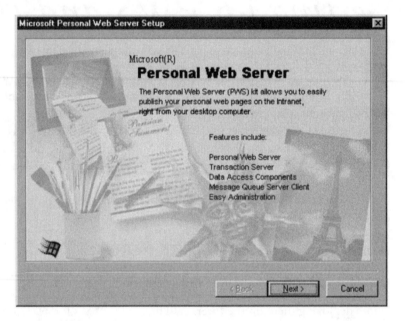

Figure D.1   The PWS setup page

For beginners, it is easiest to accept the defaults recommended by the installation program.

2 To launch PWS, click Start->Programs->Microsoft Personal Web Server-> Personal Web Manager.

You should see the Personal Web Manager screen (figure D.2).

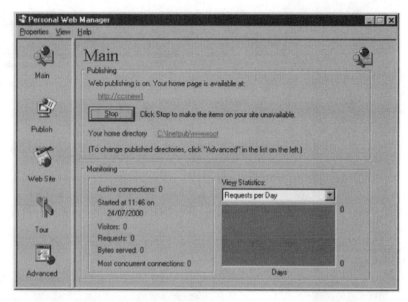

Figure D.2   Personal Web Manager screen

D.1.3   Starting and stopping PWS

To start the web server, click Start. The web server is automatically started after installation, so you will not see the button. You should see Stop instead. Clicking Stop stops the web server.

D.1.4   Testing PWS

You should now be able to see the PWS web server in action! Launch your favorite browser (Internet Explorer 5.0 in this example) and enter http://localhost.

If PWS is installed correctly, you should see the welcome page (figure D.3).

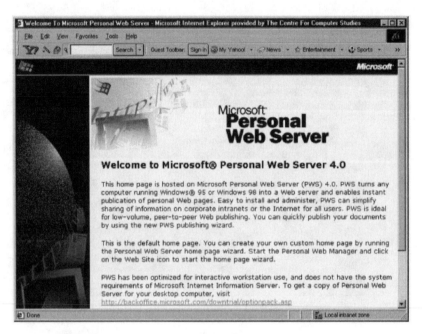

Figure D.3   The Personal Web Server welcome page

Up to this point, you cannot use the web server to serve WML decks because the MIME types for WAP have not been set up (see the section on Creating new MIME types in Windows 95/98 on how to set the new MIME types).

D.1.5   Setting default documents

When you enter a URL without a file name, as you did in the previous section (http://localhost), the web server attempts to look for a *default document*. PWS allows you to set a list as the default document. In the WAP environment, we suggest that your default document be an ASP document that is able to detect the type of browser that the client is using. Upon detecting the browser type, the ASP document can perform a redirection to the appropriate content (WML for WAP device and HTML for web browser). The techniques for detecting the browser type are discussed in part VI.

To set the default document, launch the Personal Web Manager and complete the following steps:

1 Click the Advanced icon on the left-hand side of the screen to open the Advanced Options dialog box (figure D.4):

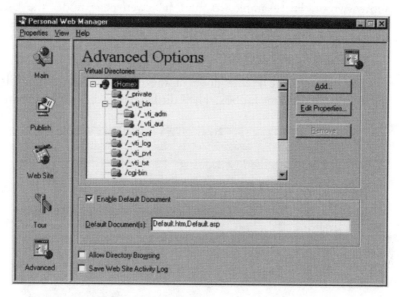

Figure D.4   Advanced options dialog box

PWS automatically assigns Default.htm and Default.asp as the default documents. This means that if the Default.htm document is found in the home directory, it is automatically sent to the web browser if the user enters an URL of the home page without a file name.

For example, if the user enters http://www.yourhost.com/, this is equivalent to http://www.yourhost.com/Default.htm.

If the Default.htm document is not found, the next document specified in the list (Default.asp) will be sent. The list of default documents are searched in this particular order and they are separated by a comma.

2 Enter/add the name of the file you want to set as the default document. For example, if you want to override the default documents specified by PWS, you can clear the list and enter your own default documents (figure D.5).

**Figure D.5
Overriding a default
document**

D.1.6   Setting the root directory

By default, the root directory of the web site is mapped to the directory c:\inet-pub\wwwroot. For example, to publish a web page under the URL http://local-host/hello.html, you would save the web page hello.html in the root directory (c:\inetpub\wwwroot).

To modify the root directory:

1   Double-click the Home node of the directory tree that is displayed in the Advanced Options list box. The Edit Directory dialog box appears (figure D.6):

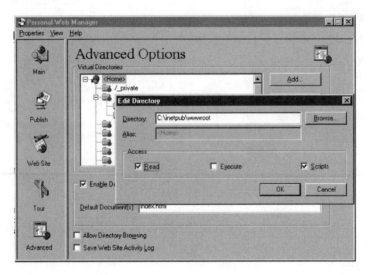

Figure D.6   The Edit Directory

2   To change the root virtual directory to another directory on the hard disk, simply enter a new directory path in the Directory: text box.

D.1.7   Creating virtual directories

To create a virtual directory, select a directory from the Advanced Options list box; then click Add. For example, if you want to create the URL http://localhost/WAP/, complete the following steps:

1   Select the Home directory; then click Add.

2   Specify the directory that you want to map to this virtual directory (d:\wap, shown next).

3   Specify a name for the virtual directory .

The Add Directory dialog box is shown in figure D.7

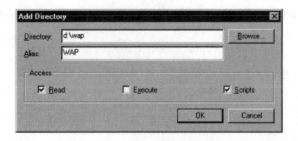

Figure D.7
The Add Directory dialog box

D.1.8 Setting permissions of virtual directories

Each virtual directory has three access rights:

- *Read*—Allows web browsers to read the files stored in this directory.
- *Execute*—Allows the web server to execute files stored in this directory. CGI applications must have this permission; otherwise, the web server cannot execute them.
- *Scripts*—Allows the web server to interpret ASP scripts.

It is important to note that you must store your ASP documents in a virtual directory that has *only* the Scripts permission enabled. ASP documents do not need the Read permission to function. Enabling the Read permission on a virtual directory that contains ASP scripts exposes you to security risk as the scripts may contain password access to databases.

D.1.9 Creating MIME types in Windows 95/98

Part III explained how to create a WAP application using WML. Once you create a WAP document, there are two ways to load it (figures D.8 and D.9):

- Directly from the hard disk
- Served from the web server

Figure D.8   Loading from the hard disk

Figure D.9   Loading from the web server

A common problem with the second approach involves the MIME type. As you are probably aware by now, a WML document requires a special WAP MIME type (`text/vnd.wap.wml`). When a web server serves a WML document, the web server attempts to send the correct MIME type in the HTTP header. If you have not specified the correct MIME type on the web server, the WAP browser receives, by default, the `text/html` MIME type. This will cause an error and the WML deck will not load correctly.

In Windows 95/98, you must add new MIME types to the operating system, not the web server.

To add a new WAP MIME type, complete the following steps:

1 From My Computer, select Folder Options from the View menu.

2 From the File Types tab, click New Type.

The Add New File Type dialog box (figure D.10) appears:

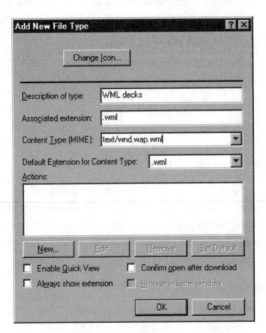

Figure D.10
The Add New File Type dialog box

3 Enter the appropriate MIME type information; then click OK.

You *need to reboot* your machine for the new MIME type to take effect.

D.2 MICROSOFT INTERNET INFORMATION SERVER 4.0

Microsoft IIS is a web server that runs on the Microsoft Windows NT server platform. IIS is increasingly becoming the web server of choice for Small and Medium Enterprises (SME) that want a reliable and affordable web solution.

D.2.1 Obtaining IIS

IIS comes free with Windows NT and is included on the Windows NT Option Pack CD. Alternatively, it can be downloaded from the Microsoft web site. The installation files can be found under the package Windows NT Option Pack.

D.2.2   Installing IIS

The installation of IIS is straightforward; simply double-click the setup.exe icon and follow the instructions on the screen. The initial setup screen is shown in figure D.11.

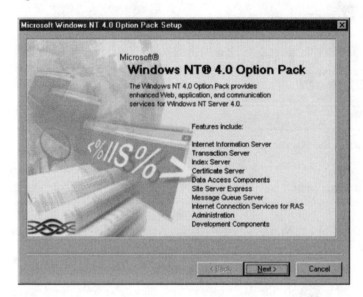

Figure D.11
The Option Pack
Setup screen

For beginners, accept the defaults recommended by the installation program.

D.2.3   Starting and stopping IIS

To manage IIS, you use the Microsoft Management Console (MMC). To launch the IIS Internet Service Manager, click Start->Programs->Windows NT Option Pack-> Microsoft Internet Information Server->Internet Service Manager. The console window (figure D.12) appears.

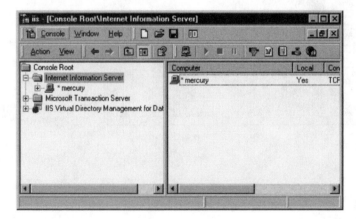

Figure D.12
The console window

To start the web service, select the web site and click Start. To stop the web service, click Stop (figure D.13).

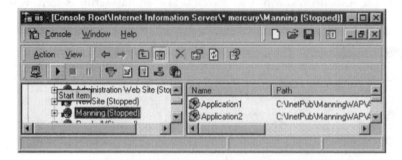

Figure D.13   Click the Start button to start the web service

D.2.4   Creating a web site

To create a web site:

1 From the console window, right-click your computer name (*mercury* in the example above) and select New->Web Site.

The New Web Site Wizard window appears.

2 From the New Web Site Wizard window, enter the web site description; then click Next (figure D.14).

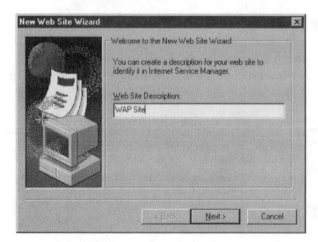

Figure D.14
The New Web Site
Wizard window

3 Assign an IP address for this web site and configure the port number to be used; then click Next (figure D.15).

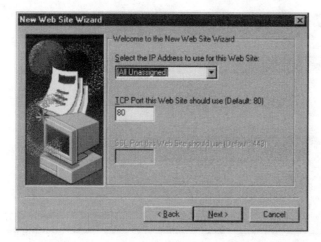

Figure D.15
Configuring the page

4 Enter the path for your home directory, then click Next (figure D.16).

Figure D.16
Entering the home directory

5   Set the access permissions for your home directory; then click Finish (figure D.17).

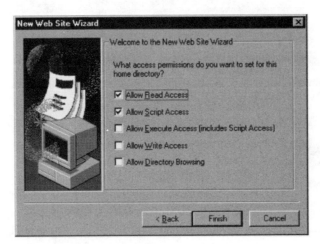

Figure D.17
Setting permissions

D.2.5   Creating virtual directories

The steps for creating a new virtual directory are similar to that of creating a new web site.

1   Select a web site; then right-click and select New->Virtual Directory. The New Virtual Directory Wizard appears

2   Enter an alias for this virtual directory (figure D.18); then click Next.

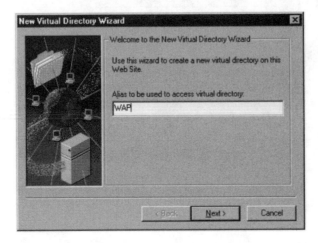

Figure D.18
Entering an alias

3 Enter the path to be mapped (figure D.19) to this virtual directory; then click Next.

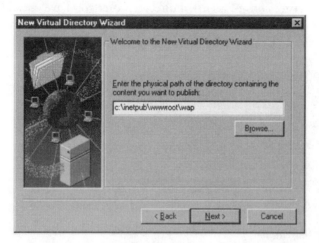

Figure D.19
The path to be mapped

4 Set the access permissions for this directory (figure D.20); then click Finish.

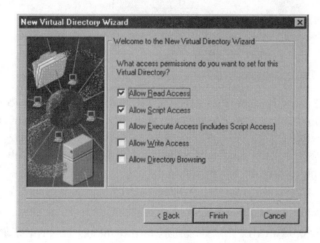

Figure D.20
Setting access
permissions

D.2.6   Setting permissions of virtual directories

To modify the permissions of a virtual directory after you have created it, right-click the web site name from the console window; then select Properties. The permissions appear on the Home Directory tab (figure D.21).

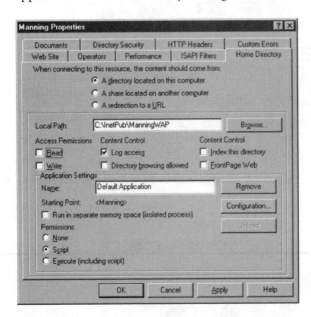

Figure D.21
Modifying permissions

The Read check box specifies whether web browsers have read access to the files stored in this directory. To disable read access to the current virtual directory, uncheck the Read check box.

The Write permission allows the client to modify the content of the web directory. This setting should be left unchecked.

Under the Permissions section, select:

- None, if you do not allow scripts or CGI applications to be executed.
- Script, if you want to run ASP scripts in this folder. This is the default permission setting.
- Execute, if you want the web server to execute CGI applications.

You must store your ASP documents in a virtual directory that has *only* the Script permission enabled. ASP documents do not need the Read permission to function. Enabling the Read permission on a virtual directory that contains ASP scripts exposes you to security risk as the scripts may contain password access to databases.

D.2.7   Configuring MIME types

Configuring MIME types in IIS is simple, as you need not add them to the operating system. To add a new MIME type to a web site, open the web site Properties dialog box and complete the following steps:

1   From the HTTP Headers tab, click File Types in the MIME Map section (figure D.22).

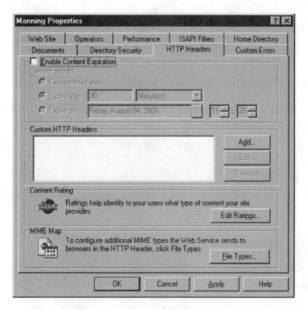

Figure D.22
The HTTP Headers tab

2   From the File Types dialog box, click New Type (figure D.23):

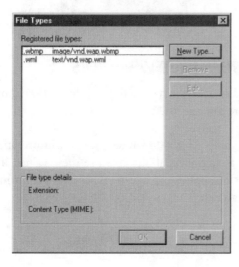

Figure D.23
The New Type button

3 From the File Type dialog box enter the appropriate file type information; then click OK (figure D.24).

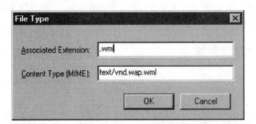

Figure D.24
Entering the file type

D.3 *TESTING YOUR CONFIGURED WEB SERVER*

Now that your web server is configured properly to serve WML documents, let's try to load a WML deck from the web server.

Save a WML document (index.wml) into the root directory of your web server (e.g., c:\inetpub\wwwroot) (figure D.25).

Use a WAP emulator to load the WML document.

If your web server is working correctly, you should see the deck loaded on the emulator (figure D.26).

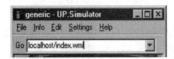

Figure D.25
Saving a document

Figure D.26
The loaded deck

D.4 *WEB SERVER ENVIRONMENT VARIABLES*

When a web client connects to a web server, it passes information about itself to the web server. This information contains the type of web client, any cookie values, type of content that the client can receive, and so on.

In order for the client (web or WAP browser) to pass information to the web server, the web server must have the capability to store these values. The web server stores these values; a server-side application can then access this information through the use of environment variables.

Table D.1 lists and describes the various environment variables accessible by the web server.

Table D.1 Environment variables

Environment variable	Description
AUTH_TYPE	The authentication method used to validate a user
CONTENT_LENGTH	The length of the query data (in bytes or the number of characters) passed to the CGI program through standard input
CONTENT_TYPE	The media type of the query data, such as text/html, text/vnd.wap.wml
DOCUMENT_ROOT	The directory from which web documents are served
GATEWAY_INTERFACE	The revision of the CGI the server uses
HTTP_ACCEPT	A list of the media types the client can accept, such as text/vnd.wap.wml
HTTP_COOKIE	A list of cookies defined for that URL
HTTP_FROM	The email address of the user making the query (many browsers do not support this variable)
HTTP_REFERER	The URL of the document the client points to before accessing the CGI program
HTTP_USER_AGENT	Information about the web browser
PATH_INFO	Extra path information passed to a CGI program
PATH_TRANSLATED	The translated version of the path given by the variable PATH_INFO
QUERY_STRING	The query information passed to the program. It is appended to the URL following a question mark (?)
REMOTE_ADDR	The remote IP address from which the user is making the request
REMOTE_HOST	The remote host name from which the user is making the request
REMOTE_INDENT	The user making the request
REMOTE_USER	The authenticated name of the user making the query
REQUEST_METHOD	The method with which the information request was issued (e.g., GET, POST, HEAD)
SCRIPT_NAME	The virtual path (e.g., /cgi/cgiprog.pl) of the script being executed
SERVER_NAME	The server's hostname or IP address
SERVER_PORT	The port number of the host on which the server is running
SERVER_PROTOCOL	The name and revision of the information protocol the request came in with
SERVER_SOFTWARE	The name and version of the server software that is answering the client request

D.5 *MIME* TYPE LIST

Table D.2 shows the complete list of MIME types that you need to set for deploying WAP applications:

Table D.2   MIME types for deploying WAP applications

Content	Extension	MIME type	Description
WML	.wml	text/vnd.wap.wml	WML deck
WMLScript	.wmls	text/vnd.wap.wmlscript	WMLScript source
WMLC	.wmlc	application/vnd.wap.wmlc	WML compiled
WMLScriptC	.wmlsc	application/vnd.wap.wmlscriptc	WMLScript compiled
WBMP	.wbmp	Image/vnd.wap.wbmp	Wireless bitmap
HDML	.hdml	text/x-hdml	HDML source

HTTP/1.1 request and response headers

This appendix presents the general structure of an HTTP/1.1 message and focuses specifically on two types of request messages: GET and POST requests. It covers all the header fields presented in the RFC 2068 document (January 1997), which is the HTTP 1.1 specification supported by WAP 1.1 used in this book. The reader should be informed that RFC 2068 was further improved to RFC 2616 (June 1999).

E.1   HTTP MESSAGE OVERVIEW

An HTTP message can be either a request sent from a client to an HTTP server or a response sent from an HTTP server to the requesting client.

If a request from an originating client (user agent) needs to pass through one or more intermediaries, such as proxies or gateways, such traversal of a request is also called a request chain. Similarly, a response chain is one in which a response message is sent from the origin server to the user client via one or more intermediaries.

You should be aware of the existence of the request/response chain because not all header fields have the same effect. Some:

- Affect only the connection between two consecutive communicating parties (user agent, intermediaries, or origin server)
- Affect connection to the end point (user agent or origin server)
- Affect all connections along a request/response chain

E.2   HTTP MESSAGE FORMAT

When discussing header fields, the syntax in table E.1 is used:

Table E.1   Syntax for header fields

Syntax	Meaning
|	Or
[ ]	Enclosed token or entity is optional
*( )	Enclosed token or entity has zero or more occurrences
CRLF	Carriage return and line feed
Token	The smallest unit of entity, e.g., a constant value such as GET

E.2.1   General format of an HTTP request message

```
HTTP-Request =      Request-line
                    *( general-header-field : [field-value]
                    | request-header-field : [field-value]
                    | entity-header-field : [field-value] )
                    CRLF
                    [Message-body]
```

```
Message-body = entity-body | encoded-entity-body-with-transfer-coding
```

Entity refers to the information or payload of a request or response. It consists of metainformation in the form of entity-header fields and content in the form of an *entity-body.* The term *transfer coding* refers to an encoding transformation that is applied to an entity body to ensure a safe transfer of the *entity-body* through the network.

Understanding the request line

```
Request-line  = Method  Request-URI  HTTP-Version  CRLF
```

- *Method*—This parameter denotes one of the following values: OPTIONS, GET, HEAD, POST, PUT, DELETE, TRACE, or other extension methods. All general-purpose servers must support the GET and HEAD methods. We will concentrate more on the GET and POST requests.

    A GET request retrieves the specified (via the Request-URI) document or the results after processing the specified document. Data may be sent to the specified URL by using a query string, which follows immediately after the specification of the Request-URI.

    A POST request is much the same as a GET request. The former, however, puts the data in the message body rather than immediately following the Request-URI. Also, a POST request consists of the header fields: Content-Type and Content-Length.

- *Request-URI*—This parameter, in which URI denotes Uniform Resource Identifier, may either be an absolute location description of the target resource where the host is part of the specification, or a nonabsolute path, where the host is specified separately by a request header field, namely Host.

Examples of a valid request line:

```
GET  http://www.wapforum.org/what/technical.htm  HTTP/1.1

POST /Protocols/rfc2068/rfc2068 HTTP/1.1
Host: www.w3.org
```

E.2.2 General format of an HTTP response message

```
HTTP-Response =     Status-line
                    *( general-header-field : [field-value]
                    | response-header-field : [field-value]
                    | entity-header-field : [field-value] )
                    CRLF
                    [Message-body]
```

Understanding the status line

```
Status-line = HTTP-Version  Status-Code  Reason
```

- *Status-Code*—This parameter is a three-digit code that indicates the result of the request sent earlier. The first digit ranges from 1 to 5, each signifying a category of status carried in the response. They are classified as:

  1*xx*   Informational
  2*xx*   Successful
  3*xx*   Redirection
  4*xx*   Client errors
  5*xx*   Server errors

- *Reason*—This parameter provides a brief text description of the status indicated by the status code explained in table E.2.

Table E.2   Status codes and reasons defined in HTTP/1.1 (RFC 2068)

Status code	Reason
100	Continue
101	Switching Protocols
200	OK
201	Created
202	Accepted
203	Nonauthoritative Information
204	No Content
205	Reset Content
206	Partial Content
300	Multiple Choices

Table E.2   Status codes and reasons defined in HTTP/1.1 (RFC 2068) (continued)

Status code	Reason
301	Moved Permanently
302	Moved Temporarily
303	See Other
304	Not Modified
305	Use Proxy
400	Bad Request
401	Unauthorized
402	Payment Required
403	Forbidden
404	Not Found
405	Method Not Allowed
406	Not Acceptable
407	Proxy Authentication Required
408	Request Time-out
409	Conflict
410	Gone
411	Length Required
412	Precondition Failed
413	Request Entity Too Large
414	Request-URI Too Large
415	Unsupported Media Type
500	Internal Server Error
501	Not Implemented
502	Bad Gateway
503	Service Unavailable
504	Gateway Time-out
505	HTTP Version Not Supported

Examples of a valid status line:

```
HTTP/1.1  200  OK
HTTP/1.1  404  Not Found
```

E.3   *HEADER FIELDS BY CATEGORY*

This section lists HTTP/1.1 header fields by the following categories:

- General
- Request
- Response
- Entity

E.3.1 General header fields

One or more of the general header fields may appear in either a request or a response message (table E.3).

Table E.3 General header fields

Header field	Description	Example

Cache-Control	Specifies a caching mechanism that applies to the entire request or response chain	`Cache-Control: no-cache`
		This example shows the origin server imposing a request that a receiving cache must not use the response to satisfy subsequent requests without successful revalidation with the origin server.
		
		`Cache-Control: no-store`
		This example shows how to prevent the retention of information in the recipient's cache, both volatile and nonvolatile.

Connection	Sender can specify options about a connection. These options will not be propagated if the recipient of the message concerned is a proxy.	`Connection: close` A sender would include the Connection header field to indicate that the connection will be closed upon the completion of the current request/response communication.
Date	Indicates the date and time at which the message originated. Typically, an origin server must include a Date header field. Exceptions are cases in which the response status code indicates there is a continuing or protocol-switching situation, some server errors occurring, or the server does not have a clock.	Date: Mon, 9 Aug 1999 09:21:33 GMT
Pragma	Specifies implementation-specific directives that may apply to any recipient along the request/response chain	Pragma: no-cache
Transfer-Encoding	Lists one or more types of transformation that apply on the message body	Transfer-Encoding: chunked
Upgrade	Allows the client to specify to the server the other application-layer communications protocols (e.g., SHTTP or future versions of HTTP) the client supports and would prefer to use if the server would switch protocol. This change of protocol applies immediately on the response message sent to the client. However, this upgrade takes place only in the current connection.	Upgrade: SHTTP/1.3

Table E.3   General header fields (continued)

Header field	Description	Example
Via	Consists of pairs of protocol and receiving host that tracks the forwarding path between user agent and origin server, both in a request and response message. Gateways and proxies use this header field to track message forwarding and to avoid request looping.	Via: HTTP/1.1 host1:8080, 1.0 host2 The example indicates that the sender sends the message to host1 at port 8080 using HTTP/1.1, which in turn forwards the message to host2 (at port 80) via HTTP/1.0. The default protocol is HTTP. If the port number is not specified, the default port number for the protocol in question is used.

E.3.2   Request header fields

The request header fields (table E.4) provide more information to the HTTP server about the request and the requesting client. One or more of the following request header fields may appear in a request message.

Table E.4   Request header fields

Header field	Description	Example
Accept	Specifies the media (MIME content types) acceptable to the client	Accept: text/html, text/*;q=0.5, image/gif The symbol * is a wild-card character. Hence, text/* indicates all subtypes of the media type, text, are acceptable. The precedence level is indicated by the quality value assigned to q.
Accept-Charset	If this field is not present in the header, the interpretation is that any character set is acceptable. If this field is present, it lists the character sets acceptable to the client, in addition to the default—ASCII, also known as ISO Latin-1 or ISO–8859–1, with a quality value of 1.	Accept-Charset: iso-8859-5;q=0.8
Accept-Encoding	Specifies the encoding types acceptable to the client	Accept-Encoding: x-compress, gzip
Accept-Language	Lists the languages acceptable to the client	Accept-Language: en, fr;q=0.7
Authorization	This field is absent from the header if the client does not need to authenticate itself with the server. Otherwise, it indicates the encryption scheme to be used together with the scheme-specific authorization data.	Authorization: Basic hUfoLr7qKLm3 The Basic scheme passes user ID and password to the server as an encoded string (e.g., using uuendcoding). Note that this is not very secure as it can be easily decoded compared to an encrypted string.
From	Specifies the email address of the human user controlling the user agent in question	From: foo@hotmail.com
Host	Specifies the domain name and port number (if not 80) to which the request is sent	Host: www.manning.com

Table E.4   Request header fields (continued)

Header field	Description	Example
If-Match	The server will perform the requested method (e.g., PUT) only if there is any entity tag listed for the If-Match header that matches an entity tag of the entity in the response that the server would have returned if there were no If-Match header.	If-Match: "abc" If the entity corresponding to "abc" is no longer a representation of the resource concerned, the status code 412 (Precondition Failed) will be returned.
If-Modified-Since	Used with the GET method to inform the server not to return the entity if the requested resource has not been modified since the specified date/time.	If-Modified-Since: Mon, 9 Aug 1999 09:21:33 GMT
If-None-Match	The server will perform the requested method only if there is no entity tag listed for the If-None-Match header that matches one in the response that the server would have returned if there were no If-None-Match header.	
If-Range	Specifies an entity tag or a date and time. It can be used together with a Range header field to make a conditional GET request in order to update a certain range of an entity instead of requesting the transfer of the entire entity.	
If-Unmodified-Since	Contains a date and time. It is used to inform the server to service the request only if the requested resource has not been modified since the specified date and time.	If-Unmodified-Since: Mon, 9 Aug 1999 09:21:33 GMT
Max-Forwards	This is used with the TRACE request method. It specifies the maximum number of times a request message can be forwarded. Each recipient, be it a proxy or gateway, should decrease the integer value of this header field before forwarding the request, unless the value is zero, in which case, the recipient must not forward the message, but must respond with an indication that it is the last recipient.	
Proxy-Authorization	Specifies authorization information of user agent or its user to identify itself to a proxy that requires authentication. The authorization information is passed to the first proxy. The latter may forward the Proxy-Authorization header to subsequent proxies if a cooperative authentication mechanism is used.	
Range	Specifies one or more ranges of bytes of an entity to be transferred from the server	Range: bytes=99-199,-5 This specification identifies the 100th to the 200th bytes as well as the last 5 bytes of the entity.

Table E.4   Request header fields (continued)

Header field	Description	Example
Referer	Specifies the location (URI) of the resource from which the Request-URI is obtained. This header value can either be expressed as an absolute URI or relative URI. In the latter case, the address value is interpreted relatively to the Request-URI.	
User-Agent	Indicates the client software that originates the request	User-Agent: Mozilla/4.0 (compatible, MSIE 4.0; Windows 95)

E.3.3   Response header fields

The response header fields provide more information to the client about the response from the origin server. One or more of the response header fields in table E.5 may appear in a response message.

Table E.5   Response header fields

Header field	Description	Example
Accept-Ranges	Specifies the range unit (or "none") accepted, in response to a range request	Accept-Ranges: bytes The example indicates server's acceptance of a byte-range request for a resource.
Age	Sender estimates the time lapse in seconds since the generation of the response by the origin server	Age: 8900
Location	Provides location other than the Request-URI for the completion of servicing the request or identification of a new resource	Location: http://www.manning.com/index.html
Proxy-Authenticate	A response with status code 407 ("Proxy Authentication Required") used by proxy to challenge authorization of a client must include this header field, which contains authentication scheme and parameters applicable to the proxy for the Request-URI concerned. It applies to only the current connection.	Proxy-Authenticate: Basic realm="timtam" The content after the colon is known as the challenge. In the example, the challenge consists of the scheme, Basic, with parameter, realm, that uses a string to identify the protected space for the resource in question. The Basic authentication scheme requires the client to specify an ID and password for each realm.
Public	Lists the methods supported by the server, which may or may not be applicable to the Request-URI. This header applies only to the server directly connected to the client. Any intermediate proxy must either remove the Public header field or replace it with one that reflects its own capabilities.	Public: OPTIONS, TRACE, GET, HEAD

Table E.5 Response header fields (continued)

Header field	Description	Example
Retry-After	A response with status code 503 ("Service Unavailable") must include this header field. A redirection response may also include this. It specifies expected period of unavailability of the requested service. It may specify the period as number of seconds or alternatively, as a date/time value.	Retry-After: 60 Note that the integer value is in seconds.
Server	Identifies the software at the origin server that handles the request	Server: NCSA/1.5.2
Vary	Lists the request header fields that fully determine, while the response is fresh, whether a cache is permitted to use the response to reply to a subsequent request without revalidation	
Warning	A warning carries additional information that may not be reflected by the response status code. It consists of a warning code, agent (i.e., server) that adds the warning, text description of the warning, and optional date when the warning is generated. A response message may contain more than one warning. It is used to warn about possible lack of semantic transparency from caching operations (e.g., staleness of cache or disconnection of cache) or transformations applied to the message body.	
WWW-Authenticate	A response with status code 401 ("Unauthorized") must include this header, which consists of at least one authentication scheme and parameters applicable to the resource specified by Request-URI.	WWW-Authenticate: Basic realm="mydir@xxx.yyy.zzz"

E.3.4 Entity header fields

The entity header fields provide metainformation about the entity body in a message (either a request or a response), or if the entity body is not present, about the requested resource. One or more of the entity header fields in table E.6 may appear in either a request or a response message. Additional entity headers other than those listed in table E.6 may be defined. This adding of header definitions does not require changing the protocol. However, the new entity headers may not be recognizable by the recipient.

Table E.6 Entity header fields

Header field	Description	Example
Allow	Lists the valid methods for the resource specified by Request-URI. The header may be used in a PUT request to inform the server of the valid methods supported by the new or modified resource. The server may return the actual methods it supports to the client using the Allow header in the response message. This header must be present in a response message with status code 405 (Method Not Allowed).	Allow: GET, HEAD, POST
Content-Base	Specifies the base URI for resolving relative URLs.	
Content-Encoding	This header field identifies one or more content coding that apply on the entity body, listed in the order in which they were applied.	Content-Encoding: gzip
Content-Language	Describes the natural languages of the intended audience.	Content-Language: en
Content-Length	Indicates the length, in octets, of the entity body the sender delivers to the recipient. If the response is in reply to a HEAD request, its value is interpreted as the size of the entity body that would have been sent had the request been a GET.	Content-Length: 330
Content-Location	Provides location other than the Request-URI which supplies the entity enclosed in the message. A cache, however, cannot assume that this location can be used to retrieve the entity for a subsequent request.	
Content-MD5	This is generated by the origin server for the purpose of integrity check of the entity body. This may be generated by a user agent or the origin server for the purpose of integrity check of the content, and is not to be generated by any intermediaries such as a proxy or gateway. However, any recipient in the request/response chain is able to check the digest value to verify its integrity.	
Content-Range	Specifies the range of bytes where the partial entity occurs in the full entity.	Content-Range: bytes 99–199/300 This message body consists of content from the 100th byte to the 200th byte of a 300-byte entity.

Table E.6 Entity header fields (continued)

Header field	Description	Example
Content-Type	Identifies the MIME media type of the entity body. It may contain additional parameters (e.g., charset) which, however, are ignored by most current browsers.	Content-Type: text/html; charset=ISO-8859-1
Etag	Specifies the entity tag for the associated entity in a response to the client.	Etag: "abc"
Expires	This header field is more commonly used in a response message. It indicates the date and time after which the content being sent is considered invalid. This infers the need to refresh the cache, if any exists.	
Last-Modified	Specifies the date and time at which the origin server believes the entity was last modified.	

E.4 USING COOKIE HEADER FIELDS

To resolve the problem of state preservation over the stateless HTTP protocol, Netscape introduced the use of cookies. This requires the use of a cookie header field. The HTTP protocol allows for additional header fields without having to rewrite the HTTP server. However, we need to modify a client browser to support the cookie header field.

The functioning of a cookie actually starts with an HTTP server. While sending the requested resource to the client, such as an HTML document, the HTTP server includes a Set-Cookie header field in its response message to the client. This Set-Cookie header field requests that the client store a small piece of information on its local storage device. The cookie information specifies a domain and a path as well as other parameters.

Subsequently, whenever the client requests resources from a specified location, any cookie whose domain and path values match the location attaches its values to the Cookie header field in the client's request message to the HTTP server.

This section presents the syntax of the Set-Cookie response header and the Cookie request header as specified in the RFC 2109 document.

E.4.1 Set-Cookie header field—from HTTP server to client browser

The full syntax of the Set-Cookie header is (table E.7):

```
Set-Cookie: name=value;
comment=c_value;
domain=d_value;
max-Age=a_value;
path=p_value;
secure;
version=v_value
```

Table E.7 The Set-Cookie parameters

Attribute	Description	Example
Name	Required. This parameter is a user-defined name that indicates the type of information (i.e., its value portion) it carries.	inquirer=sam In the example, the *name* of the cookie is inquirer and it is assigned the value, sam.
Comment	Optional. Allows origin server to document its intended use of the cookie.	comment="library inquiry session"
Domain	Optional. Specifies the domain to which the cookie will be sent whenever the client sends a request to the domain with its trailing name matching the value of this parameter. An explicitly specified domain value starts with a dot and contains at least one embedded dot. The default is the domain of the server that sends the Set-Cookie header.	domain=.manning.com
Max-Age	Optional. Specifies the lifetime of the cookie in seconds. The default behavior is to discard the cookie when the user agent exits.	max-age="180"
Path	Optional. Indicates the path, as well as all its subdirectories, in the specified or default domain for which the cookie is valid. The default is the path to the requested resource, which originated the Set-Cookie header. A valid path value is a prefix of the Request-URI.	path=/books/category
Secure	Optional. If this keyword is present as part of the Set-Cookie header value, it indicates that the cookie content must be communicated over a secure HTTP connection.	secure
Version	Required. For this version specified in RFC 2109, the value is 1.	version="1"

E.4.2 Cookie header field—from client browser to HTTP server

The syntax of the Cookie header that contains one cookie is:

```
Cookie: $Version=v_value;
cookie_name1=n_value1[;$Path=p_value1][;$Domain=d_value1]
```

The header must contain at least one cookie name and value pair. Multiple cookies may be delimited by a comma or a semicolon. Also, for each cookie sent, the path and domain values may be specified in the header if they are included explicitly as attributes in the corresponding Set-Cookie response header.

Below are two examples of a Cookie request header:

- Cookie:$Version="1"; inquirer="sam";$Path="/books"

- Cookie:$Version="1";
  inquirer="sam"; $Path="/books";
  iden="s19980101"; $Path="/books";
  subject="science"; $Path="/books/category"

A P P E N D I X   F

Java servlet packages

The Java Servlet API has evolved to version 2.2, and the final draft for version 2.3 has emerged. This appendix presents mainly Java Servlet API 2.2 that the examples in this book refer to. In particular, two packages of interest to us are javax.servlet and javax.servlet.http.

In the javax.servlet package, we will list in full the GenericServlet abstract class and `Servlet` interface, while in the javax.servlet.http package, we will present the details of the HttpServlet abstract class, and the `HttpServletRequest`, `HttpServletResponse`, and `HttpSession` interfaces.

For a complete listing of the servlet APIs, visit http://java.sun.com/.

F.1   THE JAVAX.SERVLET PACKAGE

The javax.servlet package consists of the interfaces and classes in table F.1.

Table F.1   javax.servlet interfaces and classes

Object	Type
GenericServlet	abstract class—implements javax.servlet.Servlet, javax.servlet.ServletConfig, java.io.Serializable
RequestDispatcher	interface
Servlet	interface
ServletConfig	interface
ServletContent	interface
ServletException	class—extends java.lang.Exception
ServletInputStream	abstract class—extends java.io.InputStream

Table F.1 javax.servlet interfaces and classes (continued)

Object	Type
ServletOutputStream	abstract class—extends java.io.OutputStream
ServletRequest	interface
ServletResponse	interface
SingleThreadModel	interface
UnavailableException	class—extends javax.servlet.ServletException

We will look into the GenericServlet abstract class and the Servlet interface in this section.

F.1.1 GenericServlet abstract class

This abstract class allows the definition of a generic, protocol-independent servlet. Details of its public methods are in table F.2.

```
/*  GenericServlet.java  */
package javax.servlet;

import java.io.IOException;
import java.util.Enumeration;

public abstract class GenericServlet
        implements Servlet, ServletConfig, java.io.Serializable {

    private transient ServletConfig config;

    /* Constructor */
    public GenericServlet () { }

    /* Other public methods */
    . . . .
```

Table F.2 Public methods of GenericServlet

Public method	Function
void destroy()	Called just before the servlet is unloaded from the memory
String getInitParameter (String name)	Returns a string value of the specified initialization parameter, *name*, or null, if the requested parameter does not exist
Enumeration getInitParameterNames()	Returns the names of the servlet's initialization parameters
ServletConfig getServletConfig()	Returns the startup configuration information for this servlet
ServletContext getServletContext()	Returns a ServletContext object, which contains information about the network service in which the servlet is running
String getServletInfo()	Returns information about the servlet, such as author, version, and copyright
String getServletName()	Returns the name of this servlet instance

void init (ServletConfig conf)
    throws ServletException
	Initializes the servlet where parameter *config* may be used to initialize the private variable, *config*, by including the following in the method's definition:
	    this.config = conf;

Table F.2   Public methods of GenericServlet (continued)

Public method	Function
void init() throws ServletException	Initializes the servlet when it is first loaded into the memory
void log (String msg)	Writes the name of the servlet and the specified message, *msg*, to the servlet log file
void log (String message, Throwable t)	Writes the servlet's name, an explanatory message, and a stack trace for a given Throwable exception to the servlet log file

abstract void service
  (ServletRequest req,
   ServletResponse res)
  throws ServletException, IOException
	Services a single request from the client

F.1.2   Servlet interface

This interface defines methods that all servlets must implement. Its public methods and their functions are explained in table F.3.

To implement this interface, you can write one of the following:

- A generic servlet that extends javax.servlet.GenericServlet
- An HTTP servlet that extends javax.servlet.http.HttpServlet

Table F.3   Public methods of the Servlet interface

Public method	Function
void destroy()	Called just before the servlet is unloaded from the memory
ServletConfig getServletConfig()	Returns startup configuration information for this servlet
String getServletInfo()	Returns information about the servlet, such as author, version, and copyright

void init (ServletConfig conf)
    throws ServletException
	Initializes the servlet where parameter *config* may be used to initialize the private variable, *config*, by including the following in the method's definition:
	    this.config = conf;

abstract void service
  (ServletRequest req,
   ServletResponse res)
  throws ServletException, IOException
	Services a single request from the client

F.2   *THE JAVAX.SERVLET.HTTP PACKAGE*

The javax.servlet.http package consists of the interfaces and classes in table F.4.

Table F.4   javax.servlet.http interfaces and classes

Object	Type
Cookie	class—implements java.lang.Cloneable
HttpServlet	abstract class—extends GenericServlet, implements java.io.Serializable

Table F.4 javax.servlet.http interfaces and classes (continued)

Object	Type
HttpServletRequest	interface—extends ServletRequest
HttpServletResponse	interface—extends ServletResponse
HttpSession	interface
HttpSessionBindingEvent	class—extends java.util.EventObject
HttpSessionBindingListener	interface—extends java.util.EventListener
HttpUtils	class

In this section, we will discuss only the first five items listed in table F.4.

F.2.1 Cookie class

This class provides the APIs to set the various values in the `Set-Cookie` HTTP header field, as well as APIs for retrieving client information from the Cookie header field of an incoming request.

This class has a constructor, `Cookie(String name, String value)`, which creates a cookie with the specified name and value.

Other methods of a Cookie class are in table F.5.

Table F.5 Methods of a Cookie class

Public method	Function
void setComment (String purpose)	Sets comment to describe usage of the cookie
String getComment ()	Returns comment describing usage of this cookie, or **null** if this cookie has no comment
void setDomain (String pattern)	After this setting, a host domain must end with the specified *pattern* before the cookie is sent to the host
String getDomain ()	Returns the valid trailing domain *pattern*
void setMaxAge (int expiry)	Sets maximum age of cookie in number of seconds. Negative values indicate that the cookie will be deleted when the user agent exits (default behavior). A zero value causes the cookie to be deleted.
int getMaxAge ()	Returns maximum age of cookie
void setPath (String URI)	After the setting, the cookie is sent to the requested resource if the latter is in the specified URI or its subdirectories. The URI must include the location path of the servlet that originated the setting of the cookie.
String getPath ()	Returns prefix of all URLs for which this cookie is valid
void setSecure (boolean flag)	Indicates to the user agent if the cookie should only be sent using a secure protocol (e.g., https or SSL)
boolean getSecure ()	Returns value (i.e., true or false) of the security requirement attribute of the cookie
String getName ()	Returns the name of the cookie
void setValue (String newValue)	Sets the value of the cookie
String getValue ()	Returns value of the cookie as a string

Table F.5   Methods of a Cookie class (continued)

Public method	Function
void setVersion (int v)	Sets the version of the cookie protocol. Sets version (v) to 0 to indicate compliance with the Netscape cookie specification and 1 to indicate compliance with RFC2109.
int getVersion ()	Returns version of protocol this cookie complies with
Object clone()	Returns a copy of this cookie

F.2.2   HttpServlet abstract class

This is an abstract class from which a subclass can extend to create an HTTP servlet suitable for deployment at a web site.

This abstract class has a constructor that does not do anything:

```
public HttpServlet () { }
```

Table F.6 lists protected and public methods in this abstract class.

Table F.6   Methods of the HttpServlet abstract class

Protected method	Function
void doDelete (HttpServletRequest req, HttpSevletResponse res) throws ServletException, IOException	Called to handle an HTTP **DELETE** request
void doGet (HttpServletRequest req, HttpSevletResponse res) throws ServletException, IOException	Called to handle an HTTP **GET** request
void doOptions (HttpServletRequest req, HttpServletResponse res) throws ServletException, IOException	Called to handle an HTTP **OPTIONS** request
void doPost (HttpServletRequest req, HttpServletResponse res) throws ServletException, IOException	Called to handle an HTTP **POST** request
void doPut (HttpServletRequest req, HttpServletResponse res) throws ServletException, IOException	Called to handle an HTTP **PUT** request
Void doTrace (HttpServletRequest req, HttpServletResponse res) throws ServletException, IOException	Called to handle an HTTP **TRACE** request
long getLastModified (HttpServletRequest req)	Returns a long integer specifying the time in milliseconds the HttpServletRequest object was last modified since midnight, January 1, 1970 GMT, or –1 if the time is not known

Table F.6   Methods of the HttpServlet abstract class (continued)

Protected method	Function

void service
    (HttpServletRequest req,
    HttpServletResponse res)
    throws ServletException, IOException
	Receives standard HTTP requests from public service method and dispatches them to specific Java methods, e.g., doGet(), that specialize in handling specific HTTP request methods

Public method	Function

void service
    (ServletRequest req,
    ServletResponse res)
    throws ServletException, IOException
	Implements a higher-level service method that is responsible for delegating the requests to Http-specific service methods via the protected service method

F.2.3   HttpServletRequest interface

This interface gets data from the client for use in the `HttpServlet.service()` method. It allows the header information in an HTTP request to be accessed from the `service()` method.

Methods of this interface are explained in table F.7.

Table F.7   Methods of the `HttpServletRequest` interface

Public method	Function
String getAuthType()	Returns authentication scheme for protecting servlet: BASIC, SSL, or null if servlet is not protected
String getContextPath()	Returns the context of the request which is part of the request URI
Cookie[] getCookies()	Returns the array of Cookie objects sent together with the request
long getDateHeader (String name)	Returns a *long* value of the specified request header, which represents a Date object Returns *−1* if the header is not found
String getHeader (String name)	Returns a *String* value of the specified request header
Enumeration getHeaderNames()	Returns all header names the request contains
Enumeration getHeaders (String name)	Returns all values of the specified request header as an *Enumeration* of String objects
int getIntHeader (String name)	Returns an integer value of the specified request header
String getMethod()	Returns the HTTP method of the request, e.g., GET, POST, etc.
String getPathInfo()	Returns any optional extra path information following the servlet path of the request URI, but immediately preceding the query string
String getPathTranslated()	Returns any optional extra path information following the servlet name but preceding its query string, and translates it to a real path
String getQueryString()	Returns the query string that is part of the request URI, but after the path
String getRemoteUser()	Returns username of the authenticated user making the request; returns *null* if the user has not been authenticated
String getRequestedSessionId()	Returns the session ID associated with the request

Public method	Function
String getRequestURI()	Returns the URI for the requested resource (servlet, in this case). The string returned starts with the protocol portion and up to the query string of the URL in the request.
String getServletPath()	Returns the part of the request URI that invokes the servlet
HttpSession getSession()	Returns the reference to the current session associated with the request. Creates a session if the request does not have one.
HttpSession getSession (boolean create)	Returns the reference to the current session associated with the request. If no session exists, returns *null* if the parameter, *create*, has a *false* value; otherwise it creates a session if the parameter has a *true* value.
java.security.Principal getUserPrincipal()	Returns a Java Security Principal object containing the name of the current authenticated user
boolean isRequestedSessionIdFromCookie()	Returns boolean result of a check to determine if the requested session ID came in as a cookie
boolean isRequestedSessionIdFromURL()	Returns boolean result of a check to determine if the requested session ID came in as a part of the request URL
boolean isRequestedSessionIdValid()	Returns boolean result of a check to determine if the requested session ID is still valid—i.e., if the request has an ID for a valid session in the current session context
boolean isUserInRole(String role)	Returns boolean result of a check to determine if the authenticated user is included in the specified role

F.2.4   HttpServletResponse interface

This interface consists of methods to allow a servlet's `service()` method to manipulate the HTTP-protocol-specific header information, and to return data to the client.

The interface defines *static final* integer values that represent the possible status codes of an HTTP response to the client. They are denoted by names that contain the prefix: `SC_` (SC means Status Code).

Table F.8 lists methods contained in the `HttpServletResponse` interface.

Table F.8   Methods of the HttpServletResponse interface

Public method	Function
void addCookie (Cookie cookie)	Adds the specified cookie to the response. It can be called multiple times to set more than one cookie.
boolean containsHeader (String name)	Checks whether the header of the response message contains a field with the specified name.
String encodeRedirectURL (String url)	Encodes the specified URL for use in the sendRedirect() method. Returns the URL unchanged if encoding is not required.
String encodeURL (String url)	Encodes the specified URL by including the session ID. Returns the URL unchanged if encoding is not required.
void sendError (int sc)	Sends an error response to the client using the specified status code and a default message.

Public method	Function
void sendError (int sc, String msg)	Sends an error response to the client using the specified status code and descriptive message
void sendRedirect (int location)	Sends a temporary redirect response to the client using the specified redirect location URL. The URL must be absolute (e.g., http://hostname/path/file.html). Relative URL is not permitted here.
void setHeader (String name, String value)	Sets a response header with the given name and value. If the header has already been set, the new value overwrites the previous one. The containsHeader() method can be used to test for the presence of a header before setting its value.
void addHeader (String name, String value)	Adds a response header field with the given name and value. This allows the specified header to have more than one value.
void setDateHeader (String name, long date)	Sets a response header field with the given name and date value. The date is specified as the time lapse in milliseconds since the epoch. If the header has already been set, the new value overwrites the previous one.
void addDateHeader (String name, long date)	Adds a response header field with the given name and date value. The date is specified as the time lapse in milliseconds since the epoch. This allows the specified header to have more than one value.
void setIntHeader (String name, int value)	Sets a response header field with the given name and integer value. If the field has already been set, the new value overwrites the previous one.
void addIntHeader (String name, int value)	Adds a response header field with the given name and integer value. This allows the specified header to have more than one value.
void setStatus (int sc)	Sets the status code for the response. This method is used to set the return status code when there is no error (e.g., status codes SC_OK or SC_MOVED_TEMPORARILY). If there is an error, the sendError() method should be used instead.

Table F.9 lists the status codes for this interface:

Table F.9   Status codes for the `HttpServletRequest` interface

public static final int	Value	Status description
SC_CONTINUE	100	The client can continue.
SC_SWITCHING_PROTOCOLS	101	The server is switching protocols according to the HTTP Upgrade header field.
SC_OK	200	The request succeeded normally.
SC_CREATED	201	The request succeeded and created a new resource on the server.
SC_ACCEPTED	202	A request was accepted for processing, but was not completed.
SC_NON_AUTHORITATIVE_INFORMATION	203	The metainformation presented by the client did not originate from the server.

Table F.9   Status codes for the `HttpServletRequest` interface (continued)

public static final int	Value	Status description
SC_NO_CONTENT	204	The request succeeded but there was no new information to return.
SC_RESET_CONTENT	205	The agent should reset the document view, which caused the request to be sent.
SC_PARTIAL_CONTENT	206	The server has fulfilled the partial GET request for the resource.
SC_MULTIPLE_CHOICES	300	The requested resource corresponds to any one of a set of representations, each with its own specific location.
SC_MOVED_PERMANENTLY	301	The resource has permanently moved to a new location, and future references should use a new URI with their requests.
SC_MOVED_TEMPORARILY	302	The resource has temporarily moved to another location, but future references should still use the original URI to access the resource.
SC_SEE_OTHER	303	The response to the request can be found under a different URI.
SC_NOT_MODIFIED	304	A conditional GET operation found that the resource was available and not modified.
SC_USE_PROXY	305	The requested resource must be accessed through the proxy given by the Location response header field.
SC_BAD_REQUEST	400	The request sent by the client was syntactically incorrect.
SC_UNAUTHORIZED	401	The request requires HTTP authentication.
SC_PAYMENT_REQUIRED	402	Reserved for future use.
SC_FORBIDDEN	403	The server understood the request but refused to fulfill it.
SC_NOT_FOUND	404	The requested resource is not available.
SC_METHOD_NOT_ALLOWED	405	The method specified in the Request-Line is not allowed for the resource identified by the Request-URI.
SC_NOT_ACCEPTABLE	406	The resource identified by the request is only capable of generating response entities that have content characteristics not acceptable according to the Accept headers sent in the request.
SC_PROXY_AUTHENTICATION_ REQUIRED	407	The client must first authenticate itself with the proxy.
SC_REQUEST_TIMEOUT	408	The client did not produce a request within the time that the server was prepared to wait.
SC_CONFLICT	409	The request could not be completed due to a conflict with the current state of the resource.
SC_GONE	410	The resource is no longer available at the server and no forwarding address is known. This condition should be considered permanent.
SC_LENGTH_REQUIRED	411	The request cannot be handled without a defined Content-Length value.
SC_PRECONDITION_FAILED	412	The precondition given in one or more of the request-header fields evaluated to false when it was tested on the server.

Table F.9 Status codes for the `HttpServletRequest` interface (continued)

public static final int	Value	Status description
SC_REQUEST_ENTITY_TOO_LARGE	413	The server refuses to process the request because the request entity is larger than the server is willing or able to process.
SC_REQUEST_URI_TOO_LONG	414	The server refuses to service the request because the Request-URI is longer than the server is willing to interpret.
SC_UNSUPPORTED_MEDIA_TYPE	415	The server refuses to service the request because the entity of the request is in a format not supported by the requested resource for the requested method.
SC_REQUESTED_RANGE_NOT_SATISFIABLE	416	The server is not able to service the byte range requested.
SC_EXPECTATION_FAILED	417	The server is not able to meet the expectation specified in the Expect request header.
SC_INTERNAL_SERVER_ERROR	500	An error inside the HTTP server, which prevented it from fulfilling the request.
SC_NOT_IMPLEMENTED	501	The HTTP server does not support the functionality needed to fulfill the request.
SC_BAD_GATEWAY	502	The HTTP server received an invalid response from a server it consulted when acting as a proxy or gateway.
SC_SERVICE_UNAVAILABLE	503	The HTTP server is temporarily overloaded, and unable to handle the request.
SC_GATEWAY_TIMEOUT	504	The server did not receive a timely response from the upstream server while acting as a gateway or proxy.
SC_HTTP_VERSION_NOT_SUPPORTED	505	The server does not support or refuses to support the HTTP protocol version that was used in the request message.

F.2.5 HttpSession interface

`HttpSession` provides a mechanism to create an association, i.e., a session, between an HTTP client and an HTTP server. The session persists for a specified time period, across more than one connection or page request from the user. A session usually corresponds to one user, who may visit a site many times. The server can maintain a session in many ways such as using cookies or rewriting URLs.

This interface allows servlets to view and manipulate information about a session, such as the session identifier, creation time, and the time it was last accessed. It allows the binding of objects to sessions, allowing user information to persist across multiple user connections.

Session information is scoped only to the current web application (`ServletContext`). Information stored in one context will not be directly visible in another.

The methods of the `HttpSession` interface are listed in table F.10.

Table F.10 Methods of the HttpSession interface

Public method	Function
Object getAttribute (String name)	Returns the object bound to the specified name in this session, or null if there is no object bound to the name.
Enumeration getAttributeNames()	Returns an Enumeration of String objects containing the names of all objects bound to this session.
long getCreationTime()	Returns the time at which this session was created, in milliseconds since midnight of January 1, 1970 GMT.
String getId()	Returns the identifier assigned to this session. An HttpSession identifier is a unique string that is created and maintained by HttpSession-Context.
long getLastAccessedTime()	Returns the last time the client sent a request carrying the identifier assigned to the session. Time is expressed as milliseconds since midnight of January 1, 1970 GMT.
int getMaxInactiveInterval()	Returns the maximum time interval, in seconds, that the servlet will keep this session open between client accesses.
void invalidate()	Causes this representation of the session to be invalid and removed from its context.
boolean isNew()	Returns true if the session has been created by the server, but the client has not yet acknowledged joining the session.
Void removeAttribute (String name)	Removes the object bound to the given name in the session's application layer data. Does nothing if there is no object bound to the given name.
void setAttribute (String name, Object value)	Binds the specified object into the session's application layer data with the given name. Any existing binding with the same name is replaced.
void setMaxInactiveInterval (int interval)	Specifies the time, in seconds, the session can remain valid without client request before the servlet engine invalidates it.

references

1 Changes from RFC 2068 to RFC 2616 (June 1999). http://www.w3.org/Protocols/rfc2616/rfc2616-sec19.html#sec19.6.3.

2 Developer news from the XML community. http://www.xmlhack.com.

3 Directory Services Markup Language Specification. http://www.dsml.org.

4 Ducharme, Bob. *XSLT Quickly.* Greenwich, CT: Manning Publications, 2001.

5 eXtensible Markup Language (XML) 1.0 2nd Ed. http://www.w3.org/TR/2000/REC-xml-20001006.

6 eXtensible StyleSheet Language Transformations (XSLT) 1.0. http://www.w3.org/TR/xslt.html.

7 Gamma, Erich, Richard Helm, Ralph Johnson, John Vlissides. *Design Patterns: Elements of Reusable Object-Oriented Software.* Reading, MA: Addison-Wesley, 1995.

8 Harold, Elliotte Rusty. *XML Bible.* Foster City, CA: IDG Books Worldwide, Inc., 1999.

9 HDML Language Reference. http://developer.phone.com/dev/ts/htmldoc/31h/hdmlref/output.

10 HDML Language Reference 3.0. http://developer.openwave.com/htmldoc/31h/hdmlref/output.

11 Hypertext Transfer Protocol—HTTP/1.1 (RFC 2068, January 1997). http://www.w3.org/Protocols/rfc2068/rfc2068.html.

12 HTTP State Management Mechanism (RFC 2109, February 1997). http://www.w3.org/Protocols/rfc2109/rfc2109.

13 Hypertext Transfer Protocol—HTTP/1.1 (RFC 2616, June 1999). http://www.s3.org/Protocols/rfc2616/rfc2616.html.

14 JavaBeans Activation Framework Specification. java.sun.com/products/javabeans/glasgow/jaf.html.

15 "JavaMail." *Java Developer's Journal* 4, No. 10 (October 1999): 8-12.

16 JavaMail API Specification. http://www.javasoft.com/products/javamail/index.html.

17 Java Naming and Directory Interface API Specification. http://www.javasoft.com/products/jndi/index.html.

18 Microsoft XML Parser/XSLT Processor Documentation. http://msdn.microsoft.com/library/default.asp?URL=/library/psdk/xmlsdk/xmlp91b9.htm.

19 Moraes, Ian. (1999). JavaMail. Java Developer's Journal. Sys-con Publications.

20 Moraes, Ian. (2000). The Use of JNDI in Enterprise Java API's. Java Developer's Journal. Sys-con Publications.

21 Standard Libraries Specification. http://www.wapforum.org/what/technical.htm.

22 Third Generation Partnership Project. Technical Specifications. www.3gpp.org.

23 "The Use of JNDI in Enterprise Java APIs." *Java Developer's Journal* 5, No. 8 (August 2000): 72-78.

24 WAP Forum. Technical Specifications. http://www.wapforum.org.

25 WAPForum. WAP-100, Wireless Application Protocol Architecture Specification. http://www.wapforum.org/what/technical.htm.

26 WAPForum. WAP-190, Wireless Application Environment Specification. http://www.wapforum.org/what/technical.htm.

27 WAPForum. WAP-191, Wireless Markup Language Specification. http://www.wapforum.org/what/technical.htm.

28 WAPForum. WAP-193, WMLScriptLanguage Specification. http://www.wapforum.org/what/technical.htm.

29 WAPForum. WAP-194, WMLScript http://www.wapforum.org/what/technical.htm.

30 Wilson, Mark and Tracey Wilson. *XML Programming with VB and ASP.* Greenwich, CT: Manning Publications, 2000.

31 WML Language Reference. http://developer.phone.com/dev/ts/htmldoc/40/wmlref.

32 WML Reference: Phone.com extensions. http://developer.openwave.com/htmldoc/41/wmlref.

33 WMLScript Language Reference. http://updev.phone.com/dev/ts/beta/docs/wmlsdev.

34 WMLScript Reference: Phone.com extensions. http://developer.openwave.com/htmldoc/41/wmlscript.

35 Xalan Java 2 Documentation. http://xml.apache.org/xalan-j/apidocs/index.html.

36 Xerces Java Documentation. http://xml.apache.org/xerces-j/api.html.

37 XML from the inside out. http://www.xml.com.

38 XML Path Language (XPath) 1.0. http://www.w3.org/TR/xpath.html.

index

VoiceXML

Rick Parfitt, Ph.D.
Softbound, 375 pages, $44.95, November 2001
ISBN 1-930110-14-6

Ebook edition w/sword, $13.50
Ebook edition available from publisher's site:
www.manning.com/parfitt

VoiceXML is a new markup language that allows access to information on the Web from a telephone. For that it requires a "voice browser" which is analogous to a web browser. Instead of keyboard input, VoiceXML uses speech recognition to process voice commands and provide information to the user by converting text into speech.

This book covers comprehensively all aspects of developing VoiceXML applications. It explains the underlying voice browser technology, and demonstrates how to set up a voice browser. All the features of VoiceXML 2.0 are explained in depth, as well as the new XML extensions for writing speech recognition grammars and marking-up text strings for speech synthesis. The book also explains how JSP, Perl, ASP, & PHP can be used to dynamically generate VoiceXML documents, as well as the many ways that VoiceXML documents can be created using the same data as HTML. A step-by-step programming guide is provided for the VoiceXML language.

The author, a speech scientist, uses his decades of experience in the areas of speech recognition and speech interface design to present effective guidelines for writing VoiceXML. Three real-world case studies are provided, which demonstrate good design and the successful use of this new technology. For anyone who wants to understand the growing impact of VoiceXML on handheld communication devices and web access, this book is a valuable resource.

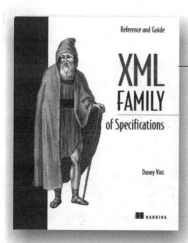

XML Family of Specifications: Reference & Guide

Danny Vint
Softbound, 700 pages, $39.95, October 2001
ISBN 1-930110-10-3

Ebook edition $17.50
Ebook edition available from publisher's site:
www.manning.com/vint

There is a growing family of XML-based standards, with an increasingly complex relationship of requirements and expectations. This comprehensive desktop reference not only addresses XML, but gives special attention to the other core standards including XSLT, Namespaces, XInclude, and Fragments. It is the single source you will need when trying to review the syntax, requirements and interrelationships between features of the complete XML family of standards. As various features have different uses depending upon your application, all topics are described from both a document and data-centric viewpoint.

It covers the latest version of the standards in complete detail as nuggets of information and relationships. A single standard is difficult enough to work with, but in the growing world of XML-based standards, there is an increasing intertwining of requirements and expectations. Here you will find the information that you want, fully indexed and cross-referenced in one location.

JSP Tag Libraries

Gal Shachor, Adam Chace, Magnus Rydin
Softbound, 656 pages, $44.95, June, 2001
ISBN 1-930110-09-X

Ebook edition
PDF files, 8 MB, $13.95
Ebook edition available only from publisher's site:
www.manning.com/shachor

If you are a JSP programmer looking to give your page developers a powerful but trouble-free environment, you will want to use JSP tags. By writing a tag library that is customized for your site you can reuse existing code, separate presentation from implementation, provide easy access to J2EE services, avoid the use of scriptlets (with which a page designer can inadvertently shut down the whole system with a single line of code), enhance the clarity of the flow of events in a page, and make it easy to see what's happening—and to find what's not (i.e., debug). Tag libraries will have a huge impact on the way people develop JSP.

We expect this book will become a bible for serious JSP developers. It is loaded with useful tags including tags to perform iterations, access databases, EJBs, email systems and JavaBeans. It comes with two full-scale use cases showing the effectiveness of tags in the context of ecommerce and of WAP applications.

XSLT Quickly

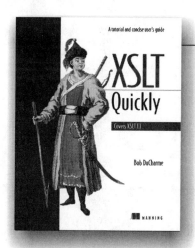

Bob DuCharme
Softbound, 320 pages, $29.95, May 2001
ISBN 1-93011-11-1

Ebook edition
PDF files, 5 MB, $11.95
Ebook edition available from publisher's site:
www.manning.com/ducharme

A step-by-step tutorial covering the basic concepts needed for the most common XSLT tasks *and* a task-oriented user's guide to more advanced techniques for XML document manipulation Part 1 is a tutorial that gets the reader up to speed in XSLT. It is short, deliberate, and covers all the basic concepts you need for the most common XSLT tasks. Part 2 is a task-oriented user's guide to more advanced techniques for XML document manipulation. It is organized by the XSLT tasks themselves—for example, converting elements to attributes or reading in multiple documents at once. The book also includes a glossary, a quick reference to XSLT syntax, and a thorough index to help you find the information you need as easily as possible. *XSLT Quickly* is designed for people who want to hit the ground running with XSLT development: web designers, Java developers, and anyone interested in the latest XML technology.

Purchase of *Dynamic WAP Application Development* includes free author online support. For more information on this feature, please refer to page xxxii.